Destructive Coordination, Anfal and Islamic Political Capitalism

Mehrdad Vahabi

Destructive Coordination, Anfal and Islamic Political Capitalism

A New Reading of Contemporary Iran

palgrave
macmillan

Mehrdad Vahabi
CEPN
University Sorbonne Paris Nord
Paris, France

https://doi.org/10.1007/978-3-031-17674-6

This Palgrave Macmillan imprint is published by the registered company Springer Nature
Switzerland AG.
The registered company address is: Gewerbestrasse 11, 6330 Cham, Switzerland

Dedicated to my mother
Regin Nadjl-Hosseini (Setareh Gilan)

Acknowledgments

In no other country than Iran, political Islam culminated in both a political and an economic revolution after overthrowing the Shah's regime in 1979. By 'revolution', I do not mean what Fernand Braudel wrote about revolution as an indicator of modernity or as Goldstone called "a radical attack on all older institutions in the name of creating a wholly new and better society" (Goldstone, 1998, p. xxxii). Political Islam in Iran brought another definition of revolution by returning to the past or to the Islamic origins. It meant Islamic revivalism. What was the impact of Islamic revivalism on capitalism and political order?

Addressing this issue requires an understanding of capitalism in general and its specific forms of booty capitalism as developed in the critical situation of the Middle East region since the establishment of the Islamic Republic of Iran particularly in the new context of the post-Cold War 'order' marked by the 9/11 disaster and the American invasion of Iraq. In this part of the world, it would be impossible to think of economic development without looking for ways to contain violence and restore the 'normal life' that has become an unattainable mirage.

While my previous books on *The Political Economy of Destructive Power* (2004) and *The Political Economy of Predation* (2015) addressed the two major problems of development in our epoch, namely destruction and predation, the present book completes the cycle by focusing on the relationship between these two and political Islam. As an economist, I am particularly interested in exploring the *economic* consequences of political Islam. This requires an insider look into the Shi'i fiqh on Islamic economics.

Thanks to specialists in Islamic and Middle Eastern studies, a burgeoning economic literature has been spawned that investigates some specific aspects of Islamic economics in banking, corporate law, and Islamic financial certificates such as Sukuk. Despite its originality and significant findings, this sub-field of economics does not hold a prestigious rank in mainstream economics. Moreover, it is often limited to Sunni sharia and excludes Shia fiqh and political Islam.

It is not excessive to say that after the verdict against Salman Rushdie, and Charlie Hebdo shooting in France, many intellectuals and publishers are fearful of touching on issues that are related to political Islam. Moreover, progressive minds are also reluctant to critically assess Islamic fiqh and its bearing on economic performance in regions impacted by political Islam to not be accused of Islamophobia. Thus, it is not surprising that almost no major economist has heard the term *Anfal*, which describes the crux of Shi'i public finance.

A thorough investigation of the roots and background of political Islam in conjunction with Islamic fiqh requires intellectual integrity and boldness or at least strong scientific curiosity. These qualities are needed particularly among economists and publishers of economic literature. A book on 'Anfal' has a 'niche' market; the title is 'weird', 'non-prestigious' for an economist, and maybe even dangerous. Who would like to take on such a hazardous intellectual journey and who would like to publish such a scientific monograph?

Like my previous books, my motivation for writing this "New Reading of Contemporary Iran" has been both moral and scientific. I was born in a country that was a source of emulation and inspiration for political Islam since 1979. It was in this country that *Velayat faqih* (the guardianship of the jurisconsult) was first established. The massacre of the Iranian secular and non-secular opposition not only in prisons (August 1988) but also in the streets (June1982, June 2009, December 2017, October 2019, June 2022) translated what *Velayat faqih* meant in terms of destruction of human life and human rights. As a public intellectual, I am personally committed to the bright and unforgettable memories of all those who dared to resist in the darkest moments of tyrannical rule at the cost of their lives.

But what was the economic consequence of political Islam? This important issue has been treated only marginally in economic literature. From an intellectual viewpoint, it is a true challenge to show how a political economy approach can contribute to our understanding of political Islam and its impact on economic performance.

The practical importance of this theoretical challenge has not been disregarded by major broadcasting channels among the Iranian diaspora such as *BBC TV Persian section* (Hard Talk) and *Iran International TV* (Shahid Tarikh or History Witness). They both conducted interviews with me regarding my findings on this issue in my forthcoming book in June and August 2022. But how did the book get published?

I was lucky enough to send my book proposal to the economics section of Palgrave Macmillan and contact Wyndham Hacket Pain as editor. Undoubtedly, he found the title of this book 'odd' but was curious enough to carefully review my prospectus. He liked it from the start and sent it to two anonymous readers, specialists in Middle Eastern and Islamic economics. The report I received was laudatory filled with insightful remarks that I zealously followed. I wholeheartedly thank Wyndham and the anonymous readers for believing in my journey and getting my manuscript into print. I would like also to thank the two project managers of Palgrave, Ms. Sujatha Mani and Ms. Dhanalakshmi Muralidharan for their efficiency and help in different stages of this work.

This was not my only lucky star; I had a few others. Let me go over them. I should first thank the economic section of the National Council of Universities (CNU) as well as the French Ministry of higher education for giving me a sabbatical semester in 2021–2022.

In addition, I must thank the French National Center for Scientific Research (CNRS) for bestowing upon me a one-year delegation at Centre d'Economie de l'Université Paris Nord (CEPN) in 2021–2022. Although I could only opt for a one-semester delegation in order to take advantage of my one-semester sabbatical leave, I was able to add two semesters and have a whole year for my research. Professor Peter Leeson invited me as a visiting researcher to his research unit at George Mason University for 2021–2022 and the late Professor Janos Kornai invited me to Corvinus University as a visiting professor for the same year. My gratitude toward both as colleagues and friends is immense.

Peter Leeson, Nicolas Da Silva, Miklos Rosta, and Claude Menard generously accepted to read one or more chapters and provided precious feedback. A smaller number of colleagues, namely Philippe Batifoulier, Bertrand Crettez, and Mandana Vahabi, reviewed the entire manuscript. I can never thank them enough for their insightful inputs.

I would like to thank two other publishing houses, Wiley and Springer Nature, for giving me permission to use my already published works.

Chapter 3 of this book is the adaptation and extension of a paper of mine which was published by Wiley:

Mehrdad Vahabi, 2009, "An Introduction to Destructive Coordination," *American Journal of Economics and Sociology*, Vol. 68, No. 2, pp. 354-386.

Section 7-1 of my book is the adaptation and extension of another paper of mine published by Springer Nature:

Mehrdad Vahabi, 2016, "A positive theory of the predatory state," *Public Choice*, vol. 168, pp. 153-175.

Finally, I have to end these long acknowledgments by reminding that even a lucky man has bad luck in life from time to time. Life also generously gave me my share of slaps in the face. A guardian angel is good for such moments. I am lucky because I have two of them. My mother, *Setareh Gilan,* to whom this book is dedicated. The second one is my whole life friend and sister, Mandana Vahabi, who never missed her 'mission' as a guardian even when she could not behave like an angel.

REFERENCES

Goldstone, Jack, 1998, "Introduction," in Goldstone Jack (ed.), *The Encyclopedia of Political Revolutions*, Washington, D.C., Congressional Quarterly Inc., xxxi-xxxviii.

PROLOGUE

The term *Anfal* in the title of this book is not familiar for the general readership and its meaning cannot be easily understood by referring to English dictionaries. What is *Anfal*?

If you launch an internet search on *Anfal*, you will encounter two main strands of literature. The first one relates to the Kurdish genocide by Saddam's regime in the late eighties, and the second is about the eight Surah (chapter) of the Koran known as 'Al-Anfal'.

As Kurdistan regional government has aptly underlined, in Kurdish society, the word *Anfal* has come to represent the entire genocide over decades. *Anfal* was the term used by Saddam Hossein to describe a series of eight military campaigns conducted by the Iraqi government against rural Kurdish communities in Iraq, which lasted from February 23 to September 6, 1988.[1]

The campaign took its name from Surah *al-Anfal* in the Koran. *Al-Anfal* literally means the spoils of war (bounties) and was used to describe the military campaign of extermination and looting commanded by Ali Hassan al-Majid, the cousin of Saddam Hossein. As President of Iraq, Saddam Hossein frequently used religious language when describing the actions of his Ba'athist regime (see Johns, 2006), portraying Arabs as true defenders of Islam and Kurds as infidels.[2] He claimed *Anfal* was a

---

[1] See https://us.gov.krd/en/issues/anfal-campaign-and-kurdish-genocide/, retrieved on 17 July 2022.
[2] See https://kurdistanmemoryprogramme.com/story-of-anfal/, retrieved on 17 July 2022.

direct punishment of the Kurds for supporting Iran in the Iraq–Iran War of 1980 to 1988. However, the Ba'athists misused what the Koran meant by *Anfal*. This word in the Koran did not refer to genocide but it was used as a code name by the former Iraqi regime for the systematic attacks against the Kurdish population. The campaign also targeted the villages of minority communities including Christians.

For rural Kurds, Saddam Hossein's massive assault during *Anfal* may have felt like the wrath of a violent deity, as his government exercised the power of life and death over them. Genocide of such a dimension was unprecedented in the modern history of Iraq.

The second strand of literature on the internet explores the etymological sources of *Anfal* in the Koran. The term was used in the first verse of the eight Surah *Al-Anfal* composing 75 verses. It refers to the spoils of the first battle of the new Muslim faith at Badr. The word also alludes to what is given as an extra sum over what is required. The message is clear: the reward of undertaking holy war (*jihad*) for God is permanently saved with God. Other than this prize, the spoils of war picked up from the Unbelievers are an extra offer for such individuals; before the Day of Judgment, the Almighty awards these to the war participants.

According to the eminent Muslim philosopher Abul Ala Maududi, the chapter was probably revealed in 2 A.H. after the Battle of Badr in 624 A.D. in what is modern-day Saudi Arabia's province of Hejaz. It was the first defensive clash between Meccans and the Muslim people of Medina after they fled from persecution in Mecca. This Surah is part of Madni Surahs (Surah Madaniyah) or Madani chapters of the Koran that were revealed at Medina after Muhammad's *hijra*[3] from Mecca. These Surahs often elaborate on moral principles, legislation, warfare, and principles for establishing the Muslim community (McAuliffe, 2006, p. 111).

The victory of Muslims in the Badr battle[4] was followed by a quarrel among the old and young warriors over dividing the spoils of war. The prophet resolved the dispute by God's revelation in *al-Anfal*. The first verse declared that the spoils of war belonged to God and the apostle. However, later revelation in verse 41 abrogated the previous one and announced that only one-fifth of the spoils belonged to God, his apostle, and the apostle's relatives.

---

[3] *Hijra* was the journey of the Islamic prophet Muhammad and his followers from Mecca to Medina on 16 July 622.

[4] Details of Badr battle are provided in Chap. 5 of the present book.

The Sunni and Shi'i theologians advocated contradictory interpretations of *Anfal*, the former narrowed down its scope and relegated all the apostle's belongings to the Islamic State, while the latter extended *Anfal*'s scope that had to be exclusively owned by the apostle and his successors, namely the Imam and the supreme jurisconsult representing the Imam in his absence (for a detailed explanation of *Anfal* in theory, see Chap. 5 of the present book).

Anfal is one of the underlying principles of Islamic public finance in addition to (1) *Kharaj* or Islamic tax on conquered lands; (2) *Moqasemat* or tributes paid by peasants; (3) *Khoms* or a tax on one-fifth of all Muslims' wealth to be devoted to special causes; 4) *Zakat* or a predictable fixed mild tax system; (5) alms; and (6) fines notably *Jizyah* or a special tax imposed on a certain erring faction from among the people of the Book (non-Muslim groups such as Jews, Christians, and the followers of Zarathustra). Historically speaking, in Sunni Islam, *Kharaj* constituted the bulk of Islamic public finance, whereas Shi'i Islam considered *Anfal* as the main source of public finance since the Safavid dynasty in Iran in the sixteenth century.

What is *Anfal* as a component of Islamic public finance? The internet search will not help you to find an answer to this question. The dearth of sources on this point is striking. *Anfal* is also disregarded in most of the literature on Islamic economics. The latter is often limited to Islamic banking, halal and haram food, or a few Islamic moral principles regarding gambling, painting, music, and so on. Surprisingly, Islamic public finance notably in the Shia fiqh has been left unnoticed and unexplored even after the victory of the Shi'i clergy in toppling the Shah's regime in Iran and establishing *Velayat faqih* (the guardianship of the Supreme Jurisconsult).

Article 45 of the constitution of the Islamic Republic of Iran explicitly stipulated *Anfal*, but the term was omitted from the English translation of the Article since economists, political scientists, jurists, and historians generally overlooked the term or considered it the equivalent of 'public property'. But as will be shown in this book, *Anfal* is not the synonym of public property; it pertains to appropriating all 'ownerless' public properties by the Imam and in his absence by the Supreme Jurisconsult. This includes all public wealth that is known as *res nullius* in Roman law including all natural resources such as seas, mountains, forests, and latent mines as well as all confiscated wealth from 'tyrants' and 'usurper' Kings who do not concede the sovereignty of Imam over the state.

In the Shi'i fiqh, *Anfal* does not belong to all Muslims or people; it belongs to the Imam or the Supreme Jurisconsult. Accordingly, *Anfal's* properties should be kept separate from the state's property belonging to all Muslims. *Anfal* is the underlying tenet of the Shi'i jurisprudence commanded the way the giant Islamic economic holdings have been organized under the Islamic Republic of Iran since the 1979 Revolution. Four major Islamic holdings that dominate the Iranian economy are as follows:

Bonyad Mostazafan (Foundation for the downtrodden) which was created a month after the 1979 Revolution through the confiscation of Pahlavi's foundation, and the properties of 53 industrialists and financiers following Khomeini's injunction labeling them as 'spoils of war'. All these 'public properties' were organized separately from the state under the personal purview of Khomeini. *Bonyad*, as part of *Anfal*, is not controlled by the state, or the parliament or any other authority except the Supreme Leader (jurisconsult).

The second major *Anfal's* holding, namely *Setad* (The Execution of Imam Khomeini's Order-EIKO), was created after the eight-year war with Iraq in 1989 to possess or control the confiscated properties of the persecuted religious minorities such as Bahai's or other 'illicit' wealth as stipulated in Article 49 of the constitution acquired through 'non-Islamic' means as well as abandoned properties during the war.

Khatam al-Anbiya Construction Headquarters (the economic organization of the Islamic Revolutionary Guard Corps-IRGC) is the third major holding. This institution was built after the end of the war during the presidency of Hashemi Rafsanjani to secure the economic and financial independence of the IRGC. Although IRGC is not part of *Anfal*, it comes under the scope of Islamic economic institutions under the exclusive purview of the Imam. The collusion between *Anfal* and the IRGC enhanced the expansion of the Supreme Leader's grip over economic and political power.

Finally, *Astan Quods Razavi* is the most important Waqf endowments based at Mashhad (a holy city in the East of Iran) in which the Imam Reza shrine, the eighth Imam of the Shi'i Twelvers, is situated. While Waqf existed before *Anfal*, it became part of the Islamic sovereign economic institutions exclusively controlled by the Supreme Leader since the 1979 Revolution.

According to *Tabnak*, a site close to the IRGC, more than 60 percent of the Iranian economy belongs to these four aforementioned Islamic economic institutions (see *Tabnak*'s report on September 24, 2019, https://www.tabnak.ir/fa/news/925637 retrieved on July 10, 2022).

Anfal in theory is conceptualized as the exclusive property of the Imam over all the 'ownerless' public properties in contradistinction from the state property belonging to all Muslims or people. The Imam's belongings overweigh the people's meager part of the public finance. This is particularly germane in a country largely dependent on petroleum revenue. *Anfal* in practice is depicted by the four major holdings supporting the Imam's privileged position based on the dispossession of the people from their public properties. *Anfal* can be considered as an enhancer of Islamic predation of public resources.

Anfal as a specific form of Islamic confiscatory regime captures one of the two principal lines of inquiry of the present book and addresses several questions that will be discussed in Chaps. 5–8 such as, What has been the impact of *Anfal* in theory and practice on the political economy of post-revolutionary Iran? To what extent is *Anfal* compatible with chronic political and economic crises in Iran? What has been the role of different types of allocative and coordinative economic mechanisms such as exchange, authority, cooperation, or coercion under *Anfal*? Can *Anfal* be explained in terms of 'Islamic socialism' or 'Islamic capitalism'? Or, should it be grasped as an original model of Shi'i economics? What have been the consequences of such public finance on the development of capitalist production and economic performance?

The second line of inquiry is more universal and explores the general conditions for the emergence of confiscatory regimes in critical situations. Chapters 2–4 introduce the concept of critical order or 'ordered anarchy' as a fertile soil for the emergence of confiscatory regimes based on the fusion of sovereignty and property. Parallel institutions prevail under an appropriative regime eschewing market and authority as dominant forms of coordination mechanisms. I will introduce 'destructive coordination' to grapple with the coordination of agents and organizations under an ordered anarchy. It will be argued that the absence of clear and delineated property rights does not preclude capital accumulation based on profit-making, since the latter can be achieved through non-market channels, for example, confiscatory measures. While an appropriative regime is opposed to a productive one, it is a source of capital accumulation. Max Weber coined 'political capitalism' or 'politically oriented capitalism' to describe profit-making through non-market means. It can also be characterized as rent-seeking activities. Confiscatory and appropriative regime goes hand in hand with political capitalism. This theoretical framework will be applied in understanding *Anfal* and Islamic political capitalism in the later chapters.

While I let the reader discover other aspects of the book, I will continue my persuasive strategy in the introduction to present the whole scope of this book and the main questions that will be addressed throughout this endeavor.

CONTENTS

LIST OF FIGURES

LIST OF TABLES

CHAPTER 1

Introduction

1.1 PROBLEM STATEMENT

Two types of crises should be distinguished: crisis as antinomic to order and as part of a specific order. The former pertains to the crisis as a transitory moment from one order to another. This meaning of crisis prevails in conventional economics in which order is generally defined as a state of equilibrium. Accordingly, the crisis is considered to be an exogenous random shock that moves the system away from its initial state of equilibrium and brings it to a new state of equilibrium. The crisis is then nothing but a transition from one equilibrium (order) to another.

The second type of crisis is not exogenous but endogenous to order in the sense that crisis becomes an order insofar as order becomes critical. In this second type, the crisis is not temporary but chronic detaining the property of autopoiesis or self-replication. Using an analogy with the human body, the former type of crisis is akin to infectious diseases and the latter to chronic diseases such as cardiovascular and bipolar disorders.

This book is about the type of economic systems that can arise from a critical order and sustain in its turn a critical order. In other words, our main line of inquiry consists of exploring a type of economic system that maintains reciprocal causation with critical order in the sense that while it feeds on critical order, it contributes to its reproduction.

© The Author(s), under exclusive license to Springer Nature Switzerland AG 2023
M. Vahabi, *Destructive Coordination, Anfal and Islamic Political Capitalism*, https://doi.org/10.1007/978-3-031-17674-6_1

A close but different question has already been addressed in the vast literature on *political* Natural Resource Curse (NRC)[1] which asks what type of natural resources can sustain critical orders such as protracted civil wars in Angola, the Democratic Republic of Congo, Liberia, Sierra Leone, Afghanistan, Burma, Colombia, Peru, Cambodia, and many other countries? It has been suggested that "lootable goods", namely goods with a high ratio of value-to-weight that can be exploited by non-qualified labor such as alluvial diamonds, gemstones, and narcotics, can sustain critical orders for a long time (Le Billon, 2001). Accordingly, opium in Afghanistan, alluvial diamonds in many African countries, and narcotics in Latin America are assumed to be the source of durable civil wars or critical orders.

In my critical survey of this literature (Vahabi, 2018), I have demonstrated the primacy of *institutional* rather than a *natural* curse in explaining the durability of political and military conflicts. The real issue is not what a good or a bad natural resource is; the crux of the matter is *what type of economic systems comprising fundamental institutions are compatible with critical orders.*

Keen (2012) identified the transformation of warfare into "business as usual" as a possible explanation of the durability of civil wars in many countries like Sudan, Sierra Leone, Nigeria, Uganda, and Afghanistan. In all these cases, the regime and the rebel were not merely adversaries, but covert allies and partners in preying on natural resources such as diamonds and narcotics, raping women, and racketing the civil population. To put it differently, both contenders were interested in waging war rather than winning the war, since the war was a continuation of economics by other means. Contrary to the NRC, Keen's analysis focused on political collusion between soldiers and rebels and not natural resources. The predatory rule tacitly accepted by belligerents could sustain critical order and determined the use of *natural* resources.

In fact, Keen discovered a form of profit-making through non-market channels that Max Weber (1922) had named "booty capitalism" which is a specific case of "political capitalism" that prevailed even before the

---

[1] The main line of inquiry of this strand of NRC consists of exploring how and why regimes richly endowed with natural resources tend to be more authoritarian and prone to civil wars than those without such resources (Wantchekon, 2002; Collier & Bannon, 2003; Jensen & Wantchekon, 2004; Humphreys, 2005; Smith, 2007; Goldberg et al., 2008; Papaioannou & Gregorios, 2008; Ross, 2009; Aslaksen, 2010; Ahmadov, 2014). See Vahabi (2018) for a critical survey of this literature.

emergence of modern capitalist production in the nineteenth century. Weber believed that political capitalism existed during antiquity in China and under the Roman Empire during wartime. However, booty capitalism can also flourish in modern times as it happened with the industrialization of the army and the rise of mass warfare. The emergence of the Military-Industrial Complex in the aftermath of the World War II rendered the warfare economy sustainable even in peacetime (Vahabi, 2004).

But what do we mean by 'economics' in a 'warfare economy'? Are all economic systems supporting a critical order reducible to warfare economics? Or warfare economics is just a variant of economic systems that are compatible with critical orders? These questions remain unanswered in Keen, and they beg further scrutiny.

Furthermore, critical orders are not reducible to protracted civil wars. Other recent examples include international terrorism, permanent political tensions at an international level related to social movements or post-revolutionary orders such as the Islamic Republic of Iran (IRI), and many other movements related to political Islam since 1979. The confrontation between political Islam and the so-called world imperialism led by the USA provides abundant illustrations. Once again, empirical evidence regarding critical orders is not enough to grapple with its rationale. We need to grasp theoretically, what a critical order means as a typical-ideal model.

The general theoretical framework of this book will be exposed in the first three chapters in which the above-mentioned questions will be addressed. The first chapter explores the twofold meaning of economic systems from a distribution and production perspective. The second chapter analytically examines critical orders as an ideal-typical model of coordination and appropriation that I will coin *destructive coordination* or *ordered anarchy*. The third chapter studies political capitalism and its different varieties embracing the so-called NRC.

After outlining my general theoretical framework, I will focus on a specific critical order that rose with Islamic revivalism including different strands of Islam both Sunni and Shiite. Among these movements, the conquest of power by the Shi'i Islam in Iran and the establishment of the Islamic Republic of Iran (IRI) in 1979 have a prominent place, although Shia constitutes only about ten percent of the total population of Muslims in the world.

Considering the role of the late Shah as one of the hegemonic powers of the Middle East and North Africa, its overthrow by a popular revolution led by Khomeini and his followers brought an immense 'revolutionary' credit for the Shi'i Islam even among Sunni insurgents. This model became a reference and a source of emulation for political Islam in general especially since the IRI behaved like an 'anti-imperialist', 'pro-Mostazafan' (defenders of the downtrodden) at a worldwide level. Politically speaking, the IRI is an emblematic figure of critical order born in crisis, feeding on the crisis, and sustaining crisis at an international level. Can we relate both the Shah's despotism and the critical order under the IRI to political NRC?

It is noteworthy that the NRC was initially conceptualized about Iran by Mahdavy (1970). The development of capitalism in Iran was financed by oil revenue during the Pahlavi dynasty. Although the Islamic leaders promised the end of reliance on oil, their dependence was reinforced during the last four decades. Thus, it might be argued that the political NRC has been allegedly the source of a constant tendency toward authoritarianism and political instability in Iran. The second objective of this book is to critically assess this thesis and argue for an institutional curse.

My general theoretical framework in the first three chapters will be mobilized to explore the Iranian case through Chaps. 5–8. Once again, we will focus on the specific economic system that supports the critical order under the IRI. Our first question will be about the institutional impact of the seizure of power by the Shi'i clergy on the economic system. This question is particularly important for Islamic economics in general since although the idea of an Islamic overhaul of the economy can easily be traced back to the 1940s, the only attempt at restructuring the whole public finance according to an Islamic economic model was made in Iran in the aftermath of the 1979 Revolution.

While political and legal scholars, sociologists, and economists grasped the importance and novelty of *Velayat faqih* (the Jurisconsult of the Vicegerent)[2] as the central feature of the Shi'i political system, they totally

[2] It is a Persian expression for the guardianship of an Islamist jurist (Faqih or jurisconsult) who is vicegerent exercising delegated power on behalf of Prophet and his righteous successors, namely the Imam. It pertains to a political system that underpins the way the Shi'i theologians govern Iran since the 1979 Revolution in Iran. In this system all political and religious authority belongs to the Shi'i clergy and particularly to the Supreme Jurisconsult who makes all the state's key decisions. The Supreme Leader as the representative of the Imam provides guardianship (Velayat) over the nation and secures the top-down Islamization of the sovereignty. Articles 5, 57, and 110 of the Constitution of the Islamic Republic of Iran describe the scope of authority and various functions of the jurisconsult of the vicegerent.

dismissed the most prominent feature of its economic model, namely *Anfal*. They all tried to reduce Islamic economics to one of the principal dichotomous models of Islamic socialism or Islamic capitalism denying any original model for the Shi'i Islam (Abrahamian, 1993, 2009; Behdad, 1989, 1994, 1995, 2006; Nomani & Rahnema, 1994, Rahnema, 1995; Nomani & Behdad, 2006; Pryor, 2009; Behdad & Nomani, 2012; Maloney, 2015; Kuran, 2018).

Accordingly, they all periodized the political economy of the IRI in two major episodes. The first covers the 'revolutionary phase' of the IRI that allegedly started with revolution and terminated with the end of the Iran-Iraq war (1979–1989). It has been a commonly held belief that during this initial phase, the IRI pursued a model of 'Islamic socialism' or 'state populism'. In this narrative, a second phase began after the war under the presidency of Hashemi Rafsanjani by implementing the IMF's adjustment and stabilization programs (1989–1997) that culminated in the privatization edict of the Supreme Leader, Khamenei in July 2006. This second phase has been characterized as 'Islamic capitalism' or a turn toward liberalization and privatization of the entire economy. The shift from 'state populism' to 'liberalism' was justified based on another widely held assumption that Islam in general regardless of its different sects enshrines the sanctity of private property.

This fallacious narrative based on wrong assumptions stems from disregarding not only the whole history of *Anfal* in the Shi'i jurisprudence but also its central place in the Constitution of the IRI and its effect on the formation of Islamic parallel economic institutions. *Anfal* as the foundation of public finance allots the entire 'ownerless' public properties (*res nullius*) to the Imam or the Supreme Jurisconsult. These public properties do not belong to all Muslims or people since the sovereignty over these resources is strictly reserved for the Imam. *Anfal* is the dispossession of people from their public properties; it institutionalizes a confiscatory regime.

Chapter 5 of the present book substantiates the history of *Anfal* in the Shi'i jurisprudence and the constitution of the IRI to explore its impact on enhancing a confiscatory regime in practice. What type of capitalism is enhanced or impeded by *Anfal*? What is privatization under *Anfal*? Does this confiscatory regime promote destructive coordination? Tackling these questions warrants a thorough investigation of *Anfal* beyond *theory* as discussed in the Shi'i jurisprudence or in the Constitution of the IRI.

This explains why Chap. 6 is devoted to examining *Anfal* in *practice*, that is, the emergence and evolution of new economic institutions such as

Bonyad Mostazafan (the foundation of the downtrodden) and *Setad Headquarters for the execution of the Imam's verdict* under the purview of the Supreme Leader.

Chapter 7 will evaluate the 'privatization' process under *Anfal* in three phases: (1) under Ayatollah Khomeini the founder of the IRI (1979–1989); (2) under the presidencies of Rafsanjani (1989–1997) and Khatami (1997–2005); (3) under the presidency of Ahmadinejad (2005–2013), particularly since the privatization edict by new Supreme Leader Khamenei in July 2006. It will be shown that massive privatization during the third phase known as the 'Islamic economic revolution' culminated in *Islamization* rather than *liberalization* of the whole economy. This is an original model irreducible to Western capitalism or Oriental socialism.

Chapters 6 and 7 highlight the specific economic system that emerged from the interplay of *Anfal* and capitalism in post-revolutionary Iran. The underlying tenets of this original economic system, characterized as 'Islamic political capitalism',[3] are based on three fundamental institutions describing the ideological/political power, the dominant form of property, and the preponderant coordination mechanism. They comprise *Velayat Faqih, Anfal,* and destructive coordination. These institutions establish a predatory economic system determining the behavioral regularities of economic agents and the typical state of the economy.

Chapter 8 will discuss these economic processes starting by comparing the Shah's regime and the IRI as two types of predatory systems (Vahabi, 2015, 2016). Although they share state predation, they will be distinguished according to their contradictory effects on production. While predation under the Shah's regime during (1962–1971) was an enhancer of production through land reform and limited diversification, predation in the IRI is an impediment to production because of regular capital flight. Capital and labor flight will be presented as the behavioral regularity of economic agents that result in the economics of hoarding as the normal state of the economy.

Chapters 6, 7, and 8 demonstrate that *Anfal* in *practice* constitutes a coherent economic system in line with *Anfal* as the basic principle of public finance in the Shi'i jurisprudence. The oil revenue serves as an

---

[3] More exactly, it is '*Shi'i* Political Capitalism' deriving from the Shi'i jurisprudence. I employ Islamic instead of Shi'i in the book's title for commodity of comprehension for the reader not familiar with the distinctions among different strands of Islam.

economic means to finance this system. Accordingly, it is not a curse of natural resources but an institutional one: Islamic political capitalism.

The epilogue will discuss the practical implications of this book by reviewing the dynamics of this economic system and inquiring about its reformability or the need for transformation. The systemic coherence questions the reformability perspective and lends credence to an institutional revolution aiming at transforming the whole system.

Chapters 4–8 provide a truly new reading of contemporary Iran as the subtitle of this book suggests. The term 'contemporary' includes mainly the last four decades of post-revolutionary Iran with some comparative references to the Pahlavi dynasty. The story told here about contemporary Iran from an economic perspective is different from all other readings because of both its original general theoretical framework and demystifying *Anfal*'s specific predatory system.

In the remaining part of the introduction, I will briefly review principal concepts introduced in different chapters and underline some of the theoretical and practical interests of topics covered in this book. I will then highlight the research method and the background of the present book by discussing its relationship with my previous works.

1.2   PRIMACY OF INSTITUTIONS OR ECONOMY: DISTRIBUTION OR PRODUCTION?

The first step to grasp crisis endogenously is to have a theory of economic system. An economic system is embedded in a social multifactorial complex including political power, ideology, religious, and legal relationships that can be classified as institutional. In short, an economic system is a social totality comprising both economic and institutional factors. Which one of these two components plays a primary role: institutions or economic factors?

This issue is a bone of contention among economists that are divided into two large groups: one that gives the pride of place to economic factors and the other to institutional factors. The former includes Classical, Neoclassical, and Marxist economics. The liberal Manchester school in the nineteenth century is the common ground of these important economic schools. Adam Smith, David Ricardo, and Karl Marx all believed in the primary role of economics, and this belief is largely shared by mainstream economics today. A second approach grants the primary role to institutional factors. Diverse institutionalist schools, from German histori-cal institutionalism, Ordo liberalism to American old and new institution-alism hold that institutional factors play a primary role in explaining economic processes. One of the theoretical interests of this book consists of reexamining this fundamental issue in defining an economic system.

My reflection on this issue is original in the sense that I do not consider the primary role of economic or institutional factors unconditionally. It depends on a distinction that I introduce among different moments of an economic process including production, distribution, exchange, and con-sumption. The term transaction often covers the sum of distribution and exchange.[4] While institutional factors assume a primary role in determin-ing 'distribution' or appropriation of resources, they are secondary in view of long-term technological change or 'productive system'. In other words, I suggest a pattern of *reciprocal causation* between institutional and eco-nomic factors. While institutional factors determine appropriation or dis-tribution of resources, and through this channel production in long term; they are determined in the very long term by technological progress (pro-duction) that incrementally changes the whole distributive system gener-ating social movements to transform institutions.

Hence, the economic system has a twofold meaning: distributive and productive. The former is captured by mode of appropriation or coordina-tion, and the latter by mode of production. Thus, the question about the primary role of economics or institutions cannot be answered before drawing a line of demarcation regarding the two different moments of economic processes: appropriation (distribution) or production.

For example, Keen's reference to 'warfare economy' involves a type of economics dominated by *politics* whereas *Anfal* economics entails the dominance of *religion*. In both cases, economics is closely related to *distri-bution* or *appropriation* rather than the *production* of resources. Unfortunately, the subtle distinction between these two spheres is often dismissed in contemporary political economy and comparative economic studies.

---

[4] In modern economic theory, 'price theory' is the exclusive field of microeconomics whereas 'revenue theory' constitutes macroeconomics. Accordingly, exchange is discussed in micro while distribution is studied in macroeconomics. Karl Polanyi's (1957/1968) usage of the term 'transactions' overlaps micro/macro division covering both distribution and exchange. On the other hand, Williamson (1985) employs the term transaction rather in a microeconomic sense.

In the Marxian materialist conception of history, the primacy of economics has a precise connotation. It pertains to *production* as the basis of society determining other aspects of social relationships such as politics, law, and ideology. Engels delivered a succinct description of this philosophy in his speech at the grave of Karl Marx on March 17, 1883:

Just as Darwin discovered the law of development of organic nature, so Marx discovered the law of development of human history: the simple fact, hitherto concealed by an overgrowth of ideology, that mankind must first of all eat, drink, have shelter and clothing, before it can pursue politics, science, art, religion, etc., that therefore the *production* of the immediate material means, and consequently the degree of economic development attained by a given people or during a given epoch, form the *foundation* upon which the state institutions, the legal conceptions, art, and even the ideas on religion, of the people concerned, have been evolved, and in the light of which they must, therefore, be explained, instead of vice versa, as had hitherto been the case (Engels, 1883/1993, emphases are added).

The mode of production is assumed to be the foundation over which the superstructure embracing politics, religion, and ideology is built. However, the example in the above citation does not support Engels's emphasis on 'production'. Eating, drinking, and satisfying all other basic needs are conditioned on the preliminary *appropriation* of resources including land, water resources, and so on before producing. Appropriation or the way resources are distributed precedes production. The 'mode of appropriation or coordination' captures the distribution of resources, whereas 'modes of production' pertain to technological progress, productive forces, and direct producers as well as social relations of production.

Broadly speaking, a distinction between distribution and production results in differentiating two levels of economic systems. Modes of appropriation or coordination describe an economic system at the distribution level. At this level, economic processes are not limited to the means of producing social wealth; they also include the conflictual power of different social groups in fighting over their share of production. The level of cohesion of these social groups and their ability to act collectively depend largely on the integrative power of moral/ideological forces that unite them together. In other words, distribution is decided by an interplay of economic, destructive (conflictual), and moral/ideological powers (Vahabi, 2004). Borrowing the system theory, the mode of coordination involves 'control processes', whereas the mode of production contains 'material processes' of production.

Productive forces are not exempt from social relationships, but they engage primarily in social relations of production. The division of labor, the organizational forms of production, the ratio of labor to capital, the degree of their substitutability or complementarity, and the intensity in the use of productive factors such as land, labor, and capital are all related to material processes of production. Leontief's input-output matrix or Marx's simple and extended accumulation schemes are based upon a two-sector economy comprising of the sector I (production of means of production) and sector II (production of means of consumption) (*Capital*, vol. 2) depict economics as material processes of accumulation. In this sphere, production determines either directly or indirectly both distribution and institutions in the very long term.

By 'very long term', I refer to Kondratieff's long waves or the Schumpeterian phases of technological innovations.[5] Although institutional changes in politics, property forms, or coordination mechanisms warrant 'long term' transformation, they often require shorter periods than the span of time necessary for major changes in technical progress such as first, second, third, and fourth technological revolutions.

The complexity of relationships between institutions and economics both at distribution and at production level cannot be reduced to the unilateral determinacy of one or the other; it is rather *reciprocal causation*. This relationship is the subject of Chap. 2.

1.3   BRINGING MORE DIVERSITY TO 'DIVERSITY OF CAPITALISMS'

A second interest of this book consists of calling our attention to a subtle difference between capitalist production and capitalist distribution leading to a further distinction between modern capitalism and political capitalism. Chapter 4 will argue that the literature on the diversity of capitalisms (Hall & Soskice, 2001; Amable, 2003) has not dwelt upon *what is common* in all types of capitalisms before differentiating its diverse variants.

This book tries to contribute to the literature on the diversity of capitalisms by focusing on the qualifier of capitalism to sort out modern capitalist

[5] In Schumpeter's literally metaphor, technological innovations are depicted as 'Sturm und Drang' (storm and stress).

production from political capitalism in distribution. Our endeavor aims at fostering the field of comparative economic studies by bringing more diversity to the 'diversity of capitalisms'.

This amplified diversity is particularly pertinent in emerging countries or countries exposed to the so-called NRC. While the term 'capitalism' is of common usage today, there is a strong tendency to conflate all types of profit-making and rent-seeking as if they all promote capitalist production without critically assessing whether certain types of profit-making might be an impediment to capitalist production. Hence, our starting point is to inquire about the qualifier of capitalist production in its historical trajectory.

The capitalist mode of *production* emerged at a certain level of techno-logical change represented by industrial revolution in England notably the use of steam power (steam engine). It was also reliant on specific social relations of production that can be summarized by four major social and organizational changes:

1. Separation of the peasants from their means of production and transformation of these means into capital.
2. The emergence of wage/salary system based on the generalization of commodity-money relationships, the transformation of labor into a commodity and the formation of free labor
3. A developed credit system or capital market.
4. The rise of modern factories and corporations with rational account-ing systems based on costs/benefits calculations. In this sense, the capitalist mode of production emerged only in the nineteenth century.

But what about capitalist *appropriation*? From a distribution viewpoint, capitalist appropriation can be defined as *profit-making in monetary terms.* In this sense, capitalist appropriation existed long before capitalist produc-tion. Braudel's long-distance trade capitalism during the fourteenth and fifteenth centuries describes capitalist appropriation that ended with the autarky of a subsistence economy. Similarly, Weber described six methods of capitalist appropriation, three of them through market mechanisms and three others through non-market channels. He coined the term 'capital-ism with a political orientation' or 'political capitalism' to identify specific forms of profit-making through non-market channels before the advent of modern capitalism. Inspired by Braudel and Weber, I have tried to eluci-date the difference between modern and political capitalism.

Modern capitalism is opposed to political capitalism in three ways:

1. Modern capitalism is capitalism in *production*, and not just in *distribution*.
2. Modern capitalism extends market mechanisms of profit-making to all spheres of economic activities because it dominates production relationships whereas political capitalism is an impediment to general market extension.
3. Modern capitalism develops private property and reinforces the demarcation between property and sovereignty to secure the dominance of the former over the latter.

By contrast, although political capitalism partially enhances the private property of privileged groups (elites or oligarchs) supported by the sovereign power, it systematically violates the sanctity of private property since it favors sovereignty over the property.

From a historical point of view, capitalism can be imagined as a building with multiple storeys in which the ground floor is composed of subsistence economy, the second of profit-making or capitalism in distribution including political capitalism, and the last storey comprising of modern capitalism or capitalist production. Can political capitalism re-emerge in a developed capitalist production? I will respond affirmatively to this question in Chap. 4 and explore diverse forms of political capitalisms both in advanced and developing countries.

1.4   *ANFAL* AND ECONOMIC REDUCTIONISM

Trained in modern economics, students of Islamic economics often tend to prove that different interpretations of Islamic teachings both conservative and radical are reducible to one of the two great modern economic systems, namely capitalism or socialism (see Nomani & Rahnema, 1994). Of course, they occasionally acknowledge some particularities of Islamic economics such as Islamic banking, or halal food but they assume that such specificities are marginal because of the economic superiority of modern systems over traditional forms of economics.

This economic reductionism is particularly misleading since it results in dismissing a closer and deeper knowledge of the Shi'i and Sunni Islamic jurisprudence, their historical evolution, and recent impact on the appropriation of resources in the wake of Islamic revivalism. It is noteworthy that although *Anfal* has been well-known to all Shi'i faqihs and was central in shaping the Shi'i public finance and new economic institutions under the IRI, it was almost totally overlooked by modern economists, legal and political scholars, and sociologists. The paucity of literature on this point reveals that economic reductionism fails to take on board institutional factors stemming from political Islam. Moreover, it discloses that the bulk of what is known as Islamic economics is limited to Sunni Islam and the Shi'i jurisprudence on economic issues has largely been left unnoticed. A third interest for the present book is to cast light on a key piece of Shi'i jurisprudence regarding economic institutions.

My investigation starts by exploring the place of *Anfal* in the Koran, the Prophet's practice and contending interpretations of the Shi'i and Sunni theologians regarding its significance in Islamic public finance. The relevance of this theoretical background will then be demonstrated in drafting and adopting the constitution of the IRI under Khomeini in 1979 as well as the recent program of "privatization" initiated by Khamenei in July 2006. The key importance of *Anfal* will not be discussed only through the lens of Islamic jurisprudence but also from a political and economic perspective. It will be shown how the conquest of political power by the Shi'i clergy and the establishment of *Velayat Faqih* (the Jurisconsult of the vicegerent) in Iran motivated a revisionist interpretation of *Anfal* by Khomeini.

Studying Islamic Fiqh and following the historical trajectory of Islamic jurisprudence is necessary but insufficient to grapple with the institutional importance of underlying tenets of Islamic economics. Cultural and ideological dimensions of religious percepts become particularly germane to institutional studies when they are supported by political power and practiced in economic activities. *Anfal* is one of these institutions that has a significant bearing on distribution since it cultivates a confiscatory regime and concentrates all 'ownerless' public properties in the hands of the Supreme Jurisconsult. *Anfal* promotes political capitalism but provokes serious obstacles to capitalist production. It violates the sanctity of private property without being able to build a new mode of production. In this sense, *Anfal* is a constant source of tension and crisis for modern capitalist production although it fosters profit-making and rent-seeking through non-market mechanisms.

Economic reductionism precludes addressing the institutional impact of *Anfal* on capitalism and its deleterious incidence on water shortages, mountains' erosion, biodiversity losses, and in short on the Iranian ecological system. This explains why privatization in the IRI has been generally considered as a shift to 'liberalization' as if the term 'privatization' automatically implies liberalization regardless of the ideological/political power in place. This book tries to demystify *Anfal* as a specific predatory system buttressed by *Velayat Faqih* that I coin Islamic political capitalism.

1.5   Critical Order: Destructive Coordination

The post-cold war epoch is replete with critical orders or situations on the frontiers of order and disorder; they do not cease to proliferate everywhere. However, disparate empirical examples such as protracted civil wars, international terrorism, Islamic revivalism engaging in contentious politics, and proxy wars are not sufficient to define critical orders. We need to conceptualize theoretically a critical order to isolate the conditions under which such kind of order emerges and evolves. The state of the art, as revisited in Chap. 3, indicates the dearth of work in this field. This book tries to fill this gap.

From an economic perspective, a critical order should be classified as a specific mode of coordination, the fourth type in addition to the market, authoritative and cooperative coordination. Like other forms of coordination, this fourth type of coordination is germane to economics as an instituted process at the distribution or appropriation level. While other principal forms of coordination can be supported by specific forms of production, critical orders are not backed up by a particular type of production. It can emerge under different types of production, but it cannot lead to an original productive system, since it is all about grabbing rather than producing.

This book starts by disentangling what a crisis means for any mode of coordination, and under which conditions a crisis transforms into a self-replicating order.

Answering the first question, we must clarify the role of coordination mechanisms. They are mediators between *fundamental institutions* (political/ideological power, property form) on the one hand, and economic processes (behavioral regulatory of agents and typical state of the economy), on the other. For example, in a classical socialist system, the fundamental institutions are (1) the monopoly of power by the Communist party; (2) the dominance of state and quasi-state property forms. Authoritative coordination is the preponderant type of coordination that mediates between these fundamental institutions and economic performance under a soviet-type economy marked by soft budget constraints and economics of shortage. Crisis ensues once authoritative coordination fails to mediate between fundamental institutions and economic performance. All institutional and economic reforms to reduce the role of authoritative coordination and increase market coordination to promote labor productivity and growth reflect this crisis.

A crisis transforms into an order once none of the principal types of coordination, namely market, authoritative, and cooperative, can dominate the others. In other words, when authoritative coordination fails to coordinate the whole system and it is not supported by the complementary role of the market and cooperative coordination, an era of critical order ushers in which none of the coordination mechanisms can perform its respective regulatory role. This can be named *disarticulation* among different forms of coordination. What is the type of appropriation and coordination under a critical order?

Critical order is 'ordered anarchy' describing a specific mode of coordination that is marked by integration through coercion. I have coined it as 'destructive coordination' because access to destructive means determines de facto rights of individuals and groups regardless of their *de jure* rights. Accordingly, the appropriation of resources is based on a *confiscatory* regime in which property rights are not clearly defined or allocated. Destructive coordination promotes state predation and profit-making through non-market channels.

The reference to 'destruction' can also be justified in terms of Roman law. Property rights in Roman law consist of three elements, namely *usus*, *fructus*, and *abusus*. The latter comprises the right to sell, donate, or destroy. This can be separated from *usus* pertaining to the right of disposing of an asset, and *fructus* relating to the right to benefit from the fruit of an asset. While *usus/fructus* might be rented, *abusus* is not transferable except by selling, donating, or destroying. *Abusus* or the right to destroy is the ultimate frontiers of ownership (Vahabi, 2004). The ability to destroy conditions de facto right of possession.

Accordingly, suicide is a sin if discretion on our life or death is assumed to belong to God. In the same vein, only the state retains the right to enforce capital punishment as a sovereign power. If customary or religious laws command the possession of women by men, then the assassination of women by men does not entail any punishment.[6]

When African slaves were brought to Europe between the eighteenth and nineteenth centuries, the captives were transformed into chattel slaves or 'commodities'. As a commodity, they had to be "dehumanized" or "animalized" (Brown, 2009, p. 1232). According to Patterson (1985), they were both legally and "socially dead". While historians are not unanimous about "social death", the imposition of legal death on them is a fact: they were at least temporarily, incorporated as "living dead" into the universe of commodities (Yazdani, 2021, p. 492). The transformation of a slave from captive or property of slaver into a commodity, susceptible to be the property of whoever buys it, required legal destruction. Then the 'abusus' on the commodity meant selling, donating, or destroying the zombie or chattel slave. In this sense, destructive coordination pertains to a type of coordination in which the allocation of resources hinges upon commanding over coercive means.

In destructive coordination, state failure exists side by side with market failure and none of them can overcome the other's defection. Although legal or formal institutions might be officially in charge of regulatory measures, the failure of the third-party (state or tribunal) enforcement displaces the center of sovereign power to *extra-legal* institutions or to the private resolution of conflicts. Accordingly, another characteristic of destructive coordination is the existence of *parallel institutions* or the juxtaposition of legal and extra-legal orders.

To sum up the general characteristics of destructive coordination, it can be said that this type of coordination is based on:

---

[6] Honor killing of women by father or husband for the cause of adultery under the IRI is a salient example. The cases are multiple. The *New York Times* (June 7, 2020) reported the decapitation of a 14-year-old daughter by her father with a farming sickle to shun dishonoring the family. According to the same report: "A 2019 report by a research center affiliated with Iran's armed forces found that nearly 30 percent of all murder cases in Iran were honor killings of women and girls. The number is unknown, however, as Iran does not publicly release crime statistics" (Fassihi, June 7, 2020). Inspired by the Islamic Sharia, the penal code under the IRI does not consider fathers or husbands to be subject of 'retaliation laws' if they murder their daughters or wives for adultery or dishonoring the family. Since 'women murdering' by de facto owners of women (namely, fathers and husbands) is not treated as a criminal act, it continues to prosper. A very recent case has been the beheading of a 17-year-old wife by her husband who paraded her head gruesomely in the streets with a smile in the provincial capital of Ahwaz in February 2022. For him, it was his religious right to do this, preserving the "honor" of the family (see *CNN*, Salem and Mostaghim, February 9, 2022).

1. Confiscatory appropriation, state predation, and profit-making through non-market channels.
2. Social integration through coercion.
3. Fusion of sovereignty and property.
4. Failure in third-party enforcement and indeterminate property rights.
5. Parallel institutions combining legal and extra-legal institutions.

The predominance of destructive coordination depends on two prerequisites:

1. Failure of all three principal modes of coordination, namely market, authoritative, and cooperative in mediating between fundamental institutions and economic processes.
2. Disarticulation among different modes of coordination.

Several examples at micro, meso, and macro levels will be provided in Chaps. 2 and 3 to illustrate the rationale of destructive coordination as an ideal-model type.

Chapters 6 and 7 disentangle the relationship between the four modes of coordination under Islamic political capitalism. I will demonstrate how giant holdings belonging to *Anfal*, the Sepah, and the Basij are mainly coordinated through destructive coordination while the share of authoritative, cooperative, and market coordination has shrunk in the economy during the last four decades.

1.6   RESEARCH METHOD

This book is a scientific monograph in economics with a multidisciplinary approach. Its content can be situated at the disciplinary edge of economics, political science, Islamic studies, law, and history. It contributes to the field of political economy and comparative analysis of economic systems.

Its method is both historical and comparative. In presenting my theoretical framework, I have followed analytical narratives. However, the use of game theory has been limited to Chap. 3 on conceptualizing destructive coordination so that the reader's access to the main message of the book should not be eschewed by technicalities. The reader who may be unfamiliar with the basic concepts of game theory can also follow the main line of argument in Chap. 3 since all the results are elaborated literally.

Furthermore, I must add that my findings on *Anfal* are based on an extensive review of the firsthand sources on the Shi'i and Sunni jurisprudence in Persian and Arabic and a thorough investigation of the minutes of debates on the Constitution of the IRI and other juridical and legal texts of the IRI.

Similarly, my study on the contemporary Iranian economy is documented by vast firsthand official documents, economic literature and data, daily newspapers, and radio programs in Persian both in Iran and abroad that are not translated into other languages. I tried to use synthetic figures that can cast light on relative weights of different economic sectors, property forms, coordination mechanisms, the formation of fixed capital, and capital flight. Although a detailed examination of different economic processes requires reliable aggregate and sectoral data to which I had limited access, the present work provides a general overview of the most important economic trends in contemporary Iran.

This book provides an original and totally new reading of the political economy of the IRI and must be considered as the first steps to future detailed research on topics introduced in this work.

1.7   Background of the Present Book

This book completes the circle of a trilogy that was started in 2004 by my book on the *Political Economy of Destructive Power* and followed by the *Political Economy of Predation* in 2015. It was impossible to grapple with the Shi'i political capitalism born in post-revolutionary Iran without having a general theoretical framework on destruction and predation.

I am cognizant of the harshness of the terms that I use to describe the political economy of Iran and the Middle East. This region has been the center of the crisis of the international order throughout the transition period from the cold war to the post-cold war era. The terms 'destruction' and 'predation' are not merely harsh, they are horrendous; but they reflect a complex reality replete with inter-intra states warfare, military occupations of several countries by the USA and its allies, military confrontations, political tensions, international terrorism, political Islam, Talibans, Al Qaida, Boko Haram, and ISIS. This image is only one side of the Janus face of the region. The reverse side is the rise of social movements and mass revolutions in Iran and Arab countries aspiring to a new and better world. The future is unpredictable and uncertain, but we are now sure that the political economy of the region cannot be written by excluding conflict, destruction, and predation. This field of study needs to embrace both wealth creation and wealth destruction, productive and appropriative activities.

I have already elaborated my theoretical framework on political economy comprising both creative (productive) and destructive efforts in 2004. Following this work, I tried to understand how destructive or conflictual activity could transform into an institution or a self-replicatory sustainable order. The synthesis of wealth production and wealth destruction in economics is the political economy of predation. This line of research brought me to suggest a distinction between *booty value* of an asset as perceived by the state in contradistinction of the *economic value* of an asset in the market or in any form of voluntary exchange. Accordingly, the frontiers of a predatory state can be defined by differentiating assets according to their booty values. Inclusive and exclusionary predatory states have also been elaborated based on their strategies in extending the state's frontiers.

In the present book, I have borrowed the results of my previous works on destruction, destructive coordination, and predation to understand how the Shi'i political capitalism emerged in the context of a critical order in contemporary Iran. In this sense, the present book closes the loop started by the previous books on destruction and predation. A careful reader can refer to the earlier works to take cognizance of certain concepts that are only defined succinctly in the present book.

References

Abrahamian, E. (1993). *Khomeinism*. University of California Press.

Abrahamian, E. (2009, Spring). Why the Islamic Republic Has Survived. *Middle East Report, 250*, 10–16.

Ahmadov, A. (2014). Oil, Democracy, and Context a Meta-Analysis. *Comparative Political Studies, 47*(9), 1238–1267.

Amable, B. (2003). *The Diversity of Modern Capitalism*. Oxford University Press.

Aslaksen, S. (2010). Oil and Democracy: More than a Cross-Country Correlation? *Journal of Peace Research, 47*(4), 421–431.

Behdad, S. (1989). Property Rights in Contemporary Islamic Economic Thought: A Critical Perspective. *Review of Social Economy, 47*(2), 185–211.

Behdad, S. (1994). A Disputed Utopia: Islamic Economics in Revolutionary Iran. *Comparative Studies in Society and History, 36*(4), 775–813.

Behdad, S. (1995). The Post-Revolutionary Economic Crisis. In S. Rahnema & S. Behdad (Eds.), *Iran after the Revolution: Crisis of an Islamic State* (pp. 97–128). London and New York.

Behdad, S. (2006). Islam, Revivalism, and Public Policy. In S. Behdad & F. Nomani (Eds.), *Islam and the Everyday World: Public Policy Dilemmas* (pp. 1–37). Routledge.

Behdad, S., & Nomani, F. (2012). Women's Labour in the Islamic Republic of Iran: Losers and Survivors. *Middle Eastern Studies, 48*(5), 707–733.

Brown, V. (2009). Social Death and Political Life in the Study of Slavery. *American Historical Review, 114*(5), 1231–1249.

Collier, P., & Bannon, I. (2003). *Natural Resources and Violent Conflict: Options and Actions.* World Bank.

Engels, F. (1883/1993, March 17). *Speech at the Grave of Karl Marx Highgate Cemetery, London.* Transcribed: by Mike Lepore. https://www.marxists.org/archive/marx/works/1883/death/burial.htm

Goldberg, E., Wibbels, E., & Myukiyehe, E. (2008). Lessons from Strange Cases: Democracy, Development, and the Resource Curse in the U.S. States. *Comparative Political Studies, 41*, 477–514.

Hall, P., & Soskice, D. (2001). *Varieties of Capitalism: The Institutional Foundations of Comparative Advantage.* Oxford University Press.

Humphreys, M. (2005). Natural Resources, Conflict and Conflict Resolution. *Journal of Conflict Resolution, 49*, 508–537.

Jensen, N., & Wantchekon, L. (2004). Resource Wealth and Political Regimes in Africa. *Comparative Political Studies, 37*, 816–841.

Keen, D. (2012). *Useful Enemies, When Waging Wars Is More Important than Winning Them.* Yale University Press.

Kuran, T. (2018). Islam and Economic Performance. *Journal of Economic Literature, 56*(4), 1292–1359.

Le Billon, P. (2001). The Political Ecology of War: Natural Resources and Armed Conflicts. *Political Geography, 20*(5), 561–584.

Mahdavy, H. (1970). The Patterns and Problems of Economic Development in Rentier States: The Case of Iran. In M. Cook (Ed.), *Studies in economic history of the Middle East* (pp. 428–467). Oxford University Press.

Maloney, S. (2015). *Iran's Political Economy since the Revolution.* Cambridge University Press.

Nomani, F., & Behdad, S. (2006). *Class and Labor in Iran: Did the Revolution Matter?* Syracuse University Press.

Nomani, F., & Rahnema, A. (1994). *Islamic Economic Systems, Studies in Islamic Society.* London: Zed books.

Papaioannou, E., & Gregorios, S. (2008). Economic and Social Factors Driving the Third Wave of Democratization. *Journal of Comparative Economics, 36*, 365–387.

Patterson, O. (1985). *Slavery and Social Death. A Comparative Study.* Harvard University Press.

Polanyi, K. (1957/1968). *Primitive, Archaic and Modern Economies.* Doubleday.

Pryor, F. L. (2009). The Political Economy of a Semi-Industrialized Theocratic State: The Islamic Republic of Iran. In M. Ferrero & R. Wintrobe (Eds.), *The Political Economy of Theocracy* (pp. 243–270). Palgrave Macmillan.

Rahnema, S. (1995). Continuity and Change in Industrial Policy. In S. Rahnema & S. Behdad (Eds.), *Iran after the Revolution: Crisis of an Islamic State* (pp. 129–149). London and New York.

Ross, M. (2009). *Oil and Democracy Revisited.* University of California-Los Angeles.

Smith, B. (2007). *Hard Times in the Land of Plenty: Oil Politics in Iran and Indonesia.* Cornell University Press.

Vahabi, M. (2004). *The Political Economy of Destructive Power.* Edward Elgar.

Vahabi, M. (2015). *The Political Economy of Predation: Manhunting and the Economics of Escape.* Cambridge University Press.

Vahabi, M. (2016, September). A Positive Theory of the Predatory State. *Public Choice, 168*(3–4), 153–175.

Vahabi, M. (2018). The Resource Curse Literature as Seen Through the Appropriability Lens: A Critical Survey. *Public Choice, 175*(3-4), 393–428.

Wantchekon, L. (2002). Why do Resource Dependent Countries Have Authoritarian Governments? *Journal of African Finance and Economic Development, 2,* 57–77.

Weber, M. (1922/1978). *Economy and Society* 1, University of California Press.

Williamson, O. (1985). *The Economic Institutions of Capitalism. Firms, Markets, Relational Contracting.* Free Press.

Yazdani, K. (2021). !8th-Century Plantation Slavery, Capitalism and the *Most Precious Colony* in the World. *Vierteljahrschrift für Sozial-und Wirtschaftsgeschichte, 108*(4), 457–503.

CHAPTER 2

Economic Systems, Modes of Production, and Coordination

2.1 Introduction

This chapter is about social order and crisis from an economic viewpoint. Standard economic theory often considers 'crisis' as an exogenous random shock that moves the economy out of equilibrium state. Frisch's (1933) apologue of the 'rocking horse' epitomizes the way random shocks could be absorbed by an internal mechanism: "If you hit a wooden rocking horse with a club, the movement of the horse will be very different from that of the club." He predicted Real Business Cycles by conceptualizing crisis as a random shock (Klein, 2006).

Using the human body as a metaphor, exogenous shocks are similar to infectious diseases. By contrast, endogenous crises are akin to chronic diseases such as diabetes and cancer. Applying this distinction in analyzing social order, an endogenous explanation of crisis requires primarily a theory of social order. What are the inherent contradictions of social order or an economic system that result in crisis?

This requires an integrative theory of order and crisis. There are two broad approaches that afford such an integrative theory. The first one is economic and the other consists of an institutionalist approach to the economic system. Marx's concept of 'mode of production' comes into the scope of the first approach while 'mode of coordination' constitutes the cornerstone of the latter approach. This explains the importance of elaborating different 'modes of coordination' and the problem of articulation

M. Vahabi, *Destructive Coordination, Anfal and Islamic Political Capitalism*, https://doi.org/10.1007/978-3-031-17674-6_2

or disarticulation among them in this chapter to understand both the sources of cohesion and crisis.

2.2   Endogenous Explanations of Social Order and Crisis

The concept of an economic system assumes that the economic activities constitute an organic whole capable of self-reproduction and self-regulation. Capitalism and socialism are emblematic figures of 'great systems' that Karl Marx tried to explain in terms of 'modes of production'.

For Marx, a mode of production includes productive forces and social relations of production. Productive forces pertain to the level of technological progress that determines the social relations of production. For instance, the hand-mill leads to feudalism, and steam-mill to capitalism: "In acquiring new productive forces men change their mode of production; and in changing their mode of production, in changing the way of earning their living, they change all their social relations. The hand-mill gives you society with the feudal lord; the steam-mill, society with the industrial capitalist" (Marx, 1847/2009, p. 42).

While the primacy of technological progress in explaining economic cycles found strong echoes in the works of eminent economists like Joseph Alois Schumpeter (1939), many Marxists considered it as economic determinism. Among them, the economist Charles Bettelheim (1976), who was one of the pioneering theoreticians of the Maoist 'cultural revolution'. The latter insisted on the primacy of 'social relations of production' over 'productive forces' and argued that the transformation of Russia to a state capitalist system was because of the predominance of such economic determinism in reading Marx. Bettelheim also accused Marx himself of being partially responsible for such an interpretation, but he particularly traced back the rise of economic determinism to dominant discourse among socialists to the writings of Karl Kautsky and other leaders of the Second International (1880–1920). Lenin's description of communism in Russia as a combination of 'Soviet power and electrification of the whole country in the 1920s' (Lenin, 1920/1976, pp. 15–16) was in line with Marx's emphasis on 'productive forces'.

Bettelheim was not alone in his emphasis on 'social relations of production' in the 1970s. In fact, Janos Kornai (1971a, 1971b) as a non-Marxist advocate of systemic approach formulated a similar criticism. He had not yet espoused an institutionalist approach in the *Economics of Shortage* as he did in 1980, but he believed that in an economic system, the 'material process' should be distinguished from 'control process' (Kornai, 1971a, 1971b).

Kornai cited Leontief's inter-branch input-output model as an illustration. While this model captured the material structure of the economy or the production-technical relations between production and consumption, the focus of economic systems theory had to be on the way the control of material processes was taking place, what kind of information served this purpose, what were the characteristics of the decision processes of economic organizations, and in sum how the decision-information-motivation structure functioned. The Leontief model described the "body" of the economy, whereas economic systems theory was centered on the "soul", the "brain", and the "nervous system".[1] This included, foremost, the "organizations and institutions [that] are functioning within the system beside the basic units of production and consumption, i.e., the firm and the household" (Kornai, 1971b, pp. 302–303). Institutions and organizations were the "soul" of economic systems. For Kornai, the 'economic system' captured the 'control process', whereas Marx's mode of production focused on 'material process'.

While Bettelheim's historical observations on the development of capitalism supported his thesis that the so-called industrial revolution was rather a consequence of a host of institutional factors impacting 'social relations of production', he never reconstructed Marxist's materialist conception of history in a way that the primacy of 'social relations of production' could be fitted into an alternative theory of 'social revolution'.

In Marx, the endogenous source of social revolution derives from the constant growth of productive forces that push away all the barriers including the 'outdated' social relations of production that turn from a source of enhancement into fetters of productive forces. Marx's theory of social crisis is eloquently explained in these terms:

At a certain stage of development, the material productive forces of society come into conflict with the existing relations of production or—this merely expresses the same thing in legal terms—with the property relations within the framework of which they have operated hitherto. From forms of development of the productive forces, these relations turn

---

[1] It is not the only place where Kornai compares economy with biology. Kornai (1983) explores the similarities between the medical sciences and economics.

into their fetters. Then begins an era of social revolution. The changes in the economic foundation lead sooner or later to the transformation of the whole immense superstructure. (Marx, 1859/1977, p. 11).

For Marx, a social crisis is rooted in the economic growth of productive forces and when these forces are impeded by existing social relations of production, an 'era of social revolution' ushers in which this contradiction will be reflected in the superstructure leading to class conflicts for transforming property relationships and political power. In his words:

The totality of these relations of production constitutes the economic structure of society, the real foundation, on which arises a legal and political superstructure and to which correspond definite forms of social consciousness. The mode of production of material life conditions the general process of social, political, and intellectual life that provides the economic basis of a society. It is not the consciousness of men that determines their existence, but their social existence that determines their consciousness. (Marx, 1859/1977, p. 11).

This approach is known as the materialist conception of history. Thus, an economic system is primarily explained by economic factors in the productive sphere that shapes the 'real foundation' on which depends all institutional (legal, political, and ideological) 'superstructure'. The driving force behind all major changes in institutions such as political regime, property relationships, and ideology is sought in the mode of production.

An institutionalist approach to economic systems reverses the line of causality by attributing the primary role to institutions. There are two levels of institutions. The first level defines fundamental institutions describing the rules governing ideological/political structure and preponderant forms of property. The impact of these institutions on economic processes is *mediated* by the second type of institution that I call 'mode of coordination'. Modes of coordination are the outcome of economic, political, and juridical factors. The concept of 'mode of coordination' captures the role of *mediating* institutions between *economic* processes and *extra-economic* fundamental institutions. This explains why this chapter is devoted to modes of coordination and economic systems.

A mode of coordination describes a specific pattern of *social integration* through exchange, reciprocity, redistribution, or coercion that determines the way wealth and rights are *appropriated* by different individuals and collective agents in accordance with their *cooperative or adversarial* (conflictual) efforts. This pattern explains how material and immaterial resources and human activities are coordinated, and how the rights of action are allotted to secure a specific type of (re)distribution of income and assets. It also highlights the priorities assigned to certain individuals or social groups in accessing certain rights of action. The emergence of a specific type of social order involves a process of conflict, compromise, and compliance among individual and social groups with different or contradictory interests. The fact that these interests are 'perceived' as contradictory or even antagonist by individuals or collective agents is more important than the objective tensions and contradictions that might arise from the weight of losses and benefits for each of them in case of adopting an alternative course of action. This explains the importance of adversarial or destructive activities in shaping and changing a given mode of coordination.

The focus of 'mode of coordination' is *not production* but rather (re)*distribution and exchange*.[2] A mode of coordination is about the appropriation mechanism including the *predatory* activity of appropriating the wealth produced by others (Vahabi, 2015a, 2015b). This is the first distinction between 'mode of coordination' and 'mode of production'.

But there are two other major distinctions. Appropriative activity is not necessarily productive, it may be a fighting or grabbing activity. It is not only the creative/productive activity but also the destructive/conflictual activity that determines the appropriation of wealth and rights[3] (Vahabi, 2004). The bargaining and conflictual power of different individuals and collective agents determine their share in (re)distribution.

Finally, a mode of coordination is decided by institutional arrangements, particularly the political and juridical rules, and structures. In this sense, Marx's economic determinacy between 'base and superstructure' is inverted since the superstructure or legal and political rules might determine the appropriative patterns. The concept of 'mode of coordination' captures the way in which the economy is embedded in society. An analysis in terms of the prevailing modes of coordination may shed light on the specific institutional arrangement through which human activities are coordinated in a particular economy.

---

[2] Commons (1970) characterized them as different forms of *transactions*. His typology of different types of transactions will be discussed later in this chapter.

[3] A recent example of destructive power is reported by *C News* on July 28, 2021: an entrepreneur destroyed 30 new apartments using a loader in Blumberg, Germany, after the client refused to pay the bill.

In an institutionalist approach, an economic system is not defined by 'mode of production'; it includes fundamental institutions, modes of coordination, typical behavior of economic agents, and typical state of economic structure. Accordingly, crises cannot be explained endogenously based on purely economic factors. They arise from failure in the mediating role of coordination mechanisms that might stem from economic or non-economic factors. The articulation versus disarticulation[4] among different modes of coordination provides an endogenous explanation of the crisis from an institutionalist perspective.

2.3   Two Levels of Defining Economic Systems

In the preceding section, I underlined the main differences between two allegedly opposed integrative theories of social order and crisis. Can they be reconciled by any chance?

Janos Kornai rejected any reconciliation. He granted the pride of place as a superstructure to politics and not economics: "while the interaction of political power, property and the modes of coordination are all important in movements between capitalism and socialism or back again, *the political dimension plays the primary role*" (2000a, 2000b, p. 33, the emphasis is added). Table 2.1. Illustrates Kornai's institutionalist approach in comparing two 'great systems', namely capitalist and socialist.

In this table, both systems are compared according to five blocs. There exists a hierarchical causal relationship among them in accordance with their relative roles in the causal chain. The first block is the primary cause; it determines the second, and so on.

There are two major shortcomings in this table that begs for scrutiny.

First, are there any commonalities between these two great systems? Kornai never dwelt upon this point although this is a fundamental question in gauging the importance of 'transformation' of one system to another. A closer look reveals that they both share commodity-market, and salary-wage relationships in the *production* field. If comparative economic analysis would have focused on *production*, the contrast was not so radical. But Kornai's comparative analysis could identify significant divergences between the two great systems because it was focused on the

---

[4] Articulation and disarticulation issues will be addressed in this chapter and Chap. 3, Section 3.7.

Table 2.1 Kornai's models of the capitalist and socialist system

Mode	Capitalist system	Socialist system
1. State/ ideology	Political power friendly to private property and market	Unfriendly power of the Marxist-Leninist party
2. Property ownership	Dominant position of private property	Dominant position of state and quasi-state ownership
3. Coordination mechanism	Preponderance of market coordination	Preponderance of bureaucratic coordination
4. Typical economic behavior	Hard budget constraints; strong responsiveness to prices	Soft budget constraints; weak responsiveness to prices; plan bargaining; quantitative drive
5. Typical economic facts	No chronic shortage; buyers' market; chronic unemployment; fluctuations in the business cycle	Chronic shortage economy; sellers' market; labor shortage; unemployment on the job

Source: Based on Kornai (Kornai, 2000a, 2000b, Fig. 2.1, p. 29)

distribution sphere.[5] In other words, economic systems can be compared at two different levels: *appropriative or productive.*

A second problem concerns Kornai's assumption regarding the primacy role of political power over economics. It is noteworthy that Kornai considers a political power friendly to private property and markets as the primary criterion. Such a political regime is not necessarily a democratic one; a despotic regime such as the late Muhammad Reza Pahlavi in Iran might also promote capitalism as long as it is friendly to private property and market institutions.

But couldn't a capitalist system develop despite an unfriendly stance toward private property and markets? While North et al. (2009) highlighted the inhibiting role of a state hostile to private property in the genesis of capitalism, they did not exclude that the spontaneous development of capitalism could gradually change the structure of the state through bargaining over shares of rents between economic and political elites. Economic rents might offer a foundation for containing violence and contribute to the emergence of an "open access society". Thus, it is unclear

---

[5] Kornai's investigation regarding the socialist system was not concentrated on technical progress until late in the post-socialist transition. His interest in Schumpeter increased over time once he started to delve into the lack of innovations in the socialist system (see particularly Kornai, 2010).

why the state rather than the economy should be considered as a primary cause in the rise of capitalism.

While Kornai's idea about the primacy of politics in capitalism is arguable, it seems to be quite germane to the socialist system. In refuting the Marxist scheme of social development in explaining the genesis of socialism, Kornai (1992, p. 364) argues persuasively that the socialist revolutions were the outcomes of wars, particularly the First and Second World Wars. The Communist party's ascent to power took place in settings of political instability and power vacuums rather than in mature capitalist states. The keys to explaining the classical socialist system are found in an understanding of political structure. The starting point is the undivided political power of the Communist party, the interpenetration of the party and the state, and the suppression of all forces that deviated from or opposed the party's policy.

Why Kornai's scheme of political primacy is applicable to socialism but not capitalism? The difference resides in the role of extra-economic power in shaping social relations of production. While capitalism as a *productive* system is unique in not relying on extra-economic power, other forms of economic systems depend on personal subordination rather than impersonal market subordination. The idiosyncratic characteristic of the capitalist mode of production is the extended development of impersonal market-monetary relationships comprising labor and capital markets. The specific feature of the socialist system is the semi-passivity of money and its replacement by the bureaucratic distribution of resources (von Mises, 1946) or what Janos Kornai coined soft budget constraints (Kornai, 1979, 1980, 1998).

Unless capitalism would have been defined in *distribution and exchange* spheres rather than *production*, it could be depicted as profit-making activities as opposed to a subsistence economy (Braudel, 1977, 1983). While the capitalist mode of production could only exist in an economy with credit-system and wage/salary relationships, profit-making activities through non-market channels including state predation and colonialism or 'booty capitalism' existed since the Roman Empire. Max Weber (1922/1978) eloquently described the latter as 'political capitalism' or 'politically oriented capitalism'. I will substantiate the distinction between market and political capitalism as two different economic systems in Chap. 4 considering that they represent two different levels of economic systems. Market capitalism elucidates the economic system at a *productive* level, while political capitalism displays the economic system at an *appropriative* level. These two different types of economic systems will be differentiated further in Chap. 4.

Acknowledging these two levels of economic systems is particularly crucial for comparative studies of economic systems. It is noteworthy that Marx had noticed this difference between production and distribution in conjunction with institutional factors. Marx (1857a, 1857b/1971, p. 96) wrote: "Production is determined by general laws of nature; distribution by random social factors, it may therefore exert a more or less beneficial influence on production; exchange, a formal social movement, lies between these two." He attributed 'production' to general laws of nature whereas distribution was linked to 'random' social factors. He mentioned a few of these random social factors:

> When one considers whole societies, still another aspect of distribution appears to be antecedent to production and to determine it, as though it were an ante-economic factor. A conquering nation may divide the land among the conquerors and in this way imposes a distinct mode of distribution and form of landed property, thus determining production. Or it may turn the population into slaves, thus making slave-labour the basis of production. Or in the course of a revolution, a nation may divide large estates into plots, thus altering the character of production in consequence of the new distribution. Or legislation may perpetuate land ownership in certain families, or allocate labour as a hereditary privilege, thus consolidating it into a caste system. In all these cases, and they have all occurred in history, it seems that distribution is not regulated and determined by production but, on the contrary, production by distribution. (Marx, 1857a, 1857b/1971, pp. 100–101)

He then endeavored to refute the primacy of distribution overproduction by insisting on the determinant role of production in settling the final result:

> Conquests may lead to either of three results. The conquering nation may impose its own mode of production upon the conquered people (this was done, for example, by the English in Ireland during this century, and to some extent in India); or it may refrain from interfering in the old mode of production and be content with tribute (e.g., the Turks and Romans); or interaction may take place between the two, giving rise to a new system as a synthesis (this occurred partly in the Germanic conquests). In any case, it is the mode of production—whether that of the conquering nation or of the

conquered or the new system brought about by a merging of the two—that determines the new mode of distribution employed. Although the latter appears to be a pre-condition of the new period of production, it is in its turn a result of production, a result not simply occasioned by the historical evolution of production in general, but by a specific historical form of production. (Marx, 1857a, 1857b/1971, pp. 101–102)

Among different scenarios, Marx forgot to include the situations in which both contending classes and nations might be destroyed simultaneously. In this case, the result does not necessarily depend on the mode of production but the intensity of warfare. However, the most interesting example in the above passage is the Germanic conquests of the Roman Empire that resulted in feudalism. Despite the Germanic lower level of economic progress, the military superiority of Germans over Romans was a source of interaction between two different modes of production that led to a new synthesis. In other words, 'conquest' played *a decisive factor in production*. But if contrary to what I think, 'conquest' might be treated as a factor of production, then the whole concept of 'mode of production' needs to be redefined in a way that it would be irreducible to productive forces and social relations of production.

Marx's illustrations do not confirm the determining role of production. It rather shows that there exists *reciprocal or cumulative causation* between distribution and production. Political, legal, and economic institutions condition appropriation of resources which in turn influence production. But the production, in its turn, decides fundamental institutions, mode of coordination, and hence, distribution. This circular movement reinforces reciprocal causation. Figure 2.1 describes the cumulative causation between modes of coordination (forms of appropriation) and modes of production.

It is noteworthy that the separation between transaction and production is 'analytical' or conceptual. In reality, they are not easily separable, since transaction structures influence productive sphere through organizational structures (Menard et al., 2021). While transactional and productive approaches concentrate respectively on exchange and technology, they are interdependent and interact with each other. Figure 2.1 simplifies the reality by isolating appropriation and production conceptually.

The whole circuit can be considered in the long and very long time. In the long term, the fundamental institutions impact distribution and

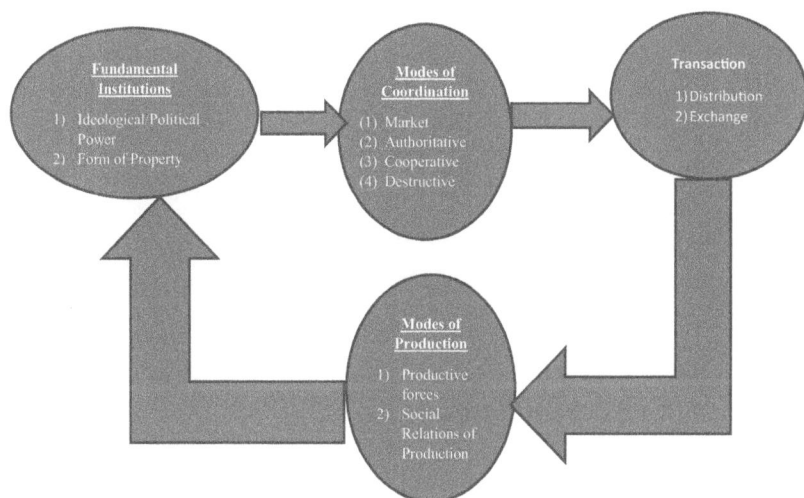

Fig. 2.1 Cumulative Causation between Mode of Coordination and Mode of Production

production through modes of coordination. In the very long term, the modes of production condition fundamental institutions and distribution through modes of coordination. The Schumpeterian technological progress and innovation is particularly relevant to the evolution of productive forces in the very long term. The Schumpeterian explication of Kondratieff long waves lends credence to the idea that the technological progress has been the underlying determinant of booms and slumps of trade cycles. However, the catalyzers of all these long waves of capitalist expansion and contraction over **20** to **25** years have often been major extra-economic, and political events such as revolutions and wars (Mandel, 1995).

Considering the cumulative causation between appropriation and production, the sources of crises should not be unilaterally situated in the mode of production. It can derive from the failure of coordination mechanism as a mediator between fundamental institutions and economic processes. The crises often start from distribution sphere and spreads to production. The significance of coordination mechanism in ascertaining social order and crisis brings us to explore its different forms in the next sections.

As explained in the previous section, a mode of coordination can be characterized by three specific features: (1) the form of social integration or the way transactions are instituted among individuals through exchange, reciprocity, redistribution, or coercion; (2) the type and form (monetary or non) of appropriation; (3) the conflictual and bargaining power as corrective or transformative mechanisms. Applying these three specifications, I distinguish four main typical or ideal modes of coordination.

2.4   Market Coordination

Social integration in market coordination is not based on personal subordination. The agents as sellers and buyers are 'free contractors'. Voluntary transactions and free labor are the basis of *horizontal relationships* between agents having equal rights in front of law. In market coordination, personal subordination is replaced by subordination to impersonal market relationships. This entails not only making huge profits but also the possibility of bankruptcies, firing and restructuring economic units that are insolvent or in difficult financial situation. The lack of personal subordination also means that the social order emerging from market coordination is not designed consciously *ex ante* by free contractors but achieved *ex post* through a spontaneous process of mutual adjustment of numerous rivalrous individual economies.

Mutual interests based on exchange provide a self-enforcing mechanism that binds together sellers and buyers. Adam Smith's metaphor of the 'invisible hand' pertains to this self-enforcing mechanism of *ex post* market coordination. However, Hayek's (1937, vol. 1, Chap. 2) caveat about the importance of *Cosmos* or some fundamental legal rules of contracting is key to grasp the functioning of the 'invisible rule'. The impersonal rule of market requires law and its extended application to all spheres of voluntary contractual relationships involving free buyers and sellers.

Acquisition through 'bargaining transactions' (Commons, 1931) is the basic appropriation mechanism in market coordination that requires at least four parties, namely two buyers and two sellers securing competitive conditions. The traditional markets (bazaar)[6] should be distinguished from modern markets. The former was not necessarily governed by prices. Barters were regulated through customs in personal markets embedded in local social networks (Polanyi, 1957/1968). Transactions in modern impersonal markets are similar to what happens in stock exchange market in which the value of every product is expressed in terms of *monetary prices*.[7] Full-fledged market relationships (like modern stock exchange) become impersonal and independent of social relationships. Market acquisition in an ideal-typical market coordination is carried out through price appropriation involving the exchange of formal legal property titles.

Two main corrective mechanisms in market coordination are 'exit and voice' (Hirschman, 1970). When you are not satisfied with a service provider or a seller's product, you can exit out of his/her shop and find out another provider or an alternative seller. Capital owners often resort to exit to achieve their goals. Capital flight has been a strong bargaining instrument in the hands of merchants and financiers throughout history against authoritarian regimes to restrain their confiscatory measures and to impose a parliament for securing their property rights. While working classes also use the threat to exit to take advantage from competition among employers, their exit power is limited since employers have the 'money' (the general equivalent of purchasing power) whereas they have only their labor force to offer. The latter needs to be transformed into money to exchange against all other products and services. Thus, if there is not an alternative job available, quitting is a very risky option for the worker. Exit as an individual means to protect one's interest is only efficacious in specific cases when demand is particularly high. Workers are more powerful as a collective force. Voice rather than exit is the main means of

---

[6] Bazaars exist in many regions particularly in the Middle East and Southeast Asia. There exists a vast literature on 'bazaar' in economics, management, anthropology, and sociology. Geertz (1978) had explored the synergy between anthropology and economics on understanding bazaars in organizing exchanges among peasants in the countryside. Fanselow (1990) distinguished homogenous, substitutable products and heterogenous, non-substitutable goods, and attributed the exchange of latter goods in the bazaar. Dana and Wright (2015) drew our attention to the elements of Bazaar Economy that can enhance our ability to manage the emerging relationships and multipolarity that underlie the new, Network Economy.

[7] This does not exclude face-to-face relationships in modern markets with highly idiosyncratic products. In modern markets, the impersonal markets are particularly relevant for generic assets, whereas in traditional markets, such type of assets were often exchanged within specific social relationships at local level.

pressure for working classes. They need to organize and fight collectively to gain an increase in salaries, to stop massive layouts, or to reduce the workers' hours, etc. In this sense, working classes have a relative advantage in voicing rather than exiting compared to capital owners. Labor voice and capital flight are two types of conflictual activities that are complementary to market coordination as corrective mechanisms.

Scream (revolution) goes beyond the dichotomous relationship between exiting from the rules and voicing within the rules (Vahabi, 2004; Vahabi et al., 2020), since it questions existing rules in order to establish new ones. Scream is not a corrective to market coordination but rather a means to transform it. Table 2.2 illustrates two different types of market coordination.

In this table, traditional markets pertain to pre-capitalist production and modern markets are associated with market capitalism.[8] The latter is related to a radical change in the extension of market relationships from products to factors of production, namely labor, capital, and land markets. The generalized form of market relationships requires the transformation

Table 2.2 Traditional and modern market coordination

Type of market coordination	Form of social integration	Type of appropriation	Form of appropriation	Corrective mechanism	Example
Traditional	Personal market relationships based on horizontal linkage (social embeddedness)	Barter and exchange based on customs	Non-monetary	Exit	Bazaar
Modern	Impersonal market relationships based on horizontal linkage (social disembeddedness)	Price appropriation through exchange of property titles	Monetary	Exit and voice particularly capital flight and labor voice	Stock exchange

Source: The author

[8] Market capitalism should be distinguished from political capitalism (see Chap. 4).

of labor power into commodity, the institution of private property on land, and the formation of capital market.

While traditional markets in pre-capitalist economies existed for exchange of products, its scope was limited to distribution and redistribution but not to production. It was only in market capitalism that market penetrated production relationships. The developed form of market economy can be characterized by two distinctive features: (1) *impersonal markets* or social disembeddedness, that is, the autonomy of market exchange from face-to-face, social relationships between transactors; (2) *price appropriation* of every product and service through 'voluntary' market exchanges. The coordinating role of price mechanism assumes monetary form of transactions.

While free labor is specific to capitalism, it did not prevail until the end of the nineteenth century. Labor exit is a relatively new historical phenomenon, whereas capital flight started from at least early modernity. Capital flight and labor voice are two principal corrective mechanisms in developed market economies (Hirschman, 1970; Vahabi, 2015a, 2015b). Our analysis shows that the evolution of a mode of coordination needs to be understood in conjunction with the evolution of production mode. Market coordination is the dominant form of coordination in the capitalist system both at distribution and productive levels.

2.5   Authoritative Coordination

This type of coordination prevails in the army, war economies, and the authoritarian states, as well as modern big corporations. In authoritative coordination, social integration is based on *personal subordination* within a hierarchical structure in which there are superiors and inferiors. The relationships between agents are organized based on *vertical linkages*. The social order stemming from this kind of coordination is organized *ex ante*. The rules of conduct in such an organized and conscious order are called *taxis* (von Hayek, 1937, vol. 1, Chap. 2). The plans of action of subordinates are decided by superiors.

As Simon (1951) argued, the employment contract is about delegation of power from employee to employer so that the latter could have the 'authority' to choose a specific range of activities to be performed by the former in return for a monetary reward (salary). Authority is not a synonym of hierarchy in this context. Authority as 'power delegation' may be from shareholders to the director of an enterprise. However, this delegation does not imply subordination of shareholders to managers.

Two types of vertical linkages should be distinguished. In economic literature particularly in organization theories, we often tend to disregard the difference between a command or authoritative system within a factory and that of the state, since different corrective mechanisms are not usually integrated in distinguishing organizational structures.

The first type of vertical linkage is within modern firms' hierarchy in which there are two parties instead of four parties as previously noted in the bargaining transactions. These two parties are on the one hand, a principal (e.g., a manager, a foreman, or any other executive agent) and on the other hand, an agent (a servant, a workman, or other subordinates). The relationship between the two parties is partly command and obedience, partly persuasions or coercion. Borrowing Simon's definition of 'authority', the boss's authority is not followed without questioning. Reasonable and unreasonable commands as well as willing or unwilling obedience need to be differentiated. Different forms of voice such as strikes, demonstrations, petitioning, etc. are used by workers to improve their working conditions or increase their salaries. The transaction between the two parties within modern firms is named 'managerial' or 'authorized' (Commons, 1924/1995, 1931). Although Williamson (1985) is correct in depicting the discretionary power of the firm's management as a 'tribunal of the last resort' in resolving conflicts over property issues, the firm's legal status as a moral person depends on the sovereignty at a national level. To put it differently, the state as an external enforcer inspects on the compliance of both parties of an employment contract to the terms of working rules and labor legislation. Moreover, partial command and obedience evolve with the level of collective action of both parties. Two-sided collective action by workers and employers results in new labor legislation based on collective bargaining. This type of authoritative coordination may be considered as *limited* since bargaining between inferiors and superiors is possible.

The second type of vertical linkage is what prevails in relationships in which the superior is a collective superior while the inferiors are individuals with almost no bargaining power. Familiar instances are the relationship within the army, or between individual citizens and the tax office or custom tariffs, the decisions rendered by courts, the decrees of fascist or Soviet-type dictatorships, and the budget-making of a corporate board of directors. In all these cases, vertical linkages are based on command and obedience without bargaining. These relationships might involve negotiations, but it would be in the form of pleading and arguments addressed to the 'goodwill' of the superior. The relationship is clearly authoritative reflecting the ideal form of command mechanism. Commons associated this type of relationship to 'rationing transactions': "[H]ere the subject person is not permitted to choose any alternative when once the superior person has decided. There is no bargaining between citizen and official, no power to withhold service or property, the psychological aspect of the transaction being that of command and obedience" (1924/1995, p. 107).

Although the term 'bureaucratic coordination' is suggested to depict this type of coordination (Kornai, 1984, 1992), I rather prefer to replace 'bureaucratic' by 'authoritative' to underline this ideal form of command mechanism.[9] Assuredly, this does not mean discarding the term 'bureaucracy' in describing this type of coordination.

While wealth and purchasing power are *rationed* for subordinates without bargaining, superiors have priority in accessing rationed resources. Commons speaks of 'rationing transactions' to describe the way wealth and purchasing power are allocated in fascist or Communist dictatorships: "Modern totalitarianism is rationing transactions imposed by those in power, the 'superiors', upon those deprived of power, the 'inferiors'" (Commons, 1970, p. 55).

The term *rationing* is sufficiently clear to echo the logic of war and a militarized economy where superior represents collective sovereignty, and all others are atomized individuals who must obey the command without bargaining. Resources are appropriated by having an administrative priority over others in accessing rationed resources. In other words, Kornaïan dichotomy between 'soft budget constraints' and 'hard budget constraints' (Kornai, 1979, 1980, 1998) might be reconsidered as a rule of appropriation under authoritative coordination. Superiors have a 'soft budget constraint' since they are released from rationing constraints, while inferiors are subject to rationing or a 'hard budget constraint'. The appropriation under authoritative coordination is not necessarily monetary. In fact, money has a semi-passive role under the Soviet-type system. Command substitutes prices in allocating resources. Administrative prices for rationed resources are not market prices. They often reflect arbitrary decisions by

---

[9] Knight (1947) and Arrow (1951/2012) also employed "authority" as an alternative mechanism of coordination to market. See also Sect. 2–10 for other typologies.

superiors and repressed inflation. As von Mises (1946) aptly noticed, bureaucracy replaces the regulatory force of money.

Superiors can fire or 'execute' inferiors, but inferiors cannot exit without heavily risking their lives. Authoritative coordination is a *non-exit* social arrangement. Moreover, bargaining or voicing dissatisfaction is also very costly. The only options are either unconditional obedience (silence) or scream. The rigidity of this type of coordination is related to the lack of corrective and transformative mechanisms. This second type of authoritative coordination is *unlimited* since bargaining is not possible. Table 2.3 illustrates two different types of authoritative coordination.

The typical form of authoritative coordination is the *unlimited* form notably what is practiced in the army, war economies, and the authoritarian states. The Soviet-type regime is a salient illustration. Historically speaking, such a politico-economic regime appeared in consequence of the last century's two world wars, in which whole societies were mobilized to serve the state (Vahabi et al. 2020). War socialism was the basis of what later transformed into Soviet-type economies, essentially *total mobilization of society's resources during peacetime*. As Lange (1958, p. 3) suggested, "I think that, essentially, it [socialism] can be described as a *sui-generis* war economy. Such methods of war economy are not peculiar to socialism because they are also used in capitalist countries in war time. They were developed in the first and second World War. In capitalist countries similar methods were used during the war, namely, concentration of

Table 2.3 Two different types of authoritative coordination

Type of authoritative coordination	Form of social integration	Type of appropriation	Form of appropriation	Corrective mechanism	Example
Limited authoritative coordination	Vertical linkage with possible collective bargaining	Administrative rationing based on command	Non-price allocation	Exit and voice	Factory, modern corporations
Unlimited authoritative coordination	Vertical linkage without bargaining	Administrative rationing based on command	Non-price allocation with limited monetarization	Loyalty or scream	The army, war economy

Source: The author

all resources on one basic purpose, which was the production of war material."

The shortage economy describes the production relationships within a war economy or what Rudolf Bahro (1978) called "non capitalist path to an industrial society" under the Soviet-type economies. Similar to market coordination, authoritative coordination cannot be grasped in abstraction from a specific economic system. It is the preponderant coordination mechanism under the classical socialist system.

2.6 COOPERATIVE COORDINATION

Mutual aid among neighbors and colleagues, comradeship, solidarity, sense of community, and priority rights for emergency public services such as ambulances and firefighters are illustrations of cooperative coordination.

Like market coordination, social integration in cooperative coordination is not based on vertical linkages but on lateral *horizontal linkages* among parallel collective units (such as tribes or a confederation of tribes). The social order originated from this kind of coordination precedes the emergence of the state and state rules. Customary and modern forms of cooperative coordination should be distinguished.

Cooperative coordination in the past was structured on what the great Arab historian of the fourteenth century, Ibn Khaldun, named the bonds of *Assabiya* that literally mean 'party spirit' (see Issawi, 1950). This term refers to tribal pride and partiality based on family and blood ties. The importance of tribal and clan relationships indicates the primacy of closed parallel social units such as kinship groups. The modern form of cooperation is not confined to closed family or tribal ties. It is based on universal human rights and solidarity among all working classes to create their self-organized social order at a world scale.

Cooperative coordination is governed by informal customary rules, traditions, social norms, and conventions based on *reciprocity* (Polanyi, 1944, 1957/1968). Polanyi's use of the term reciprocity relates to an overarching social pattern. In that, it differs from modern usage that refers to bilateral interaction. Reciprocity in the past entails a relation based on gift for gift between two parties that alternatively assumes the role of a donor and a recipient (Mauss, 1967). However, a donor does not expect to be a recipient of gift in return. In other words, it is not akin to a market exchange in future contracts. Moreover, reciprocity entails unilateral donations without any counterpart. Polanyi (1944) and Leeson and Stringham (2007) provide examples of archaic stateless societies based on 'reciprocity' or primitive communism. There also existed a pure destructive reciprocity called Potlatch that was simultaneously the gift and the opposite of the principle of reciprocity. The ultimate goal of Potlatch was to offer a gift that cannot be reciprocated (Bataille, 1967), for example by decapitating one's own slaves or burning entire villages or cities (Vahabi, 2011b, pp. 82–85).

The modern meaning of cooperative coordination maintains reciprocity, but its focus is on communal ownership independent (if not opposed to) of the state. An Israeli Kibbutz represents an organization based on cooperative coordination. Working classes' productive, consumption, and credit cooperatives provide a few examples of modern cooperative coordination. Citizens' welfare as opposed to welfare state is another salient illustration explored in Vahabi et al. (2020). While the welfare state is closely related to total warfare, social welfare is not. Fraternal social welfare organizations based on cooperative coordination in the USA predate the New Deal and the rise of welfare state. Similarly, the French welfare system was born as *citizen* welfare and not as *state* welfare. In fact, welfare programs were initiated in 1871 during the Paris Commune by workers under the name of *la sociale* and were recreated as self-managed citizen groups in 1945 before being displaced by government welfare programs (Vahabi et al., 2020).

Voluntary cooperatives appeared, enjoying more or less real self-government during revolutionary periods like Paris Commune in 1871, Soviets in Russia in 1905 and 1917, Worker's cooperatives in Spain during the civil war (Bookchin, 1977), and many other examples. This, however, proved to be temporary. In Soviet-type economies, rural and urban cooperatives were transformed into state-owned firms through forced collectivization. Cooperative coordination exemplifies anarchy and not mayhem or chaos, that is, a society without a state, but not one without rules (Bush & Mayer, 1974; Hirshleifer, 1995).[10]

Cooperative coordination provides collective or communal appropriation of resources. Contrary to market coordination, economic processes are not autonomous of social relationships. Social embeddedness of economic relationships is enhanced under cooperative coordination. The

---

[10] A recent model of stateless society based on entrepreneurial communities has been developed by Spencer Heath MacCallum (2003) and Duke Calvin (2021).

equity principle favors distribution on the basis of social needs among less privileged groups. While the ownership belongs to the community, the *ususfructus* rights can be granted to specific economic units on a contractual basis for a definite period. In principle, the form of appropriation is not monetary and monetary prices do not play a regulatory role in allocating resources. However, monetary appropriation is not totally excluded.

Since full employment is a fundamental objective, 'exit' as a corrective mechanism is not common. Similarly, the role of 'voice' and the emergence of proposals and criticisms from below is not a corrective mechanism in cooperative coordination but a sign of active participation of cooperative members in self-management. Table 2.4 provides two different types of cooperative coordination.

Customary cooperative coordination was a *closed* cooperation limited to blood and family relationships. There was no exit. Its members lacked individual identity and rights, but they belonged to a social unit and could take advantage of social care based on reciprocity. Moreover, punishment and sanctions were generally collective rather than based on individuals. The economic processes were socially embedded.

The rise of capitalist relationships disintegrated such closed units and enhanced individual universal rights. Modern cooperation is a product of capitalist development and an alternative to social disembeddedness. They

Table 2.4 Two different types of cooperative coordination

Type of cooperative coordination	Form of social integration	Type of appropriation	Form of appropriation	Corrective mechanism	Example
Customary	*Assabiya* (family and blood ties)	Communal based on reciprocity (gift vs. gift)	Non-monetary based on custom and tradition	Voice as a working rule	Tribal societies
Modern	Voluntary cooperation based on individual rights and non-state rules	Communal based on reciprocity and self-management	Non-monetary	Voice as a working rule	Workers' cooperatives, citizen's welfare (the French *la sociale*)

Source: The author

are based on *open and voluntary cooperation* among working classes. The French self-managed citizens' welfare during the Paris Commune in 1871 (known as *la sociale*) and in 1945 exemplified this modern type of social care (Vahabi et al. 2020). This type of cooperation builds upon an alternative order that can be named anarchy since it replaces state rules by self-managed direct democracy of associated cooperatives at municipal or at a confederation level.

While customary cooperation was supported by primitive communal production, the modern type cannot develop without self-managed communal property. Their emergence during the revolutionary periods is often related to dual powers, but their transitory nature and subsequent withering away reflect the absence of condition for communal production.

2.7   DESTRUCTIVE COORDINATION

Contrary to the three previous modes of coordination, destructive coordination is almost entirely neglected in the economic literature with only one exception.[11] Janos Kornai (1984) once referred to this type of coordination under the title of 'aggressive coordination'.

The main idea behind destructive coordination is that destructive or conflictual power is not only a source of disorder and chaos, but it may also generate order and social integration. To illustrate this point, we need to refer to an everyday fact of life. We have all encountered people in our everyday life and in our profession who are not particularly performant in what they do, but they can be a pain in the neck if we do not come to terms with them. These people have special ability to bother others and if they are not totally incompetent in their profession to be discredited right away, they can impose themselves on collectives since most people try not to enter into a conflictual relationship with them. In a sense, they are accepted among their coworkers because people often wish to shun conflicts, disputes, and various types of annoyance. *Social integration through coercion* is the gist of destructive coordination. I first introduced this type of coordination in Vahabi (2009): it is social coordination through

---

[11] At an empirical level, there are a few studies on destructive coordination. For example, destructive coordination has been examined in descriptions of social organization among French ragpickers (Lupton, 2011), in ethnic minorities in France (El Karouni 2012), and in the economic history of Ivory Coast since colonialism (Dago, 2012).

intimidation, threat, and the use of non-institutionalized coercive means to appropriate goods, assets, and rights of others.

According to Kornai, 'aggressive coordination' is characterized by three specific features: "(a) There exists a vertical relationship between a super-ordinated and one or several subordinated individual(s) or organizations(s)...(b) The motivation is established by force on part of the superordinated towards the subordinated in order to achieve the desired transformation or transaction. This is a willful force-not acknowledged by law and morality...(c) The transaction may be either monetarized or not...For this reason it is mostly not lasting but of occasional nature" (1984, p. 308).

Kornai identified a major distinction between a 'bureaucratic coordination' and an 'aggressive coordination', namely a *non-institutionalized* coercion in the latter. From this observation, he deduced that 'aggressive coordination' is occasional and not lasting. In fact, Kornai is mistaken in depicting this type of coordination as 'occasional'. The willful unsup-ported force by law is not necessarily non-institutionalized and occasional. Such kind of force might derive from 'parallel institutions' (Paxton, 1998, 2004; Vahabi, 2010) or a 'state within a state' (Albats, 1994; Benigo, 2012). By parallel institutions, I do not mean, formal and informal institu-tions, but formal state and extra-legal sovereign power. The latter is not necessarily informal, it may be formal, but it functions beyond the law, rules, and regulations. More exactly, parallel institutions are not those that are informal but those that operate outside the structures of a formal state. In this case, the parallel institutions described are not organized by formal state but by a sovereign power that acts extra-legally. Acting extra-legally does not mean to be 'illegal'. Quite the contrary, these parallel institutions symbolize the 'law in action'; they are law in their arbitrariness. Whatever they decide is the law, in the sense that whatever they say restrain others and are assumed to be binding for others but not for them. They even decide whom should be excepted and whom should be subject to the rules.

Another concept which is particularly used in the case of Turkey is 'deep state' (Filkins, 2012). It pertains to a presumed secret network of military officers and their civilian allies trying to preserve the secular order based on the ideas of Mustafa Kemal Atatürk from 1923. The concept is also applied to Pakistan and Egypt. The problem with this concept is that the identification of 'deep state' is not easy. I will not use this concept in conjunction with parallel institutions in Iran because the sovereign institu-tions that are not part of formal state are clearly identifiable. But as 'revolutionary and Islamic' institutions under the purview of the Supreme Leader, they act extra-legally. In this sense they are exogenous to the formal state but endogenous to extra-legal sovereign power.

Parallel institutions are not limited to relationships between the formal state and extra-legal sovereign power. It also pertains to situations in which the formal state's failure to act as an external enforcer, creates a room for informal parallel rules that replace the state's authority and are interiorized by private agents.

Contrary to Kornai's first condition, a destructive coordination is not just a vertical relationship between a superior and an inferior. Parallel institutions entail double parallel 'hierarchical' structures belonging to 'normative' and 'prerogative' states. A caveat is to nuance the use of 'hierarchy' in the context of parallel institutions.

Parallel institutions imply constant violation of law and order in the name of some higher value such as 'revolutionary ideal', 'Islamic values', etc. while repressing all other political forces in the name of law and order. To put it differently, the hard core of power under parallel institutions does not abide to law; it constantly resorts to extra-legal means such as coups, hostage taking, and holdups to promote its interests. But at the same time, it mobilizes law particularly a 'state of emergency' to control, repress, and constrain any other political force (see Piryaei, 2018). An emblematic figure is the Islamic Republic of Iran that relies on the concept of 'Expediency' (*maslahat nezam*). According to Khomeini, the founder of the Islamic Republic of Iran, the existence of the Islamic state was so crucial for the survival of Islam that if the 'expediencies' of ruling (*maslahat nezam*) required contravention of Islamic norms, the latter had to be suspended on Islamic grounds (Schirazi, 1997; Fujinaga, 2018).

Formal hierarchical relationships between an inferior and a superior are not respected in this type of coordination with multiple centers of power who consider themselves beyond the law. The existence of parallel institutions contradicts the state of law and undermines any established order. In such an organization, members are loyal only to the 'leaders' (Fuhrer, Imam, the Supreme Leader) who is above the law. Order supported by anarchy, or an *ordered anarchy* prevails under parallel institutions. In a sense, supporters of parallel institutions hate formal hierarchy and bureaucracy. They act as 'anti-establishment' and behave as 'revolutionaries'.

Paramilitary organizations in Fascist Italy with the 'Black Shirts' and Nazi's Germany with the 'SA', the Guardians of Revolution (Sepah) and the paramilitary forces of Basiji under the Islamic Republic of Iran are a few examples of such parallel institutions. For Paxton, the American historian and political scientist, parallel institutions were one of the major characteristics of fascism.[12] The concept describes a collection of institutions that are state-like in their organization but are not officially part of the 'normative state'. This is different from what Dunmore (1980) called 'parallel institutions' pertaining to multiple levels of decision-making within the same state, for example the difference between central government policy-making in ex-Soviet Union and the industrial ministries as executants of that policy during 1945–1953. According to Paxton (2004), parallel institutions entertain a rather complementary and not contradictory relationship.[13] This should be distinguished from another concept namely 'parallel power'.

The latter is coined by Bookchin (1991), the American anarchist, who described a dual power[14] structure being composed of the municipal confederations based on a bottom-up organic institutions of popular power and the nation state. For Bookchin, the two sources of power are diametrically opposed to each other. Although 'parallel institutions' are not radically opposed, they entertain contradictory relationships as well. The decisions taken by one hierarchy (normative state) are often violated by the second (prerogative state). In this sense, 'parallel institutions' are close to what is named the 'state within a state'. Initially, this concept depicted constant interferences of the ecclesiastical hierarchy in the process of decision-making by the formal state. However, the term was also used by

---

[12] Paxton (1998, pp. 19–20) states: "The Vichy regime was certainly not fascist at the outset, *for it had neither a single party nor parallel institutions*. As it became transformed into a police state under the pressures of war, however, parallel institutions appeared: the *Milice* or supplementary police, the 'special sections' in the judiciary, the Police for Jewish Affairs" (emphasis is added).

[13] The "parallel state" concept entered Turkish political jargon in late 2013. Turkey's former Prime Minister Recep Tayyip Erdoğan has employed the term to accuse Fethullah Gulen's followers (occupying senior bureaucratic and judicial positions) of fomenting a coup to topple down the 'legitimate' government. This is not necessarily what is meant by parallel state in Paxton (2004).

[14] Lenin (1917/1964, p. 38) pioneered the concept of 'dual power' referring to a particular situation in April 1917 when the Provisional Government existed alongside another government "so far weak and incipient, but undoubtedly a government that actually exists and is growing—the Soviets of Workers' and Soldiers' Deputies." Trotsky (1932, Vol 1, Chap. 11) substantiated the dual power in 1917, and emphasized that the two power could not be reconciled: "The two-power régime arises only out of irreconcilable class conflicts—is possible, therefore, only in a revolutionary epoch, and constitutes one of its fundamental elements."

Albats (1994) to stress the role of Soviet secret police. According to her, most KGB leaders, including Lavrenty Beria, Yuri Andoropov, and Wladimir Kryuchkov competed for power with the Communist party and manipulated Communist leaders. Benigo applies the same concept to describe the policy of Iraqi Kurds to build a state within a state.

What is the appropriation regime under parallel institutions? The great demarcation between sovereignty and property cannot be maintained under parallel institutions. The extra-legal force of the prerogative state is contradictory with 'sanctity of private property' resulting in indeterminate arbitrary property rights. A *confiscatory regime* is in order under destructive coordination. Those who are leaders or close to the prerogative state are privileged groups in appropriating assets while others have only conditional rights and limited security to possess resources. Acquisition is predatory by its nature under destructive coordination. This point has been captured in Pareto's classification of two types of activities: "The efforts of men are utilized in two different ways: they are directed to the *production or transformation* of economic goods, or else to the *appropriation* of goods produced by others" (Pareto, 1927/1971, p. 341). Appropriative activity includes all the different types of predatory methods, such as expropriation, confiscation, piracy, grabbing, and so forth.[15] Destructive coordination is consistent with political capitalism as an economic system since it promotes profit-making through non-market mechanisms.

Although transactions may be monetarized under destructive coordination, the predatory appropriation of resources depends more on access to coercive power than on exchange and monetary acquisition.

Finally, political and economic crisis is the normal state of destructive coordination. In fact, the emergence of parallel institutions is the outcome of a critical situation in which other coordination mechanisms such as market and authority fail to insure their mediating role. A self-reproducing critical order (or an ordered anarchy) stems from destructive coordination in which internal and external conflictual relationships are institutionalized. A destructive coordination is born in crisis, lives in crisis, and ends in crisis. 'Permanent revolution' involving repeated tentative coups against normative state by prerogative state is the normal state of destructive

---

[15] The same distinction had been suggested long time ago by Plato (2013. P. 27) in *Sophist*: "Acquisition may be effected either by *exchange* or by *conquest*: in the latter case, either by force or craft. Conquest by craft is called hunting."

coordination. In a sense, scream rather than exit and voice is the rule. Different rival groups and oligarchs are both enemies and partners.

A destructive coordination may also arise out of civil wars. The literature on economics of conflict has explored the situations in which conflict constitutes an *institution in itself*. While David Keen has never employed the concept of destructive coordination, he extensively contributed to our knowledge of such type of coordination by unraveling the puzzle of situations 'when waging wars is more important than winning them' (Keen, 2012). War enemies as economic beneficiaries of the war might be implicit partners. Keen's investigation on civil wars in different historical episodes in Sierra Leone, Sudan, Nigeria, Uganda, the Democratic Republic of the Congo, Philippines, Indonesia, and even Vietnam and today's Afghanistan furnish cases of 'useful enemies and useless allies'. Demystifying the alliance between Revolutionary United Front (RUF) rebels and government forces to form a military junta in Sierra Leone in the May 1997 coup, Keen (2012, pp. 4, 12–21) highlights the background of an enduring covert cooperation between soldier-rebel (or 'sobel') to exploit diamonds, raping women, looting, and *intentionally* victimizing civilians. While Clausewitz considered war as a continuation of politics in another form, the 'sobel' figure lends credence to the idea that war is a continuation of economy in another form. Destructive coordination is the economic rationale of warfare activities.

I provide two short examples to illustrate what I mean by *predatory* nature of brutal acquisition in destructive coordination.[16] The two examples are about (1) land; (2) ragpicking.

How is the land appropriation coordinated under destructive coordination? The land is grabbed from the earlier owners or users. Enclosures during the 'primitive accumulation of capital' in England (Marx, 1867/1978, Chap. 26), forced collectivization in Russia and other Eastern European countries (Iordachi & Bauerkàmper, 2014), and colonialization of North America through coercive acquisitions of the Native American's land (Vahabi, 2016) are a few cases of *land grabbing*.

Since land grabbing leads to a radical re-arrangement of ownership and rights, many authors have treated it as a form of *land reform* (Bhattacharya,

---

[16] Chapter 3 will provide other illustrations to compare the four basic forms of coordination.

Mitra, and Ulubaşoğlu 2019[17]). But land reform should not be lumped together with land grabbing. One example of land reform is Homestead Act in the USA on May 20, 1862, that cannot be conflated with forced acquisition of Native American's land. Another case of land reform is a *peasant revolution* such as France during 1790–1792: using violence to destroy feudalism in the countryside by expropriating aristocratic land-lords and distributing their land without indemnification among peasants (Markoff, 2006; Plack, 2013). While the use of violence is common to both peasant revolutions and enclosures, they do not share the same ratio-nale. The difference between them resides in the fact that the former leads to a separation of property and sovereignty whereas the latter results in a fusion of property and sovereignty.

As Tyrou and Vahabi (2021) have suggested, *land grabbing* is the use of coercive means to appropriate land in the interests of those who have concentrated political or economic power *leading to a fusion of sovereignty and property*. By contrast, *land reform* is the appropriation of land in the interests of those who do not have concentrated economic or political power *leading to a separation of property from sovereignty*.

This theoretical distinction might be supported by empirical evidence provided by Bhattacharya et al. (2019). The authors distinguish between 'pro-poor' reforms and 'non-pro-poor' (elite) reforms[18] (ibid, pp. 53, 57, 58, 59). The non-pro-poor 'reforms' are what we call land grabbing since they enhance the fusion of political and economic power by the elite. Land reforms are then limited to pro-poor reforms that weaken the elite and strengthen the demarcation between property and sovereignty. The authors construct a unique and extensive annual dataset that codifies "372 major land reform enactments across 165 countries during a period of more than a century, 1900–2010. We also identify that 140 of the 372 land reforms were pro-poor given the stated objective of the law" (Ibid, p. 65).

Reconsidering the authors' distinction in terms of land grabbing and land reform, 232 cases can be categorized as land grabbing and 140 cases

---

[17] While the authors do not discuss enclosures and colonialism, they consider forced col-lectivization in Russia and other East European Communist regimes as 'land reform'.

[18] The main distinction is not between 'pro-poor' or 'non-pro-poor' but rather the replace-ment of 'land rent' by 'profit'. Land reforms often resulted in the betterment of middle or well-to-do peasants rather than poor peasants. However, favored layers of peasants enhanced profit-making rather than land rent. In other words, the difference is between the use of property title on land to gain land rent or to invest on land to derive profit from land.

as land reforms. The predatory nature of land grabbing is clearly manifested in this example.

The second example is nicely illustrated by Lupton (2011, Chap. 3) on ragpicking. Until 1960, ragmen formed an independent society in France, a state within a state, out of the boundaries and jurisdictions of the state. They would pick rags (that would be initially used to produce paper), bones (for the production of glue), metal scraps in the streets and sold these secondary materials to earn a living. Their society was based on destructive coordination as they would fight between themselves over the territory that was the very source of their subsistence. In France, women would take the lead, and rooms in cafés were dedicated to these brawls among women (hence the French expression "se battre comme des chiffonières").

Their society was coded, and based on reciprocity and solidarity. When women would prepare pancakes, there was always enough for all the ragpickers' children. The state had never been able to register this population, living in the outskirts of law and order. Ragpickers would intentionally never marry so as not to be administratively framed. The state was also intrigued by this society living without any governmental assistance. The state realized this came from the precious waste they picked and sold. Waste was a goldmine that had to be conquered. Several restrictions were put into place to register ragmen to no avail. It was only in 1960 that a French law prohibited ragpicking. Table 2.5 provides the specific features of destructive coordination.

Table 2.5 Destructive coordination

Coordination type	Form of social integration	Type of appropriation	Form of appropriation	Corrective mechanism	Example
Destructive coordination	Ordered anarchy with parallel institutions, or state within a state	Confiscatory regime	Non-monetary with the primacy of coercion and monetary	Institutionalization of conflict and scream	Primitive accumulation of capital in England, religious and military foundations in Iran since 1979

Source: The author

The dominance of market, authoritative, cooperative, or destructive coordination is linked to specific economic systems. As noted earlier, market coordination is preponderant in market capitalism, while authoritative coordination is dominant in the classical socialist system. Cooperative coordination was dominant in tribal societies, the Israeli Kibbutz, and the French citizen welfare. However, we have not yet created an economic system principally coordinated by modern cooperative coordination. This may be named modern Communist anarchy. Destructive coordination might prevail in political capitalism but is not limited to this economic system. The fusion of sovereignty and property under destructive coordination contradicts the legal foundations of market capitalism. However, it can impede or strengthen capitalist mode of production in practice. Table 2.6 summarizes the relationship between economic systems and dominant forms of coordination.

The difference between market and political capitalism will be explored in Chap. 4. Coordination mechanisms mediate between fundamental institutions and economic processes. Hence, we need to clarify the linkages among different coordination mechanism and different forms of property.

In my approach, there is a direct relationship between forms of appropriation and the full control over the asset's services. By full control of assets, I refer to the way discretionary power regarding property rights (*ususfructus* and *abusus*) is distributed to specific agents such as the state, parallel institutions, private sector, self-managed communal entities, etc. In this context, the property rights are defined in *distribution* sphere. Accordingly, private property is different from the state property since the property rights are allocated to the state and not citizens. Modes of coordination constitute different forms of appropriation in *distribution* sphere.

Appropriation is defined in a radically different way within a mode of *production*. According to Karl Marx (1867/1978, Chap. 26), private

Table 2.6 Economic systems and dominant forms of coordination

Dominant form of coordination	Type of economic system
Market coordination	Market capitalism
Authoritative coordination	Classical socialist system
Cooperative coordination	Tribal system
Destructive coordination	Political capitalism

Source: The author

ownership entails the *separation of direct producer from its means of production*. In this sense, there exists a fundamental difference between a free laborer who is separated from his means of production under capitalism and a peasant family who is not separated from its means of production under the subsistence economy. By the same token, a slave is not separated from its means of production, it is rather part of the means of production. Private production prevails in the capitalist mode of production whereas it is absent in the subsistence economy.[19] However, from this *productive* perspective, the state property within a capitalist economy is still private in so far as the separation between direct producers and means of production remains intact.

Table 2.7 provides a comparison between different modes of coordination with regard to different types of appropriation and different forms of property as defined in *distribution* sphere with considerable impact on *production*. Coordination mechanisms play a key role in determining the organization of production.

Although I differ from Kornai in understanding modes of coordination (see section 9 in this chapter), I support his 'affinity thesis' (Kornai, 1990). Borrowing the Weberian concept of affinity, Kornai distinguished between 'weak' and 'strong' linkages among different types of coordination and property forms. Accordingly, market coordination has a *strong linkage* with private property whereas it entertains a *weak linkage* with state

Table 2.7 A comparison among different modes of coordination and property ownerships

Coordination type	Type of appropriation	Form of property
Market	Price appropriation	Private
Authoritative	Administrative rationing	State
Cooperative	Communal	Communal
Destructive	Confiscatory	Indeterminate property rights of parallel institutions

Source: The author

---

[19] This is radically different in the Neoclassical school. For example, Leon Walras (1874/2003) assumes that everybody owns a specific form of capital, being personal capital (labor), immobile capital (land) or just capital (machines and equipment).

property. Similarly, authoritative coordination (or bureaucratic coordination in Kornai's terminology) has a strong linkage with state property and a weak linkage with private property. Table 2.7 can be reinterpreted in terms of affinity thesis. Market price appropriation is closely related to private property. Administrative rationing in authoritative coordination can be directly associated to state property. Cooperative coordination entertains close relationship with communal property.

Destructive coordination is based on a *confiscatory* regime with indeterminate and unclearly defined property rights. Salient illustrations are parastatal military and religious foundations under the auspices of parallel institutions. Examples abound: Bonyad, Setad, Khatam headquarters under the Islamic Republic of Iran (Vahabi, 2010, 2014a, 2014b), Military business (Milbus) in Pakistan (Siddiqa, 2007), and military control of economy in Egypt (Springborg, 2013). Afghanistan, Iraq, Lebanon, Libya, and Syria in the early twenty-first century offer additional examples.

2.8   POLITICAL ECONOMY OF COORDINATION

In studying a mode of coordination, the research task consists of elaborating the *political economy of coordination* assuming an interplay of sovereignty and property. The use of violence and conflictual efforts are as important as productive or exchange activities in appropriating resources. A mode of coordination determines how agents' efforts are distributed among *grabbing* versus *exchange or transformative* activities. This is in dire contrast with the political economy as apprehended by English Classical school and its critics such as Karl Marx.

In fact, English Classical school is based on the separation of property and sovereignty. This point is explicitly acknowledged in Jean Baptiste Say's preface to his *Treatise on Political Economy*:

> For a long time the science of *politics*, in strictness limited to the investigation of the principles which lay the foundation of the social order, was confounded with *political economy, which unfolds the manner in what wealth is produced, distributed, and consumed*...Since the time of Adam Smith, it appears to me, these two very distinct inquiries have been uniformly separated the term *political economy* being now confined to the science which treats of wealth, and that of *politics*, to designate the relations existing between a government and its people, and the relations of different states to each other. (Say 1821/1964, p. XIV-XV)

This passage outlines two principles: (1) a field separation between 'economics' and 'politics' ever since Adam Smith,[20] which precludes the treatment of sovereignty by economics; and (2) the confinement of economics to the study of wealth or property. This separation persisted in both England and America as emphasized by John Commons:

> Economic science, in England and America, began with the separation of property from sovereignty, on the assumption that private property was a natural, primordial right of individuals, independent of sovereignty which might artificially and unjustly interfere with it. But this was a substitution of justification for fact, as is often the method of argument in economics and politics. Property rights were justified on the ground that the object of property was a product of labor, and belonged, therefore, by right to him who had embodied his labor in it by giving to nature's materials the quality of usefulness. Having this natural right of ownership of his own product, he had the right to exchange it for the products of other labors. (1970, p. 41)

It will be shown in Chap. 4 that the demarcation between property and sovereignty was a direct outcome of the great revolutions notably the British Glorious Revolution (1688), the American Independence War (1776), and the French Revolution (1789). The new science of political economy at the time reflected this separation and argued for the primacy of property over sovereignty based on labor theory.

Karl Marx also followed this tradition in his 'contribution to a critique of the political economy'. The sovereignty issue is almost absent in his analysis of the mode of production of capitalist system in *Das Capital*. His research program as presented in *Grundrisse* (Marx, 1973) relegated an analysis of the state and the world market to future studies. In the same vein, Frederick Engels (1877/1966, 1887/1968) argued for the primacy of productive activities over violent appropriation or grabbing of resources

---

[20] I have argued elsewhere (Vahabi, 2012, pp. 153–54) that contrary to Say's view, Smith insists on the *political* dimension of political economy and asserts that the primary object of the political economy of every country "is *to increase the riches* and *power* of that country" (1776/1961, Book II, Chapter V, paragraph 31). However, the difficulty of introducing 'wars and conflicts' in economics may be related to Smith's 'invisible hand': if the hand works, it coordinates agents peacefully and there will be no room for conflicts. The result would be a Nirvana market economy. In line with the Doux-Commerce thesis of Adam Smith and David Hume, a recent economic literature tries to capture how market institutions tend to resolve conflict between strangers (Seabright, 2010; Hirschman, 1977a, 1977b/2013; Cronk & Leech, 2013; Garnett Jr. et al., 2014).

on the assumption that nothing can be appropriated unless it has already been produced.

This is only partially true since natural resources particularly land may be grabbed without preliminary production. Land grabbing (e.g., through colonialism) provides economic inputs for producing outputs. In his polemics with *Eugen Dühring*, Engels (1877/1966) aptly remarked the importance of industrial production of warfare technology. Undoubtedly, the industrialization of destructive means radically changed the techniques of warfare. But Engels did not dwell upon the precedence of *military* revolution to *industrial* revolution (Parker, 1988). As Marx conceded, violence as an economic force preceded capitalist production. Thus, the primacy of production over violent appropriation is not unconditional. Moreover, allocation of resources to fighting activities provokes a resource diversion from production and exchange[21] diminishing the productive potential of those civilizations who had a comparative advantage in grabbing activities.

While the primacy of production to brutal force is not proven in all economic systems, capitalist production is based on free labor and voluntary contractual relationships. Theoretically speaking, market capitalism does not depend on brutal force to produce. The primacy of production to coercive acquisition of resources is justified in this specific mode of production. Thus, the political economy of capitalist production is concentrated on property (wealth production) and not sovereignty. By contrast, *the focus of political economy of coordination is appropriation* or the process of distribution and redistribution involving both property and sovereignty.

2.9   COMPLEMENTARITY AND ARTICULATION PROBLEM

The four modes of coordination provide a complete classification in the sense that each of them is an ideal-typical form, independent from other types. The direct control of many micro, meso, or macro processes is performed by one of the basic forms or some combinations of them. However, the typology introduced in this chapter is not inclusive, nor the only way to classify all other conceivable modes. Other types of coordination might

---

[21] Collier (1999, p. 171) dissects the three economic costs of conflict as diversion, disruption, and destruction. Anderton and Carter (2009, pp. 21–23) discuss and graphically analyze Collier's three categories of the economic costs.

be added.[22] In fact, pre-capitalist societies provide a fertile field of investigation about numerous other types of coordination. In formulating the present typology, I have followed two principal criteria. The first is the logical one in the sense that none of them can be described as a special case of another type. The second is the applicability to the focus of this particular book, namely destructive coordination notably in its recent versions in conjunction with the Islamic rule. The suggested typology will be mobilized to highlight the effective functioning of a type of coordination that is only marginally explored in the economic literature.

A typical or ideal model is of course an abstraction that selects a group of closely related elements from real-world mixed systems. There is no real social system that can be exclusively coordinated by only one of these modes of coordination; rather, any given society may be analyzed in terms of a certain combination of these modes of coordination. Different modes of coordination entertain a *complementary* relationship with each other. For instance, the internal mechanism of a privately owned modern corporation under capitalism blends co-management, authoritative coordination, and monetary reward. Simon (1997) and Schlicht (1998) explain the internal mechanism of capitalist firms as a dovetailing of monetary reward (exchange), authority (command) and custom. Similarly, a cooperative self-managed Israeli Kibbutz undertakes market coordination to procure inputs from its suppliers and sell its outputs to buyers.

The combination of different modes of coordination is organic and not mechanical. It requires an *articulation* among different modes based on the predominance of one main form of coordination. For example, in market capitalism, market, authoritative, cooperative, and destructive coordination coexist with each other, but impersonal markets dominate other modes of coordination. The hierarchy of big modern corporations, the development of an impersonal bureaucracy under a pluralist electoral system, as well as the trade union's bureaucracy are examples of authoritative coordination under capitalism.

Fraternity societies, workers' mutual aids, diverse forms of self-organized cooperative organization, or participative democracy at

---

[22] In addition to his triad (exchange, redistribution, and reciprocity), Polanyi (1944) mentioned 'householding' as another mode of coordination. Kornai (1992, pp. 94–95) added 'family coordination' to his previous list (Kornai, 1984). The problem with the 'family coordination' is the very concept of 'family' since if it refers to blood relationship or kinship, it is already incorporated in Polanyi's 'reciprocity' or cooperative coordination.

municipal or national levels reflect cooperative coordination under capitalism. Destructive coordination on the basis of parallel institutions is also present under market capitalism particularly in cases of collusive relationships between the state and private sector such as Military-Industrial Complex. However, these various modes of coordination constitute a capitalist economic system under the predominance of market coordination. Why can market coordination assume such a predominant role? The answer to this question cannot be found by referring to any natural superiority of market coordination to other types of coordination.

Two factors are key to understand the predominance of any specific mode of coordination: (1) the institutional prerequisites particularly the political and juridical system that support a coordination; (2) the relationship between modes of coordination and modes of production. Considering the predominance of market coordination, the great demarcation between sovereignty and property provided such an institutional prerequisite. Moreover, market exchange could extend to all fields of economic activity when the *productive* system came under market coordination. Thus, the articulation issue hinges upon two major determinants: the institutional prerequisite and productive mode. In Marx's analysis, there exists a hierarchy between the two factors: first the basis (productive mode), then the superstructure (institutional prerequisite). The order is inverted in my analysis of the modes of coordination. To make it extremely simple and hence caricatural to some extent, it may be said that coordination (appropriation) precedes production, but without integrating production into the picture, articulation issue cannot be explained. This explains why major institutional or productive crises can cause disarticulation.

Contrary to other modes of coordination, the dominance of destructive coordination cannot be supported by a specific productive mode. In fact, destructive coordination cannot be dominant without a major crisis in other principal modes of coordination, notably in market, authoritative, and cooperative coordination. In a sense, the predominance of destructive coordination requires a *disarticulation* rather than an *articulation* between different modes of coordination. I will dwell more upon this point in the next chapter.

Finally, one of the most important issues is the dynamics of modes of coordination. The four main modes of coordination evolve through time. They may transform from one form into the other. For example, cooperative coordination (Form 3) may change to a commercial enterprise (Form 1) or an authoritative body (Form 2). In fact, workers' cooperatives experienced both types of transformation. For example, many workers' cooperatives or mutuals in France were conducted under cooperative coordination during 1789–1871. After the termination of Paris Commune in 1871, these cooperatives were transformed either into a state-dependent institution or commercial enterprises (Dreyfus, 2001; Da Siva, 2020). Vahabi et al. (2020) show how the French self-managed citizen welfare (*la sociale*) in 1945 was transformed into a welfare state through a three-stage reform process manifesting itself in 1946, 1967, and 1996. This was a transition from cooperative coordination (Form 3) to an authoritative coordination (Form 2).

As mentioned above, Lupton (2011, Chap. 3) describes social organization among French ragpickers before the interdiction of ragpicking by the state in 1960 as a combination of 'destructive coordination' (Form 4) and 'reciprocity' (Form 3). However, it transformed into 'authoritative coordination' (Form 2) since 1960 when the state took the control of ragpicking. Not so long after, private companies took over household waste management (now known as the behemoths Veolia and Suez). This was a transition from Form 2 to market coordination (Form 1).

Another example that casts light on the transformation of 'destructive coordination' (Form 4) to 'authoritative coordination' (Form 2) is the ex-Soviet Union during the thirties. Forced collectivization and the Great Purge in the Russian Communist party under Stalin in the thirties (1936–1938) developed parallel institutions (the Party and the security agency NKVD) and a confiscatory regime. Destructive coordination (Form 4) was the dominant form in this period, but it changed to 'authoritative coordination' (Form 2) in the aftermath of the Second World War.

There is a paucity of historical research regarding the transformation of modes of coordination and the type of conflict and bargaining they have generated. State predation and conflictual activities over appropriation of resources cannot be fully documented without such investigation. The political economy of coordination is a multidisciplinary field that requires the analysis of sovereignty and property together.

2.10   OTHER RELATED CLASSIFICATIONS

Modes of coordination include not only *allocation* of natural resources among human beings but also *social relationships* among people. However, the Walrasian ideal-type impersonal market assumes away the problem of social coordination among decentralized agents. *Crieur de prix* is a fictive agent who resolves the problem of coordination by centralizing all the information about buying and selling intentions of decentralized agents. Individual agents acquire perfect knowledge about the whole economic situation, thanks to this fictive agent and avoid any transaction out of equilibrium since they proceed to exchange only when *crieur de prix* announces the equilibrium prices for all markets. The *tatonnement process* describes the way the equilibrium prices are discovered. Market prices are not the basis of transactions. Transactions are only possible when equilibrium prices are achieved. Market is supposed to be institutionally neutral; it is only an allocative mechanism of scarce resources. Mainstream economics reasons in terms of *allocation* rather than *coordination*. But if this fictive centralizing agent disappears, how are decentralized transactions be coordinated?

The way market transactions are organized among decentralized agents with changing local, dispersed, fragmented, and tacit knowledge is an issue that has been brought back to economics by the Austrian economists. We are indebted to von Hayek (1937, 2014) in grasping the importance of *division of knowledge* reflected in real monetary market prices and not necessarily equilibrium prices. Assuming decentralized partial and imperfect knowledge about the changing conditions of market economy raises the coordination problem among decentralized agents who should decide under uncertainty regarding the way other agents behave and decide.

Hayek's contribution to our discipline is now acknowledged even by the advocates of Walrasian general equilibrium who distinguish between perfect and imperfect 'information'. However, the term used by Hayek is not 'information' but 'knowledge'. The difference between the two is not minor if we look into *Sensory Order* (Hayek 1952/ 2017). Hayek insists on the need to distinguish between a physical and a phenomenal world, between the external world of objective facts and the inner world of our subjective experience. The physical world provides only 'stimuli' for nervous system (the 'neural order'), and the latter gives rise to the sensations of our subjective experience. Our perception or our subjective understanding of 'data' often deviates from 'objective data'. In this perspective, there is no objective 'information', and knowledge acquisition is a never-ending process.

In analyzing this knowledge problem, Hayek (1937/2014) differentiates between two aspects of knowledge acquisition: (1) how *individuals* acquire knowledge in a changing world; (2) how a group of agents can coordinate with their imperfect and partial knowledge? This is the *social* dimension of the knowledge problem. According to Hayek, the second aspect is the crux of economics as a social science whereas an inquiry regarding the acquisition of knowledge by *individuals* is a task of cognitive psychology and not any other field of social sciences including economics.

However, the formal analysis in economics did not follow Hayek with regard to the empirical foundations of individual cognitive capacities. It adopted a priori assumptions at individual level regarding rationality and maximizing behavior. Hayek's *knowledge* problem was translated into *information* problem.[23] Imperfect or asymmetry of information is assumed to be the sources of market failures. Market coordination does not fail if perfect information or rational expectations are possible. But there is no need for 'coordination' if information is perfect and all the agents are supposed to share the correct representation of the external world.

In addition to *allocation* mechanism, mainstream economics has employed the term 'adjustment mechanism' to describe the dynamics of resource allocation when the system is out of equilibrium for any external shock. *Adjustment* depends on the type of signals required to restore equilibrium. Two types of signals are price or non-price (quantity) signals that constitute the principal sources of information. Allocation or adjustment mechanisms do not address social coordination.

The issue of social coordination was seriously addressed by Karl Polanyi (1944). He conceived the economy as an 'instituted process'. Accordingly, the economic order could stem from specific institutional arrangements. He distinguished three forms or 'patterns of transactions or social integration'. In his terminology, coordination or social integration was a pattern of 'transaction'. These three principal forms of transactions were 'exchange, redistribution, and reciprocity' (1944, 1957/1968). The first one refers to social organization through exchange and markets. This form of transaction requires a specific institution, namely, a system of price-making markets. The second refers to a social organization in which all resources are directed to a center and then redistributed to all members of the

---

[23] Arrow characterized information as an intangible commodity with three specific features: (1) indivisibility, (2) uncertainty, and (3) inappropriability. He analyzed communication as an issue of transmission between a sender and a receiver based upon signals. Price and non-price signals allocate the information as a specific commodity in market or other alternative allocation mechanisms (for a survey of Arrow's theory of information, see Vahabi, 1997).

society. It requires some kind of religious or political center, such as the state, that appropriates resources and then redistributes them. The third refers to social organization through 'reciprocity'. It requires parallel coexisting social units such as tribes with kinship relationships.

Polanyi's triad corresponds to what I described as market, authoritative and cooperative coordination. I am inspired by his classification and his understanding of 'transaction' since it is not reduced to market transactions and includes different forms of distribution and redistribution. But unfortunately, he does not scrutinize the *appropriative* dimension of transactions depending on the bargaining and conflictual power among different social groups. Paradoxically, while Polanyi's historical research supports extensively the role of coercion in social integration (Polanyi, 1965), his concept of 'transaction' precludes conflicts and destructive coordination.

Polanyi's 'transaction' forms also inspired North (1977). However, he continued to understand market as an 'allocation system' and reduced all 'other allocation systems in history' to market allocation. In fact, North distinguished voluntary market transactions from involuntary transactions (like feudalism or slavery) throughout history. But he extended market logic to all involuntary transactions in which agents bargain as if they were in a voluntary transaction. North (1981, p. 202) wrote: "The relationship that concerns Meckling and Jensen is a voluntary one; it should be noted that in my framework it may be voluntary or involuntary (such as is slavery)." North's reference to slavery was built on Barzel's (1977) classic article on the topic.[24]

Barzel (1977) had tried to show that slavery evolved as a contractual relationship between a master and slave, arguing that a master will gain by transferring certain rights to a slave in return for more output, within the context of principal-agent schemes for motivation structure. This line of reasoning extends the meanings of 'voluntary exchange' and 'mutual gain from trade' far beyond their usual connotations. For example, from this perspective a robbery can be defined as an 'implicit contract' between victim and robber, in which the robber agrees to save the victim's life in return for a certain amount of money. As I have shown elsewhere (Vahabi, 2011a), this is in line with an extension of Coase Theorem (Coase, 1960) to a "coercive exchange", or what North (1990b) called "Political Coase

---

[24] North (1990a, p. 32) later redefined slavery as an "implicit contract between a master and a slave". To North, slavery exemplified policing agents.

Theorem". This approach supports market reductionism in mainstream economics.[25] The diversity of coordination modes is disregarded in favor of market 'allocation' or 'adjustment' that replaces all other forms of coordination.

A third approach was followed by Kornai in 1992, although he previously had advocated a line of inquiry close to Polanyi in 1984. In other words, we have two Kornai: Kornai (1984) and Kornai (1992). While he was initially inspired by Polanyi's transactional approach (Kornai, 1984), he later redefined 'coordination mechanisms' according to *system paradigm* (Kornai, 1992). By system paradigm, I refer to Ludwig von Bertalanffy's (1950) early works in the field of 'organismic' biology as well as Duffy and Neuberger's work (1976) on economic systems as a process of Decision-Information-Motivation (DIM) structure.

Kornai's references to organismic biology may be traced back to the early seventies (Kornai, 1971a, 1971b) in which he depicted coordination mechanism as the 'nervous system' in 'control' of real economic systems (body). Reconsidering different modes of coordination, Kornai (1992, p. 91) adopted later DIM structure to explain the rationale of coordination in each case: "Each mechanism has its own range of characteristics: who the participants are, what relation there is between them, what communications flow between them to further the coordination, and what motivations encourage the participants to take part in the coordination process."

The first criterion specifies the type of horizontal or vertical relationships that prevail among the agents to determine whether decisions are made hierarchically or not. The second is communications flow or information channels. Finally, the third is the motivation structure that incentivizes agents to coordinate. This is exactly DIM systemic structure. Based upon these three criteria, Kornai (1992, Chap. 6) distinguished five main types of mechanisms: (1) bureaucratic coordination, (2) market coordination, (3) self-governing coordination, (4) ethical coordination, and (5) family coordination.

---

[25] It advocates even more vigorously market reductionism than the modern modelers of Walrasian general equilibrium. For example, Arrow adhered to Knight's typology of different systems of social choice comprising custom, authority, and consensus (1947, pp. 308–310), but focused on consensus. He (1951/2012) subdivided the latter into the two categories of voting and the market. Arrow's impossibility theorem addressed non-market decision-making. However, contrary to North, he never extended voluntary market transactions to involuntary or coercive exchange.

This typology radically diverges from the previous one on several points. In the preceding classification, two mechanisms (number 3 and 5) were missing. Instead, there was an additional one, namely 'aggressive coordination' (Kornai, 1984) that is not included in 1992. But the most important issue is that the underlying criteria for classifying coordination as control mechanism have changed from Kornai, 1984 to Kornai, 1992.

In the recent version, the term 'control process' "underlines the fact that the coordination mechanism controls the activity of those taking part in it" (Kornai, 1992, p. 95). The control is broadly defined without any reference to the relationship between property and sovereignty. Interestingly, Lindblom (1977) also referred to coordination as 'control mechanisms', but he gave the pride of place to the interplay of economics and politics.

It is true that Kornai (1984) did not explicitly speak of politics, but he distinguished 'bureaucratic' from 'aggressive' coordination on the basis of whether the coercion is institutionalized or not. Moreover, Kornai (1984) pigeonholed different forms of coordination according to the type of transaction (monetary or not). In the new typology, the transaction type is entirely dismissed. Coordination in Kornai's systemic approach is not primarily determined by the type of bargaining and conflictual relationships related to the appropriation issue.

2.11   Conclusion

An endogenous theory of social crisis warrants an understanding of the inner dynamic of social order. Two broad approaches have been distinguished in explaining this dynamic: economic and institutional.

The Marxian concept of 'modes of production' provides an economic explanation of social crisis based on productive forces. In this approach, institutional factors play a secondary role. By contrast, in an institutionalist perspective, modes of coordination as mediators between fundamental institutions and economic performance are the key to explain both social order and social crisis. A social crisis arises when coordination mechanisms fail to ensure their mediating role.

In Marxian approach, production is assumed to be determinant in shaping the whole economic system, whereas in an institutionalist approach there exists a reciprocal causation between production and distribution. The latter can be resumed in terms of appropriation relying on multifactor interactions among economic, destructive, and ideological forces. While in the long term, distribution (appropriation forms) decide production, in the very long-term, production or technological change determine distribution. Social crises arise from failure in dominant forms of appropriation to coordinate agents and allocate resources.

Economic systems might be classified at two levels: distribution and production. Coordination mechanism is one of the underlying tenets in defining a typology of different economic systems from an appropriative viewpoint.

A mode of coordination describes a social order with its specific (1) type of appropriation, (2) the interplay between property and sovereignty, and (3) conflictual and cooperative efforts regarding the distribution or redistribution of resources.

I distinguished four main modes of coordination, namely market, authoritative, cooperative, and destructive coordination. While any economic system cannot be reduced to just one form of coordination and is characterized by a constellation of all different coordination mechanisms, there exists a dominant form of coordination allowing the articulation of all forms of coordination. For example, in tribal societies cooperative coordination prevailed. In modern times, market coordination has been preponderant in the capitalist system, whereas authoritative coordination has been dominant in the socialist system.

In a social crisis, none of these coordination mechanisms is dominant. In this sense, crisis is marked by disarticulation among different modes of coordination. Under such circumstances, a particular type of coordination might arise which is specifically adapted to crisis. I called it 'destructive coordination'. While the first three forms of coordination have been extensively identified and discussed in the literature, there is a dearth of analysis regarding the last one since it is often assumed that crisis and order are irreconcilable. Destructive coordination is based on the fusion of sovereignty and property, parallel institutions, and confiscatory regime. From an economic viewpoint, destructive coordination enhances a predatory regime based on profit-making through non-market channels. Political capitalism is an economic system that is compatible with such type of coordination.

The focus of this book is the destructive coordination and its relationships with institutions related to the Islamic rule, and political versus market capitalism. The next chapter will conceptualize this type of coordination before tackling its relationship with political capitalism and Islamic rules.

REFERENCES

Albats, Y. (1994). *The State Within a State, the KGB and Its Hold on Russia-Past, Present and Future*. Farrar, Strauss, Giroux.

Anderton, C. H., & Carter, J. R. (2009). *Principles of Conflict Economics, A Primer for Social Scientists*. Cambridge University Press.

Arrow, K. (1951/2012). *Social Choice and Individual Values*. Yale University Press.

Bahro, R. (1978). *The Alternative in Eastern Europe*. New Left Books/Verso.

Barzel, Y. (1977). An Economic Analysis of Slavery. *Journal of Law and Economics, 20*(1), 87–110.

Bataille, G. (1967). *La part maudite précède de la Notion de dépense*. Les Editions de Minuit.

Benigo, O. (2012). *The Kurds of Iraq: Building a State Within a State*. Lynne Rienner.

Bettelheim, C. (1976). Class Struggles in the USSR: First Period 1917–1923, New York and London: Monthly Review Press.

Bhattacharya, P., Mitra, D., & Ulubaşoğlu, M. (2019). The Political Economy of Land Reform Enactments: New Cross-National Evidence (1900–2010). *Journal of Development Economics, 139*, 50–68.

Bookchin, M. (1977). *The Spanish Anarchists: The Heroic Years, 1868–1936*. Free Life Editions.

Bookchin, M. (1991, October). Libertarian Municipalism: An Overview. *Green Perspectives*, No. 24, Burlington, VT.

Braudel, F. (1977). *Afterthoughts on Material Civilization and Capitalism*. Johns Hopkins University Press.

Braudel, F. (1983). *Civilization and Capitalism 15th–18th Century, vol. 2, The Wheels of Commerce*. Book Club Associates.

Bush, W., & Mayer, L. (1974). Some Implications of Anarchy for the Distribution of Property. *Journal of Economic Theory, 8*, 401–412.

Calvin, D. (2021). *Entrepreneurial Communities: An Alternative to the State*. Book Villages.

Coase, R. (1960, October). The Problem of Social Cost. *The Journal of Law and Economics, III*, 1–44.

Collier, P. (1999). On the Economic Consequences of Civil War. *Oxford Economic Papers, 51*(1), 168–183.

Commons, J. (1924/1995). *Legal Foundations of Capitalism* (With a New Introduction by Jeff Biddle & Warren J. Samuels). Transaction Publishers.

Commons, J. R. (1931). Institutional Economics. *American Economics Review, 21*, 648–657.

Commons, J. (1970). *The Economics of Collective Action*. University of Wisconsin Press.

Cronk, L., & Leech, B. L. (2013). *Meeting at Grand Central: Understanding the Social and Evolutionary Roots of Cooperation.* Princeton.

Da Siva, N. (2020). Mutualité et capitalisme entre 1789 et 1947: de la subversion à l'intégration. *RECMA, 357,* 36–51.

Dago, J. (2012). *L'Investissement Direct Etranger en Côte d'Ivoire, Economie Politique et Changement Institutionnel.* l'Harmattan.

Dana, L., & Wright, R. (2015). Bazaar Economies, Modern Networks and Entrepreneurship. In Wright, R. (ed.), Wiley Encyclopedia of Management, 2015 - Wiley Online Library. https://doi.org/10.1002/9781118785317.weom030005

Dreyfus, M. (2001). *Liberté, Égalité, Mutualité: mutualisme et syndicalisme, 1852-1967.* Éditions de l'Atelier.

Dunmore, T. (1980). *The Stalinist Command System: The Soviet State Apparatus and Economic Policy, 1945-1953.* Macmillan.

El Karouni Ilyess. (2012). "Ethnic Minorities and Integration Process in France and the Netherlands: An Institutionalist Perspective", *American Journal of Economics and Sociology,* 71, p. 151–183.

Engels, F. (1877/1966). *Herr Eugen Dühring's Revolution in Science (Anti-Dühring),* International Publisher.

Engels, F. (1887/1968). *The Role of Force in History, a Study of Bismarck's Policy of Blood and Iron.* International Publisher.

Fanselow, F. (1990). The Bazaar Economy or How Bizarre is the Bazaar Really? *MAN, New Series, 25*(2), 250–265.

Filkins, D. (2012, March 12). The Deep State. *The New Yorker.* Retrieved January 6, 2022.

Frisch, R. (1933). Propagation Problems and Impulse Problems in Dynamic Economics. In *Economic Essays in Honour of Gustav Cassel* (pp. 171–205). George Allen & Unwin.

Fujinaga, A. F. (2018). Islamic Law in Post-Revolutionary Iran. In A. M. Emon & A. Rumee (Eds.), *The Oxford Handbook of Islamic Law.* Oxford University Press.

Garnett, R. F., Jr., Lewis, P., & Ealy, L. T. (Eds.). (2014). *Commerce and Community: Ecologies of Social Cooperation (Economics as Social Theory).* Routledge.

Geertz, C. (1978). The Bazaar Economy: Information and Search in Peasant Marketing. *American Economic Review, 68*(2), 28–32.

Hirschman, A. (1970). *Exit, Voice, and Loyalty.* Cambridge University Press.

Hirschman, A. (1977a). A Generalized Linkage Approach to Development, with Special Reference to Staples. *Economic Development and Cultural Change, 25,* 67–98.

Hirschman, A. O., (1977b/2013). *The Passions and the Interests: Political Arguments for Capitalism before Its Triumph.* Princeton University Press.

Hirshleifer, J. (1995). Anarchy and Its Breakdown. *Journal of Political Economy*, *103*, 25–52.

Iordachi, C., & Bauerkämper, A. (Eds.). (2014). *2014, The Collectivization of Agriculture in Communist East Europe, Comparison and Entanglements*. Central European University Press.

Issawi, C. (1950). *An Arab Philosophy of History; Selections from the Prolegomena of Ibn Khaldun of Tunis (1332–1406)* (Translated and arranged by Issawi). John Murray.

Keen, D. (2012). *Useful Enemies, When Waging Wars Is More Important than Winning Them*. Yale University Press.

Klein, L. (2006). Ragnar Frisch's Conception of the Business Cycle. In S. Strom (Ed.), *Econometrics and Economic Theory in the 20th Century*, Cambridge Collections Online, Cambridge University Press.

Knight, F. (1947). Human Nature and World Democracy. In *Freedom and Reform* (pp. 308–310). Harper and Bros.

Kornai, J. (1971a). *Anti-Equilibrium, On Economic Systems Theory and the Tasks of Research*. American Elsevier Publishing Company, Inc.

Kornai, J. (1971b). Economic Systems Theory and General Equilibrium Theory. *Acta Oeconomica*, *6*(4), 297–317.

Kornai, J. (1979). Resource-Constrained Versus Demand-Constrained Systems. *Econometrica*, *47*(4), 801–819.

Kornai, J. (1980). *Economics of Shortage*. North-Holland.

Kornai, J. (1983). The Health of Nations: Reflections on the Analogy between the Medical Sciences and Economics. *Kyklos*, *36*(2), 191–212.

Kornai, J. (1984). Bureaucratic and Market Coordination. *Osteuropa Wirtschaft*, *29*(4), 306–319. Reprinted in: Kornai Janos (1990). *Vision and Reality, market and state, contradictions and dilemma revisited*. Routledge, pp. 1–19.

Kornai, J. (1990). The Affinity between Ownership Forms and Coordination Mechanisms: The Common Experience of Reform in Socialist Countries. *Journal of Economic Perspectives*, *4*(3), 131–147.

Kornai, J. (1992). *The Socialist System. The political economy of Communism*. Princeton University Press and Oxford University Press.

Kornai, J. (1998). "The place of the soft budget constraint in economic theory," *Journal of Comparative Economics*, Vol. 26, pp. 11–17.

Kornai, J. (2000a). What the Change of System from Socialism to Capitalism does and does not Mean? *The Journal of Economic Perspectives*, *14*(1), 27–42.

Kornai, J. (2000b). *Ten Years After 'The Road to a Free Economy': The Author's Self-Evaluation*. Paper for the World Bank 'Annual Bank Conference on Development Economics-ABCDE', April 18–20, Washington, DC.

Kornai, J. (2010). Innovation and Dynamism: Interaction between Systems and Technical Progress. In G. Roldand (Ed.), *Economies in Transition, Studies in Development Economics and Policy* (pp. 14–56). Palgrave Macmillan.

Lange, O. (1958). The Role of Planning in Socialist Economy. *Indian Economic Review, 4*(2), 1–15.

Leeson, P., & Stringham, E. (2007). Is Government Inevitable? Comment on Holcombe's Analysis. In E. Stringham (Ed.), *Anarchy and the Law, the Political Economy of Choice* (pp. 371–376). Transaction Publishers.

Lenin, V. I. (1917/1964, April). The Dual Power. In *Collected Works* (Vol. 24, pp. 38–41). Progress Publishers.

Lenin, V. I. (1920/1975–1979). "Report on the Work of the Council of People's Commissars" (December 22, 1920). In *Collected Works* (Vol. 36). Progress Publishers.

Lindblom, C. E. (1977). *Politics and Markets: The World's Political Economic Systems*. Basic Books.

Lupton, S. (2011). *Économie des Déchets. Une Approche Institutionnaliste*, Collection "Ouvertures économiques", Bruxelles, De Boeck.

MacCallum, S. H. (2003). The Entrepreneurial Community in Light of Advancing Business Practices and Technologies. In MacCallum, Spencer Heath, D. Klein, & F. Foldvary (Eds.), *The Half-Life of Policy Rationales*. New York University Press. chapter 12.

Mandel, E. (1995). *Long Waves of Capitalist Development: A Marxist Interpretation* (2nd revised ed.). London and New York: Verso.

Markoff, J. (2006). Violence, Emancipation, and Democracy: The Countryside and the French Revolution. In G. Kates (Ed.), *The French Revolution, Recent Debates and New Controversies* (2nd ed., pp. 165–197). Routledge.

Marx, K. (1847/2009). *The Poverty of Philosophy*. Progress Publishers, 1955; Transcribed: by Zodiac for Marx/Engels Internet Archive (marxists.org) 1999; Proofed: and corrected by Matthew Carmody, 2009.

Marx, K. (1857a–8/1964). *Pre-capitalist Economic Formations*. Translated by Jack Cohen, https://www.marxists.org/archive/marx/works/1857/precapitalist/ch01.htm

Marx, K. (1857b/1971). Introduction to a Contribution to the Critique of Political Economy. In *A Contribution to the Critique of Political Economy*, translated from the German by S. W. Ryazanskaya, Appendix I, London: Lawrence & Wishart, pp. 81–111. https://www.marxists.org/archive/marx/works/1859/critique-pol-economy/appx1.htm

Marx, K. (1859/1977). *A Contribution to the Critique of Political Economy*. Progress Publishers. Retrieved from https://www.marxists.org/archive/marx/works/1859/critique-pol-economy/preface.htm.   Accessed July 15, 2019.

Marx, K. (1867/1978). *Capital, a Critique of Political Economy* (Vol. 1), Progress Publishers.

Marx, K. (1973). *Grundrisse*. Vintage Books.

Mauss, M. (1967). *The Gift: Forms and Functions of Exchange in Arabic Societies.* Norton.

Menard, C., Kunneke, R., & Groenewegen, J. (2021). *Network Infrastructures: Aligning Technologies and Institutions.* Cambridge University Press.

North, D. (1977). Markets and Other Allocation Systems in History: The Challenge of Karl Polanyi. *Journal of European Economic History, 6,* 703–716.

North, D. (1981). *Structure and Change in Economic History.* W.W. Norton and Company.

North, D. (1990a). *Institutions, Institutional Change and Economic Performance.* Cambridge University Press.

North, D. (1990b). A Transaction Cost Theory of Politics. *Journal of Theoretical Politics, 2*(4), 355–367.

North, D., Wallis, J., & Weingast, B. (2009). *Violence and Social Orders: A Conceptual Framework for Interpreting Recorded Human History.* Cambridge University Press.

Pareto, V. (1927/1971). *Manual of Political Economy.* A.M. Kelley.

Parker, G. (1988). *The Military Revolution, Military Innovation and the Rise of the West, 1500–1800.* Cambridge University Press.

Paxton, R. (1998). The Five Stages of Fascism. *The Journal of Modern History, 70*(1), 1–23.

Paxton, R. (2004). *The Anatomy of Fascism.* Alfred A. Knopf.

Piryaei, S. (2018, March). *State of Perpetual Emergency: Legally Codified State Violence in Post-Revolutionary Iran and the Contemporary U.S.* PhD Thesis in Comparative Literature, University of California Riverside.

Plack, N. (2013). The Peasantry, Feudalism, and the Environment, 1789–93. In P. McPhee (Ed.), *A Companion to The French Revolution* (pp. 212–227). Wiley Blackwell Ltd.

Plato. (2013). *Sophist* (Benjamin, J., Hazelton, P.A. Trans.). An Electronic Classics Series Publication. http://www2.hn.psu.edu/faculty/jmanis/plato/sophist.pdf

Polanyi, K. (1944). *The Great Transformation.* Farrar and Rinehart.

Polanyi, K. (1957/1968). *Primitive, Archaic and Modern Economies.* Doubleday.

Polanyi, K. (1965). *Trade and Market in the Early Empire; Economies in History and Theory.* Free Press.

Schirazi, A. (1997). *The Constitution of Iran: Politics and the State in the Islamic Republic.* I.B. Tauris.

Schlicht, E. (1998). *On Custom in the Economy.* Clarendon Press.

Schumpeter, J. A. (1939). *Business Cycles: A Theoretical, Historical, and Statistical Analysis of the Capitalist Process.* McGraw–Hill Book Company Inc.

Seabright, P. (2010). *The Company of Strangers: A Natural History of Economic Life,* Revised Version. Princeton University Press.

Siddiqa, A. (2007). *Military Inc. Inside Pakistan's Military Economy.* Pluto Press.

Simon, H. (1951). A Formal Theory of the Employment Relationship. *Econometrica, 19*(3), 293–305.

Simon, H. (1997). Organizations and Markets. In H. Simon (Ed.), *An Empirically Based Microeconomics* (pp. 217–240). Cambridge University Press.

Springborg, R. (2013). Learning from Failure: Egypt. In T. Bruneau & F. C. Matei (Eds.), *The Routledge Handbook of Civil-Military Relations* (pp. 93–109). Routledge.

Tyrou, E., & Vahabi, M. (2021). *A Critical Survey on Land-Grabbing: Land as a Source of Power and Profit*. Manuscript.

Vahabi, M. (1997). A Critical Survey of K.J. Arrow's Theory of Knowledge. *Cahiers d'Economie Politique, 29*, 35–65.

Vahabi, M. (2004). *The Political Economy of Destructive Power*. Edward Elgar.

Vahabi, M. (2009). An Introduction to Destructive Coordination. *American Journal of Economics and Sociology, 68*(2), 353–386.

Vahabi, M. (2010). "Ordres contradictoires et coordination destructive: le malaise iranien" (Contradictory Orders and Destructive Coordination: The Iranian Disease). *Revue Canadienne d'Etudes du Développement (Canadian Journal of Development Studies), 30*(3–4), 503–534.

Vahabi, M. (2011a). Appropriation, Violent Enforcement and Transaction Costs: A Critical Survey. *Public Choice, 147*(1), 227–253.

Vahabi, M. (2011b). Economics of Destructive Power. In D. Braddon & K. Hartley (Eds.), *The Elgar Handbook on the Economics of Conflict* (pp. 79–104). Edward Elgar., Chapter 5.

Vahabi, M. (2012). Political Economy of Conflict - Foreword. *Revue d'Economie Politique, 122*(2), 151–167.

Vahabi, M. (2014a). Soft Budget Constraint Reconsidered. *Bulletin of Economic Research, 66*(1), 1–19.

Vahabi, M. (2014b). "Contrainte budgétaire lâche et le secteur paraétatique" (Soft Budget Constraints and Parastatal Sector). In M. Makinsky (Ed.), *L'économie réelle de l'Iran* (pp. 147–176). L'Harmattan.

Vahabi, M. (2015a). *The Political Economy of Predation: Manhunting and the Economics of Escape*. Cambridge University Press.

Vahabi, M. (2015b, December 22). Jaygah Sepah dar Eqtesad Iran (The Place of Sepah in the Iranian Economy). *Mihan*, No. 6. Retrieved December 11, 2021, from http://mihan.net/1394/10/01/562/ (in Persian).

Vahabi, M. (2016, September). A Positive Theory of the Predatory State. *Public Choice, 168*(3–4), 153–175.

Vahabi, M., Batifoulier, P., & Da Silva, N. (2020). A Theory of Predatory Welfare State and Citizen Welfare: The French Case. *Public Choice, 182*(3–4), 243–271.

Vahabi, M., Philippe, B., & Nicolas, D. S. (2020). The Political Economy of Revolution and Institutional Change: The Elite and Mass Revolutions. *Revue d'Economie Politique, 130*(6), 855–889.

von Hayek, F. (1937, February). Economics and Knowledge. *Economica, New Series, 4*(13), 33–54.

von Hayek, F. (2014). In B. Caldwell (Ed.), *The Collected Works of F.A. Hayek, Vol. 15-The Market and Other Orders*. Chicago University Press.

von Hayek, F. (1952/2017). *The Collected Works of F.A. Hayek*. Vol. 14-The Sensory Order and Other Writings as the Foundation of Theoretical Psychology (V. J. Vanberg, Ed.). University of Chicago Press.

von Mises, L. (1946). *Bureaucracy*. Yale University Press.

Walras, L. (1874/2003). *Elements of Pure Economics or the Theory of Social Wealth* (William Jaffé, Trans.). Routledge.

Weber, M. (1922/1978). *Economy and Society* 1, University of California Press.

Williamson, O. (1985). *The Economic Institutions of Capitalism. Firms, Markets, Relational Contracting*. Free Press.

CHAPTER 3

Conceptualizing Destructive Coordination

3.1 Introduction

The social crisis is often described as anarchy and mayhem representing a rupture in the social order. But crisis might become chronic or sustainable if it transforms into a specific type of order. Under such circumstances, the crisis in order transforms into order in crisis. It may be called 'ordered anarchy' but since that expression has been previously used for depicting a stateless Communist or market society, I coined another expression, namely destructive coordination.

Our purpose in this chapter is to conceptualize the destructive mode of coordination. In a sense, the present chapter is a continuation of the preceding chapter (see Sect. 2.6) by focusing on one of the specific modes of coordination that can prevail only in a critical situation in which other modes of coordination (market, authoritative, and cooperative) are not preponderant.

As previously noted, *it is social coordination through intimidation, threat, and the use of coercive means*[1] to appropriate goods, assets, and

This chapter is the adaptation, and extension of my paper: Mehrdad Vahabi, 2009, "An Introduction to Destructive Coordination," *American Journal of Economics and Sociology*, Vol. 68, No. 2, pp. 354-386.

[1] The movie "On the Waterfront" directed by Kazan nicely illustrates *destructive coordination* in the job market.

rights of others. In this type of coordination, resources and human efforts are allocated to *appropriate* what other people produce. Strictly speaking, non-institutionalized coercion refers to coercion unsupported by the law or the state. Yet in a broader sense, it also embraces coercion used by rival, contending parallel institutions.[2]

A 'state of exception' as described by Agamben (2005) fits into this broader definition of non-institutionalized coercion. It lends credence to the foundational role of organized violence that precedes the emergence of law. The term 'destructive' refers to the conflictual and aggressive nature of a relationship that entails physical or moral destruction.[3] Moreover, appropriation through piracy, confiscation, etc. connotes ownership of resources by disregarding, violating, annihilating, or excluding the property rights of others. Accordingly, the term 'destructive' also captures the establishment of the right to destroy or *abusus* as the ultimate boundary of property rights.

This type of coordination has been almost entirely neglected in mainstream economics, although some of its important empirical dimensions have been addressed by literature on the sustainable crisis or durable conflicts and civil wars. David Keen (2012) and his associates extensively contributed to our understanding of situations in which "waging wars is more important than winning them" (Keen, 2012). They provide salient illustrations of protracted military conflicts during which contending parties are both adversaries and partners.

In studying the destructive mode of coordination, it is useful to commence by considering simple illustrations. Hence, in the second part, destructive coordination will be discussed and compared with other types of coordination using two examples: traffic circles (roundabouts) and prisons. In the third part, appropriation through pirating will be discussed as a further mechanism of destructive coordination. Biopiracy (blood patenting) will be first examined to clarify the relationships between *destructive coordination* and the institutionalization of property rights. Then, we will tackle the question of rivalrous or complementary relationships between different modes of coordination and focus on the disarticulation among them in the absence of a dominant mode. It will be argued that destructive coordination should be conceived as a mechanism

---

[2] See Sect. 2.6 regarding what I mean by parallel institutions.

[3] For a more systematic analysis of 'destructive power' and its different forms including threat power and coercive means, see Vahabi (2004).

that emerges in a period marked by parallel institutions. It may persist but may also provide the soil where the other modes of coordination may take root.

3.2   THEORETICAL BACKGROUND

Destructive coordination as a form of social integration is about cooperating to coerce. The resource *appropriation* in this type of *coordination* is predatory based on grabbing or confiscatory activities. This type of coordination has been neglected in mainstream economics for a long time, although 'grabbing' activity as an *appropriation* mechanism has received some attention in Rational Conflict theory since the early fifties. In fact, economic theory first endeavored to integrate *rational* (and not real or 'social') conflicts as a source of appropriation.

Haavelmo (1954) pioneered a canonical general equilibrium model of the allocation of resources among appropriative and productive activities. The model was further developed, during the last four decades, in a variety of ways by game theoretical models of rational conflict (Boulding, 1962; Schelling, 1963), and different strands of new political economy (Hirshleifer, 2001) within a partial equilibrium framework. Their goal was to understand *rational* conflict which did not entail *real destruction*.

Rational conflict refers to *threat power* and can be defined as a bargaining procedure without any real clash or conflict between the parties that are both partners and adversaries (such as negotiations on nuclear power, commercial negotiations within the GATT or WTO, and negotiations between institutionalized trade unions and employers' organizations on wage and work conditions) (Vahabi, 2015a, 2015b, Chap. 4). This literature is in line with 'Coase Political Theorem', that is, using Coase bargaining mechanism in settling conflictual relationships without any destruction (Vahabi, 2011, 2015a, 2015b).

A second version of conflict theory was developed by the founders of the Public Choice School, notably by Bush (1972), Bush and Mayer (1974), Olson (1965, 1982), and Tullock (1972a, 1972b, 1974a, 1974b) in order to tackle genuine political violence. They studied not only *threat power* but also *real* conflictual situations such as revolutions, wars, and terrorist activities. Their goal was to extend the Neoclassical assumptions to other fields of social science such as politics. They thus endeavored to incorporate *real* conflicts in the Neoclassical analysis and provided a theoretical framework for a new political economy. Real conflicts are not neutral and have a clear impact on economic performance since they come within the scope of rent-seeking activities.

The theoretical background of 'cooperating to coerce' (Cowen & Sutter, 2007) should be sought in the theory of anarchy pioneered by Bush (1972) and introduced through two afore-mentioned edited volumes of Tullock (1972a, 1972b, 1974a). Two relevant edited volumes of Stringham (2005, 2007) which include a republication of some seminal papers in this field are valuable additions to this trend of thought. Unless anarchy is understood as chaos and mayhem, it can be conceived of a society without a state but not without rules (Coyne, 2005). The main issue is then whether an 'ordered anarchy' (i.e., a social order without a state) is possible.

Although earlier criticisms of anarchy (Tullock, 1972a, 1972b, 1974a; Nozick, 1974) are almost unanimous that government is at least inevitable even if unnecessary, many libertarian anarchists suggest other alternatives. As Moss (1974) correctly underlines, an 'ordered anarchy' not only entails a *pure market economy* but also a *stateless Communistic* society. Rothbard (1973, 1977), Leeson (2009, 2014), Geoloso and Leeson (2020), and many other free-market economists are advocates of a recent version of 'private-property' anarchism. Polanyi (1944), Leeson and Stringham (2007) provide examples of archaic stateless societies based on 'reciprocity' or primitive Communism. The importance of these two forms of 'ordered anarchy' notwithstanding, there is a third form of 'ordered anarchy' which has been neglected in economic literature. I call this 'destructive coordination'. *In this case, state failure or sovereignty crisis is more important than a lack of state.*

Parallel institutions and contradictory orders (Vahabi, 2010) may lead to an ordered anarchy where aggressive behavior and the use of coercive means constitute the 'rule of the game'. The focus of Public Choice literature is not such kind of 'ordered anarchy', and a few contributions that deal with the problem of 'cooperation to coerce' result in the reemergence of government (Tullock, [1972a, 1972b] 2005; Gunning, [1972] 2005; Hogarty, 2005; Cowen & Sutter, 2007; Rutten, 2007; Holcombe, 2007). More importantly, in exceptional cases where such an order is considered to be viable (Friedman, 2007), state monopoly is opposed to a private market system of 'multiple police'.

In other words, 'ordered anarchy' in the framework of Public Choice School is presently reduced to a pure market system that may also include (or exclude) coercion. Our contention is that 'ordered anarchy' should be extended to include destructive coordination that is irreducible to either a pure market or a stateless cooperative order.

Finally, there is a recent theoretical literature on *coercive exchange* or appropriation by force that is neither random nor 'mutually beneficial'. This type of appropriation is explored in 'pillage games' (Jordan, 2006) and 'jungle exchange' (see Houba et al., 2017) in which economic agents resort to capture assets. Piccione and Rubinstein (2007) define a *jungle* as a set of individuals who have preferences over a bunch of desirable goods and entertain a transitive strong power relationship (it is irreflexive, asymmetric, complete, and transitive). Moreover, the use of power is assumed to be costless in the jungle. The more powerful individuals can capture goods of others without incurring any cost. Those who are less powerful cannot flee.

Accordingly, a jungle equilibrium is defined as a feasible allocation of goods such that no agent desires to capture goods possessed by a weaker agent. Similar to the two fundamental theorems of Pareto in welfare economics, the authors derive two fundamental theorems of Jungle economics: first, a jungle equilibrium is Pareto optimal. Second, under certain conditions, each Pareto-optimal allocation corresponds to a power relationship for which the allocation is a jungle equilibrium.

A recent development of the model assumes symmetric power among agents and shows that in such a setting, jungle equilibria are neither always unique nor Pareto-optimal (Crettez, 2020). This literature explores conditions of an 'ordered anarchy' with or without asymmetric power relationships. The 'ordered anarchy' is not necessarily anarcho-capitalist or Communist.

In the following parts, we will first study destructive coordination as a particular form of *social* integration through two simple illustrations. Then we will focus on the *economic* dimension of this coordination as an appropriative confiscatory mechanism.

3.3   DESTRUCTIVE COORDINATION IN A ONE-SHOT GAME: TRAFFIC CIRCLES

A simple illustration of destructive coordination in comparison with other modes of coordination is provided by the way car drivers may coordinate with each other in traffic circles.

Different modes of coordination allocate the right to use the road in different manners as depicted below.

Market coordination: special tolls may be set to obtain the permission to drive in districts leading to such traffic circles during the day (i.e., Teheran's 1992 'traffic project').

Authoritative coordination: several traffic lights are installed on the circle to monitor and enforce the priority of drivers according to official prescriptions (i.e., *Place d'Italie* in Paris).

Cooperative coordination: the voluntary attention and compliance of drivers toward other drivers render such coordination possible. The rules of politeness and civility also work in this direction. Respecting these rules does not need third-party enforcement. The state of social brotherhood during the 1979 Revolution in Iran contributed to such instances of coordination even in the absence of police monitoring and official prescriptions. In everyday life, the priority given to ambulances and firefighters is a salient illustration of cooperative coordination. Another example is the Paris Ring-road. While the code of conduct accords the priority to those entering the ring-road, everyone respects the customary rule of 'each one in its turn'.

Destructive coordination: some drivers adopt an aggressive way of driving (by rushing into others and 'pushing' them out of way, honking, and nipping in and out of traffic) to force others to give them the lead. In such cases, they willfully infringe upon the rights of others or 'impose' their proper rights which otherwise would be violated despite the fact that there exists a 'code' which clearly defines the rules and priorities.

It is noteworthy that in a destructive coordination, even the drivers who have the priority must behave aggressively to impose their rights. Hence, to drive aggressively is not just an attitude chosen by 'bad' drivers who do not have the priority. Every driver, irrespective of being 'bad' or 'good', should adopt an aggressive behavior to guarantee his/her rights or to infringe the rights of others.

Aggressive driving increases the probability of accidents. However, borrowing the terminology of the 'incomplete contract' literature (Hart, 1995), the problem is that although the offense of the transgressor is 'observable', it cannot easily be 'verified' by the third party (i.e., the insurer or the court) given the multiple entry/exit situation in a complex traffic circle such as *Place Charles de Gaulle* in Paris. If both parties are insured, if there is no severe corporal damage, and if the accident is not so costly as to require a detailed damage survey that may identify the offender, the insurance companies may apply systematically the rule of 50/50 to share the damage costs of the accident due to the *non-verifiability* problem.

The systematic application of the 50/50 rule may encourage aggressive driving. Let us suppose that there are two types of drivers: aggressive and non-aggressive. If the probability of an accident is θ, then the benefit of an aggressive driver who can overtake others, and shorten his waiting time in the traffic circle, in terms of the price of time saved would be B $(1-θ)$, and the cost in terms of time spent in the traffic and the car insurance surcharge would be C θ.

The net benefit of an aggressive strategy, then would be: B $(1-θ)$ - C θ, whereas a non-aggressive driver will save C θ if there is no accident. The real issue is thus to shorten the waiting time in a traffic circle and 'grab' the price of time saved by adopting an aggressive behavior. The game between these two categories of drivers is a special case of the 'Chicken or Hawk-Dove game' of Maynard Smith (1982).[4] It is a non-cooperative and non-repeated game, with no dominant equilibrium strategy if it is played simultaneously. A simple illustration of the game with the following matrix of payoffs between two players A_1 and A_2 with two possible pure strategies, namely A (aggressive strategy) and P (pacifist strategy) clarifies the point (Fig. 3.1.).

Mainstream game theory would distinguish three Nash equilibria here: (Aggressive, Pacifist), (Pacifist, Aggressive), and a mixed strategy Nash equilibrium where each player plays aggressively with a probability of 1/3 (Hargreaves Heap & Varoufakis, 1995, p. 198). (**4, 0**) and (**0, 4**) are two

		Player A₁	
	Strategy	A	P
Player A₂	A	-1, -1	**4, 0**
	P	**0, 4**	1, 1

Fig. 3.1 Traffic circle game

[4] There are three basic types of games that have been extensively discussed in game theory, namely the *Chicken* or *hawk-dove*, *coordination*, and the *prisoners' dilemma* games (Rasmusen, 1992; Hargreaves Heap & Varoufakis, 1995). The *Chicken* or *hawk-dove* game is also known as the *anti-coordination* game (Binmore, 1990).

pure strategy Nash equilibria,[5] but they have the defect of asymmetry. How can the players know which equilibrium is the one that will be played out? Even if they could have communicated before the game started, it would not be clear how they could obtain an asymmetrical result. The game contains a mixture of conflict and cooperation. Both parties will benefit if they can avoid simultaneous aggressive behavior (with -1, -1 payoffs), so there are benefits from some sort of cooperation.

On the other hand, there are also conflictual interests because depending on how the conflict is avoided, the benefits of cooperation will be differently distributed between the two players. If for example, the conflict is avoided because A_2 adopts a 'pacifist' strategy while A_1 chooses an 'aggressive' strategy, then A_1 will have four benefits and A_2 zero and vice-versa. The game is accordingly called *anti-coordination*. This well-known game provides a good illustration for disorder or anarchy. But under what conditions could we have an 'ordered anarchy'?

Inspired by the Anarchy Research Program of the Public Choice, Osborne (2005) argues that individuals can adopt a strategy known as 'contingent cooperation'. Osborne's model postulates that even in one-shot games, individuals can communicate before interacting, thereby enabling them to detect signals about the likelihood that the other party will cooperate. Undoubtedly, the problem of multiple equilibria in the *anti-coordination* game will be solved if the players play *sequentially*. Every player has an advantage to move *first*, since the first mover can adopt an

---

[5] We can calculate the probability of adopting each strategy in the *mixed* strategy equilibrium by players in our example. In the mixed strategy equilibrium, A_2 must be indifferent between *Pacifist* (P) and *Aggressive* strategies (A). This requires that A_1's probability of *Aggressive* strategy, which we denote by ψ, be such that

π (Pacifist) = $(\psi) . (0) + (1 - \psi) . (1) = (\psi) . (-1) + (1 - \psi) . (4) = \pi$ (Aggressive)

From this equation, we can conclude that $1 - \psi = 4 - 5\,\psi$, so $\psi = 0{,}75$. The Chicken game discussed in our example is simpler than the movie *Rebel Without A Cause*, in which the players race toward a cliff and the winner is the player who jumps out of his car last. The pure strategy space in the movie game is continuous and the payoffs are discontinuous at the cliff's edge, which makes the game more difficult to analyze technically. Technical difficulties arise in some models with a continuum of actions and mixed strategies. Sometimes these difficulties can be avoided by clever modelling as in Fudenberg and Tirole's (1986) version with asymmetric information. As strategies, they specify the length of time firms would continue to *Stay* (instead of *Swerve*) given their beliefs about the type of the other player, in which case there is a pure strategy equilibrium. For an analysis of the Chicken game in the context of evolutionary game theory, see Larry Samuelson, 1997, pp. 104–105.

aggressive strategy and force the other to adopt a pacifist strategy (4, 0; or 0, 4) so that a situation of (-1, -1) be avoided.

Plainly, it implies that drivers entering in a traffic circle from the right-hand side (in the case of a right-hand side priority rule which exists in most countries like France) should choose an aggressive strategy to 'impose' their rights. This result holds true for every incumbent driver who has the possibility to move first. Drawing upon this basic textbook game, I would like to emphasize the conditions under which even a one-shot *anti-coordination* game finds its equilibrium solutions. Put differently, our endeavor is to show how coercion and aggressive behavior can lead to a particular order: 'ordered anarchy'.

Note that this type of coordination is at work due to the *third-party failure* (insurance companies or courts) to implement the rules. For example, when the insurance companies are not legally bound to reimburse the insured in a short period after the accident, they are not motivated to incur the additional costs of a detailed damage survey necessary to identify the driver at fault. In France, the Badinter Law and conventions decreed in July 1985 (Chabas, 1995) radically modified the situation by binding insurance companies to reimburse the victims of car accidents within a six-month period. A more detailed investigation by insurance companies in case of serious car accidents limits the adoption of aggressive strategy and weakens destructive coordination. Thus, the law provides a *credible commitment* to *protect* 'good' or pacifist drivers against aggressive drivers by having insurance companies that can reprimand them through monetary sanctions.

The traffic circle example casts light on destructive coordination in a one-shot or non-repeated case. Our second example illustrates the logic of destructive coordination in a repeated game.

3.4   Destructive Coordination in a Repeated Game: Prison

Different modes of coordination can be distinguished in different types of prisons. *Authoritative coordination* is common in military prisons for *national* soldiers and officers at fault.[6] In this type of prison, the relation-

---

[6] We are not referring here to the 'indefinite detention of *non-citizens* suspected of terrorist activities' decreed by the Bush administration, and practiced in Guantanamo and Abu Ghraib prisons after the attacks of 9/11 in the midst of what it perceived to be a 'state of exception' (see Agamben, 2005; Szurek, 2004).

ships among prisoners and between prisoners and guards are regulated by official prescriptions and strict administrative regulations.

Cooperative coordination usually prevails in political prisons under authoritarian or totalitarian regimes. Political prisoners support and take care of each other especially the weaker ones (those who are ill or recently and severely tortured receive special treatment and attention from other prisoners in the cell). Prisoners act collectively to display their distinct identity as 'political' opponents of the regime and boost their morale against the prison authorities who continuously try to crush their resistance.

Market coordination is used in case of affluent or renowned prisoners (for instance, Paris Hilton in her short captivity in June 2007) in ordinary or criminal prisons who can bargain special treatment and protection with guardians against monetary reward. Privatization of prisons or their management can strengthen such kind of coordination.

Destructive coordination is the dominant form of coordination in many criminal public prisons throughout the world. A more general philosophical reflection concerning the 'prison' as the continuation of the medieval dungeon for 'surveillance and punishment' (Foucault, 1975; Deleuze, 1996) reveals the destructive nature of the institution in itself.[7] Putting human beings in a cage like animals (Netz, 2004) and destroying their vital space of life leads to adverse consequences such as reproduction of criminal activities, high rate of suicide, mental disease, drug addiction, sexual assault, and sexually transmitted infections (STIs) (Coid et al., 2002; Stewart, 2007).

These destructive dimensions of the prison as an institution notwithstanding, I refer to destructive coordination in a more specific way. The latter is based on the predominance of violence between guards and prisoners as well as among prisoners themselves.[8] Accordingly, the 'law of the

---

[7] Foucault (1975) documents the generalization of 'prison' as an institution all over the world since the eighteenth century and underlines the relationship between politics and repressive technology.

[8] There are also situations in which a mixture of different modes of coordination is at work. For example, when in the absence of a political prison, political prisoners as well as military convicts are kept in jail with criminals under military supervision. Dostoyevsky's personal experience in the prison fortress at Omsk, Western Siberia, for a four-year term of penal servitude (1850-1854) for his part in the Petrashevist conspiracy is a good illustration. The full horror of his experiece of prison is given vivid utterance in his masterpiece, *The House of the Dead*, which depicts coexisting modes of coordination particularly destructive, cooperative, and authoritative one.

jungle' reigns among the various gangs of prisoners, particularly when governors and guards, far from protecting prisoners, mistreat them. While practices employed in Guantanamo would have been illegal on US soil, they were authorized by an appeal to a 'state of emergency' (Agamben, 1998), yet the results of detailed investigations about prisons in the USA and France revealed that "every prison has its own Guantanamo" (Mouloud, 2006).[9]

Nevertheless, the 'jungle' has its own 'codes and laws', and one of its inviolable articles is what we also find among the Mafia: "It is a fundamental rule for every man of honour never to report a theft or crime to the police" (Gambetta, 1996, p. 119). As Taylor (2003) reports regarding rape victims in English prisons, many suffer in silence because being labeled a 'grass' guarantees hostility or violence from other prisoners; and some may consider suicide as the sole option.

An overcrowded and impoverished prison environment with severe sexual deprivation and frustration is a fertile soil for harsh territorial conflicts. Furthermore, a recent detailed study about the experience of imprisonment in various countries has found that the number of prison cells has increased, rather than decreased after major political changes such as the collapse of the Soviet bloc, the Apartheid system, or the Haiti dictatorship: "All international studies have clearly shown that the construction of new establishments, has increased, rather than diminished demand for incarceration" (Artières & Lascoumes, 2004, p. 35, my translation). In the absence of 'public' protection, aggressive behavior permeates all relationships among prisoners. Even when an inmate is confronted with an aggressive and stronger prisoner, it is advisable to act aggressively and accept the cost of giving a 'signal' of not being a coward.

Everyone will better seek 'private' protection by joining a 'gang'—and pay for it in terms of sexual intercourse, drug trafficking, etc. Even if an inmate is not personally capable of reacting aggressively to violence, his/her gang will respond in kind. Retaliation emerges, thus, as a way to regulate conflicts. Contrary to the traffic circle example, in a repeated game situation such as in a criminal prison, having the initiative to *move first* is not sufficient to determine the equilibrium position, since *retaliation* is possible (Kreps, 1990). In this case, costly 'signalling' and creating the

---

[9] The movie "Mauritanian" in 2021 provides a vivid description of Guantanamo Bay detention camp, based on a true story of Muhammad Ould Slahi who was detained in that prison for 14 years (from 2002 to 2016) without charge.

'reputation' of being a 'tough guy or woman' is a prerequisite of rendering one's threat credible.

The length of detention is a key factor for revealing the value of the 'signal' since those approaching the end of their sentence have a strong tendency to avoid conflicts. Furthermore, the type of crime for which the prisoner is detained, and the number of incarcerations are other important criteria on which the hierarchy in the prison is established. "If a hierarchy exists in UK prisons, it may be linked to *length of sentence* (long and short term or remand), to the *age* (old and young) of the predominantly male population, and *type of offence* (sex, drugs, robbery or any other violence-related act). The older long-term or life prisoners (including sex offenders) are likely to have power and influence within the prison system, whereas the younger short-term or remand prisoners with drug problems or convicted of non-violent offences are likely to be more vulnerable and compliant, especially those who are in the prison for the first time or who will be found innocent" (Stewart, 2007, p. 53).

Providing three "Cases in Anarchy", Hogarthy (2005) discusses a prisoner-of-war camp (Andersonville) during the American Civil War. In his example, the prisoners do not act cooperatively, and are engaged in aggressive behavior. He identifies an initial coalition of 'raiders' and a second one of 'regulators' who defend themselves against the raiders. The benefits of predatory or 'grabbing' activity in the prison are once again a major issue for the raiders. Nevertheless, their pleasure is more than pure grabbing, but rather gaining a dominant position: "In the outer world, they had been insignificant, eternally existing in dread of discipline. Here the only discipline consisted of that which they administered" (Hogarthy, 2005, p. 106). Of course, in Hogarthy's illustration, the temporary domination of the raiders is overcome with the aid of the 'pre-existing' provisional government. In the following discussion, I try to analyze a situation where an 'ordered anarchy' can emerge in the presence of the state failure to guarantee public protection.

The territorial conflict between prisoners in terms of game theory should be represented in an extensive form due to the dynamic character of the game. If A_1 and A_2 are respectively the stronger and the weaker prisoners, then their strategies (aggressive or pacifist) and the payoffs related to them are as follows (Fig. 3.2.):

The upper number stands for the benefits of the stronger prisoner (A_1), and the lower one represents the benefits of the weaker one (A_2). If A_1 adopts an aggressive strategy, A_2 may adopt either an aggressive strategy or

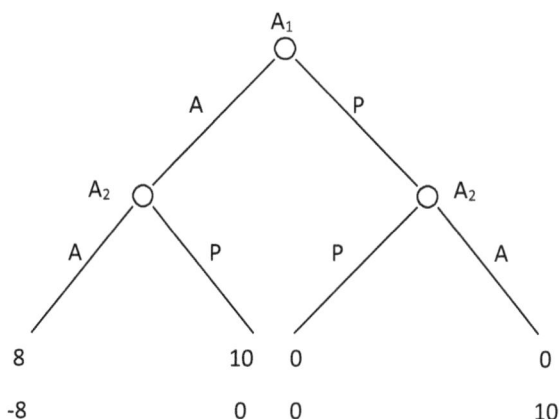

Fig. 3.2 Territorial conflict in prison

a pacifist strategy. Although an aggressive strategy is costly for A_2 (-8) compared to a pacifist strategy (0), A_2 should adopt an aggressive strategy to give a 'signal' that he is 'tough'.

This will pay off in the long term, since A_2's credible commitment to retaliate persuades A_1 to adopt a pacifist strategy if A_1 anticipates that the outcome of a war of attrition will be mutually destructive. In such case, A_2 will prefer to behave pacifically despite the fact that otherwise he will gain more (ten instead of zero), since he will be menaced by further retaliation of A_1 that will cost him (-8) if he sticks to his reputation as 'tough'. Signaling to build a 'tough' reputation will transform, step by step, the initial aggression/aggression situation with payoffs (8, -8) to a final pacifist/pacifist situation with payoffs (0, 0).

All prisoners do not necessarily serve a lifetime sentence, and it is realistic to suppose that the dynamic game has a finite horizon with a last period of exit for the prisoners. Approaching the liberation date, prisoners have a strong stake to avoid conflict so that their detention will not be prolonged. The expected intertemporal payoffs of aggression and non-aggression compared to a pure pacifist strategy can be formulated as follows:

Expected intertemporal benefits of aggression and

$$nonaggression = \int_0^T Ae^{-rt} Ae \, dt + \int_T^t Pe^{-st} dt \qquad (3.1)$$

$$Expected\ benefits\ of\ a\ pacifist\ strategy = \int_{0}^{t} Pe^{-rt} dt \qquad (3.2)$$

(A) stands for an aggressive behavior and (P) stands for a pacifist behavior. (T) is the moment when the weaker party stops fighting and loses its reputation to reply to tit for tat. If (α) denotes the signal of the initial combat, then in a two-period game, the expected benefits of being aggressive would be

$$\alpha 8 + (1-\alpha)10 > \alpha 0 + (1-\alpha) \qquad (3.3)$$

It can be assumed that the probability of being aggressed (α) evolves with the length of detention. At the beginning of detention, the probability of aggression is at its maximum, since the newcomer is not part of a gang, and his combat value is not tested. Then, given that prisoner as part of a gang or individually tries to build a reputation of a 'tough guy', he (or his gang) will respond to aggression with aggression even if it costs him (or his gang) highly. The reputation effect weakens the probability of aggression by the incumbent prisoners.

Consequently, the probability of aggression will decrease up to a point where the date of liberation approaches. In this last period, the possibility of aggression will increase once again but not as high as the initial period, since the previous combats and the length of detention provide a signal that one cannot mess about with the 'tough guy' over a certain tolerance threshold. These three phases are illustrated in the following graphic (Fig. 3.3).

The peace between prisoners is then nothing but a 'balance of terror'. The dynamic of this extensive game is not like the typical Rosenthal's (1981) centipede game.[10] It is a *sequential equilibrium* in which every

---

[10] The solution of such a dynamic game of complete and perfect information is given by backward induction (see Kreps, 1991, pp. 77-79). At the last node, player A_2 will choose a pacifist strategy even if A_1 adopts an aggressive strategy, since given the imminent date of liberation, the adoption of a strategy of aggression by A_2 will cost him more. Hence at the next-to-last node, A_1 chooses to adopt an aggressive strategy given that his payoff will be more if A_2 behaves pacifically, and so on till the first node. Then it can be 'predicted' that A_1 will begin by adopting an aggressive strategy and A_2 will respond by a pacifist strategy. This is, of course, a pretty bad prediction given the importance of building a reputation of a 'tough guy' by A_2. To rectify this bad prediction, one should introduce the *belief* of each player about the way the other player may behave with a given probability. This brings us to another type of equilibrium which Kreps (1990, pp. 536–543) analyzes under the title of 'Reputation redux: Incomplete information'.

Agression
probability

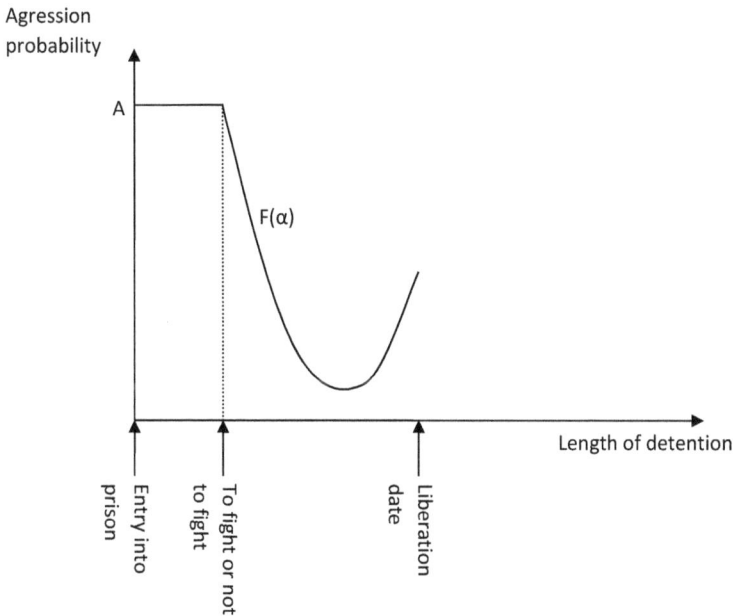

Length of detention

A

F(α)

Entry into
prison

To fight or not
to fight

Liberation
date

Fig. 3.3   The probability of aggression and imprisonment

player adopts his strategy on the basis of a *belief* he may have about the way
the other player may behave with a certain probability. Thus, it includes
the possibility that each player's information set (for instance, A₁'s) is *out
of equilibrium* or *off the play* given the way the belief is formed.

The possibility of choosing an out-of-equilibrium move by a player
implies the fragility of equilibrium and can be represented by a particular
type of sequential game called 'a trembling-hand perfect equilibrium'
(Kreps, 1990, section 12.7). This type of sequential game captures the
reputation effect. The depiction of the dynamic of the 'balance of terror'
within the prison in terms of trembling-hand equilibrium highlights the
fragile character of a non-aggressive situation.

Note that in this example, destructive coordination is closely linked to
the nature of the prison as a social institution that destroys the vital space
of prisoners. Apart from this fundamental institutional failure, the lack of
'public' *protection* and the need for 'private' *protection* nurture destructive
coordination. The perpetuation of this type of coordination is thus related

to an *institutional vacuum* or sovereignty crisis within prisons that justifies the existence of gangs and guarantees compliance to the 'parallel' codes of prisoners.

3.5   DESTRUCTIVE COORDINATION
AND PREDATORY APPROPRIATION

How are resources (goods and services) and human efforts allocated in destructive coordination compared to other types of coordination? This is, from an economic point of view, the thrust of the matter. To answer this question, Pareto's distinction between two different 'allocation mechanisms',[11] namely the productive and the appropriative ones is useful. Borrowing Pareto's distinction, the appropriation mechanism in destructive coordination should be characterized as predatory. It includes all sorts of predatory methods such as expropriation, confiscation, piracy, grabbing, etc.

In the preceding two examples, we highlighted the importance of grabbing activity. Aggressive behavior in the traffic circle case guarantees the shortening of the waiting time or the grabbing of the price of time saved. In the prison example, raiders' predatory activity is not only paid off by significant material benefits but also by gaining a dominant position. In both cases, social integration through coercion appropriates resources in a predatory way. Although pure *economic* or appropriative dimension of destructive coordination has been stressed in the previous examples, our focus was mainly on the specific *social* coordination as an 'ordered anarchy'.

Since property rights are part of the law-and-order package, an inquiry about the type of social order precedes the analysis of property rights and economic allocation. The latter shall now be developed. A simple illustration regarding the way destructive coordination appropriates a given resource in comparison with other types of coordination will clarify this point.

---

[11] North (1977) also interprets Polanyi's 'forms or patterns of integration' as 'markets and other allocation systems'. He suggests an explication of different 'allocation systems' in terms of transaction costs (see section 2.9).

3.6   Biopiracy: *Res Nullius* and Privatization

Consider the example of a 'contested' or an 'invaluable good' (Radin, 1996; Arrow, 1997), namely blood. Although the practice of blood transfusion started 500 years ago, it was not until the twentieth century that blood became a widely sold body 'product'. Blood was the first human body 'part' to be commercialized. In fact, there are different allocation mechanisms in the case of blood.

Cooperative coordination: Richard Titmuss (1971) strongly advocated an entirely voluntary system for blood donations, excluding monetary rewards for the donors. In his opinion, blood should be a *gift, not* a *commodity* and the act of donation should confirm a citizen's commitment to the principle of reciprocity. "Short of examining …the institution of slavery—of men and women as market commodities—blood as a living tissue may now constitute in Western societies one of the ultimate tests of where the 'social' begins and the 'economic' ends" (Titmuss, 1971, p. 158). The United Kingdom system of supplying blood for transfusion on the basis of a voluntary and unpaid collection was his model. This model was a reproduction of the first modern blood bank at Cook County Hospital in Chicago in 1927, invented by Oswald Hope Robertson, which was inspired by the experience of battlefield transfusion (Hess & Schmidt, 2000).

Market coordination was introduced in 1955 and then legalized in the USA in 1966 after a court ruling which ordered that blood was a product like any other. The dispute had started when two commercial blood banks in Kansas City, Missouri, had charged a non-profit community blood bank with conspiracy "to hamper, restrict and restrain the sale and distribution of blood in interstate commerce" (Cited in Kimbrell, 1995, p. 134). It should be highlighted that the American system was not one of undiluted market coordination; rather it was a mixed system, comprising both commercial and non-commercial blood banks, and utilizing various modes of payment. According to Titmuss' estimates at the time, about one-third of the US supply came from paid blood donors, most of them poor, homeless, often alcoholics or drug addicts. In West Germany more than one-third of the blood was coming from paid blood donors. In Japan, virtually all blood was commercially distributed because giving blood was shunned as an infringement of the personal sphere, and all blood was imported.

Authoritative coordination: in this system, the blood allocation is managed by the state, rather than by commercial blood banks. Here the donors were sometimes paid. Two salient but different examples are (i) the former

USSR where approximately 50% of the blood collected this way, and donors fetched a high monetary reward; and (ii) Sweden, where all blood was (and is) gathered and paid for by the state, rather than by commercial blood banks. An authoritative coordination without any payment to the donor, and even without the donor's consent has recently been made possible through a new definition of death. Following the recommendation of the Harvard Medical School committee in 1968, the American Medical Association, the American Bar Association, and a White House commission all endorsed, in 1981, that death was the moment when brain activity rather than heart and lung function stopped permanently. Within a short time, most states had passed legislation in the same vein. Given new technologies in artificial circulation and respiration, patients who were, according to this new definition, 'dead' could be kept functioning for months, even years. These 'neomorts' or 'living cadavers' could then be used as 'storage systems' or 'research tools' for testing drugs and new medical procedures, or for providing scarce organs and blood. Hospitals could allocate the organs from the 'neomorts' according to a waiting list to patients without payment. If such harvested organs or blood is provided for free, this would be an instance of rationed or administrative coordination. If, on the other hand, harvesting was done without compensation, and the crop sold in the market for organs and blood, this would be *destructive coordination*.

Count Dracula (Stoker, 1897/1997) and vampires illustrate nicely a kind of *destructive coordination* of blood. The Transylvanian Count sucks 'unpaid' and 'non-donated' blood. His action is comparable to piracy or coercive appropriation of blood. The same type of coordination can be found through harvesting the 'dead' in developed countries by tightened definition of death, or through biopiracy in under-developed countries. We have already mentioned the importance of a change in the definition of death. The appropriation of 'neomorts' blood without donors' consent is related to the fact that there is no authority or defined property rights over a cadaver. We are confronted with a *non-property* or *res nullius* situation. To rectify this *institutional vacuum* that provides the opportunity for appropriation, people in developed countries are informed that in the absence of a clear disapproval of organs donation during their lifetime, their cadaver may be used for clinical purposes.

Biopiracy provides another instance for destructive coordination in blood appropriation. The term 'biopiracy' was coined in the early 1990s by Pat Mooney, Executive Director of ETC Group, a Canadian NGO formerly known as the Rural Advancement Foundation International (RAFI), "to cover the unauthorized and uncompensated expropriation of traditional knowledge. This includes the patenting of seeds and trees, healing herbs, and the selling of human body tissue" (Tedlock, 2006, p. 257). Many other definitions and interpretations have been ascribed to the concept[12] (see Hamilton, 2006, p. 159) among which the one suggested by Shiva (2001) is particularly relevant. For it calls into question the legitimacy of 'intellectual property rights' (IPR) as a way to 'plunder' rather than 'protect' biological resources and products that have been used over centuries in non-industrialized cultures.

In fact, in 1994, the WTO developed a global patent system based on the US legal concept of intellectual property rights. Under this new legal regime, known as the Trade Related Aspects of Intellectual Property Rights Agreement (TRIPS), individuals and groups who claim to have 'discovered' or 'invented' something are given a monopoly over the commercial development of their innovation over a limited time period (usually 20 years). Anything that is *not protected by intellectual property rights* is considered to be in 'the public domain'. Many examples of biopiracy have been cited. The following are a few of the well-known cases: the 'seed wars' or the 'international controversy over the ownership of germplasm and other related issues' of the 1980s (Juma, 1989), the patenting of living organisms (Bright, 1994; Kimbrell, 1995), the W.R. Grace patent on a fungicide derived from the seeds of the Neem tree—*Azadirachtin*

---

[12] The notion of biopiracy has been severely criticized recently as an alarmist exaggeration or a misguided reading of the IPR (Taubes, 1995; Zaitlen & German, 2000a, 2000b; Chen, 2006). Obviously, this notion will always be controversial, since the dispute about whether someone should be called a 'pirate' or 'promoter of science' and 'public good' is really about who has the power. St. Augustine's reflections regarding the 'pirate and emperor' are illuminating: "For elegant and excellent was the pirate's answer to the great Macedonian Alexander, who had taken him: the king asking him how the durst molest the seas so, he replied with a free spirit, 'How darest thou molest the whole world? But because I do what a little ship only, I am called a thief: thou doing it with a great navy, art called an emperor'" (quoted in Pérotin-Dumon, 1991, p. 196). One can easily imagine that after 'patenting' the traditional knowledge of the Indian people about the Neem tree (its scientific name *Azadirachtin Indica* is derived from the Persian words *Azad Darakht* which means free tree), the giant pharmaceutical corporations accuse them later of 'pirating' the 'patented' knowledge which is basically their own knowledge. Of course, if science looks for 'shared conventions' to claim 'neutrality', then there will never be a science about piracy and *a fortiori* regarding biopiracy.

Indica[13] (Hamilton, 2006, pp. 164–168), the launch of a new strain of 'trailing' Busy Lizzie by the multinational biotech giant Syngenta (Barnett, 2006), the possible extinction of the Rosewood tree and the production of Chanel No. 5 (Amazon News, 2002). Biopiracy also includes blood patenting and several cases have been reported.

The first case was reported in August 1993 by the RAFI regarding the US government's attempt to patent a cell line derived from a 26-year-old Guyami woman (Western Panama). The cell line, a type of culture that can be maintained indefinitely, came from a blood sample obtained by a researcher from the US National Institutes of Health in 1990. The application claimed that the cell might prove useful for the treatment of the Human T-lymphotropic virus, or HTLV, which is associated with a form of leukemia and a degenerative nerve disease. Despite the intervention of the President of the Guyami General Congress who asked the US to withdraw its claim and repatriate the cell, the GATT did not forbid the patenting of human material. Facing strong opposition by a growing number of NGOs, the US finally dropped its claim in November 1994 (Bright, 1994).

But this was not the end of the story. In January 1994, two similar cases were brought to light by a European researcher. The Swiss NGO activist Miges Baumann discovered that the US National Institutes of Health had filed 'invention' applications on cell lines derived from the Hagahai people[14] and the Solomon Islanders. These cells might also be useful in curing

[13] Chen (2006, p. 5) who has adamantly decided "not to praise the biopiracy narrative, but to bury it" alludes to the Neem tree story. Astonishingly, however, he keeps silent about the fact that the patent was revoked since the 'inventive step' could not have been proved, and according to the European Patent Convention, it did not also meet the 'morality' criterion. While Chen generously recommends that 'traditional knowledge' should be kept within the 'public domain' (p. 24), he expresses his profound regrets about the "novel and economically senseless solution of proprietary status for traditional knowledge of biological properties and applications". But what about an unjustified claim of 'novelty' for issuing a patent when there already exists 'traditional knowledge' about the so-called invention as in the case of the Neem tree? "It may be enough simply to ensure that alleged facts of biopiracy do not form the basis for patents under existing intellectual property laws" (p. 28). He prefers to be 'socialist' with regard to the utilization of 'traditional knowledge' in the South, but an ardent partisan of 'private property' when it comes to patenting for the North.

[14] Zaitlen and German (2000a, p. 66) contest the notion of biopiracy, since "'life'—such as the transgenic mouse, the Mo cell line, and Brazzein sweetener—are human inventions…It had to be invented before our patent laws would allow Harvard to patent it in the first place." Apart from the unjustified notion of 'patenting human cells', one finds no clue whatsoever why the Hagahai blood cell or the traditional knowledge of the Indian people about the Neem tree should be regarded as an 'invention' of the US government or pharmaceutical corporations.

HTLV. The story of this so-called invention of the Hagahai cell line could be traced back to the early 1990s when the Genetic Institute of the University of Javeriana in Colombia gathered tissue samples from hundreds of Columbian indigenous people and sent 2305 blood samples to the US National Institutes of Health. The US National Institutes of Health then patented the cell in March 1995.

However, it abandoned the patent under the pressure of public outcry in late 1996. Of course, even today the Hagahai cell line is available to the scientific public for $290 per sample at the American Type Culture Collection (ATCC). Another case of biopiracy in August 1996 concerned the doctor accompanying a US research team in Brazil who asked hunters from the Karitiana tribe for samples of their blood under false pretexts. When questioned about the motivation for taking samples, the doctor denied any intention of commercializing the blood. However, later it was revealed that the blood was commercialized and sold $500 per sample on the internet by Coriell Cell Repositories, a not-for-profit scientific institution, in Camden, New Jersey (Tedlock, 2006, p. 257).

Patenting blood, like other forms of biopiracy such as expropriation of traditional knowledge of indigenous people, patenting of seeds, healing herbs, and selling of human body tissue, *institutionalizes private property through the abolition of property rights*. The origin of private property is not necessarily frugality, 'invention' or free exchange, but appropriation through colonialism, pirating, and other violent means. This was true during the so-called primitive accumulation of capital in England (Marx, 1867/1978, Vol. 1, Chap. 26), and it is also true in the age of fully fledged capitalism. Private property should begin with a state of no property (*res nullius*)[15] as if one finds or 'discovers' something that has never been lost,[16] or has never belonged to anyone so that it becomes 'appropriable'.

---

[15] During the eighteenth and nineteenth centuries, the state of no property was claimed by England over the 'free international seas' to legitimize its naval hegemony and pirating activities. Sovereignty is a territorial-land concept which has never been applied over the seas. As Pérotin-Dumon (1991, p. 203) rightly remarks: "There is no authoritative definition of international piracy." Presently, the state of no property (*res nullius*) is posited for outer space by the new "US National Space Policy" (2006) so that the monopoly of the US should be justified: "The United States rejects any claims to sovereignty by any nation over outer space or celestial bodies, or any portion thereof, and rejects any limitation on the fundamental right of the United States to operate in and acquire data from space".

[16] The French comedian Coluche used to define 'theft' as 'finding something that has never been lost'.

Patenting life and plants assumes such a state of 'free access' or *res nullius*. As noted earlier, according to the TRIPS legislation, anything that is *not protected* by intellectual property rights is considered to be in the 'public domain', which means it can be exploited by anyone without any concern for the wishes of the original (knowledge) holders and without sharing any monetary or non-monetary rewards with them.

The inclusion of Intellectual Property Rights (IPR) into the text of the WTO agreements was a direct result of pressure from US industries dependent on IPR, not least of which were the pharmaceutical and agro-chemical companies (Correa, 2000). Bromley (1992) rightly notes that 'public domain' is not an appropriate concept for describing an 'open access regime' in which there is no property (*res nullius*). "The essence of any property regime is an authority system that can assure that the expectations of rights holders are met...When the authority system breaks down—for whatever reason—then common property (*res communes*) degenerates into open access (*res nullius*)" (Ibid., p. 12). Open access results from the absence—or the breakdown—of an authority system whose very purpose is to assure compliance with a set of behavioral conditions with respect to the natural resources or human life. To address this problem, the TRIPS legislation requires *each nation state to create patents for all life forms in its territory.*

This legislation assumes the inseparability of property from sovereignty since the separation between them blurs the frontiers between 'common property' and 'open access'. The latter implies the absence of property rights which means that resources belong to those who can control them by force: might creates right. The reason is that among different types of property rights, the one which cannot be contracted away is *abusus*, while both *usus* and *fructus* can be contracted without causing any damage to the very right of ownership. Thence *the ultimate boundary of ownership is the right to destroy.* Ownership also starts by the sovereign power that protects and hence could destroy. The institutionalization of private property requires the exclusion or expropriation of others from the right to control. Blood patenting is a prerequisite of commercializing cell lines. Thus, destructive coordination of blood allocation through cell line patenting or dead 'harvest' is a *transitional phase* to build the necessary institutional arrangements for private property and market coordination.

3.7 DESTRUCTIVE COORDINATION
AND DISARTICULATION PROBLEM

Social order is too complex to be represented by a single 'idealized' coordination mechanism. It is rather the outcome of a particular constellation of different modes of coordination. The rivalrous or complementary relationships between different types of coordination is thus the major issue of every social order. To illustrate the point, Schlicht (1998)[17] cites Titmuss' blood allocation example.

Titmuss (1971) stresses the rival uses of exchange and gift in blood donation. Many persons donate blood voluntarily but cease to do so if a commercialized system is introduced whereby donors receive money for their donation. But why is this so, asks Arrow (1972) in his paper about Titmuss' book, and finds no answer to his question: "Why should it be that the creation of a market for blood would decrease the altruism embodied in giving blood? I do not find any clear answer in Titmuss" (1971, p. 351). Arrow is more in favor of a 'mixed system' in blood allocation such as the type developed in the US and maintains his position 25 years later when he reviews Radin's book (Arrow, 1997, p. 762).

Schlicht, however, finds an answer to this question: "Without a blood market, the individual donor will donate out of moral obligation ('If nobody donates, there would be no blood to help the injured'). With a market, this argument loses force, *because the price mechanism now provides another means to secure blood supply* ('If there is insufficient blood supply, the price must be raised'). Without a market, blood donations appear indispensable. The introduction of a blood market creates an improved possibility for obtaining blood and thereby destroys the moral obligation to make donations. Duty is substituted by money in a lumpy way" (Schlicht, 1998, p. 228).

In Schlicht's answer, the dilemma '*gift* versus *exchange*' is explained in terms of an institutional arrangement (price mechanism) at work. If there is a market, then the price mechanism takes care of a shortage in 'blood supply' by raising the price level. Nevertheless, the price mechanism is not sufficient to resolve the problem of 'quality', since adverse selection due to

---

[17] Schlicht (1998, pp. 217-41, 276–77) is inspired by Polanyi's *integration forms* though he employs 'modes of control' as a synonymous expression to delineate different types of coordination, namely 'exchange, command, and custom' (in his terminology) within a firm or a society.

asymmetric information between buyers and sellers is present in the blood market. In fact, Titmuss (1971) emphasizes several types of failure with regard to the market appropriation of blood among which the 'bad' quality of blood is noteworthy. The blood sold by paid donors is drawn almost exclusively from the neediest layers of the population including the sick, and addicts. Accordingly, a major risk of infection through transfusion becomes imminent. Hence, the market failure requires a complementary mechanism such as *reputation* or special *regulation* to guarantee the quality of blood collected by commercial blood banks. It is not surprising then that since the Federal Trade Commission (FTC) decision in 1966 concerning the classification of blood as a 'commodity', the use of paid donors for whole blood used in transfusions declined in the US "from about 80% of all transfused blood in 1966 to less than one per cent in 1991, due to ethical concerns about buying and selling and in part to fears that blood from paid donors is a potential source of infection" (Kimbrell, 1995, p. 135).

The *cooperative coordination* of blood appropriation is not exposed to the infection risk, since unpaid donations come from all layers of the population, and the voluntary nature of procurement precludes untruthfulness with regard to the quality of blood. But why, as Schlicht suggests, does an improvement in obtaining blood through market appropriation destroy the moral obligation? The reason should be sought in the *pervasiveness* of market relationships. In the presence of commercialized blood, free blood donations also become 'commodity' to some extent, since it can be sold at market prices. One simple illustration is blood products. In 1991, over 13 million plasma extraction procedures were performed in the US. Over 95% of the donors were paid. Voluntary donor centers like the Red Cross provided another 2 million liters of plasma, collected for free from donors "but *often sold at market prices* in the plasma products market" (Kimbrell, Ibid.). But why should one provide a 'gift' that would be sold at market price? In other words, the reciprocity logic becomes subordinated to the market logic. Moreover, there exists in some cases a 'crowding out effect' between market and cooperative motivations in the sense that if the blood can be 'bought', the intrinsic motivation for donating blood might weaken. The organic combination of different modes of coordination leads to the *domination* of one of them. The pervasiveness of the market coordination subordinates the logic of reciprocity by reducing its proportions and feasibility, and by destroying its particular institutional arrangement.

At a psychological and cognitive level, Schlicht notes the importance of 'the clarity principle': "If there are several reasons for doing something, this creates 'overjustification'; one possible motive will be selected, and all others will be discounted" (Schlicht, 1998, p. 228). This *psychological* explanation at an individual level should be completed by an *institutional* analysis at an aggregate level. The integrative effect of every type of coordination is conditioned by the presence of definite institutional arrangements, such as symmetrical organizations (reciprocity), central points (redistribution), and market systems (exchange). The articulation among different forms of coordination requires the domination of one of them due to the *coherence* of institutional arrangement that supports a particular type of coordination.

But what happens in the case of an *institutional vacuum*? To continue with the example of the paper, what happens in the case of 'blood patenting'? We find no answer to this question in Titmuss, Arrow, or Schlicht, since they do not discuss biopiracy. To address this problem, the Convention on Biological Diversity (CBD) recognizes that genetic resources are *nationally sovereign* resources. When genetic resources become conceived of as 'sovereign resources', it becomes possible to see them as something other than 'common heritage' or in IPR terminology, as part of the 'public domain' from which we can all benefit for free. But as already mentioned, this means that the TRIPS legislation requires each nation state to create patents for all life forms found in its territory. Of course, one can imagine the implication of this legislation for many African countries which do not even have sufficient financial funds to hire lawyers or juridical experts to represent them in the WTO!

As argued before, biopiracy is a form of destructive coordination that appropriates resources and human efforts belonging to others. Destructive coordination is the emblematic type of coordination that usually prevails under conditions of institutional vacuum, as illustrated by the examples given in this paper. By 'institutional vacuum', we do not mean a situation devoid of institutions or amorphous institutions. It refers to a transitional period where the old institutions and organizations of coordination cease to function, but the requisite for new systems of coordinative institutions have still not been developed sufficiently. An institutional vacuum is generally linked to sovereignty crisis, or generalized parallel institutions where *protection* of one's life and entitlements is often more important than *production or transaction*. It may be conceived as a state where the rules confined to pockets of Guantanamo's in some prisons govern an entire region or society.

The post-revolutionary Iran has been witnessing the dominance of destructive coordination with *Bonyads* (religious and military Foundations) as its particular economic institution. This type of coordination at a macro level can be called 'the Iranian Disease', a pandemic more dangerous than 'the Dutch Disease' for economic growth (see Vahabi, 2010). Protection costs rather than transaction costs become accordingly the determining factor in the allocation of resources and human efforts.

Bargaining, reciprocity, and third-party intervention (state or some other form of central power) would then assume a secondary role compared to bi-party conflictual relationships. Predatory appropriation is a *transitional* phase, giving rise to more tightly defined definite rights (not only property rights, but also communal rights also—the entire system of rights may crystallize). A transitional phase may not be necessarily 'transitory', or short. It may stretch over centuries as in the case of 'primitive accumulation of capital'. Under such circumstances, there is no *dominant* mode of coordination. In this sense, we may even speak of *disarticulation*. However, disarticulation does not necessarily imply chaos. A special kind of order or 'ordered anarchy' may be maintained through intimidation, threat, and aggressive means that prepare the way for new institutional arrangements and corresponding constellation of property rights.

3.8   Conclusion

Four results can be drawn from this chapter. The *first* is that besides market, authoritative, and cooperative coordination, there exists another type of coordination: destructive coordination. As my illustrations of traffic circles and prisons show, destructive coordination is supported by parallel institutions, and is regulated through intimidation, threat, and the adoption of aggressive attitudes or means.

Two general conditions are required for the existence of destructive coordination: (i) there should be a game that contains a mixture of conflict and cooperation, where adversaries should also behave as partners. In both examples, destructive coordination is not the outcome of a zero-sum game; (ii) there should be a third-party failure (the state or the insurer), and hence a failure of external enforcement. In the traffic circles case, the non-verifiability condition by the insurer or the state prompted the failure. In the prison case, the absence of public protection entailed destructive coordination. Yet an order or equilibrium was established through aggression (noninstitutionalized violence or coercion) that can be depicted as 'ordered anarchy'.

The *second* result is that the aggressive behavior is not the result of the players' wicked nature or motivation (good or evil). Players must necessarily adopt an aggressive behavior—not only in order to infringe upon the rights of others but also to impose their own rights on others or to build a reputation for toughness. To put it differently, aggressiveness as behavioral regularity is derived from the rules of the game (or institutional arrangement) in case of destructive coordination.

The *third* result is that at an economic level, the proper appropriation mechanism of destructive coordination is through piracy, confiscation, robbery, predation, etc. Destructive coordination is essential in the *abolition* as well as in the *emergence* of property rights due to its role in defining a*busus*. Private as well as state ownership assumes that property rights are institutionalized and are well defined so that the ultimate boundary of ownership, namely the right to destroy (*abusus*) is also legally clarified and enforced. But the primary role of destructive power in resource appropriation implies extra-legal, ambiguous, undefined, or non-institutionalized (or insufficiently institutionalized) property rights. Booties in warfare and looting, or confiscated properties in a revolution are what may be called 'indeterminate' properties.

The essence of any property regime is an authority system that can assure that the expectations of rights holders are met. When the authority system breaks down—for whatever reason—then common property (*res communes*) degenerates into open access (*res nullius*). Although they can be transformed into 'public', 'personal', 'private', 'combinatorial', or other types of property ownership, their initial status remains indeterminate. In 'indeterminate' properties, entitlements to property rights depend on the discretionary power of the coercive authority.

The biopiracy example identifies the importance of destructive coordination as a *transitional* phase in the institutionalization of definite property rights. Under destructive coordination, the question of sovereignty overwhelms the problem of property, and protection rather than production or transaction occupies the pride of place. This example highlights how *destructive coordination* (blood patenting) can transform into *market coordination* (blood commercialization) in the presence of the US liberal state and giant pharmaceutical multinationals.

Finally, the analysis of the articulation among different types of coordination leads us to grasp the domination of one type of coordination over the others. However, parallel institutions that enhance disarticulation among different modes of coordination provide a fertile soil for the preponderance role of destructive coordination.

REFERENCES

Agamben, G. (1998). *Homo Sacer: Sovereign Power and Bare Life*. Stanford University Press.
Agamben, G. (2005). *State of Exception*. The University of Chicago Press.
Amazon News. (2002, July 18). *Rosewood, a Sweet Aroma that Could Fade Away*.
Arrow, K. J. (1972). Gifts and Exchanges. *Philosophy and Public Affairs, 1*(4), 343–362.
Arrow, K. J. (1997, June). Invaluable Goods. *Journal of Economic Literature, XXXV*(2), 757–765.
Artières, P., & Lascoumes, P., (dir.) (2004). *Gouverner, enfermer, La prison, un modèle indépassable?* Presses de Sciences Po.
Barnett, A. (2006, August 27). Special Report: The New Piracy. *The Observer*, p. 9.
Binmore, K. (1990). *Essays on the Foundations of Game Theory*. Basil Blackwell.
Boulding, K. E. (1962). *Conflict and Defense: A General Theory*. Harper and Brothers.
Bright, C. (1994, November). Who owns indigenous peoples' DNA? *World Watch, 7*(6), 8.
Bromley, D. W. (1992). The Commons, Common Property, and Environmental Policy. *Environmental and Resource Economics, 2*, 1–17.
Bush, W. (1972). Individual Welfare in Anarchy. In Tullock G. (ed.), 1972, pp. 5–18; see also, Stringham E. (ed.) [2005], Chapter 2, pp. 10–23.
Bush, W., & Mayer, L. (1974). Some Implications of Anarchy for the Distribution of Property. *Journal of Economic Theory, 8*, 401–412.
Chabas, F. (1995). *Les accidents de la circulation*. Dalloz.
Chen, J. (2006). There's No Such Thing as Biopiracy...and It's a Good Thing Too. *McGeorge Law Review, 37*, 1–32.
Coid, J., Babbington, P., Brugha, D., Jenkins, R., Farrell, M., Lewis, G., & Singleton, N. (2002). Ethnic Differences in Prisoners: Criminality and Psychiatry Morbidity. *British Journal of Psychiatry, 181*, 473–480.
Correa, C. (2000). *Intellectual Property Rights, the WTO and Developing Countries: The TRIPS Agreement and Policy Options*. Zed Books.
Cowen, T., & Sutter, D. (2007). Conflict, Cooperation and Competition in Anarchy. In E. Stringham (Ed.), *Anarchy and the Law, The Political Economy of Choice* (pp. 315–321). Transaction Publishers.
Coyne, C. (2005). Social Interaction Without the State. In E. Stringham (Ed.), *Anarchy, State and Public Choice* (pp. 49–59). Edward Elgar.
Crettez, B. (2020). Pareto-Minimality in the Jungle. *Public Choice, 182*, 495–508.

Deleuze, G. (1996). *"Post-scriptum sur les sociétés de contrôle", dans Pourparlers* (pp. 240–247). Minuit.

Foucault, M. (1975). *Surveiller et punir.* Gallimard.

Friedman, D. (2007). Law as a Private Good: A Response to Tyler Cowen on the Economics of Anarchy. In Stringham E., pp. 284–291.

Fudenberg, D., & Tirole, J. (1986, July). A Theory of Exit in Duopoly. *Econometrica, 54*(4), 943–960.

Gambetta, D. (1996). *The Sicilian Mafia.* Harvard University Press.

Geoloso, V., & Leeson, P. (2020). Are Anarcho-Capitalists Insane? Medieval Icelandic Conflict Institutions in Comparative Perspectives. *Revue d'Economie Politique, 130*(6), 957–974.

Gunning, P. (1972/2005). Towards a Theory of the Evolution of Government. In Stringham E., pp. 60–66.

Haavelmo, T. (1954). *A Study in the Theory of Economic Evolution.* North-Holland.

Hamilton, C. (2006). Biodiversity, Biopiracy and Benefits: What Allegations of Biopiracy Tell Us About Intellectual Property. *Developing World Bioethics, 6*(3), 158–173.

Hargreaves Heap, S. P., & Varoufakis, Y. (1995). *Game Theory, a Critical Introduction.* Routledge.

Hart, O. (1995). *Firms, Contracts, and Financial Structure.* Clarendon Press.

Hess, J. R., & Schmidt, P. J. (2000, January). The First Blood Banker: Oswald Hope Robertson. *Transfusion, 40*, 110–113.

Hirshleifer, J. (2001). *The Dark Side of the Force, Economic Foundations of Conflict Theory.* Cambridge University Press.

Hogarthy, T. (2005). Cases in Anarchy. In Stringham E. (Ed.), *Anarchy, State and Public Choice*, (pp. 98–112). Cheltenham and Northampton: Edward Elgar.

Holcombe, R. (2007). Government: Unnecessary but Inevitable. In Stringham E. (ed.), pp. 354–370.

Houba, H., Luttens, R. I., & Weikard, H.-P. (2017). Pareto Efficiency in the Jungle. *Review of Economic Design, 21*(3), 153–161.

Jordan, J. (2006). Pillage and Property. *Journal of Economic Theory, 131*(1), 26–44.

Juma, C. (1989). *The Gene Hunters: Biotechnology and the Scramble for Seeds.* Zed Books.

Keen, D. (2012). *Useful Enemies, When Waging Wars Is More Important than Winning Them.* Yale University Press.

Kimbrell, A., (1995, July/August), "The Body Enclosed, The Commodification of Human 'Parts'", *The Ecologist*, Vol. 25, No. 4, pp. 134-141.

Kreps, D. M. (1990). *A Course in Microeconomic Theory.* Princeton University Press.

Kreps, D. M. (1991). *Game Theory and Economic Modelling.* Oxford University Press.

Leeson, P. T. (2009). The Laws of Lawlessness. *Journal of Legal Studies, 38*, 471–503.

Leeson, P. T. (2014). *Anarchy Unbound: Why Self-Governance Works Better than You Think*. Cambridge University Press.

Leeson, P., & Stringham, E. (2007). Is Government Inevitable? Comment on Holcombe's Analysis. In E. Stringham (Ed.), *Anarchy and the Law, the Political Economy of Choice* (pp. 371–376). Transaction Publishers.

Marx, K. (1867/1978). *Capital, a Critique of Political Economy* (Vol. 1), Progress Publishers.

Moss, L. (1974). Private Property Anarchism: An American Variant. in Tullock G. (ed.), 1974, pp. 1–31; see also, Stringham E. (ed.) [2005], Chapter 12, pp. 123–152.

Mouloud, L. (2006). "Chaque Prison a Son Petit Guantanamo..." *Journal l'Humanité*, le 21 décembre.

Netz, R. (2004). *Barbed Wire: An Ecology of Modernity*. Wesleyan University Press.

North, D. (1977). Markets and Other Allocation Systems in History: The Challenge of Karl Polanyi. *Journal of European Economic History, 6*, 703–716.

Nozick, R. (1974). *Anarchy, State, and Utopia*. Basic Books.

Olson, M. (1965/1980). *The Logic of Collective Action, Public Goods and the Theory of Groups*. Harvard University Press.

Olson, M. (1982). *The Rise and Decline of Nations: Economic Growth, Stagflation, and Social Rigidities*. Yale University Press.

Osborne, J. (2005). Jungle or Just Bush? Anarchy and the Evolution of Cooperation. In Stringham E. (ed.), pp. 24–35.

Pérotin-Dumon, A. (1991). The Pirate and the Emperor: Power and the Law on the Seas, 1450–1850. In J. D. Tracy (Ed.), *The Political Economy of Merchant Empires* (pp. 196–227). Cambridge University Press.

Piccione, M., & Rubinstein, A. (2007). Equilibrium in the Jungle. *Economic Journal, 117*(522), 883–896.

Polanyi, K. (1944). *The Great Transformation*. Farrar and Rinehart.

Radin, M. J. (1996). *Contested Commodities*. Harvard University Press.

Rasmusen, E. (1992). *Games and Information, An Introduction to Game Theory*. Blackwell.

Rosenthal, R. (1981). Games of Perfect Information, Predatory Pricing, and the Chain-Store Paradox. *Journal of Economic Theory, 25*, 92–100.

Rothbard, M. (1973/1996).*For a New Liberty: Libertarian Manifesto*. Fox and Wilkes.

Rothbard, M. (1977). *Power and Market: Government and the Economy*. Sheed, Andrews and McMeel, Second Edition.

Rutten, A. (2007). Can Anarcy Save Us from Leviathan? In Stringham E. (Ed.), *Anarchy and the Law, the Political Economy of Choice*. New Brunswick, NJ: Transaction Publishers.

Samuelson, L. (1997). *Evolutionary Games and Equilibrium Selection*. The MIT Press.

Schelling, T. (1963). *The Strategy of Conflict*. A Galaxy Book, Oxford University Press. Scheuer [1994], *Focus*, pp. 99–101.

Schlicht, E. (1998). *On Custom in the Economy*. Clarendon Press.

Shiva, V. (2001). *Protect or Plunder? Understanding Intellectual Property Rights*. Zed Books.

Smith, M. (1982). *Evolution and the Theory of Games*. Cambridge University Press.

Stewart, E. C. (2007, February). The Sexual Health and Behaviour of Male Prisoners: The Need for Research. *The Howard Journal of Criminal Justice, 46*(1), 43–59.

Stoker, B. (1897/1997). *Dracula*. Norton and Company.

Stringham, E. (Ed.). (2005). *Anarchy, State and Public Choice*. Edward Elgar.

Stringham, E. (Ed.). (2007). *Anarchy and the Law, The Political Economy of Choice*. Transaction Publishers.

Szurek, S. (2004). Guantanamo, une prison d'exception. Artières Ph. et Lascoumes P. (dir.), pp. 201–223.

Taubes, G. (1995, November 17). Scientists Attacked for 'Patenting' Pacific Tribe. *Science, 270*, 1112.

Taylor, S. (2003). *Rape in Prison: A Need for Support Systems and Prison Sex*. http://www.stetay.com

Tedlock, B. (2006). Indigenous Heritage and Biopiracy in the Age of Intellectual Property Rights. *Explore, 2*(3), 256–259.

Titmuss, R. (1971). *The Gift Relationship: From Human Blood to Social Policy*. London and New York.

Tullock, G. (Ed.). (1972a). *Explorations in the Theory of Anarchy*. Center for the Study of Public Choice.

Tullock, G. (1972b/2005). The Edge of the Jungle. In Stringham (ed.), pp. 36-48.

Tullock, G. (Ed.). (1974a). *Further Explorations in the Theory of Anarchy*. University Publications.

Tullock, G. (Ed.). (1974b). *The Social Dilemma: The Economics of War and Revolution*. University Publications.

Vahabi, M. (2004). *The Political Economy of Destructive Power*. Edward Elgar.

Vahabi, M. (2010). "Ordres contradictoires et coordination destructive: le malaise iranien" (Contradictory Orders and Destructive Coordination: The Iranian Disease). *Revue Canadienne d'Etudes du Développement (Canadian Journal of Development Studies), 30*(3–4), 503–534.

Vahabi, M. (2011). Appropriation, Violent Enforcement and Transaction Costs: A Critical Survey. *Public Choice, 147*(1), 227–253.

Vahabi, M. (2015a). *The Political Economy of Predation: Manhunting and the Economics of Escape*. Cambridge University Press.

Vahabi, M. (2015b, December 22). Jaygah Sepah dar Eqtesad Iran (The Place of Sepah in the Iranian Economy). *Mihan*, No. 6. Retrieved December 11, 2021, from http://mihan.net/1394/10/01/562/ (in Persian).

Zaitlen, R., & German, J. B. (2000a, June). Of Mice and Men. *Modern Drug Discovery, 3*(5), 63–66.

Zaitlen, R., & German, J. B. (2000b, July/August). "Of Mice and Men" (Part II). *Modern Drug Discovery, 3*(6), 67.

CHAPTER 4

Political Capitalism, its Varieties, and Islam

4.1   INTRODUCTION

In Chap. 2, I showed that an institutionalist approach provides an endogenous explanation of social order and crisis by giving the pride of place to the concept of coordination mechanism in describing economic systems at the *distribution* level. A specific constellation of different modes of coordination determines an economic system in which one coordination mechanism dominates the other. In the same vein, the origins of endogenous social crises were related to the failure of these coordination mechanisms to ensure their mediating role between fundamental institutions (political power and dominant form of property) and economic performance. Moreover, I linked the durability of crisis or the emergence of ordered anarchy to a specific mode of coordination, that is, destructive coordination. Chapter 3 showed that destructive coordination prevails when there exists a disarticulation among different modes of coordination.

Modes of coordination are relevant to understanding different regimes of appropriation, but they do not capture the productive sphere. Accordingly, we need to understand each economic system at two levels: *distribution* and *production*. This distinction is necessary to clarify the interplay of economic and non-economic factors and their combined effect on shaping social orders. The two-level definition of economic

© The Author(s), under exclusive license to Springer Nature   105
Switzerland AG 2023
M. Vahabi, *Destructive Coordination, Anfal and Islamic Political
Capitalism*, https://doi.org/10.1007/978-3-031-17674-6_4

systems is particularly pertinent in the case of capitalism which is now the world-wide system dominating the world market and globalization.

From an institutionalist viewpoint, we need to scrutinize the meaning of capitalism as an economic system at two different levels. Capitalist *production* is a very recent reality emerging in the nineteenth century compared to capitalist appropriative rationale in *distribution* that started during antiquity.

By capitalist appropriation, I mean an economic system based on monetary profit-making as opposed to a subsistence economy. This definition of capitalism is shared by Braudel and Weber, and it can be applied to all those profit-making activities based on the use of market or non-market channels. In this sense, long-distance trade capitalism of luxurious goods and booty-capitalism (stemming from marketization of spoils of war) were forms of pre-modern capitalism. The development of Weberian 'political capitalism' was not dependent on the sanctity of private property rights or the dominance of market coordination. This type of capitalism was also more adapted to political and social crises and wartime situations. Profit-making and rent-seeking from colonialism, and the slave trade are a few historical examples. Similarly, the fusion of property and sovereignty could even enhance political capitalism. But capitalist predatory acquisition is not limited to pre-modern capitalism. Profit-making through non-market channels, such as 'revolving doors' among politicians and businessmen, abound in present-day America, Russia, and China, and many other countries.

However, capitalist production could not emerge before the ripening of a host of economic and institutional prerequisites. Capitalist production is based on the generalization of market or commodity-monetary contractual relationships in all markets including factor markets. The transformation of the labor force into a commodity, the formation of free labor, and the development of the capital market notably the credit system have been determinants in the genesis of capitalist production. Impersonal markets coordinate capitalist production and competition is the driving force of markets and capital accumulation. Confiscatory regimes, the absence of the sanctity of property rights, and monopolistic legal privileges of sovereign institutions hinder competitive market economies. Thus, while destructive coordination enhances predatory acquisition of assets, it impedes capitalist production. The outcome of this contradictory dynamic of creating barriers in production versus enhancement in capital accumulation is unpredictable.

This chapter substantiates the distinction between the capitalist system at the two levels of distribution and production. Such clarification is particularly important in analyzing 'diversities of capitalisms'. The burgeoning literature in comparative economic systems often overlooks the sphere in which diversity is examined. In fact, before discussing diversity, we need to scrutinize what commonalities are at work that renders diversities the possibility to be classified as different varieties of the same family.

Finally, I will explore the relationship of Islam with capitalism and the sanctity of private property. It is often assumed that Islam is supportive of private property and its jurisprudence is compatible with the requirements of modern capitalism. These claims will be critically assessed in this chapter in light of different tendencies in Islam particularly the Sunni and the Shi'i. Our investigation about a specific variant of political capitalism that I have coined 'Islamic political capitalism' starts in this chapter. The Shi'i and Sunni Islamic jurisprudence regarding private property and capitalism is the first step in our journey to grapple with the reality of Islamic political capitalism throughout the remaining chapters of this book.

4.2   The Term Capitalism and Diversity of Capitalisms

Political capitalism assumes varieties of capitalism unless we understand it as something entirely different from capitalism. Holcombe (2018, p. 3) advocates the latter position: "political capitalism is not capitalism, so the name is pejorative and inappropriate for the economic system that has produced such a high level of material well-being everywhere it has been implemented. But there may be a tendency for free-market economies to move toward political capitalism." If political capitalism is not a variant of capitalism, why does the author refer to capitalism? The only possible answer is that the author implicitly assumes non-pejorative capitalism, or a good one, which he names 'free market economies' to distinguish from the bad political capitalism. Thus, the problem is first about the usage of the word 'capitalism' rather than scrutinizing its 'political' version.

The term 'capitalism' has been loaded with political content in support of the Marxist model of the present economic system even though Marx himself used it only a few times (see Beaud, 2018).[1] It was long banned by the economists of the early twentieth century, like Charles Gide, Alfred Marshall, Edwin Seligman, and Gustav Cassel. For example, in the sixth edition of *Principles of Political Economy* (1898/2018), Charles Gide wrote: "This is the new social regime that socialists name capitalism." According to Fernand Braudel (1983, Vol. 2, p. 238), the word capitalism caused many people embarrassment since the Russian Revolution of 1917 to the point that "A reputable historian, Herbert Heaton, has suggested simply abolishing it: '[Of all] the "isms" … the greatest noisemaker has been capitalism. That word, unfortunately, has acquired such a motley of meanings and definitions that one may justly plead that capitalism, like imperialism, is a term that should be cut out of the vocabulary of every self-respecting scholar'."

Braudel added that even the well-known Marxist, "Lucien Febvre himself felt it could be dropped, since it had been over-used". Other terms were alternatively used to describe this new regime: 'open society', 'industrial society', 'developed economy', 'free market economy'. Holcombe's reluctance to use the term capitalism instead of 'free market economies' might also be grasped with regard to his political orientation.

From a purely economic viewpoint, the problem with these alternative terms is that they do not accurately characterize the economic relationships in a developed market economy with a credit and a marketized free labor system in which profit-making activity is the principal drive. As Schumpeter has shown, capitalism is not reducible to a 'market economy'. The term capitalism is now used by many Nobel Prize economists who are not Marxists. Williamson's (1985) masterpiece *The Economic Institutions of Capitalism: Firms, Markets, Relational Contracting* is a salient illustration. Despite the vast adoption of the word capitalism by economists, its

---

[1] According to Braudel (1983, Vol. 2, p. 237) and Axel Honneth (2018), Marx never used the word. Contrary to these authors, Inikori (2017, p. 139) believes that Marx invented the term capitalism. Following Küttler (2008, p. 250-1), both claims can be refuted. In fact, Marx used the term capitalism twice in the three volumes of *Das Kapital*. Küttler documents that Marx only started employing the noun capitalism in the late 1870s and early 1880s to describe a mode of production and society. Küttler's contention might be slightly nuanced in light of Krätke (2020, p. 2). The latter quotes Marx (1857a, 1857b) in 'Conspectus of Bakunin's *Statism and Anarchy*' in which he employed 'capitalism' as a shorthand term of the 'capitalist mode of production'. I thank the historian Kaveh Yazdani for sharing with me his unpublished notes on this issue.

meaning is often ambiguous in the recent literature on the varieties of capitalism.

For example, Hall and Soskice (2001) explore varieties of capitalism without clarifying what they mean by capitalism throughout their whole edited volume. They suggest a dichotomous opposition between two types of capitalism, namely 'liberal market economies' and 'coordinated market economies' based on specific firms' behavior. Following Williamson (1985), they distinguish the governance structure in these two major varieties. The former using market mechanisms favors investment in transferable assets, while the latter employing non-market mechanisms privileges specific assets. Both variants are examined in terms of 'market economies' as if capitalism is simply market economy.

Similarly, Bruno Amable (2003) studies varieties of capitalism but never explains what he means by 'capitalism'. He selects five fundamental institutional areas, namely institutions of product, labor, and financial markets as well as the welfare state and education sector. Given the multiplicity of criteria, he shuns a dichotomous opposition and ends up by identifying five types of capitalism: (1) the market-based model, (2) the social-democratic model, (3) the Continental European model, (4) the Mediterranean model, (5) the Asian model. The first model is akin to that of Hall and Soskice's 'liberal market economies'. But the other ones have all a geographical denomination.

In the same vein, Esping Andreson (1990) distinguishes three types of welfare capitalism, namely conservative, liberal, and social-democratic, without dwelling on the qualifier 'capitalism'. One of the commonalities of Esping Anderson (1990), Hall and Soskice (2001), and Amable (2003) is that they do not explain the institutional varieties of capitalism by reference to capitalist appropriative rationale, namely *different forms of profit-making*. By contrast, Max Weber (1922/1978) conceptualized his dichotomous opposition of 'market' versus 'political' capitalism based on different forms of *profit-making* activity.

4.3   WEBER: MARKET VERSUS POLITICAL CAPITALISM

Werner Sombart and Max Weber were among the first authors who used the term capitalism in academic milieu. Sombart's (1902) use of the term in *Der Moderne Kapitalismus* (*Modern Capitalism*) might be related to his engagement in the socialist movement. Weber, however, as a non-Marxist also used the term in 1905 in analyzing the protestant ethics as the spirit of capitalism. Since 1905 until his later works in 1922, Weber distinguished 'political capitalism' from 'market capitalism'. The former was coined by Weber to depict the economic and political system in ancient Rome. He also called it 'politically oriented capitalism'. Weber opposed political capitalism to market or modern 'rational' capitalism of the nineteenth century. It is noteworthy that Weber extended his teacher's tradition, Theodor Mommsen, in applying the term capitalism to describe economic realities before the end of the eighteenth century, namely before the industrial mode of production.

Marx was categorically against such a usage since he reserved the term for a specific 'mode of production' based on generalized commodity-monetary relationships, free labor, and credit system. According to Marx (1857–8/1964), *personal* subordination in pre-capitalist economic formations was replaced by *impersonal* subordination to market relationships under capitalist production. The supra-economic force was not required to extract surplus value in this new system. Weber (1922/1968, p. 165) shared with Marx his description of modern or rational capitalism: "It is only in the modern Western World that rational capitalistic enterprise with fixed capital, free labor, the rational specialization and combination of functions, and the allocation of productive functions on the basis of capitalistic enterprises, bound together in a market economy, are to be found."

In Weber's opinion, modern market capitalism is rational for two principal reasons. First, it relies upon 'voluntary' relationship of free labor within the capitalist type of organization rather than brutal force or personal subordination. Second, rational business enterprises are based on capital accounting (see Love, 1991). However, Weber also referred to capitalism during Antiquity and the Middle Ages all over the world for thousands of years wherever the possibilities of exchange and money economy and money financing have been present. Could the term capitalism be extended to those periods? And if so, in what sense?

Reconsidering this issue, Fernand Braudel (1983, pp. 238–239) averred: "Well this is really a question of terminology. I need hardly point out that no historian of *ancien régime* societies, *a fortiori* of ancient civilizations, would ever, when using the term capitalism, have in mind the definition Alexander Gerschenkron calmly gives us: 'Capitalism, that is the modern industrial system'. I have already indicated that capitalism in the past (as distinct from capitalism today) only occupied a narrow platform of economic life. How could one possibly take it to mean a 'system' extending over the whole of society? It was nevertheless a world apart, different from and indeed foreign to the social and economic context surrounding it. And it is in relation to this context that it is defined as 'capitalism', not merely in relation to new capitalist forms which were to emerge later in time. In fact, capitalism was what it was in relation to a non-capitalism of immense proportions. And to refuse to admit this dichotomy within the economy of the past, on the pretext that 'true' capitalism dates only from the nineteenth century, means abandoning the effort to understand the significance - crucial to the analysis of that economy - of what might be termed the former topology of capitalism."

Braudel employed the term capitalism to depict *commercial capitalism* based upon 'long-distance trade' long before the rise of industrial capitalism. This type of capitalism represented a different rationale compared to the subsistence or household economy (*oikonomia*) and resulted in the separation of household and enterprise.

What was common between the old and the modern types of capitalism? According to Weber, they could be defined by reference to qualitatively different forms of profit-making. He distinguished six forms of profit-making, three of them (number 3–5) were attributed to political capitalism. "3. It may be orientation to opportunities for predatory profit from political organizations or persons connected with politics. This includes the financing of wars or revolutions and the financing of party leaders by loans and supplies. 4. It may be orientation to the profit opportunities in continuous business activity which arise by virtue of domination by force or of a position of power guaranteed by the political authority. There are two main sub-types: colonial profits, either through the operation of plantations with compulsory deliveries or compulsory labor or through monopolistic and compulsory trade, and fiscal profits, through the farming of taxes and of offices, whether at home or in colonies. 5. It may be orientation to profit opportunities in unusual transactions with political booties" (Weber, 1922/1978, p. 164). In summary, they were *all non-market predatory ways of profit-making* or 'booty capitalism'. In the past, they existed during the war times, and declined where large areas such as China and later Roman Empire have been pacified.

Most of the great magnates of the late Roman Republic like Caesar, Pompey, Lucullus, Brutus, or Antony enriched themselves through political capitalism. A salient example is the way Crassus benefited from repeated fires in Rome. Observing how extremely subject the city was to fire and falling down houses, and their standing so near together, he bought slaves that were builders and architects, and when he had collected these to the number of more than 500, he made it his practice to buy houses that were on fire, and those that were in the neighborhood at a price close to nothing (Love, 1991, pp. 165–168). The profit was made by using slave or unfree labor. Crassus also enriched himself by taking advantage of the Sullan proscriptions, buying apparently whatever booty and spoils were available at rock-bottom prices. Political capitalism contributed to the transformation of booties into commodities. It enriched the Roman political, military, and economic elites. But the accumulated wealth could not be transformed into 'capital' since political capitalism promoted slavery and not market capitalism.

4.4   Political Capitalism and Crony Capitalism

Is political capitalism different from crony capitalism? The answer is both yes and no in the sense that while crony capitalism overlaps political capitalism, the latter cannot be reduced theoretically and historically to crony capitalism. To ascertain the relationship between them, we first need to scrutinize what is meant by crony capitalism.

Crony capitalism, the expression coined by George Taber in 1980 to describe the Philippine economy under the autocrat Ferdinand Marcos, has also been widely used in the press to characterize an economic system based on rent-seeking by individuals and businesses with political connections and influence (Taber, 2015).

Its two major characteristics are (1) dispensation of selective privileges regarding tax exemption, grants, and other forms of government assistance to suppress open competition in a free market; (2) social connections and networking among private/public beneficiaries. Razo (2021) builds a model to explain how crony networks can induce large-scale effects that can both propagate risk of predation and incentivize private protection to withstand it.

Crony capitalism moved beyond Philippine shores and acquired regional currency during the 1997–1998 Asian Financial Crisis, when American officials such as Bill Clinton (2005), Robert Rubin (2003), and notably Lawrence Summers (1998), then a deputy Treasury secretary, employed the Philippine-coined terms "cronyism" and "crony capitalism" to lay the blame for the Asian crisis on the cozy collusion between government and business (see Kristof, 2011).

In this sense, crony capitalism was grasped as the opposite of the "developmental state" (like Singapore), while the latter also symbolized the close relationship between government and industry (Bello, 2000, 2004). In reality, drawing a demarcation line between political cronyism and development state is impossible. As Hau (2017) aptly noted: "Successful developmental states (…) are unable to escape being tarred by the label of 'crony capitalism,' as seen in the *Economist*'s Crony Capitalism Index (2014) ranking Hong Kong (1), Malaysia (3), and Singapore (5)—the three countries that experienced the East Asia Miracle—*above* the Philippines (6) in the list of countries where 'politically connected businessmen are most likely to prosper'."

After the 2008 financial crisis, many analysts and journalists transposed crony capitalism to the USA. It was often considered as a politically corrupt and inefficient system generated by lobbying activities of private sector and their influence on the state representing a deviation from free-market capitalism. In this sense, there exist commonalities between political and crony capitalism since they both build on profit-making through non-market mechanisms. However, political capitalism as conceptualized by Max Weber is not a deviation of capitalism; it precedes historically market capitalism and develops capitalist rationale of profit-maximizing from a distributive viewpoint although it might hinder capitalist productive relationships. Booty capitalism, colonialism, and predatory activities based on private/state collusion cannot be characterized as 'crony capitalism' but they constitute main forms of political capitalism.

Moreover, crony capitalism has often a negative connotation pertaining to corruption, patron-clientelist relationships, plunder, and depletion of a country's resources for the sake of personal and political benefits of the dictator and his family. It has been introduced to emphasize the failure of a state-led (authoritarian) development. Crony capitalism has been characterized as an anti-developmental state. Political capitalism does not necessarily assume inefficient political apparatus and breaches the conceptual opposition between crony capitalism and developmental states. Thus, we explore the general characteristics of political capitalism in the next section.

4.5 General Characteristics of Political Capitalism

Political capitalism is not limited to Antiquity. It also existed in the Medieval period, early modern Europe, and persisted after the rise of modern capitalism all over the world.

Borrowing upon Braudel (1977), human activity in the economic sphere might be described as a three-storey building in which the first level is composed of 'material life' or subsistence, non-market activities. This is what the Ancient Greeks meant by *Oikonomia*. The term was composed of two words: *oikos*, which is usually translated as 'household'; and *nemein*, which is best translated as 'management and dispensation' (Leshem, 2016). The second storey is 'market economy' including daily market exchanges and local trade, and finally the third floor is 'capitalism' by which Braudel understands long-distance trade, high profits, and the emergence of monopolies. The last floor is what the Ancient Greeks named *Chrematistic* or profit-making activities. Although we now employ the term 'economics' deriving from *Oikonomia* for describing profit-making activities, we clearly mean the opposite, namely *Chrematistic*. The enterprise or Company[2] rather than the household is the main subject of economic inquiry.

Similar to Weber, Braudel characterized 'capitalist' activities by *profit-making* rationale. He referred to highly profitable long-distance trade and banking activities as capitalist long before the emergence of industrial capitalism. Depicting the activities of big merchants, he wrote: "It is no accident that throughout the world a group of large merchants stands out clearly from the mass of ordinary dealers and this group is, on the one hand, very small and, on the other, always connected with long-distance trade, among its other activities...Need I comment that these capitalists...were friends of the prince and helpers or exploiters of the state?...Who doubt that these capitalists had monopolies at their disposal or that they simply had the power needed to eliminate competition nine times out of ten?" (Braudel, 1977, 56–57).

According to Braudel, the ascendancy of merchant capitalism in the Western economies was related to its close relationship with the state. This observation is in tune with Weber's 'politically oriented capitalism'. The alliance between merchants and the prince was a driving force of political capitalism in the third storey of profit-making economy in the West. In this alliance, the big merchants had a leading role compared to the prince. In fact, during the thirteenth century, the merchant republics of Italy or the Low countries were spearheaded by the merchants as a 'class' influencing the state.

---

[2] See sections 3.4 and 3.7 for the importance of Company as a legal identity in the development of market capitalism.

By contrast, according to Gernet (1962), big merchants in Song China never acted collectively despite their common interests since the state was constantly depriving them or any other rival force from acting collectively to undermine the dominant power of central administration. In a sense, while the rise of Western capitalism was supported by fragmented states and the primacy of property over sovereignty, in China and many other parts of the world sovereignty reigned over property. In the latter case, the state-merchant or the politico-capitalist class played a major role in profit-making activities. Political capitalism enhances a collusion of political and economic elites, but its driving force might be either property owners or power holders.

Moreover, even in the West, the transition from the third storey (commercial capitalism) to a fourth storey of modern industrial capitalism required the intervention of brutal force of the state, enclosure, colonialism, and 'triangular trade' (Findlay, 1990) to accumulate colossal amounts of capital. Although the emergence of industrial capitalism in the West concentrated economic power in the hands of the bourgeoisie, the political power still belonged to the landed aristocracy dominant in the state apparatus. The interaction between two different magnates of economic and political power took a long historical period during which the bourgeoisie could 'buy' the state.

The metaphor of the three-storey-floor building should not be interpreted as if each inferior floor is superseded by the superior one. For example, political capitalism may derive from developed forms of capitalism in which big monopolies tend to control the state (Holcombe, 2015). Furthermore, the floors often coexist simultaneously and in parallel. The President Eisenhower's warning in 1961 regarding the dangers of the Military-Industrial Complex might be regarded as the emergence of political capitalism in a permanent war economy in the aftermath of the Second World War. In other words, the genesis and development of capitalism involve both market and political capitalism while their relationships might be contradictory, complementary, or partially complementary and partially contradictory.

Three major channels lead to the emergence and development of political capitalism.

1. **Spoils of war**: warfare and revolutions often provide the origins of political capitalism particularly because they breed war economy and markets for spoils. Political capitalism is also dubbed 'booty

capitalism' (Weber, 1922/1978, vol. 1; Vahabi, 2004). While in the pre-capitalist societies, the war economy was directly related to the wartime, in market capitalism, the war economy as a branch of economic activity persists even during the peace time. Moreover, the industrialization of war and the emergence of 'total warfare' mobilize the whole economy and society at the service of the state (Vahabi et al., 2020). Accordingly, destructive activity offers a large market for reconstruction. In this sense, market capitalism expands the scale of booty capitalism. Contrary to the thesis of 'Doux commerce', raid and trade entertain a complementary rather than a contradictory relationship (Vahabi, 2016).

2. **Colonialism**: Empire-building, territorial expansion, and colonialism entail the coercive acquisition of natural resources and control over labor force. The dispossession of the native residents of vast territories from their natural resources and enslavement of part or the whole population were principal factors in generating the world market since the fifteenth century. Colonialism played a contradictory role with regard to market capitalism. On the one hand, it enhanced the *material* basis for market capitalism through the expansion of world market, and on the other hand, it impeded the *institutional factors* for the development of market capitalism since it promoted political capitalism in the colonies by conflating sovereignty and property.

3. **Confiscatory regimes in the presence of market and monetary relationships**: Absent of security for property rights, the state transforms into a 'private property' of the tyrant, the Imam, or oligarchs. Tribute (*Kharaj*) and tax-farming, coercive transactions, monopoly of specific commodities or whole economic sectors, and regulatory activities of the state can be all sources of profit-making by privileged and protected groups in the society. Rent-seeking through a confiscatory regime in the presence of market and money relationships results in political capitalism, but it strongly hinders the development of market capitalism.

These three channels do not provide an exhaustive list of all methods breeding political capitalism. Indeed, the use of political power to achieve economic gains coevolves with the evolution of market capitalism and the scope of state's interference in the economy.

The impact of political capitalism on market capitalism has not been the same at different stages of economic development. Before reviewing the complex interplay of political and market capitalism, we need to isolate universal characteristics of political capitalism throughout the history. Following Weber, I define political capitalism as specific forms of profit-making or rather *rent-seeking*. It assumes the following general characteristics:

1. Broadly speaking, political capitalism can be characterized as non-market predatory mechanisms of profit-making in monetary terms. The profit is extracted from *distribution* sphere through *appropriative* activities in different modes of production wherever market, money relationships, and financing exist.
2. The institutional prerequisite of political capitalism is the conflation of sovereignty and property.
3. Political capitalism requires a collusion of state and private sectors on the basis of rent-seeking activity. Political capitalism is inconceivable without a predatory state in which the state bureaucracy is a booty for the political class.
4. Political capitalism enhances a strong tendency toward bureaucratization within market relationships.
5. From a sociological viewpoint, political capitalism promotes the interests of a small group of elites against the interests of majority of the people.

These universal characteristics adopt specific features in individual cases. An empirical investigation about political capitalism needs to explore its specific features before and after the rise of modern capitalism in different countries.

During Antiquity, political capitalism was closely related to the wartime economies, and booty acquisition. Weber depicted political capitalism under ancient conditions as 'patrician' since it was carried by the dominant classes of the day. The militarism of ancient burghers played a crucial role, ensuring that the dominant classes were the bearers of a capitalism that exploited warrior virtues and martial/political competences rather than entrepreneurship, hard work, or technical inventiveness. By contrast, the incipient market-oriented capitalism in the *latifunida* and in some urban production developments can be characterized as 'plebian' because it was supported by non-dominant classes. This 'plebian' capitalism lacked the impetus to expand beyond a certain point. The major arena for private capital formation became instead the sphere of political capitalism. Contrary to the republican era, the later emperors, like Nero attacked private latifundists in Africa and elsewhere, a policy that contributed to a greater centralization of government for which a more bureaucratic administration was required. In this sense, it had an important inhibiting effect on the development of market capitalism. Weber considers political capitalism as one of the major sources of the Roman Empire's decline (see Love, 1991, Chap. 6).

While political capitalism became the predominant force in antiquity, its ascendency cannot be attributed to an inherent 'superiority' over market capitalism. We cannot postulate an intrinsic tendency of development in this direction. In fact, political capitalism may be present without completely forestalling the development of market capitalism as during early modern Europe or even today. The political and juridical institutions including our routines of thought, perceptions, norms of behavior as well as the economic system determine the relationship between political and market capitalism.

For example, while Marx scrupulously reserved the term 'capitalism' for the modern industrial capitalism based on free labor and credit system, he (1867/1978, Chap. 26) paradoxically furnished an explanation about the genesis of capitalism in England starting in the late fifteenth and early sixteenth century in terms of 'primitive accumulation of capital'.[3] This original accumulation was orchestrated by the absolutist state through taxation, expropriation of land, the enclosure act, colonialism, and triangular trade. Marx's analysis of primitive accumulation in England and the role of the absolutist state come within the scope of political capitalism as defined by Weber. However, in this case, political capitalism was not an impediment to market capitalism, but rather an enhancer of its development. Perry Anderson (1974) disagreed with Marx's analysis of the absolutist state and distinguished two different trajectories in the Eastern and Western Europe with regard to the impact of absolutist states in developing capitalism. Historical evidence regarding the relationships between political and market capitalism in the transition from feudalism to capitalism in the West indicates both contradictions and complementarities.

[3] Marx credited Smith (1776/1961) for being the originator of the concept. Mingardi (2018) challenges this contention.

4.6   MARKET CAPITALISM AND GREAT DEMARCATION

The British Glorious Revolution (1688), the American Independence War (1776), and the French Revolution (1789) all contributed to a fundamental institutional change that made possible the rise of modern capitalism. This institutional leap was initially juridical and political, and it can be summarized by a *great demarcation* between sovereignty and property (Vahabi et al. 2020, pp. 866–868). Without this legal and political foundation, modern capitalism could not be born. It was not 'capitalist mode of production' that preceded the political and juridical 'superstructure'. It was rather the other way around: *the demarcation between sovereignty and property gave rise to the predominance of property, and the advent of market capitalism.*

John Locke (1690/1952) pioneered the conceptualization of this change by insisting on the 'sanctity of private property'. Locke did not mean the 'sanctity' of private property of the King over the state, or the security of property rights for feudal wealth-holders. He was explicitly referring to the labor's right of private property over its product. This right could not be secured without finishing with the state as the 'private property' of the tyrant.

In his Chapter 3, on "Method I. John Locke", Commons (1931/1961, Vol. 1) pointed out that Locke united Law, Economics, and Ethics in a single concept 'Labor'. The issue arose in his justification of the revolution of 1689. It was against the doctrine of a divine right of political power that Locke set up the "natural right of life, liberty, and property", derived from the right of labor to its own product: "Locke set forth the labor theory of value, not mainly as a foundation for economics, but mainly as a justification of a revolution that supplanted rights of sovereigns by rights of property" (Ibid, p. 52).

Before the great demarcation, the state was the Crown's private property, and it was transformed into *Sovereign* power by the revolution. As Commons explained in *Sociology: Syllabus*: "Sovereignty involves three conceptions: coercion, order and right. These together constitute the state. Absolutism, despotism [is] not a true state" (1899–1900/1965, p. 356). Similarly, the French Revolution abolished privately owned forms of power, such as feudalism, seigneurialism, and venal public office, and dismantled the Crown domain, thus making the state purely sovereign. On the other hand, property was defined by rules specific to itself, not by extraneous political factors. This, in short, confirmed the autonomy of the sphere of property (Blaufarb 2016).

In the first chapter, we distinguished traditional from modern markets. The predominant coordination mechanism in market capitalism is impersonal markets. The transition from personal to impersonal modern markets requires the great demarcation. This demarcation put an end to juridical monopolies, unsecured property rights, confiscatory regime, and superiority of sovereignty over property. The 'sanctity of private property' and the role of the state as enforcer of property rights paved the way for flourishing impersonal markets and corporation as a legal identity. Recent studies on the impact of institutions on economic growth demonstrate that property rights can be a growth enhancer if they are not only well defined, private and secure, but also "generalized" in the sense that they can be applied to all agents in the economy and not just to a privileged subset (see Ogilvie & Carus, 2014).

Two caveats are warranted in discussing the demarcation of property and sovereignty. The first one is that 'demarcation' means *autonomy* and not necessarily *separation*. The autonomy implies the independence of 'enterprise' from the 'state'. The evolution of the enterprise since its separation from the household,[4] and the emergence of the joint stock company strengthened this demarcation. The invention of company as a moral person with an independent juridical identity living 'immortally' furnished the basis for the predominance of property. The birth of joint stock company with mobile capital based on reunifying dispersed assets, and hardly confiscable by the absolutist state was a salient illustration of demarcation.

However, the *demarcation* is not synonymous to *separation*. A joint stock company derives its status as a moral person by reference to sovereignty. "Sovereignty is inseparable from property. It is the sanction of sovereignty that make property what it is for the time being in any country, because physical force, or violence, is the last and final appeal when the other sanctions are deemed inadequate to control individuals" (Commons, 1970, p. 41). The role of the state as a third-party external enforcer confirms the inseparability of property and sovereignty. It is noteworthy that in enforcing property rights, the intervention of the brutal force guarantees the external conditions of production, even though it is not required

---

[4] This refers to a transition from *Oikonomia* to *Chrematistic* resulting in the separation between household (a real person) and company (a juridical person), see section 4.2.

in organizing the production. Herein lies one of the principal differences of political capitalism with market capitalism.

A second caveat is regarding the demarcation of property and sovereignty. Contrary to the natural right philosophy, property rights have nothing eternally sacred, and they change through time. The Fourteenth Amendment of the American constitution (adopted in 1868) provides a good illustration. According to this amendment, property meant *use-value*, not *exchange-value*. Commons (1924/1995, Chap. 2) devoted a whole chapter to show how the meaning of property gradually changed from *use-value* to include *exchange-value* decided not by the executive or legislative powers but by the Supreme Court in 1890. Following the primitive definition of property as the mere exclusive holding of objects for one's own use, a property was considered to be taken from the owner under the power of *eminent domain* which took *title* and *possession*. However, if the owners were deprived of the power to fix the prices, this did not mean the violation of property rights. On the contrary, if property is defined with respect to the *exchange-value*, then depriving the owners of their property does not necessarily mean taking under the eminent domain. The owners are deprived of their property whenever they cannot set the price under the police power which takes its exchange-value. According to this new definition of property, the distinction between sovereignty and property is blurred under both *eminent domain* and *police power* (the state's power to fix the price). Similarly, the exchange-value of property is absent if either the owner or expected purchasers are forbidden access to markets where they can sell and buy the property. Hence, the Fourteenth Amendment was reinterpreted in 1897 in a way to extend liberty of access to markets as part of the new definition of property.

The evolution of the meaning of property has resulted in two different things: "One is Property, the other is Business. The one is property in the sense of things owned, the other is property in the sense of exchange-value of things. One is physical objects, the other is marketable assets...In the course of time this exchange-value has come to be known as 'intangible property,' that is, the kind of property whose value depends upon right of access to a commodity market, a labor market, a money market, and so on" (Commons, 1924/1995, pp. 18–19). In this sense, the exchange-value is not 'physical' or *corporeal* but *behavioristic*. The right of action creates a market value for the asset. This point has been captured by the property rights approach: the economic or consensual value of an asset is not determined by its physical properties, but rather by the allowed rights of action over the asset. "(T)he value of what is being traded depends upon the allowed rights of action over the physical good and upon the degree to which these rights are enforced" (Demsetz, 1964, p. 18).

The tension between the need for demarcation and the inseparability of property and sovereignty explains a *permanent tendency* in market capitalism toward political capitalism. The *new* political capitalism, born as a prelude to market capitalism or as a tendency originating from market capitalism itself, is different from *past* political capitalism. The general commonalities of new and past political capitalism notwithstanding, they fundamentally differ with regard to productive process of capitalist system.

The new political capitalism is limited to *(re)distribution* domain and does not extend to *productive* sphere, although it develops monopoly power, violates competition, and extends authoritative mode of allocation. Accordingly, the relationships between political and market capitalism are both complementary and contradictory. Political capitalism as a permanent tendency in market capitalism is as universal as market capitalism itself and cannot be attached to certain regions in the world.

The concept of political capitalism has recently been used to characterize two different economic situations. Holcombe (2018, p. 52) employs it to describe the evolution of recent American capitalism,[5] while Milanovic (2018, Chap. 3) refers to political capitalism in analyzing the post-socialist transition in China, and ten other Asian and African countries with a colonial and feudal (or semi-feudal) background. In my theoretical framework, they are both correct in underlining the presence of political capitalism in today's USA and China. However, their theoretical framework narrows the scope of application of the concept. We will review both in the following sections.

4.7   Varieties of Political Capitalism: The North American Case

The ancient political capitalism existed during antiquity in Rome and China in the wartimes. The fusion of property and sovereignty prevailed before the modern revolutions. The new political capitalism emerged

---

[5] Holcombe implicitly suggests the election of Ronald Reagan as a turning point by citing Hacker and Pierson: "In a study of political capitalism, Hacker and Pierson's view is that American capitalism as an economic system has increasingly evolved into political capitalism since the election of Ronald Reagan" (2018, p. 52).

within the context of a new era marked by the transition from personal to impersonal markets and the great demarcation of property and sovereignty. A major source of new political capitalism is the development of regulatory functions of the modern state since the progressive era.

Borrowing Weber's concept of political capitalism, Kolko (1963, 1965) described the American political and economic systems during the Progressive Era dating from 1900 to 1916 as political capitalism. The ascent of big corporations based on concentration and centralization of capital had resulted in violating free competition and creation of market power by monopolies and oligopolies. It was generally believed that the government's intervention was necessary to regulate business in defense of consumers' individual rights. The Progressive Era disseminated the ideology that the state had to go beyond protecting individual rights, to assume a managing or regulating function to eschew the concentrated market power of corporations.

Kolko (1965) challenged this belief by furnishing abundant empirical evidence including the powerful railroad industry. He examined the origins and early history of the Interstate Commerce Commission (ICC) with regard to the regulation of this industry. Kolko demonstrated that the purpose of the Act of 1887 was simply to lend stability to railroad cartels which the expansion of the industry had rendered chronically unstable. Concerning the Elkins Act of 1903, he also showed that the Act had its origins in the legal department of the Pennsylvania Railroad and was the product of railroad pressures throughout. By the eve of the First World War, the Commission was succeeding in the course on which it had been set in 1887: cartelizing the railroad industry without pooling. This was a clear example of collusions and cartelization. The rules and regulations were decided in reality by those who had deemed to be regulated: "It is business control over politics (and by 'business' I mean the major economic interests) rather than political regulation of the economy that is the significant phenomenon of the Progressive Era" (Kolko, 1963, p. 2).

Holcombe (2015, pp. 41–66; 2018, pp. 9–10) acknowledges the pioneering work of Kolko (1963) in applying the concept of political capitalism to the American economic history. He adds other manifestations of political capitalism such as Eisenhower's warnings about (1961) Military-Industrial Complex (Holcombe, 2015, p. 41), government bailouts of firms following the recession of 2008, subsidies to firms with political connections, the Microsoft's political connections to maintain its profitability, and even Federal Reserve policy of supporting the banking industry

(Holcombe, 2018, pp. 10, 41–42). He defines the new political capitalism in these terms: "Political capitalism is an economic system in which business controls government more than government controls business" (Holcombe, 2015, p. 61).

Holcombe's concept of political capitalism is concurrent with Luigi Zingales (2015, 2017) on a political theory of the firm and the increasing importance of 'revolving doors' in the recent American business. He also argues that the interaction of concentrated corporate power and politics is a threat to the functioning of the free-market economy as well as to democracy. A major issue is to gauge to what extent can the power of firms in the marketplace be transformed into political power. Another problem is to measure to what extent the political power gained by firms will be used to hinder competition and maintain their incumbent monopoly power.

These questions were already discussed in Berle and Means (1932) classical work. Zingales (2017, p. 117) wrongly assumes that "the overwhelming political power of business was first tamed during the Progressive Era and later by the New Deal". However, he (2017, pp. 121–124) aptly notes that *between 1997 and 2012, profits are principally derived from barriers to entry and competition rather than from capital accumulation.* This confirms the significance of the market power of big corporations and their connections with the White House, the Congress, and the Senate.[6] In other words, the rules of regulatory activities of the government are decided by those actors that are supposed to be regulated.

Big corporations employ a combination of economic innovation and political influence to maintain their market power in their rivalry with other competitors (Philippon, 2019).[7] Efficient lobbying as a strong means of competition is an art of avoiding juridical barriers to bribe without being accused of bribing. Revolving doors is the outcome of this intricate mechanism of the so-called unethical but yet legal behavior: "In the last decade, the 'revolving door' phenomenon - defined as such when the heads of state agencies, after completing their bureaucratic terms, enter the very sector they have regulated - has intensified, and has been widely

[6] Zingales (2017, pp. 122–124) provides many examples such as the extension of the copyright of the Walt Disney Co. on Mickey Mouse, or Google during the Obama administration.

[7] Philippon (2019) provides a vivid description of the increase in market power of big enterprises in the USA during the last 20 years in comparison with the European free-market development.

documented as having negative effects on the economy" (Brezis & Cariolle, 2019, p. 595). The authors document its presence in many sectors including the pharmaceutical, telecommunication, and defense. Zingales (2015) underlines its significance, particularly in the finance sector. According to an OECD report (2009), the revolving door has been one of the major causes of the 2008 crisis. Vukovic (2021) demonstrates the 'political bailouts' by exploring the relationship between political connections and corporate bailouts during 2008–2009.

These studies cast light on the emergence of new political capitalism which is an outcome of the control that business exerts on government. The concentrated power of corporations or the power of property dominates sovereignty. The insightful illustrations and analysis of Holcombe regarding the presence of political capitalism in the American today's economy notwithstanding, his theoretical framework suffers from two major shortcomings.

First, Holcombe tries to deny the relationship between the emergence of political capitalism and a predatory state in the American case. In doing so, he reduces predatory states to 'monarchies and dictatorships' as if Liberal democratic states are not predatory, or that they cannot degenerate to autocratic states.[8] "Political capitalism is more than just a reversion to a predatory model of the state that draws a parallel between capitalism and predatory governments like monarchies and dictatorships" (2018, p. 70).

One of the conditions of political capitalism is the presence of a state in which the bureaucracy has transformed into a booty for the political class. This entails the conversion of the state into a corporation. Revolving doors and the collusion between the state and financial circles or big oligopolies afford abundant illustrations with regard to the predatory role of the state in the USA.

James Galbraith correctly described the predator state in the USA at the beginning of the new century: "The Predator State is an economic system wherein entire sectors have been built up to feast on public systems built

---

[8] Holcombe (2018, p. 70) kindly refers to my paper on a positive theory of predatory state (Vahabi, 2016) but he erroneously considers that I have developed a "framework for analyzing North's predatory state". As a matter of fact, I have done exactly the opposite, since I have characterized North's theory of the state as 'contractual' and tried to develop a 'predatory' approach to the state that contradicts the contractual perspective. In my opinion all the states including Liberal democratic are predatory although they might be welfare-enhancing or welfare-degrading.

originally for public purposes and largely serving the middle class. The corporate republic simply administers the spoils system. On a day-to-day basis, the business of its leadership is to deliver favors to their clients. These range from coal companies to sweatshop operators to military contractors (…) Everywhere you look, regulatory functions have been turned over to lobbyists. Everywhere you look, public decisions yield gains to specific private persons. Everywhere you look, the public decision is made by the agent of a private party for the purpose of delivering private gain. This is not an accident: it is a system. In the corporate republic that presides over the Predator State, nothing is done for the common good" (2009, pp. 146–147).

Second, Holcombe (2015, p. 61) pretends that "Political capitalism is an economic system in which business controls government more than government controls business". This holds true in the American case, but not for all forms of political capitalism. As emphasized by Weber, political capitalism has been historically an outcome of the interference of politicians, political parties, and military officials in profit-making. Milanovic (2019) focuses on government's control over business to characterize political capitalism in China.

4.8   Varieties of Political Capitalism: The Chinese Case

Milanovic (2019) explores political capitalism in 11 Asian and African countries with a colonial and feudal background, namely China, Vietnam, Malaysia, Laos, Singapore, Algeria, Tanzania, Angola, Botswana, Rwanda, and Zimbabwe. Among them, China is by far the most important country, and it is regarded as the prototype of the system of political capitalism.[9]

Quoting Weber on political capitalism, Milanovic endeavors to clarify why the Chinese economy provides an illustration of this type of system. He starts by arguing that in reality 'Communism' was nothing but a system of transition from feudalism to indigenous capitalism in countries that were less developed and often colonized or dominated by the West. "Communism is the functional equivalent of the rise of the bourgeoisie in

---

[9] According to Milanovic (2019, p. 125), political capitalism in Africa has been strengthened because of the Chinese strong economic ties with this continent. He particularly underlines China's first successful intervention in engineering the removal of Robert Mugabe from power in Zimbabwe in 2017.

the West" (2019, pp. 75–76). Speaking concretely, the Communist movement in the Orient was a left-wing and nationalist movement for the modernization of backward societies by combining two objectives: a social revolution to put an end to the power of landlords and other magnates, and a political revolution to overthrow foreign rule.

Contrary to Communism, other pro-independence parties such as the Congress party in India were by definition nationalist but did not advocate social transformation. To support his critical assessment of Communism as the equivalent of domestic bourgeoisie in the West, Milanovic underlines the fact that "communism was more successful in less-developed countries" (2018, p. 82). It was the least successful in more developed industrial countries such as East Germany and Czechoslovakia and more successful in poor agricultural countries like China and Vietnam.

Milanovic is correct in arguing that Communism in practice should not be grasped within the 'standard Western influenced conception of history', namely as an antithesis of capitalism. In fact, Communist movement accomplished what Rudolf Bahro (1978) called 'the non-capitalist path to an industrial society'. Bahro was speaking of the East Germany and not China since the Communist movement accomplished the industrialization and modernization mission of capitalism without capitalists. The two pillars of what Karl Polanyi (1944) called 'grand transformation', namely the transition from agriculture to industry and from countryside to the urban life were furnished by Communist revolutions. This included not only those countries with a colonial and feudal background but also countries with a certain level of capitalist development like Russia, East Germany, and Czechoslovakia.

The common point among all these countries was that the Communism appeared as a result of mass warfare during the two world wars. While in some countries, colonialism and feudalism were the major targets, in some other tsarism, fascism, and feudal remnants were principal sources of opposition. But the so-called socialist system was nothing but the prolongation of war economy during peacetime.[10] Thus, my major objection to Milanovic's contention is that modernization mission of the communist movement cannot be limited to countries with a feudal and colonial role. The industrialization of Russia through the Stalinist forced collectivization is not less important than the Chinese industrialization. But communism

---

[10] See section 1.4 for the relationship between this type of economy and authoritative coordination.

or state socialism cannot be characterized as 'political capitalism'. Neither in Stalin's Russia nor in Mao's China, the state bureaucracy was not a booty for the political class to conduct monetary profit-making.

Milanovic also concedes that state socialism was not political capitalism. He cites Deng Xiaoping as the "founding father of modern political capitalism, an approach rather than an ideology-that combined private-sector dynamism, efficient rule of bureaucracy, and a one-party political system" (2019, p. 91). Chinese 'modern political capitalism' starts with Deng's reforms from the late 1970s to the mid-1990s embracing three major characteristics: (1) Efficient bureaucracy (administration); (2) Absence of the rule of law; (3) Autonomy of the state (2019, pp. 91–96).

The first characteristic assumes that "the bureaucracy needs to be technocratic and the selection of its members merit-based if it is to be successful, especially since the rule of law is absent" (Ibid., p. 91). The author cites China, Vietnam, Malaysia, and Singapore as examples of a highly efficient and technocratically savvy bureaucracy in charge of the system. The description seems to be highly atguable. First, Singapore cannot be lumped together with China. As Csaba (2022, pp. 679–680) persuasively argues, Singapore with its meritocratic bureaucracy is rather one of the four countries (others are South Korea, Taiwan, Hong Kong) that form a model of 'development state'. By contrast, China lacks administrative meritocracy and detains a state bureaucracy serving as a booty for the political class. This does not contradict 'political capitalism' as defined by Weber, but it is not in line with Milanovic's understanding of 'modern political capitalism' which has to possess an efficient meritocratic bureaucracy. "The strong selling point of political capitalism is state efficiency-the fact that it can bring private actors to build something that improves peoples' ordinary lives in tangible, material ways" (ibid., p. 127).

If political capitalism is a particular system of profit-making, why should it necessarily bring improvement in peoples' ordinary lives? On the contrary, political capitalism often enhances private interests of special groups detrimental to public welfare. The only reason that explains why Milanovic gives pride of place to the 'efficiency' criterion is that he necessarily ties political capitalism to a transition from state socialism to capitalism. In fact, he does not see that *political capitalism is not a form of market capitalism*; it is a totally different economic system.

The second characteristic is the absence of a binding rule of law. This does not mean the laws are absent; they are both present and absent, since they can be applied discriminately depending upon the state's discretionary power to punish an 'undesirable' political actor, or business competitor. For example, the rules are absent when Xi Jinping requires to extend his presidency beyond the two terms. This indetermination about the law enforcement extends the arbitrariness of the state's decision and makes interventionism a rule rather than an exception.

The state autonomy is the third characteristic. According to Milanovic, the leading idea of Deng was to increase the economic efficiency while exerting the state's control over business to shun business's political empowerment. "It was not, however, the size of the private sector that Deng wanted to limit but its political role—that is, its ability to impose its preferences on state policy" (2019, p. 92). The ability to control the private sector is what distinguishes modern political capitalism in China in contradistinction with political capitalism in USA where business controls government.

Interestingly, while Holcombe and Milanovic diverge on the definition of modern political capitalism regarding whether the business controls government or the other way around, they both miss a fundamental characteristic of political capitalism, namely the *state predation*. Magyar (2016) and Madlovics and Magyar (2021) address this missing link by applying the concept of predatory state (Leeson, 2007; Vahabi, 2016) to the Russian, Ukrainian,[11] and Balkan models of *predatory capitalism*. Indeed, if we revise the first characteristic of Milanovic to integrate this point, we need to ask why have not Russia[12] under Putin or Hungary during Orban been characterized as political capitalism?

Finally, it is noteworthy that contrary to Holcombe, Milanovic (2019, Chap. 2) totally disregards the symptoms of political capitalism in the USA. In his opinion, political capitalism is limited to countries marked by a feudal and colonial background, notably China whereas the USA is "the emblematic country of liberal meritocratic capitalism" (ibid., p. 98). In my opinion, Holcombe and Milanovic are both correct in underlining the presence of political capitalism in the USA and China. But the list can also

---

[11] For the state predation by an oligarchy in Ukraine under Kravchuk, Kuchma, and Yanukovych, see Mitchell, 2012; Lawson, 2019, pp. 174–195. Systemic looting of state finances was a common feature. After the uprisings of 2013–2014, it has been revealed that the estimated amount of corruption during Yanukovych (2010–2014) has been around $100 billion while GDP was $150 billion annually and total tax revenue worth 17–18 billion annually (Lawson, 2019, p. 187).

[12] Csaba (2022, p. 680) considers Russia under Putin as political capitalism but does not characterize Hungary under Orban as such (ibid., p. 684).

be extended to Russia and many East European countries, as well as many countries in the MENA region.

4.9   VARIETIES OF POLITICAL CAPITALISM: THE NATURAL RESOURCE CURSE

The term 'natural resource curse' (NRC) was coined by economic geographer Richard Auty in 1993. It has been defined as "the perverse effects of a country's natural resource wealth on its economic, social, or political well-being" (Ross, 2015, p. 240). The curse can either be *economic* or *political* in nature. The former is considered to be "one of the stylized facts of our times" (Wright, 2001, p. 1), meaning that economies in resource-rich countries tend to grow more slowly than their resource-poor counterparts.

The *political* resource curse was initially explored in pioneering works by Mahdavy (1970), Karl (1997), Collier and Hoeffler (1998), and Ross (1999); research in that area has flourished over the past decade (Morrison, 2007; Cuaresma et al., 2011; McGuirk, 2013). Studies in that vein have explored how and why regimes richly endowed with natural resources tend to be more authoritarian and prone to civil wars than those without such resources.

In early research, natural resources included both extracted and produced commodities; more recent research has tended to exclude agricultural products and focus only on *extracted* resources. That narrow definition was adopted to explore whether resources correlate with unfavorable political outcomes such as violent conflicts. Presently, natural resources often encompass petroleum, gemstones, other types of minerals and narcotics. For Ross (2012), the resource curse is overwhelmingly related to crude oil endowments and the curse is particularly relevant to undeveloped and developing countries.

Economists investigating the poor performance of many countries endowed with rich natural resources have often assumed a 'world with no government' when government behavior is actually the key element.[13] Some economists may not have neglected the role of government, but have adopted a public goods approach to the state, implying a politically

---

[13] In recent literature, a particular attention is granted to the relationship between the taxation of natural resources and fiscal capacity that clearly indicates the importance of the government behavior (see e.g., Peres-Cajias et al., 2020; Savoia & Sen, 2021).

neutral government maximizing collective interests. The behavior and motivation on the part of politicians become particularly important when the state is assumed to behave *predatorily* rather than as a maximizer of broader social goals. I have conducted an extensive critical survey on the natural resource curse (Vahabi, 2018a, 2018b)[14] that integrates a predatory state into the analysis of how natural resources are related to economic performance. My study shows that there is not such a thing as 'natural resource' curse. If there is any curse, it is *institutional*.

Reviewing *economic* and *political* dimensions of NRC through the appropriability lens shows that NRC is a *consequence* of political capitalism in the presence of institutions promoting state predation and rent-seeking from extractive sectors of the economy. The integration of colonies or peripheral economies in the world market through the exportation of natural resources has a double contradictory impact on the development of market capitalism.

On the one hand, it extends market capitalist relationships by enhancing labor market, commodity-money relationships, and capital accumulation. On the other hand, it gives an autonomous role to a centralized state in the periphery or colonies that can share part of the natural resource revenue with major global corporations. The latter effect is an impediment to one of the major institutional prerequisites of market capitalism, namely the demarcation between sovereignty and property. In fact, sovereignty becomes the source of property resulting in big 'political enterprises' managing highly lucrative natural resources. The emergence of political capitalism derives from dispossession of peoples from public resources by those who control the state. In this sense, it is rather an appropriative than a productive regime.

One interesting illustration is the management of natural resources notably in the fields of oil, petrochemical, and gas during the second Pahlavi dynasty in Iran. They were all big political enterprises under the strict personal control of the Shah and opaque to any other official authority. The National Iranian Oil Company (NIOC) was never transformed into a ministry until the Iranian 1979 Revolution. This was a state within a state that 'belonged' to the Shah personally.

[14]This paragraph and the preceding ones are drawn from Vahabi (2018a, 2018b, pp. 394–396). I would like to thank Springer for giving me the permission to use that paper.

In an interview, Ali-Akbar Moinfar (2019), the first Iranian minister of petroleum,[15] explained the situation before the creation of the oil ministry in these terms: "During the Shah's period, the National Iranian Oil Company (NIOC) was a state within a state. It was independent from the state and worked directly under the Shah's personal supervision, and for this reason someone like Dr. Manouchehr Iqbal who was the prime minister for many years was nominated as CEO of the NIOC without having any background in oil industry, whereas Hoveyda[16] who was a less important political personage became the Prime Minister. Iqbal oversaw reporting only to the Shah. In addition to the NIOC, other companies were gradually established such as the National Petrochemical Company (NPC), and the National Iranian Gas Company. These companies were also supposed to have a board of directors and a CEO but had to be under the Shah's personal supervision. All these organizations had a general assembly presided by the Prime Minister and a few ministers. But it was clear that this was a separate type of organization over which the Shah could overlook. Things related to the Organization of the Petroleum Exporting Countries (OPEC) were concentrated in the ministry of finance. The Iran's representative in OPEC was not an oil expert either. In fact, the Iran's representative was for many years Dr. Jamshid Amuzegar who served once as the minister of interior and for a while as the minister of finance.[17] He later became the Prime Minister and entertained personal contact with the Shah. The OPEC's secretariat was also located in the ministry of finance. Thus, there was a dispersion in the NIOC" (Interview with Ahmadi, 2019, pp. 17–18).

Hence, parallel institutions did not start with the establishment of *Velayat Faqih* in 1979.[18] It already existed during the Shah's regime. It was a heritage of political capitalism in which the Shah's despotic power

[15] Ali-Akbar Moinfar was the first oil minister of the Islamic Republic of Iran under the provisional government of Mehdi Bazargan for a short period from September 29, 1979, to May 28, 1980. He died in January 2, 2018.

[16] Amir Abbas Hoveyda, the longest-serving Prime Minister of Muhammad Reza Shah Pahlavi, was in office from January 27, 1965, until August 7, 1977. After the Iranian 1979 Revolution, he was arrested and briefly 'tried' by the Revolutionary Court and executed because of 'waging war against God' and 'spreading corruption on earth'.

[17] He also became the Prime Minister during the critical period of August 7, 1977, to August 27, 1978. He resigned at that date. He also was the leader of the Shah's mono-party system, that is, Rastakhiz Party, during his tenure as Prime Minister of Iran.

[18] Chapter 6 will be devoted to substantiating these parallel institutions in the economic sphere in conjunction with *Anfal*.

could convert into immense privileges in economic activities and property holding. The role of political enterprise has been examined in other countries such as Indonesia, Nepal, and Bangladesh (Mobarak & Purbasari, 2005, 2006).

Concurrently with this type of accumulation, the sociological composition of bourgeoisie altered. Generally speaking, different layers of bourgeoisie in market capitalism are originated in commercial, financial, industrial, agricultural, and service sectors. However, one of the distinctive features of political capitalism in countries dependent on the natural resources is the formation of an almost inexistent type of bourgeoisie in the Western market capitalism, namely *bureaucrat bourgeoisie.*

The vast literature on the staple trap, the Dutch disease, rent-seeking, and institutional failures has addressed both the state predation and the inefficiencies of specific capitalist development in economies marked by NRC in terms of non-diversification, the weakness of the manufacturing sector, the importance of the service sector, the extension of rentier activities, etc. (Vahabi, 2018a, 2018b). In their totality, they describe specific inefficiencies of a variant of political capitalism that arise from dependency on natural resources. Contrary to what Milanovic (2019) assumes, political capitalism need not be economically efficient or having a meritocratic bureaucracy. The Russian political capitalism reflecting NRC variant is also replete with inefficiencies. The efficiency criterion is not required to characterize political capitalism, but state predation is one of its underlying pillars.

4.10   ISLAM AND CAPITALISM

Weber (1905/1985) pioneered a new line of research by arguing that the rise of modern 'rational' capitalism in Western Europe could be partially attributed to the Protestant ethics particularly the Calvinist emphasis on worldly 'calling', labor, and frugality. If Protestantism was an enhancer of modern capitalism, could Islam be considered as an impediment to capitalist development?

To put it differently, why did capitalism triumph in modern times in Europe, and not in the Muslim countries (among others)? Weber (1922/1978) suggested that Islam as a religion of warriors fostered an ethic unfavorable to the spirit of capitalism. Turner (1974) rejected Weber's contention on this issue but adhered to his view that the Islamic cultural complexity hindered industrial capitalism primarily because it lacked the economic and political requirements of capitalism, namely rational, formalized law, autonomous cities, an independent bourgeois class, political stability based on freedom of governmental interference with business, money economy, and a free labor market.

Rodinson (1973) started his investigation on Islam and capitalism by asking Weber's principal question. However, he added a second question: Why has European capitalism been able to penetrate the Muslim world so easily?

Before dealing with these questions, he deemed indispensable to scrutinize what he meant by capitalism. He quoted several authors including Marx, Sombart, and Max Weber to distinguish two different usages of the term capitalism (Rodinson, ibid., pp. 4–7, 246).

The first one referred to capitalism as a specific form of society or a 'social formation' in which institution or a mentality defined as capitalist is predominant. This description has been applied to Western European and the American societies. The second definition described a specific 'capitalist sector' or a specific mentality in combination with other forms of production and mentalities. In the latter case, capitalism was not the dominant form, but it existed as complementary to pre-capitalist forms of production. "These are at least forms of that pre-capitalist commercial capital and usurer's capital which theoreticians like Max Weber regard as 'a capitalism of various forms'" (Rodinson, 1973, p. 7).

While Rodinson (1973, p. 246) approvingly quoted Weber for having combined both definitions of capitalism, he never noticed that Weber had distinguished 'political' from 'market' capitalism in the same passages he was quoting. Instead, he refuted Weber's thesis regarding the incompatibility of Islam with capitalistic 'rational' methods by underlining the fact that the society in which Islam was born, the society of Mecca, was already a center of capitalistic trade. The inhabitants of Mecca, belonging to the tribe of Quraysh, fructified their wealth through trade and loans at interest in a way that Weber would call 'rational'. Rodinson (1973, pp. 28–29) claimed that the society of Mecca "was indeed an 'unembedded' economy, to employ Karl Polanyi's terminology and this to the maximum possible extent. Economic activities were carried out in a framework of economic roles that were grouped *in lasting economic organizations, namely, trading companies, and the structure of relations between these companies was in no way 'embedded' in a non-economic context such as the clan*" (emphasis is added).

Accordingly, Islam had never been an impediment to the development of capitalism as claimed by many Western scholars including Weber and Turner. However, Rodinson's claim is not supported by historical evidence. Corporations or "lasting economic organizations" are not authorized in the classical Islamic Jurisprudence. In fact, Timur Kuran (2005) has identified one of the major reasons of the Middle Eastern relatively late development of market capitalism in the Islamic law regarding corporations. Classical Islamic law recognized only natural persons; it refused to accept the corporation as a perpetual legal person. The very mechanisms that blocked the emergence of large and perpetual commercial trading companies also excluded the emergence of banks. The lack of banks and corporations delayed the transition from personal to impersonal markets under Islam.

But why could the corporation develop under Christianity and not Islam? According to Kuran (2018, p. 1323), "Whereas Christianity was born within a state that projected immense power, Islam emerged in a stateless region inherited by feuding tribes, sedentary or nomadic. Its spectacular success in gaining Arabian converts stemmed partly from the benefits that the peoples of seventh century Western Arabia achieved from political centralization under a single legal system".

The new centralized state under the leadership of the Prophet Muhammad deprived the potential groups from the organizational means that could destabilize the achieved order. This explains why the concept of the corporation was excluded from the emerging Islamic legal system. By contrast, after the collapse of the Western Roman Empire in 476, the new fragmented states of the Western Europe were too weak to eschew incorporations. Accordingly, different social groups such as religious orders, guilds, and cities were able to organize themselves as a corporation.

But why did the absence of corporations persist in the Middle East? Kuran (2001) sought the sources of persistence in waqf system. In fact, until the Industrial Revolution, the Islamic unincorporated trust known as waqf assumed the same role as corporations in the West to provide public goods.

The waqf properties could not be confiscated by the Sultan and this offered a credible commitment mechanism to incentivize property owners to convert real estate into a waqf. In return for this economic safety, the property owners instead of the state provided social services or public goods. But why the waqf system could not be imitated by other organizations? The Community building was central to Islam's mission and had not to be relegated to any other religious or non-religious groups. Therefore, early Muslim jurists had no use for a concept liable to facilitate factionalism. Waqf was an exception because it accomplished community building with financial sources of property owners and not Sultan.

The Khalifate system was financed by *Kharaj* and provided public goods indirectly through waqf system. Both *Kharaj* and waqf were generated by a confiscatory regime. The corporation was banned since it could weaken the sovereignty in favor of property. Kuran (2005) provided the historical evidence for the birth of the first predominantly Muslim-owned joint stock company of the Ottoman Empire: the Sirkat-i-Hayriye marine transportation company, literally the 'Auspicious Company'. The company was initiated by sultan Abdulmecit who became the largest shareholder of its 2000 tradable shares. Other partners were high government officials, almost all Turks, and a handful number of Armenian financiers.

Since the term 'Company' did not exist in Turkish, sultan used a neologism by combining the French pronunciation of 'compagnie' with the English word 'Company' to coin '*Kumpanyie*'. The company started when the legal infrastructure was in course of installation comprising commercial courts that had to enforce the French commercial code. The sultan's motivation for establishing this new organizational form that was alien to the Sunni Islamic law was that he had grasped that Islamic commercial law was not adequate for creating banks, mass transportation companies notably railroads and manufacturing sectors. "A traditional Islamic partnership becomes null and void at the withdrawal, incapacitation, or death of even a single partner. Wherever commerce was conducted under Islamic law, this vulnerability had discouraged investment in large and long-lasting ventures. Authorized to issue tradable shares, Sirket-i Hayriye could survive changes in membership; the shares of exiting partners would simply switch hands, without recontracting. As significant, however, is that Sirket-i Hayriye was not declared a corporation. Established as an unincorporated joint-stock company, it lacked legal personhood" (Kuran, 2005, p. 786).

During almost half a century, the 'Kumpanyies' established under the Ottoman Empire were mostly foreign corporations with headquarters in London and Paris. Their commercial disputes were also settled in foreign courts. The Ottoman corporations belonged to non-Muslim owners who were under the foreign legal protection. It was only after 1908 that the Ottoman parliament passed a law of corporations, and the domestic Muslim 'Kumpanyies' could flourish within a new civil juridical system.

Paradoxically, the Islamic law was not a barrier to install 'Kumapnyie' in Iran. The Shi'i Ulema not only did not resist the adoption of this new organizational form but also participated actively in its establishment during the 'Politics of Reform' under the Qajar dynasty (1858–1880) particularly the era of Mirza Hossein Khan Moshir od-Dowleh Sepahsalar. The latter was the Prime Minister (grand vizir) of Iran (Persia) (1871–1873) during the Qajar dynasty under King Naser od-Din Shah Qajar. The rise of market capitalism with a new bourgeois class composed of merchants and financiers investing in manufacturing started in this reform period of 1858–1880 a few decades before the Persian Constitutional Revolution in 1906–1907. The Shi'i faqihs supported this ascending domestic bourgeoisie in their advocacy of 'Kumapnyie' to establish banks, railways, and manufacturing companies with their own capital and the State's help.

The Iranian historian Fereydoun Adamiyat (1972, pp. 323–324) wrote: "The increase in the central state's power ensuring a relative security, introducing new political institutions, and supporting the rights of merchants, were all the factors that contributed to the accumulation of capital and collective economic activities. It was exactly at this time that 'Company' and 'Sherkat' in the new commercial sense were created. This is noteworthy that in Ottoman empire the recognition of the governing principles of Company and its legal personality became a hot controversial issue involving strong disputes since it opposed the Islam Fiqh. In Iran such a dispute never existed, since in dire contrast to Ottoman, the Shi'i Faqihs supported the establishment of Company. For example, the Mujtahid Tabriz invested personally in the Azerbaijan Company of Transport. In any rate, the state was supportive of the merchants' initiative in installing domestic trade Company."

Among the first Persian companies was the Company for exporting opium to Europe and China. The creation of Company significantly augmented the volume of the Iranian opium exports to China and England (Adamiyat, ibid., p. 325). The merchants of Bushehr also established a company for domestic and international trade with Europe. Haj Amin al-Zarb, one of the major big capitalists, used 'Company' to invest in manufacturing, notably in Porcelain manufacturing, crystal making, and silk spinning. He also initiated a railway Company that connected Bandar Mahmud Abad to Amol and invited the Belgian engineers to Iran for conducting the operation. In almost all projects for establishing railway Companies to Qom, Mashhad, Azerbaijan, and many other cities, three social groups were active: merchants, wealthy urban notables, and Ulema (see Adamiyat, ibid., pp. 326–334). The idea of using 'Company' organizational structure to establish domestic banks was also defended firmly by the same social groups, but the King was not supportive and considered the project too risky to engage.

Thus, the Shi'i faqihs did not follow the Sunni faqihs in opposing 'Kumapnyie'. Kuran's (2005) insightful observation regarding the late introduction of the corporation in the Middle Eastern menu of organizational option cannot be related only to the Islamic law. In Iran, the tyranny rather than the Shi'i fqihs was a major obstacle. The Qajar kings were not always supportive of domestic merchants in their projects for creating banks, railways, or manufacturing sectors although the era of the 'Politics of Reform' (1858–1880) enhanced the position of domestic bourgeoisie. The Shi'i Ulema were rather an ally of domestic merchants than the tyrant and foreign imperial powers that they considered as a real threat to their religious and cultural hegemony in Iran.

Considering the position of the Shi'i' faqihs, could it be maintained that even if Rodinson's claim was not correct for the Sunni Islam, it was applicable to the Shi'i Islam? I will respond to this question after introducing a central piece of Shi'i public finance which has been totally ignored not only by Rodinson but also by almost all Western scholars in economics, politics, sociology, and law.

This central piece is *Anfal* that will be thoroughly explored first in Shi'i jurisprudence and the constitution of the Islamic Republic of Iran (IRI) at a *theoretical* level in Chap. 5. Then, *Anfal* in practice will be studied in conjunction with different modes of coordination in Chaps. 6 and 7. I will argue that the specific variant of Islamic political capitalism has shaped under the Islamic Republic of Iran thanks to *Anfal*.

4.11   Conclusion

In this chapter, we extended our definition of the economic system at two different levels as formulated in Chap. 2 by distinguishing capitalist *production* from capitalist *distribution*. Mode of coordination is the key concept to depict the latter.

While Marx emphasized capitalism as a new mode of *production* grounded on free labor and credit system, Weber favored the *distribution* sphere in defining capitalism as an economic system characterized by different forms of monetary profit-making. Accordingly, he introduced a distinction between market and political capitalism.

Borrowing Braudel's metaphor of three storey-building, the first floor stands for *Oikonomia* or material life (subsistence economy), the second refers to 'market economy', and the third floor represents *Chrematistics* based on long-distance trade and profit-making. Capitalist production constitutes the fourth floor including labor and credit markets and the generalization of commodity-monetary relationships. While the fourth storey is marked by industrial capitalism, the third layer is composed of commercial and usury capital.

Political capitalism as non-market predatory ways of profit-making exists at this third level and it entertains a contradictory or/and a complementarity relationship with market capitalism. Spoils of war, colonialism, and confiscatory regimes in the presence of market and monetary relationships come within the scope of political capitalism.

While political capitalism preceded market capitalism, it can stem from the latter because of centralization and concentration of capital and the influence of oligopolies over the state. The control of the business over government is a recent path of political capitalism as experienced in the USA (Kolko, 1963, 1965; Holcombe, 2015, 2018). This path is illustrated by 'revolving doors' and 'political enterprises'.

But political capitalism might also derive from the government's control over the business. This second path can be either economically efficient (e.g., in the Chinese case as explored by Milanovic, 2019) or inefficient. The latter can be seen in Russia, and many Eastern European countries (Madlovics & Magyar, 2021). In this chapter, we argued that the whole NRC can be characterized as an inefficient type of recent political capitalism. The birth of giant political corporations like oil and gas companies (NIOC) in Iran since the late Muhammad Reza Shah Pahlavi, and (Gazprom) in Poutine's time, are the outcomes of political capitalism deriving from state predation.

Finally, we reviewed two broad perspectives regarding the relationship between Islam and capitalism. While Weber insists on the incompatibility of Islam and capitalism, Rodinson advocates the compatibility between them. According to Kuran (2005), Islamic jurisprudence has been an impediment to the development of corporations, banks, and impersonal markets under the Ottoman Empire. Kuran's assessment might be valid for Sunni Islam, but the Shi'i jurisprudence was not opposed to the development of 'Kompanyie'. The question is whether Rodinson's thesis regarding the compatibility of Islam with capitalism is valid for Shi'i jurisprudence. We will examine this thesis both theoretically and practically.

Chapter 5 demonstrates at a theoretical level that *Anfal* as the underlying tenet of the public finance in the Shi'i jurisprudence and the constitution of the IRI discredits Rodinson's thesis. Islamic economics as described in *Anfal* impedes market capitalism, although it can enhance political capitalism.

Chapter 6 explores *Anfal* in the practice of the IRI. This chapter explains how *Velayat Faqih* and *Anfal* established the fundamental institutions of Islamic political capitalism.

References

Adamiyat, F. (1972). *The Politics of Reform in Iran 1858-1880, in Persian.* Entesharat Kharazmi.

Amable, B. (2003). *The Diversity of Modern Capitalism.* Oxford University Press.

Anderson, P. (1974). *Lineages of Absolutist State.* Verso.

Bahro, R. (1978). *The Alternative in Eastern Europe.* New Left Books/Verso.

Beaud, M. (2018). L'indiscernable début du capitalisme. *Revue internationale de la philosophie, 285,* 279–275.

Bello, W. (2000). The Asian Financial Crisis: Heroes, Villains, and Accomplices. In W. Paul & R. L. Edwin (Eds.), *Principled World Politics: The Challenge of Normative International Relations* (pp. 181–190). Rowan and Littlefield Publishers, Inc.

Bello, W. (2004). *The Anti-Developmental State: The Political Economy of Permanent Crisis in the Philippines, by Walden Bello, Herbert Docena, Marissa de Guzman, and Marylou Malig.* Department of Sociology, University of the Philippines and Focus on the Global South.

Braudel, F. (1977). *Afterthoughts on Material Civilization and Capitalism.* Johns Hopkins University Press.

Braudel, F. (1983). *Civilization and Capitalism 15th–18th Century, vol. 2, The Wheels of Commerce.* Book Club Associates.

Brezis, E., & Cariolle, J. (2019). The Revolving Door, State Connections, and Inequality of Influence in the Financial Sector. *Journal of Institutional Economics, 15*(4), 595–614.

Clinton, B. (2005). *My Life* (Vol. 2). Vintage Books.

Collier, P., & Hoeffler, A. (1998). On the Economic Causes of Civil War. *Oxford Economic Papers, 50,* 563–573.

Commons, J. (1899–1900/1965). *A Sociological View of Sovereignty by John R. Commons [1899–1900].* Augustus M. Kelley, Bookseller.

Commons, J. (1924/1995). *Legal Foundations of Capitalism* (With a New Introduction by Jeff Biddle & Warren J. Samuels). Transaction Publishers.

Commons, J. R. (1931). Institutional Economics. *American Economics Review*, *21*, 648–657.

Commons, J. (1970). *The Economics of Collective Action*. University of Wisconsin Press.

Csaba, L. (2022). Illiberal Economic Policies. In S. Holmes et al. (Eds.), *Routledge Handbook of Illiberalism* (pp. 674–691). Routledge.

Cuaresma, J., Oberhofer, H., & Raschky, P. (2011). Oil and the Duration of Dictatorships. *Public Choice, 148*(3/4), 505–530.

Demsetz, H. (1964). The Exchange and Enforcement of Property Rights. *Journal of Law and Economics, 7*, 11–26.

Findlay, R. (1990, March). The 'Triangular Trade' and the Atlantic Economy of the Eighteenth Century: A Simple General Equilibrium Model. *Essays in International Finance*, No. 177, Princeton University, Department of Economics.

Galbraith, J. (2009). *The Predator State, How Conservatives Abandoned the Free Market and Why Liberals Should Too* (Paperback ed.). Free Press.

Gernet, J. (1962). *Daily Life in China on the Eve of Mongol Invasion, 1250–1276*. Stanford University Press.

Gide, C. (1898/2018). *Principes d'Economie Politique* (6th ed.) Hachette-livre BNF.

Hall, P., & Soskice, D. (2001). *Varieties of Capitalism: The Institutional Foundations of Comparative Advantage*. Oxford University Press.

Hau, C. (2017). What Is Crony Capitalism? *Emerging State Project (EPS) Grips*, Retrieved July 7, 2022, from http://www3.grips.ac.jp/~esp/en/event/what-is-%E2%80%9Ccrony-capitalism%E2%80%9D/.

Holcombe, R. (2015). Political Capitalism. *Cato Journal, 35*(1), 41–66.

Holcombe, R. (2018). *Political Capitalism, How Economic and Political Power Is Made and Maintained*. Cambridge University Press.

Honneth, A. (2018). 'Capitalism' - Economy, Society or a Form of Life? Greatness and Limits of Marx' Theory of Society,' Lecture Delivered at the Hamburger Institut für Sozialforschung 4.5.2018, https://www.youtube.com/watch?v=BB6epE9YVz0

Inikori, J. (2017). The Development of Capitalism in the Atlantic World: England, the Americas, and West Africa, 1400–1900. *Labor History, 58*(2), 138–153.

Karl, T. L. (1997). *The Paradox of Plenty: Oil Booms and Petro-States*. University of California Press.

Kolko, G. (1963). *The Triumph of Conservatism: A Reinterpretation of American History, 1900–1916*. The Free Press of Glencoe.

Kolko, G. (1965). *Railroads and Regulation 1877-1916*. Princeton University Press.

Krätke, M. (2020). Capitalism. In M. Musto (Ed.), *The Marx Revival. Key Concepts and New Interpretations*. Cambridge University Press.

Kristof, N. (2011, 27 October). *Crony Capitalism Comes Home*. The New York Times. Retrieved July 7, 2022, from https://www.nytimes.com/2011/10/27/opinion/kristof-crony-capitalism-comes-homes.html.

Kuran, T. (2001). The Provision of Public Goods under Islamic Law: Origins, Impact, and Limitations of the Waqf System. *Law and Society Review, 35*(4), 841–897.

Kuran, T. (2005). The Absence of the Corporation in Islamic Law: Origins and Persistence. *The American Journal of Comparative Law, 53*(4), 785–834.

Kuran, T. (2018). Islam and Economic Performance. *Journal of Economic Literature, 56*(4), 1292–1359.

Küttler, W. (2008). *Kapitalismus. Historisch-Kritisches Wörterbuch des Marxismus 7.1* (pp. 238–272). Argument-Verlag.

Lawson, G. (2019). *Anatomies of Revolution*. Cambridge University Press.

Leeson, P. T. (2007). Anarchy, Monopoly, and Predation. *Journal of Institutional and Theoretical Economics (JITE), 163*, 467–482.

Leshem, D. (2016). What did the Ancient Greeks mean by Oikonomia? *Journal of Economic Perspectives, 30*(1), 225–231.

Locke, J. (1690/1952). *The Second Treatise of Government* (Edited with an introd. by Thomas P. Peardon). The Liberal Arts Press.

Love, J. (1991). *Antiquity and Capitalism: Max Weber and the Sociological Foundations of Roman Civilization*. Routledge.

Madlovics, B., & Magyar, B. (2021). Post-Communist Predation: Modeling Reiderstvo Practices in Contemporary States. *Public Choice, 187*(3-4), 247–273.

Magyar, B. (2016). *Post-Communist Mafia State: The Case of Hungary*. CEU Press.

Mahdavy, H. (1970). The Patterns and Problems of Economic Development in Rentier States: The Case of Iran. In M. Cook (Ed.), *Studies in economic history of the Middle East* (pp. 428–467). Oxford University Press.

Marx, K. (1857a–8/1964). *Pre-capitalist Economic Formations*. Translated by Jack Cohen, https://www.marxists.org/archive/marx/works/1857/precapitalist/ch01.htm

Marx, K. (1857b/1971). Introduction to a Contribution to the Critique of Political Economy. In *A Contribution to the Critique of Political Economy*, translated from the German by S. W. Ryazanskaya, Appendix I, London: Lawrence & Wishart, pp. 81–111. https://www.marxists.org/archive/marx/works/1859/critique-pol-economy/appx1.htm

Marx, K. (1867/1978). *Capital, a Critique of Political Economy* (Vol. 1), Progress Publishers.

McGuirk, E. (2013). The Illusory Leader: Natural Resources, Taxation and Accountability. *Public Choice, 154*, 285–313.

Milanovic, B. (2019). *Capitalism Alone, the Future of the System that Rules the World*. Belknap Press of Harvard University Press.

Mingardi, A. (2018). P.T. Bauer and the Myth of Primitive Accumulation. *Cato Journal, 38*(2), 613–630.

Mitchell, L. (2012). *The Color Revolutions*. University of Pennsylvania Press.

Mobarak, A. M., & Purbasari, D. (2005, July 9). *Political Trade Protection in Developing Countries: Firm Level Evidence from Indonesia.* Available https://ssrn.com/abstract=770949 or https://doi.org/10.2139/ssrn.770949

Mobarak, A., & Purbasari, D. (2006). *Corrupt Protection for sale to Firms: Evidence from Indonesia. Unpublished Working Paper.* University of Colorado at Boulder.

Morrison, K. (2007). Natural Resources, Aid, and Democratization: A Best-Case Scenario. *Public Choice, 131*(3/4), 365–386.

Ogilvie, S., & Carus, A. W. (2014). Institutions and Economic Growth in Historical Perspective. In P. Aghion & S. N. Durlauf (Eds.), *Handbook of Economic Growth* (Vol. 2, pp. 403–513). North Holland, Chapter 8.

Peres-Cajias, J., Torregrosa-Hetland, S., & Ducoing, C. (2020). Resource abundance and public finances in five peripheral economies, 1850–1939. *Lund Papers in Economic History*, No. 216, Department of Economic History, Lund University.

Philippon, T. (2019). *The Great Reversal: How America Gave Up on Free Markets.* Harvard University Press.

Polanyi, K. (1944). *The Great Transformation*. Farrar and Rinehart.

Razo, A. (2021, January). Network Structure and Performance of Crony Capitalism Systems Credible Commitments Without Democratic Institutions. *Public Choice, 189*, 115–137.

Rodinson, M. (1973). *Islam and Capitalism* (Trans from the French by Brian Pierce, First American ed.). Penguin Books Ltd.

Ross, M. (1999). The Political Economy of the Resource Curse. *World Politics, 51*(2), 297–322.

Ross, M. (2012). *The Oil Curse: How Petroleum Wealth Shapes the Development of Nations.* Princeton University Press.

Ross, M. (2015). What Have We Learned about the Resource Curse? *Annual Review of Political Science, 18*, 239–259.

Rubin, R. E. (2003). *In an Uncertain World: Tough Choices from Wall Street to Washington.* Random House.

Savoia, A., & Sen, K. (2021). The Political Economy of the Resource Curse: A Development Perspective. *Annual Review of Resource Economics, 13*, 203–223.

Smith, A. (1776/1961). *An Inquiry into the Nature and Causes of the Wealth of Nations.* Methuen.

Sombart, W. (1902). *Der moderne Kapitalismus*. Duncker& Humblot.

Taber, G. (1980, April 21). A Case of Crony Capitalism. *Time Magazine.*

Taber, G. (2015, November 3). The Night I Invented Crony Capitalism. Knowledge @ Wharton. Retrieved July 7, 2022, from http://knowledge.wharton.upenn.edu/article/the-night-i-invented-crony-capitalism/.

Turner, B. (1974). *Weber and Islam: A Critical Study*. Routledge and Kegan Paul.

Vahabi, M. (2004). *The Political Economy of Destructive Power*. Edward Elgar.

Vahabi, M. (2016, September). A Positive Theory of the Predatory State. *Public Choice, 168*(3–4), 153–175.

Vahabi, M. (2018a). The Resource Curse Literature as Seen Through the Appropriability Lens: A Critical Survey. *Public Choice, 175*(3-4), 393–428.

Vahabi, M. (2018b, March). *Coercive State, Resisting Society, Political and Economic Development in Contemporary Iran, Dr Sadighi Lecture Series*. International Institute of Social History and Leiden University. https://socialhistory.org/en/events/lecture-political-and-economic-development-contemporary-iran

Vahabi, M., Batifoulier, P., & Da Silva, N. (2020). A Theory of Predatory Welfare State and Citizen Welfare: The French Case. *Public Choice, 182*(3–4), 243–271.

Vahabi, M., Philippe, B., & Nicolas, D. S. (2020). The Political Economy of Revolution and Institutional Change: The Elite and Mass Revolutions. *Revue d'Economie Politique, 130*(6), 855–889.

Vukovic, V. (2021). The Politics of Bailouts: Estimating the Causal Effects of Political Connections on Corporate Bailouts During the 2008–2009 US Financial Crisis. *Public Choice, 189*, 213–238. https://doi.org/10.1007/s11127-020-00871-w

Weber, M. (1905/1985). *The Protestant Ethic and the Spirit of Capitalism* (Talcott Parsons, Trans.). Unwin.

Weber, M. (1922/1978). *Economy and Society* 1, University of California Press.

Williamson, O. (1985). *The Economic Institutions of Capitalism. Firms, Markets, Relational Contracting*. Free Press.

Zingales, L. (2015). Presidential Address: Does Finance Benefit Society? *The Journal of Finance, 70*(4), 1327–1363.

Zingales, L. (2017). Towards a Political Theory of the Firm. *The Journal of Economic Perspectives, 31*(3), 113–130.

CHAPTER 5

Anfal and Islamic Economics

5.1 Introduction

In this chapter, we explore those elements of Islamic economics that enhance a confiscatory regime and are compatible with destructive coordination. I am not suggesting that Islam is consubstantial with destruction or destructive coordination. Akin to Judaism and Christianity, Islam embraces a host of principles and guidelines about daily life for believers that promote cooperation, reciprocity, and solidarity. This chapter does not study Islam in general, it only focuses on those rules and precepts in Islamic economics that are in tune with destructive coordination knowing that such kind of coordination has its specific self-reproducing inner logic.

Social integration through coercion does not necessarily rely upon any religion. However, the interplay of sovereignty and property has been strongly influenced by major monotheistic religions throughout history. The religious institutions have played a key role in the emergence of sovereign powers and provided the initial grammar of politics and *reasons of state*. Considering the significant role of religion in defining the *legitimate* forms of sovereign power and appropriation, it is germane to investigate its impact on different forms of coordination.

The choice of Islam in this study is closely related to the emergence of a critical social order in all regions affected by the rise of political Islam since the Iranian Revolution of 1979. The Islamic triumph in Iran became a source of inspiration and a model of emulation to the Afghan Mujahideen,

M. Vahabi, *Destructive Coordination, Anfal and Islamic Political Capitalism*, https://doi.org/10.1007/978-3-031-17674-6_5

the Houthi Movement in Yemen, the Shi'is of Kuwait, Lebanon, and Iraq, and the opposition forces of Pakistan, Syria, Algeria, Egypt, Nigeria, Mali, Somalia, Malaysia, and Mozambique.[1] This model has been presented as an Islamic alternative to both Occidental capitalism and Eastern Communist system. From an economic point of view, the idea of restructuring entire economies according to Islamic principles has been on the Islamic agenda since the 1940s. However, as Kuran (2018, p. 1313) aptly averred: "The only attempt at comprehensive restructuring was made in Iran, where Islamists gained full political control in the aftermath of the 1978-1979 revolution that overthrow the Pahlavi monarchy."

While many Iranian economists have persuasively argued that the post-revolutionary Iran has never abandoned the capitalist development (Amuzegar, 1992; Behdad, 1989, 1994, 1995, 2006; Behdad & Nomani, 2012; Nomani & Behdad, 2006; Pryor, 2009; Rahnema, 1995), they never identified the most prominent feature of the Islamic economics that impedes the advance of market capitalism. In fact, the emergence of 'Imam's property' or *Anfal* embracing all resources and assets known as *res nullius* has been the major invention of the Islamic revolution that has been left unnoticed by specialists in Islamic economics. In this chapter, I will show that *Anfal* in the Shi'i Islam justifies a confiscatory regime by dispossessing people from all 'ownerless' public properties (*res nullius*) and transferring them to the restrictive property of the Imam.

In a sense, *Anfal* realized in economic sphere what *Velayat Faqih* (the jurisconsult of the vicegerent) accomplished in political sphere. While the latter dispossessed people from their political sovereignty, the former dispossessed them from all public properties known as *res nullius*. A lot of ink has been spread on *Velayat Faqih* but *Anfal* is still concealed under a false appearance of 'statist ideology'. To unmask this institutionalized dispossession of people from their sovereignty over *res nullius* is the main contribution of this chapter.

The term *res nullius* is Latin meaning 'nobody's thing/property'. It is derived from private Roman law according to which *res* refers to anything that can be owned including a slave but not a free citizen or any subjects having rights. *Res nullius* comprises all *ownerless property* that might be acquired by means of occupation. The concept is still used in modern civilian legal system. Colonialism has repeatedly mobilized this concept to

---

[1] This is also true about the recent Taliban's triumph as a source of inspiration for other Islamist insurgents and global jihad (see the *Economist*, August 28,–September 3, 2021).

justify the occupation of unclaimed territories as well as vast territories in North America and Australia that were inhabited by indigenous peoples but Europeans claimed as newly discovered land.

Anfal is one of the underlying tenets of the Islamic public finance in addition to (1) *Kharaj* or Islamic special tax on conquered lands; (2) *Moqasemat* or tributary share paid in crops by peasants tilling on the conquered lands of Islam; (3) *Khoms* or the required religious obligation of any Muslim to contribute one-fifth of his/her acquired wealth from certain sources to specific causes; (4) *Zakat* or a predictable, fixed, and mildly progressive tax system; (5) alms; and (6) fines. The meanings of *Anfal*, its sources and scope, as well as its expenditures are controversial issues among different schools of Shi'i and Sunni Islam.[2]

Koran, Hadith, reports and traditions, juristic consensus, and Ijtihad[3] are regarded as the means to support the validity of any Islamic rules. In this chapter, I start by introducing *Anfal* in different Surahs (or chapters) of Koran, its meaning, and the historical context in which it appeared. Several apparent textual contradictions in Koran will be discussed and divergent interpretations between Shi'i and Sunni Islam will be highlighted.

While the Sunni Islam established the Caliphate system after the Prophet and accorded a central place to *Kharaj* from the conquered lands, the Shi'i Islam was mainly concerned with private affairs such as marriage, divorce, and trade until the rise of the Twelver Shi'is school as the official state religion during the Safavid dynasty. A radical change took place in the Shi'i faqihs' position regarding *Kharaj* and *Anfal* under the Safavid. The seizure of power by the Shi'i clergy in the Iranian revolution of 1979 ushered in a new era of Imam's sovereignty and property. An important shift occurred in the way *Anfal* was previously interpreted by the Shi'i theologians such as Sadr (1961). The constitution of the Islamic Republic of

---

[2] In the Sunni Islam, *Anfal* constitutes a marginal fraction of the public finance of the Islamic government. Chaudhury (1992, 1999, Chap. 13) includes seven sources of revenue for the Islamic state, namely (1) Az-zakat, (2) Al-Ushr, (3) Al-Khoms, (4) Al-Jizyah, (5) Al-Fai, (6) Al-Kharaj, (7) Miscellaneous sources. Only the fifth (*Al-Fai*) refers to *Anfal*. The author underlines the fundamental differences between the Islamic public finance and the modern fiscal system based on Wealth tax, Income tax, Customs Excise, Sales tax, Gift tax, Capital Gains tax, and Property tax. We will come later to '*Al-Fai*' and the controversial issue of *Kharaj* in the Sunni and Shi'i Islam (see section 3–4).

[3] *Ijtihad* is a legal Islamic term referring to independent reasoning in addressing and solving a legal issue. Since the nineteenth century, the Shi'i Islam emphasized *Ijtihad* rather than tradition or reports.

Iran reflects this shift. We will then concentrate on the recent Islamic practices notably the way *Anfal* is introduced in the constitution of the Islamic
Republic of Iran. Our review of the economic section of the constitution
will show that, paradoxically, the Article 45 on *Anfal* has been totally disregarded by economists specialized in the Iranian economy.

5.2   Anfal in Koran and the Battle of Badr

The term *Anfal* first appeared in the eight Surah (chapter) of Koran titled
Al-Anfal or Spoils[4] (Koran, 2014, pp. 116–122). This Surah is composed
of 75 verses. The first verse is related to the battle of Badr (624 CE), the
first holy war led by the Prophet Muhammad. This battle was a turning
point for the early Muslim community (*ummah*) from a defensive to an
offensive position, since the Prophet Muhammad who had emigrated
from Mecca to al-Medina shifted to a new strategy of reconquering Mecca
by defeating Quraysh. Its importance in the Islamic consciousness is
marked by the fact that it is the only battle mentioned by name in Koran.

The exact date of the battle is a subject of contention. According to one
of the most reliable historical sources, namely al-Tabari (838-923) at least
three different dates have been suggested: March 15, March 17, and
February 28, but all agree on the year 624 (Al-Tabari & Jarir, 1987, vol.
7, pp. 26, 27, 38). A very short account of the event should start by the
fact that Muhammad had been informed that Abu Sufyan ibn Harb[5] was
coming from Syria in a great caravan belonging to Quraysh containing
money and merchandise. He called the Muslims, both *Emigrants* and

---

[4] The written compilations or manuscripts of the holy book of Islam, the Koran spanned
several centuries. It was first compiled into a book format under the first Caliph, Abu Bakr
Siddiq. With the expansion of the Islamic Empire, recitations were proliferated in far-flung
areas. The Koran was recompiled for uniformity in recitation under the auspices of the third
Caliph, Uthman ibn Affan (Esposito, 1995). That explains why the Koran as it exists today
is also known as Uthmanic codex. *As Peters (1991, p. 297) pointed out, the order of Surahs was
decided in a mechanical fashion according to their length to avoid redactional bias. Chronological
rearrangement of Surahs has been an arduous task. I use Dawood's translation of Koran which
is particularly scrupulous about the order of Surahs and proper translation accessible in today's
English language.*

[5] A leader and merchant from the Quraysh tribe of Mecca. He was a prominent opponent
turned companion of the Islamic prophet Muhammad.

Ansar,[6] to go against them, saying, "This is the caravan of Quraysh, containing their wealth; so go out against it, and it is to be helped that God will give it to you as booty" (Al-Tabari & Jarir, 1987, vol. 7, p. 35).

Abu Sufyan was informed about Muhammad's intention to intercept the caravan, and he sent a messenger to Quraysh summoning them to come out and fight to protect their property. However, Abu Sufyan could finally turn away his caravan from the road where Muhammad and his army were beseeched to intercept it. He then informed Quraysh that the caravan was safe and there was no need to go to a confrontation with Muhammad's army but Quraysh under the leadership of Abu Jahl b. Hisham was determined not to retreat particularly because all the family leaders had participated either personally or sent someone to represent them in the battle (al-Tabari, ibid., pp. 38–45). The unification of different families of Quraysh and their advantage in terms of number of combatants might have been one of the major reasons for their resolution to confront Muhammad and his army at Badr.

The exact number of Muhammad's army is not known, but all the accounts converge on a figure close to more than 310 warriors, whereas Quraysh had gathered, three times more, that is 950 fighters. "Abu Jafar [al-Tabari] says: The total number of the emigrants who were present at Badr and who were given a share and awarded by the Messenger of God was eighty-three according to Ibn Ishaq (Ibn-Humayd-Salamah). The total number of al-Aws who were present and received a share was sixty-one, and the total number of al-Khazraj who were present was one hundred and seventy, according to Ibn Ishaq. The total number of Muslims martyred on that day was fourteen men, six of them were Emigrants and the rest were Ansars. The polytheists, so al-Wqidi asserts, consisted of nine hundred and fifty fighters, and their cavalry consisted of a hundred horses" (al-Tabari, ibid., p. 83).

The majority of Muhammad's warriors were from Ansar (231 warriors) compared to Emigrants who were 83.[7] The victory of the Prophet's army seemed to be a miracle, and in fact, Muhammad attributed it to God and

[6] The ninth Surah 'Al-Tawbah' (Repentance) (Dawood, 2014, pp. 122–136) defines the Emigrants (*Muhajirin*) as Muslims who had left their homes and emigrated with Muhammad from Mecca to al-Medina. The Helpers (*Ansar*) were Muslims of al-Medina who supported the Prophet in the time of the distress. They gave shelter to his followers or *Emigrants*.

[7] There are other accounts according to which they were 77 Emigrants and 236 Ansar (for a total of 313) (see al-Tabari, ibid., p, 39). But all reports confirm that Ansar constituted the bulk of Muhammad's army.

not Muslim's warriors. Many passages in al-Tabari refer to the help of angels: "The angels did not fight on any day except the day of Badr, on the other days they were assistants and helpers, but they struck no blows" (al-Tabari, ibid., p. 61).[8]

The Prophet, his family, and Abu Bakr were sheltered at a place close to Badr so that they could survive in case of military defeat (al-Tabari, ibid., pp. 48, 53, p. 84). But Muhammad was supervising and leading the war closely. To incentivize his warriors, he went to them and "promised every man that he could keep all the booty he took, and then said, 'By him in whose hands Muhammad's soul rests, if any man fights them today and is killed, fighting steadfastly and with resignation, going forward and not returning back, then God will cause him to enter paradise" (al-Tabari, ibid., p. 55). The prophet also promised to reward those who killed or took captives from the enemy.

The battle was waged by young Muslims who were strongly motivated by the Prophet's promises. The elderly Muslims did not participate in war and guarded the Prophet. Reports are not unanimous about the number of captives and deaths from Quraysh. Most reports say that 70 people were killed and 70 were taken captive (al-Tabari, ibid., pp. 34, 65, 81). However, it is also reported that when the Prophet returned to al-Medina, the "polytheist captives [who] were with the Messenger of God…were forty-four…There was similar number of dead" (al-Tabari, ibid., p, 65). Does it mean that some of the captives were killed before Muhammad's return to al-Medina? It is doubtful that 26 captives had been killed after their arrest since Muhammad's policy was to use captives for ransoming. Apparently, Abu Bakr had also recommended ransoming whereas Umar advocated the assassination of captives (al-Tabari, ibid., p. 81).

After the triumph in the battle, the younger Muslims came to the Prophet to capture the booties of war. The older Muslims protested and

---

[8] Other passages mention that angels also contributed to take captives from Quraysh (al-Tabari, ibid., pp. 69-70). Another sign of God's help was the rain, since it rendered the wadi-bed soft for Muhammad's army while its effect on Quraysh was that they were not able to advance easily. Thus, Muhammad's army could get to the water before them and captured the nearest well of Badr (al-Tabari, ibid., p. 47). The control of wells by Muhammad's troop was one of their sources of victory, since the Prophet ordered to fill all wells except the one kept by his army. They built a cistern next to their only well that was filled with water. Consequently, "When Quraysh halted, a number of them advances until they reached the cistern…Everyone who drank was killed that day, with the exception of Hikm b. Hizan" (al-Tabari, ibid., p. 49).

asked for an equal share. They argued that they were not afraid to participate in the battle but stayed with the Prophet to guard and protect him.
In fact, "While the Muslims were taking captives, the Messenger of God
was in his shelter. Sa'ad b. Muadh was standing at the door, girt with his
sword, along with a few of the Ansar, guarding the Messenger of God,
since they were afraid that the enemy would round and attack him" (al-
Tabari, ibid., p. 56). It is reported that eight people were guarding the
Prophet and his family, three of them were Emigrants and five of them
from Ansar (al-Tabari, ibid., p. 84).

Thus, they were entitled as much as the young Muslims to have their
share (Mahamed, 2012, p. 83; Hosseini & Sadeghi Fadaki, 2019,
pp. 22–24). Al-Tabari (ibid., p. 63) also reports on Muslims' differences
regarding the division of the booty: "Those who had collected it said, 'It
is ours. The Messenger of God promised every man that he could keep the
booty he took.' Those who were fighting and pursuing the enemy said, 'If
it had not been for us, you would not have taken it. We distracted the
enemy from you so that you could take what you took.' Those who were
guarding the Messenger of God for fear that the enemy would attack him
said, 'By God, you have no better right to it than we have. We wanted to
kill the enemy when God gave us the opportunity to made them turn their
backs, and we wanted to take property when there was no one to protect
it but we were afraid that the enemy might wheel around and attack the
Messenger of God.'" In brief, the differences boiled down to how the
booties of war had to be divided between Muslims present or absent in the
battle. The main issue was to whom belonged the property of the booties of war?

Settling differences among Muslims, the Prophet asked God's guidance. The first verse of *Anfal* defined the rule of conduct: "They ask you
about the spoils. Say: 'The spoils belong to God and the Apostle.
Therefore, fear God and end your differences. Obey God and His apostle
if you are true believers" (Dawood, 2014, p. 116).

Thus, *Anfal* refers to the spoils of war that belong to God and the
Apostle. It was to the Prophet as the owner of *Anfal* to decide how the
booties had to be shared. This was a radical change from what was traditionally practiced in the war: the booties of war belonged to the warriors
who collected them in the battle. When an enemy's soldier was assassinated, his horse, coats of mail, sword, helmet, ring, and other personal
belongings belonged to the fighter who had killed him. By contrast, *Anfal*
allocated the property rights to God and the Apostle. The Prophet

Muhammad decided to distribute the booties of war equally among all Muslims present or absent in the battle of Badr (see al-Tabari, ibid., p. 64). But he could decide other ways to spend or divide the booties.

It is noteworthy to underline that textually speaking, *Anfal* always refers to 'the spoils of war' in Koran. This holds true not only for the first verse of *Anfal* but also in the case of verse 41 on 'Khoms': "And know that if you gain any spoils one-fifth of them shall belong to God, the Apostle, his kin, the orphans, the destitute, and the traveller in need: if you truly believe in God and what We revealed to Our servant on the Day of Salvation, the day when the two armies met" (Dawood, 2014, p. 119). This verse seems to contradict the first verse, since God and the Apostle are regarded as the owner of only one-fifth of the spoils implying that four-fifths belong to the Muslim community. This apparent contradiction has been the subject of many interpretations by the Sunni and the Shi'i theologians to which we will come later in section 4-2. However, despite this contradiction, both verses of *Anfal* pertain to spoils of war.

Furthermore, the sixth verse of the fifty-ninth Surah on 'Exile' (*Al-Hashr*) (Koran, pp. 375–376) treats another type of *Anfal* that is known as 'Fai'. The latter includes all the territories or spoils of war that are acquired without the use of violence or warfare. For example, the victory of Muhammad's expedition against the Jews of Banu al-Nadir or the territories and properties that have been captured without resistance from Banu Qurayza residing in al-Medina and its vicinity such as Khaybar and Fadak. The sixth verse of 'Exile' states: "It was by God's leave that you cut down or spared their palm-trees, so that He might humiliate the ungodly. As for those spoils of theirs which *God has assigned to His apostle*, you spurred neither horse nor camel to capture them: but God gives *His apostles authority over whom He will*; and God has power over all things" (Dawood, 2014, pp. 375-76). This verse does not limit the apostle's authority over 'one-fifth' of the spoils. He has authority over all the spoils.

However, the seventh verse of 'Exile' allegedly contradicts the preceding verse since the ownership of the spoils is *not limited to God and the Apostle*: "The spoils taken from the town-dwellers and assigned by God to *His apostle shall belong to God, to the Apostle and his kin, to orphans, to the destitute and to the traveller in need*; they shall not become the property of the rich among you. Whatever the Apostle gives you, take it; and whatever he forbids you, abstain from it. Fear God; God is stern in retribution. They shall also be for the poor among the *muhajirin* [Emigrants] who have been driven from their homes and their possessions, who seek God's grace and pleasure and who help God and His apostle; these are the true believers" (Dawood, 2014, p. 376). In this verse, the scope of ownership is extended to the apostle's kin, to orphans, to the destitute, and to the traveler in need. Again, how we can reconcile this contradiction?

5.3   Contradictory Verses on *Anfal*

As discussed above, there are two apparent contradictions in Koran regarding *Anfal*: (1) the first and the forty-first verses of the eight Surah on *Anfal*; (2) the sixth and the seventh verses of the fifty-ninth Surah titled 'Exile' (*Al-Hashr*).

Three solutions have been suggested to solve the first contradiction.

1. According to some Sunni theologians (see Tabarsi, 1973; Razi, 1992; Tusi, 1984), the forty-first verse on *Khoms* (one-fifth) contradicts the first verse on *Anfal*. In the first place, the spoils belonged to God and the apostle, but with the new revelation, that order was abrogated[9] and now only one-fifth of the spoils belong to God and his apostle.

2. Most Shi'i theologians deny any true contradiction between the two verses. They maintain that the first verse of *Anfal* clarifies the principle of ownership of *Anfal* belonging to God and the Apostle, while the forty-first verse on '*Khoms*' determines the way *Anfal* should be *spent*. The latter commands that the Islamic sovereign should spend one-fifth of *Anfal* for specific groups and the rest should be distributed among warriors (Tabatabei, 1995, vol. 9. p. 10; Montazeri, 1987, vol. 4, p. 10). Contrary to the Sunnis, the Shi'is do not limit *Anfal* to the spoils of war, and 'one-fifth' is supposed to be applied to Muslim's acquired wealth from certain sources in general not limiting to the spoils. According to certain Shi'i faqihs, the booties of war also belong to the Prophet and if in the forty-first verse four-fifth of the booties are devoted to warriors, this was to reward the warriors' efforts (Schirazi, 1997, vol. 7, p. 82). The Shi'i theologians refer to a few facts and certain reports from Imams to support their claims. For example, the Prophet did not distribute the booties of the war after the victory over Mecca and the battle of Hunain[10] (Ghartabi, 1973, vol. 8, p. 4; Montazeri,

---

[9] In Islamic Fiqh, the term is '*Naskh*' meaning abrogation or nullification. When a new verse contradicts and replaces the old one, it is a '*Naskh*'.

[10] A valley near Mecca.

1987, vol. 4, p. 10). In other words, the Shi'i theologians distinguish between the *ownership* of *Anfal* and its *expenditures*. According to them, the property of *Anfal* belongs to the apostle as indicated in the first verse. But the Prophet can spend it in different ways: to devote four-fifth to warriors, to donate it partly to his kin, to spend it entirely for the needs of Muslims, etc. The verse on 'Khoms' is related to the *expenditure* and not the *ownership* of *Anfal*. In this sense, the two verses are not contradictory.

3. A third solution is to distinguish between the two types of spoils. The spoils of war that are acquired through violence and warfare, and those that are captured without violence. The latter constitute *Anfal*, while the former type is not part of *Anfal*. Accordingly, the verse on 'Khoms' relates to spoils that are not part of *Anfal* and do not belong to the apostle (Ghartabi, 1973, vol. 8, p. 4). This interpretation narrows down the scope of *Anfal* to 'Fai', that is, the spoils that are captured without resorting to warfare and violence.

Two solutions have been suggested to explicate the contradiction between the sixth and seventh verses of the fifty-ninth Surah titled 'Exile' (*Al-Hashr*).

1. The first interpretation often advocated by the Sunnis maintains the distinction between two types of spoils. Accordingly, the sixth verse considers the apostle as the owner of 'Fai' or spoils of war that are acquired without resorting to violence. *Anfal* is reduced to 'Fai'. By contrast, the seventh verse names other owners in addition to the apostle since the spoils are captured by violence and warfare and are not part of *Anfal*.

2. The second interpretation held by the Shi'is adopts a broad definition of *Anfal* covering both types of spoils but suggests a distinction between the *ownership* and the *expenditures* of *Anfal*.

In sum, these contradictions have been resolved either by narrowing or by broadening the scope of *Anfal*. Sunnis support a *stricto* sensu definition of *Anfal* limited to the booties of war or even the booties acquired without the use of violence (known as 'Fai'). This interpretation acknowledges the contradictions as true ones. By contrast, Shi'is defend a broad definition of *Anfal* as properties existing in excess or without any specific owner belonging to the prophet and to the Imams or Vali Faqih (the jurisconsult of the vicegerent) after them. Shi'is do not see any true contradictions among the verses.

The difference between the two approaches is also manifested in the way the term *Anfal* is defined. Etymologically speaking, *Anfal* derives from the root *Nafl* meaning the booty or donation or something in excess (Babookani et al., 2018, p. 407). For example, praying in excess of the required praying for any Muslim is named '*Nafeleh*'. Similarly, someone's small children are called '*Nafeleh*' since they are 'in excess' or prolongation of one own's children.

In a sense, spoils are 'gifts' from God and the apostle in excess of what true believers deserve as warriors of Islam, since the Muslim's reward is the accomplishment of his/her duty towards God. "He that fights for God's cause fights for himself. God needs the help of none. Those that have faith and do good works, We shall surely cleanse of their sins and require according to their noblest deeds" (Koran, the sixth verse of the 29th Surah titled 'The Spider').

5.4   ANFAL AND THE PROPHET'S PRACTICES

The importance of textual references to the Koran notwithstanding, it is important to inquire how the Prophet dealt with *Anfal* in practice. Two cases should be mentioned: (1) the surrender of Banu al-Nadir's properties and (2) the property of Fadak.

Lands and Properties of Banu al-Nadir

A major item of *Anfal* is the conquered land. The first piece of land that came under the ownership of the Prophet as *Anfal* was those of Banu al-Nadir. The Banu al-Nadir were a Jewish Arab tribe which resided in northern Arabia at the oasis of al-Medina until the seventh century. The tribe declined to convert to Islam as Muhammad had commanded it to do. As a consequence, the tribe was expelled from al-Medina (Sahih Muslim, 1765). The Banu al-Nadir then planned the Battle of the Trench together with the Quraysh. They later participated in the battle of Khaybar.

Similar to other Jews of al-Medina, the Banu al-Nadir bore Arabic names, but kept aloof from the Arabs, conversed in a distinctly Jewish dialect of Arabic. They were engaged in agriculture, usury, and trade in armor and jewels, entertaining commercial relations with Arab merchants of Mecca. Their fortresses were located half a day's march to the south of

Medina (Vacca, 2012). Banu al-Nadir were wealthy and lived in some of the best lands in al-Medina (Stillman, 1979).

Muhammad besieged the Banu al-Nadir in July 625 and ordered them to surrender their property and leave al-Medina within ten days. The tribe decided to put up resistance, hoping also for help from the Banu al-Qurayza, despite opposition within the tribe (Vacca, 2012). The al-Nadir could not succeed in their resistance when the promised help failed to materialize and when Muhammad ordered the burning and felling of their palm trees. They were forced to surrender after the siege had lasted a fortnight. Under the conditions of surrender, their immovable property was forfeited, and nothing left to them but what they could take away on camels with the exception of weapons (Vacca, 2012). After two days of bargaining, the tribe departed with a caravan of 600 camels (Stillman, 1979, p. 14). Most of Banu al-Nadir found refuge among the Jews of Khaybar, while others emigrated to Syria (Vacca, 2012).

Upon expulsion of the Banu al-Nadir, Muhammad is said to have received a revelation of the Surah 'Exile' (*Al-Hashr*). The Banu al-Nadir's wealth was captured without violence and according to the sixth verse of 'Exile', God bestowed it upon the Prophet. Muhammad divided Banu al-Nadir land between *Muhajirin* (Emigrants), that is, his companions who had emigrated with him from Mecca. Until then, the emigrants had to rely upon the Medinese sympathizers (*Ansar*) for financial assistance. The Prophet did not give anything to *Ansar* (Helpers) except to two of them who were poor (Mesbahi Moghaddam et al., 2011, pp. 202–203). Muhammad reserved a share of the seized land for himself, which also made him financially independent. He and his family's annual expenditures were financed from this wealth. The rest was partly used to provide horses and weapons in order to wage holy wars.

Fadak

Fadak, an ancient small town in the northern Hijaz, near Khaybar was a garden oasis, a tract of land in northern Arabia; it is now part of Saudi Arabia. Situated approximately 140 km (87 mi) from Medina, and inhabited, like Khaybar, by a colony of Jewish agriculturists, Fadak produced dates and cereals; handicrafts also flourished, with the weaving of blankets with palm-leaf borders (Veccia, 2012).

When the Muslims defeated the people of Khaybar at the Battle of Khaybar; the oasis of Fadak was part of the bounty given to the Prophet

Muhammad. Fadak owes its fame in the history of Islam to the fact that it was the object of an agreement and a particular decision by the Prophet, and that it gave rise to a disagreement between Faṭimah, the daughter of the prophet Muhammad, and the caliph Abu Bakr, the consequences of which were to last more than two centuries.

Muhammad led the march on Khaybar oasis on 7 May AH/629 CE with approximately 1500 men and 100–200 horses. Primary sources including the *Sirah Rasul Allah* (Biography of the Prophet) of Ibn Ishaq describe the conquest of Khaybar, detailing the agreement of Muhammad with the Jews to remain in Fadak and cultivate their land, retaining one-half of the produce of the oasis (Ibn Ishaq, 2004). This agreement was distinct from the agreement with the Jews of Khaybar, which essentially entailed the practice of sharecropping. Muhammad retained the revenues of the Fadak region for the poor as *Sadaqa*, travelers in need, and for his family (Sunan Abi Dawood Book 19, Number 2961).

Upon the death of Muhammad, the disagreement between his daughter Fatimah and Abu Bakr started. She declared that Fadak, like Muhammad's share of the produce from Khaybar, should come to her as her father's heiress. Abu Bakr, on the other hand, maintained that their attribution should remain exactly as Muhammad had settled it, since it was a question of *Sadaqa* (namely, 'public property' used for benevolent purposes, like the *Zakat*). According to the caliph, the Prophet had announced that he was heirless; what he left would be *Sadaqa*. Ali ibn Abi Talib, the first Shi'i Imam and the fourth rightly guided caliph, supported his wife Fatimah, and this question of inheritance aggravated his opposition to Abu Bakr (Veccia, 2012).

Hazleton (2010, pp. 71–73) described the dispute between Fatimah and Abu Bakr as follows. Fatimah "sent a message to Abu Bakr asking for her share of her father's estate -date palm orchards in the huge oases of Khaybar and Fadak to the north of Medina. His response left her dumbfounded. *Muhammad's estate belonged to the community, not to any individual*, Abu Bakr replied. It was part of the Muslim charitable trust to be administered by him as Caliph. [...] There was no denying the populist appeal of the message Abu Bakr sent by denying Fatimah's claim: the House of Muhammad was the House of Islam, and all were equal within it" (Emphasis added).

It is reported that the caliph used a fatherly tone in his conversation with Fatimah but remained firm. He invited her to produce witnesses to testify to the claim which she alleged to have been made by her father.

However, as she could only produce her husband and a woman named Umm Ayman, Abu Bakr considered their evidence inadequate, nevertheless admitting that an appropriate income must be guaranteed for the Prophet's family. The rejection of Faṭimah's claim appeared to be an injustice in the eyes of the S̲h̲i'i Muslims. After the failure of her claim, Faṭimah was unwilling to meet Abu Bakr again, and it was only after her death, some months after that of the Prophet, that Ali consented to recognize the election of Abu Bakr and renounced the claims to Fadak (Veccia, 2012).

Various primary sources contend that Fadak was gifted by Muhammad to Fatimah, drawing on the Koran as evidence. These include narrations of Ibn Abbas who argued that when the Koran's verse on giving rights to kindred was revealed,[11] Muhammad called to his daughter and gifted the land of Fadak to her (Mesbahi Moghaddam et al., 2011, p. 203; Shahid Jamal Rizvi, 2014, p. 143). By contrast, according to Sunnis, based upon verses 6–7 of 'Exile' (*Al-Hashr*), Fadak was clearly a case of 'Fai', meaning properties of the unbelievers surrendered to the Muslims without war. It was not to be distributed like spoils among the soldiers, but the whole of it was for Allah and His apostle. Hence, Muhammad himself used to manage 'Fai' as the head of the Islamic government. In this sense, it could not be bequeathed to his daughter as a *personal* belonging (Chaudhry, 1999, Chap. 13).

When Umar became Caliph, Ali again claimed Fatimah's inheritance, but was denied with the same argument as in the time of Abu Bakr. However, Umar restored the estates in Medina to Abbas ibn Abd al-Muttalib and Ali, as representatives of Muhammad's clan, the Banu Hashim. According to Veccia (2012), these two men quarreled bitterly, each maintaining his own right of possession, and Umar left them to sort out the matter by themselves. It seems that they partitioned the oasis, and that one condition had been imposed by Umar, namely that Fadak had to remain a *Sadaqa*. Therefore, in the Caliph's view, Ali and al-Abbas had merely been the *administrators of a charitable foundation*.

Mu'awiyah, the first Umayyad Caliph did not return Fadak to Fatimah's descendants. The same treatment was kept intact by later Umayyad Caliphs until Umar ibn Abd al-Aziz seized power. Fadak was granted to Fatimah's descendants by an edict given by Umar II, but this decision was renounced by later caliphs. Umar II's successor, Yazid ibn Abd al-Malik (known as

---

[11] "And give the relative his right" (Koran, Surah Isra, verse 26).

Yazid II) reversed his decision, and Fadak was again made 'public trust'. Fadak was then managed this way until the Umayyad Caliphate expired.

In year 747 CE, a huge revolt against the Umayyad Caliphate occurred. The Umayyad's were eventually defeated by the Abbasid army under the rule of Abu Abbas Abdullah al-Saffah in year 750. The last Umayyad Caliph, Marwan II, was killed in a lesser battle a few months after the Battle of the Zab, thus ending the Umayyad Caliphate. Historical accounts differ on what happened to Fadak under the early Abbasid caliphs. There is, however, consensus among Islamic scholars that Fadak was granted to the descendants of Fatimah during Al-Ma'mun's reign as Caliph (831–833 CE). Al-Ma'mun even decreed this to be recorded in his *(diwans)*. Al-Ma'mun's successor, Al-Mutawakkil (847–861) recaptured Fadak from the progeny of Fatimah, decreeing it to be used for the purposes initially outlined by Abu Bakr. Al-Muntasir (861–862), however, apparently maintained the decision of Al-Ma'mun, thus allowing Fatimah's progeny to manage Fadak (Al-Samhudi, 2001). What happened hereafter is uncertain, but Fadak was probably seized by the Caliph again and managed exclusively by the ruler of the time as his private property.

The two illustrations that I offered in this section raise a fundamental question: to whom belong *Anfal* (or *Fai* as part of it)? Does it belong to the Prophet or to the *Umma* (Muslim community)? Here is an important line of demarcation between Sunnis and Shi'is. The former considers that *Fai* (booties acquired without resorting to violence) belongs to Muslim community but is under the guardianship of the Prophet, whereas the latter believe that *Anfal* is owned and managed by the Prophet. In this sense, *Anfal* is the specific property of the Prophet and not the Muslim community.

5.5   The Place of *Anfal* in the Islamic Public Finance

Anfal does not have the same place in the Sunni and the Shi'i Islam. In the Sunni public finance, *al-Kharaj* constituted the bulk of public finance of the Caliphate system. By contrast, *Anfal* was a tiny part of the public finance (Mesbahi Moghaddam et al., 2011. p. 205).

Al-Kharaj means tribute or 'agricultural tax' received from land which Islamic jurists dubbed '*Kharaj* land'. In practice, it was a tribute imposed on non-Muslim owners of the lands. However, once the lands were declared as *Kharaj* land, *Kharaj* Tax continued to be paid by the tiller regardless of whether the initial owner was minor or adult, free or slave, Muslim or non-Muslim (*Zimmi*). In other words, even if the initial owner embraced Islam or sold his land to a Muslim, *Kharaj* had to be paid. The amount of *Kharaj* was fixed either per unit of land in the form of cash or share of the harvest in kind. Historically, it has been charged either on a fixed or on a proportional basis. The fixed *Kharaj* levied at a fixed amount per unit of land, while proportional *Kharaj* was measured in the form of a definite fraction of the produce, for example one-half or one-third (Chaudhry, 1992, 1999).

At the era of early Islam, *Kharaj* was levied on the conquered lands of the Jews, Iraq, Iran, Syria, Egypt, and other provinces of the Islamic empire. It was legitimized on the basis of the verses 7 to 10 of the 59th Surah on 'Exile' (*Al-Hashr*). Another source of legitimation was the Prophet's practice who gave the conquered lands of Khaybar to the Jews who were previous owners of these lands on a contractual basis according to which they had to pay half of the produce to the Islamic State. For Choudhury (1999, Chap. 13), the *Kharaj* system was set up so efficiently that the revenue from *Kharaj* increased before the death of Umar ibn al-Khaṭṭab (the second Rashidun Caliph) to an impressive level of 12.80 crore[12] Dirham in Iraq, in Egypt it augmented to 1.20 crore Dinar, and in Syria it amounted to 1.40 crore Dinar.

During the rise of Muhammad, there was no Islamic sovereignty. It emerged as a result of holy wars and *Kharaj* provided the financial foundation of the new Islamic State. This system could not exist if *Anfal* as the property of the Prophet and his descendants or Imam's would have to be expanded. The Caliphate system eschewed any parallel institutions and integrated all financial resources in the state's public funds. This explains why Abu Bakr insisted on the Prophet's Hadith that he was heirless entailing the ownership of the Islamic community over Muhammad's estate.

Accordingly, the Sunnis strictly narrowed down the scope of *Anfal* to the spoils of war. Shaikh Mahmoud Shaltoot, Bayzawi, Siooti, Maraghei, Aloosi, and Seyyed Ghotb have advocated this strict interpretation of *Anfal* (see Noori, 1990). Still, other faqihs argued for reducing the scope of *Anfal* to those spoils of war that have been abandoned by the enemy. For example, a camel or weapons that have been left behind by the

---

[12] Crore is equal to ten million. Specifically, a unit of value equal to 10 million rupees or 100 lakhs.

non-believer warriors. In this interpretation, *Fai* replaced *Anfal*. Others referred only to 'one-fifth' of the spoils and not all of it. Still certain faqihs confined *Anfal* to the coats of mail of the assassinated non-believer soldiers. In Ghartabi's *Comprehensive Exegesis* (1973) that embraces almost all the reports and quotations of Sunni faqihs, *Anfal* is reduced to four components.

1. All things that are abandoned by non-believers where the war has taken place and are captured by the Islam's warriors.
2. One-fifth of the spoils of war.
3. One-fifth of the spoils distributed at the Prophet's discretion to incentivize warriors who can contribute to the triumph of the holy war. This rule is particularly advocated by Shafi'i, Maliki, and Hanafi's Schools of the Sunni Islam.
4. Those additional spoils that are bestowed upon some warriors by the apostle. This point is particularly supported by Razi (1992).

Contrary to the Sunnis, the Shi'is extended the scope of *Anfal*. But this happened by the time Shi'ism was summoned to guide national life in Iran in the sixteenth century under the Safavid dynasty when the latter adopted the Twelver Shi'is school as a religion in its rivalry with the Ottoman Sunni empire (Momen, 1985). Before that time, Shi'ism existed as a scholastic relic insensitive to politics. For a long time, it was mainly occupied by personal and private affairs including marriage, divorce, and funerals, leaving public interests and public affairs to the Sunni faqihs. The ascent of Shi'ism to the state religion radically changed the position of Shi'i faqihs. They were now solicited to pronounce themselves on public affairs, the property issues, and particularly *Kharaj* or the tribute (tax) levied on the non-Islamic lands.

The key figure among the Shi'i theologians who collaborated actively with the Safavid dynasty during the Shah Ismail and particularly the Shah Tahmasp was Muhaqqiq al-Karaki. The cornerstone of the Shi'i understanding of *Anfal* was laid by his teachings. Karaki (1510/1992) tried to delineate the frontiers between '*Kharaj* land' and *Anfal*. He was strongly echoed and repeatedly cited during the late Qajar dynasty in the nineteenth century by theologians, especially by Shaikh Morteza Ansari Shushtari (1886-7/1990) in *Al Makasib* on the Islamic commercial law.

Karaki's collaboration with the Safavid dynasty opened a new era in the Twelver Shi'is in which the political apathy was replaced by active involvement in politics and the 'Islamization' of kingdom. Of course, Karaki was not the first Shi'i faqih who had collaborated with a dynasty. During the Shi'i Iranian dynasty of Al Buyid,[13] many faqihs were engaged in official positions. This dynasty was an interlude between the rule of the Abbasid Caliphate and the Seljuk Empire. Karki was influenced, in his turn, by the faqihs of this period.

Karaki (1510/1992, pp. 15, 44) considered the donations and gifts of the Safavid's Kings halal despite the fact that they were financed by *Kharaj*. He accepted them personally for which he was sharply criticized by a few faqihs such as Shaikh Ibrahim Qatifi. To grasp the importance of this radical political shift in the attitude of the Shi'i faqihs during the Safavid, it suffices to remember one of the salient features of Shi'ism, namely Mahdism, or the Return of the hidden Imam, the Mahdi, and the rehabilitation of the universe. According to the Shi'is, after the era of the four Rightly Guided Caliphs, all other governments are 'usurping' and 'despot' (*Jaer*) until the Return, and the ultimate, global sovereignty of the righteous. In the meanwhile, a strong tendency grew among the Shi'is to consider just government as an ideal which is impossible to achieve before the age of the Return.

However, as Enayat (1982, p. 26) aptly mentioned: "All this does not mean that Shi'ism never compromised with the powers that be. On the contrary, for the best part of their history, Shi'i theologians and jurisconsults displayed an impressive ingenuity in devising practical arrangements with the rulers...But what distinguishes Shi'i pragmatism in such cases from its Sunni counterparts is that these arrangements were often in the nature of ad hoc dispensations which never abrogated or diluted the basic Shi'i doctrinal position that all temporal authority in the absence of the hidden Imam is illegitimate." Enayat's statement should be nuanced with the foundation of the Islamic Republic of Iran in 1979, since the establishment of *Velayat Faqih* or the jurisconsult of the vicegerent (Khomeini, 1970) diluted that basic Shi'i's doctrinal position. It was now believed by many Shi'i faqihs that the 'usurping' kings are replaced by a 'just government' during *intizar* (waiting period for the Return).

While Karaki did not conquer the power like Khomeini, he was named as the great Mujtahid or the 'Fully qualified *faqih*' by the Shah Tahmasip from whom the Safavid King derived his legitimacy to the throne. The

---

[13] Al Buwayhid (or Al Buyid) were of Daylamite origin and they ruled over Iraq and central and Southern Iran from 934 to 1062.

King considered himself as the 'deputy of Mujtahid' recognizing the legitimacy of the faqih as the source of sovereignty (Rajabi, 2009, p. 58). In a sense, Karaki might be regarded as a precursor of the idea of *Velayat Faqih* since he was arguing that a just *faqih* or a 'fully qualified Imam' could represent the Hidden Imam during his absence (Nowroozi & Nemati, 2017). The concept of Islamization of political norms or 'Islamic constitutionalism' (*Saltanat Mashrooeh*) could be traced back to Karaki (Eftekhari, 2004, pp. 279–293). Karaki's collaborative position toward the Safavid had a decisive impact on his fatwa regarding *Kharaj* and *Anfal*. Indeed, the major controversial issue between him and his Shi'i contenders was 'Kharaj' (Abadi & Hossein, 1973, p. 462).

Karaki (1510/1992) started by classifying different types of lands. He distinguished '*Kharaj* lands' from *Anfal* lands. The former refers to the territories conquered by the Safavid Empire; it is the outcome of 'forced conquest' (*maftuhe onveh*) by Muslims through war waged on the basis of the Imam's authorization. To illustrate Kharaj lands, Karaki (ibid, p. 61) cited Arabic Iraq, Khorasan, Levant, and Ray (or Ragha). All non-Muslim communities as well as Muslims who worked on these lands in operation had to pay a tribute or an agricultural tax (*Kharaj*). The tax was two sorts. The first was either cash in gold and silver proportional to the land's size, or in kind based on a fixed percentage of the agricultural product. The second form was coined 'Moqasemeh' (sharing or partnership). The *Kharaj* lands were non-communal property of all *Muslims* and could not be owned by private owners. They came within the scope of public law and not civil law. The income derived from *Kharaj* lands belonged to the public and had to be kept in the Muslims' Public Treasury (*Beit al-mal*). By contrast, *Anfal did not belong to all Muslims but only to the Imam* (Karaki, Ibid, p. 61; Ansari Shushtari, 1886-7/1990, vol. 4, p. 169). Moreover, *Anfal* lands were exempt from *Kharaj*.

Three major issues need to be addressed here:

1. If the authority who rules on *Kharaj* lands is a 'usurping Caliph' or a tyrant king then would *Kharaj be* halal or haram? Should the Muslims pay *Kharaj*?
2. Who would decide that a land is a *Kharaj* land? Could the tyrant or usurping Caliph determine which land is a *Kharaj* land?
3. What are the specific features of *Anfal* lands in contradistinction with *Kharaj* lands?

It was on the first problem that Karaki (1510/1992) wrote his book to argue that *Kharaj* had to be paid to the Safavid dynasty. This was a revisionist position in the eyes of many faqihs and the Shi'i community who considered the Kings as 'usurper' and 'tyrant' and believed that paying tribute or *Kharaj* to them would be haram or mixed with haram. It was an extremely sensitive issue for the Shi'i faqihs to justify socially or religiously the acceptance of the King's donations, gifts, or financial aid to meet their daily subsistence. Karaki broke with this 'obstinate' (*lejaj*) position, and adopted a totally different opinion. He not only accepted the King's donations (Karaki, ibid., p. 15) but argued that Kharaj had to be paid to the government by Muslim and non-Muslim communities. The "denial of *Kharaj* and *Moqaemeh* and non-remittance of them to the tyrant is haram since these are duties of the tillers" (Ansari Shushtari, 1886-7/1990, p. 169).

However, who could decide whether a given parcel of land is '*Kharaj* land' or not? Is the King's verdict sufficient to recognize a land as *Kharaj* land? This is a second issue. The answer to this question is negative. Only the Imam or the Muslim qadis has the authority to declare a land *Kharaj* land, otherwise the tyrant or usurping King may appropriate *Anfal* lands under the pretext of *Kharaj* land. Accordingly, it is the religious obligation of the tillers to ask the Imam's or the Muslim qadis whether the land is *Kharaj* or not. They are obliged to pay the tribute once the Imam declare the land to be *Kharaj* land.

This distinction between two separate spheres of authority, that of the King or governor and that of the Imam or qadi is not specific to Shi'ism. It also exists in the Sunni Islam. As Calder (2010) showed in the case of the Ottoman empire, there was a broad distinction between affairs of government and affairs of the Sharia: the Sultan conducted wars, organized the army, administered the country, looked after the welfare of its inhabitants, established communications, suppressed the wicked, and so on. The qadi had to undertake matters of marriage, divorce, sale, and Waqfs. The two spheres were never combined except during the four Rightly Guided Caliphs. "Two spheres of authority-that relating to the Sharia which was the sphere of authority of the judges, and that relating to governmental matters which was the sphere of authority of the actual powers. The distinction is not new and is present in Mawardi who has (too often) been seen as a statement of Caliphal absolutism" (Calder, 2010, pp. 159–160). Parallel institutions stem from this double power structure in Islam; it is particularly accentuated in Shi'ism once it becomes politicized since it claims a broad definition of *Anfal* and the Imam's authority over the delineation of property rights.

Finally, what are *Anfal* lands in contradistinction with *Kharaj* lands? Three distinctive features are mentioned (Ansari Shushtari, ibid., pp. 189-194):

1. All the spoils including lands that are waged without the Imam's permission belong to *Anfal* and are not considered as *Kharaj* land.
2. The conquered land through warfare that is authorized by the Imam may be *Kharaj* land if and only if the lands are in operation or cultivated. In such cases, one-fifth of the spoils belong to the Imam and the rest belongs to all Muslims. However, if the conquered lands through force and warfare are *barren*, and not in operation or cultivated, they are part of *Anfal* and do not constitute *Kharaj* lands.
3. All lands conquered without using violence are part of *Anfal*.

Compared to the Sunni Islam, Shi'ism advocates a broad definition of *Anfal* detrimental to *Kharaj* share. While the Sunni public finance gives the pride of place to *Kharaj* as 'non-communal property of all Muslims', the Shi'i public finance grants the lion share of public wealth to *Anfal* as 'the Imam's property'. The former is the source of Muslims' Public Treasury (*Beit al-mal*), while the latter provides the Imam's Treasury.

5.6 Examples and Definition of *Anfal* in the Shi'i Islam

We showed in the preceding section that the Shi'i Islam advocates a broad definition of *Anfal* that is not limited to the spoils of war. But what is its definition and its concrete illustrations according to the Shi'is?

An early literature on *Anfal* in the tenth and eleventh centuries does not contain any precise definition of the concept but solely a host of examples. Among this strand of work, two should be cited:

1. *Al-Muqni'ah* (*The Legally Sufficient*) (1989) written in the tenth century by al-Shaikh al-Mufid (948–1022).
2. *Al-Iqtisad (Economics)* (1955) written in the eleventh century by al-Shaikh Tusi (995–1067), the most eminent student of al-Mufid, and the founder of Shi'i jurisprudence.

Both faqihs were prominent scholars of the Twelver Shi'i school and lived under the Al-Buyid dynasty. In their works, *Anfal* is explained through illustrations referring to different Hadith without any precise definition.

Al-Mufid (1989, p. 279) wrote: "During the Messenger of God's lifetime, *Anfal* belonged to him and after his departure, it only belongs to the Imam representing him; and *Anfal* refers to any conquered land without using the warfare as well as to barren lands,[14] a heirless inheritance, seas, and mines, etc." In this passage, al-Mufid attributed the ownership of *Anfal* not only to the Prophet but also to the Imams coming after him. In this sense, he advocated the institutionalization of *Anfal* under the Imam as a religious authority. However, he did not clarify the criterion according to which *Anfal* could be defined. Moreover, he did not speak of the spoils to characterize *Anfal*. In fact, he only included *Fai* (conquered land without resorting to violence) in *Anfal*.

Tusi (1955, p. 284) also followed his teacher in defining *Anfal*: "*Anfal* belonged to the Messenger of God, and after him, it belongs to his representatives. Anfal is meant any land which is not conquered by the army's attack, or any land surrendered voluntarily by the people residing in it, as well as the summit of mountains or barren lands, etc." Again, there is no definition but a series of examples. Other eminent theologians pursued the same path by scrutinizing and detailing a comprehensive list of elements that can be pigeonholed as *Anfal*. The detailed list might contain 15 items as below (see Noori, 1990; Mesbahi Moghaddam et al., 2011; Mahamed, 2012; Babookani et al., 2018).

1. Barren lands
2. All lands that have no owner
3. Forests
4. Reed beds
5. Seas, lagoons, and lakes
6. Rivers
7. Sea bores

---

[14] Barren lands pertain to lands previously cultivated that are abandoned afterward by their owners. Shi'i theologians often distinguish between 'principal' and 'incidental' barren lands, the former referring to abandoned lands at a permanent basis is regarded as part of Anfal whereas the latter is the outcome of some specific events such as wars are not viewed as a component of Anfal.

8. Mines both 'apparent' and 'latent'. In Islamic jurisprudence, the former pertains to the mines that can be exploited without much exploration with unqualified labor, for example salt mine. The latter are those mines that need industrial exploration and the use of qualified labor such as petroleum.
9. The summit of mountains, but also some faqihs add the slope of a mountain and what are in it.
10. Riverbed and valleys
11. Land belonging originally to non-believers that are abandoned by them and surrendered to Muslims both when non-believers do not reside there anymore or even when they still reside there.
12. All spoils of war that Muslims acquire in a war that has not been authorized by the Imam. However, if the war has the Imam's permission, only one-fifth of the booties would belong to the Imam and the rest can be kept by warriors.
13. All the confiscated properties of the tyrants or usurping kings whether they are immovable assets (known as *Qataya* in Islamic Jurisprudence) such as gardens and palaces or movable (coined as *Safaia* in Islamic jurisprudence) such as precious objects.
14. All spoils of war taken by Muslims in the war against non-believers should be handed to the Imam to be divided among them. Before the division, the Imam can appropriate part of the booties in order to spend it for the sake of Islam or Muslims. This levy over the spoils by the Imam for public interests is part of Anfal (in Islamic jurisprudence, it is named *Safval-mal*).
15. The inheritance without any heir

This long list indicates that according to the Shi'i jurisprudence all natural resources are part of *Anfal* and belong to the Imam. In economics, natural resources constitute public wealth, but the specific feature of the Shi'i economics is that 'public wealth' are part of *Anfal* and as such it belongs to the Imam. There is, however, a bone of contention among the Shi'i faqihs over the ownership of mines. Three approaches can be distinguished on this issue.

1. Some faqihs consider all mines belong to *Anfal* regardless of whether they are located on the Imam's lands or on lands owned by private persons (Kulayni, 1988, vol. 1, p. 538). Shaykh al-Mufid (1989,

p. 278) and Shaykh Tusi (1955, p. 419) also advocate that mines are absolutely the property of the Imam.

2. Some faqihs support that the mines do not belong to *Anfal*. Al-Hilli (al-Muhaqqiq) (1988) maintains that there are strong doubts regarding the ownership of mines by the Imam. The rules of Sharia are more conducive to the idea that all people should equally share them. As reported by Babookani et al. (2018, p. 413), Allamah Al-Hilli (1250-1325) and al-Amili (1505-1558) also defended the idea that mines are not part of *Anfal* and they should be equally shared by all people.

3. A third position suggests a distinction between apparent and latent mines. The former belongs to all Muslims while the latter is part of *Anfal*. This position is a combination of the preceding positions advocated by Ahmad Ibn Muhammad Ardabili (1500-1585) (Babookani et al., ibid., p. 413).

The lack of a precise definition of *Anfal* is largely accountable for the divergence among the Shi'i faqihs. In fact, the earliest definition of *Anfal* was formulated by Al-Hilli (al-Muhaqqiq) (1988, p. 136): "*Anfal* is everything that the Imam, similar to the Prophet, deserves to own." In other words, *Anfal* includes all exclusive properties of the Imam meaning the properties over which Imam has an *uncontestable monopoly*. As a consequence, *Khoms* (one-fifth) should be distinguished from *Anfal*, since in the case of *Khoms* the property is shared and does not belong exclusively to the Imam. In conformity with this definition, the spoils of war cannot be pigeonholed as *Anfal* since they should be shared. Thus, the Shi'i faqihs classify the spoils under the Jihad whereas 'public wealth' is regrouped under *Anfal*.

After defining *Anfal*, Al-Hilli (al-Muhaqqiq) (1988, pp. 210-211) explains its five components: "Anfal includes five things: First, all lands that are captured by Muslims without warfare or lands that are surrendered by non-believers to Muslims or sometime when non-believers abandon their lands and emigrate to other places. In all these cases, the land belongs to the Imam. Second, barren lands either those lands whose owners are assassinated or lands that have never been owned by anybody such as deserts and Sahara that are not cultivated by any owner. Third, sea bores and large river banks such as Nile, Euphrates or vast seas that are flourishing but have no owners and have considerable economic interests. This also belongs to the Imam. The Imam has a discretionary power over them and can even hand a share of it to anybody he considers adequate. Fourth, the summit and the slope of mountains as well as whatever exists in them, river-beds, forests and reed beds located in them and have some value belong to the Imam. Fifth, the properties and precious palaces of tyrants and usurping kings that are confiscated by Muslims belong to the Imam if they are not seized properties. Similarly, all the spoils captured without warfare before being divided among Muslims such as horses of good breed or expensive garments belong to the Imam. In the same vein, all spoils captured by Muslims in a war that has not been authorized by the Imam belong to the Imam."

These examples clearly show that Anfal extends over all things that are 'ownerless' (*res nullius*). All 'ownerless' natural resources and valuable objects belong exclusively to the Imam. However, Al-Hilli (al-Muhaqqiq) does not consider the inheritance of a heirless person as part of *Anfal* since that can belong to all Muslims and not the Imam. In other words, that inheritance should go to the Muslims' Public Treasury and not the Imam's House. In fact, while the bulk of natural resources or public wealth belongs to *Anfal*, they are not 'public property' since in the Shi'i Islam the latter pertains to properties that should be shared equally among Muslims whereas *Anfal* exclusively belongs to the Imam.

This definition also clarifies the principal difference between the Shi'i and the Sunni Islam regarding *Anfal*. The question is to whom belongs *Anfal:* Does it belong to all Muslims (*umma*) or to the Imam? The Sunnis consider that they belong to the people and that the Islamic ruler may only act as a 'representative' of the people in allocating them. By contrast, the Shi'is believe that *Anfal* embracing 'public wealth' belongs to the Imam. The Imam does not act as the 'representative' of the people since the latter is not the owner of public wealth.

It is not the people's sovereignty that defines the role of Imam; it is Imam's sovereignty as the vicegerent of jurisconsult (*Velayat faqih*) that decides people's rights and obligations. While Muslims should *believe* in the good intentions of the Imam to secure 'public good' because of their religious faith, they have no right to control the God's representative on the earth. *Anfal* extends the rationale of *Velayat faqih* to economics and the way public treasury should be tailored. Imam has no obligation to spend *Anfal* in the interests of all Muslims (and people[15] *a fortiori*). Since Imam is supposed to represent the 'public good' in the name of Islam, he is above and beyond secular public law. His discretionary power is not limited by public law. The personal dictatorship of the Imam stems from his status as the source of sovereign power. All the institutions under the purview of Imam are out of the control of executive, parliamentary, and juridical powers. While the Assembly of experts has the right to design the Supreme Leader, its role is interpreted in terms of 'discovering' and not 'deciding' who the Supreme Leader should be. This means that the Assembly of experts is not considered something like a Senate that has some control over the Imam's intentions and over *Anfal* properties. Accordingly, the dispossession of the people from their public wealth is intrinsically assumed in the concept of *Anfal*. *Anfal institutionalize a confiscatory regime and is entirely compatible with destructive coordination.*

From a purely financial viewpoint, the question raises whether the revenue from *Anfal* goes to the Muslims' Public Treasury (*Beit al-mal*) or to the Imam's Treasury (*Beit al-Imam*)? In the Sunni Islam, the income from public wealth should finance the states' funds or the Muslims' Public Treasury, but in the Shi'i Islam the public wealth should ideally be directed to the Imam's House. Then the Imam will decide how that income will be allocated to different types of public, private, or personal (for the Imam and his kin) expenditures.

5.7   *Anfal* and the Constitution of the Islamic Republic of Iran

The seizure of power by the Shi'i clergy in Iran in 1979 ushered in a new era in which *Velayat Faqih* (the jurisconsult of the vicegerent) replaced the Shah's despotic power. The new state was defined as the Islamic Republic intending to invent an alternative economic system different from both the Western capitalism and the Eastern socialism. This third path was

---

[15] I refer to 'all Muslims' and not people or citizens in general since only Umma or Muslims have "rights" under an Islamic rule. Atheists or believers of faiths who are not officially recognized by Shi'i Islam such as Baha'is have no right and are persecuted (Pistor-Hatam, 2019). The accepted religious groups such as Jews, Christians, and followers of Zarathustrianism have rights under the Islamic rule if they pay their special tax 'Jasiah'. Although Jasiah is not practiced under the Islamic Republic of Iran, these 'minority religions' as well as Sunnis have no political power and are strongly discriminated.

called the Islamic economy. The preparation and adoption of the constitution of the Islamic Republic passed two steps.

The draft constitution published by the provisional government of Mehdi Bazargan in June 1979 was the first step. A preliminary version of this draft was written by Hassan Habibi on January 22, 1979, in conformity with Khomeini's order when he was in exile in Paris. This draft was sent to Iran by Khomeini on February 1, 1979. It was revisited by a group of jurists including Nasser Katouzian, Abdul-Karim Lahiji, Muhammad Jafar Jafari Langroudi, and Hassan Habibi under the supervision of Ahmad Sadr Haj Seyyed Javadi, the Interior Minister of the provisional government of Bazargan. The result of their work was sent to Qom by Khomeini to collect the Grand Ayatollahs'[16] comments. After revising the draft based on the faqihs' recommendations, it was handed to a commission under the supervision of the provisional government. Abul-Hassan Bani Sadr (the first Iranian President), Mehdi Bazargan (the first Prime minister of the interim government), and Morteza Mottahari (a prominent Shi'i faqih and a student of Khomeini) were members of this commission (Schirazi, 1997, Chap. 2). They prepared a new blueprint that was adopted by the Supreme Council of the Islamic revolution and handed again to Khomeini. Khomeini introduced some slight modifications in this blueprint and the final outcome was published as 'Draft constitution of the Islamic Republic of Iran' on June 14 and June 16, 1979. In this draft, there was no allusion to *Velayat Faqih* and the discretionary power of the Supreme Leader.

It was during the discussion of this draft by the 'Assembly of Experts' and the adoption of the final version of the constitution that *Velayat Faqih* was introduced. This was the second step during which the 'Assembly of Experts' was convocated instead of a much promised 'Constitutional Assembly' by Khomeini and Bazargan. Despite the opposition from the members of the interim government, Khomeini and other ruling clergies decided to renege their earlier promises and confer the adoption of the new constitution to the 'Assembly of Experts' dominated by the Shi'i clergy. The draft was replaced by a totally new constitution of the Islamic Republic of Iran that was adopted by referendum on December 2 and 3, 1979.

This radical change has been explored extensively by political scientists and jurists with regard to the political and juridical system (for a detailed

---

[16] They are called *Marjah Taqlid* or the source of emulation for their Muslim followers who imitate them in religious matters.

review see Schirazi, 1997). However, the economic dimension of this radical change was almost completely disregarded by economists, political scientists, and jurists. There are three important articles on economic issues that reflect this radical change in the adopted constitution: Articles 44, 45, and 49.

There had not been any allusion to *Anfal* in draft constitution, but it was stipulated in Article 45 of the final constitution replacing Article 46 in draft constitution. Interestingly, none of the specialists on the Islamic economics has noticed this major change, and while Article 44 was (and still is) a constant subject of discussion,[17] Article 45 on *Anfal* has never received any attention. Paradoxically, decoding Articles 44 and 49 is impossible without grasping the importance of *Anfal* in Article 45. This section will first review the incorporation of *Anfal* in Article 45, and then explore its impact on the Islamic economy as reflected in Articles 44 and 49.

Anfal and Article 45

Before discussing the constitution, it is important to underline the new interpretation of *Anfal* by Khomeini, the Supreme Leader of the Islamic Republic and a conceptualizer of *Velayat Faqih* as well as Hossein-Ali Montazeri, once designated successor to Khomeini in the aftermath of revolution until their clash in1989. The latter was also a theorist of *Velayat Faqih* and played an influential role in formulating the political and economic sections of the constitution. Montazeri's (1984, 1987) viewpoint on *Anfal* and on the 'unity of the Imam and people's property' shaped Articles 44 and 45.[18]

Khomeini's (2000) original contribution to the literature on *Anfal* was rather political than theological. He was the architect of *normalizing* and *rationalizing Anfal* in terms of exercising modern sovereign power. He endeavored to make it a normal practice that could be attributed to any state. Knowing that *Anfal is the dispossession of public properties from the people* and monopolizing it by the Imam, Khomeini tried to soften the

[17]For example, Malonney (2015, p. 133) explicitly stated that the constitutional provision "most relevant" for Iran's post-revolutionary economic development was Article 44. She never ever mentioned *Anfal* in Article 45 although she maintained that Khomeini had no economic program (2015, p. 96). Of course, Malonney wrote what other Iranian specialists had repeatedly written about the economic section in the constitution of the IRI.

[18]Muhammad Reza Mahdavi Kani (2000) also contributed to the same trend in understanding *Anfal*.

emphasis on *Anfal* as the *exclusive property of the Imam*. Instead, he concealed the unrestricted discretionary power of the Imam under the feigned appearance of a statist discourse as if the Imam's authority under the Islamic Republic was on par with that of any other modern head of the state. This was a political strategy to appropriate the bulk of natural resources (*res nullius*) for the Imam without provoking the people's sensitivity against the newly despotic power of the Supreme Leader. Imagine for a second that the Imam would have announced to the people who had just overthrown the Shah's autocratic regime that 'mineral deposits' (oil and gas), as well as the mountains and seas such as Damavand, Caspian, etc., belonged to the Imam and not the people. What a shock that could have been on that revolutionary people? Indeed, even the Shah had never claimed to be the sole owner of all natural resources or *res nullius*.

Khomeini (2000, p. 27) claimed that *Anfal* verdict was basically derived from a 'rational' assumption and not from a religious belief: "It is true that barren lands and all ownerless properties including land, sea, and sky (atmosphere) are under the authority of the head of government in all states regardless of their specific type of government, and other states cannot invade them. Moreover, the inhabitants of the same country cannot take them without the permission of the ruler. Islam has not brought anything new in this field contrary to what the rational reasoning implies." In this passage, Khomeini speaks of *Anfal* as a statesman and not a theologian. According to him, *Anfal* includes all 'ownerless' properties or *res nullius* embracing all three dimensions of the state space in the modern sense of the term, namely territorial, sea, and air (atmosphere). But this whole line of reasoning is sophistry.

Anfal cannot be justified on a purely rational basis, or as a necessary consequence of exercising the sovereign power. Since all modern states are based on the principle of the *people's sovereignty*, the people and not the state are the owner of public property; the state act only on behalf of people in supervising and managing public property. In the Shi'i Islam, there is also a line of demarcation between public property and *Anfal*. While "the owner of public property is the whole Islamic umma" (Mesbahi Moghaddam et al., 2011, p. 201), *Anfal* belongs only to the Imam and not the people. However, the Imam's property is not a personal but a statutory one.

To put it differently, the Imam's children and his kin are not the heirs of *Anfal*, but *Anfal* as the institutional property of the Imam should be transferred to the next Imam. The Imam can spend *Anfal* as he sees it fit and is not bound to spend them for all Muslims, since the people are not the owner of *Anfal*. This is based upon the Shi'i's jurisprudence and cannot be derived from the rational assumption regarding the exercise of the sovereign power. If *Anfal* belonged to all people and not the Imam, it would have been dissolved in public property in general. But in that case, why should it be mentioned in the constitution at all?

In fact, the draft constitution only mentioned *public property* and totally dismissed *Anfal* in Article 46: "Underground resources, seas, mineral deposits, forests, marshland, lakes and other public waterways as well as barren lands and pasturelands are *public properties* and their utilization is decided by laws" (emphasis added).[19] The final version of constitution radically revised this early version and introduced *Anfal* in Article 45 replacing the preceding Article 46. It now reads: "*Anfal* and public wealth, such as barren lands or abandoned land, mineral deposits, seas, lakes, rivers and other public waterways, mountains, valleys, forests, marshland, natural forests, unenclosed pastureland, legacies without heirs, property of undetermined ownership, and public property recovered from usurpers, shall be at the disposal of the Islamic government to act in accordance with the public interest. Law will specify detailed procedures for the utilization of each of the foregoing items."[20] Interestingly, the term *Anfal* does not appear in the official English translation of Article 45. Instead, we read: "Public wealth and property"[21] as if *Anfal* is synonym of 'public property'. It indicates the lack of knowledge on *Anfal* at national and international levels to the point that it could be totally dismissed in English translation. This was also in line with Khomeini's strategy to normalize or rationalize *Anfal* as any public property represented by the state.

This 'rationalized' version of *Anfal* conflated it with public property, in general, and brought both of them under the 'property of Islamic government'. Accordingly, they extended the scope of Anfal to include not only the Imam's property but also properties belonging to all Muslims ('umma' in Islamic terminology). *In this way, the scope of people's dispossession from public wealth and properties extended in proportion to the increase in the Supreme Leader's discretionary power over all resources.*

---

[19] *Minutes of the discussions of the Majles on the final version of the Constitution of the Islamic Republic of Iran*, vol. 4, p. 9.

[20] This is the author's translation. For an alternative official translation see PURL: https://www.legal-tools.org/doc/4205c7/ retrieved on September 10, 2021.

[21] See *Iran (Islamic Republic of)'s Constitution of 1979 with Amendments through 1989*, constituteproject.org, retrieved on June 28, 2021.

Moreover, conflating *Anfal* and public property in general could shun disputes among the Shi'i faqihs on what should be included or excluded from *Anfal*. For example, the Shi'i theologians are not unanimous whether 'mineral deposits' and 'property of undetermined ownership' are part of *Anfal*. But lumping together *Anfal* and public property, in general, provides an excuse to eschew the dispute on whether those elements are *Anfal* or not. The discussion regarding Article 45 demonstrates these points.

The minutes of the discussions of the Assembly of Experts on the final version of the constitution of the Islamic Republic are available online (PDF format) in four volumes in Persian.[22] The new Article 45 replacing the preceding article 46 of the draft was discussed in the 55th session of the Assembly of Experts on October 29, 1979 (see *Minutes*, vol. 3, pp. 1499-1516).[23] The session was presided by the deputy-President, Seyyed Muhammad Hossein Beheshti. In that session, Mr. Sobhani objected that "property of undetermined ownership is not part of *Anfal*" (Minutes, vol. 3, p. 1514) and Beheshti replied: "We refereed to Anfal and public wealth" (ibid., p. 1515). Similarly, another deputy, Mr. Heydari also objected that "It is written here *Anfal*, but barren lands are two types, principal and derisory. Principal barren lands are part of *Anfal*, but derisory barren lands that were previously cultivated and in operation and then fell into barren lands, for example due to the war, are not part of *Anfal*" (Minutes, p. 1515). Again, Beheshti, replied: "As we previously responded, the article refers to public wealth including both *Anfal* and those that are not *Anfal*" (ibid., p. 1515). In other words, the clause "Anfal and public wealth" eschewed any objection regarding the exact perimeters of *Anfal* by saying that the article included both *Anfal* and non-*Anfal*.

The Minutes show that at one point, Mr. Ali Khamenei (the present Supreme Leader) underlined the ambiguity of the Article 45 by reminding

---

[22] From now on, we refer to these discussions as 'Minutes'.

[23] https://www.shora-gc.ir/fa/news/2098/%D8%B5%D9%88%D8%B1%D8%AA-%D9%85%D8%B4%D8%B1%D9%88%D8%AD-%D9%85%D8%B0%D8%A7%DA%A9%D8%B1%D8%A7%D8%AA-%D9%85%D8%AC%D9%84%D8%B3-%D8%A8%D8%B1-1%D8%B1%D8%B3%DB%8C-%D9%86%D9%87%D8%A7%DB%8C%DB%8C-%D9%82%D8%A7%D9%86%D9%88%D9%86-%D8%A7%D8%B3%D8%A7%D8%B3%DB%8C-%D8%AC%D9%85%D9%87%D9%88%D8%B1%DB%8C-%D8%A7%D8%B3%D9%84%D8%A7%D9%85%DB%8C-%D8%A7%DB%8C%D8%B1%D8%A7%D9%86 retrieved on February 10, 2022.

that *Anfal* were the property of the Imam whereas the article has been drafted in a way to nuance this point as if the Imam was just managing the property: "Why shouldn't we refer to the 'Public Treasury of Muslims' (*Beit al-mal*) instead of being 'at the disposal of' the government'? If what is referred to are part of the Public Treasury, then we shouldn't clarify to whom the property belongs as if we mean by being 'at the disposal of' that others are owners whereas the Imam who is the owner has only the power to use or has the priority" (Minutes, ibid., p. 1515). In reaction to this very important objection, Beheshti promptly shortened the discussion by saying that "The so-called Public Treasury differs from these cases in the Islamic culture, and the Public Treasury cannot be referred to in the case of these properties. In any way, the gentlemen have proposed the end of discussions and those who are for this proposal, please raise your hands" (Minutes, ibid., p. 1515).

Ali Khamenei was right in asking why the 'Public Treasury of Muslims' (*Beit al-mal*) had not been named as the fund in which *Anfal* and public wealth had to be kept. The problem was that *Anfal* did not belong to the 'central treasury of the state' as stipulated in Article 53 of the constitution but to the 'House of the Imam' (*Beit al-Imam*). To illustrate this point, it suffices to focus on 'public property recovered from usurpers' to which refers Article 45. This point is substantiated in Article 49. As discussed in section 5-5, the Shi'i faqihs are unanimous in considering that all the confiscated properties of the tyrants or usurping kings are part of *Anfal* after deducting those properties that should be returned back to their legitimate owners if they were illicitly taken. But how these properties were managed? Khomeini issued an injunction in the aftermath of the revolution in which he referred to the assets of the late Shah and 53 industrialists in exile as 'spoils'. The term employed by Khomeini had a clear religious connotation, he was categorizing them as part of *Anfal* belonging to the Imam. Accordingly, they were *not nationalized* but 'kept and controlled separately from state properties under the Guardianship of the Jurist' (Saeidi, 2004, p. 484).

Khomeini decided to manage these assets by creating a foundation, namely *Bonyad Mostazafan va Janbazan* (BMJ, Foundation of the Downtrodden and War Veterans). This was the inception of big holdings constituting the most powerful para-governmental sector. This sector reports only to the Supreme Leader as the one who owns it. Its activities are totally opaque, and the Majles Shoorai Islami (the so-called Islamic Parliament) as well as the executive power has no authority over it. It constitutes a parallel institution besides the formal state sector. The income derived from this sector does not go to the central treasury of the state since it belongs to the 'House of the Imam' (*Beit al-Imam*). Thus, Ali Khamenei was putting the finger at the right place, predicting that those assets in Article 45 would belong to him as the next Supreme Leader.

Anfal *and Article 44*

Article 44 did not exist in draft constitution. It was formulated by the 'Assembly of Experts' to describe the Islamic economy as an alternative to both the Western capitalism and the Eastern socialism (see Makarem Schirazi, *the Minutes*, vol. 3, p. 1546). The discussion on this article was one of the longest since it took three sessions, namely sessions 55, 56, and 57 starting on October 29 and ending by October 31, 1979. Chronologically speaking, this article was discussed and adopted after the adoption of Article 45 on *Anfal*. All sessions were again presided by the deputy-president, Seyyed Muhammad Hossein Beheshti. Interestingly enough, similar to Article 45, Ayatollah Hossein-Ali Monatzeri played a key role in drafting and leading the discussion on this article.[24] The Minutes of the discussions (vol. 3, pp. 1523–1568) afford a vivid picture of the deep differences, divisions, and conflicts among the deputies on this article although they only cover discussions in the afternoon while morning discussions regarding the initial drafts by commissions are not recorded. Thus, we do not have access to a complete picture of each session.

Reviewing the minutes, it becomes clear that there were several blueprints about the way this article had to be formulated. Beheshti was for a very short description of the Islamic economy as drafted in the first two lines of the adopted final article:

"The economy of the Islamic Republic of Iran is to consist of three sectors: state, cooperative, and private, and is to be based on systematic and sound planning."

According to Beheshti, further elaboration of these sectors had to be left to the law. This position was not that of Montazeri and many other deputies. At least, two detailed proposals were suggested in the morning discussions (see the Minutes, vol. 3, pp. 1543–1547, particularly the

---

[24] My guess is that Montazeri was directly connected to the Supreme Leader, Khomeini, in leading the discussion. Beheshti's tactful attitude toward Montazeri throughout sessions on different economic issues indicate that he was occupying a strategic position.

interventions of Khamenei at p. 1543 and those of Makarem Schirazi and Beheshti at pages 1546–1547). One of them was supported by Montazeri, Rabbani Schirazi, Zyaei, and some other deputies and the second proposal was defended by Makarem Schirazi, Taheri Isfahani, and several others. Montazeri tried to combine them and propose a unified formulation. He was not always successful in achieving unity and his authority was challenged a few times during sessions (see the Minutes, vol. 3, pp. 1556–1559). Montazeri explicitly expressed his bitterness at the start of the third session regarding these disputes (see the Minutes, vol. 3, p. 1556).

The initial formulations of Article 44 during the first two sessions were aimed to present a radically new picture of the Islamic economy from capitalist and socialist systems. But they could not achieve the majority vote and were rejected one after the other. In fact, while the extension of the state sector was not contested, there was no unanimity among the deputies about whether the private sector should be limited or not. Moreover, the only novel point in the proposals regarding Article 44 was about the role of *cooperatives* in conjunction with *Anfal* and state intervention. But this was also ambiguous as Khamenei persuasively argued in his once and for all intervention during the session 56: "It seems that the main point is about the cooperative sector which is a new thing, and is supposed to be invented here or if it already exists, we need to adopt and legalize it. However, this part is the weakest and the shakiest part of the article…we need to separate this point and elaborate it and put aside the other two sectors. It should be clarified if the cooperatives' properties can be inherited? Or do they belong to the state? Are they transferable?" (Khamenei, ibid., p. 1541).

Khamenei considered cooperative as the main point of Article 44 since in its initial formulation it was closely related to *Anfal*:

> The state should do its best to act in managing *Anfal* and public wealth mentioned in Article 45 through cooperatives (The minutes, vol. 3, p. 1523 and p. 1532).

Khamenei also suggested to emphasize the role of the Supreme Leader in the Islamic economy. His talk on Article 44 was consistent with his speech on Article 45, since he was characterizing the originality of the Islamic economy in terms of *Anfal* and the Imam's role as owner and guardian of public properties. But no one wished to spell out this truly original Islamic economic principle. In fact, Khomeini himself tried his best to 'rationalize' *Anfal* as properties controlled by the *state* without identifying the role of the Imam as the owner of *Anfal*. Accordingly, the deputies reached a new conclusion at the third session on October 31, that they had to abandon their initial intention. Instead of specifying the rupture of the Islamic economy from the prevalent capitalist economy during the Shah, *they decided to indicate the continuity*. They acknowledged unanimously that Article 44 had nothing new to offer compared with what existed previously during the Shah's regime. This point was acknowledged by all parties to the discussion.

For example, Hojjati Kermani asked: "Could you explain what is different here regarding the state sector that this article adds and that had not existed previously during the Shah's regime?" (Minutes, ibid., p. 1560). Beheshti replied: "In my opinion, this article has nothing different from what existed in the previous regime with respect to the system, regulations, and practice. I do not find anything new (Hojjati Kermani—I say the same thing) ...we had said new things in other articles. I believe we have already adopted new articles in which the specific features of the Islamic economy had been elaborated ... but I do not see anything new in this article" (ibid., p. 1560). In the same vein, Rabbani Schirazi explained: "If we analyze this article without considering other articles, it repeats what already existed in the previous regime. But if we respect all newly adopted articles, then the difference becomes clear...Our new rules particularly those related to public properties and *Anfal* mark the difference, since they confer all the authority to the state. For example, barren lands cannot be taken tomorrow and owned by some people; similarly, pasturelands, forests, and other natural resources including mineral deposits cannot be captured by anybody...under the pretext that they were located in their lands. These were the sources of capitalist exploitation that we blocked in the preceding articles" (ibid., p. 1561). In other words, Article 44 was seen as an article that only described the external expression of the Islamic economy. This was not different from what existed during the Shah regime. However, Article 45 could reflect the inner nature of this new economy. *Anfal* was the distinctive feature of the Islamic economy. The deputies also emphasized the abolition of *Riba* (usury or bank interest) or other illegitimate sources of revenue in Article 49 as another major difference.

In the final version of Article 44, all references to Anfal in conjunction with cooperatives were removed. The article reads as follows:

The economy of the Islamic republic of Iran is to consist of three sectors: state, cooperative, and private, and is to be based on systematic and sound planning.

The state sector is to include all large-scale and mother industries, foreign trade, major minerals, banking, insurance, power generation, dams and large-scale irrigation networks, radio and television, post, telegraph and telephone services, aviation, shipping, roads, railroads and the like; all these will be publicly owned and administered by the State.

The cooperative sector is to include cooperative companies and enterprises concerned with production and distribution, in urban and rural areas, in accordance with Islamic criteria.

The private sector consists of those activities concerned with agriculture, animal husbandry, industry, trade, and services that supplement the economic activities of the state and cooperative sectors.

Ownership in each of these three sectors is protected by the laws of the Islamic Republic, in so far as this ownership is in conformity with the other articles of this chapter, does not go beyond the bounds of Islamic law, contributes to the economic growth and progress of the country, and does not harm society.

The [precise] scope of each of these sectors, as well as the regulations and conditions governing their operation, will be specified by law.[25]

While the deputies finally conceded that this article had nothing new to offer in a comparative perspective with the Shah's capitalist regime, they did not acknowledge that it was a major revision from what existed in the Shi'i conventional description of the property regime. Article 44 starts with describing three 'sectors' of economic activities and not three 'forms of property'. Many deputies confused the term 'sectors' with 'forms of property' and assumed that private, state, and cooperative sectors described three forms of property (see Minutes, vol. 3, pp. 1538–39 and 1541–42). Beheshti tried to dissipate this confusion by underlining the term 'sector' instead of 'property' (ibid., p. 1538). Many deputies considered that the article needed to be amended by incorporating a precise definition of the property regime in the Islamic economy. This path was not followed, but Makarem Schirazi mentioned at one place that the article did not mention different types of property since it assumed that there were "two types of property" (Minutes, vol. 3, p. 1536). A *dyadic* instead of a *tripartite* property regime was a revision of the conventional Islamic economy.

---

[25] *Iran (Islamic Republic of)'s Constitution of 1979 with Amendments through 1989*, constituteproject.org, retrieved on June 28, 2021.

To grasp the importance of this radical change, it would be worthwhile to review the influential work of the Iraqi eminent Shi'i theologian, Muhammad Baqir Sadr (1961/1978) on the Islamic economics. In his book, Sadr distinguished three forms of property: state, public, and private (Sadr, 1961, pp. 63–141). According to him, state and public ownerships were under the auspices of the Islamic ruler over what is known in Islamic law as *Anfal*. He defined *Anfal* in terms of natural resources (notably land, water, and mineral deposits), and spoils of war including the confiscated properties by the state. While Sadr considered that public and state properties were similar in the sense that they both belonged to the state, their expenditures were different. The state could use public property in a non-exclusive way to serve all public users such as schools and hospitals. However, the state might alternatively decide to use the state property to benefit specific target groups, for instance by providing preferential assistance and subsidies.

While Sadr's description of *Anfal* was ambiguous with regard to the exclusive rights of the Imam over 'ownerless' things (*res nullius*), he maintained a *tripartite* property regime with *private, public, and state properties*. The constitution of the Islamic Republic totally dismissed this tripartite description by fusing 'public' and 'Imam's property' (*Anfal*) into the state property. This was in line with Montazeri's (1987, vol. 1, p. 93) position regarding the 'unity of the public and the Imam's property'. According to him, since the Imam's property over *Anfal* is not personal but statutory, and his authority regarding the guardianship and expenditure of public wealth extends over those assets that belong to all Muslims, the Imam's property and the public property should be lumped together under the Islamic government. Accordingly, there is no need to distinguish 'public property' from *Anfal* (the Imam's property) reducing the property forms to two main types: the state and private property relationships. This was enacted in Article 45. Article 44 is consistent with Article 45 in assuming two types of property (state and private) and three sector economic activities.

Contrary to this viewpoint, in the traditional Shi'i jurisprudence, the distinction between the public and the state property is essential since while the Imam has discretionary power over the use of *Anfal* including its partial transfer to specific groups or individuals, the other types of public property and wealth belonging to all Muslims should only be spent for *all Muslims*. Blurring this distinction extends the Imam's authority over the whole public wealth and creates n what Montazeri (1987, vol. 1,

p. 92) called 'Faqih Mabsoot al-Yad' (Faqih with the long arm or expanded authority). As a consequence, the Imam would become even less 'controllable' with this expanded authority.

Therefore, the 'unity' thesis had two principal advantages for the newly established Velayat Faqih: (1) keeping silence about the Imam's property over *Anfal*; (2) extending the Imam's discretionary power over the whole public wealth and property. In this sense, the dyadic property regime enhanced the dispossession of the people by the Imam from their public wealth and properties. While the income from all the assets was supposed to finance the Muslims' Public Treasury (*Beit al-mal*), in practice the incomes were distributed to two specific parallel institutions. A fraction of the incomes (*Anfal*) was used for the creation of para-governmental sector and another part funded the formal state sector. The final outcome of *Anfal* in practice was the emergence of Islamic foundations or large holdings such as *Bonyad Mostazafan va Janbazan* (BMJ, Foundation of the Downtrodden and War Veterans) that constituted the para-governmental sector.

While in theory, the 'unity' thesis prevailed, in practice the whole process of the Islamization of the Iranian economy during the last three decades consisted of separating *Anfal* from the state sector leading to a growing para-governmental sector independent from the state, and totally free from any control by the executive, legislative, and juridical powers. This sector belongs to the Imam and reports to him regarding its activities. This resulted in a system of parallel institutions in economy that will be discussed in Chap. 6.

5.8   Anfal: The Missing Point in the Economic Literature

As discussed in the preceding sections, *Anfal* is the most prominent source of revenue in the Shi'i Islamic public finance. Strangely enough, economists, political scientists, and jurists have not explored it even tangentially. The lack of familiarity with the Shi'i economic literature may be considered as one of the reasons for this lack of attention. But another reason resides in the fact that academics have tried to review all Islamic economics in the light of Western mainstream economics. Their main line of inquiry has been to verify whether Islam is rather compatible with the capitalist private system or the state socialist system. In other words, they have often explored Islamic economics from the lens of the Western economics or the established economic systems rather than its own rhetoric and practices.[26]

To the best of my knowledge, there are not many who have referred to *Anfal* in academic journals. I have identified one exception: Sohrab Behdad (1989, p. 192; 1994, p. 788)[27] who has referred to *Anfal* a few times. In two cases, he was just summarizing the ideas of an Iraqi Shi'i faqih, Muhammad Baqr Sadr (1961), concerning *Anfal*. He wrote: "According to Sadr, ... state and public forms of ownership are exercised by the Islamic Ruler over what Islamic law calls *Anfal*. Anfal, in Islamic jurisprudence includes natural resources and spoils of war. The most important examples of Anfal are land, mineral deposits and water. Properties confiscated by the state for whatever reasons, will also come under this category" (Behdad, 1989, p. 192). He repeated the same summary in another paper (1994, p. 788).

But to whom *Anfal* belongs? What is its importance in the Islamic economics? Behdad did not tackle these questions since he could not see the relevance of this concept in understanding the Islamic economics. That explains why he never looked into *Anfal* in the constitution of the Islamic Republic of Iran and totally disregarded Article 45. While he mentioned articles 44, 47, and 49 (Behdad, 1995, p. 105, 2006, p. 26), he dismissed the relationship between *Anfal* and these articles. Why was it so? Because Behdad reduced *Anfal* to the 'state property' and accepted uncritically Khomeini's 'rationalizing' discourse on *Anfal* (see section 3-6).

In his reading of the Islamic economics, the whole issue was reduced to classify them in three approaches with regard to the private property: 'laissez-faire', 'populist', and 'populist-state control' (Behdad, 1989, p. 189). He added in a footnote (number 134, p. 795) that he employed the term 'conservatism' to designate laissez-faire economic approach, in contrast to the terms liberal, suggesting a policy of state intervention, and radical, meaning some form of socialism.

[26] For example, Ehsani (2009) denies any specific characteristic of Shi'i Islam, reducing it to 'cooperative sector' and dismissing *Anfal*: "Although vague, Khomeini's positions on the economy were above all nationalist, insisting on self-reliance and independence, and had a strong developmentalist slant. In practice, the 'Islamic' aspects of the economy remain limited to a 'cooperative sector', which has never exceeded a minute fraction of the gross domestic product, and the replacement of interest in finance with 'investment profits'" (2009, p. 27).

[27] In his comprehensive survey on "Islam and Economic Performance", Timur Kuran (2018, pp. 1313-1314, 1317, 1354, 1358) repeatedly referred to Behdad regarding the Islamic economy in the post-revolutionary Iran.

This classification is also puzzling. Behdad was transposing the terms employed in the American political culture to the Shi'i Islam. He disregarded the fact that *Anfal* was not the state property in the modern sense of the term. The modern state is theoretically a representative of the people's sovereignty; it is nothing more than an *agent* who acts on behalf of the people as *principal*. It is not the state but the people who are assumed to be the true owners of public properties, whereas in *Anfal* all public properties related to *res nullius* are assumed to be the *Imam's property*. Furthermore, *Anfal* is based on the pre-capitalist lack of demarcation between sovereignty and property, while Liberalism advocates the end of tyranny, securing property rights by establishing a great demarcation between sovereignty and property. The defense of capitalist private property is not conservatism but radical in contrast to *Anfal* or the Imam's property. While *Anfal* is the dispossession of the people from their public properties by the Imam, Behdad is applauding for it as a 'radical' measure since it belongs to the state! The statist ideology misleads Behdad in not seeing what is concealed under *Anfal*.

Following the same line of reasoning, Behdad demarcated two phases in the evolution of the political economy of the Islamic Republic of Iran: the first phase started from the outbreak of the 1979 Revolution until the end of the eight-year war with Iraq in 1989. The second phase began with the first presidential term of Hashemi Rafsanjani in 1989 and notably the start of negotiation with the World Bank and the IMF in 1992. "With the death of Khomeini, the Islamic Republic began a process of transformation… The search for an ideal Islamic society, the struggle for establishing the rule of the mustaz'afin (oppressed) had come to its dead end. Instead, a pragmatic coalition of conservatives and reformed populists was formed. The experts of the World Bank and the International Monetary Fund were invited to serve as the source of guidance, and they were happy to oblige" (Behdad, 2006, p. 29). In Behdad's viewpoint, these two periods echoed the historical evolution of the original Islam from a rebellious Islam during Muhammad and Abu Dharr to Pax Islamicus of the Umayyads and Abbasids dynasties.

The first phase was characterized by a 'statist-populist orientation' (Behdad, 1994, p. 787, 1995, p. 105). Transposing the recent terminology of 'populism' and 'statism' to Muhammad's time, Behdad interpreted *Anfal* as a trace of 'Islamic populism' in support of 'Islamic revivalism': "It was the collectivism of the band of warriors of Islam, who distributed the booty of the war among their ranks and left some for the newly formed state of Islam only when the Prophet presented them with God's words (Sura Al-Anfal). This is the Islamic populism that has the power of mobilizing the poor and destitute, the unemployed and the low wage urban workers" (2006, p. 30). It seems that Behdad was not cognizant of contradictions between the verses 1 and 41 of *Anfal* and the Muslims' disputes in dividing the spoils of Badr. As previously mentioned in the first three sections of the present chapter, *Anfal* was not about "the collectivism of the band of warriors", but the Prophet's discretionary power.

Following Behdad, Kuran also dubbed the first period of the Islamic Republic of Iran (1979–1989) as "Islamic Socialism" (2018, p. 1313) entailing a staunchly egalitarian system seeking redistribution in favor of the oppressed masses and state ownership of major productive assets. This characterization missed the most prominent feature of the Islamic economics that was established during this phase, namely *Anfal* or the Imam's property. *Anfal* was neither statism nor 'socialism' but pre-capitalist ownership of the Imam. The dispossession of the people from their public property was concealed under the ideological cover of 'statist-populism' or 'Islamic socialism'.

In line with this type of reasoning, many Iranian leftist activists such as Fedayan Aksaryat (Majority)[28] supported Khomeini's 'statist-populist' policy as an anti-imperialist struggle for 'social justice'. The tragedy was that during this period the economic foundation of Velayat Faqih, namely the para-governmental sector was institutionalized[29] in the name of social justice. The discourse on the 'unity between the people and the Imam's property' found an echo in terms of social justice among many populist leftist activists.

The second phase was defined as 'pragmatism' and the start of economic and cultural 'liberalism'. As Rahnema and Behdad (1995, p. 15)

---

[28] This was a Marxist-Leninist (but not pro-Soviet) guerrilla organization during the Shah's regime with a strong popular sympathy in 1979. After the revolution, the organization was split into several groups. The majority of its members advocated a pro-Soviet line and supported the Islamic Republic of Iran because of its anti-Imperialist and egalitarian position.

[29] Interestingly enough, Behdad (1995, pp. 105, 112–113, 115, 126) referred to this sector a few times but did not see its relationship with *Anfal*. In his eyes, the para-governmental sector was part of 'statist-populist' strategy to provide popular support for the new regime: "Moreover, this faction of the Islamic Republic supported the establishment of various revolutionary foundations in an attempt to create grassroots support for an Islamic regime and to confront the radical opposition to the Islamic Republic" (Behdad, 1995, p. 105).

contended: "cultural liberalism added to economic liberalism could be taking the Islamic Republic back to the norms of pre-revolutionary Iran." Kuran (2018, p. 1313) also cited Behdad (1994) regarding the second phase, and called it "Islamic capitalism", during which a market system regulated by Islamic norms and regulations prevailed.

To quote Behdad (1994, p. 811), "the IMF and the World Bank have become the source of guidance for the readjustment process. Foreign investment is now being viewed by the Islamic Republic as the means for saving the economy. The large enterprises that were nationalized are being offered wholesale to whoever wants to buy them. There is no longer any claim for establishing an Islamic economy." This was a totally wrong description and forecast about the political economy of the Islamic Republic. Foreign direct investment in Iran was not spawned and it still is one of the lowest in the world, and the large nationalized enterprises were never 'sold to whoever wanted to buy them'. They were sold to para-governmental sector. In other words, not only the constitutional 'unity' between *Anfal* and the state sector never realized in practice, but also the share of *Anfal* increased in the same proportion as the share of the state sector shrank. This was not a 'liberal phase' but the enhancement of the Islamization of the economy or the uncovering of the concealed Imam's property. The Islamic foundations 'bought' the bulk of the state properties during Mahmoud Ahmadinejad's presidential terms (2005–2013) and claimed later in 2020 to possess even the mountain Damavand[30] as part of *Anfal*.

5.9   Shi'i Islam and Islamic Political Capitalism

Now, we can return to the question raised at the end of previous chapter. How do we ascertain Rodinson's thesis regarding the compatibility of Islam and capitalism? Kuran deemed that the Sunni's jurisprudence hindered the development of modern capitalism under the Ottoman Empire. But what about the Shi'i Islam?

My contention is that the Shi'i jurisprudence is even a stronger impediment to market capitalism than the Sunni jurisprudence. The Shi'i faqihs supported 'Kumpanyie' to weaken the king's position, but they always advocated *Anfal* which was in dire contrast to any demarcation between

---

[30] Regarding Bonyad's claims on the mountain Damavand, see https://www.zeitoons.com/78754. For more details, see next chapter.

sovereignty and property. While in the Sunni jurisprudence *Anfal* is derisory and public properties belong to all Muslims, in the Shi'i jurisprudence all ownerless natural resources belong to the Imam.[31] Rodisnon never explored *Anfal* in the Shi'i fiqh before or after the 1979 Iranian revolution. Therefore, he could write: "The precepts of Islam have not seriously hindered the capitalist orientation taken by the Muslim world during the last hundred years, and nothing in them is really opposed to a socialist orientation, either (…) Similarly, the precepts of Islam have nowhere created a social or economic structure that was radically new" (Rodinson, 1973, p. 186). The Shi'i clergy proved him wrong: *Anfal* or the dispossession of public properties by the Imam was their radically new creation in public economics that could not be invented by any other political or economic force in Iran in 1979. This unique invention was neither capitalist nor socialist, it was a product of the pre-capitalist Shi'i economics that strongly enhanced political capitalism in the post-revolutionary Iran.

Contrary to the Islamic 'revolution' (better to say, revivalism), modern revolutions in the seventeenth and the eighteenth centuries radically altered the relationships between political and market capitalism and provided fundamental institutional changes for the predominance of the latter.

The political economy of the Islamic Republic of Iran represents continuity rather than rupture with the political economy of Muhammad Reza Shah Pahlavi with respect to the persistence of a variant of political capitalism based upon the oil revenue. However, there are two major differences between *Anfal* and the Shah's control over the oil, gas, and petrochemicals.

The Shah was allegedly 'loyal' to the underlying tenet of the 1905–1906 constitutional revolution according to which the people were sovereign over public properties including natural resources although he violated people's rights in practice by imposing his personal control and creating parallel institutions that were alien to the principle of supervision by an impersonal state. In Chap. 4, we noticed that Khomeini also endeavored to dissimulate *Anfal* as a form of state property. However, he overtly rejected people's sovereignty and advocated *Velayat Faqih* in dire contrast to the constitutional revolution.

Anfal is the Imam's property over *res nullius* that includes all natural resources. It is based on the dispossession of the people from their public

---

[31] See Chap. 4 on *Anfal*.

properties. The Pahlavi dynasty never ever pretended to be the legitimate owner of all natural resources. The only political force in Iran that could put forward such a claim was the Shi'i faqihs. They vindicated such unlimited property ownership in the name of God, the Prophet, and his legitimate successors. This is the first major difference between the two regimes.

As argued before, *Anfal* is not reducible to capitalism or statism, it is a specific Shi'i invention in which the Imam owns all natural resources. This is the rule of a clergy caste over the whole Muslim society. Paradoxically, this pre-capitalist institution could survive due to the integration of the Iranian economy in the world capitalist market through the natural resources. The relative independence of the state provides the economic foundation for the resilience of the Islamic economy. However, the fusion of sovereignty and property implies a secondary role for property in comparison with sovereignty. In other words, property is important as long as it can be a source of reproducing authoritative resources.

In this context, *political* efficiency is considered to be more important than *economic* efficiency. The political, cultural, and ideological tensions between the ruling Shi'i faqihs and the Western powers hinder foreign direct investment and economic growth. This is a second major difference between the Shah's regime that could promote a more diversified industrial economy than *Velayat Faqih* due to its less contentious relationship with the Western powers. Considering the significance of political tensions, the economic trajectory of the Islamic Republic hinges more and more upon an appropriative regime in which the commodification of natural resources plays a primary role.

The economic foundation of *Anfal* should be sought in this variant of political capitalism that we call the 'Islamic political capitalism'. Contrary to liberal market capitalism in which market coordination prevails, destructive coordination is preponderant under the Islamic political capitalism[32] since *Anfal* as the dispossession of people from their public properties by the Imam is based on a confiscatory regime. Destructive coordination prevails under a confiscatory regime. Table 5.1 illustrates a comparative study of the political economy of these two types of capitalism.

The political economy of the Islamic Republic of Iran is an emblematic figure of the Islamic political capitalism that will be explored in light of *Anfal* in the next chapter.

---

[32] For a detailed analysis regarding the relationship between *Anfal* and destructive coordination, see Chap. 6.

Table 5.1 Comparative analysis of liberal market capitalism versus Islamic political capitalism

Type of capitalism	Dominant type of property	Dominant form of coordination	Example
Liberal market capitalism	Private	Market coordination	U.S.A. (1945–2008)
Islamic political capitalism	*Anfal*	Destructive coordination	The Islamic Republic of Iran

5.10   Conclusion

In this chapter, we identified two elements in the Islamic public finance that are in tune with a confiscatory regime: *Kharaj* in the Sunni Islam and *Anfal* in the Shi'i Islam. While *Kharaj* constituted the bulk of the Caliphate system of public finance, *Anfal* was supposed to provide the required finance for the Imamate system. Our textual and historical investigation about *Anfal* showed that it started since the Prophet first holy war in Badr and continued all throughout the Islam history. In the Sunni Islam, the scope of *Anfal* has been narrowed down to the spoils of war.

However, the Shi'is advocate a very broad definition of *Anfal* embracing all 'ownerless' properties (*res nullius*). Contrary to the Sunnis, the Shi'is support the idea that *Anfal* belong to the Imam and not all Muslims. The conceptualization of *Anfal* as one of the underlying tenets of the Islamic economy was developed by the Shi'i faqihs under al Buyid and particularly during the Safavid and Qajar dynasties. However, it truly flourished during the most recent version of the Imamate system, namely *Velayat Faqih* in Iran since the 1979 Revolution. Although, Khomeini and his associates presented it as a 'rational' consequence of any form of government and tried to camouflage this concept under a 'statist-populist discourse', *Anfal* is nothing but the dispossession of the people from their public properties and wealth by the Imam.

While the Iranian post-revolutionary economy has never abandoned capitalist development, *Velayat Faqih* added a truly new economic element: *Anfal* or the Imam's property over *res nullius*. This original Islamic public finance impedes the development of market capitalism but leads to a new variant of political capitalism, namely Islamic political capitalism. In the next chapters, I will elaborate the emergence and development of this specific type of political capitalism under the IRI since 1979 until now.

REFERENCES

Abadi, K., & Hossein, S. A. (1973). *Vaghayieh al-saneen va al-awam (The events of the years and masses)*. Entesharat Elsamieh.

Al-Mufid, M. I. M. I. N. (1989). *Al-Muqni'ah (The Legally Sufficient)*, 2nd edn. Daftar Entesharat Islami.

Al-Samhudi, N. a.-D. A. b. A. (2001). *Wafa al-Wafa bi akhbar Dar al-Mustafa (The Fulfillment of Faithfulness on the Reports of the City of the Chosen One), edited and annotated by Qasim Al-Sammarai in five volumes*. Al-Furqan Islamic Heritage Foundation.

Al-Tabari, A. J., & Jarir, M. B. (1987). *The History of al-Tabari, the Foundation of the Community* (Vol. VII). State University of New York Press.

Amuzegar, J. (1992). The Iranian Economy Before and After the Revolution. *Middle East Journal, 46*(3), 413–425.

Ansari Shushtari, M. (1886–7/1990). *Makasib (Islamic Commercial Law)* (vol. 4, Translated in Persian by Seyyed Muhammad Djavad Zehni Tehrani). Hazeq (in Persian).

Babookani, E. A. A., Saadi, H., & Tabeebi Jabali, M. (2018, Summer). Pajooheshay Fqih-i. *Persian, 2*, 405–427.

Behdad, S. (1989). Property Rights in Contemporary Islamic Economic Thought: A Critical Perspective. *Review of Social Economy, 47*(2), 185–211.

Behdad, S. (1994). A Disputed Utopia: Islamic Economics in Revolutionary Iran. *Comparative Studies in Society and History, 36*(4), 775–813.

Behdad, S. (1995). The Post-Revolutionary Economic Crisis. In S. Rahnema & S. Behdad (Eds.), *Iran after the Revolution: Crisis of an Islamic State* (pp. 97–128). London and New York.

Behdad, S. (2006). Islam, Revivalism, and Public Policy. In S. Behdad & F. Nomani (Eds.), *Islam and the Everyday World: Public Policy Dilemmas* (pp. 1–37). Routledge.

Behdad, S., & Nomani, F. (2012). Women's Labour in the Islamic Republic of Iran: Losers and Survivors. *Middle Eastern Studies, 48*(5), 707–733.

Calder, N. (*2010*). *Islamic Jurisprudence in the Classical Era*. Cambridge University Press.

Chaudhry, M. S. (*1992*). *Taxation in Islam and Modern Taxes*. Impact Publications International.

Chaudhry, M. S. (1999). Retrieved August 29, 2021, from www.muslimtents.com.

Dawood, N. J. (2014). *The Koran* (Translated with notes by N.J. Dawood). Penguin Books.

Eftekhari, A. (2004, Summer). "Shari sazi ghodrat siasi; daramadi bar jaygah amnyat dar andisheh va amal foghahay shia dar asre safavi" (The Islamization of the Political Power; A Prelude to the Place of Security in the Thought and

Deed of the Shi'i Faqih During the Safavid Era). *Faslnameh Motaleeat Rahboordi, 7*(2), 275–298 (in Persian).

Ehsani, K. (2009, Spring). Survival Through Dispossession: Privatization of Public Goods in the Islamic Republic. *Middle East Report, 250,* 26–33.

Enayat, H. (1982). *Modern Islamic Political Thought.* University of Texas Press.

Esposito, J. L. (1995). The Islamic World: Past and Present. *Oxford Islamic Studies Online.* Retrieved August 27, 2021.

Ghartabi, M. i. A. (1973). *Tafsir Ghartabi (Ghartabi's exegesis)* (Vol. 8). Markaz Etellat va Madarek Islami. http://dl.islamicdoc.com/site/catalogue/457506

Hazleton, L. (2010). *After the Prophet: The Epic Story of the Shia-Sunni Split in Islam.* Anchor Books.

Hosseini, S. R., & Sadeghi Fadaki, S. J. (2019). "Anfal", *Daerotal-maref Koran Karim* (The Encyclopedia of the Koran) in Persian, *5,* 15–24. (in Persian).

Ibn Ishaq. (2004, June 25). The Earliest Biography of Muhammad. https://web.archive.org/web/20040625103910/http://www.hraic.org/hadith/ibn_ishaq.html#khaybar#khaybar

Karaki, Ali ibn Hossein ibn Abdol-Ali Ameli. (1510/1992). *Ghat al-lejaj fi tahghigh hal al-Kharaj (Ending with Obstinacy Regarding an Inquiry into the Solution of Tribute Issue).* Moasseseh Nashr Islami.

Khomeini, R. (1970). *Velayat Fqih.* Daftar Nashre Falagh. Translated in 1981, *Islam and Revolution, Writings and Declarations of Imam Khomeini.* Mizan Press.

Khomeini, R. (2000). *Ketab Al-Bey (The Book of Sale)* (Vol. 3). Moassesseh tanzeem va nashr asar al-Imam al-Khomeini.

Kulayni, M. I. Y. (1988). *Al-Kafi (Extant)* (Vol. 1, 4th ed.). Dar al-kotob al-islamieh.

Kuran, T. (2018). Islam and Economic Performance. *Journal of Economic Literature, 56*(4), 1292–1359.

Mahamed, A. (2012, Spring). "Tafsir Tatbeeghi Ayeh Sharifeh Anfal" (*A comparative interpretation of the honorable verse of Anfal*). *Faslnameh Motalleat Tafsiri, 3*(9), 81–104. (in Persian).

Mahdavi-Kani, M. R. (2000). *Anfal va asar an dar Islam (Anfal and its effects in Islam).* Qom: Bostan ketab Qom (in Persian).

Maloney, S. (2015). *Iran's Political Economy since the Revolution.* Cambridge University Press.

Mesbahi Moghaddam, S., Ghyasi, M., & Nakhli, S. R. (2011, Fall). "Osool va siasathay hakem bar masraf Anfal va daramadhay hasel az an dar dowlat islami," (*The Governing Principles and Policies Regarding the Expenditure of the Income Originated from Anfal in the Islamic State*), *Faslnameh pajoohesh-hay eghtesadi Iran, in Persian, 48,* 193–221 (in Persian).

Momen, M. (1985). *An introduction to Shi'i Islam, the history and doctrines of Twelver Shi'ism.* Yale University Press.

Montazeri, H.-A. (1984). *Al-Khoms va Al-Anfal (Khoms and Anfal)* (2nd ed.). Mossasseh al-nashr al-Islamie.

Montazeri, H.-A. (1987). *Darasat fi velayet al-faqih va feqhe al-dowlah al-islamieh (Studies on Velayat faqih and the Jurisprudence of the Islamic State)* (Vol. 1, 4). Al-markaz al-alemi il-darasat al-islamieh.

Nomani, F., & Behdad, S. (2006). *Class and Labor in Iran: Did the Revolution Matter?* Syracuse University Press.

Noori, H. (1990). Hookomat islami and naghsh *Anfal (The Islamic Government and the Role of Anfal)*, *Hawza*, in Persian, Numbers 37 and 38.

Nowroozi, M. D., & Nemati, M. (2017). Roykardi moghaysehi beh andisheh siasi 'Muhaqqiq Karaki' va Agustine (*A Comparative Approach to the Political Ideas of Muhaqqiq Karki and Saint Augustine*), two parts, *Faslnameh Hokomat Islami*, Number 80 (in Persian).

Peters, F. E. (1991). The Quest of the Historical Muhammad. *International Journal of Middle East Studies, 23*(3), 291–315.

Pistor-Hatam, A. (2019, Winter). Religious Minorities in the Islamic Republic of Iran and 'The Right to Have Rights'. *Iran Namag, 3*(4).

Pryor, F. L. (2009). The Political Economy of a Semi-Industrialized Theocratic State: The Islamic Republic of Iran. In M. Ferrero & R. Wintrobe (Eds.), *The Political Economy of Theocracy* (pp. 243–270). Palgrave Macmillan.

Rahnema, S. (1995). Continuity and Change in Industrial Policy. In S. Rahnema & S. Behdad (Eds.), *Iran after the Revolution: Crisis of an Islamic State* (pp. 129–149). London and New York.

Rahnema, S., & Behdad, S. (1995). Introduction. In R. Saeed & S. Behdad (Eds.), *Iran after the Revolution Crisis of An Islamic State* (pp. 1–18). London, New York.

Rajabi, M. H. (2009, Spring and Summer). "Arae Faqihan asr Safavi darbareh-I tamool ba hookomatha" (*The Faqihs' Viewpoints on the Relationship with Governments During the Safavid era*). *Tarikh va Tamadoon Islami, 5*(9), 53-80. (in Persian).

Razi, F. (1992). *Tafsir Kabir (The Great exegesis)* (Trans to Persian by Asghar Halabi). Tehran (in Persian).

Rodinson, M. (1973). *Islam and Capitalism* (Trans from the French by Brian Pierce, First American ed.). Penguin Books Ltd.

Sadr, M. B. (1961/1978). *Iqtisade ma (Our economics)* (Trans to Persian in two volumes, vol. II). Entesharat-e Islami (in Persian).

Saeidi, A. (2004). The Accountability of Para-Governmental Organizations (Bonyads): The Case of Iranian Foundations. *Iranian Studies, 37*(3), 479–498.

Sahih Muslim. *The Book of Jihad and Expedition*, Book 32, Hadith 1765. Retrieved August 29, 2021, from https://sunnah.com/muslim:1765.

Schirazi, A. (1997). *The Constitution of Iran: Politics and the State in the Islamic Republic*. I.B. Tauris.

Shahid Jamal Rizvi, S. (2014, November 10). *Khutba E Fadak (The Fadak Speech)* Vol.2. Koran O Itrat Foundation (in Persian).

Stillman, N. (1979). *The Jews of Arab Lands: A History and Source Book.* Jewish Publication.

Tabarsi, F. I. H. (1973). *Majma Al-bayan* (*Speech collection*) (Vol. 6, Trans to Persian by Ahmad Behshti and Moosavi Dameghani). Farhani (in Persian).

Tabatabei, S. M. H. (1995). *Al-Mizan* (*The Measurement*), Vol. 9 (*on Anfal and Repentance*) (Trans to Persian by Mosavi Hamedani, Seyyed Muhammad Bagher). Jame Modaresseen Hozeh Elmieh Qom (in Persian).

Tusi, M. I. H. (1955). *Al-Iqtisad (Economics).* Ketabkhaneh Jamee Chehl Sotoon.

Tusi, M. I. H. (1984). *Al-Mabsoot (Comprehensive Study of the Shi'i Fqih)* (Vol. 2). Mortazavi.

Vacca, V. (2012). Nadir, Banu'l. In P. Bearman, Th. Bianquis, C.E. Bosworth, E. van Donzel, W.P. Heinrichs (Eds.). *Encyclopedia of Islam Online.* Brill Academic Publishers. Retrieved August 29, 2021, from http://dx.doi.org.myaccess.library.utoronto.ca/10.1163/1573-3912_islam_SIM_5714

Veccia Vaglieri, L. (2012). Fadak. In P. Bearman, Th. Bianquis, C.E. Bosworth, E. van Donzel, W.P. Heinrichs (Eds.). *Encyclopaedia_of_Islam Online.* Second edition. Brill Academic Publishers. Retrieved August 29, 2021, from http://dx.doi.org.myaccess.library.utoronto.ca/10.1163/1573-3912_islam_SIM_2218

CHAPTER 6

Anfal in Practice and Islamic Political Capitalism

6.1   INTRODUCTION

In this chapter, we explore the formation of Islamic political capitalism under the Islamic Republic of Iran (IRI) through *Anfal*'s progression and institutional complementarity since 1979 until the privatization decree in 2006.

In Chap. 5, we discussed the place of *Anfal* in Koran and its further institutionalization as part of the public finance in both the Sunni and the Shi'i Islam. Article 45 of the constitution of the IRI stipulates the most recent legal expression of *Anfal*. Although in the traditional Shi'i jurisprudence *Anfal* is the specific property of the Imam over all 'ownerless' public properties (*res nullius*), its enactment in Article 45 is based on a revisionist interpretation according to which there is no need to distinguish 'state property' from *Anfal* (the Imam's property).

This is known as the 'unity thesis' advocating the unity of the Umma and the Imam's property (Montazeri, 1987, vol. 1, p. 93). Based upon the unity thesis, Article 44 of the constitution maintains that state property embraces both types of public properties, namely those that belonged to the Imam (*Anfal*) and those belonging to all Muslims. A major advantage of this statist discourse was to dissimulate the fact that *Anfal* did not belong to all Muslims, it only belonged to the Imam. The public announcement of the Shi'i's jurisprudence in the middle of revolution in 1979 could have resulted in discrediting the new regime since it clearly meant

© The Author(s), under exclusive license to Springer Nature   195
Switzerland AG 2023
M. Vahabi, *Destructive Coordination, Anfal and Islamic Political
Capitalism*, https://doi.org/10.1007/978-3-031-17674-6_6

that the Shah's property should be replaced by the Imam's property (*Anfal*) which was even more extended than the Shah's belongings. Thus, the constitution, which was adopted on December 3, 1979, did not distinguish between the 'state' and the so-called non-state public properties.

This distinction was only introduced on July 1, 2006, when the new Supreme jurisprudent,[1] Khamenei, decreed the 'General policies pertaining to Article 44 of the constitution of the Islamic Republic of Iran'.[2] This decree included 92 Articles and 90 footnotes. It was adopted in the public session of the Islamic Consultative Assembly[3] (Majlis Shoorai Islami or the Iranian parliament) on January 28, 2008, and approved by the Expediency Discernment Council of the System[4] (Majma Tashkhis-e Maslahat Nezam) on June 14, 2008. This order was known as the 'Privatization' decree since the Supreme Leader had mandated the state to sell off 80% of all state-owned enterprises. The goal was to 'privatize' all the industries cited in Article 44 of the constitution by the end of the fourth Five-Year Development Plan. According to an Iranian parliamentary commission on privatization, the total value of the whole state assets amounted to 1500 thousand billion Iranian Rials (approximately 150 billion dollars)[5] (Mousavi Nik, 2009, p. 2). Hashemi Rafsanjani (2007), the ex-Iranian president and the head of the Expediency Discernment Council, has called the privatization program "an economic revolution". Many Iranian economists, political scientists, and sociologists considered the privatization as a clear sign of *liberalization* of the Iranian economy in the post-war period (Behdad, 2006; Ehsani, 2013; Abazari & Zakeri, 2019; Valadbaygi,

---

[1] The Supreme Jurisconsult is also called the Supreme Leader. In this book, the two terms will be used interchangeably.

[2] See Iran Data Portal, https://irandataportal.syr.edu/the-general-policies-pertaining-to-principle-44-of-the-constitution-of-the-islamic-republic-of-iran

[3] It is also called Iranian Parliament, and for brevity Majlis. It is the national legislative body of Iran that was composed of 272 seats until February 18, 2000, elections. The number of seats increased to 290 representatives since then.

[4] This is an administrative assembly appointed by the Supreme jurisprudent every five years. It was originally created to resolve conflicts between the Islamic Consultative Assembly (Majlis) and the Guardian Council. The latter is charged with interpreting the Constitution, supervising elections, and approving the candidates for the Assembly of Experts, the President and the Majlis as well as ensuring the compatibility of the adopted laws by the Majlis with the Islamic principles and the Constitution (see Vahabi, 2010).

[5] There are other estimations about the total value of assets. According to Mohsen Rezai (July 5, 2006), the total amount has been 1000 thousand billion Rials.

2021). Interestingly, none of them related the decree of July 2006 to *Anfal*.

In fact, evidence suggests that the privatization program dissimulated the appropriation of the state properties by the Imam and other non-state sovereign institutions such as the Islamic Revolutionary Guard Corps (IRGC or the *Sepah*). Khamenei's decree was nothing but the institutionalization of the separation of *Anfal* from the state sector, and the transfer of state assets to *Anfal*.

In this sense, the privatization program was an "Islamic economic revolution". The occupation of the American Embassy in Tehran and the hostage crisis on November 4, 1979, that resulted in the removal of the provisional government of Mehdi Bazargan was the culmination of the Islamic political revolution. The Supreme jurisprudent's decree in July 2006 completed the *political* revolution with an *economic* revolution. This revolution was for the *Islamization* rather than *liberalization* of the Iranian economy. The final outcome of the privatization program was the extension of *Anfal* that was opposed to the sanctity of the private property since *Anfal* is based on the fusion of sovereignty and property.

The economic revolution was organized under the two terms of Ahmadinejad's presidency particularly during the period 2005–2011. He was heftily supported by the Supreme jurisprudent, *Sepah* and *Basij* (the para-military forces of the Supreme Leader) because he acted as an instrument of them to appropriate state assets. Khamenei's support for the presidency of Ahmadinejad against his contenders, namely Hashemi Rafsanjani and Mousavi,[6] was for implementing the Islamic economic revolution. This revolution was neither for the extension of the 'private' nor 'state' sectors but for his own specific property rights as the Imam. The immense increase of the oil revenue in the first term of Ahmadinejad's presidency

---

[6] Mir-Hossein Mousavi served as the seventy-ninth and last Prime Minister of Iran from 1981 to 1989. He was known as an advocate of a statist program during the Khomeini's era and then became one of the two so-called Reformist candidates along with Mehdi Karoubi against the administration of incumbent President of Iran Mahmoud Ahmadinejad for the 2009 presidential election. According to official results, he did not win the election, and following alleged vote-rigging and manipulation, his campaign sparked a long protest that eventually turned into a national and international movement against Ahmadinejad's government and the Supreme jurisprudent Ali Khamenei. Mousavi chose green as his campaign color, and his opposition 'reformist' movement was known as the Green Movement. Although he insisted on his loyalty to the Constitution of the Islamic Republic of Iran, he, his wife, and Mehdi Karroubi were detained at their residence and are currently under house arrest

(2005–2009) that amounted to 700 billion dollars was channeled to beef up *Anfal* and the *Sepah*.

In the interregnum between *Anfal* in Khomeini's era (1979–1989) and its unprecedented extension in Khamenei's time (2005 until now), the economic holdings belonging to *Anfal* and the Sepah took roots and enlarged their fields of activities by actively participating in the post-war economic reconstruction. The two terms presidencies of Hashemi Rafsanjani and Khatami (1989-2005) experienced limited privatization, renegotiation about foreign direct investment, and intense factional political rivalries that terminated the exclusion of the so-called reformist tendency from power[7] and marginalization of Hashemi Rafsanjani as well as other traditional Shi'i Faqihs. A new coalition of oligarchs emerged that included principally the Imam, the Shi'i clergy loyal to Khamenei, and the Sepah. Thus, *Anfal* in practice can be periodized in three phases: (1) *Anfal* in Khomeini era (1979–1989); (2) *Anfal* and the transition period (1989–2005); (3) *Anfal* under Khamenei (2005–now).

The third phase, marked by Khamenei's privatization decree in July 2006, is the culmination of the Islamic economic revolution that will be substantiated in the next chapter. In this chapter, we explore its preparation through the first two phases of *Anfal* (1979–2006). Before explaining these two phases, it is necessary to discuss the general rationale of *Anfal*'s progression and its contribution to the formation of new economic institutions since 1979.

6.2   INSTITUTIONAL COMPLEMENTARITY AND GENERAL PATTERN OF *ANFAL*'S PROGRESSION

Anfal is possible only under a specific political system, namely *Velayat Faqih* (the jurisconsult of the vicegerent). They are complementary core institutions of the Shi'i Imamate. While *Velayat Faqih* has been under the scrutiny of recent social and religious studies, *Anfal* has been almost totally disregarded in social sciences. This might perhaps be explained by the fact that we have difficulties to understand its *novelty* compared to other dominant forms of economic institutions such as market, state, and hybrid organizations. The first step to understand *Anfal* is to acknowledge

---

[7] In addition to house arrest of the two 'reformist' candidates Mousavi and Karoubi and Mousavi's wife, Zahra Rahnavard, the ex-president Muhammad Khatami's images have also been forbidden to display in any journal or media since 2009.

its novelty as a specific institution of Islamic political capitalism in our time. However, *Anfal*'s impact on the economy cannot be grasped without addressing a second issue: What is its relationship with other institutions? This brings us to examine institutional complementarity.

While institutional complementarity is often cited to explain institutional *stability* rather than *change* (Pagano, 2011), in this case the complementarity of the core institutions of Islamic political capitalism casts light on major institutional innovation. New economic and political institutions were born in the wake of *Velayat Faqih* and *Anfal*. They have reshaped the behavior of economic actors such as business firms and interest associations. To explore the impact of these changes, we need to specify not only the way *Anfal* has been organized but also its linkages with other economic, military, and ideological institutions.

The fusion of sovereignty and property in *Anfal* furnishes the foundation of Islamic political capitalism. *Anfal* is the major source of public finance in the Shi'i Islam. While modern direct and indirect taxes are based on *income* and *added value* of traded products, the source of *Anfal* is the appropriation and accumulation of public *assets*. *Anfal* comes within the scope of appropriative rather than productive regime. Thus, productive activity and industrial profit are not the sources of *Anfal*. Its value depends on the total accounting market value of the assets transferred as booties regardless of the type of economic activity. This nominal accounting value of assets increases in an economy with chronic inflation and depreciating national currency (Rial) in terms of dollar. The higher value of the assets does not necessarily include 'added value'; they might have even lost value because of depreciation and non-renewal of the fixed capital. The maximization of the *financial value* rather than the *added value* of the assets is the objective of the sovereign institutions. Hoarding of assets both as idle and as financial capital in all economic sectors is the economic rationale for creating big holdings to manage *Anfal*'s undertakings in a modern capitalist economy.

In this case, mergers and acquisitions do not follow productivity or profitability but financial return through confiscatory policies by *Anfal* and *Sepah*.[8] This seems like the American economic growth during 1989–2001which was led by US corporations and private equity firms

---

[8] For a detailed examination of this point, see Chap. 6 and 'patrimonial development' in Chap. 7, section 7-4.

giving pride of place to financial return.[9] However, there exists a fundamental difference between the Iranian and the American case since the financial return in the former hinges upon the preponderant place of confiscatory policies in appropriating financial assets and not maximizing the private shareholders' assets. The colossal increase of assets belonging to the state and *Anfal*'s economic institutions in the aftermath of confiscatory measures clearly support this point.

On October 22, 2017, Seyyed Rahmattolah Akrami as Acting Minister of Economic Affairs and Finance of President Rouhani announced that the state's wealth amounted to 183,000,000 billion tomans (see khabaronline.ir/news/719612, retrieved on July 10, 2022). According to the Iranian Central Bank's statistics, the Iranian total GDP in 2017 has been 694, 08 thousand billion tomans (see Tabnak on June 14, 2018, https://www.tabnak.ir/fa/news/925637, retrieved on July 10, 2022). This means that the state's wealth has been 27 times more than the annual budget. *Tabnak*, a site close to the Sepah, reported on September 24, 2019, that more than 60% of the Iranian economy belong to four economic institutions, namely *Bonyad Mostazafan* (Foundation for the downtrodden), *Setad* (The Execution of Imam Khomeini's Order-EIKO), *Khatam al-Anbiya* Construction Headquarters (the economic organization of IRGC), and *Astan Quods Razavi* (see https://www.tabnak.ir/fa/news/925637 retrieved on July 10, 2022). These institutions are all related to *Anfal*.

Accordingly, *Anfal* penetrates all economic activity and has a strong replicatory effect. It extends and increases its share detrimental to the shares of formal state and the private sector. This self-reproducing tendency is particularly accentuated by *Anfal*'s political aspect. From a political viewpoint, *Anfal* is a source of authoritative resources. It reproduces the Imam's domineering position in the politics and economics. Hoarding of assets may be inefficient economically but efficient politically. Adopting the Coasean bargaining mechanism (Coase, 1960), the Imam will not

[9] The average annual American economic growth (1989–2001) generated by search for maximizing financial return was around 3 to 3.5%, much lower than the average annual economic growth of 5% during the Thirty Glorious years (1945–1973). Nevertheless, this growth was also supported by an important technological progress in ITC that economized on the costs of using capital as a factor of production increasing the so-called capital productivity. Contrary to the American recent economic growth, in the Iranian case, the 'capital productivity' significantly diminished (see Chap. 7). This is another major difference between the Iranian and American case.

necessarily allocate property rights to the most profitable options since assets considered as authoritative resources are primarily allocated where they can result in politically efficient deals with allies or sanctioning potential contenders.[10] The giant holdings of *Anfal* such as *Bonyad Mostazafan* (Foundation for the downtrodden) have linkages with economic, military, and ideological institutions such as Islamic banks, the Sepah, and Imam Khomeini's Publications. A coalitional dynamic explains the rule-making processes that govern institutional change.

The general pattern of *Anfal*'s progression is like cancerous cells starting with genetic changes interfering with the orderly process.[11] By 'cancerous cells', I mean institutions and organizations related to *Anfal* growing steadily by swallowing public budget and public properties and resulting in an ever-shrinking provisions of public goods and services to citizens by the formal state with colossal debts.

To keep with the metaphor, these cells grow uncontrollably and create a tumor which can be either benign or malignant. The former can grow but will not spread whereas the latter can spread to other parts of body. As a cancerous tumor grows, the bloodstream or lymphatic system may carry cancer cells to other parts of the body. During this process, the cancer cells grow and may develop into new tumors. This is known as *metastasis*.[12] Most types of cancer have four stages to reach to metastatic cancer (Yokota, 2000).

- **Stage I.** This stage is usually a cancer that has not grown deeply into nearby tissues. It also has not spread to the lymph nodes or other parts of the body. It is often called early stage cancer.

---

[10] I thank Peter Leeson for a discussion about *Anfal* from a Coasean perspective to clarify why the Imam's monopoly regarding property rights on *res nullius* is not economically efficient.

[11] I am not suggesting that social processes are identical to biological processes. However, the progression patterns can be similar. In fact, epidemiological models can be a source of inspiration to grasp the contagion in financial crisis. Since the 1990s, economists have drawn on the epidemiology of emerging infectious diseases to explain the diffusion of shock through an increasingly complex financial system. The commonalties notwithstanding, differences between biological and financial systems should not be disregarded (Peckham, 2013). In this section, our emphasis is only on the patterns of progression between cancerous cells and *Anfal* without transposing biological interactions to social relationships.

[12] See https://www.cancer.net/navigating-cancer-care/cancer-basics/what-cancer

- **Stage II and Stage III.** In general, these two stages are cancers that have grown more deeply into nearby tissue. They may have also spread to lymph nodes but not to other parts of the body.
- **Stage IV.** This stage means that the cancer has spread to other organs or parts of the body. It may be also called advanced or metastatic cancer.[13]

This scheme can be applied to *Anfal.* Continuing with the cancer analogy, Stage I describes the interim period between the formation of the provisional government of Mehdi Bazargan on February 4, 1979, and Iran hostage crisis on November 4, 1979, that resulted in the resignation of Bazargan and the establishment of the IRI. Excluding Stage I, the three phases of *Anfal* correspond to Stage II, III, and IV in the progression of cancerous cells.

If we assume enterprises as 'economic cells', then *Anfal* is like cancer for public properties. It starts by a *genetic change* of enterprises managing public properties, since the giant holdings running *Anfal* such as *Bonyad* or *Setad* (The Execution of Imam Khomeini's Order-EIKO) do not belong to people. In fact, *Anfal* contradicts the underlying principle of modern public finance, namely the people's sovereignty. The key point about *Anfal* is that the Supreme Jurisconsult rather than people is assumed to be the owner of 'ownerless' public properties. This explains the total opacity of these holdings that are exempt from any public accountability to government or parliament and is only accountable to the Supreme Leader personally. These holdings are embedded in the economy and society through two principal channels that are similar to 'lymph' and 'blood' vessels in spreading cancerous cells. The first channel is social protection that functions as 'lymph' vessels and the second channel is banking system that is similar to 'blood' vessels.

Social security is similar to 'lymph nodes' containing immune cells that can help fight infection by attacking and destroying germs that are carried in through the lymph fluid. *Bonyad Moastazafan* (the Foundation for the downtrodden) and other religious foundations are often created as Islamic

---

[13] Some cancers also have a stage 0 (zero). This stage describes cancer in situ or in place. Stage zero cancers are still located in the place they started. They have not spread to nearby tissues. This stage of cancer is often curable and the entire tumor can be removed usually. For different stages of cancer's progression, see: https://www.cancer.net/navigating-cancer-care/diagnosing-cancer/stages-cancer

charities for social protection of the martyrs' families, veterans of the revolution and war. They constitute a parallel system to the official social security. While this network of Islamic charity entertains a clientelist relationship with social supporters of the regime to secure its political stability, it preys on state resources causing colossal debts for the state.

The banking sector is like 'blood vessels' in any modern economy. Like cancer, the progression of *Anfal* has been through a parallel banking system composing of Islamic loan funds and Islamic financial institutions that not only undermine the Iranian Central Bank (ICB) and drastically augment liquidity but also prey massively on people's savings (Ahmadi Amooei, 2018).

The progression of cancerous cells also hinges upon what is called the 'Grade' of malignant tumor. Cancer grade is recorded by the pathologist using the letter "G" with a number from 1 to 3 for most cancers and from 1 to 4 in some. In general, the lower the tumor's grade, the better the prognosis.

The "G" is particularly relevant in cancer staging or its progression. The grade describes how much cancer cells look like healthy cells. If the cancer looks very different from healthy tissue, it is called a poorly differentiated or a high-grade tumor. The cancer's grade may help predict how quickly cancer will spread. In *Anfal* case, the "G" depends on the institutional complementarity or coalition between *Anfal* and other core institutions of the sovereign power notably Sepah. The so-called privatization decree in 2006 became possible through this alliance between *Anfal* and Sepah.

The 'Grade' or the spread of cancerous cells of *Anfal* highly increased under the two terms of Ahmadinejad's presidency and then during the newly president of the 13th government, Ebrahim Raisi. In the recent period, the international sanctions strengthened the stronghold of *Bonyad*, *Setad*, and *Khatam al-Anbiya*[14] Construction Headquarters (the economic organization of IRGC) on the petroleum and gas fields. This is the culmination of *Anfal*'s progression comparable to advanced or metastatic cancer. From an economic viewpoint, it means the effective appropriation of public properties by the Supreme Jurisconsult, the formation of Islamic political capitalism with preponderant destructive coordination.

---

[14] For brevity, we will use *Khatam* instead of *Khatam al-Anbiya*.

The progression has been to the point that in July 2020, Bonyad overtly claimed its property rights over Mount Damavand[15] (see the site *Zeitoons* July 22, 2020, https://www.zeitoons.com/78754; and *Aftab News*, July 28, 2020). Supported by the Shi'i jurisprudence on *Anfal* (see Chap. 5), Bonyad legally claimed the ownership of the summit and the slope of Mount Damavand and whatever existed in them. This has not been a purely hypothetical juridical claim, the sale of pumice stones extracted from Mount Damavand to the neighboring countries has been one of the major sources of income for Bonyad *from* non-oil exporting products.

The commodification and sale of 'ownerless' natural resources (*res nullius*) under *Anfal* is the source of an unprecedented disastrous destruction of ecological system in Iran that is not less lethal than metastatic stage of cancer. We now review the three phases of *Anfal*'s progression.

6.3   PHASE 1: *ANFAL* IN KHOMEINI ERA (1979–1989)

The first phase of *Anfal* (1979–1989) starts by the confiscation of the late Shah's properties. While the Shi'i faqihs diverge on some of items that should be included in *Anfal* (e.g., latent or apparent mines as well as heirless inheritance), they are unanimous in considering that all the confiscated properties of the tyrants whether they are immovable assets (known as *Qataya* in Islamic Jurisprudence) such as gardens and palaces or movable (coined as *Safaia* in Islamic jurisprudence) like precious objects are part of *Anfal* (see section 4-5). *Anfal* as sealed in Article 45 includes 'public property recovered from usurpers'. The Shah and the Iranian big bourgeoisie loyal to him were considered by the new regime as 'usurpers'. Article 49 of the constitution substantiates this component of *Anfal*: "The government has the responsibility of confiscating all wealth accumulated through usury, usurpation, bribery, embezzlement, theft, gambling, misuse of endowments, misuse of government contracts and transactions…and other illicit means and sources in accordance with the law of Islam."[16]

Khomeini as the first Supreme jurisprudent of the Islamic Republic confiscated the properties of *Bonyad Pahlavi* (Pahlavi foundation) and the assets of 53 industrialists and financiers in exile in the aftermath of

---

[15] Mount Damavand is the highest peak in Iran and Western Asia, and the highest volcano in Asia, at an elevation of 5609 metres. At a world-wide level, it is the 12th most prominent peak in the world and the 2nd most prominent in Asia after Mount Everest.

[16] See http://en.wikipedia.org/wiki/Constitution_of_the_Islamic_Republic_of_Iran

revolution. While according to Article 45 of the constitution, all 'public properties' including *Anfal* should be managed as 'state property', Khomeini decided *not to nationalize* these assets. His injunction on February 28, that is, seven days after the victory of the 1979 Revolution, addressing the 'Council of the Islamic Revolution'[17] clearly indicated that he opted to keep and control the confiscated assets separately from state properties under his guardianship as the jurisconsult of the newly Islamic state. This was the start of *parallel institutions* in the post-revolutionary Iranian economy.

Khomeini wrote: "By this injunction, the Council of the Islamic Revolution has the mission to confiscate all the movable and immovable properties of the Pahlavi dynasty and all its various branches, agents and associates who illicitly profited from public treasury of Muslims for the interests of the needy population, workers, and low-income employees. Their movable assets should be deposited to the banks under a specific number in the name of the *Council of the Islamic Revolution or under my own name.* Their immovable assets such as real estates and lands should be registered and confiscated so that they could be used for the interests of deprived layers of all classes. I also order to all the Committees of Islamic Revolution[18] all over the country that they should deposit to banks whatever they have seized from these *booties* under a specific bank account number. They must indicate to the state that these *booties* do not belong to it but to the Council of the Islamic Revolution which is in charge of these assets. The state agents as well as all persons who have seized any of these assets should deliver them immediately to the Committees or to the banks under a specific account number. Those who do not follow these rules will be penalized" (Rahman Zadeh Heravi, 2018, p. 521; emphases are added).

---

[17] The Council of the Islamic Revolution (Shoorai Inqelab Islami) was a group selected by Ayatollah Ruhollah Khomeini to manage the Iranian Revolution on January 10, 1979, shortly before his return to Iran. The decisions of the council were undisclosed to the public until early 1980.

[18] Committees of Islamic Revolution (Komitehaye Inqelab Islami) were law enforcers in Iran in the wake of the 1979 Revolution. They were also in charge of enforcing Islamic regulations with regard to the 'Islamic moral code of dressing and behavior'. While they were founded as one of the revolutionary military organizations in 1979, they were eventually merged with Gendarmerie and Shahrbani to form Law enforcement of the Islamic Republic of Iran (NAJA) in 1991.

Clearly speaking, Khomeini dealt with the confiscated assets as 'booties' and part of *Anfal*. It was not by chance that he commanded that they had to be kept under *his own name* or the Council separately from the state properties. In other words, while Article 45 of the constitution lumped together *Anfal* and state property in general, Khomeini strictly separated *Anfal* from state property in practice. Not only *Anfal* did not extend state sector, but also undermined its authority and financial resources.

Following Khomeini's injunction, *Bonyad Mostazafan* (Foundation for the Downtrodden) was established on March 5, 1979. Under the auspices of Khomeini, a board of director was initially nominated that was composed of Khomeini's closest associates, namely Seyyed Ali Khamenei (the present Supreme jurisprudent), Akbar Hashemi Rafsanjani, Muhammad Hossein Beheshti, Abdolkarim Mousavi Ardabeeli, Ahmad Jalali, Ali Asghar Masoudi, and Ezaatolah Sahhabi. While the Supreme Leader was and is the real owner of the Foundation, he appointed an individual to control this conglomerate for five years. Since 1979, the Foundation's heads were as follows: Seyyed Ali-Naghi Khamoushi (March 1979–September 1980), Muhammad-Ali Rajaei (September 1980–September 1981), Mir-Hossein Mousavi (December 1981–September 1989), Mohsen Rafiqdoost (September 1989–July 1999), Muhammad Foruzandeh (July 1999–July 2014), Muhammad Saeedi-Kia (July 2014–July 2019), and Parviz Fattah (July 2019–Now).[19] Following the outbreak of the Iran-Iraq war, the Foundation official name was changed into the "Foundation for the Downtrodden and Veterans" (Bonyad Mostazafan va Janbazan (BMJ)).

Many authors have studied BMJ and other similar Bonyads as 'parastatal' or 'para-governmental' foundations (Harris, 2013; Maloney, 2000, 2015; Mousavi Nik, 2009; Nili and associates, 2015; Rahman Zadeh Heravi, 2018; Saeidi, 2004; Vahabi, 2010, 2014, 2015a, 2015b, 2018b). However, the relationship between these foundations and *Anfal* has been overlooked. Parastatal economic institutions exist almost all over the world and are often based on a collusion between the state and private sectors

---

[19] See Bonyad's website www.irmf.ir and https://irannewsupdate.com/news/economy/mostazafan-foundation-a-pillar-of-khameneis-economic-empire-in-iran/

extending either the state or private sector through subcontracting.[20] *Anfal* should be distinguished from parastatal sector in its conventional sense, since it derives from the Imam's sovereign power undermining the formal state as a representative of people's sovereignty.

Considering BMJ as the first phase of *Anfal*, we will start by exploring its organizational structure as giant holdings from an economic viewpoint, and then the way these assets were partially spent on Islamic charities to secure political stability through clientelist relationships. It will be shown that these charities have nothing to do with an Islamic version of the 'welfare state'. Finally, institutional complementarities of *Anfal* with Islamic charitable funds (known as 'Islamic banks') will be highlighted.

6.4   Holding Structure of BMJ[21] and Islamic Charities

BMJ is a powerful economic bloc consisting of six different organizations each undertaking several related groups of companies as subsidiaries. The organizations include Civil Development and Housing, Recreation and Tourism, Industries and Mines, Agriculture and Transportation and Commerce (the official website of Bonyad, www.irmf.ir/2013). In 1982, BMJ embraced 400 enterprises exceeding the number of firms owned by the private sector that was 111 at the time and increased to 128 in the following year (Sodagar, 1990, pp. 465–467).

By the late 1980s, BMJ's assets, totaled more than 20 billion dollars, owning some 140 factories, 470 agricultural related companies, 100 construction firms, 64 mines, and 250 commercial companies (see https://

---

[20] I am not completely denying the analogy between Bonyads and a specific variant of parastatal sector in the advanced market economies. The sectoral activities of the Military Industrial Complex (MIC) come within the scope of 'destructive creation'. As Galbraith (2004, Chaps. 7 and 11) and Weber (2001, Chap. 2) rightly noted the blurred frontiers between 'public' and 'private' sectors was also an undeniable fact in case of the MIC. The similarities between the MIC sector in the advanced market economies and the Iranian Foundations with regard to the secrecy, non-accountability, and inseparability of 'public' and 'private' sectors, as well as the influence over foreign policy are striking (see Caldicott, 2002).

[21] The BMJ was renamed as *Bonyad-e Mostazafan* (the Foundation for the downtrodden) and a separate holding was created under the title of *Bonyad-e Janbazan* (the Foundation for the martyrs). We systematically employ BMJ to homogenize our references in different chapters.

www.ifmat.org/bonyad-mostazafan-report/).[22] In 1989, *BMJ* had over 800 companies and financial firms; all of them were confiscated.

Many of these enterprises were insolvent but kept working allegedly under different charitable excuses, notably job creation for the regime's sympathizers. Although financially insolvent, these bankrupt enterprises provided the opportunity for rent-seeking since they could have access to preferential bank credits and hard currency with state exchange rate due to their privileged status as an enterprise belonging to BMJ (see Encyclopedia Iranica, 1987, pp. 360–61; Maloney, 2000, pp. 151–152; Saeidi, 2004, pp. 488–490; Vahabi, 2015a, pp. 276–285). The revelations of many scandalous corruption cases in the BMJ resulted in the closure of many enterprises. Although by the end of 1990s, the number of enterprises and factories under the BMJ diminished to 400 (Klebnikov, 2003; Katzman, 2006), when Muhammad Foruzandeh replaced Mohsen Rafiqdoost in July 1999 as the head of Bonyad, he announced that 80% of its 350 companies were losing money (Saeidi, 2004, pp. 495-98). While the number of Bonyad's enterprises varied during time, the BMJ constituted the largest non-state sector holding in the Iranian economy, second in size only to the National Iranian Oil Company (Smith, 1997; Maloney, 2000). According to an estimation, the BMJ was the biggest holding company in the Middle East and its workforce exceeded 200,000 employees (GlobalSecurity.org, September 7, 2011).

BMJ's assets and income do not finance Muslims' Public Treasury (*Beit al-mal*) but the Imam's Treasury (*Beit al-Imam*). This is the basis of a parallel 'public' treasury system, one belonging to the Supreme Leader and the other to all Muslims or 'people'. The former is only accountable to the jurisconsult, and benefits from tax exemptions since Bonyads are professedly Islamic 'charitable' (non-profitable) organizations (IMF Staff Country Report, 1998, p. 26). They also enjoy preferential bank credits, subsidies, and special 'quasi-budgetary redistribution' (Coville, 2002; Vahabi & Coville, 2017).

BMJ is not the only Islamic charity organization under the Supreme Leader's direct supervision. Some of them existed even before the 1979 Revolution and many others after the revolution. For example, the Imam Khomeini Relief Committee (IKRC) had its origins in pre-revolutionary Iran where Ayatollah Khomeini's loyalists organized underground charitable networks to provide relief to Muslim or clergy political prisoners and

---

[22] The same figures are also reported in Abrahamian (2008, p. 178).

finance other acts of subversion. On March 5, 1979, less than a month after the revolution, Khomeini formally established the IKRC. The IKRC also operates as the Islamic Republic's primary aid distribution network outside of Iran's borders, where it works as a sort of world-wide organization to disseminate goodwill among foreign populations and spread political Islam. The Supreme jurisprudent coordinates with Iran's Ministry of Foreign Affairs and the Office for Expansion of Relations with Iranians Abroad to direct IKRC's external charitable activities, distributing aid through a network of in-country offices, distribution centers, and educational institutes. The IKRC maintains offices dedicated to welfare, culture, and education in Lebanon, Syria, Afghanistan, Azerbaijan, Tajikistan, Iraq, and Comoros, and additionally conducts the so-called philanthropic activities in Chechnya, the Palestinian territories, Bosnia, Kosovo, Somalia, and Sierra Leone.[23]

To name a few prominent charities that were established after the revolution, we can cite the Alavi Foundation, Martyrs Foundation, Pilgrimage Foundation, Housing Foundation, Foundation for War Refugees, and Foundation for Imam Khomeini's Publications. According to Amuzegar (1993, p. 100), together they employed more than 400,000 people. Their combined budgets were as much as half that of the central government. What is more, the long-existing shrines such as those of Imam Reza in Mashhad (Astan Quods Razavi), Fatemeh in Qom, and Abdul-Azim in Ray together owned as much as $8 billion of real estate (Abrahamian, 2008, p. 178). They were states within the state—or rather, clerical fiefdoms accountable only to the Supreme jurisprudent. What is the objective of these charities?

6.5   *ANFAL* AND ISLAMIC 'WELFARE STATE'

The Imam should use *Anfal* to create its own community or Umma. He is the Shepherd, the benefactor that guides the herd of Muslims as 'minors'. The Muslim community, as the followers of Imam, is not defined within a national border or on the basis of citizenship; it is composed of Muslims all over the world. A Lebanese or a French Muslim following the Imam is part of the Umma whereas a disobedient Iranian who does not follow the Imam is not part of the community. Moreover, as Thomas

[23] See   https://www.unitedagainstnucleariran.com/ideological-expansion/imam-khomeini-relief-committee retrieved on November 20, 2021.

Marshall (1963) suggested, 'welfare state' corresponds to an advanced phase of *citizenship* after the first two phases of *legal* and *political* citizenships. As Esping-Andersen (1990, p. 21) averred: "social citizenship constitutes the core idea of a welfare state...Above all, it must involve granting of social rights." Social citizenship is inconceivable in the absence of the people sovereignty. In this sense, *Anfal* and welfare state are antinomic.

This is not what Abrahamian (2009) and Harris (2012, 2017) have claimed about the "welfare state" in the post-revolutionary Iran. In their opinion, the Islamic Republic of Iran is politically stable not because of oil revenue, ideological orientation, and patron-client networks. Its resilience is rooted in its state-building project involving the creation of a "welfare state" (Abrahamian, 2009) that reflects a "social revolution politics"[24] (Harris, 2017). Abrahamian totally overlooks the role of Bonyads (Foundations) in state predation and maintains that they constitute 'small welfare states': "Some of these foundations [the Mostazafin (Oppressed), Martyrs', Housing, Alavi and Imam Khomeini Relief Foundations] also lobby effectively to protect university quotas for war veterans and together they provide hundreds of thousands with wages and benefits, including pensions, housing and health insurance. In other words, *they are small welfare states within the larger welfare state*" (2009, p. 14; the brackets and emphases are added).

This apologetic line of defense for the IRI and *Anfal*'s institutions was initially introduced by the Tudeh Party of Iran (an Iranian pro-Soviet Communist party) during the period 1979–1988. This political formation described Khomeini as an anti-imperialist equalitarian leader struggling for social justice, and 'non-capitalist development path'. They considered themselves as 'followers of Imam's line'. The arrest of Tudeh Party's leadership and the execution of many militants and leaders of that party in 1988 discredited this political line. However, the apologetic attitude

---

[24] Skocopol (1982) initially characterized the Islamic revolution in Iran as a 'social revolution'. This was echoed not only in Harris (2017) but also in Keshavarzian (2007, p. 280). Interestingly, none of them explained how a 'social revolution' can dispossess people from their sovereignty and establish *Velayat Faqih* (the jurisconsult of vicegerent)? This might be better characterized as 'reactionary' or 'anti-revolutionary' compared even to the slogans of the Iranian Constitutional Revolution at the beginning of the twentieth century. Moreover, if the expression 'social revolution' can be attributed to any "rapid transformation of a country's state and class structures, and of its dominant ideology" (Skocopol, 1982, p. 265), then political Islam is as much carrier of a social revolution as Fascism.

toward the Islamic regime was followed by a tendency among the left intellectuals in the name of social justice.

In the recent period, Kevan Harris characterized the IRI as "Martyrs' welfare state" (Harris, 2012) and completely dismissed the rent-seeking as a theoretical explanation of its activities. His explanation emphasized a Polanyian protective reaction against modern capitalism embedding economics in society through 'social revolution'. Harris's perspective on social protection fundamentally dismisses two important facts underlined by Pierson.

First, social protection systems are not imposed exogenously to modern capitalist system, they are a fundamental part of modern capitalism. As Pierson persuasively argued, the limits of traditional scholarship on the welfare state consisted in disregarding the role of employers in shaping and reshaping social policy. Most work on the politics of social policy has proceeded with the (often implicit) assumption that "employers everywhere and always simply opposed any extension of the welfare state, and those employers today would demolish it entirely if they only could" (2000a, p. 795). Contrary to the Polanyian perspective, welfare state is not synonym of 'decommodification' process. In the case of so-called martyrs' welfare state, the rise of such a regime preceded the eight-year war with Iraq. It was closely related to stop 'social revolution' or to terminate with workers' strike committees and their intervention in management and control over production. Khomeini's 'welfare policies' for martyrs of revolution and *Mostazafan* (the downtrodden) should be assessed within specific workers-employers relationship under Islamic corporatism. The so-called martyrs' welfare system was a means to protect capitalist mode of production from the threat of a social revolution as spontaneously developed in workers' movements during 1979–1982 (for a detailed discussion, see Chap. 7, Sect. 7.7). While traditional corporatism could not protect employers' interests in the aftermath of revolution, Islamic corporatism had to fill the vacuum to protect employers' interests.

Second, the traditional scholarship on the welfare state often ignored the importance of political democracy in the analysis of social protection. Pierson (1996, 2000) argued that 'political parties did matter' and showed that political democracy was key to the development of social protection. In Harris, people's sovereignty and *a fortiori* political democracy are evacuated in discussing welfare state.

While I totally agree with Harris that the creation of a host of Islamic charitable organizations has contributed to the political stability of the regime, his apologetic attitude toward the Islamic Republic of Iran seems not to be supported by theoretical and empirical evidence. From a theoretical viewpoint, Harris completely disregards *Anfal* in all of his works. This is clearly related to his research strategy to keep silence on the sensitive political issue of the Supreme Jurisconsult.[25] Unless *Anfal* is taken on board, theoretical explanations in terms of rent-seeking, religious orientation, and patron-client networks would of course be irrelevant! But if this core institution is assumed away, how *parallel institutions* in public finance might be explained theoretically?

From an empirical viewpoint, the Islamic sovereign institutions were not only involved in 'state building', but they were also *preying* on the formal state's assets and resources. The colossal debts of the state, as well as those of the official social security, commercial banks, and state education system, are causally related to the increasing economic shares of giant holdings of *Anfal* and Sepah as well as their institutional linkages and networks including Waqf, diverse Islamic charities, Islamic banks, Islamic propaganda, Islamic filmmaking, religious seminaries, and publishing houses. With no public account, no governmental or parliamentary inspection or control over their expenses, no shareholders, and no well-defined legal status, these holdings have been operating autonomously from the government (Mousavi Nik, 2009, p. 11).

The so-called martyrs' welfare state has been built upon predation of state funds and rent-seeking. It provides a parallel system of social protection based on charity and assistance by *Anfal*'s economic institutions under the purview of the Supreme Leader. Accordingly, the post-revolutionary social protection in Iran is divided in two separate parallel systems: an official state insurance system and a parallel non-insurance Islamic charity. The latter is non-accountable to the state executive and parliamentary powers and is exclusively supervised by the Supreme Leader. The *Anfal*'s holdings provide its financial resources creating a parallel 'public' treasury or more exactly the Imam's personal treasury.

The official social security system is on the verge of bankruptcy (16 over 17 pension funds are insolvent) wrestling with colossal debts (*Radio*

---

[25] This silence is also present in his paper regarding the rise of the subcontractor state in Iran (Harris, 2013) in which the Supreme jurisprudent is only cited one or two times for his 2006 privatization decree (2013, pp. 46, 55) as if he played no role in shaping politics of 'pseudo-privatization' or the inter-factional struggles for the transfer of the state assets to the so-called parastatal sector.

Zamaenh, April 12, 2022[26]). These two parallel systems entertain contradictory and not complementary relationships. While the state is heftily indebted to the official social security system and has no power to control the Islamic charities, it is supposed to 'assist' Islamic charities financially. The state annual budget allocates financial resources to these 'charities'. Figure 6.1. shows the parallel system of pension funds in Iran.

A major crisis of the whole social security is caused by this parallel system and all efforts to "coordinate and provide a unitary comprehensive social security system" during Khatami's presidency and then Rafsanjani in

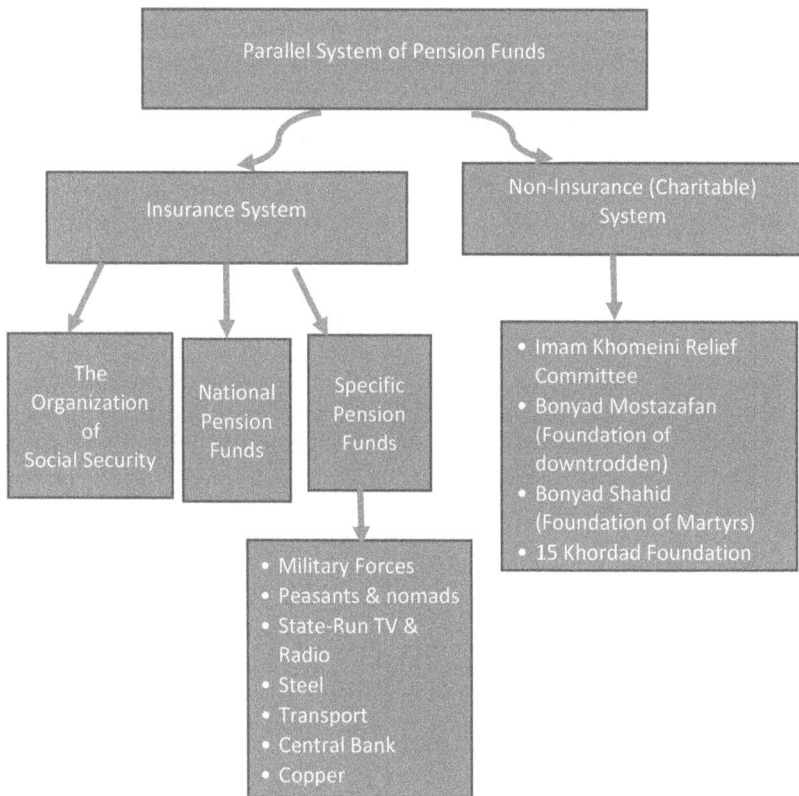

Fig. 6.1   A Parallel System of Pension Funds in Post-Revolutionary Iran

[26] See https://www.radiozamaneh.com/711417 retrieved on April 12, 2022.

the Expediency Council since 2013 have failed because of the impossibility to bring the two parallel systems under a unitary system of governance and coordination. All stakeholders of Islamic charities repel any control over their rent-seeking activities and their lion's share of state resources by official state authorities. The recent edict of the Supreme Leader in April 2022 also maintained the fundamental structure of the system intact. The result needs no comments: the state's debt to the national social security funds amounts to 400 trillion tomans (20 billion American dollars) (see *Radio Zamaenh*, April 12, 2022).

Due to unaccountability and total opacity of its activities, widespread corruption (a salient empirical evidence of rent-seeking activities) in the BMJ and its diverse branches has been reported frequently. One of the major episodes that received extensive press coverage at an international level involved Rafiqdoost's brothers and many other directors of the BMJ. These revelations ensued after a parliamentary investigation in 1995–1996 headed by the conservative deputy Ali Movahedi Savoji. While the details of the parliamentary report were never publicly announced, journalists could have access to some information according to which the parliamentary investigation had unraveled numerous cases of corruption such as serious failings in the BMJ's charitable activities on behalf of veterans, illicit sales, and transfers of property (see *The Economist*, ep 25, 1993; *The New York Times*, Jan 8, 1995; *Financial Times*, Jul 17, 1997; Saeidi, 2004, pp. 495–98; Maloney, 2015, pp. 242–243). This led to the replacement of Mohsen Rafiqdoost,[27] one of the founders of Sepah, by the former Defense Minister Muhammad Foruzandeh in July 1999.

Moreover, Bonyad's assets have always been used as an authoritative resource in line with the strategic political and military considerations of the Islamic system. I provide two examples. The first one is the "15 Khordad Foundation", an Islamic charity foundation that has been supplementary office to the Foundation of Martyrs and Veterans. It is also exempt from taxes and reap huge subsidies from the regime, while providing limited and inadequate charity to the poor. This Foundation has been particularly active in boosting $500,000 the bounty it had offered for the killing of British author Salman Rushdie to $3.3 million from $2.8

---

[27] Rafiqdoost is known for serving as the driver of Ayatollah Ruhollah Khomeini, the leader of Iran's Islamic Revolution, from the Tehran International airport to his place of residency on February 1, 1979, when he triumphantly returned back to Tehran on an Air France flight from Paris after 14 years in exile. He also served as Minister of the IRGC from 1982 to 1989.

million, after protests around the world over alleged insults to the prophet Muhammad. The 15 Khordad Foundation reportedly would pay the higher bounty to whoever acts on a fatwa issued by Iran's late leader Ayatollah Ruhollah Khomeini on February 14, 1989, which called for the death of Rushdie, the author of "The Satanic Verses", because the novel was considered blasphemous to Muslims.

The second example concerns the organizational connections between the Revolutionary Guard and the BMJ during Rafiqdoost's direction that confirms the substantial involvement of the latter in weapons procurement and production: "the Bonyad's heavy presence in legitimate mining and chemicals production allegedly camouflage IRGC [the Revolutionary Guard] chemical weaponry plants. In addition, German intelligence sources contend that the Bonyad [BMJ] has utilized a network of sham enterprises to acquire inputs for the Revolutionary Guard's defense industry, including its biological, chemical, and nuclear weapons as well as its missile development. In addition, the foundation apparently undertakes international endeavors that transgress the traditional definition of trade— the BMJ is commonly cited as a generous supporter and active political patron of the Lebanese terrorist organization, Hezbollah...In addition, state control over the industrial sector meant that 'the commercial bourgeoisie became the most active faction of the ruling class.' This, of course, represents another potent link between the bazaar and the *bonyads*: they are 'the only winners' in the Islamic Republic's lackluster economic history" (Maloney, 2000, pp. 159–160).

It is noteworthy that during 1979–1989, Sepah has not been involved extensively in economic activity. Sepah became engaged in economic activities after the end of war and particularly since the first term presidency of Hashemi Rafsanjani (1989–1993). Thus, the alliance of Bonyads with Sepah at the time was not on an economic base and could not strongly augment the 'Grade' or the rapidity of progression of *Anfal* in economic sphere.

In sum, although Bonyads act as Islamic charities to secure a clientele relationship with their social base, they are principally organizations to appropriate public properties for the restrictive property of the Supreme Leader and for the sake of its political power and stability.

6.6   *ANFAL*'s Progression in its First Phase and Islamic Banks

The *Anfal*'s progression in its first phase (1979–1989) was principally through Islamic charities. The Islamic banks were developed during the second (1989–2005) and third phases (2006–now) of *Anfal*'s progression.

The Islamic loan funds (Qarz al-Hasaneh), preceding the birth of Islamic banks, existed long before the revolution in the sixties. They were often created as a joint initiative of the clergies like Muhammad Behsehti and the Iranian traditional merchants (Bazaari) like Mir-Muhammad Sadeghi to develop the influence of political Islam incrementally through mutual aid and cultural activities.

On the eve of the 1979 Revolution, the number of Islamic loan funds was 200. This number quadrupled two years later and reached to 800 in 1981. Its constant increase is shown in Table 6.1.

The evolution of Islamic loan funds was not only quantitative but also qualitative. Before the revolution, they were acting as funds granting small loans to needy layers of population but could not open deposit account and create liquidity. Considering their petty capital size and the non-banking nature of their activity, Islamic loan funds were not under the Iranian Central Bank (ICB) supervision. But they were controlled by the police force and the Ministry of Interior since the Shah's regime was particularly sensitive to the political network that could be developed by these funds.

Table 6.1 Number of Islamic loan funds (1979–2014)

Year	Number of funds	Anfal's progression phase
1979	200	First phase
1981	800	Idem
1984	1400	Idem
1985	1650	Idem
1987	2250	Idem
2001	5000	Second phase
2014	7000	Third phase

This table was created by the author based on Ahmadi Amooei's figures regarding Islamic loan funds (2018, p. 29)

However, the situation radically changed after the revolution because most of these funds belonged to the traditional conservative Bazaari related to the *Jami'at Mo'talefhh Islami* (Islamic Coalition Party)[28]who were Khomeini's supporters before the revolution. The leaders of this political group became politically and economically influential under the Islamic Republic of Iran. For example, seven days after the victory of revolution, on February 18, 1979, *Mo'talefhh* undertook the control of the chamber of commerce. Seyyed Ali-Naghi Khamoushi, one of the leaders of *Mo'talefhh* who served as the first head of the BMJ by Khomeini's order, became president of the Iran Chamber of Commerce, Industries and Mines from 1984 to 2007. He said in an interview with Ahmadi Amooei (2018, p. 36) that his presidency of the Chamber of Commerce was supported by Muhammad Beheshti.

Mir-Muhammad Sadeghi was also among the high-ranked members of *Mo'talefah*. As a Bazaari and ardent supporter of Khomeini, he actively participated in creating Islamic loan funds before and after the revolution. Shortly after the revolution, he was appointed to manage a new organization, *Sazman Iqtesad Islami* (the Organization of the Islamic Economics) that was the *first Islamic bank*, acting as a sort of Central Bank for the Islamic loan funds. The creation of this organization was a first step in establishing a parallel system in the banking sector particularly because funds continued to operate outside the purview of the Iran's Central Bank.

Moreover, several major loan funds that belonged to Islamic sovereign institutions including the BMJ (such as Bank Sina, later known as Sina Financial and Investment Holding company), Sepah (such as Ghavamin loan funds), and Basij (such as Basijan loan funds) were no more under the control of the Ministry of Interior. They became completely independent from the formal state's inspection and gradually started to function as 'banks' in the sense that they accepted bank deposits, created money, and

---

[28] Mo'talefah refers to Jami'at Mo'talefeh Islami or the Islamic Coalition Party dating back to 1963 when a handful of petite-bourgeoisie and Baazari men formed an association advocating Islamic fundamentalism. Because of their opposition to the Shah's regime and support for Ayatollah Khomeini, almost all members of this small group were arrested and imprisoned for some years before the 1979 Revolution. Later many of them joined the Islamic Republic Party (IRP) and held high positions in the post-revolutionary governments and played important roles in the economy of the country. After the demise of the IRP, the group revived itself as an independent association. Mo'talefah represents the older generation of Islamic fundamentalists and is one of the main pillars of the more conservative wing of the IRI.

increased the total liquidity. Although the parallel institutions in the banking sector developed later, its origin should be sought in the Khomeini's era during the nationalization of domestic banks and insurance companies by the provisional government of Mehdi Bazargan.

In a long interview with the economic journal, *Tejarat Farda*, Ali Akbar Moinfar (2014), the first oil Minister of the IRI, reported that despite the Banking Nationalization Act, Khomeini decided to make an exception for the Islamic bank. He issued a decree on the establishment of the Islamic Bank of Iran in April 1979. Bazargan and several members of the interim government, including Finance Minister Bani Sadr, were not supportive of this bank. Moinfar also joined the opposition arguing that this decision was the origin of parallel institutions in the banking sector. After Khomeini's decree, the statute of the Islamic Bank was submitted to the Central Bank and the 'Money and Credit Council' for approval. The Council approved the statute on May 9, 1979. Finally, the interim government agreed that the Islamic Bank could exist on one condition: the term 'Bank' had to be replaced by 'Organization'. Thus, the Islamic Bank was rebaptized as the 'Organization of the Islamic Economics' (*Sazman Iqtesad Islami*).

While the interim government resisted the explicit naming of Islamic Bank, it was born at the heydays of the revolution by transgressing the law on the nationalization of all banks. Accordingly, the BMJ had its own Islamic Bank that could create liquidity, and issue cheque books without being under the ICB's purview. This point has been confirmed by two official authorities of the BMJ before 1989, namely Mazaheri and Shahsavar Khojasteh: "Perhaps we can say that the first private bank after the revolution under the Islamic Republic of Iran was created in Bonyad [BMJ]. Although this bank was not under the supervision of the Central Bank, we tried to comply to the ICB's general regulations. However, since there was no law supporting the establishment of private banks or financial private credit institutions, we could not proceed to have legal deposits. The chequebooks that were issued could only be used within the financial and credit institutions of the Foundation [BMJ] as a sort of payment order" (Ahmadi Amooei, 2018, p. 87, brackets are added).

Could Islamic banks be regarded as the 'first private banks' under the IRI? It is rather a hoax to label them 'private banks' when the empirical evidence clearly demonstrates their relationship with the sovereign institutions. Following the standard macroeconomics, many Iranian economists

(Nili and associates, 2015; Nili 2017[29]) repeatedly have suggested the 'independence of the ICB' for controlling the ever-increasing liquidity without seriously addressing this parallel banking system. In fact, the ICB has no inspecting authority over Islamic banks and the liquidity creation cannot be stopped with the ICB independence. While Islamic banks were born in the middle of nationalization, they were particularly developed with the decrees on private banks and Article 44. We will further explore this issue in the second phase of *Anfal*.

To sum up the first phase of *Anfal*, Table 6.2 recapitulates *Anfal*'s juridical status, its domain, its progression channel, and the rapidity of its progression ('Grade' by analogy to the cancer metaphor) due to coalitional alliance.

According to Article 45 *Anfal* was juridically lumped together with state sector, while in practice it was kept separately from the state sector under the guardianship of the Supreme jurisprudent and spawned parallel institutions. The main progression channel was the BMJ and Islamic charities. Islamic banks were nascent and rare in the first phase; they played only a marginal role in *Anfal*'s progression. The rapidity of progression was low despite *Anfal*'s alliance with Sepah since the latter was not extensively involved in economic activities. Their alliance was rather on political, military, and ideological bases.

In this initial phase, *Anfal*'s economy was embedded in social relationships through Islamic charities. We now study the second phase of *Anfal*.

Table 6.2   First phase of *Anfal* (1979–1989)

Juridical status	Domain of Anfal	Channel of progression	Rapidity of progression
Article 45: Inseparability of *Anfal* from the state property (Unity thesis)	Confiscation of the late Shah's properties and 53 industrialists and financiers	BMJ giant holding and Islamic charities for social protection	Low

[29] Masoud Nili has been one of the top economic advisors of the President Hassan Rouhani. He has been recommending the independence of the CBI since 2013 and recently in 2017 (see the site of Agah Group: http://agahgroup.com/necessity-cbi-independence/ retrieved on December 1, 2021).

6.7   PHASE 2: *ANFAL* AND THE TRANSITION PERIOD (1989–2005)

Ruhollah Khomeini, the first Supreme jurisprudent of the IRI, passed away on June 4, 1989, after accepting a truce with the Iraqi government to end an eight-year war when the near-collapse of the Iranian army forced him to "swallow poison"[30] as he metaphorically described the ceasefire.

The vulnerability of political situation in terms of future leadership was never so critical. By 1988, the Iranian GDP per capita hanged in the vicinity of 54% of its 1976 level. The war had shrunk per capita income by 45%, inflation was approaching 29%, and direct and indirect war damages amounted to somewhere close to $1 trillion (Maloney, 2015, pp. 194–195). As *Los Angeles Times* wrote: "In many ways, Khomeini could not have died at a worse time. The situation is complicated by current deliberations over constitutional reforms, which have not been finalized and which officially needed Khomeini's approval. Without an obvious heir-apparent and without final agreement on the reforms, the theocracy faces a highly volatile period" (Schanche, 1989).[31]

In fact, Khomeini had fired his heir-apparent, the Ayatollah Hossein Ali Montazeri, in the spring, when the latter contested his order of massacring political prisoners in summer 1988.[32] His succession was a major challenge for all political factions. At the time of his death, Khamenei, the present Supreme Jurisconsult was the Iranian president and Hashemi Rafsanjani was the Parliament Speaker. None of them had religious credentials sufficiently enough to alone inherit the mantle of "Supreme jurisprudent". Moreover, none of the eminent Shi'i faqihs had Khomeini's charisma and popularity. There was allegedly a tendency to fill the political vacuum of Khomeini's succession by nominating an eminent theologian such as Muhammad-Reza Golpaygani or by creating a council of faqihs. However, the coalition of a troika composed of Ali-Akbar Hashemi Rafsanjani,

---

[30] Khomeini described the acceptance of a truce in these terms: "I reiterate that the acceptance of this issue [truce] is more bitter than poison for me, but I drink this chalice of poison for the Almighty and for His satisfaction" (Khomeini, cited in Moin, 1999, p. 269, bracket is added).

[31] We do not know the exact day of his decease, since the IRI's leaders controlled all public announcements to eschew any political crisis.

[32] For a history of this massacre as a crime against humanity, see Mohajer, 2020.

Seyyed Ali Khamenei, and Ahmad Khomeini[33] who had actively partici-pated in the removal of Ayatollah Hossein Ali Montazeri as Khomeini's heir changed the scenario.

When the 60 members of the Assembly of Experts, the official body to elect the Imam's successor, gathered in 1989, Hashemi Rafsanjani orches-trated a scenario according to which Khomeini had named Khamenei as a potential heir to himself in his personal conversation with him and his son. Cognizant of his feeble religious credentials compared to other eminent faqihs, Khamenei warned the Assembly against his nomination as Khomeini's successor predicting that the Shi'i clergy would not accept his leadership.[34] Finally, when the votes were casted only 14 out of 60 mem-bers of the Assembly voiced against his nomination as the new Supreme jurisprudent (for an official story of the succession, see Jebrayli, 2018).

In August of the same year, Hashemi Rafsanjani was elected as the new president of Republic succeeding Khamenei. Thus, while Khamenei was elected as a contested/contestable Supreme Jurisconsult, Hashemi Rafsanjani was elected as a powerful president.[35] It took 16 years for the new Supreme Leader to isolate the pragmatist and the so-called reformist factions of the government in order to consolidate his power. By 'transi-tion period (1989–2005)', I mean the period during which the status of the Supreme Jurisconsult had to be reconsolidated. Major institutional changes that happened in the meanwhile should be highlighted briefly to clarify the context in which *Anfal* spawned during this transitional period.

The nomination of Khamenei marked a major change: the predomi-nance of 'political' considerations over 'religious' credentials. It was not Khamenei's religious status in the traditional Shi'i hierarchy but rather his

---

[33] Ahmad Khomeini was Khomeini's son who supported Khamenei to succeed his father in order to be part of the leading circle. But he was gradually removed from his positions during the leadership of Khamenei and died on March 16, 1995, at the age of 49 for unclear reasons.

[34] See the video of the Khamenei's speech in the Assembly of Experts in 1989 at *BBC Persian* on June 3, 2020, https://www.bbc.com/persian/iran-52913328

[35] Hashemi Rafsanjani ran for presidency almost uncontested. The Council of Guardians approved only one among eight other candidates running against Rafsanjani. He was Abbas Sheibani, a former agricultural minister, who according to *Reuters*, was merely "a name to fill out the ballot sheet" (Hall, 1989). Maloney described Rafsanjani's victory in these terms: "Rafsanjani moved into the presidency with an ease that belied the factional divisions that had beset Iran for the previous decade. At the outset, his new position appeared an enviable one. Constitutional revisions had strengthened the office, curtailing the parliament's author-ity while empowering the executive branch" (Maloney, 2015, p. 197).

position in the inter-factional political rivalries that decided his ascendancy to the position of Supreme Jurisconsult. The revolution brought the Shi'i clergy to the summit of political power in order to overthrow its traditional hierarchy by the new institutions that were born with its triumph. The seizure of the power by the Shi'i clergy pushed the religious seminaries toward centralization under the ruling faqihs.

Historically, this happened first by the proclamation of Twelver Shi'ism as state religion under the Safavids that made the establishment of state-run religious institutions a necessity. The head of these institutions became the *Sadr*, a function that was already established within the Sunnite Iranian tradition (Floor, 2001). The general question of the legitimacy of political power and the spiritual guidance of the community of believers in the absence of the Twelfth Imam entailed a gradually increasing role for the Ulema, who de facto began to assume the prerogatives of the Hidden Imam. The Ulema has always tried to keep their independence from the state's centralizing effect. *Ijtihad* or independent reasoning among the body of Ulema could survive because of this multiplicity of Shi'i faqihs who were not subjugated to the rationale of a centralized state. Every eminent faqih as a source of emulation also had his own financial autonomy based on the voluntary contributions of his followers.

With the establishment of theocratic state in Iran, the clergy has become completely dependent on the Supreme Jurisconsult for having access to a well-paid job, a political position, or for functioning as a judge (Khalaji, 2011). More importantly, the entitlement to lead the Friday prayers (Stewart, 2001) during the occultation of the Mahdi, the right to collect the religious alms (*Zakat*) and taxes (*Khoms*), which contributed to the financial independence of the Ulema and the right to declare *Jihad* (the holy war) now belong to the Supreme Leader. However, as Brunner aptly noted: "In 1989 a constitutional amendment had been passed on Khomeini's initiative to the effect that the rank of *Marjah Taqlid* [source of emulation] was no longer mandatory for the wali-e faqih [Supreme Jurisconsult] and the rahbar-e enqelāb [Supreme Leader of the revolution] and that the minimal qualification as mojtahed [qualified theologian] is now sufficient (*Qānun-e asāsi-e jomhuri-e eslami-e Irān* [the constitution of the Islamic Republic of Iran], arts. 5, 107, and 109). Thereby, at least in Iran, the clerical hierarchy, that under Khomeini had encompassed the religious and political spheres, again bifurcated. Because of the *Velayat-e Motlaqeh Faqih* [Absolute rule of the jurist], to which allusion is made in the Iranian Constitution (art. 57), the traditionally religious office of Marjah [the source of emulation] is even subjected to politics. Khamenei and the Ulema who support him have repeatedly made it clear that the welāyat-e faqih [jurisprudence of vicegerent] is a God-given institution not dependent on any other form of legitimation, and that the wali-e faqih [jurisconsult of vicegerent] is above the Sharia and even above the constitution" (all brackets are added).

Only obedient faqihs supportive of the Imam can now survive and have followers. The supremacy of politics over religious principles concentrates all power in the hands of Supreme Jurisconsult and the new institutions supporting his authority. One of these new institutions is the Sepah (IRGC) that has been created as a parallel institution to the official army in which the Islamists had no trust. Its formation was a legacy of forceful liquidation of domestic opposition and the war against Iraq. The end of war raised a fundamental issue: How to buy the consent of the Sepah and its para-military force (Basij) in the post-war era to overcome their bitter feelings of being betrayed by the rich Bazaari who made colossal profits from the war economy?

Two important measures were adopted. The new Supreme Leader instituted a formal ranking system into what had been a flat Sepah organization. The introduction of a genuine hierarchy began the process of inculcating the notion of perquisites, privileges, and status for the senior leadership of the Sepah into its institutional culture. This measure was completed by a second when President Hashemi Rafsanjani in the 1992–1993 initiated the idea of involving 'revolutionary organizations' such as the Sepah in business transactions as a way to generate independent income. In this way, the Sepah became a stakeholder in the post-war economic reconstruction (Sazegara, 2006). Khamenei's alliance with the Sepah rather than the traditional Shi'i clergy prepared his ascendancy during the transition period.

The legitimacy of Khamenei's authority was not rooted in popular support or religious credentials. It was based on new Islamic institutions notably two centers of power: (1) a newly dominant group of Ulema serving as judges in the judiciary system or high official authorities in parallel Islamic institutions; (2) the Sepah, the Basij, and their giant economic holdings such as *Khatam*. The second phase of *Anfal* spawned within the context of an extended network of newly created economic institutions belonging to the Supreme Jurisconsult and the Sepah. However, its inception can be traced back to Khomeini's order on establishing a new institution, that is, *Setad* (The Execution of Imam Khomeini's Order-EIKO) shortly before his decease on April 26, 1989.

6.8   *SETAD*: THE EXTENSION OF *ANFAL* AND ESTABLISHMENT OF A NEW GIANT HOLDING

Khomeini's two-paragraph injunction maintained that *Setad* had to manage or sell properties confiscated or "supposedly abandoned during the chaotic years following" the 1979 Islamic Revolution or the eight-year war with Iraq. The order also referred to Article 49 of the constitution regarding the confiscation of all 'illicit' properties. This was an extension of *Anfal* in practice, since the scope of its implementation went beyond the seizure of the late Shah's belongings and 53 big capitalists. The properties that had to be confiscated or managed were composed of:

1. the so-called illicit properties (Article 49) belonging to business people and Iranians living abroad regardless of their cult including Shi'i Muslims and persecuted religious and political minorities such as Bahais.
2. 'ownerless' (or heirless) abandoned assets either because of the 1979 Revolution or the eight-year war.

Again, the confiscated properties (group 1) *were not nationalized,* and the state was not named as the custodian of 'ownerless' assets (group 2). They were all kept independently from the state and the Shi'i traditional hierarchy under the personal tutelage of the Supreme Jurisconsult. Consequently, the transferred assets and income were not handed to the Public Treasury but to *Beit al-Imam* (the Imam's House). The new jurisconsult, Khamenei, was now in possession of *Anfal*'s extended assets embracing both the cumulated assets of *Bonyads* in Khomeini's era and the newly transferred assets to *Setad*. In this sense, *Anfal* is the *institutional* property of the jurisconsult and not his *personal* belonging and cannot be inherited by his heirs. However, the jurisconsult can donate part of *Anfal*'s properties to his family in his lifetime.

Setad prolonged the logic of *Bonyads* in two ways. First, it transformed confiscatory measures into a permanent institution. In 1984, Majlis (the Iranian parliament) created a special category of tribunals in all Iranian provinces devoted to property confiscations, dubbed 'Article 49 courts'.

However, it could not perpetuate its functioning without Khomeini's order of April 1989. Thanks to this injunction, those tribunals continue to operate today (see Stecklow et al., 2013 and Vahabi, 2015a, p. 278). One of the latest rulings of the special court for Article 49 was the confiscation of the Bahai properties in the village of Ivel in Mazandaran province in 2019: "Concerning the appeal of the Execution of Imam [Khomeini's] Orders and Faramarz Rowhani against court order number 98–84, dated 13 Aban 1398 [4 November 2019], issued by the Special Court for Article 49 of the Constitution in the Province of Mazandaran, by virtue of which the residents of Ivel and the Execution of Imam [Khomeini's] Orders ask for a final settlement of the assets left behind without supervision by the locals belonging to the perverse sect of Baha'ism, which comes to about 10 acres and the land of *khaneh sara*, approximately 500 m², and so on, in light of the usual investigation and inquiry, [those assets] were associated with the previous regime and the perished Hoveyda,[36] who moved and settled here with intent to spread the ideologies of this sect, and usurped these lands, and, as indicated in the court order, due to the illegality of the assets left behind by the perverse sect in the Village of Ivel, a decision was issued in favour of the Execution of Imam [Khomeini's] Order to assign the lands to the locals who have small holdings" (see the ruling in Archives of Bahai Persecution in Iran, August 1, 2020, the brackets are added, https://iranbahaipersecution.bic.org/index.php/archive/court-appeal-tehran-special-court-article-49-constitution-confirms-ruling-confiscate-bahai retrieved on November 19, 2021).

Article 49 is the Damocles sword of the IRI that hangs over all property-holders and undesired minority groups labeled as potential 'usurpers'. A six-month *Reuters* investigation, published in three parts on November 11, 12, 13, 2013, has found that "*Setad* built the empire on the systematic seizure of thousands of properties belonging to ordinary Iranians; members of religious minorities like Vahdat-e-Hagh, who is Baha'i, as well as Shi'ite Muslims, business people and Iranians living abroad" (Stecklow et al., 2013).

While strengthening the American sanctions against the IRI created the profitable business of money laundering, converting private businessmen into the middlemen of the regime to evade embargo's multiple obstacles

---

[36] The reference is to Amir Abbas Hoveyda who served as Prime Minister of Iran from January 27, 1965 to August 7, 1977. He was executed by the 'Revolutionary Court' of the IRI on March 15, 1979.

to sell oil, Article 49 became a strong juridical means to control them. This Damocles sword was used by different political factions to have their shares of booties in pillaging public properties. From time to time, rivalry among factions for the lion share resulted in the revelations regarding 'corruption' of big businessmen and their execution. The severity of death sentence was a way to dissimulate political capitalism in action. A victim of this political rivalry was the Iranian businessman Mahafarid Amir Khosravi, also known as Amir Mansour Aria, executed on May 24, 2014 (see Vahabi, 2015a, p. 285). But fortunately, not all victims of factional political rivalries were executed even though their death sentence had been announced. Babak Zanjani is an example of a middleman of the IRI who called himself an 'economic Basij' in the tribunal and was sentenced to death, but his execution was postponed because the judiciary authorities could not allegedly recuperate the stolen money from the Ministry of Petroleum kept abroad.[37]

Moreover, Khomeini's 1989 injunction extended the domain of *Anfal* to the so-called abandoned or ownerless properties (*res nullius*). This was in conformity with Khomeini's (2000, p. 27) definition of *Anfal* that included "barren lands and all ownerless properties including land, sea, and sky (atmosphere)". Concretely speaking, if a property or piece of land has been left behind by someone after his/her death without any heirs or, for example, property that has been freed by customs but remains without an owner, then such types of properties must be managed somehow. If the lack of ownership is confirmed through the order of the court, then the property is given to *Setad*. According to testimonies collected by *Reuters*

---

[37] Babak Zanjani, a businessman that used to help the Ahmadinejad administration to evade sanctions, was later arrested and sentenced to death during the presidency of Hassan Rouhani for embezzlement on March 6, 2016 (*Newsweek*, March 14, 2016). Zanjani was accused of withholding $2.7 billion of government money owned by the Ministry of Petroleum in his accounts abroad. In the court, he called himself the "economic basij" and boasted about his financial contributions to different leading figures. In fact, he was bribing the ruling elite (Dabashi, 2016) and the judiciary system never revealed whether the money was returned to Iran. In his polemics with the judiciary power, President Hassan Rouhani said: "I said this three years ago, if you arrest someone and execute them, it doesn't make things right. We are not after executions, we're after the money. Where is the money?" (*Iran International*, November 13, 2019, https://old.iranintl.com/en/iran/rouhani-judiciary-where-money retrieved on December 3, 2021). Article 49 may or may not be implemented with or without execution depending on whether the leaders had their lion shares (see also Forozan, 2016, pp. 149–150; Erdbrink, 2013 for the role of Zanjani's collaboration with Sepah to evade sanctions).

in 2013, *Setad* has amassed a giant portfolio of real estate by claiming in Iranian courts, sometimes falsely, that the properties are abandoned. The organization now holds a court-ordered monopoly on taking property in the name of the Supreme Jurisconsult, and regularly sells the seized properties at auction or seeks to extract payments from the original owners. Here is one testimony:

"An Iranian Shi'ite Muslim businessman now living abroad…attempted two years ago to sell a piece of land near Tehran that his family had long owned. Local authorities informed him that he needed a "no objection letter" from Setad. The businessman said he visited Setad's local office and was required to pay a bribe of several hundred dollars to the clerks to locate his file and expedite the process. He said he then was told he had to pay a fee, because Setad had "protected" his family's land from squatters for decades. He would be assessed between 2% and 2.5% of the property's value for every year. Setad sent an appraiser to determine the property's current worth. The appraisal came in at $90,000. The protection fee, he said, totaled $50,000… Several other Iranians whose family properties were taken over by Setad described in interviews how men showed up and threatened to use violence if the owners didn't leave the premises at once" (ibid.).

Most of the so-called abandoned or ownerless properties were real estate. In 2013, *Reuters* was able to identify about $95 billion in property and corporate assets controlled by *Setad*. Real estate with $52 billion constituted the bulk of *Setad*'s properties. The organization regularly conducted large auctions of its real estate, at least 59 as of November 2013. In one auction in May 2013, "nearly 300 properties" where for sale, "the required opening bids totaled about $88 million" (Stecklow et al., November 12, 2013). According to the estimation of Rahman Zadeh Heravi (2018, p. 550), the surface of land possessed by *Setad* exceeds the size of *Khaleseh* (land owned by the state) before the revolution.

In expanding its corporate holdings, *Setad* has acquired 37 companies both private and public, covering nearly every sector of Iranian industry including investments in major banks, an insurance company, a brokerage, power plants, energy and construction firms, a refinery, a cement company, soft drinks manufacturing as well as large number of shares in the Iranian largest telecommunications company. The value of its corporate holding amounted to $43 billion in 2013. *Setad* imposed its confiscatory methods to control many businesses in which it held very small stakes. Two illustrations cast light on its strategy.

The first one is Parsian Bank, the largest non-state bank in Iran in 2006. *Setad* bought 16% of its ownership in 2007 and transformed its behavior by pushing for nominating new managers and a new strict dress code (Stecklow et al., November 11, 2013). Another example has been reported by the *Daily Telegraph* of Britain (Mcelroy, May 2, 2013) regarding the rapacity of Rey Investment Co., a subsidiary holding company of *Setad* to become the "sole representative of BMW in Iran".

In an interview with the *Fararu news agency of Iran*, Ali Nouriyani, the managing director of Nouriyani Enterprises, which has served as Iran's exclusive trade partner with Germany's auto and printing industries, revealed that he was pressured to sell his stake in his auto dealership to Khamenei's Shah Abdol Azim charity (Rey Investment Co.) (Ghosh, 2013). As *International Business Times* underlined, the chairman of Rey Investment Co. at the time was Muhammad Reyshahri, a former intelligence minister, that was appointed directly by Khamenei having the power to credibly threat any private business.[38] Setad followed the BMJ in extending *Anfal* through confiscatory measures. They both gave Khamenei financial independence from parliament and the national budget, and thus "insulating him from Iran's messy factional infighting" (Stecklow et al., November 12, 2013).

Setad and BMJ are closely akin in the sense that Setad also is a giant holding functioning as a so-called charitable (non-profit) organization under the direct purview of the Supreme Jurisconsult with no public account, total opacity, and no control by the state or the Iranian parliament. Some general and scattered information about its organizational structure and its activities can be accessed through its official site.[39] Its organigram suggests that it is composed of two foundations:

(1) *Tadbir Economic Development Group* founded in 2000 as the economic group of Setad to "set up an investment management firm". In 2010, it took control of Rey Investment Co, valued by the US Treasury Department at $40 billion at the time (Stecklow et al., November 12, 2013). Now it is a stockholder of many oil and non-oil companies (Nowroozi, 2016), but this has particularly been developed during Ahmadinejad's presidency (2005–2013), that is, the third phase of *Anfal*.

---

[38] Reyshahri reportedly received this plum job as a reward for conspiring to remove Khamenei's rival, Ayatollah Hossein Ali Montazeri, as Khomeini's apparent heir.
[39] See https://en.wikipedia.org/wiki/Execution_of_Imam_Khomeini%27s_Order

(2) *Barakat foundation* created on December 11, 2007, that "has the duty of eliminating poverty and empowering poor communities". It did not exist during the transition period, but it later contributed to promote Setad's penetration in pharmaceutical sector, a sector that like agriculture was less under the American's sanctions and could evade them more easily. Moreover, medical treatment, drugs, hospitals, and health sector in general were and are the most profitable products and services in Iran. Coronavirus has been one of the major sources of income for Barakat foundation. According to the *Tasnim News Agency*, related to the Sepah, Southwest Asia's largest factory producing face masks in Iran was opened by Muhammad Mokhber, director of the Setad in April 2020. "The factory has the capacity to produce 4 million masks per month" (*Tasnim*, April 14, 2017).[40] Moreover, *ISNA News* reported that the production line of 'Corona Immediate Diagnosis Kit' has also been inaugurated by Setad on November 17, 2020.[41]

When Khamenei described vaccines coming from Britain and the United States as "completely untrustworthy" during a televised speech in Tehran on January 8, 2021, many interpreted his intervention as a political reaction to the American's sanctions. Iran's Red Crescent Society confirmed that it had canceled the delivery of 150,000 doses donated and produced by Pfizer after Khamenei's comments (Areeb Ullah, *Middle East Eye*, January 8, 2021[42]). The result of this policy has been disastrous since Iran has struggled to stem the worst virus outbreak in the Middle East. Khamenei's decision on banning the import of American and British vaccines might be better understood from an economic viewpoint if we take on board the fact that Barakat foundation has been promoting its vaccine called *COVIran Barakat* (*Mehr News Agency*, March 15, 2021[43]). The promised Barakat vaccine had to fill up the coffers of Setad and the Supreme Leader had to think about his economic and political interests as the owner of *Anfal*.

To sum up, it can be said that the extension of *Anfal* in the transition period was followed by Khomeini's injunction in 1989 on

[40] See https://www.tasnimnews.com/en/news/2020/04/14/2243571/iran-opens-largest-mask-factory-in-southwest-asia retrieved on December 5, 2021.
[41] https://www.isna.ir/news/98060402209/ retrieved on December 2021.
[42] See https://acquiaprod.middleeasteye.net/news/covid-iran-rejects-pfizer-vaccine--khamenei-ban-uk-us retrieved on December 5, 2021.
[43] See "Iran to kick off production of 3mn doses of COVIRAN", https://en.mehrnews.com/news/171121/Iran-to-kick-off-production-of-3mn-doses-of-COVIRAN

institutionalizing confiscatory measures stipulated in Article 49 and the guardianship of 'ownerless' properties. This resulted in creating a second giant conglomerate, that is, Setad complementary to BMJ. Although Setad like BMJ was legally named a charitable foundation and spread through charitable networks, *Anfal*'s progression in this second phase was strongly enhanced by Islamic banks.

6.9   *ANFAL*'s PROGRESSION IN ITS SECOND PHASE AND ISLAMIC BANKS

The second phase of *Anfal*'s progression was principally through Islamic banks. These banks were the outcome of a transformation of major ex-Islamic loan funds. As Table 6.2 indicated, the number of Islamic loan funds doubled from 2250 in 1987 to 5000 in 2001. This spectacular increase was related to the adoption of a new law authorizing the creation of private banks in March 2000, and the related Article 98 of the Third Five-Year Development Plan.

The 'Money and Credit Council' elaborated the specific measures of establishing private banks on December 10, 2000. The creation of private banks preceded the decree of Khamenei on Article 44 of the constitution in July 2006. It was enacted by the end of the first term of Khatami's presidency. The creation of private banks under Khatami accentuated the rivalry of Islamic loan funds that were acting independently from the ICB to challenge these banks and push for transforming into Islamic banks. Major Islamic loan funds related to *Anfal* (BMJ and Setad), or to the Sepah and the Basij were finally succeeded in transforming officially into Islamic banks. Then, they bought the shares in private banks to dominate the whole banking system. I will try to describe this process below.

It should be first reminded that on the eve of revolution, the total number of state, private, mixed, and foreign banks amounted to 35 with 8300 branches (Rahman Zadeh Heravi, 2018, p. 490). After the revolution, all domestic private banks and insurance companies, except the Islamic Bank (then renamed as the Organization of the Islamic Economics) were nationalized and many of them were fused together. The implementation of Banking Nationalization Act in 1982 had reduced the number of banks to nine (six commercial and three specialized) and the number of branches to 6581 (Kurtis & Hooglund, 2008, p. 195).

With the law on private banks, a few private banks were established, namely Bank Parisan (2002, 160 branches), Bank Karafrin (2001, 52 branches), Bank Saman (2002, 132 branches), Bank Iqtesad Noveen (2001, 680 branches), Bank Pasargad (2005, 296 branches), and Bank Sarmayeh (2005). President Khatami supported most of these banks as a source of new economic dynamic. The Islamic sovereign institutions under the Supreme Leader's control challenged private banks to impede the political influence of the 'reformist' President Khatami in order to enhance the position of the parallel Islamic loan funds. In practice, the latter were not acting only as 'loan funds' but rather as de facto banks accepting checking and saving deposits. However, they were functioning independently from the ICB. More precisely, they had their own central bank, that is, the Organization of the Islamic Economics. These loan funds had to transfer 3–5% of all their deposits to this organization boosting its financial capacity to the point that it could hinder any economic or financial state's policy (Ahmadi Amooei, 2018, p. 37). Moreover, the director of the organization, Mir-Muhammad Sadeghi was strongly opposed to President Khatami and the 'reformist' political faction.

Muhammad Djavad Vahhaji, the vice-President and inspector of monetary and banking institutions of the ICB throughout the eighties described the relationship between Islamic loan funds and the ICB in these terms: "The Central Bank had always a negative assessment about the Islamic loan funds. This assessment was based on the information and documents that have been communicated from all over the country to the Central Bank. Widespread frauds in these funds and Islamic economic institutions prevailed as they were acting beyond their limits. They had started to create money and had given cheque books to some of their members. Furthermore, considering the war conditions and the state's control over the exchange rate, they were able to enter into the official and free currency markets to neutralize the state's policies by using their huge currency reserves" (ibid., pp. 37–38).

It should be highlighted that in 1991, upon the proposal of the Ministry of Interior, the council of ministers and the governor of the ICB decided to cancel the supervision of the Central Bank over the activities of these funds for the reason that these funds were merely doing charities. This legal vacuum provided a golden opportunity for the funds to grow rapidly between 1991 and 2002, and some of them could profit from this situation to spawn fraudulent activities. The scandalous cases have been extensively documented by Ahmadi Amooei (2018, Chap. 5). The pattern of fraud was almost the same in different provinces such as Isfahan, Mashhad, Mazandaran, and Tehran. The funds were acting as banks collecting people's deposits, and promising loans with much lower interest rates than commercial banks. However, in granting loans, people had to be registered in a waiting list according to a calendar. For a couple of months, a fraction of depositors could have their requested loans with low interest. However, the majority of people on the waiting list could never have a loan since the funds were insufficient to cover all the promised loans and after a while, they were declared bankrupt. But why people were so attracted by these funds?

The reason should be sought in the official banking sector's failures in providing credit supply to households and enterprises, the financial insolvency of most of commercial banks due to the state's colossal debts to them. The Islamic loan funds profited from the liquidity shortage and critical banking situation to offer loans with low interest rates. There was no monetary control over their activity while they detained 30% of country's total liquidity (see Naseri, 2006[44]; Ahmadi Amooei, 2018, p. 140).

To put it differently, the ICB had no control over 30% liquidity creation. This caused a revision of the 1991 decision and the adoption of a new law in 2004 on 'Adjusting the non-organized monetary market' according to which the creation and activities of funds had to come under the ICB purview. The implementation of the law required specific instructions that had to wait until 2009 (*Daftar Mot'alat Iqtesadi Markaz Pajoheshhay Majles, the Research Centre of Islamic Legislative Assembly*, April 2008). However, in 2009 under the Presidency of Ahmadinejad who was opposed to the ICB, the control of the latter over these funds was abandoned. Thus, from a legal point of view, Islamic loan funds had never been effectively restrained. After many failed attempts to control them, it became clear that the only possible avenue to come to terms with these funds within the political framework of the IRI was to give them the lion share of 'private' banks. Khatami's power struggle with loan funds confirmed this point.

Confronted with a chain of scandalous frauds in many loan funds, Khatami was persuaded to impose some sort of control over funds'

---

[44] In 2004, the Office of Planning and the Budget Organization of the Khatami government announced that the foundations, along with other quasi-state bodies, controlled more than 35% of the financial flow and business in the country, while the shares of the cooperative and the private sectors accounted for 45.8% and 19.8%, respectively (Naseri, 2006).

activities. This was a very difficult task for him at least for two reasons. First, none of the Iranian presidents could be against the Islamic banking in principle. Loan funds represented an ideologically alternative banking system namely Islamic banking without *Riba* (usury) while maintaining interest rate in the name of Islamic principle of *Mudarabah* (passive partnership in capital investment). Moreover, funds were supported by Khatami's most resolute political opposition, namely the traditional conservative right-wing faction organized around *Mo'talefeh*. In the absence of the ICB's control, the only legal channel to control funds was the Ministry of Interiors. But how could the Ministry control those funds belonging to the same forces that were supposed to enforce law?

A good illustration was Ghavamin funds that belonged to the 'forces of order' (NAJA). As Mazaheri mentioned in his interview with Ahmadi-Amoeei (2018, p. 106), Ghavamin's fraudulent activities were always apparent, since all the money that people had to pay to officials in order to get their passports was deposited in its funds. Since Ghavamin could not be controlled by any means, Khatami had no other way than to establish it as an Islamic bank in 2000. He then channeled smaller funds including bankrupt and fraudulent ones to join it. For example, when the two major funds in Isfahan, namely Al Tay Parvin and Muhammad Rasulullah,[45] went bankrupt and the economic consequences of their scandalous activities grew to a political and security issue, it was negotiated that Ghavamin funds could undertake these smaller funds in return for the ICB's recognition of its conversion into an Islamic Bank (Ibid, p. 98).

The story of Ghavamin holds true for all the powerful loan funds. These included the Mehr Credit and Finance Institution, affiliated with the Basij

---

[45] The founders of these two funds were composed of a religious circle studying Koran. The funds started in Isfahan in 2000 with 500,000 depositors from Isfahan and outside of it. Any depositor was eligible to receive a loan twice its deposited amount after four months with 4% interest rate while banks were offering 16% interest rate for granting loans. The depositors had to be registered on a waiting list and be served in turn. A group of economic professors at the University of Isfahan prepared a report about these two funds in which they clearly demonstrated the inflationary impact of their activities and provided many details concerning the deposits. In fact, half of the depositors had deposited very small amounts, almost less than 2 million tomans while few of them had deposited high amounts, more than 450 million tomans. They were all hoping to receive loans, but only one-third of them could receive promised loans. To give the exact figures for Al Tay Parvin, 80,000 people over 230,000 members were granted loans. The same ration held for Muhammad Rasulullah. Two-thirds of depositors lost their deposits while a third of them were served (cited by Ahmadi Amooei, 2018, pp. 95–96).

Cooperative Foundation; the Sina Credit and Finance Institution, affili-
ated with the BMJ; and the Ansar and the Samen al-a'em-e Credit and
Finance Institutions, affiliated with the Sepah Cooperative Foundation
(Forozan, 2016, p. 155). Ebrahim Sheibani,[46] the 16th governor of the
ICB (2003–2007), explained the crux of the problem with strong funds:
"I would like to draw your attention to a fact and few figures. Loan funds
of Basijian has 463 branches, loan funds of Ansar al-Mujahideen has 200
branches, loan funds of Tavoon has 144 branches, loan funds of Ghavamin
has 100 branches, and loan funds of Ali Ibn Abi Talib has 59 branches. We
have no problem with small loan funds of mosques; they obey us [ICB].
The truth of the matter is that we have problems with those that we cannot control them...The big funds do not want to come under the ICB
purview, since the ICB give orders and if it sees their activities are fraudu-
lous, it will close them. The problem is that funds do not wish to lose their
ruling position. 463 branches mean a bank. The forces of order, who is
supposed to be our protector, has its own loan funds, i.e., Ghavamin with
100 branches" (Ibid, pp. 128–129, bracket is added).

Two other important cases are *Ansar* and *Mehr*. They came under the
purview of the ICB as part of a deal with the commander of the Sepah in
return for their transformation into banks (*Sarmayeh* December 30,
2007). It is noteworthy that the Mehr Credit and Finance Institution has
more than 700 branches across Iran. One of the Mehr's subsidiaries is the
Mehr-e Eqtesad-e Iranian Investment Company, which has been the top-
ranking winner of significant shares on the Iranian Stock Exchange following the privatization initiative in July 2006.[47] These two institutions
obtained the ICB's authorization to become banks following the approval
of the Money and Credit Council (Omidvar, 2009).

As mentioned earlier, BMJ was the birthplace of the first Islamic Bank.
However, Islamic banks could not develop in the first phase of *Anfal*.

---

[46] He also held the longest tenure (19 years) as a member of the board of governors in
ICB's history. Before his appointment as the governor, he was the deputy of economic affairs
and the secretary general of the ICB from 1989 to 2003. In 2007, Sheibani resigned due to
conflicts with President Ahmadinejad over economic policies.

[47] Mehr-e Eqtesad-e Iranian Company invested more than US$1.5 billion in the stock
market and owned, partially or entirely, shares in major companies. These include Mobarak-e
Steel, Zinc Mines Development Company, Parsian Bank, Sadra, Alborz Insurance, Iran
Telecommunication, Tabriz Tractor Company and Iralkow (Bahadori, 2010). The ease with
which these shares have been acquired was a subject of many complaints, particularly that of
Tabriz Tractor deal (see Forozan, 2016, pp. 156–157).

They penetrated and dominated the banking system in the second phase of *Anfal* with the help of BMJ, Setad, the Sepah, the Basij and other sovereign economic institutions. In fact, the law on private banking in 2000 benefited primarily these institutions. The banking system can be compared to blood vessels and the progression of *Anfal* during the transition period (1989–2005) was carried out through these vessels, notably by loan funds, Islamic banks, and Islamic financial institutions.

6.10   ALLIANCE OF *ANFAL* AND SEPAH

It is now a well-known fact that the Sepah (IRGC) has large stakes in the Iranian economy covering a vast range of investments from constructing dams and roads to exploiting oil, gas, and running banks and financial institutions. It is also commonly known that the Sepah is considered as 'revolutionary army' in parallel to an official army (*Artesh*) that plays a secondary role and has not the same privileges in the Iranian economy. The Sepah and its diverse giant financial and economic holdings are part of the Islamic sovereign institutions that are exempt of public accountability and public control. They only report to the Supreme Jurisconsult and run a shadow economy for the so-called security reasons in total opacity to evade sanctions (Wehrey et al., 2009; Vahabi, 2010, 2015b, 2018a, 2018b; Forozan, 2016). There are two points that are missing or treated tangentially in the economic and political literature on the Sepah: (1) what are the specific mechanisms of profit-making or the type of capitalism promoted by the Sepah? (2) what is the relationship between the Sepah's involvement in the economy and *Anfal*'s economic institutions such as BMJ and Setad. This section will focus on these two points.

Generally speaking, the existing literature on the political economy of the IRI conflates *Khatam* (Sepah's biggest economic and financial conglomerate) and major religious foundations such as BMJ and Setad as if they are one and the same thing. For example, the *Guardian* reports: "Now, in a reflection of the regime's continuing evolution, the IRGC (Islamic Revolutionary Guard Corps- i.e., Sepah) is the dominant force, particularly through Bonyad Mostazafan, the Foundation of the Oppressed" (Borger and Tait, 2010). The authors assume that (1) the Sepah is the dominant force; (2) the BMJ (the Foundation for the downtrodden) is a channel of the Sepah's economic undertakings.

Similarly, Wehry et al. (2009, p. 57) averred: "Two important bonyads, which are not directly controlled by the IRGC but are indirectly influenced by it, are the Bonyad Mostazafan (Foundation of the Oppressed or The Mostazafan Foundation) and the Bonyad Shahid va Omur-e Janbazan (Foundation of Martyrs and Veterans Affairs)." In this passage, the authors also claim that the Sepah is more powerful economically than Bonyads, and the latter are influenced by the Sepah.[48] The question is that whether the economic institutions related to *Anfal* and Sepah share the same rationale?

If we follow the arguments in Chap. 5 on *Anfal* and its comparatively different significance in the Sunni and Shi'i jurisprudence, the response would be negative. In the Shi'i Islam, *Anfal* constitutes the bulk of public finance whereas in the Sunni Islam, it has only a marginal place. For the latter, the scope of *Anfal* is narrowed down to *Fai*, that is, properties of the unbelievers surrendered to the Muslims without war. But if spoils of war are captured through violence and warfare, then the Imam owns only *Khoms* (one-fifth) of the booties and the rest belongs to warriors. Accordingly, in the Sunni Islam, the bulk of public finance is tribute (*Kharaj*) rather than *Anfal*. The Prophet is supposed to be 'pacificator' to appropriate *Fai*, otherwise warriors would have a higher share of booties. The post-Prophet Islamic empire developed on the basis of *Kharaj* and *Anfal* played a derisory role. This was in tune with the requirements of a 'territorial empire' (Mann, 1986, p. 142; Vahabi, 2004, p. 107) in which the military conquest is institutionalized, and the prophet assumes the role of pacificator and protector. By contrast, the 'early empire of domination' was based on military influence without sufficient economic and politically integrative power. In the latter case, the ruler had to act as a warrior or 'armed Prophet'. This corresponded to the period when the Prophet, residing in Medina, launched a war of conquest against Mecca.

Contrary to the Sunni Islam, the Shi'i faqihs were often in 'opposition' and not in power. Except during the Safavid dynasty, they were not generally concerned about the expansion of a territorial empire. In their opposition to 'usurpers' and 'tyrants', Shi'i faqihs emphasized on the share of *Anfal* and extended its scope to all 'ownerless' resources (*res nullius*)

---

[48] Other sources implicitly conflate these two types of sovereign economic institutions, for example: "Other than its own cooperatives and firms, the Sepah and the Basij continued to amass economic dividends through their informal links with other revolutionary and governmental institutions, such as the Foundation of the Oppressed and the Ministry of Defence and Armed Forces Logistics, both headed by former members of the Sepah" (Forozan, 2016, p. 144).

belonging to the Imam or the Supreme Jurisconsult. The contesting Imam in the Shi'i Islam had to be an 'armed prophet'.

In the IRI, *Anfal* is assumed to be the principal source of public properties. Bonyad and Setad represent *Anfal*, but the Sepah's economic undertakings are not part of *Anfal* although they need the Supreme Leader's authorization to enjoy their assets and income. The rationale of Sepah's properties is tribute (*Kharaj*). In the present institutional set up of the IRI, *tribute* granted to the Sepah is complementary to *Anfal* which constitutes the bulk of public finance. This is what I call 'coalition' entailing an increasing share of both *Anfal* and *Kharaj* at the expense of diminishing share of the formal state. However, the competition between *Anfal* and *Kharaj* might accentuate when available resources for public treasury are restrained.

In such situations, two options are theoretically conceivable: (1) maintaining the primacy of *Anfal* over *Kharaj* and reducing the share of *Sepah* and *Basij*; (2) imposing the primacy of *Kharaj* over *Anfal* and 'nationalizing' the share of *Anfal*.

The first option is less probable in politically unstable situations, since the IRI depends more and more on its repressive forces. Furthermore, the expansion of the IRI's regional influence also empowers the Sepah both politically and economically. However, this expansion has been a source of division inside the Sepah. The extraterritorial branch, the *Quds* force of the Sepah under the late General Qasem Soleimani[49] has gained a special status in the whole structure of the *Sepah*. According to a confidential conversation among the leaders of the Sepah, revealed by *Radio Farda* on February 10, 2022,[50] the Supreme Leader had ordered to give 90% of the Sepah's budget to the *Quds* force.

The internal tensions among different leaders of the Sepah are numerous and often related to their share of the economic booties. The *Quds* force has a considerable share and is extensively involved in corruption. The same document exposed several cases of corruption at a large scale

[49] From 1998 until his assassination in 2020, Qasem Soleimani was the commander of the *Quds Force*, an IRGC division primarily responsible for extraterritorial and clandestine military operations. In his later years, he was considered by some analysts to be the right-hand man of the Supreme Leader of Iran, Ali Khamenei, as well as the second-most powerful person in Iran behind him.

[50] See Radio Farda, February 10, 2022, https://www.radiofarda.com/a/leaked-tape-unveiling-corruption-in-highest-level-of-irgc/31697618.html retrieved on February 17, 2022.

involving billion of dollars with the high-rank officers of the Sepah as beneficiaries. Among them, the tape names the triumvirate of the late Qasem
Soleimani, Hossein Taeb,[51] and Muhammad Bagher Ghalibaf.[52] Not only
the Supreme Leader and his son, Mojtaba Khamenei, and the Beit al-
Imam (the Imam's House or staff) are informed about the corruption,
but they also profit from the internal divisions of the Sepah to control the
Sepah. However, the reliance of the Supreme Leader on the repressive
forces makes him particularly vigilant not to reduce the size of economic
booties for the Sepah and the Basij. Hence, the second option is not probable either, unless a unified leadership inside the Sepah could challenge the
ultimate authority of the Supreme Leader in the future.

This option is in line with what happened to the Sunni Islam during the
rise of Islamic territorial empire. Maintaining an Islamic empire warranted
a fundamental restructuring of public finance by narrowing the size of
Anfal. The Shi'i Islam might experience the same trajectory as the Sunni
in the future if it wins an established regional hegemony with a unified
leadership in the Sepah. To put it differently, the coalition of *Anfal* and
the Sepah will become particularly fragile and unstable in the presence of
political stability or a regionally 'peaceful' situation.

The divergence of *Anfal* and *Kharaj* notwithstanding, what are the
commonalities between them? Basically, they both hinge upon *a specific
variant of 'political capitalism' (or 'capitalism with a political orientation')
flourishing in the context of political crisis*. My thesis is that political stability, and the end of parallel institutions undermine the alliance between
Anfal and the Sepah. The Sepah's comparative advantages in profit-making
through non-market means in the second phase of *Anfal* are as follows:

(1) *The economic privileges of the Sepah as a revolutionary force.* The
political and economic privileges of the Sepah compared to the
official Iranian Army (*Artesh*) are justified on the basis of its mission

---

[51] He is an Iranian Shi'i cleric and senior Islamic Revolutionary Guard Corps official who
is currently the head of the IRGC's Intelligence Organization

[52] He is an Iranian 'fundamentalist' and former military officer who held office as the
Mayor of Tehran from 2005 to 2017. Ghalibaf was formerly Iran's Chief of police from 2000
to 2005 and commander of the Revolutionary Guards' Air Force from 1997 to 2000. He
announced his run for a third time in the 2017 election. However, he withdrew on May 15,
2017, in favor of Ebrahim Raisi's candidacy. In the 2020 Iranian legislative election, the
'Osolgrayan' (Principlists) regained the majority in the legislature, and Ghalibaf was elected
as the new Speaker of Iran Parliament.

to save the 'ideals of the revolution' and to keep contact with popular forces such as *Basij* (see the interview of the deputy commander of the *Khatam* headquarter, Abdul Reza Abedzadeh with the *Sharq* newspaper, Zandi, 2006). According to the President Hashemi Rafsanjani, the Sepah's contribution to the economy was enshrined in Article 147 of the constitution because of its emphases on 'Construction Jihad'[53] and 'Islamic justice': "Article 147. In time of peace, the government must utilize the personnel and technical equipment of the Army in relief operations, and for educational and productive ends, and the Construction Jihad, while fully observing the criteria of Islamic justice and ensuring that such utilization does not harm the combat-readiness of the Army" (PURL: https://www.legal-tools.org/doc/4205c7/).   Hashemi Rafsanjani's policy consisted of engaging the Sepah in economic activities so that it becomes a partner in the post-war economic reconstruction. This was also helpful in cutting the defense budget and reducing subsidies, because the Sepah and the Basij could maintain and even augment their budgets through non-military national reconstruction projects. They were granted priority in having state contracts for infrastructure reconstruction particularly in constructing dams and roads.

As I suggested previously (Vahabi, 2015b, 2018b), the Sepah's engagement in economic activities can be periodized in two phases: (1) 1989–2005; (2) 2005–2013. The first phase covers the presidential terms of Hashemi Rafsanjani and Khatami, and the second phase includes the two terms of Ahmadinejad's presidency. Whereas in the first phase, the Sepah was mainly active in the construction of dams and roads, since Ahmadinejad's election it has conducted large-scale industrial projects in oil and gas, thereby gaining an upper hand in an industry once dominated by foreign companies and a joint consortium of Iranian and foreign partners (*Sarmayeh,* October 25, 2007). We will explore the second phase in the next section.

---

[53] The Construction Jihad was established in the aftermath of the revolution as an Islamic 'revolutionary' institution to extend the regime's authority in the countryside by contributing to rural development particularly in building infrastructure. It also collaborated with the Sepah on land seizures and gradually acted as the IRGS's de facto 'corps of engineers' with regard to military operations during the eight-year war. It finally became subordinate to the Sepah (see Maloney, 2015, p. 305 and Katzman, 1993, p. 41).

During the first phase, the Sepah and the Basij followed two major objectives. First, they created the armed forces' cooperative foundations, including the Cooperative Foundation of the Sepah (*Bonyad Taavon-e Sepah*) in 1986 and the Cooperative Foundation of the Basij (*Bonyad Taavon-e Basij*). The two cooperative foundations were established to serve the economic and housing needs of their personnel. They also provided job opportunities for their veterans. Second, the Sepah's engineering firm, *Khatam*, established in 1990, undertook a sizable number of developmental and industrial projects. It appropriated the lion share of the state contracts at national and municipal levels for reconstruction. Its total personnel were 55,000 in 2004–2005, among them 40,000 from the Sepah and 15,000 from the Basij. The total amount of Sepah's income before Ahmadinejad's presidency has been estimated at $12 billions (Vahabi, 2015b).

It was during the Khatami presidency that the Sepah's economic activities started to flourish. As Hassan-Yari (2005) reported, Khatami paid tribute to the Sepah in his meeting with Sepah commanders in March 2000 for defending Iran and protecting the country's reconstruction plan. In 2003, "the Khatami administration increased the annual budget of revolutionary organisations by 14%. According to the estimate reported by the Office of Planning and the Budget in the Majles, of the 22 trillion rial allotted to the revolutionary organisations, 20 trillion belonged to the General Headquarters of the Sepah [*Khatam*] and the *Artesh* (*BBC Persian*, 24 July 2004)" (cited in Forozan, 2016, p. 145, the bracket is added).

Although Khatami supported the economic engagement of the Sepah, he was concerned about its exemption from the official state's oversight. As a 'revolutionary institution', the Sepah was an independent body under the Supreme Jurisconsult's purview. So, Khatami tried to impose a sort of financial oversight on the Sepah by subjecting it to government taxation. In line with the president, the sixth Majles dominated by the so-called reformist faction could revoke tax exemptions for the Sepah and the Basij. However, the government could never enforce this law, and its requirement was totally dismissed by allocating ever-increasing budget to these institutions. Finally, the seventh Majles with a Fundamentalist majority revised all the decisions of the preceding Majles.

(2) *National security and the Sepah's economic privileges.* As mentioned earlier, Khamenei used the Sepah to consolidate its power as the

new Supreme Leader by marginalizing pragmatists and 'reformists'. In return, the Sepah and the Basij were compensated by a
high share of economic contracts exclusively granted to them in all
economic sectors. This exchange was carried out in the name of
'national security'.

The primacy of 'national security' in economic transactions was first
manifested in closing the Imam Khomeini Airport by the Sepah one day
after its inauguration in the presence of President Khatami on May 8,
2004. The Sepah occupied the airport through its tanks, armories, and Air
Force claiming that the Turkish company, Tepe-Akfen-Vie (TAV) that had
the construction contract of the airport had close ties with Israeli companies in various arenas, including the military industry. The Sepah's claim
was allegedly supported by a communique issued by the *Markaz
Pajoheshhay Majles, the Research Centre of Islamic Legislative Assembly* a
day after the conclusion of the deal with the Turkish company (Farahmand,
September 21, 2004). The Sepah announced that it would prevent the
landing of aeroplanes should the TAV deal were not annulled.

Following the Sepah's intervention, the seventh Majles with its
Fundamentalist majority forced the impeachment of Khatami's
Transportation Minister Ahmad Khoram, hastening the impotency of the
Khatami administration (*BBC Persian*, October 30, 2004). The new
Fundamentalist Majles concomitantly passed a twin bill opposing the gov-
ernment's allocation of telecommunication and aviation contracts to two
Turkish consortia, TAV and Turkcell. The bill required the government to
seek the Majles' approval before contracts could be delegated to foreign
companies in the telecommunications and aviation industries (Farahmand,
September 21, 2004). Accordingly, the TAV contract was canceled, and
the government had to pay a heavy fine to the Turkish company.

Although the Sepah justified its military intervention in the name of
'national security', the evidence clearly indicates that economic drive was
the main reason. Many authors have underlined that one of the major
motives was that *Khatam* had lost the bid on the airport contract to the
Turkish company (Wehrey et al., 2009, p. 74; Ehteshami, 2010, p. 32).
Moreover, "according to Minister of Transportation Ahmad Khoram,
prior to the airport fiasco the Sepah had demanded the handover of 2000
hectares of the airport's lands for the establishment of a Sepah airfield. The
Sepah's demands, nonetheless, were rejected by the Ministry of
Transportation on the grounds that they did not correspond with

international conventions on the separation of military and civilian airports (*Aftabnews* 2 July 2012)" (cited by Forozan, 2016, p. 146).

This experience gave a lesson to all official state authorities that in dealing with the Sepah, the 'no bid contract' should be the rule since the presence of *Khatam* as a bidder entails the *securitization* of the commercial contact. The examples abound. Zandi (2006), Wehry et al. (2009, p. 62–63) and Forozan (2016, pp. 148–150) cite several illustrations of no-bid contracts, among them the Asaluy-e to Sistan and Baluchestan pipeline and the South Pars oilfields. In these cases, Abdul Reza Abedzadeh conceded that *Khatam* was offered government contracts without engaging in a formal bidding process. He justified it by claiming that the government had taken cognizance of the quality of the Sepah's job and was willing to reward the contract without bidding (*Sharq*, August 13, 2006).

(3) *Shadow economy and the Sepah.* The role of the Sepah in running a shadow economy has been underlined by many politicians and journalists. Mehdi Karrubi, speaker of the sixth Majles during President Khatami, implicitly suggested that the Sepah was operating sixty illegal jetties in Iran without government's permission. Another parliamentarian in the same Majles, Ali Ghanbari, also indirectly accused the Sepah of delivering one-third of the imported good through underground economy and illicit jetties (Sazegara, 2006). The *Guardian* has also reported that: "The IRGC's control over a string of jetties along the Gulf coast, as well as terminals in Iranian airports, allows it to move commodities in and out without paying any duty" (Borger and Tait, 2010).

Black market activities are organized in multitude ways. One avenue has been the exportation of state subsidized gasoline outside the country through facilities such as the Martyr Rajai Port Complex in Hormuzgan province (Wehrey et al., 2009, p. 65). Others are the distribution of banned commodities in Iran, including alcoholic beverages and narcotic at a large-scale lending credence to the allegations of the Sepah's involvement in illegal smuggling activities. According to the *Economist* (August 27, 2009), the net value of the Sepah's alleged engagement in smuggling of goods such as alcohol, cigarettes, and satellite dishes has been estimated $12 billion a year on the black market.

In sum, the economic involvement of the Sepah during the second phase of *Anfal* (1989–2005) entails three forms of profit-making based on non-market means, namely 'revolutionary and populist' credentials, the exploitation of the mantle of 'national security', and the organization of a shadow economy of illicit jetties with 'free zone' trades and black markets of banned goods. This is a specific political capitalism closely related to the rise of political Islam in the context of political crisis. The coalition of the Sepah and *Anfal* promotes a strand of *Islamic political capitalism that feeds on political crisis.*

The symbiotic relationship between BMJ, Setad and Khatam has been emphasized by almost all authors in the field. One illustrative example is the sale of the 51% of shares of Iran Telecommunication, worth US$8 billion, to the Etemad-e Mobin consortium that has been dubbed as the biggest deal in the history of the Iranian stock market. The consortium was composed of three companies, two of which, the Mobin Electronic Development Company and Shahriar-e Mahestan, were subsidiaries of the Sepah Tavoon Foundation; the third company, the Etemad Development Company, was affiliated with *Setad* (*Etemaad*, September 28, 2009).

In the same vein, BMJ also became a partner of this big contract through the Sepah: "In an action which further testified to the Sepah's link with the Foundation of the Oppressed [*BMJ*], the consortium reached out to the Sina Bank, a subsidiary of the Foundation of the Oppressed [*BMJ*], for prepayment of 20% of the deposit required for the transfer of the Iran Telecommunication shares. In exchange, the Sina Bank was given ownership of 5% of the Iran Telecommunication shares as a new member in the consortium (2009). Not only did the Sepah protect its economic dividends in the face of parliamentary pressures, but it also managed to reward the foundation, its extended client. The incident was another indicator of the power of the state bourgeoisie in the business sphere" (Forozan, 2016, p. 158).

The Sepah, BMJ, and Setad are not 'state bourgeoisie'; they constitute oligarchic power of parallel institutions that grow at the expense of the formal state's properties including Iran Telecommunication which belonged to the state sector before being 'privatized'.

In light of the empirical evidence on Islamic political capitalism, I suggest distinguishing between two types of political capitalism: one which spawns in a war economy or under political crisis, and the other growing in peacetime or under political stability. Booty capitalism (Weber, 1922/1978; Vahabi, 2004, 2015a) and political Islam are variants of the former.

Borrowing the medical terminology regarding the rapidity of progression of cancerous cells or its 'Grade', we can conclude that the coalition of the Sepah and *Anfal* in the second phase of *Anfal*'s progression was high.

To sum up the second phase of *Anfal*, Table 6.3 recapitulates *Anfal*'s juridical status, its domain, its progression channel, and the rapidity of its progression (Grade) due to the coalitional alliance. The first phase of *Anfal* is also incorporated in the table so that the two phases can be compared.

According to Article 49 of the IRI constitution, *Anfal* was juridically the source of a confiscatory regime against 'illicit' properties in general. Khomeini's injunction in April 1989 regarding the guardianship of the

Table 6.3   First and second phase of *Anfal*

Phase of Anfal	Supreme Jurisconsult	Source of legitimacy	Juridical status	Domain of Anfal	Channel of progression	Rapidity of progression
First phase: 1979-1989	Ruhollah Khomeini	Charismatic leader of revolution: Political and religious	Article 45: Inseparability of Anfal from the state property (unity thesis)	Confiscation of the late Shah's properties and 53 industrialists and financiers	BMJ, Islamic charities for social protection, and coalitionary political alliance with Sepah, Basij, etc.	Low
Second phase: 1989-2005	Seyyed Ali Khamenei	New parallel Islamic institutions: Political but not religious	Article 49 and Khomeini's injunction in April 1989	Universal confiscatory regime and guardianship of 'ownerless' properties	BMJ, Setad, Islamic charities, Islamic banks, and coalitionary political and economic alliance with Sepah, Basij, etc.	High

Source: the author

Supreme Jurisconsult over 'ownerless' properties extended *Anfal* further and led to the creation of a second giant holding, that is, *Setad*.

The main progression channel in the second phase was Islamic loan funds that were transformed into Islamic banks and Islamic financial institutions. The rapidity of progression was high, thanks to *Anfal*'s coalitional political and *economic* alliance with Sepah's conglomerates, *Khatam*.

6.11 CONCLUSION

In this chapter, we explored the first two phases of *Anfal* under Ruhollah Khomeini (1979–1989) and then during his successor time, Seyyed Ali Khamenei (1989–2005). Since *Anfal* is the specific property of the Imam, and in his absence, that of *Vali Faqih* (the Supreme Jurisconsult), the sources of jurisconsult's legitimacy are particularly important.

When Khomeini (1970/1981) wrote his book on *Velayat faqih* (the jurisconsult of the vicegerent), he imagined a Shi'i faqih in power overthrowing the 'usurping tyrant'. The religious ruler had to combine two types of qualifications, religious and political. Opposing the Shah's reforms in the sixties regarding land reform, women's suffrage, and the state's control over Waqf, Khomeini lacked religious credentials because he was not yet a source of emulation (*Marjah Taqlid*). However, the eminent faqihs of the time granted him the title so that he could safely emigrate to Iraq. In 1979, he appeared as the charismatic leader of the Islamic revolution in Iran, and the only political figure that could carry the mantle of *Vali faqih* satisfying both the traditional Shi'i criteria and political exigencies.

But a question had to be answered once a faqih could seize power: between Islamic orthodoxy and raison d'état, which one should have the primacy in governing? Khomeini's advocacy of *Velayat-e motlaqeh-ye faqih* (the absolute rule of the jurist), enshrined in Article 57[54] of the constitution, provided a clear response to this question in 1988. In his doctrine, the existence of the Islamic state was so crucial for the survival of Islam

---

[54] "Article 57. The powers of government in the Islamic Republic are vested in the legislature, the judiciary, and the executive powers, functioning under the supervision of the absolute wilayat al-'amr and the leadership of the Ummah, in accordance with the forthcoming articles of this Constitution. These powers are independent of each other." https://www.iranchamber.com/government/laws/constitution_ch05.php#:~:text=Article%2057%20The%20powers%20of%20government%20in%20the,Constitution.%20These%20powers%20are%20independent%20of%20each%20other, retrieved on December 20, 2021.

that if the 'expediencies' of ruling (*maslahat nezam*) required contravention of Islamic norms, the latter had to be suspended on Islamic grounds (Schirazi, 1997; Fujinaga, 2018). Consequently, the jurisconsult should not necessarily be among the sources of emulation; he could be only a *Mujtahid* but politically qualified to run the Islamic state. The expediency issue was particularly important to set the stage for the succession of Khamenei as the new Supreme Leader, since the political and religious exigencies bifurcated in his case. Khamenei's source of legitimacy was political and not religious.

The concept of 'expediency' (*maslahat*) was historically emerged during the Sunni Khalifate. The concept has been interpreted in a host of ways by jurists with two extremely opposite positions. On the one extreme, more prudent faqihs authorized the primacy of state exigencies when scripture was silent. On the other extreme was Khomeini's position that resulted in the creation of 'Expediency Discernment council of the System' (Majma'-e Tashkhis-e Maslahat-e Nezam). While the 'Council of Guardians' could curtail the authority of the Majles (Iranian parliament) by screening and rejecting 'un-Islamic laws', the Expediency council had the discretionary power to veto its decision by referring to the expediency of the Islamic state.

The expediency measure entails contradictory implications: "On the one hand, it gives potentially limitless discretion to unelected authoritative interpreters of Islam (Leader, Guardian Council, Expediency Council), and as such is yet another tool strengthening these unelected, hence non-democratic, institutions. On the other, it provides an instant 'workaround' for inconvenient scriptural commandments, which means that if the people demand reforms which are deemed un-Islamic, the government has the power to accommodate them" (Fujinaga, 2018, p. 612). While it is theoretically conceivable that the unelected institutions comply with popular demands because of the system's expediency, in practice this is impossible unless the Supreme Leader approves them. Thus, expediency consideration is a pro-leader force, and hence democratically deficient.

Expediency principle has also been applied in *Anfal*'s case. While in the Shi'i jurisprudence, *Anfal* as the exclusive property of the jurisconsult must be distinguished from public properties of all Muslims, it was conflated with *state* sector in the first phase (1979–1989) because of political expediency. The same expediency measure warranted the conflation of *Anfal* with *private* sector in its third phase (2005–now). This will be shown in the next chapter. *Anfal* in practice does not come within the scope of statism or liberalism. It is part of Islamic predatory economics contributing to the enhancement of Islamic political capitalism.

From confiscating the late Shah's properties and his close associates to the establishment of a universal confiscatory regime embracing all 'owner-less' properties, *Anfal* resulted in the creation of giant holdings such as BMJ and Setad preying on state's assets. Like cancer that spreads through lymph and blood circulation, *Anfal*'s progression became possible through Islamic charities in social protection and Islamic banks. The speed of progression was particularly increased in the second phase of *Anfal* (1989–2005) by a coalition with the Sepah once the latter actively inter-fered in the Iranian economy through its giant conglomerates such as Khatam. This transitional period strengthened politically and economi-cally the new Leader and paved the path for the 2006 privatization edict.

REFERENCES

Abazari, Y., & Zakeri, A. (2019, February 24). Three Decades of Coexistence of Religion and Neoliberalism in Iran. *Critique of Political Economy* (in Persian).

Abrahamian, E. (2008). *A History of Modern Iran*. Cambridge University Press.

Abrahamian, E. (2009, Spring). Why the Islamic Republic Has Survived. *Middle East Report, 250,* 10–16.

Ahmadi Amooei, B. (2018). *Iqtesad siasi sandooqhay qarz al-hasaneh va mossasat etebari, sooghoot yek ideology (The Political Economy of the Islamic Charitable Funds and Financial Institutions, the Demise of an Ideology)*. Ketab Parseh. (in Persian).

Amuzegar, J. (1993). *Iran's Economy under the Islamic Republic*. Tauris.

Bahadori, F. (2010, January 5). *Modir 'Amel-e Mo'aseseye Mali va E'tebari-ye Mehr Taqir kard* (The Director of the Mehr Credit and Finance Institute was changed), Donya-e Eqtesad. Retrieved December 11, 2021, from www.donya-e-eqtesad.com/news/590033/ (in Persian).

Behdad, S. (2006). Islam, Revivalism, and Public Policy. In S. Behdad & F. Nomani (Eds.), *Islam and the Everyday World: Public Policy Dilemmas* (pp. 1–37). Routledge.

Borger, J., & Tait, R. (2010). The Financial Power of the Revolutionary Guards. www.guardian.co.uk/world/2010/feb/15/financial-power-revolutionary-guard; retrieved 11 August 2022.

Caldicott, H. (2002). *The Nuclear Danger, George W. Bush's Military-Industrial Complex*. The New Press.

Coase, R. (1960, October). The Problem of Social Cost. *The Journal of Law and Economics, III,* 1–44.

Coville, T. (2002). *L'Economie de l'Iran Islamique: Entre ordre et désordres*. L'Harmattan.

Dabashi, H. (2016, March 10). Babak Zanjani and the Complicity of Iran. Aljazeera.   https://www.aljazeera.com/opinions/2016/3/10/babak-zanjani-and-the-complicity-of-iran/

Ehsani, K. (2013). The Politics of Property in the Islamic Republic of Iran. In S. Amir Arjomand & N. Brown (Eds.), *The Rule of Law, Islam, and Constitutional Politics in Egypt and Iran* (pp. 153–178). SUNY Press., Chapter 5.

Ehteshami, A. (2010). *Dynamics of Power in Contemporary Iran*. Emirates Centre for Strategic Studies and Research.

Encyclopedia Iranica. (1987). "Bonyad Chahid," Costa Mesa, Mazda, pp. 360–361.

Erdbrink, T. (2013, October 4). To This Tycoon, Iran's Sanctions Were Like Gold. *The New York Times*. Retrieved December 10, 2010, from https://www.nytimes.com/2013/10/05/world/middleeast/to-this-tycoon-iran-sanctions-are-like-gold.html.

Farahmand, M. (2004, September 21). "*Monaghesheh-ye Majles va Dowlat-e Iran bar sar-e dow sherkat-e torkiyeh-ie* (The Quarrel between the Majles and the Government Regarding Two Turkish Companies). *BBC. Persian*. Retrieved December 13, 2021, from www.bbc.co.uk/persian/business/story/2004/09/040921_mf_turkcell.shtml. (in Persian).

Floor, W. (2001). *Safavid Government Institutions*. Mazda Publishers.

Forozan, H. (2016). *The Military in Post-Revolutionary Iran, the Evolution and Roles of the Revolutionary Guards*. Routledge.

Fujinaga, A. F. (2018). Islamic Law in Post-Revolutionary Iran. In A. M. Emon & A. Rumee (Eds.), *The Oxford Handbook of Islamic Law*. Oxford University Press.

Galbraith, J. K. (2004). *The Economics of Innocent Fraud, Truth for Our Time*. Houghton Mifflin Company.

Ghosh, P. (2013, May 5). Iran's Supreme Leader Ayatollah Khamenei...A Multi-Billionaire and BMW Car Dealer? *International Business Times*. Retrieved December 5, 2021, from https://www.ibtimes.com/irans-supreme-leader-ayatollah-khamenei-multi-billionaire-bmw-car-dealer-1233899.

Hall, E. (1989, July 12). Iran Names Two for Presidential Poll; Rafsanjani favourite. *Reuters*.

Harris, K. (2012). *The Martyrs Welfare State: Politics of Social Policy in the Islamic Republic of Iran*. PhD dissertation, The John Hopkins University, Baltimore, Maryland, August.

Harris, K. (2013). The Rise of the Subcontracting State: Politics of Pseudo-Privatization in the Islamic Republic of Iran. *International Journal of Middle East Studies, 45*, 45–70.

Harris, K. (2017). *A Social Revolution Politics and the Welfare State in Iran.* University of California Press.

Hashemi Rafsanjani, A. A. (2007, December 29). *Etemad* (in Persian).

Hassan-Yari, H. (2005, August 5). Iran: Defending the Islamic Revolution—The Corps of the Matter. *RadioFreeEurope, RadioLiberty.* Retrieved December 13, 2021, from http://www.rferl.org/content/article/1060431.html (in Persian).

Jebrayli, S. Y. (2018). *Revayat Rahbari, monasbeat jomhooryat va islamyat dar intekhab Valieh Faqih (The Story of Leadership, the Relationship between Republic and Islam in Electing the Supreme Jurisprudent).* Intesharat Islami. (in Persian).

Katzman, K. (1993). *The Warriors of Islam: Iran's Revolutionary Guard.* Westview Press.

Katzman, K. (2006, August 6). Iran's Bonyads: Economic Strengths and Weaknesses. *Emirates Center for Strategic Studies and Research.*

Keshavarzian, A. (2007). *Bazaar and State in Iran, the Politics of the Tehran Marketplace.* Cambridge University Press.

Khalaji, M. (2011). *Nazm-e Novin-e Rohaniat Dar Iran (The New Order of the Clerical Establishment in Iran).* H&S Media (in Persian).

Khomeini, R. (1970). *Velayat Fqih.* Daftar Nashre Falagh. Translated in 1981, *Islam and Revolution, Writings and Declarations of Imam Khomeini.* Mizan Press.

Khomeini, R. (2000). *Ketab Al-Bey (The Book of Sale)* (Vol. 3). Moassesseh tanzeem va nashr asar al-Imam al-Khomeini.

Klebnikov, P. (2003, July 21). Millionaire Mullahs. *Forbes.*

Kurtis, G., & Hooglund, E. (Eds.). (2008). *Iran, A Country Study.* Washington DC.

Maloney, S. (2000). Agents or Obstacles? Parastatal Foundations and Challenges for Iranian development. In P. Alizadeh (Ed.), *The economy of Iran: The dilemma of an Islamic State* (pp. 145–176). I.B. Tauris Publishers.

Maloney, S. (2015). *Iran's Political Economy since the Revolution.* Cambridge University Press.

Mann, M. (1986). *The Sources of Social Power, vol. 1, A History of Power from the Beginning to A.D. 1760.* Cambridge University Press.

Marshall, T. (1963). *Sociology at the Crossroads and Other Essays.* Heinemann.

Mcelroy, D. (2013, 2 May). Iran's Ayatollah Khamenei Embroiled in German Car Dealer Row. *The Daily Telegraph.* Retrieved December 5, 2021, from https://www.telegraph.co.uk/news/worldnews/middleeast/iran/10034051/Irans-Ayatollah-Khamenei-embroiled-in-German-car-dealer-row.html.

Mohajer, N. (2020). *Voices of a Massacre: Untold Stories of Life and Death in Iran, 1988.* Oneworld Publications.

Moin, B. (1999). *Khomeini: Life of the Ayatollah.* I.B. Tauris & Co.

Moinfar, A. A. (2014, 24 January). Interview Regarding the Nationalization of the Banks and Industries Under the Provisional Government of Bazargan. *Tejarat Farda,* No. 74.

Montazeri, H.-A. (1987). *Darasat fi velayet al-faqih va feqhe al-dowlah al-islamieh (Studies on Velayat faqih and the Jurisprudence of the Islamic State)* (Vol. 1, 4). Al-markaz al-alemi il-darasat al-islamieh.

Mousavi Nik, S. H. (2009). *Gozar az Iqtesad dowlati be shebh dowlati (The Transition from State to Parastate Economy)*. The Research Centre of Islamic Legislative Assembly, November, Serial number 9915, subject code 220 (in Persian).

Naseri, S. (2006). *30 Darsad-e eqtesad-e Iran dar ekhtiar-e bonyadha ast* (The Foundation's Control Over 30 percent of the Economy), *Sarmayeh*, June 10, No. 195. Retrieved December 11, 2022, from www.magiran.com/npview.asp?ID=1096929 (in Persian).

Nili, M., & Associates. (2015). *Iqtesad Iran be koja miravad? Kholaseh tarh motaleati tahleel avamel taseergozar bar amalkard myan moddat iqtesad Iran (Where the Iranian Economy Is Going? A Summary of Study Project Regarding the Analysis of Factors Impacting the Performance of the Iranian Economy in Medium Term)*. Intesharat Donyai Iqtesad (in Persian).

Nowroozi, S. (2016). Does the Problems of oil Contracts Solve with EIKO. *BBC News, Perisan Section*, October 6. Retrieved December 5, 2021.

Omidvar, K. (2009, September 23). *Sepah-e Pasdaran-e Iran bank mizanad* (The Iranian Revolutionary Guards Corps Opens Bank). *BBC News Farsi*. Retrieved December 11, 2021, from www.bbc.co.uk/persian/business/2009/09/090923_ka_bankansar_sepah.shtml, (in Persian).

Pagano, U. (2011). Interlocking Complementarities and Institutional Change. *Journal of Institutional Economics, 7*(3), 373–392.

Peckham, R. (2013). Contagion: Epidemiological Models and Financial Crises. *Journal of Public Health, 36*(1), 13–17. 2014, March.

Pierson, P. (1996, January). The New Politics of the Welfare State. *World Politics, 48*, 143–179.

Pierson, P. (2000). Increasing Returns, Path Dependence, and the Study of Politics. *The American Political Science Review, 94*(2), 251–267.

Rahman Zadeh Heravi, M. (2018). *Negahi be Iqtesad Siasi Iran az Daheh 1340 ta 1395 (A Glimpse over the Political Economy of Iran from 1961 until 2016)* (1st ed.). Nashr Akhtaran. (in Persian).

Rezai, M. (2006). "Mohsen Rezai dar jam-e khabarnegaran : 100 hezar Milliard Toman az malekyat-e dowlat beh mardom va bakhsh khosousi vagozar mishavad" (Mohsen Rezai Among Reporters: 100 Thousand Billion Tomans of State Property will be Transferred to the People and the Private Sector), Fars News Agency, July 5 (14 Tir 1385). http://www.farsnews.net/newstext,php?nn=8504140273 (in Persian).

Saeidi, A. (2004). The Accountability of Para-Governmental Organizations (Bonyads): The Case of Iranian Foundations. *Iranian Studies, 37*(3), 479–498.

Sazegara, M. (2006, July 23). "Sepah va seh enheraf" (The IRGC and three aberrations). Retrieved December 2, 2021, form http://www.sazegara.net/persian/archives/2006/07/060723_154435.html (in Persian).

Schanche, D. (1989, June 4). Ayatollah Khomeini dies at 86: Fiery Leader Was in Failing Health Following Surgery. *Los Angeles Times*.https://www.latimes.com/archives/la-xpm-1989-06-04-mn-2499-story.html

Schirazi, A. (1997). *The Constitution of Iran: Politics and the State in the Islamic Republic*. I.B. Tauris.

Skocopol, T. (1982, May). Rentier Sttae and Shi'a Islam in the Iranian Revolution. *Theory and Society, 11*(3), 265–283.

Smith, B. (1997, January 18). Dual Control. *The Economist, 342*(8000).

Sodagar, M. (1990). *Rooshd ravabet sarmayehdari dar Iran (The Development of the Capitalist Relationships in Iran)*. Shooleh Andisheh. (in Persian).

Stecklow, S., Dehghanpisheh, B., & Torbati, Y. (2013). Khamenei Controls Massive Financial Empire Built on Property Seizures. Three Parts. *Reuters Investigates*, 11, 12, 13 Nov., http://www.reuters.com/investiates/iran

Stewart, D. (2001). Islamic Juridical Hierarchies and the Office of Marji' al-Taqlid. In L. Clarke (Ed.), *Shi'ite Heritage: Essays on Classical and Modern Traditions* (pp. 137–157). Binghamton.

Tasnim, Maqsood az Anfal chist? (What does it mean Anfal)? 12 September 2017. Retrieved January 9, 2022, from https://www.tasnimnews.com/fa/news/1396/06/21/1516015, (in Persian).

Vahabi, M. (2004). *The Political Economy of Destructive Power*. Edward Elgar.

Vahabi, M. (2010). "Ordres contradictoires et coordination destructive: le malaise iranien" (Contradictory Orders and Destructive Coordination: The Iranian Disease). *Revue Canadienne d'Etudes du Développement (Canadian Journal of Development Studies), 30*(3–4), 503–534.

Vahabi, M. (2014). "Contrainte budgétaire lâche et le secteur paraétatique" (Soft Budget Constraints and Parastatal Sector). In M. Makinsky (Ed.), *L'économie réelle de l'Iran* (pp. 147–176). L'Harmattan.

Vahabi, M. (2015a). *The Political Economy of Predation: Manhunting and the Economics of Escape*. Cambridge University Press.

Vahabi, M. (2015b, December 22). Jaygah Sepah dar Eqtesad Iran (The Place of Sepah in the Iranian Economy). *Mihan*, No. 6. Retrieved December 11, 2021, from http://mihan.net/1394/10/01/562/ (in Persian).

Vahabi, M. (2018a). The Resource Curse Literature as Seen Through the Appropriability Lens: A Critical Survey. *Public Choice, 175*(3-4), 393–428.

Vahabi, M. (2018b, March). *Coercive State, Resisting Society, Political and Economic Development in Contemporary Iran, Dr Sadighi Lecture Series*. International Institute of Social History and Leiden University. https://socialhistory.org/en/events/lecture-political-and-economic-development-contemporary-iran

Vahabi, M., & Coville, T. (2017). Introduction: L'Economie Politique de la République islamique d'Iran. *Revue Internationale des Etudes du Développement,* *229,* 11–32.

Valadbaygi, K. (2021). Hybrid Neoliberalism: Capitalist Development in Contemporary Iran. *New Political Economy, 26*(3), 313–327.

Weber, M. (1922/1978). *Economy and Society* 1, University of California Press.

Weber, R. (2001). *Swords into Dow Shares, Governing the Decline of the Military-Industrial Complex.* Westview.

Wehrey, F., Green, J., Nichiporuk, B., Nader, A., Hansell, L., Nafisi, R., & Bohandy, S. R. (2009). *The Rise of the Pasdaran, Assessing the Domestic Roles of Iran's Islamic Revolutionary Guards Corps.* Rand Corporation.

Yokota, J. (2000). Tumor Progression and Metastasis. *Carcinogenesis, 21*(3), 497–503.

Zandi, R. (2006, June 8). Qarardad-e bozorg miyan-e Vezarat-e Naft va Sepah-e Pasdaran mon'aqed shod (A Big Contract Was Signed Between the Oil Ministry and the IRGC). *Sharq.* Retrieved December 12, 2021, from wwwmagiran. com/npview.asp?ID=1095191

CHAPTER 7

Privatization Decree: Liberalization or Islamization?

7.1 Introduction

Khamenei's decree on 'General policies pertaining to Article 44 of the constitution of the Islamic Republic of Iran' in July 2006 promulgated the sale of 80% of all state-owned enterprises (SOEs) enshrined in the constitution and their transfer to "private, cooperative and non-government public sectors" by the end of the Fourth Five-Year Plan (2011–2015).

All economists, political scientists, jurists, and journalists studying the political economy of the Islamic Republic of Iran (IRI) interpreted this decree as a fundamental revision of Article 44 of the constitution stipulating the nationalization of all the key industries, foreign trade, transport, and communication system. This was only partially true. From *Anfal* viewpoint, the main objective of the decree was not a revision of Article 44, but Article 45.[1] In fact, the new Supreme Leader's decree ushered in a third phase of *Anfal* marking the termination of the 'unity thesis' advocated by Khomeini and Montazeri in the first phase of *Anfal*.

Reviewing Article 45 in Section 5–6, we highlighted the conflation of *Anfal* and state property. While *Anfal* in practice was kept independently from the state under the personal purview of the Supreme Jurisconsult, it was juridically lumped together with the state property. The July 2006 decree's principal message was the introduction of 'non-state public

---

[1] See Chap. 5, Sect. 5.6 on Article 44 and Article 45 of the constitution of the IRI.

© The Author(s), under exclusive license to Springer Nature Switzerland AG 2023
M. Vahabi, *Destructive Coordination, Anfal and Islamic Political Capitalism*, https://doi.org/10.1007/978-3-031-17674-6_7

property' in contradistinction with state property. This was the end of the 'unity thesis' according to which *Anfal* or the jurisconsult's property should be lumped together with public properties of all Muslims as 'state property'. Under Khamenei, this statist interpretation of Article 45 was replaced by an allegedly 'liberal'[2] interpretation in which *Anfal* has been reintroduced as part of 'privatization' process.

It might be claimed that the first Supreme Leader (Khomeini) was a 'statist-populist' whereas the second Supreme Leader (Khamenei) is a 'liberal'. However, this impression is totally fallacious. Khomeini and Khamenei were both ardent advocates of *Anfal* which had nothing to do with either 'statism' or 'liberalism', but they adopted different political strategies to enhance the Islamic economics. In the first phase of *Anfal*, Khomeini's political strategy consisted of dissimulating the nascent *Anfal* under the popular label of Islamic charity or the dominant discourse of the time, namely 'statist-populist' policy[3] seducing the radical, and leftist opposition. In 2006, Khamenei did not need to cling to this statist discourse, since the state had cumulated colossal debts and commercial state banks were almost bankrupt. The 'privatization' program was partially presented as debt cancellations and a solution to curb the state's debts by selling off the insolvable state enterprises to other non-state sectors. In this new context, *Anfal* was now conflated with the private sector.

All the economic and political analysts of the so-called 'privatization' program, with no exception, have arrived at a very similar conclusion: the big winner of 'privatization' *was not private sector*, but rather 'non-state public sector' (see, among many others, Harris, 2013; Maloney, 2015; Nili & Associates, 2015). Eminent political figures representing different political factions of the IRI also echoed this point. For example, Hashemi Rafsanjani (2008) criticized the Ahmadinejad's government for not applying Article 44 to attract Iranian private assets to invest in Iran instead of Dubai. Ali Akbar Nateq Nouri (2008), a top conservative cleric who run against Khatami in the presidential elections of 1997, also contended that assets were transferred from "an open to a shadow government" (Dareini, August 31, 2008, *Worldnews*). In the same vein, the Research Centre of

---

[2] Some Iranian economists, political scientists, and sociologists prefer the term 'neoliberal'.

[3] This term was often used by many radical and leftist economists who had a strong sympathy for 'popular anti-imperialist' and so-called equalitarian tendencies of the IRI during 1979–1989.

Islamic Legislative Assembly called the privatization process as "The transition from state to parastate economy" (Mousavi Nik, November 2009).

Although 'non-state public sector' is an ambiguous expression begging for further scrutiny, it is true that the giant conglomerates belonging to *Anfal*, the Sepah, the Basij, and other religious and military foundations were the principal beneficiaries of the so-called privatization decree. Several reports from two official authorities corroborated the fact that privatization was not about increasing the share of private sector in the economy. The first one was the 'Special parliamentary Commission to Overview the Implementation of Article 44' which released four reports on privatization outcomes during 2006–2010 in the late 2010. According to its reports, only 13.5% of the state properties were transferred to the private sector.[4] The second authority was the 'Judiciary's Inspection Organization' that also released a report on the same issue in 2012 and announced that the private sector only owned 5% of the total state properties (Nili & Associates, 2015, p. 538).

Despite the contradictory figures, both authorities converged on one point: the share of private sector of the privatization process was totally marginal. Many economists attributed this result to the absence of necessary logistics and material conditions for private capital to take advantage of privatization decree. "In the current situation, the domestic private sector is not sufficiently talented to handle a huge part of Iran's economy through privatization … The government should pave the way for foreign investment and seriously think about investment by Iranians living abroad" (*Siyasat-e Ruz*, cited by Maloney, 2015, p. 336). But these recommendations were pure naivety in light of repeated failures of the post-war governments in attracting strategic foreign investors and the Iranian's diaspora to invest in Iran. The real issue was to study whether material conditions for the development of an independent private sector could be met in the presence of parallel institutions.

Reviewing preliminary waves of privatization can disentangle the tensions and contradictions of the privatization process resulting in the transfer of the state property to *Anfal* and other Islamic sovereign institutions. While *Anfal* progressed in the name of 'statism' in its early stage, it arrived at its maturity and preponderant position in the political economy of the

---

[4] "The private sector is defined as a sector composed of all companies and associations in which 80 percent of their shares belong directly or indirectly through legal persons to natural persons" (Najafi Khah, 2016, p. 123).

IRI through 'privatization' process. *Khamenei's decree was about further Islamization rather than liberalization of the Iranian economy.* It culminated in an economic Islamic revolution that can be characterized as the third phase of *Anfal.*

Accordingly, in this chapter, we first study the previous privatization campaigns, their failures, and their respective shares in transferring the state assets to non-state sectors during Hashemi Rafsanjani and Khatami presidencies. Then we will focus on objectives, process, and outcome of Khamenei's 'privatization' decree taking on board historical world-wide experiences of privatization since 1979. Identifying 'non-state public sector' as the principal beneficiary of 'privatization', we will scrutinize the confusing definitions of this sector under the IRI's jurisprudence to unravel the lion's share of *Anfal* and the Sepah in preying on governmental assets. Finally, it will be shown how the dominance of Islamic political capitalism has resulted in shrinking role of market, authoritative, and cooperative coordination in comparison with destructive coordination.

7.2   Privatization Background Under Rafsanjani and Khatami

The privatization programs were initially launched after the war during the 'Adjustment Program' and the 'Stabilization Program'. These programs were introduced by Ali Akbar Hashemi Rafsanjani (1989–1997) during his two terms presidency as the first and second quadrennial programs. The two programs contained a 'privatization' policy.

As far as legislation and propaganda are concerned, privatization was one of the goals of the First Five-Year Plan (1989–1994), and initially there was much optimism about the growth of a truly private sector. Inspired by the Chinese economic reform, Rafsanjani aimed at reforming the economy during the reconstruction period to strengthen the Islamic political system. The privatization issue was raised in the Economic Council and eventually led to a statute according to which privatization had to be implemented. It started in 1990–1991 by selling off 400 of 3000 state-owned enterprises (SOEs) (Maloney, 2015, p. 205). Many big state enterprises were excluded from privatization due to the constitutional restrictions. This privatization scheme provoked much enthusiasm. Pragmatists and traditional conservative bazaar merchants were coalesced against the statist tendency represented by the ex-Prime Minister Mousavi.

The privatization policy was supported by other measures such as relaxing the Article 81[5] of the constitution on foreign investment, acquiring short-term foreign loans, and inviting the Iranian diaspora to invest in Iran. Accordingly, in 1992, the Finance Ministry announced new measures for external buyouts of the total ownership of the Iranian firms by foreign companies and offering indemnification against nationalizations and protection for capital repatriation.[6] The first period of privatization, 1990–1994, was carried out by virtue of the First Development Plan's authorization, with total sales of public assets worth 1.7 trillion rials (Amuzegar, 2007, p. 62).

Avowedly, the Majlis passed a law authorizing the government to sell the state enterprises in different ways. The statute proposed three means by which state entities could be handed over: the stock market, auctions, and negotiations (Ahmadi-Amooei, 2004, p. 222). Since at the time the Tehran Stock Exchange (TSE) was even more inefficient and less developed, they included formulas for setting stock values of firms in order to determine their true value prior to being transferred. Because the auditing process of state-owned companies was unreliable and many of these state-owned enterprises were unprofitable, it was decided to set up a subsidiary stock exchange alongside the TSE which had a lower bar for entry. But the idea never materialized.

The auction method also remained on paper, and only the third method based on negotiations was widely adopted. Since the transfer process or privatization was selective and at the discretion of those in power; the Rafsanjani family and his relatives seized the lion's share of the first stage of privatization. But this led to widespread condemnation of the person of Rafsanjani as well as his cabinet. Masoud Roghani Zanjani, while defending Rafsanjani against these accusations and the manner which privatization measures were implemented, asserts:

---

[5] Article 81 of the constitution of the IRI stipulates: "The granting of concessions to foreigners for the formation of companies or institutions dealing with commerce, industry, agriculture, services or mineral extraction, is absolutely forbidden," https://ca.search.yahoo.com/yhs/search?hspart=trp&hsimp=yhs001&type=Y149_F163_202167_110321&p=Article+81+of+the+constitution+of+the+Islamic+republic+of+Iran

[6] *New York Times*, 1992, "Iran allows foreigners to buy its companies," June 29, section D, p.4, https://www.nytimes.com/1992/06/29/business/iran-allows-foreigners-to-buy-its-companies.html

There was an idea that some people were looting and pillaging the country, and these people had brought their personal and private affairs into the process of privatization. Privatization was supposed to proceed at a very fast pace, but this social issue prevented it from moving forward. Immediately after the wave of social protests and complaints about the implementation of the economic adjustment plan, the traditional right reacted by proposing a massive plan for a coupon-based sale of state-owned factories and units. Mr. Ali-Naghi Khamoushi, the chairman of the Chamber of Commerce, was the architect and promoter of this plan. ... Conservatives and the right wing, despite having vested interests in the privatization process, began to criticize the government. They wanted to take advantage of this situation politically and to weaken Mr. Hashemi (Rafsanjani), otherwise they would have benefited the most from privatization (Ahmadi-Amooei, 2004, p.232).

The mass or coupon-privatization suggested by the chairman of the Chamber of Commerce and one of the influential leaders of *Mo'talefeh*, Khamoushi, was pursued at a later stage during the Ahmadinejad's presidency under the title of 'Justice share'.[7] The privatization procedure, however, had to be stopped in the winter of 1992 due to widespread reports of flagrant corruption, cronyism, and no-bid sales of moneymaking enterprises to selected groups at below-market prices. "A new ministerial decree with added safeguards against abuses proved to be equally flawed. The Majlis in mid-summer 1994 put a temporary end to all privatization efforts until previous infractions were rectified" (Amuzegar, 2007, p. 62).

The conservative bazaar merchants' support for Hashemi Rafsanjani's government declined as early as the summer of 1992, soon after the opening of the fourth Majles. The objection of Nateq Nouri against government's proposal for a reinterpretation of the Article 81 in June 1992 was a clear indication. He criticized the government for disregarding the priority for domestic interest in accordance with the "preservation of Islamic principles and values". The traditional conservative faction was totally dissatisfied with the privatization and liberalization process since its interests were not served by Rafsanjani's government. The tension particularly accentuated "when the Central Bank floated the rial in March 1993, it became much more difficult for Iran's merchant community to secure the huge profits that they had enjoyed under the previous multiple exchange rate system" (Pesaran, 2014, p. 86).

---

[7] See next section for 'Justice share'.

Pesaran's point is valid with some nuances. It was not 'Iran's merchant community' that benefited from multiple exchange rates during 1979–1989. As Keshavarzian (2007, p. 273) persuasively argued, the IRI differentiated between revolutionary or 'committed' bazaaris and those who were supposedly not, with only the former gaining access to resources controlled by the state. While bazaaris constituted a relatively coherent group independent from the state during the Shah's regime, they lost their internal solidarity and group identity under the IRI because of individual-level patronage. The bazaar merchants advocated a mercantilist doctrine giving the pride of place to trade, commerce, and private property with a 'watchman' state. Paradoxically, the most eminent representatives of bazaar who were supposed to be ardent advocates of 'free market exchange rate' voiced against it because they entertained privileged relationships with Khomeini, permitting them to benefit from state monopoly to enrich themselves.

The period of 1979–1990 in the Iranian economy is of key importance to explore the development of a type of *government-dependent market*. A careful examination of this period shows that long before the eight-year war which depleted the state coffers and forced the Islamic rulers to borrow money from IMF and the World Bank, *state monopoly strengthened the private market*. To better understand this, let us take a closer look at those years and especially the passage of the law on the nationalization of foreign trade in 1979.

With the law enacted, the Ministry of Commerce compiled a list of all goods traded internationally. Pursuant to that, procurement and distribution centers were established which were required to classify all such goods in ten import categories. Procurement and distribution of chemical products, iron and steel products, metals, machinery, foodstuff and agricultural products, and the oversight of each was entrusted to the respective ministry. The 'commodity provision and distribution centers' had a board of directors that was a combination of private sector experts and so-called revolutionary brigades. These centers were active until 1990–1992; that is, until the beginning of Mr. Rafsanjani's presidency and the preparation of the First Five-Year Plan of the IRI. During the period 1979–1990, the entire foreign trade of the country was carried out by these centers, and they became one of the sources of corruption and rent collection.

It is worth noting that with the coming to power of Mr. Mousavi's government (1981–1989), the Ministry of Commerce was in the hands of Mr. Al-Ishaq and Mr. Asgarowladi for some time, whose close ties with the

Tehran bazaar were known to all. According to Ezatullah Sahabi, Mr. Al-Ishaq and Mr. Asgarowladi "placed the supporters of '*Mo'talefeh*' and the bazaar merchants in the production and distribution centers and they too had their own specific ideas, that the government has a duty to serve and should not make profits. So, they imported goods with government currency (at official rates far below the market's), added one or two tomans, and then released it to the market and merchants. The merchants then sold these goods at market prices and pocketed the huge difference between the state and market currency exchange rate. We have witnessed a number of cases among clothing retailers, stationery sellers, etc., who bought their products at the government currency exchange rate of seven tomans to a dollar and then sold them at a price of sixteen, eighteen, twenty or twenty-seven tomans to a dollar, because the price of the dollar was rising sharply. This is how rents were collected" (Ahmadi Amooei, 2004, pp. 23–4).

In this manner, the same people who were staunch opponents of state intervention in the economy gained the most from the state monopolies in the market. The *Mo'talefeh* and *Anjoman Hojjatieh* were the pioneers of a trend that became widespread throughout the life of the Islamic Republic with regard to the relationship between the state and the market: the emergence of new markets and their expansion alongside and in parallel with state monopolies and regulations. This also explains why these advocates of 'free market' were also against the removal of multiple exchange rate system by Rafsanjani. Of course, all bazaaris could not enjoy from multiple exchange rate if they were not among the privileged group close to the Islamic rulers.

Clearly, *a private sector thrived, thanks to preponderant state monopolies in trade and industry which is a characteristic unique to the Iranian market economy under the IRI*. While in many colonial companies of Western countries, as well as low- and middle-income countries around the world, public-private monopolies generated a thriving private sector, the state sector was not preponderant in trade and industry. Such specific characteristics of market economy cannot be found in many economies in which the state sector is the dominant form of property relationships (Vahabi & Mohajer, 2021).

In the political economy of the IRI, the private sector is by no means absent; it is very much alive. The private sector, however, acts essentially as an agent, a middleman, a broker, or a subcontractor of those Islamic sovereign institutions (often called 'parastatal') that are extra-legal and that have ties to state monopolies and rents. This can be called a dependent private sector. From a political viewpoint, this explains why separating the political factions within the Islamic Republic into 'left' and 'right' would be meaningless. Those on the 'left' are proponents of a statist economy in line with those on the 'right' who are supporters of that faction of the private sector that has ties to Islamic sovereign institutions benefiting from government monopolies.

Rafsanjani's privatization plan was ended in 1993 because of rising political opposition in the Fourth Majles and the critical economic situation. The country's oil income decreased, domestic prices escalated, the rial depreciated further, and the Central Bank was placed under increasing pressure to pay off its short-term loans. As Table 7.1 indicates, by the end of 1993, total foreign debt had reached over US$23 billion, and the level of dependence on short-term capital inflows in particular was said to be unprecedented (Pesaran, 2000, p. 87).

The debt's crisis in 1993 was a turning point in Rafsanjani's privatization plan (Ahmadi Amooei, 2004, pp. 210–213). While the Supreme Leader supported his candidacy for a second presidential term in March 1993, he emphasized the importance of 'social justice' echoing the criticisms formulated by both the statist and mercantilist factions of the government according to which the debt's crisis and high inflation rate were both the upshot of the liberalization policy.

The conflict between the pragmatists and the traditional conservatives over the looting and seizure of state property in the name of privatization eventually led to the intervention of the Supreme Leader and a solution that would transcend political camps to preserve the interest of the entire system. This solution was the transfer of state property to the Islamic

Table 7.1   Foreign debt, 1989–1993, in billions of US dollars at constant prices

Year	Total external debt (in billions)	Short-term debt (in billions)	Short-term debt to total external debt (%)
1989	4.3	2.1	49
1990	6.2	4.7	76
1991	10.9	7	64
1992	16	11.9	74
1993	23	17.6	77

Source: International Monetary Fund (April 2010)

sovereign economic institutions, an array of entities (foundations and institutions) affiliated with *Anfal* and the Iranian Revolutionary Guards Corps (IRGC). The priority, of course, was with the 'revolutionary' and 'pro-downtrodden' institutions (Adeli, 2004, pp. 474–75).

Consequently, the second phase of privatization under Rafsanjani (1995–1997) was carried out under the Second Plan's mandate according to a special Majles law "limiting the transfer of public assets—totaling 1.8 trillion rials—only to workers and war veterans on specially favored terms. In the third period, 1998–99, some 3.1 trillion rials changed hands under annual budget laws as well as the Second Plan's statutory authorization" (Amuzegar, 2007, p. 62).

The failure of the first wave of privatization under Rafsanjani (1990–1993) clearly demonstrated that privatization was not for strengthening a private sector independent from the Islamic sovereign economic institutions. The fourth Majles law on privatization provided the basis of privatization decree in July 2006.

Contrary to Rafsanjani, Khatami gave the primacy to 'political' rather than 'economic' reform. Nevertheless, the privatization policy was followed during the Third Five-Year Plan notably in energy, water, power, and banking sectors. Similar to Rafsanjani, Khatami endeavored to enhance a private sector independent from the Islamic sovereign power by foreign investment promotion and the Iranian's capital abroad. Considering the decline of oil price below 10 dollars/barrel in late 1998, followed by a historic drought in Iran, and the pressure of 'debt crisis' persisting since Rafsanjani's time, Khatami launched an 'Economic Recovery Plan'. In line with the Supreme Leader's critical assessment of Rafsanjani's liberalization policy, Khatami prioritized 'social justice' but included an embrace of foreign investment. Moreover, in the wake of victory of so-called reformists in the sixth Majles, many Iranians who emigrated or smuggled the borders during the brutal years of the IRI in the 1980s started to consider returning back to the country at least for short periods of time. This led to "a flow of individuals and capital that has mushroomed since the 1997 election" (Maloney, 2015, p. 305).

Khatami's government actively supported private banks and granted a few contracts to foreign companies including the two previously cited contracts with the Turkish companies, TAV and Turkcell.[8] We have already discussed the outcome of these partial privatizations in the previ-

[8] See Chap. 5.

ous chapter, particularly the crisis of Islamic loan funds, the rise of Islamic banks, and the Sepah's intervention in closing the Imam Khomeini's airport. In fact, the rise of the Sepah and its active intervention in the economy, as well as the intensification of domestic repression, a series of political assassinations of political leaders, journalists, and intellectuals steamed off the initial enthusiasm for reversing the labor and capital flight.

Thus, privatization during Rafsanjani and Khatami did not serve to strengthen an independent private sector and the market coordination, but instead, it increased the weight and authority of the so-called parastatal or Islamic sovereign economic institutions. Moreover, as Table 7.2 indicates the total property transfer from state to non-state sectors (principally 'parastatal sector') during Hashemi Rafsanjani and Khatami amounted to only 11% of the total privatizations. The bulk of privatization was carried out during Ahmadinejad's presidency or the third phase of *Anfal*.

In other words, the privatization decree was issued in 2006 as part of Islamic economic revolution to enhance *Anfal* and the Sepah's interests; the development of a dependent privileged private sector was subordinated to the needs of the so-called non-state public sector.

Table 7.2 Transfer of property from state to non-state sectors

President	Presidential term	Percentage of property transfer
Hashemi Rafsanjani	August 3, 1989 to August 2, 1997	6.9%
Muhammad Khatami	August 2, 1997 to August 3, 2005	4.1%
Mahmoud Ahmadinejad	August 3, 2005 to August 3, 2013	89%

Source: Harris (2013, p. 57)

7.3   Khamenei's Privatization Decree: Objectives, Process, and Outcomes

There exists a vast literature on privatization inspired by two different historical experiences. The first one relates to the privatization in the advanced capitalist countries since Margaret Thatcher conservative liberal reforms in 1979 culminating in the Washington consensus. Its program can be resumed in what is known as 'holy trinity': privatization, liberalization, and stabilization. The second experience concerns the post-socialist transition since 1989–1991 (Megginson & Netter, 2001).

Major differences between these two cases must be addressed, among them the socio-economic and institutional setup in which the privatization process was launched. In the former, there existed a full-fledged market including not only product and labor but also capital market and stock exchanges at a world-wide level. Moreover, ripe socio-economic conditions for entrepreneurial activities, a bourgeois class with historically rich political and cultural traditions, and all institutional requirements for the primacy of property over sovereignty were reunited together. Therefore, it was possible to employ standard privatization methods of large SOEs, namely negotiated direct asset sale to outside strategic investors, competitive bidding in tenders for corporate shares, and public issue of new joint stock corporations' shares through an initial public offering (IPO).

In the second experience, the privatization was initiated within a completely different socio-economic and institutional setup, that is, soviet-type economies. It targeted two fundamental changes: the dominance of private sector instead of a preponderant state sector and the replacement of authoritative coordination by market coordination. These changes were often accompanied by a third fundamental institutional change at political level, namely the end of monopoly of power by the Communist party (Kornai, 1992).

Shock therapy and gradualism have been two major trajectories in privatization process. The former was followed in many ex-Soviet-type economies such as Russia and Poland. The rapid privatization of the state sector and macroeconomic stabilization policies were adopted to control mega inflation[9] (Dornbusch, 1991) or sometime hyperinflation,[10] but these policies could not shun 'transformational recession' (Kornai, 1994). At the beginning of the post-socialist transition, it was widely held that the 'holy trinity' would be sufficient to produce an efficient market. Kornai emphatically argued that it was equally important to harden the 'soft budget constraints'[11] of state enterprises. In his opinion, the 'organic development' of a private market economy required a 'magic square' instead of a 'holy trinity': "There is close causal relations between healthy development of private sector, hardening of the budget constraint, forceful restructuring of production, and as the ultimate result, the growth of labor productivity" (Kornai, 2000, p. 10). This explains his skeptical assessment of shock therapy.

In the absence of a full-fledged capital market, and the lack of considerable amount of private saving, several 'non-standard' schemes of privatization were adopted (Andreff, 2017) that were based on coalition among powerful economic and political oligarchs, negotiation between different stakeholders, and invitation of foreign capital to invest. The most important patterns have been: (1) top-down asset sale or capitalism from above: privatization through the embourgeoisement of the ex-Nomenclature including the ex-Communist party apparatchiks known as 'Kremlin capitalism'; (2) insider privatization also known as 'management-employee buyouts' (MEBO): the transfer of property rights to the ex-appointed directors (Nachalniks) of socialist enterprises and their employees at book prices lower than market prices; (3) mass or 'coupon' privatization: 'Mass' refers to the universal and uniform opportunity for citizens to acquire the property divested by the state, but does not imply that all, or most, of the state assets will be involved in the mass privatization program. It was based

---

[9] The expression is coined by Dornbusch (1991, p. 177) pertaining to high inflations that are more than 1% monthly (435% annually) over several months. Most of post-socialist countries experienced 'mega inflation'.

[10] Cagan (1956, p. 25) defined 'hyperinflation' as a monthly inflation rate of 50%. According to Hanke and Kruz (2013), the third wave of hyperinflation occurred in a few Central and East European countries during the post-socialist transition and especially in many newly independent republics of ex-Soviet Union (see Vahabi, 2020).

[11] The expression 'Soft budget constraint' (SBC) was coined by Janos Kornai (1979) to describe the behavior of directors of the soviet-type enterprise that could spend more than its revenue expecting an *ex post* bailout by a paternalist socialist state. By contrast, he argued that in general, a capitalist firm is subject to hard budget constraint (HBC) since it will not be systematically bailed out in case of insolvency (for an analysis of different strands of economic literature on the SBC, see Vahabi, 2001, 2014a, 2014b).

on a populist vision of creating a 'popular' capitalism; (4) outsider privatization: it was often the sell off state properties to foreign capital notably
strategic investors; (5) restitution: it entailed redress by the state for expro-
priations of property deemed unjust in the soviet-type economies. It
embraced either a return of physical assets (in the Czech Republic) or
compensation certificates redeemable in the form of shares (Hungary).

The second trajectory of post-socialist transition consisted of gradual
transformation of socio-economic conditions for the growth of market
relationships, and the rise of a new class of entrepreneurs alongside the
state sector capable of challenging the state sector by its cutting-edge
competitive power (Kornai, 1990b). The state sector had to restructure to
be able to face market competition. This path has been described as 'capitalism from below'. The Hungarian 'New Economic Mechanism' (NEM)
on January 1, 1968, was an illustration of gradual transformation in the
past, and the Chinese economic reforms since 1979 mark the recent experience of gradualism.

Considering these two major experiences of privatization, it is noteworthy to inquire which one of them served as a model for the July 2006
'privatization' program under the IRI, and what were the specific socio-
economic and institutional setup in which the program was launched?

The Iranian so-called 'privatization' allegedly followed the post-socialist
transition model and its non-standard privatizing methods even though it
had been launched in a capitalist economy (see Nili & Associates, 2015).
Moreover, it was inspired by the shock therapy rather than gradualism
since it was focused on privatizing 80% of the state properties. Privatization
was never introduced in Iran as a process of ending with big monopolies
or strengthening market competition. While many commonalities can be
underlined between the Iranian and Russian 'privatization' regarding asset
grabbing by 'financial-Industrial groups' related to petroleum and gas and
state predation, they began from completely different starting points. In
Russia, the principal economic obstacle to privatization was the state sector, while in Iran, it was *Anfal* and other giant holdings related to the
Islamic sovereign power. But what is *Anfal?*

Anfal is the exclusive property of all 'ownerless' resources (including
natural resources) by the Supreme Jurisconsult. It is based on the dispossession of people from their public properties. In this sense, *the privatization process in Iran started in 1979 and not in 2006*. However, the exclusive
property of the Supreme Leader was not subject to market discipline and
competition because it was based upon the fusion of property and

sovereignty. *Thus, privatization process was blocked and would be blocked if Anfal maintained.* This holds true for other economic institutions of sovereign power such as the Sepah, the Basij, and Astan Quods Rasavi. The so-called privatization program was not aimed at dismantling *Anfal* to enhance private sector by demarcating property from sovereignty. It was a project to transfer the state properties to the so-called non-state public properties under the pretext of curbing the state's huge debts. When the sale of 80% of the state properties was announced, the state had never been richer in the whole Iranian history since the time when the income from the sale of petroleum became the principal source of the state's revenue.

As Fig. 7.1 clearly illustrates, the oil revenues during Ahmadinejad were three times more than the sum of oil revenues during both Rafsanjani and Khatami taken together. In fact, Ahmadinejad's two terms presidency (2005–2013) covered the super-spike crude prices attaining $150–$200.

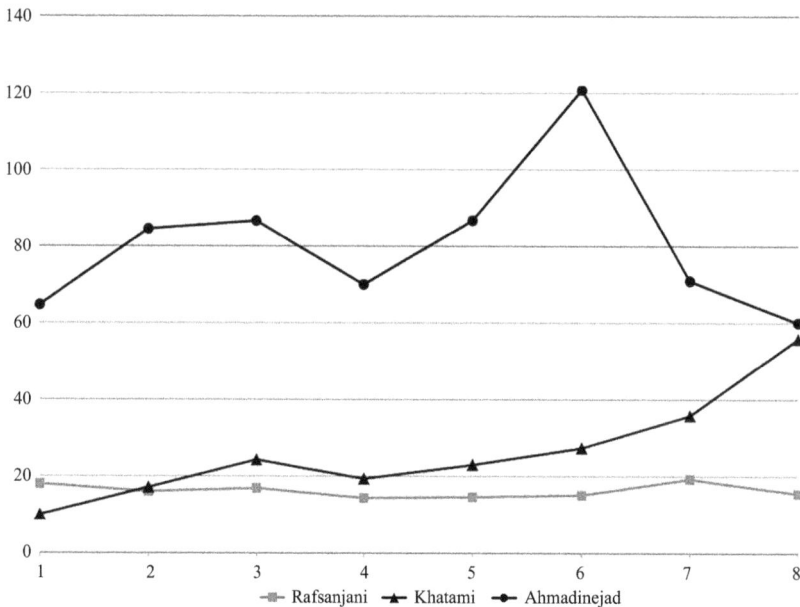

Fig. 7.1 Value of Iran's oil exports ($US billion). (X-axis shows the first to eighth years of each president's term). Source: IMF, World Economic Outlook Database, October 2012 (author's estimate for the last year of Ahmadinejad's term)

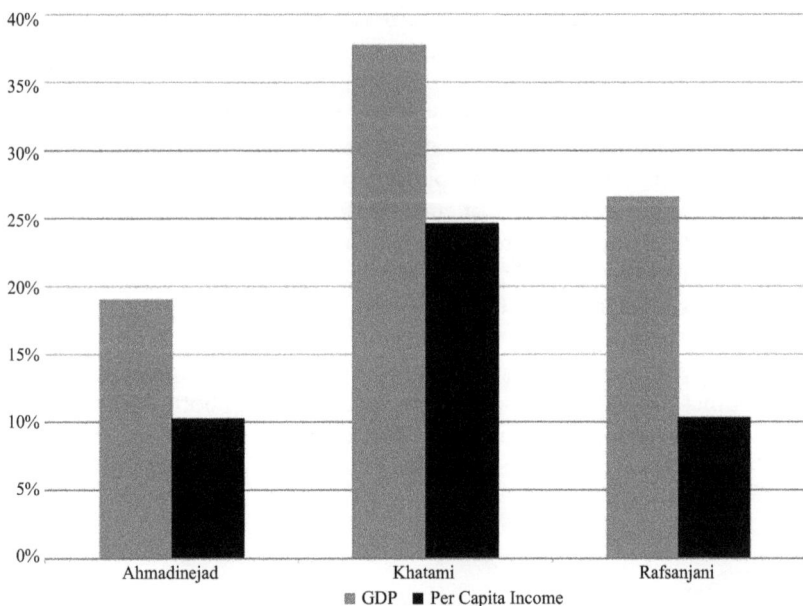

Fig. 7.2 Iranian current account balance ($US billion). (X-axis shows the first to eighth years of each president's term). Source: IMF, World Economic Outlook Database, October 2012

> Indeed, of more than $700 billion that Iran has earned through oil exports in the past thirty years, nearly 40% was during Ahmadinejad's second term (Maloney, 2015, p. 502).

Paradoxically, the income per capita in this period was the lowest compared to that of Rafsanjani and Khatami periods as shown in Fig. 7.2. While economic performance during all three presidents furnishes strong evidence of reliance on oil revenue (the so-called natural resource curse), Ahmadinejad's one provided the most striking illustration of this curse. Despite the colossal increase in oil rent, the state's debt increased drastically. Al Yaseen underlined that "according to the ICB's latest report [in 2013], the state's debts to the Central Bank have amounted to 20 thousand billion tomans. Comparing this figure with the state debts in 2007, it becomes clear that the state's debts have augmented to more than 10,5 thousand billion tomans" (2014, p. 225, the bracket is added).

In fact, the higher the state's oil revenue, the higher the state's expenditures, and considering that the latter increased more than the former, the upshot was more debts for the state. This paradox cannot be explained by the Dutch disease since the increase in oil price largely exceeded the costs of importation. The institutional rather than 'natural' curse offers a more plausible explanation. The rise of debts can be attributed to the predatory activities of parallel institutions that devoted more efforts to grab the increased oil rents through capital flight[12] and lobbying. The lobbying targeted the allocation of higher budgets for religious and military institutions as well as securing the lion's share of state contracts (at municipality and central levels) for BMJ (*Bonyad Mostazafan va Janbazan*), Setad, the Sepah, and the Basij as subcontractors with no-bidding. To put it differently, state debts were the consequence of state predation by parallel institutions, and they become in turn a cause of appropriation of the state's assets by parallel institutions in the name of 'privatization'.[13]

The bulk of privatization, 89%, was implemented during Ahmadinejad's presidency when the oil revenue had tripled. This revenue was channeled to Islamic parallel institutions through the transfer of corporate holdings. The privatization did not curb the state's chronic debts. The debts' size constantly rose during the decade 2011–2021 amounting to 1500 thousand billion tomans on November 22, 2021, as reported by the Research Centre of Islamic Legislative Assembly. Parallel to this increase, the budget allotted to the religious institutions also augmented incessantly: "The Iranian media have reported in February 2021 that 7252 billion tomans

---

[12] Capital flight will be explored in the next chapter.

[13] The privatization decree was accompanied by liberalization policies targeting at reducing or eliminating subsidies for a vast array of goods and services particularly refined petroleum. Liberalization was often forced to the government because of chronic deficits. The price of refined petroleum tripled during Rouhani's presidency in November 2019 (*Financial Times*, November 16, 2019). It provoked mass protestations in many provinces all over Iran which were violently repressed by the military forces and the Basij by the order of the Supreme Leader. The price liberalization of petroleum has recurrently been on the government's agenda with increasing budget deficits. The state's deficit in 2020 has been equivalent to half of the total annual budget forcing again the government to cut subsidies on energy and many other basic consumer goods. While ordinary household's budget is *hard*, the Islamic parallel institutions' budget is *soft*, the latter is not subject to the abolition of subsidies. Furthermore, these institutions still do not pay any taxes. The focus of this chapter is on privatization and not redistributive policies. Although we do not explore it in this book, it comes within the scope of political economy of soft and hard budget constraints of different sectors in the post-revolutionary Iranian economy (see Vahabi, 2014b).

have been allotted to 42 religious' institutions" (*Radio Zamaneh*, November 21, 2021[14]).

According to Mousavi Nik's report on privatization in November 2009, the total value of the whole state assets that had to be privatized amounted to 1500 thousand billion Iranian Rials (approximately 150 billion dollars)[15] (2009, p. 2). From 2004 to August 6, 2009, the assets of 264 SOEs valued at 544 thousand billion rials (approximately 54.4 billion dollars) were divested through three non-standard privatizing methods, namely debt cancellations, Justice share, and other methods.

1. *Debt cancellations*: the first method has been the IRI's invention in the sense that the state reimbursed part of its debts to its creditors through direct transfer of government assets instead of 'cash' payment. And 12.5% of property transfer was implemented through this type of divestment. The 'non-state public sector' was the major beneficiary of this method of privatization due to its bargaining power in its relationship with the state sector.

2. *Mass or 'coupon' privatization through 'Justice shares'*: this method was introduced as a means to promote 'social justice' through privatization. During the first two years of Ahmadinejad's presidency, 6 million people, including pensioners, state employees, and the registered low-income deciles of the population, received the equivalent of $2.5 billion in stock in various public corporations under the rubric of 'Justice shares'. However, since there were no reliable statistics regarding low-income deciles, Ahmadinejad's administration employed "politically connected distributive institutions, such as the conservative Imam Khomeini Relief Foundation, the Basij militia and pensioners, as its database for doling out stocks and dividends. Recipients have been handed stocks worth an average of 20 million rials ($220), hardly a remedy for severe poverty" (Ehsani, 2009, p. 32).

The shares were distributed to people free of charge, but their property was left undefined and undetermined for ten years, meaning that people could not know the shares belonged to what specific enterprise and they could not sell them during this period. This was

---

[14] https://www.radiozamaneh.com/section/economy/ retrieved on December 22, 2021.
[15] There are other estimations about the total value of assets. According to Mohsen Rezai (July 5, 2006), the total amount has been 1000 thousand billion rials.

a separation of 'property' from 'management' (Nili & Associates, 2015, pp. 536–37). While the state was no more the owner, it remained the manager of distributed assets. The 'Justice share' constituted 68.5% of the transfer over the period 2004–2009 (Mousavi Nik, 2009, p. 4). It was a 'transitional' mechanism keeping the state's management without state property. In this sense, Justice share resulted in 'parastatal' or semi-state sector that should be distinguished from 'non-state public sector' embracing BMJ, Setad, Khatam, etc. 'Parastatal' enterprises are those "enterprises that are managed by the state while more than 50% of their assets do not belong to the state" (Mousavi Nik, 2009, p. 14). According to this definition, divestment through Justice share promoted the parastatal sector. Contrary to the parastatal sector, the non-state public sector is not managed by the state.

3. *Other methods* pertained to all other ways of property transfer that had not been included in debt cancellations and Justice share. Since the first two methods transferred the property to 'parastatal' and 'non-state public' sectors, the potential true privatization could only exist among this last category. Other methods embraced 19% of transfer during 2005–2009. However, as indicated previously, the share of true privatization was officially estimated between 5% and 13.5%. This last category consisted of transferring shares through stock exchange. In fact, the privatization decree explicitly stipulated stock exchange as the mechanism of property transfer compared to other mechanisms notably bidding and direct negotiations that were used during Rafsanjani's first wave of privatization from 1990 to 1993. Figure 7.3 illustrates the share of each mechanism over the period 1990–2000.

Figure 7.3 clearly demonstrates that the state assets were principally transferred through the stock exchange (70%) compared to negotiations (21%) and bidding (9%). However, it should be reminded that an estimated 85% of Iran's stock exchange was dominated by state agencies or the non-governmental public sector (Ehsani, 2009, p. 32).

Figure 7.4 shows that the bulk of divestment was carried out during the period 2006–2011.

Three types of shares were used: preferential, gradual, and in block. The preferential shares were used for insider privatization also known as 'management-employee buyouts' (MEBO). Gradual shares were given to

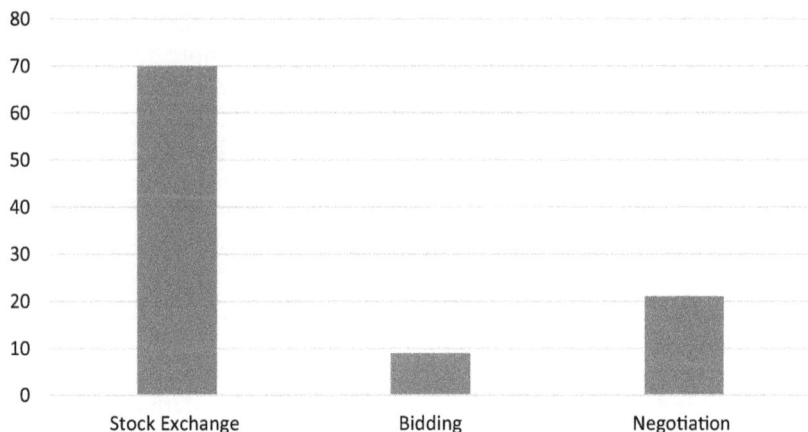

Fig. 7.3 Share of each mechanism in transferring the state assets in terms of 2004 constant price for the period 1990–2000 (%)

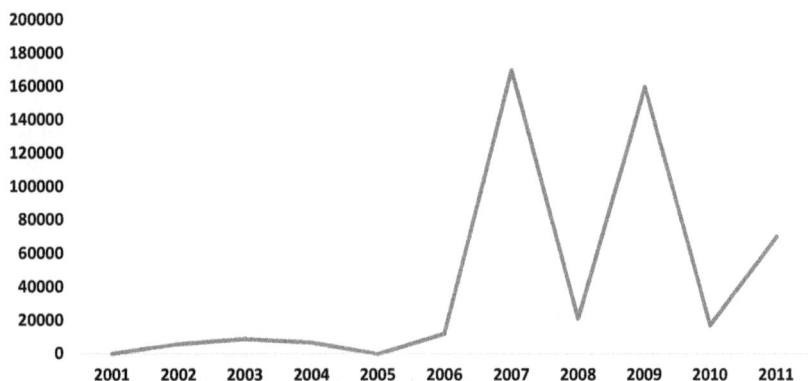

Fig. 7.4 The value of divested state assets in terms of 2004 constant price for the period 2001–2011 (billion rials)

dispersed external buyers. Block shares were used to transfer the SOEs properties to concentrated buyers.

Three characteristic features distinguished this last category of privatization. First, the sale through block shares or to concentrated buyers was preponderant. Second, the majority of the shares were transferred to a few

Table 7.3 Different types of privatizations and its beneficiaries

Type of privatization	Period 2005–2009 (percentage)	Period 2001–2011 (percentage)	Beneficiaries
Debt cancellations	12.5	25	Non-state public sector
Justice share	68.5	40	Parastatal sector
Other methods	19	35	Non-state public sector and private sector (5–13.5)

big holdings. Third, the principal buyers were parastatal organizations and non-state public corporations, among them, were the Social Security Investment Company (SHASTA) and the Iranian Mehr Investment Company (affiliated to credit and financial Mehr corporation, the ex-Basij cooperative bank). They acquired 46% of the block shares (Mousavi Nik, 2009, p. 12). Hence, even SOEs sold through stock exchange did not go entirely to the private sector. SOEs valued at 36,979 billion rials (3.7 billion US dollars) were divested through block shares to 'non-state public sector'.

Although the privatization campaign was officially launched in July 2006 by the Supreme Leader, it was informally started since the second term of Khatami's presidency in 2001. Nili and Associates (2015) provide figures for all types of privatizations during the period extending from 2001 to 2011. Table 7.3 illustrates the final outcome of different privatization methods and its beneficiaries during this period.

Table 7.3 clearly demonstrates that what is known as 'privatization' was the transfer of state property to parastatal and non-state public sectors. The share of Justice share shrank to 40% in 2011 as Ahmadinejad had initially announced while the shares of debt cancellations and other methods increased. Consequently, the principal beneficiary of 'privatization' was the non-state public sector. But who is 'non-state public sector'?

7.4 Confusing Definitions of Non-state Public Sector

All economic and political analysts of the privatization decree in Iran are unanimous that the real beneficiaries of this policy have been the organizations and corporations belonging to the 'non-state public sector'. A newly Persian expression *Khosolati* has been widely in use that captures this reality. The term is a mixture of 'private' (Khososi) and 'state' (dowlati) referring to the fact that the winners belong to both 'private' and 'state' spheres and at the same time to none of them, since they are principally composed of the extra-legal economic institutions related to the Supreme Jurisconsult. In this sense, the new owners are not part of the formal state, nor part of the private sector. This term has been contested by some scholars in social science since they believe that *Khosolati* is nothing but a special form of private property. But what is meant by 'private property'?

Two broad approaches should be distinguished in defining 'private property'. A productive approach was formulated by Karl Marx. In his theoretical framework, private property in the *production process* means the separation of direct producers from their means of production. This separation is incorporated in the commodification of products and is spawned through social division of labor. Accordingly, capitalism is defined as extended market relationships in which labor power is also transformed into commodity. In this sense, state property is also private property insofar as direct producers are separated from their means of production.

There exists a second contractual approach in which property rights are defined in the *process of appropriation*. Different institutionalist schools such as old American Institutionalism of Commons and Veblen, as well as the recent Property Rights School and Transaction Costs Economics, have contributed to this approach despite their fundamental divergences. The contractual approach considers property rights as residual claimancy over the flow of income and the fiat power to exclude[16] (Hart, 2017). To simplify the complicated story of property rights, it can be said that the agency who has the right to exclude is assumed to be the property owner. In this context, there is a great difference between private, state, and *Anfal* property since the right to exclude belongs to a specific agent in each case.

The difference between a *productive* and a *contractual* approach to property rights is crucial in classifying the type of property. For example, while in a Marxian approach, 'state' property in any capitalist economy is deemed to be 'private', in a contractual approach, state property cannot be conflated with private property. It might be argued that in a productive perspective, *Khosolati* is a form of private property, but this cannot erase

---

[16] The emphasis on fiat power to exclude is based upon incomplete contracts. Oliver Hart (2017) has formalized incompleteness of contractual relationships and has demonstrated that ownership of non-human assets is a source of bargaining power when contracts are incomplete (see Vahabi, 2002).

the difference between *Khosloati* and private property from a contractual viewpoint. Having distinguished these two broad perspectives, we need to explore further 'non-state public sector'. To which category of property does it belong?

Article 45 of the constitution of the IRI reduced all public properties to 'state property' because of 'unity thesis' conflating *Anfal* and state property. There was no allusion to public property in contradistinction from state property in Article 44. The privatization decree reversed the situation and treated 'non-state public property' as a sub-category of 'private property' rather than 'state property'. In his critical assessment of 'General policies pertaining to Article 44 of the constitution of the Islamic Republic of Iran', Najafi Khah (2016), a legal expert of the IRI legislation, has persuasively argued that in this decree "institutions belonging to the non-state sector are treated on the same foot as private and cooperative sectors, and the transfer of state property to them is pigeonholed as privatization. When the SOEs are transferred to the private and cooperative sectors, the privatization policy is implemented as a means to downsize the state sector and increase the private sector, whereas when the SOEs are transferred to institutions and organizations of non-state public sector, privatization policy entails deregulation of economic activities in the public sector. Although even in the latter case, the state property is transformed into non-state public property, the property is not transferred to the private or cooperative sectors enshrined in the Article 44; the property of these enterprises remains public ... In this decree, the non-state public sector is treated in the same way as private and cooperative sectors. The law is replete with ambiguities and confusions" (2016, p. 116).

The source of these ambiguities and confusions resides in the fact that the IRI legislation defines the 'non-state public property' on an *accounting* rather than *economic* basis. More exactly, 'state property' and 'non-state public property' are defined in Articles 4 and 5 of the 'Public Audit Act' (https://rc.majlis.ir/fa/law/show/91384) enacted by the Iranian parliament on August 23, 1987.

Article 4 states: "A state enterprise is a specific organizational unit that is created by law as a corporation or is nationalized or confiscated by the order of law and recognized as such, with more than 50% of its assets belonging to the state." Article 5 stipulates that "non-state public institutions are specific organizational units that are created or will be created by law to execute public tasks and services. Note: the list of these institutions and organizations is proposed by the state in compliance with the law and regulations and is enacted by the the Islamic Consultative Assembly (Majles)." This definition suffers from fundamental shortcomings and results in contradictory orders. Here, I focus on four major failures.

First, the privatization decree treats 'non-state public sector' in the general context of privatization, while 'Public Audit Act' is not concerned with 'private sector'. It disentangles different public entities, notably the state and non-state public organizations from an accounting viewpoint. It is not clear how 'Public Audit Act' can cast light on the relationship between 'non-state public sector' with 'private sector'?

Second, Article 5 does not provide a general definition of 'non-state public organization'. This type of public organization is defined by a list of *specific cases* or applications. The list is never exhaustive and can be amended along the enactment of new laws and regulations. It suffices that the government submits a new list and if approved by the parliament, new organizations will be pigeonholed as such. However, the list can also be amended by the Supreme Leader. The organizations might be completely heterogeneous since they are not defined according to a universal principle.

Third, contrary to the note of Article 5, most of 'non-state public organizations' such as BMJ, Setad, Khatam, and the Imam relief Committee have never been subject to the Majles preliminary approval. As 'revolutionary' institutions under the direct purview of the Supreme Leader, they did not need such approval.

Fourth, the initial governmental list of non-state public organizations was enacted in 1994 and amended afterward by the virtue of new adopted laws among them the 'Law on Stock Exchange Market of the IRI' on November 22, 2005 (https://rc.majlis.ir/fa/law/print_version/97786). Article 5 of this law defines stock exchange as 'non-state public institution'. The stock exchange market regulates the organized capital market. Its role in capital market is akin to that of the Central Bank in the monetary market or to the Central Insurance of the IRI in the insurance market. However, while the law has defined the Central Bank and the Central Insurance as 'state enterprises', the stock exchange is characterized as 'non-state public organization'. There is no explanation why they are treated differently.

Another interesting example is the library of Ayatollah Mar'ashi Najafi which is named as 'non-state public institution', whereas it is not open to public and belongs to the person of Ayatollah Mar'ashi Najafi. The status of 'non-state public institution' has many advantages and privileges including exoneration from tax payment, access to different types of subsidies and credit lines. It is allotted to an institution or organization based on *political* considerations regardless of the *economic* rationale. From a legal point of view, the identity of different types of public enterprises is distinguished by their *accounting* status in 'Public Audit Act'.

Reviewing 'Public Audit Act', a line of demarcation can be drawn between 'non-state public organizations' that are subject to public audit and those that are excluded from it because of specific rules and regulations. Among the first category are the Social Security Organization and its affiliated enterprises, municipalities, rural and urban councils, and some banks. According to a recent interview of *Fars News* with Mehrdad Bazrpash, the President of 'Supreme Audit Court of Iran' (SAI), the Supreme Court is committed to inspect the financial accounts of aforementioned non-state public institutions (see www.qudsonline.ir retrieved on December 30, 2021). However, there is a second category of non-state public institutions enshrined in Note 6 of Article 72 that are not subject to public audit. Although these institutions are not specifically named, the Note 6 refers to the rules and regulations that exclude them from public audit. These institutions are those that are under the purview of the Supreme Leader and are independent from the government including BMJ, Setad, the Sepah, the Basij, Astant Quods Razavi, and many others.[17]

But what is the nature of property relationships in these institutions? *Anfal* does not belong to 'public', it is the restrictive property of the Imam or the Supreme Jurisconsult. The economic undertakings of Khatam also do not belong to public, they are owned by the Sepah. In fact, all of them are the outcome of dispossession of people from their public properties. Generally speaking, 'non-state public sector' is an ambiguous category that dissimulates the *private property of an oligarchy of Islamic sovereign institutions*. The privatization decree benefited principally this oligarchy.

[17] See for a complete list: https://fa.wikipedia.org/wiki/%D8%B3%D8%A7%D8%B2%D9%85%D8%A7%D9%86%E2%80%8C%D9%87%D8%A7%DB%8C_%D8%B2%DB%8C%D8%B1_%D9%86%D8%B8%D8%B1_%D8%B1%D9%87%D8%A8%D8%B1%DB%8C_%D8%AF%D8%B1_%D8%A7%DB%8C%D8%B1%D8%A7%D9%86 retrieved on January 1, 2022.

7.5   Privatization Decree and the Third Phase of *Anfal*'s Progression (2006–Now)

The preceding sections showed that the privatization decree (2006–2011) enhanced *Anfal* and marked its third phase since it ended with the 'unity thesis' and institutionalized the separation of *Anfal* from the state property. This does not imply that privatization necessarily promotes *Anfal*.

In the absence of foreign investment and the return of Iranians' capital abroad, *Anfal* thrived because of privatization. *Anfal* could not prosper if privatization was accompanied by foreign investment and free capital flow. *Anfal*, privatization, and openness of the Iranian economy constitute what I name the *impossible trinity of Anfal*. This expression is inspired by what is known in international economics as 'impossible triangle' or 'impossible trinity'[18] (see Boughton, 2003; Krugman & Obstfeld, 2003). Figure 7.5 illustrates the impossible trinity of *Anfal*.

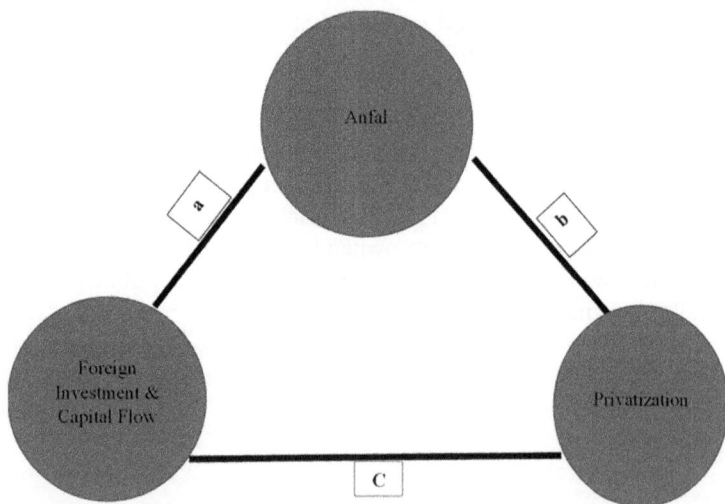

Fig. 7.5   The impossible trinity of *Anfal*

[18] The 'impossible trinity' (also known as the impossible trilemma or the Unholy Trinity) is an expression in international economics that states that it is impossible to have more than two of these three policy positions: (1) a fixed foreign exchange rate; (2) free capital movement or absence of capital controls; and (3) an independent monetary policy. This is originally formulated by Mundell and Fleming.

By 'foreign investment and free capital flow', I mean economic open-ness toward Western countries, primarily USA, and to a lesser degree toward European countries. China and Russia are not included even though Iran's economic relationships and commercial transactions with both countries radically increased since the American sanctions. It is note-worthy that while China, Russia, the European Union, and England did not abandon Joint Comprehensive Plan of Action (JCPOA) after Trump's withdrawal, they could not alter American's decisions or curb American's 'maximum pressure' policy on the Iranian economy since May 2018. Moreover, *Anfal* stands for parallel economic institutions belonging to the Supreme Leader that are not part of the official state sector.

The impossible trinity of *Anfal* states that it is impossible to have more than two of the three following policy positions: (a) *Anfal* and economic openness; (b) *Anfal* and privatization; (c) privatization and economic openness.

Policy positions (b) and (c) define two opposite strategies regarding privatization. Strategy (c) consists of combining privatization and relaxing Article 81 of the constitution leading to the erosion of *Anfal*'s position. This strategy was followed to some extent under the presidencies of Hashemi Rafsanjani and Khatami with some contradictions and inconsis-tencies. This strategy of privatization enhancing 'private sector' was thwarted by a coalition between the Supreme Leader and the Sepah. By contrast, strategy (b) promotes an alternative privatization for the interests of *Anfal* and the Sepah. Paradoxically, the American sanctions and the imposition of a closed economy on Iran during Ahmadinejad's presidency and then the withdrawal of Trump's administration from the 'Iran's nuclear deal' (JCPOA) reinforced strategy (b).

This point has been documented extensively. The *Sharq* newspaper reported that the Minister of Oil, Rostam Qassemi, had emphatically announced that the Khatam headquarter had to replace large foreign com-panies (Zandi, 2011). More recently, Forozan (2016) compared the nega-tive and positive impact of sanctions on the Sepah's economic activities and concluded that the benefits exceeded the costs incurred by 'smart' sanctions: "The fact that the Sepah benefited from the international sanc-tions against Iran does not imply that the sanctions have been completely ineffective. Arguably, the Sepah has been hit by the 'smart' sanctions, such as those that target foreign trade, Iranian banking, and oil exports, and the Sepah's affiliated companies, business dealings and assets. Nonetheless, the deleterious impacts of these sanctions have been offset by the incentives given to the Sepah to fill the vacuum left by the foreign companies which previously invested in Iran's oil and gas sector. Since the aforementioned ban on foreign companies has come into effect, the Sepah has taken advantage of its proximity to the state and has thereby been the recipient of large economic contracts in oil and gas. In the words of the Supreme Commander of the Sepah: 'In the current climate of international sanctions, contracts cannot be handed over to foreign companies that only seek to maximise their profit' (*Jaras*, 2011). He went on to say that 'it is illegal for the Sepah to enter in contracts smaller than 1 billion US dollars' (*Jaras*, 22 April 2011)" (2016, pp. 149–150).

Anfal's economic institutions have been involved in oil and gas exploitation since the end of the 1980s and had partnership with major European oil companies. They strengthened their presence during the sanctions. For example, Behran Oil was a subsidiary of the Bonyad. It established a joint company with the French energy giant, Total, named 'Beh Total'. According to Total's 2016 annual report, it sold its entire stake in the joint venture amounting to 50% in December 2012. Beh Total was renamed 'Beh Tam' since Total ended its partnership. Total did not completely severe its ties with Beh Tam. "As part of the 2012 sales agreement, Total agreed to license the trademark 'Total' to Beh Tam for a 3 year period for the sale of the Iranian Company's lubricants in Iran. Total E&P Iran (TEPI), a wholly owned affiliate of Total, received royalty payments from Beh Tam, in 2014 (almost 1 Million USD). Since 2015, royalties were suspended due to procedures that have been brought up by the Iranian tax authorities against TEPI" (https://www.ifmat.org/bonyad-mostazafan-report/ retrieved on January 7, 2022). Beh Tam extended its activities in oil fields since the US sanctions.

Thus, the third phase of *Anfal* is characterized by its extension to the petroleum and gas sectors. Insofar as *Anfal* was conflated with the state sector under the 'unity thesis', it was not important whether 'ownerless' natural resources belonged to the Supreme Leader or the state. However, once the 'privatization' of the state enterprises was launched, it became particularly important to delineate the Supreme Leader's property from 'all Muslims' property. The question was now whether the petroleum fields belonged to *Anfal* or to the state?

As discussed in Chap. 5, the Shi'i faqihs have contradictory positions on (1) whether mines in general belong to *Anfal* (2) or only one of the two types of 'latent' and 'apparent' mines is reserved for *Anfal*. This issue is particularly important in the case of petroleum, since if 'latent' mines are deemed to be part of *Anfal*, it would signify that the oil revenue does not belong to 'all Muslims' but to the Supreme Leader. While this issue has been extensively debated at a theoretical level in the seminaries during the last 15 years, it was never officially enacted as a law. However, another aspect of *Anfal* came to the surface during Rouhani's presidency in July 2020 that was shocking for the public opinion: the summit and slope of mountains such as Mount Damavand and what exist in it belong to *Anfal* and can be appropriated by the Bonyad.

The Mineral Company of Damavand (*Sherkat ma'adani Damavand*) is one of the subsidiary companies of the Bonyad, under the purview of Iran-based Somic Engineering and Management Company of Bonyad. It is the biggest mine extracting and selling pumice stones. The company is situated in the village Gazaneh (https://gazaneh.com/) close to Malayer, both villages are known for their mineral stones extracted from Damavand. According to the ecological activist, Ismail Kahrom, 500 camions carry the soil and stone extracted from Damavand daily leading to the total erosion of the second most prominent summit in Asia after Mount Everest within 200 years. The value of each camion has been estimated at 110 thousand tomans (almost 43 USD) in 2015. The pumice stones are exported to Russia, Turkey, Pakistan, Syria, Iraq, Afghanistan, and the Emirates (*Zeitoons* July 22, 2020; and *Aftab News*, July 28, 2020, retrieved on December 22, 2021). The stones are sold in USD six times more in Iraq and its revenue constitutes one of the Iran's major non-oil exporting products. *Anfal*'s ownership of 'ownerless' resources accentuated the commodification and destruction of non-renewable resources.[19]

To sum up the three phases of *Anfal*, Table 7.4 recapitulates *Anfal*'s juridical status, its domain, its progression channel, and the rapidity of its progression (Grade) due to the coalitional alliance. The first and second phases of *Anfal* are also incorporated in the table so that the three phases can be compared.

As Table 7.4 indicates, the speed of progression was very high because of coalition between *Anfal* and *Khatam* headquarters in replacing foreign oil and gas companies. In the preceding chapter, we underlined three major channels of the Sepah in rent-seeking through Islamic political

[19] The role of *Anfal* and the Sepah in destroying the environment, mountains, forests, and pastures warrants a separate systematic investigation (see, for example, https://irannewsupdate.com/news/general/the-role-of-irans-irgc-in-destroying-the-environment-forests-and--pastures/ retrieved on January 8, 2022).

Table 7.4 The three phases of *Anfal*

Phase of Anfal	Supreme Juriscomsult	Source of legitimacy	Juridical status	Domain of Anfal	Channel of progression	Rapidity of progression
First phase: 1979–1989	Ruhollah Khomeini	Charismatic leader of revolution: political and religious	Article 45: Inseparability of *Anfal* from the state property (unity thesis)	Confiscation of the late Shah's properties and 53 industrialists and financiers	BMJ, Islamic charities for social protection, and coalitionary political alliance with Sepah, Basij, etc.	Low
Second phase: 1989–2005	Seyyed Ali Khamenei	New parallel Islamic institutions: political but not religious	Article 49 and Khomeini's injunction in April 1989	Universal confiscatory regime and guardianship of 'ownerless' properties	BMJ, Setad, Islamic charities, Islamic banks, and coalitionary political and economic alliance with Sepah, Basij, etc.	High
Third phase: 2006–now	Seyyed Ali Khamenei	New parallel Islamic institutions: political but not religious	Khamenei's decree on 'General policies pertaining to Article 44 of the constitution of the Islamic Republic of Iran'	Extension through privatization, exploitation of oil and gas, and commodification of 'ownerless' natural resources	Coalition with the Sepah and the Basij particularly in oil and gas	Very high

capitalism. The control of petroleum and gas fields forms a fourth principal channel. Finally, the 'revolving doors' between the Sepah's high-rank officials and the giant economic foundations provide a fifth channel. An investigation on the political background of directors of BMJ and Setad demonstrates that they were often recruited from the Sepah (see Boroujerdi & Rahimkhani, 2018).

Furthermore, the Sepah's high-rank officials dominate the executive and legislative powers. In both Ahmadinejad's and Raisi's cabinets, ministers with a background in the Sepah constitute the bulk of ministers. The Sepah's ascent in controlling the state is decisive in the dynamics of coalition with *Anfal*. In fact, the increasing power of the Sepah breeds competition between its economic undertakings and *Anfal*'s institutions. The Sepah's interpretation of *Anfal* clearly shows that it supports the 'unity thesis' advocated by Khomeini and Montazeri to integrate *Anfal* in the state.

For instance, a site run by the Sepah, *Tasnim*, has published many articles on *Anfal* and its place in the Shi'i Islam. It defines *Anfal* in the following terms: "All ownerless properties that are under the state's control in all systems are named *Anfal* in the Islamic fiqh" (*Tasnim*, September 12, 2017). The paper quotes Ayatollah Khomeini to support the idea that *Anfal* belongs to the state. Moreover, the paper adds the new spatial dimension of the state that should belong to *Anfal* as part of the state's domain: "The outer space which is beyond personal property rights in which planes, and helicopters fly or the power for the electricity transfer through high-voltage cables (HV), as well as underground spaces that are not owned by individuals in which the municipalities decide to build tunnels or subways, are all part of *Anfal*." The paper also cites other modern illustrations of *Anfal* such as "the sea and ocean depths that can be used for transferring gas and oil pipelines or by submarines, and any undersea discoveries including mines". All these cases are named to emphasize that they belong *to the state* rather than *the Imam* under the Islamic title of *Anfal*. The implication of such an interpretation is huge: *Anfal* should be totally integrated in the state and the 'security considerations' will necessarily bring the Sepah's control over these assets.

While there is not yet such open tension between the Sepah and *Anfal*, once the privatization decree was issued, any emphasis on the 'unity thesis' prevalent during Khomeini's era would undermine *Anfal* and strengthen the Sepah's[20] authority over 'ownerless' natural resources (*res nullius*). In my opinion, one of the major critical issues in the post-Khamenei era will be the property rights of *Anfal*: to whom will it belong? To the Supreme Leader or to the State? The Sepah has stakes in allocating these rights to the state. In other words, the coalition between *Anfal* and the Sepah that culminated in the Islamic economic revolution concentrating the economic power in the hands of the Supreme Leader has paved the road to its demise. Now that *Anfal* has swallowed most of the public treasury, the question is whether it would be transformed into the state's new public treasury?

7.6   *Anfal* and Authoritative Coordination

The state sector was preponderant in the aftermath of the 1979 Revolution and during the eight-year war with Iraq (1979–1989). In conformity with Article 44 of the constitution, all basic and large-scale industries, foreign trade, banking, insurance, energy, dams and large-scale irrigation, radio and television, the post, telegraph and telephone, roads and railroads, airlines, shipping, etc. were officially concentrated in the hands of the state. Ehsani (2009, p. 27) noted that public-sector employment more than doubled after the revolution, from 1.7 million in 1976 to 3.5 million in 1986. According to his sources, within three years of the revolution, one in six Iranians above the age of 15 belonged to one state and revolutionary body or another. However, despite this extensive intervention of the state in all economic sectors and job creation, its authority as well as its centralized and hierarchical structure was undermined by two major tendencies: (1) the spontaneous revolutionary initiatives; (2) the development of an Islamic parallel system.

The former prevailed in all factories and enterprises whose owners had fled the country. Workers exercised their control over production line and

---

[20] Other potential tensions and rivalries must not be ignored. One of them is the competition between the Sepah's and the Basij's economic networks to control the assets of the state. The Iran Telecommunication deal was illustrative of such a competition. Both the Basij affiliated organization, the Mehr-e Iqetsad Iranian Investment Company, and the Sepah's subsidiary Etemad-e Mobin consortium were interested to purchase shares in Iran Telecommunication. Initially, in September 2009, it was the Basij affiliated company that tried to buy 51 percent of the shares of Iran Telecommunication. However, the Privatization Organization decided to transfer the shares to the other rival group affiliated to the Sepah's consortium and as a result Etemad-e Mobin won the deal (Forozan, 2016, pp. 158–159).

employment policies, and even were forced in some cases to undertake the management of 'abandoned' enterprises. The revolutionary upheaval paralyzed the official army and the state bureaucracy. Cooperative coordination replaced authoritative coordination during the first years of revolution (1979–1982). The Islamic forces opposed and repressed this spontaneous new form of coordination since its inception. However, they did not reinforce authoritative coordination since they developed their parallel 'revolutionary' institutions undermining centralized and hierarchical structure of the state. Hence, the authoritative coordination could not function despite the unprecedented extension of the state sector's size and scope in the wake of revolution and war.

The dual structure of the IRI perpetuated the crisis of authoritative coordination. The authority of the president of the Islamic republic was systematically dismissed by *Velayat Faqih* (the jurisconsult of the vicegerent), and the Islamic courts supplanted civil tribunals. This period corresponds to the first phase of *Anfal* during which the multiplication of Islamic charities decentralized the Social Security Organization. The hierarchical structure of the state also was undermined because of parallel Islamic system.

The authority of newly born 'Islamic revolutionary institutions' overshadowed the state's official hierarchy. Moreover, the creation and growth of the Komitehs, the Sepah, and the Basij undermined the authority of gendarmerie, *Shahrbani* (the police force remaining from the Shah's epoch), and the army. The same holds true for the newly 'revolutionary administration' such as 'Construction Jihad' that challenged the ministries. The Islamic loan funds and *Sazman Iqtesad Islami* (the Organization of the Islamic Economics) overlooked the Iranian Central Bank's authority in creating money. The state's authority was officially questioned when it could not collect taxes from the institutions under the direct purview of the Supreme Leader. The executive and legislative powers were unable to conduct a public inspection on the financial activities of these institutions. The public treasury was enfeebled by the Supreme Leader's treasury situated in Beit al-Imam (the House of the Supreme Leader). The state's downsizing started under Hashemi Rafsanjani and continued during Khatami. But the state's debt crises persisted to augment even during the unprecedented increase in oil revenues.

In the second phase of *Anfal*, giant holdings of Bonyad and Setad were reinforced through confiscatory regime and the Sepah started to interfere in the economy. Parallel to the privatization of the banking system and the reduction of state property in banking and insurance sector, the large Islamic loan funds were transformed into the Islamic banks and dominated the banking and insurance system. In other words, the decreasing share of the state sector was captured by *Anfal* and the Sepah.

Anfal's progression was detrimental to authoritative coordination in every sense. The privatization decree in July 2006 downsized the state sector to 20% of what it represented during the first phase of *Anfal*. Not only the size of state sector shrank, but also its hierarchical and centralized provision of public goods and services were negatively impacted. The reformist movement to reconstruct a republican authority in harmony with the Supreme Leader's discretionary power came to a deadlock and demonstrated its impotence and sterility. As Malonney (2015, p. 312) aptly pinpointed, the reformist president Khatami entered the presidency like a lion, and he left like a lamb. It was his unforgettable words that in the IRI, the president of the republic is nothing but a 'logistic provider'. The same story repeated for President Rouhani.

To sum up, the crisis of authoritative coordination started by the 1979 Revolution, but it became institutionalized because of *Velayat Faqih* and the appropriation of public properties by *Anfal*. The 'revolutionary' and 'Islamic' credentials of newly born parallel institutions perpetuated the state sector's crisis and impeded any reform to restructure this sector and re-establish authoritative coordination.

7.7   *ANFAL* AND MARKET COORDINATION

Impersonal market coordination hinges upon the private sector activities. As Kornai (1990a) pointed out there exists a strong linkage or a natural affinity between market coordination and private property. Thus, an inquiry regarding the share of private sector is crucial in measuring the place of market coordination in the economy. What is the share of private sector in the Iranian economy?

An official estimation suggests that the state and parastatal sectors control two-thirds of the Iranian economy, the private sector constitutes the remaining third (*Ettelaat*, October 29, 2006). Although the privatization decree in July 2006 was the first major attempt at privatization since the inception of the IRI, its implementation did not increase the share of private sector more than 5–13.5%. As discussed in the preceding section, in the absence of foreign investment and Iranian's capital abroad, the privatization enhanced mainly the share of *Anfal*, the Sepah, and the Basij.

According to Ehsani (2009, p. 30), "The state dominates the Iranian economy, and ironically this domination has been increasing since 2005. Currently there are more than 500 major state-owned corporations, which in turn are comprised of more than 16,000 subsidiaries. In recent years, state corporations have taken up to a 76% share of the total national budget and two thirds of the GDP."

This estimation calls for scrutiny since it is rather the sum of both the state sector and supra-legal parallel institutions (the so-called non-state public sector) that dominate the Iranian economy. The estimation for the private sector comprising 24% of the remaining share seems plausible. Moreover, the privatization did not enhance the role of private property in the manufacturing sector. In fact, many private buyers bought the SOEs, fired the workers, changed the land-use title of the property, sold the assets, and speculated on the real estate (*Sharq*, August 16, 2006). They were not interested in maximizing industrial profit but rather on dismantling existing enterprises and selling the assets in speculative markets.

In other words, while the state property diminished throughout the post-war period, the private sector could not gain its share. In the same vein, the failure of authoritative coordination did not strengthen market coordination; it only reinforced the position of Islamic parallel institutions. Market coordination thrived principally as a broker for these institutions. The upshot has been a 'dependent' market acting as subcontractor of *Anfal*, the Sepah, and the Basij. I call this specific type of market, *political* market.

For example, while state monopoly over the foreign trade shunned the private sector's intervention in organizing import-export during 1979–1990, those bazaar merchants who had personal ties with Islamic leaders could benefit colossally from multiple exchange rates.[21] A dependent 'political' market was developed to maximize rent-seeking. *Political markets* mushroomed in the context of *Anfal* and the parallel economic institutions. The US sanctions also resulted in a parallel political market profiting from activities related to detouring the sanctions.[22] The Sepah's intervention in the economy also promoted subcontracting of private

---

[21] This point has been elaborated in Sect. 7.2.

[22] Sanctions had asymmetrical effect on different groups of population. According to Olmsted (2013), akin to the case of Iraq and Gaza, American sanctions and embargo negatively impacted female employment, particularly the lives of women from the lowest paid segment of Iranian society.

enterprises working for it. Almost 5000 subcontracting enterprises relied on Khatam's deals (Vahabi, 2015). While Khatam headquarters directly undertook big deals more than one billion dollars, they often subcontracted smaller deals to private enterprises in return for commissions. The subcontracting system flourished after the Islamic economic revolution in 2006.

But what are 'political' markets? They are a type of market that relies on supra-economic coercive allocation mechanisms including state monopoly or privileges granted by the sovereign power or other leading political formations. The fusion of property and sovereignty feeds political markets. They are different from impersonal market coordination in two major respects.

First, instead of *price appropriation* of every product and service through 'voluntary' market exchanges, *coercive allocation* prevails. The asset transfer is not necessarily based on price; it can be free of charge without using price mechanism and resorting to means such as confiscation, no-bidding contracts, and free loans and credit.

Second, political markets are not *impersonal*, they are strongly relational and exist only based on personal or institutional *trust*. The reputational capital or the proximity to political authority is the first condition for cutting a deal. The investment is not only pecuniary but also non-pecuniary. Adherence to the traditional code of behavior and informal customary rules are part of investment in reputational capital. Political, religious, and family backgrounds support reputational capital, but it is the constant investment in this specific type of intangible capital that is indispensable for perpetuating active participation and networking in the circles of trusted ones. Political markets are compatible with caste system and inter-group marriages.[23]

What are the advantages and disadvantages of political markets? Their most important advantage is that they economize on transaction costs since they are based on informal, non-legal contacts that do not incur most of Oliver Williamson's (1985) *ex ante* and *ex post* transaction costs. However, while transaction costs for parties involved in political markets are almost nil, they provoke infinite transaction costs for transactors in impersonal markets. Those who are not part of the trusted ones, should pay all sorts of transaction costs when they enter in market coordination

---

[23] See Boroujerdi and Rahimkhani (2018) on the importance of inter-group marriages among the IRI leading figures.

and even then, they will not be sure of protecting their assets because they can be confiscated under arbitrary pretexts. Political markets engender high inefficiency for market capitalism because of highly increasing transaction costs for the whole economy.

Moreover, in the presence of political markets, the markets are both *totally unfettered* ('liberalized') and at the same time *over-regulated*. Coville (2013) disentangles more than 50 types of required permissions to launch an enterprise in Iran and highlights institutional obstacles impeding a performant market. High transaction costs prevail in the Iranian economy (Renani, 2010),[24] while political markets are exempt of such costs. In this sense, political markets enhance and hinder market relationships. Generally speaking, they are a source of allocative and productive inefficiency. The Islamic economic revolution generalized political markets in product, monetary, and capital markets.

In capital markets, as previously reported, 85% of Iran's stock exchange is dominated by pension funds, the Social Security Organization, various foundations, and municipalities (Ehsani, 2009, p. 32).[25] The same holds true for monetary market. The *Fraru* site (May 12, 2009) reported that while the government was supposed to allocate 50% of the foreign currency reserve's fund to the private sector according to the Second Five-Year development plan (1995–1999), the share of private sector stemming from foreign exchange currency reserve in 2008 amounted to less than 20% compared to the increasing shares of the government and the non-state public sectors.[26]

---

[24] Renani (2010) attempts to measure one sort of transaction costs, namely enforcement costs by comparing the data regarding the number of unfunded checks issued by physical and legal persons in 1992 and in 1976 (before the 1979 Revolution). He finds out that the number has been 45 times higher in 1992.

[25] This state-led stock exchange was used to finance state's budget deficits during the last years of Rouhani's presidency (2019–2020) by mobilizing citizens' private savings based on false promises of high 'secured' returns on their equities even though the economy was in recession with a negative economic growth rate of minus 6.78 (https://www.macrotrends.net/countries/IRN/iran/economic-growth-rate#, retrieved on January 10, 2022).

[26] Another dimension of marginalization of the private sector in monetary market is the dissolution of the board of trustees of the 'Foreign Exchange Reserve' as an independent body composed of government and the ICB's officials for approving the requested loans by private sector in 2008. Forozan (2016, p. 152) shows that the dissolution of the board of trustees was initiated by the 'quasi-governmental bodies, such as the Sepah' to use foreign currency at their own discretion without any public scrutiny or audit.

The product market is also dominated by political markets with oligarchic privileges over import-export of different products such as oil, sugar, iron, petrochemicals, luxury cars, etc. No-bidding contracts, oligopolistic or monopolistic position in the market, tax exoneration, privileged access to hard currency, easy bank credits, and a soft budget constraint describe different dimensions and particular features of political markets.

The situation in labor market is different. Wage and salary system and monetary relationships are the two fundamental underlying pillars of production relationships in Iran. Borrowing Marxian terminology, market capitalism dominates 'mode of production' in Iran. However, the capitalist process of production is not merely economic, it equally involves a myriad of political and ideological factors. Burawoy's concept of 'factory regime' is useful to grapple these multifactor relationships.

A factory regime is basically determined by the relationship between factory and the state. Burawoy (1985, pp. 12–13, 25–26, 85–121) distinguished three types of regimes: (1) an early 'manufacture despotism' based on the economic coercion in the labor market as described by Marx in *Capital* volume 1. The English manufacturing system in the early nineteenth century provides a prototype. (2) A more developed form of 'manufacturing consent' or 'hegemonic regimes' of monopoly capitalism has been classified as a second prototype. It is based on the consent or compromise between workers and employers that accompanies limited worker autonomy. Such a regime is the outcome of state's intervention to guarantee minimum subsistence levels and collective bargaining rights so that workers become insulated from the labor market and employers are incentivized to resort to more persuasive measures of labor control. Comparisons of the USA with England, Japan, and Sweden have illustrated the impact of national varieties in hegemonic regimes. However, in all these cases, the state apparatus has been kept separate from factory hierarchy. (3) A third prototype is 'bureaucratic despotic' factory regime in the Soviet-type economic systems in which the state apparatus is fused together with factory hierarchy in dire contrast to hegemonic regimes in the advanced capitalist system. This regime has been based on repressive mechanisms and bureaucratic state intervention in the factory and the economy.

The factory regime in post-revolutionary Iran experienced several phases, but the prevalent form since 1982 has been a new prototype that cannot be reduced to any of Burawoy's three afore-mentioned models. I name this fourth prototype 'Islamic corporatism'. It is generally believed that corporatist arrangements "are always the result of a state initiative, and their deployment represents a strong state *strategy* for managing political conflict" (Foweraker, 1987, p. 58). Schmitter (1974) nuanced this approach by suggesting a distinction between two sub-systems of corporatism, namely 'state corporatism' and 'societal corporatism'. Islamic corporatist arrangements have not been the outcome of formal state, but a 'strategy of domination' implemented by newly created Islamic parallel institutions that tried to manage political conflicts.

Islamic corporatism is not derived from *economic* interests but from *political* imperatives. It is carried out by Islamist workers related to the sovereign parallel institutions that represent an *exclusive* mode of mediating the capital-labor conflict. These parallel institutions at factory level (Islamic labor Councils, Islamic labor Associations) and at national level (*Khaneh Ka*rgar, Workers' house) are similar to fascist movements among workers and peasants in Italy, Germany, and Spain under Franco. They try to represent both the 'establishment' and the 'anti-establishment' oppositional force in the enterprise: they represent 'establishment' against any *independent labor movement* and act as the leading force of 'opposition' against 'liberal capitalist class' at the factory level for the interests of *Mostazafan* (the 'downtrodden').

Any independent worker organization is banned and brutally repressed in this type of factory regime. In a sense, the employment contracts are not based on 'free' but rather on 'forced' labor, since independent collective action of workers, strikes, and any other forms of voicing are unauthorized. However, this does not imply the absence of 'wildcat strikes' and contestations against the employers. The 'opposition' may be initiated by independent labor movements, but the Islamist forces often intervene to act as 'leaders' of the 'anti-neoliberal' and 'anti-capitalist' force to transform them from within and change them to a pro-sovereign movement with some partial 'economic' demands. This point will be further explored in the next section.

As discussed in Chap. 4, political capitalism does not constitute a distinctive socio-economic system in *production*, but it impacts *distribution* sphere in several ways. Islamic political capitalism has particularly embedded the Social Security system through *Anfal,* and Islamic charities as explained in Chap. 6. Moreover, it has accentuated several forms of discrimination in labor market among them gender marginalization in employment. The issue has been studied in the feminist literature from a class-gender perspective (Hoominfar & Zanganeh, 2021). Behdad and Nomani (2012) have studied the rate and pattern of women's exclusion and their incorporation in the market between 1976 and 2006 from an economic viewpoint.

An edited volume by Bahramitash and Salehi Esfahani (2011) endeavors to nuance the idea that the process of Islamization has negatively impacted the 'veiled employment'. They believe that development and Islamization have been reconciled under the IRI. In Chap. 5, the editors disentangle the sources of unemployment among women and suggest that it is not caused by the Islamization process but rather due to women's higher education. A similar strategy has been followed at a theoretical level by Carvalho (2013) who modeled veiling among Muslim women as a commitment mechanism that limits temptation to deviate from religious norms of behavior. The analysis suggests that veiling is a strategy for integration, enabling women to take up outside economic opportunities while preserving their reputation within the community.

The problem with this type of argument is that it shows how 'veiling' could be a source of social integration of young Muslim's women without inquiring what other problems and contradictions would be created by such contradictory type of 'integration'. For example, Sattari (2020) shows that a new type of employment has emerged under the IRI, namely women driving women: drivers of women-only taxis. This is an increase in 'veiled' employment based on 'segregated taxis'. This type of women 'segregated' integration abounds: segregated buses, segregated classrooms, segregated festivities, etc. The same holds true for the advocates of Islamic modernity. If 'higher unemployment' among women is not due to Islamization but higher education, then why should educated women be more subject to higher unemployment under the IRI? In other words, why is the disconnection between education and employment in the Iranian qualified labor market particularly accentuated in the case of 'veiled employment'?

7.8   *Anfal* and Cooperative Coordination

Cooperative coordination emerged as a result of workers' participation in the revolutionary process in the second half of summer of 1978. Bayat (1987, pp. 85–87) illustrated the trend of economic-political demand transformation of Iranian working class, from May 1978 to January 1979. Until October 1978 about 55% of the demands were still in an economic form. "The state's strategy at this point was to stop political demands by making economic concessions. Thus, in six months, the wages of all workers rose on average by 25%. Some sectors, such as metal and construction, obtained a 60% pay-raise (Bank Markazi Iran, 1979, p.25). The pay-rise was combined with payment of other benefits such as housing, child benefit and overtime" (Bayat, 1987, p. 88).

The turning point in workers' movement was the oil strike in October–November 1978 on which Sweezy and Magdoff (1979, p. 17) commented in these terms: "There have been few spectacles in recent history so inspiring and heart-warming as that of 70,000 oil workers, far and always the best paid and most privileged segment of the working class, bringing to a complete halt the huge production and refining complex which is the Iranian Oil Industry, and doing it not for better pay or special privileges, but in support of the quintessentially *political* demand of the whole Iranian people that the Shah and all he stands for must go." The list of demands which was submitted by Ahwaz staff workers on October 29th, 1978, included 12 demands of which 3 of them were *political*: "(1) End martial law; (2) Full solidarity and cooperation with the striking teachers; (3) Unconditional release of all political prisoners ..." (Turner, 1980a, p. 282).

This was the birth of a new political force challenging the Shah's personal regime. The workers created the strike committees that turned into *Shora* (workers' councils), a new center of power. According to Goodey (1980), these councils that were not limited to the petroleum sector established a 'dual power' exercising workers' control over production at the factory level[27] and paralyzing the Shah's regime at national level (Turner, 1980b). The councils were also formed in countryside, schools, hospitals, army bases, government offices, press, radio, and television, to ensure people's control and advance the revolution (Azad, 1980). To this long list the rise of councils among ethnic and peasant movements in Kurdistan and Turkmen Sahara in the wake of revolution should also be added. The strikes in the petroleum sector played a leading role in the movement from below because of its 'destructive power' (Vahabi, 2004) or what Jafari (2013) called 'disruptive power', that is, the potential ability to cause disruption in productive and reproductive activities of the society. The oil workers counter-power gave rise to three institutions that underpinned an alternative pole of authority parallel to the absolute monarchy: the Committee for the Coordination of Strikes in the oil industry, the Council

---

[27] Rahnema (1992) has questioned 'workers' control' over production and suggested 'workers' participation' in management.

of the Islamic Revolution which represented Khomeini's authority, and the neighborhood Committees that were in charge of local fuel distribution and security, and were later transformed into Komitehs, a new revolutionary organization that was under Khomeini's influence (Jafari, 2018).

Cooperative coordination prevailed in most of the factories during the first three years of the revolution (February 1979 to January 1982). It can be characterized by (1) a revolutionary situation marked by a general crisis of the state and private sectors ushering in an era of political vacuum in which the old institutions were paralyzed, but the new ones were not yet strong enough to replace them. (2) The workers' councils (Shora) emerged as an outcome of workers' collective action in economic and political affairs. (3) They exercised their control over production and employment policies. (4) In the absence of genuine trade unions, the workers' councils also led workers' economic demands regarding wages, working hours, housing conditions, and labor legislation in general. (5) The councils represented all workers regardless of their status (blue or white collar), industrial group, skill, and gender.

As Bayat (1987, pp. 109–112) has persuasively argued, the origins of workers' councils can be traced back to two sources. First, in the abandoned enterprises where the managers or the owners had left, there was an incentive for workers to take the initiative to control the production and employment so that the enterprise could continue to function. Second, in the enterprises in which the employer was present, the workers' councils stemmed from a more combative attitude. Workers had a new perception about their entitlement to the factory's ownership and the way society had to be run in the context of revolutionary situation. This new feeling of entitlement was strongly shared among petroleum workers who considered themselves as guardians of 'national interest' against the British and American oil companies that had supported the coup d'état against Mossadegh's government in 1953 and helped the late Shah's return to the power. Moreover, many workers identified the old factory regime with the Shah's despotism and advocated the democratization of the productive unit as an alternative way to 'bureaucratic despotic' factory regime in which the Shah's secret police (SAVAK) interfered in repressing any independent labor movement in close collaboration with the employer.

Three forces should be distinguished in the oil industry in the aftermath of the revolution reflecting the general pattern of power relationships between labor and capital in almost all big and medium-size enterprises.

1. The labor councils that represented an independent workers' movement for self-management or cooperative coordination. The councils endeavored to coordinate their activities at a national level by late February or early March 1979. The emblematic figure of this coordination was 'General Council of the Petroleum Industry Employees' (*Shora-e Sarasari-ye Karkonan-e Sanat-e Naft*) that reunited representatives of the councils in the oil, gas, and petrochemical industries at national level (Jafari, 2021, pp. 269–270). The emergence of these grassroots organizations in the oil industries and their coordination at a national level was a major obstacle to the state-building process of Islamist forces after the collapse of the Shah's regime. The councils had a dual relationship with the new regime. While they were distrustful toward the 'reformist liberal' provisional government led by Bazargan, they were strongly under the ideological influence of the charismatic figure of the Islamic revolution, Ayatollah Khomeini. Khomeini's populist discourse on *Mostazafan* (the 'downtrodden') and the Islamic justice addressed workers, urban and rural poor population for whom he was the leader of the revolution.

2. The technocrat managers of enterprises that could not accept the interference of workers' councils in management. They were supported by the provisional government of Bazargan and its representatives in the oil industry: first, Hassan Nazih who served as the head of the National Iranian Oil Company between February and September 1979 and then Ali Akbar Moinfar who replaced Nazih and served briefly as the first oil Minister of the IRI from September 1979 until the occupation of the American Embassy on November 4, 1980. The provisional government was against the councils. It published a communique in the early March 1979 regarding the nature and tasks of the councils as being separate from executive bodies such as factory management. The councils' task was described in terms of Koran's order 'summoning to the good, bidding what is right, and forbidding what is wrong' *(amr bil maroof & nahi anil munkar)* (Koran, *Ale Imran*, 104).[28] To put it differently, the councils had to register the grievances and wishes of the workers, categorize them and relay them to the officials, and promote the unity between workers and executive branches.

---

[28] See http://www.islamic-laws.com/AmrBilMaroof.htm

3. Khomeini, the Council of the Islamic Revolution, and the Islamic Republic Party were not directly opposed to the workers' councils. They had strong influence among many Muslim workers who were supposed to be the social base of the Islamic revolution namely *Mostazafan* (the 'downtrodden') against the 'liberal, capitalist' managers and the atheist Communists. Khomeini and other leading Shi'i clergy were for the transformation of the independent labor councils to the Islamic labor councils. The Islamic councils and the Islamic labor associations (*Anjomanhay Islami*) had to confront both the 'liberal-capitalist' managers and the leftist tendencies, particularly the Communist groups. The Islamic forces combined ideological hegemony and physical repression to transform the workers' independent movement into Islamic labor councils. Physical repressive measures were used against the leftist activists and independent workers' representatives who were 'purged' or arrested and executed.

The Article 9 of a law enacted on the establishment of extraordinary tribunals against 'counter-revolutionary crimes' on July 4, 1979, targeted individuals who "disrupt the business in the country's workshops and factories or encourage workers to stop working or closing the workshop or factory" threatening them to be jailed for a period of two to ten years.[29] Moreover, the newly created Islamic army, the Sepah, the Islamic Komiteh, and the Islamic labor associations were mobilized to enforce repressive measures.

The importance of repressive measures notwithstanding, Khomeini's ideological hegemony and its strategy based on monopolizing power in the hands of Islamic associations played a more influential role in defeating cooperative coordination. Three phases can be identified in the evolution and final extinction of cooperative coordination. These phases are distinguished on the basis of Islamist ideological influence and its institutionalization in the labor movement during February1979 to January1982.

1. The first phase starts from the victory of insurrection against the Shah's regime on February11, 1979, until the occupation of the American Embassy on November 4, 1979.
2. The second phase covers the period since the hostage crisis until the inception of the Iran–Iraq war on September 22, 1980.

[29] See http://rc.majlis.ir/fa/law/show/98141 retrieved on January 18, 2022.

3. The third or last period embraces September 1980 until January 30, 1982, when the Council of the Oil Industry Employees was banned and 140 workers were arrested, some of them executed and others sentenced to long-term imprisonment.

Jafari (2021) has also suggested three phases in the evolution of workers' councils. While his periodization is close to mine,[30] I diverge on the underlying criterion. He emphasizes on the physical repression or the offensive/defensive position of labor movement whereas I favor *ideology* rather than *coercion* to capture the domination of Islamic labor councils. In fact, in my periodization the occupation of the American Embassy, and not the assault on Kurdistan, constitutes a turning point in the success of Islamic corporatist strategy. The Islamist 'anti-Liberal, anti-Imperialist' slogans were part of their hegemonic strategy to become the exclusive mediator in capital-labor conflict at factory and national levels.

For example, it was in the wake of the hostage crisis that the Islamic labor council of the petroleum workers in Kharg island issued a communique in which they called themselves "Khomeini's soldiers awaiting his order" and stopped the oil flow to be transported to the USA (see Jafari, 2021, p. 271). The war with Iraq spelt the end of the cooperative coordination. The nationalist sentiment, the dislocation of workers from the south, and closure of oil fields exposed to the Iraqi assault created a situation in which the Islamist forces totally disbanded any independent labor movement as a source of disruption in war effort helping the enemy. By the end of war, nothing was left from cooperative coordination in the enterprises.[31]

---

[30] Jafari's three periods are: (1) February to August 1979 (from the victory of anti-Shah insurrection to the first major assault against the opposition in Kurdistan); (2) September 1979–September 1980 (marked by the 'defensive posture' of the councils under the 'heavy attacks from both Moinfar and the pro-Khomeini forces'); (3) September 1980 to early 1982 covering the period from the inception of war until the disbanding of the Council of the Oil Industry Employees (2021, pp. 265–266, 267–278).

[31] The 1990 labor legislation specified that only one of the three types of labor associations, namely the 'Islamic labor councils', 'guild societies', and 'workers representatives', can represent in any workplace. The Islamic labor councils were reserved only for enterprises with more than 35 employees. Smaller enterprises could dispose of workers 'representatives' and 'guild councils'. "In each of these three labour-organization types, workers can elect their representatives only with the consent of the employers and they also need to be approved by the Ministry of Labour and Social Affairs. This practice hence rules out independent trade unions and free collective bargaining at firm or industry level" (Karshenas, 2021, p. 7).

The period 1982–1989 was characterized by the extension of national-ized sectors under the hegemony of Islamist organizations culminating in a new factory regime, namely 'Islamic corporatism'. In this type of corpo-ratism, political imperatives determine the mode of regulating economic issues such as setting the minimum wage. This explains the creation of Supreme Labor Council (SLC) that decides the minimum wage at national level. The SLC is a tripartite organization presided by the Minister of Labor and composed of three representatives from the Islamic labor coun-cils, three from the employers' associations, and three appointed by the government. The end of cooperative coordination did not enhance authoritative coordination; it promoted Islamic corporatism reinforcing parallel Islamic institutions.

7.9   ANFAL AND DESTRUCTIVE COORDINATION

As emphasized in Chap. 2, any socio-economic system is a constellation of four principal modes of coordination in which one dominates the others. Destructive coordination dominates the system if cooperative, authorita-tive, and market coordination are in *crisis*. Moreover, every mode of coor-dination provides a special form of appropriation and has natural affinity with a specific form of property. Thus, assessing and measuring the place of destructive coordination requires an investigation of two factors: (1) the structure of property rights and (2) the state of articulation or lack of articulation among different modes of coordination.

I will argue that destructive coordination always dominated the politi-cal economy of the IRI since 1982. This domination was initially *political* in the first phase of *Anfal* deriving from the crisis in other modes of coor-dination. It grew into *economic* domination through the extension of *Anfal* in its second and third phases. To show this point, we will explore the structure of property rights and the articulation of different modes of coordination in each phase of *Anfal*.

The property structure in the first phase of *Anfal* (1979–1989) tra-versed two stages. The first stage (1979–1982) was characterized by the predominance of public appropriation of resources including both com-munal and public confiscation of the abandoned properties by the Shah and the 53 big industrialists and financiers. While the latter were promptly transferred to *Bonyad Mostazafan* as part of *Anfal* in conformity with Khomeini's order, the workers' control over the abandoned enterprises ended in 1982. Since then, the state property was preponderant in the economy because of Article 44 of the constitution and the warfare economy. The private sector was downsized during this phase but concentrated in the hands of privileged bazaar merchants.

Authoritative coordination entertains strong linkage with state property. Although the state property was preponderant in the first phase of *Anfal*, paradoxically authoritative coordination did not flourish. This is easily understandable since the old state institutions were paralyzed because of revolutionary situation. Cooperative coordination emerged as an alternative to authoritative and market coordination. But it only lasted for three years (1979–1982) and then replaced by Islamic corporatism.

Market coordination has natural affinity with property ownership. Parallel with confiscations and capital flight, impersonal market coordination entered into a critical situation. However, state monopoly over foreign trade and multiple exchange rates for the American dollar provided an exceptional opportunity for those bazaar merchants who had close ties with religious leaders. They could maximize their commercial rents by buying imported products at official rate and selling them at market rate. Accordingly, *political markets* prospered.

Destructive coordination based on confiscatory appropriation maintains strong linkage with *Anfal*. The size of *Anfal* in its first phase was estimated 8–10% of GDP concentrated in Bonyad giant holding. Its assets composed of the late Shah's property and big Iranian capitalists. The share of *Anfal* was already considerable at this stage but still smaller than the state sector. However, destructive coordination could dominate because of crisis in both market and authoritative coordination, and the extinction of cooperative coordination in 1982, on the one hand, and the extension of parallel Islamic institutions, on the other hand. The domination was rather *political* than *economic*. Table 7.5 illustrates the *political* domination of destructive coordination in the first phase of *Anfal*.

Table 7.5 Political domination of destructive coordination (1979–1989)

Coordination type	Property form	Property size	State of coordination (critical, normal, dominant)
Authoritative	State	Preponderant	Critical
Market	Private	Drastically downsized	Critical
Cooperative	Public or communal	Preponderant (1979–1982), totally marginalized since then	Critical
Destructive	*Anfal*	Considerable but smaller than state property	Dominant (political)

The property structure of the second phase of *Anfal* (1989–2005) can be characterized by the downsizing of the state sector, the rapid increase of *Anfal* and the Sepah's intervention in the economic activity. According to some estimation, this sector consisted of 35–40% of GDP during this phase. Private sector also augmented in the banking, insurance, real estate, and agricultural sectors, but its increase was derisory compared to *Anfal*, the Sepah, and the Basij. The private sector's promotion hinged upon subcontracting for the latter. Political markets grew more rapidly than impersonal market. The domination of destructive coordination was not exclusively *political*; it was also supported by *economic* growth of *Anfal*. Table 7.6 captures these changes.

Finally, the 'privatization' of the 80% of the state property in the third phase of *Anfal* (2006 to until now) was reaped off by the so-called non-state public sector or more precisely *Anfal*, the Sepah, and the Basij. The size of the latter was estimated 55% of GDP. The private sector also augmented its share (5–13.5% according to the official estimates), but became totally subservient to the latter sector. Political markets prospered in parallel with the domineering position of the Islamic religious and military oligarchy. Table 7.7 shows this dominant role of destructive coordination both from an *economic* and *political* perspective.

Reviewing the three phases of Anfal, we conclude that the domination of destructive coordination was reinforced throughout the political economy of the IRI perpetuating the crisis of authoritative, market, and cooperative coordination.

Table 7.6 Political and economic domination of destructive coordination (1989–2005)

Coordination type	Property form	Property size	State of coordination (critical, normal, dominant)
Authoritative	State	Preponderant but decreasing	Critical
Market	Private	Slightly increasing	Critical
Cooperative	Public or communal	Marginalized	Critical
Destructive	*Anfal*, the Sepah, the Basij	Increasing proportional to the shrinking state sector	Dominant (political and economic)

Table 7.7 Political and economic domination of destructive coordination (2006–now)

Coordination type	Property form	Property size	State of coordination (critical, normal, dominant)
Authoritative	State	Considerable	Critical
Market	Private	Increasing	Critical
Cooperative	Public or communal	Marginalized	Critical
Destructive	Anfal, the Sepah, the Basij	Preponderant	Dominant (political and economic)

7.10 Conclusion

In this chapter, we showed that the outcome of privatization decree was Islamization rather than liberalization. Mass scale privatization since July 2006 resulted in the transfer of the bulk of state properties to *Anfal*, the Sepah, and the Basij in the absence of an open economy. *Anfal* and other Islamic parallel institutions progressed by preying on the state resources comprising of both corporate assets and the oil revenue. The colossal increase of oil revenue during Ahmadinejad's presidential terms enhanced this transfer while the formal state's budget deficit rose incessantly.

The reliance of the Iranian economy on oil revenue increased proportional to the progression of *Anfal*'s share in the economy. The so-called natural resource curse is nothing but 'institutional curse'. What is this institutional curse?

The curse is Islamization of the Iranian economy. By Islamization, I mean the establishment of a specific system of political economy that can be named Islamic political capitalism. This is a variant of political capitalism, and its coherence can be explained by the causal relationship between its three fundamental institutions in three spheres, namely ideological/political, property relationship, and dominant mode of coordination.

The first underlying institution is political and ideological, that is, *Velayat Faqih* or the jurisconsult of the vicegerent that replaced the Shah's despotism after the 1979 Revolution. *Velayat Faqih* derives from a specific interpretation of the Shi'i Islam introduced by Ayatollah Khomeini (1970) and Montazeri (1987) that can be traced back to the Safavid dynasty in the sixteenth century. The constitution of the IRI has tailored this political/ideological form of power in which the power is concentrated in the hand of the Imam or the Supreme Jurisconsult. The people's sovereignty is superseded by the Imam's authority.

The second fundamental institution is property relationship that is directly caused by *Velayat Faqih*. *Anfal* or the restrictive property of the Imam over all 'ownerless' properties (*res nullius*) constitutes the bulk of Shi'i public finance. However, this property does not belong to 'public' in the modern sense since the sovereignty does not belong to the people but to the Imam. In modern terms, *Anfal* is the exact opposite of 'public property'; it consists in dispossessing people from their public properties by the Imam or the Supreme Jurisconsult.

Finally, *Anfal* as a confiscatory regime engenders destructive coordination. The critical situation of authoritative, market, and cooperative coordination gave rise to Islamic parallel institutions and the domination of destructive coordination. The latter domination, in its turn, perpetuates the crisis of other forms of coordination.

The coherence of Islamic political capitalism basically depends on this specific hierarchical chain of causality between *Velayat Faqih, Anfal,* and destructive coordination. The causal relationships among these three fundamental institutions are illustrated in Fig. 7.6.

Partial privatizations under Hashemi Rafsanjani and Khatami introduced incoherence and contradictions in the system because they intended to involve foreign capital and the Iranian capital abroad in privatizing. According to '*Anfal* Impossible Triangle', privatization in the context of open economy could have strengthened private sector hindering *Anfal*'s progression.

Anfal's promotion was also enhanced by its coalition with the Sepah and the Basij. It has attained its summit during its third phase by officially delineating its properties from the state property and swallowing it. However, this coalition can be destabilized politically or financially leading

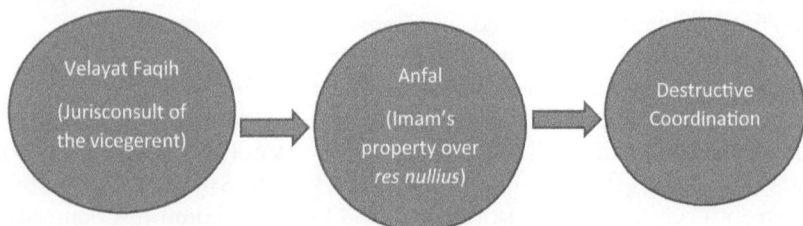

Fig. 7.6 Islamic political capitalism

to tensions regarding the respective shares of each institution in preying state resources. The 'unity thesis' (presenting *Anfal* as part of 'state' property) that initially provided a justification for *Anfal* is now the best pretext for its 'nationalization' or for dispossessing the Supreme Jurisconsult from his institutional properties in the name of Article 45 by the Sepah. Will we be witnessing this assumption in the post-Khamenei era? The answer to this question belongs to the future. But we can say that if *Anfal* changes into state property, the system will also lose its coherence. In other words, the dispossession of *Anfal* from the Supreme Leader and its transfer to other private owners or the state sector would undermine the system's coherence.

References

Adeli, H. (1383/2004). Mosahbeh ba Ahmadi Amooei. In A. Ahmadi (Ed.), *Eghtesaad Siasi Jomhouri Eslami, moshabeh ba Ezatollah Sahabi, Mohsen Norbakhsh, Hossein Adeli, Masoud Roghani Zanjani, Masoud Nili, Mohammad Ali Najafi (The Political Economy of Islamic Republic, interviews with Ezatollah Sahabi, Mohsen Norbakhsh, Hossein Adeli, Masoud Roghani Zanjani, Masoud Nili, Mohammad Ali Najafi)* (2nd edn.). Game Noo.

Ahmadi Amooei, B. (2004). Interview with Engineer Ezatullah Sahabi. In *The Political Economy of the Islamic Republic* (pp. 9–58), Gam-e No. (in Persian); Interview with Dr. Mohsen Nourbakhsh. In *The Political Economy of the Islamic Republic* (pp. 59–140), Gam-e No. (in Persian); Interview with Dr. Massoud Roghani Zanjani. In *The Political Economy of the Islamic Republic* (pp. 141–232), Gam-e No. (in Persian); Interview with Hossein Adeli. In *The Political Economy of the Islamic Republic* (pp. 435–495), Gam-e No. (in Persian).

Al Yaseen, A. (2014). *Tarikhcheh barnameh rizi tooseh dar Iran (The History of Development Planning in Iran)*. Markaz Nashr Sahar. (in Persian).

Amuzegar, J. (2007, Fall). Islamic Social Justice, Iranian Style. *Middle East Policy, 14*(3), 60–78.

Andreff, W. (2017). Post-Soviet Privatization in the Light of Coase Theorem: Transaction Costs and Governance Costs. In A. Oleinik (Ed.), *The Institutional Economics of Russia's Transformation*. Taylor and Francis. Chapter II.4, pp. 191-212.

Azad, S. (1980). "Workers' and Peasants' Councils in Iran," *Monthly Review*, October, pp. 14–29.

Bahramitash, R., & Salehi Esfahani, S. (2011). The Transformation of the Female Labor Market. In R. Bahramitash & S. Salehi Esfahani (Eds.), *Veiled Employment, Islamism and the Political Economy of Women's Employment in Iran* (pp. 123–165). Syracuse University Press., Chapter 4.

Bank Markazi Iran. (1979). Annual report, cited in Bayat, A., 1987, Workers and Revolution in Iran: A Third World Experience of Workers' Control, London: Zed.

Bayat, A. (1987). *Workers and Revolution in Iran: A Third World Experience of Workers' Control*. Zed.

Behdad, S., & Nomani, F. (2012). Women's Labour in the Islamic Republic of Iran: Losers and Survivors. *Middle Eastern Studies, 48*(5), 707–733.

Boroujerdi, M., & Rahimkhani, K. (2018). *Postrevolutionary Iran: A Political Handbook*. Syracuse University Press.

Boughton, J. (2003). On the Origins of Fleming-Mundell Model. *IMF Staff Papers, 50*(1), 1–9.

Burawoy, M. (1985). *The Politics of Production: Factory Regimes under Capitalism and Socialism*. Verso.

Cagan, P. (1956). "The Monetary Dynamics of Hyperinflation", in Friedman, .59 Milton (ed.), Studies in the Quantity Theory of Money, Chicago: Chicago. University Press, 25–117.

Carvalho, J.-P. (2013). Veiling. *The Quarterly Journal of Economics, 128*(1), 337–370.

Coville, T. (2013). How to Transform a Rent-Seeking Economy: The Case of Iran. In H. E. Chehabi, F. Khosrokhavar, & C. Therme (Eds.), *Iran and the Challenges of the Twenty-First Century Essays in Honour of Muhammad-Reza Djalili*. Mazda Publishers.

Dareini, A. A. (2008, August 31). Iranian Conservative Attacks President on Economy. *Worldnews*. Retrieved December 18, 2021, from https://article.wn.com/view/2008/08/31/Iranian_conservative_attacks_president_on_economy/.

Dornbusch, R. (1991). Experiences with Extreme Monetary Instability. In S. Commander (Ed.), *Managing Inflation in Socialist Economies in Transition* (Economic Development Institute of the World Bank, EDI Seminar Series) (pp. 175–196). The World Bank., chapter 8.

Ehsani, K. (2009, Spring). Survival Through Dispossession: Privatization of Public Goods in the Islamic Republic. *Middle East Report, 250*, 26–33.

Forozan, H. (2016). *The Military in Post-Revolutionary Iran, the Evolution and Roles of the Revolutionary Guards*. Routledge.

Foweraker, J. (1987). Corporatist Strategies and the Transition to Democracy in Spain. *Comparative Politics, 20*(1), 57–72.

Goodey, C. (1980, June). Workers' Councils in Iranian Factories. *MERIP Reports*.

Hanke, S., & Krus, N. (2013). World Hyperinflations. In R. Parker & R. Whaples (Eds.), *Routledge Handbook of Major Events in Economic History* (pp. 367–377). Routledge., chapter 30.

Harris, K. (2013). The Rise of the Subcontracting State: Politics of Pseudo-Privatization in the Islamic Republic of Iran. *International Journal of Middle East Studies, 45*, 45–70.

Hart, O. (2017). Incomplete Contracts and Control. *American Economic Review, 107*(7), 1731–1752.

Hashemi Rafsanjani, A. A. (2008, December 11). Rafsanjani Criticizes Government Bodies for not Implementing Article 44. *Fars New Agency*. (in Persian).

Hoominfar, E., & Zanganeh, N. (2021). The Brick Wall to Break: Women and the Labor Market Under the Hegemony of the Islamic Republic of Iran. *International Feminist Journal of Politics, 23*(2), 263–286.

International Monetary Fund. (2010, April). *World Economic Outlook Database.* Online. Available at: www.imf.org/external/pubs/ft/weo/2010/01/weo-data/index.aspx. Retrieved December 27, 2021.

Jafari, P. (2013, Fall). Reasons to Revolt: Iranian Oil Workers in the 1970s. *International Labor and Working-Class History, 84*, 195–217.

Jafari, P. (2018). Fluid History: Oil Workers and the Iranian Revolution. In T. Atabaki, E. Bini, K. Ehsani, & K. (Eds.), *Working for Oil: Comparative Social Histories of Labor in the Global Oil Industry* (pp. 69–98). Palgrave Macmillan.

Jafari, P. (2021). The Showras in the Iranian Revolution, Labour Relations and the State in the Iranian Oil Industry, 1979–82. In P. Brandon, P. Jafari, & S. Müller (Eds.), *Worlds of Labour Turned Upside Down Revolutions and Labour Relations in Global Historical Perspective* (pp. 252–285). Brill, chapter 9.

Karshenas, M. (2021). *Minimum Wages, Labor Market Institutions, and the Distribution of Earning in Iran.* The Economic Research Forum, Working Paper No. 1478 August.

Keshavarzian, A. (2007). *Bazaar and State in Iran, the Politics of the Tehran Marketplace.* Cambridge University Press.

Khomeini, R. (1970). *Velayat Fqih.* Daftar Nashre Falagh. Translated in 1981, *Islam and Revolution, Writings and Declarations of Imam Khomeini.* Mizan Press.

Kornai, J. (1979). Resource-Constrained Versus Demand-Constrained Systems. *Econometrica, 47*(4), 801–819.

Kornai, J. (1990a). The Affinity between Ownership Forms and Coordination Mechanisms: The Common Experience of Reform in Socialist Countries. *Journal of Economic Perspectives, 4*(3), 131–147.

Kornai, J. (1990b). *The Road to a Free Economy: Shifting from a Socialist System: The Example of Hungary.* W.W. Norton.

Kornai, J. (1992). *The Socialist System. The political economy of Communism.* Princeton University Press and Oxford University Press.

Kornai, J. (1994). Transformational Recession: The Main Causes. *Journal of Comparative Economics, 19*(1), 39–63.

Kornai, J. (2000). *Ten Years After 'The Road to a Free Economy': The Author's Self-Evaluation.* Paper for the World Bank 'Annual Bank Conference on Development Economics-ABCDE', April 18–20, Washington, DC.

Krugman, P., & Obstfeld, M. (2003). *International Economics, Theory and Practice* (6th ed.). Addison Wesley.

Maloney, S. (2015). *Iran's Political Economy since the Revolution*. Cambridge University Press.

Megginson, W., & Netter, J. (2001, June). From State to Market: A Survey of Empirical Studies on Privatization. *Journal of Economic Literature, 39*(2), 321–389.

Montazeri, H.-A. (1987). *Darasat fi velayet al-faqih va feqhe al-dowlah al-islamieh (Studies on Velayat faqih and the Jurisprudence of the Islamic State)* (Vol. 1, 4). Al-markaz al-alemi il-darasat al-islamieh.

Mousavi Nik, S. H. (2009). *Gozar az Iqtesad dowlati be shebh dowlati (The Transition from State to Parastate Economy)*. The Research Centre of Islamic Legislative Assembly, November, Serial number 9915, subject code 220 (in Persian).

Najafi Khah, M. (2016, Winter). "Marz-e myan bakhsh omomei va bakhsh khosousi dar hoghogh Iran ba takeed bar barnameh khosousi sazi va broon separi," (*The Delineation of the Public and Private Sector in the Iranian Law with the Emphasis on the Privatization Program and Outsourcing*). *Faslnameh elmi-pajooheshi Shapa, 21*(4), 101-133 (in Persian).

Nili, M., & Associates. (2015). *Iqtesad Iran be koja miravad? Kholaseh tarh motaleati tahleel avamel taseergozar bar amalkard myan moddat iqtesad Iran (Where the Iranian Economy Is Going? A Summary of Study Project Regarding the Analysis of Factors Impacting the Performance of the Iranian Economy in Medium Term)*. Intesharat Donyai Iqtesad (in Persian).

Olmsted, J. (2013). Gender and Globalization. In Bahramitash, Roksana and Salehi Esfahani, Salehi (Eds.), 2011, *Veiled Employment, Islamism and the Political Economy of Women's Employment in Iran* (pp. 25–52). Syracuse University Press, Chapter 1.

Pesaran, H. (2000). Economic Trends and Macroeconomic Policies in Post-Revolutionary Iran. In P. Alizadeh (Ed.), *The Economy of Iran: The Dilemmas of an Islamic State*. I.B. Tauris & Co.

Pesaran, E. (2014). *Iran's Struggle for Independence, Reform and Counter-Reform in the Post-Revolutionary Era*. Routledge.

Rahnema, S. (1992). Work Councils in Iran - The Illusion of Worker Control. *Economic and Industrial Democracy, 13*(1), 69–94. https://doi.org/10.117 7/0143831X92131004

Renani, M. (2010). *Bazaar ya na-bazaar (Market or non-Market)*, Third Edition (first edition: 1997, Second edition: 2005). Moasseseh aali amoozesh, pajohesh modiriyat va barnamehrizi (in Persian).

Rezai, M. (2006). "Mohsen Rezai dar jam-e khabarnegaran : 100 hezar Milliard Toman az malekyat-e dowlat beh mardom va bakhsh khosousi vagozar mishavad" (Mohsen Rezai Among Reporters: 100 Thousand Billion Tomans of State

Property will be Transferred to the People and the Private Sector), Fars News Agency, July 5 (14 Tir 1385). http://www.farsnews.net/newstext,php?nn=8504140273 (in Persian).

Sattari, N. (2020). Women Driving Women: Drivers of Women-Only Taxis in the Islamic Republic of Iran. *Women's Studies International Forum, 28*, 102324. www.elsevier.com/locate/wsif

Schmitter, P. (1974, January). Still the Century of Corporatism? *Review of Politics, 36*, 102–110.

Sweezy, P., & Magdoff, H. (1979). Iran: New Crisis of American Hegemony. *Monthly Review, 30*(9), 1–24.

Turner, T. (1980a). "Iranian Oil workers in the 1978-79 Revolution," in Nore, P. and Turner, T. (eds.), Oil and Class Struggle, London, Zed Press, 272–292.

Turner, T. (1980b). "How We Organized Strike that Paralyzed Shah's Regime (Firsthand Account by Iranian Oil Worker)," in Nore, P. and Turner, T. (eds.), Oil and Class Struggle, London, Zed Press, 293–303.

Vahabi, M. (2001). The Soft Budget Constraint: A Theoretical Clarification. *Recherches Economiques de Louvain (Louvain Economic Review), 67*(2), 157–195.

Vahabi, M. (2002). From the Walrasian General Equilibrium to Incomplete Contracts: Making Sense of Institutions. *Economie et institutions (Economics and Institutions), 1*, 99–143.

Vahabi, M. (2004). *The Political Economy of Destructive Power.* Edward Elgar.

Vahabi, M. (2014a). Soft Budget Constraint Reconsidered. *Bulletin of Economic Research, 66*(1), 1–19.

Vahabi, M. (2014b). "Contrainte budgétaire lâche et le secteur paraétatique" (Soft Budget Constraints and Parastatal Sector). In M. Makinsky (Ed.), *L'économie réelle de l'Iran* (pp. 147–176). L'Harmattan.

Vahabi, M. (2015, December 22). Jaygah Sepah dar Eqtesad Iran (The Place of Sepah in the Iranian Economy). *Mihan*, No. 6. Retrieved December 11, 2021, from http://mihan.net/1394/10/01/562/ (in Persian).

Vahabi, M. (2020, August 10). Neoliberalism and Inflation Control. Akhbar-Rooz. (akhbar-rooz.com) نئولیبرالیسم و مقابله با تورم محمداد وهابی - اخبار روز - سایت سیاسی خبری چپ (in Persian).

Vahabi, M., & Mohajer, N. (2021). A Critical Reflection on Neoliberalism. *Critique, 48*(4), 461–503.

Williamson, O. (1985). *The Economic Institutions of Capitalism. Firms, Markets, Relational Contracting.* Free Press.

Zandi, R. (2011, August 8). Sardar Qassemi barnameh-ye Vezarat-e Naft ra e'lam kard (General Qassemi Announced the Oil Ministry's plan. *Sharq*. Available at: http://old.sharghdaily.ir/news/90/05/17/7693.html. Retrieved January 7, 2022.

CHAPTER 8

Islamic Political Capitalism and Economics of Predation

8.1 INTRODUCTION

The Islamic political capitalism is an economic system based on three fundamental institutions, *Velayat faqih*, *Anfal*, and destructive coordination. Our study confirms the general pattern of Kornai's description of any economic system. He summed up three major characteristics of any economic system: (1) political structure and related dominant political ideology, (2) property relationships, and (3) coordination mechanisms. Moreover, he emphasized that there exists a hierarchical causal chain between these three principal constituents of an economic system: the first determines the second, and the second, in turn, conditions the third (Kornai, 1992, pp. 360–365). He adds two other blocks: "The first three … sum up the fundamental features of each system: what characterizes political power, the distribution of property rights, and the constellation of coordination mechanisms. Once these are in place, they largely determine the fourth block, the type of behavior typical of the economic actors, and the fifth block, the typical economic phenomena" (Kornai, 2000, p. 29).

Applying this scheme to the classical socialist system, Kornai identified three characteristic institutions: (1) undivided power of the Marxist-Leninist party, (2) dominance of state property, (3) preponderance of bureaucratic (authoritative) coordination. These institutions determined (4) the behavioral regularity of socialist enterprises, namely soft budget constraints, and weak responsiveness to prices, among many others; and (5) chronic shortage economy as normal state of the system.

Following Kornai, I will identify the fourth and fifth blocks of the Islamic political capitalism. It will be argued that the fourth bloc or behavioral regularity of Islamic enterprises is capital and labor flight. Finally, the normal state of the system is cash hoarding and patrimonial development.

Table 8.1 compares Islamic political capitalism with a classical socialist system according to Kornai's five main blocks. Iranian post-revolutionary economic system is sometimes wrongly described as close to a classical socialist system because of preponderant state and parastatal sectors (Mazaheri, 2018; Ghaninejad, 2022; Tabibian, 2022[1]). Table 8.1 illustrates the typical differences between the two systems. It is noteworthy that Table 3.1 (Chap. 5) underlined the differences between Islamic political capitalism and a liberal market economy to dissipate fallacious interpretations of the Iranian economic system as 'neoliberal'.

Table 8.1 A comparative study of the classical socialist system with the Islamic political capitalism

Blocks	Classical socialist system	Islamic political capitalism
1. Political/ideological	Undivided power of the Communist party	*Velayat faqih* (jurisprudence of the vicegerent)
2. Dominant form of property	State property	*Anfal* (the Imam's property over *res nullius*)
3. Preponderant form of coordination	Authoritative (bureaucratic) coordination	Destructive coordination
4. Behavioral regularity of economic actors	Soft budget constraints and weak responsiveness to prices	Capital and labor flight
5. Normal state of the economy	Economics of shortage	Economics of hoarding

[1] The Persian weekly economic journal, *Tejarat Farda*, has devoted a special issue (number 442, January 29, 2022) on 'The Iranian version of Polit bureau'. The issue discusses the President Ebrahim Raisi's economic policy regarding agricultural sector and other markets. In this issue the Iranian liberal economists like Ghaninejad and Tabibian have expressed their concern about the imposition of a centralized planning in Iran with the consequences of a shortage economy and repression of markets including black markets. Ghaninejad compares the Iranian economy under the 13th Government with the Soviet economy in the 1970s. See https://www.tejaratefarda.com/ retrieved on February 10, 2022.

This chapter will review blocks 4 and 5, namely the typical behavioral regularity of agents and typical economic phenomena of the Islamic political capitalism.

Kornai's institutional analysis of the economic systems reverses the line of argument in materialist conception of history as elaborated by Marx (1859/1977, p. 11).[2] He grants the pride of place as superstructure to politics and not economics: "While the interaction of political power, property and the modes of coordination are all important in movements between capitalism and socialism or back again, *the political dimension plays the primary role*" (Kornai, 2000, p. 33, the emphasis is added).

Modes of coordination in conjunction with political/ideological structure and property relationships shape social forms of integration and appropriation. They characterize the *(re)distributive* system. Productive and conflictual power are both influential in determining the appropriation of resources. Unless the definition of economics is narrowed down to wealth-producing activities, the primacy of politics over economics cannot be postulated. However, it is impossible to grab more than what is produced.

The final impact of every economic system on production determines its dynamic efficiency or the level of productivity. A predatory economic regime may enhance or impede production and economic growth. Constant grabbing without any positive impact on productive capacity will finally lead to economic collapse. This happens when the formation of fixed capital is bypassed by capital depletion due to predation. While predation determines production, production in its turn conditions predation. This is a reciprocal or *cumulative causation*.[3] Politics conditions economics, but economics in its turn decides politics. The relevance of this cumulative causation is particularly crucial in the case of Islamic political capitalism in which predation largely opposes to production and results in systemic failure of capital accumulation.

What do I mean by 'predation'? I will not dwell upon this point in detail in this chapter as I have already elaborated my definition of 'predation' as a complex and multidimensional action in a preceding book on the *Political economy of predation* (Vahabi, 2015) and several other papers (Vahabi, 2016, 2020). Based on these works, I suggest three dimensions

---

[2] See Chap. 2 for more explanation.
[3] See Chap. 2 for more explanation regarding cumulative causation.

for 'predation'. The first one is that it is a specific type of *behavior* particularly aggressive and often violent describing the relationship between prey and predator. Moreover, it is about an 'energy recycling' from prey to predator in general that can be defined as an *appropriative allocation mechanism* in social relationships between prey and predator. Pareto (1971/1927, p. 341) captured this point[4] when he distinguished productive from appropriative activity. Finally, predation is also conceived of a relationship between prey-predator in an 'imaginary construction' characterized by lawlessness or Hobbesian jungle in which a third-party enforcer is absent. Economists opposed this imaginary construction to a market economy with clearly delineated and defined property rights. The bulk of economic literature and economic textbooks is about the economic value expressed in terms of relative prices in the context of market economy.

But what is the value of an asset produced by agent A that is grabbed by agent B? In other words, what is the value of an asset captured as a 'booty' in a Hobbesian jungle without clearly defined and delineated property rights? This issue is often dismissed or treated tangentially in economic literature. However, the same problem also occurs in a market economy whenever allocation of resources is carried out through coercive means. For example, what are asset values as 'seen by a state'[5] in the context of coercive relationships? They are not the same as the economic values of assets in consensual transactions. Economics of predation can only be built upon a theory of booty value of assets in contradistinction with economic value of assets.

---

[4] Plato pioneered the exploration of predation as closely related to coercive appropriation. In *Sophist*, Plato (2013, p. 27) had already distinguished two types of techniques or crafts, one *productive*, creating its proper object, and the other *extractive*, based on coercive appropriation of what the others have produced. He wrote: "Let us define piracy, man-stealing, tyranny, the whole military art, by one name, as hunting with violence" (Plato, 2013, p. 85). Following Plato, violent hunting or prey-predator relationships embrace all types of private and state predation. Thus, violence has the double face of Janus: protective and predatory (Tilly, 1985). The former enhances production, while the latter hinders production but promotes coercive extraction.

[5] The title of James Scott's book (1998), *Seeing Like a State*, is clearly relevant to what I suggest below in distinguishing the booty value of an asset (as seen by a state) from the economic value of the same asset in a consensual relationship.

8.2 Economic and Booty Value of an Asset[6]

Coercive 'appropriation' refers here to 'capture by force' or involuntary redistribution, including state confiscation, expropriation, extortion, and theft. Other modes of appropriation, such as acquisition by market transaction, donation, inheritance, and option value of financial assets, assume voluntary transactions.[7] According to the property rights approach, the economic or consensual value of an asset is not determined by its physical properties, but rather by the allowed rights of action over the asset. "(T)he value of what is being traded depends upon the allowed rights of action over the physical good and upon the degree to which these rights are enforced" (Demsetz, 1964, p. 18). There are two important concepts in Demsetz' definition of economic value, namely 'right' and 'enforcement'. If the mere possession of an asset could imply an economic right over that asset, then the distinction between a consensual and an involuntary transaction would be entirely irrelevant. In this sense, Barzel's (1997) distinction between 'economic' and 'legal' property rights is confusing: "Whoever actually drives the car over which I have legal rights has economic rights over it, be it myself, a person I authorized to use it, or a thief though if it is a thief, the state will help me to recover it" (Barzel, 2015, p. 2). Barzel's confusing distinction is related to the fact that in line with the University of Washington branch of property rights, he assumes that involuntary transactions might be treated as voluntary transactions.[8] He applies this assumption in analyzing slavery (Barzel, 1977). However, according to Hohfeld's (1913) theory of jural relations, a 'right' to something for one person implies that at least one other person must have a corresponding 'duty' not to interfere with her possession and use thereto (Hodgson, 2015). What is the thief's 'right' over a stolen asset that implies an 'obligation' for others? Claiming property rights over an asset on the basis of using it is not synonymous with having a property 'right' because a "property claim becomes a property right only when it is socially or legally recognized as such, signifying the voluntary acceptance and enforcement of

---

[6]This section is the adaptation and extension of my paper: Mehrdad Vahabi, 2016, "A positive theory of the predatory state," vol. 168, pp. 153–175.

[7]In organization theory, 'appropriation' often refers to post-contractual opportunist behavior within voluntary transactions (Klein et al., 1978). This type of 'appropriative' activity does not fall within the scope of involuntary (coercive) transactions.

[8]For a detailed critical survey of this school, see Vahabi (2011).

concomitant duties of noninterference" (Cole & Grossman, 2002, p. 325).[9]

The second point in Demsetz' definition is 'enforcement'. Indeed, a property right is a socially enforced entitlement to a specified use of an economic asset (good or resource). The right of action depends on the degree of rights' enforcement. For example, the extent to which auto theft is prohibited determines the value of a car. If the law is lenient about auto theft, and private protection devices are not allowed (or restricted), the car price will fall below the social value of the automobile. By a socially enforced entitlement, I do not necessarily mean state enforcement, since, as Ellickson (1991, 1993) has clearly shown, property rights preceded the state. Borrowing Stringham's (2015) critical assessment of 'legal centralism', the state is not the only definer and enforcer of rights. In fact, a predatory state actually does the opposite, since it can take property, making any property rights less secure. In this sense, Hodgson (2015, p. 6) is not right in claiming that "property in its truest sense has another prerequisite—the political authority of the state". There are two problems with Hodgson's definition of 'property rights': first, property rights precede the state; second, his definition puts a unilateral emphasis on formal state entitlement, and hence, it mystifies the state and disregards the predatory laws and predatory states.[10]

In sum, economic property rights include exchanges through voluntary transactions only (or by economic means) and preclude involuntary reallocation of resources through supra-economic force. What is the difference between these two types? Coercive appropriation assumes a predatory relationship in which the reallocation of assets from the predator's viewpoint depends on two factors: (1) appropriability (the predator's ability to appropriate assets determines the benefits of appropriation) and (2)

---

[9] See also Hodgson's (2015) trenchant critique of Barzel's confusing distinction between economic and legal property rights.

[10] A good illustration is the way Germany's Fascist state robbed Jews (1933–1945) (Dean, 2008). The Nazi authorities tried not only to seize all Jewish property but also to give those confiscations at least a veneer of legality. Hence, robbing the Jews proceeded in two steps: (1) Aryanization of the economy and (2) the confiscation of Jewish property by the state. Aryanization preceded and prepared the way for 'legal' confiscation, converting various forms of Jewish wealth into bank accounts or investments that could be assessed accurately by the German Ministry of Finance and then easily confiscated by the state. According to Hodgson's definition of property rights, the Jews' properties had to be regarded as their 'possessions' and the 'property' of the state's looters as soon as the Fascist state adopted the Jewish confiscation law. This legalistic interpretation is misleading since it mystifies the state.

resistance (the prey's resistance to thwart appropriation or escape decides the costs of appropriation). The difference between the benefits and costs of appropriation defines the *booty value* of an asset. What matters for any agent interested in coercive appropriation, including a state, is not the economic value of an asset but the asset's booty value. The booty value of an asset depends on its exit option. This option is determined by two factors: (1) the degree of difficulty of appropriating an asset and (2) the ability of an asset to escape appropriation. From an anti-predatory perspective, the more an asset is mobile and invisible (i.e., either having hidden ability or easy to be hidden or disguised), the more resistant it is to confiscatory (appropriative) policies. Although mobility and invisibility are two different properties, they share a common quality in the context of predation: inaccessibility to those tracking it down. Here, the term mobility includes the invisibility of or the ability to hide an asset. Movable assets can exit more easily than unmovable ones, and assets can be more or less classified into 'fugitive' and 'captive' according to their higher or lower booty value.

A second confusion in the literature is to treat 'mobility' as synonymous with 'inappropriability'. I have distinguished them in the following manner. Appropriability pertains to the state's ability to prey; mobility refers to the prey's ability to escape. 'Mobility' of an asset provides a means to escape, but does not necessarily imply a lesser ability of the state to appropriate.

In discussing the 'exit option' we need to clearly distinguish two distinct criteria: (1) *appropriability* (predator) and (2) *mobility* (prey). *Appropriability* determines the *benefits* of predation and *mobility* decides the *costs* of predation.

1. *Appropriability: idiosyncratic assets* (e.g., human capital or investment in physical capital) are hardly appropriable whereas *generic assets* (e.g., landed property) are easily appropriable. *Concentrated* assets are more easily appropriable than *diffused* ones.
2. *Mobility:* some assets are movable (i.e., capable of escaping from a given state space), since they can be easily *hidden* (e.g., potatoes) or displaced *geographically* (the high ratio of value-to-weight, e.g., alluvial diamonds). Movability also refers to the possibility of *altering political (authority) allegiance* without any physical (geographical) displacement, for example, the vassals' rebellion against princes in Germany during High Middle Ages.

Geographical location and physical characteristics of assets as well as institutional factors are relevant in appropriability and mobility. For example, appropriability depends not only on asset specificity, concentration, or dispersal of assets but also on state accessibility of assets and asset measurability. In the same vein, mobility depends not only on the ease in geographical displacement and invisibility but also on porous national frontiers, nomadic or sedentary structure of the population, and the ability to alter political allegiance (Vahabi, 2015, 2016, 2018).

Considering the two criteria, appropriability and mobility, all assets may be regrouped into four major categories with regard to their booty values: (1) *pure captive assets* that are both appropriable and unmovable (like landed property); (2) *mixed captive assets* that do not satisfy the mobility criterion but are non-appropriable by mere use of coercive means (like investment in physical capital, a branch of a car industry, or Kimberlite diamond that needs industrial extraction); (3) *mixed fugitive assets* that satisfy the mobility criterion but are appropriable (e.g., precious manuscripts); and (4) *pure fugitive assets*[11] that satisfy both mobility and non-appropriability criteria (e.g., human capital or alluvial diamond that can be easily extracted by non-qualified labor). Table 8.2 recapitulates different types of assets distinguished based on their booty value in conjunction with state space.

In reality, state space is not decided by public goods and services that are non-excludable and non-rivalrous, but rather by *pure captive assets*. While pure fugitive assets (category 4) are out of the state space, and pure captive assets (category 1) belong to the state space, the 'mixed captive assets' as well as the 'mixed fugitive assets' (categories 2 and 3) are *intermediary assets* and have ambivalent positions regarding the state space. They can become part of a state space or undertake political exit; everything depends on the outcomes of the bargains between the state and the owners of these assets.

---

[11] Fugitive assets should not be confused with 'fugitive property', a term employed by legal scholars to define resources that have no definite boundaries and are not easily identified. Examples of fugitive property are water, natural gas, underground deposits of crude oil, and wild animals. These assets should be put under 'restraint' before ownership can be claimed. Consequently, it is difficult to determine who has property rights over them. The legal system is confronted with issues concerning the trade-off between the costs of administrating these property rights and the benefits of having these property rights clearly defined and delineated (Cooter & Ulen, 2012, Chap. 6, pp. 119–126; 128–138). In our theoretical framework, fugitive assets capture both mobility and non-appropriability. For example, oil and other minerals are regarded as captive and not fugitive assets. Best's work (2004) provides a literally critical appraisal of legal formalism concerning the disputes over the rendition of fugitive slaves and underlines the role of personhood to property.

Table 8.2 Types of assets and state space

Type of assets	Mobility (including hidden ability)	Appropriability	State or non-state space	Examples
1. Pure captive assets	No	Yes	State space	Landed property, timber, artisanal extraction of oil
2. Mixed captive assets	No	No	Ambivalent	Physical capital investment (a branch of a car industry), industrial extraction of oil
3. Mixed fugitive assets	Yes	Yes	Ambivalent	Kimberlite diamonds, commodities, merchandise
4. Pure fugitive assets	Yes	No		Alluvial diamonds. human-specific assets, 'famine' goods (e.g., potatoes)

Source: This table is a modified version of Vahabi (2015, p. 244 and 2016, p. 161)

In this table, one can note that 'pure escape assets' do not only belong to experts or privileged groups of society. Poor people might possess such type of assets. An emblematic figure is 'famine goods'. They include oats, barley, fast-growing millets, and buckwheat that are tolerant of poor soils, high altitudes, and short growing seasons. These are both *movable (hidden)* and *non-appropriable*, and typically belonged to poor and stateless people like fugitives and refuges of Zomia in the vast mountainous region of mainland Southeast Asia (Scott, 2009). Furthermore, some rich people like merchants, bankers, and industrialists often own 'mixed escape goods' that are *movable but appropriable*. They could use their exit power to exact concessions from the state. In this sense, they were not 'out' of the state, but could threaten not to be 'in' the state.

There are three major strategies to extend the state space: (1) *predatory competition* or the use of aggressive force of the state depending on the size of the army; (2) *price competition* or the use of protective force of the state by offering better or the same quality of protection for less tax;[12] (3) *mixed competition* or the use of both aggressive and protective force of the state to *discriminately* protect certain assets. The first type of competition is particularly efficient in the case of captive assets, while the second one is particularly adapted to pure fugitive assets. Mixed competition is warranted for encompassing mixed (pure or fugitive) assets.

Based on above-mentioned strategies, two types of predatory states might be distinguished.

1. *An inclusive predatory state*: a state that not only uses aggressive force of the state to include pure captive assets but also adopts an inclusive strategy regarding mixed and pure fugitive assets. Examples are the Young American Republic during 1850–1900 (Vahabi, 2016), Chile after the coup d'état against Allende during the rule of General Pinochet and Iran during the Shah's agrarian reform (1962–1971). In this type of predatory state, coercive appropriation enhances economic development.

2. *An exclusionary predatory state*: a state that mainly employs its aggressive force to include not merely pure captive assets but also other types of assets. Since brutal force is highly costly to enchain fugitive and mixed assets, an exclusionary predatory sate might be defined as a type of state that adopts an exclusionary strategy regarding mixed and pure fugitive assets. A recent illustrative example is political Islam. Not only the ISIS, which is an embryonic form of state, but also more developed and sophisticated *Velayat faqih* under Islamic Republic of Iran are good cases in point. In this type of state, predation often impedes economic development.

   Considering the importance of petroleum revenue as a source of state predation both under the Shah's regime and the Islamic Republic of Iran, we will more extensively dwell upon its booty value.

8.3   Oil as a Mixed (Pure) Captive Asset

In my theoretical framework, oil is considered as a *mixed captive asset*. It is *captive* since it is an immovable mineral resource, but it is *hardly appropriable* because its exploitation at a large scale depends upon industrial

---

[12] In public economics, this second type of competition is known as Tiebout's (1956) competition referring to tax reduction as an interjurisdictional competition by provincial states.

extraction requiring specific investment in know-how, machinery, and equipment. Artisanal refining or subsistent distillation of crude petroleum over a specific range of boiling points is also possible for the local use. This type of extraction might be organized based on traditional knowledge skills with little reliance on high-end technology at a small scale. In this sense, oil is a *pure captive asset*. However, the use of artisanal refining for oil theft aiming at capital accumulation is highly costly since it often constitutes a source of colossal water, land, and air pollution. In recent years, artisanal refining has become widespread in southern Nigeria with increasing oil theft. This method is associated with severe environmental pollution and serious adverse health effects for the workers as it is clearly reflected by the ISIS experience in Iraq, Syria, and Libya (*Iraq Nineveh Governorate*, December 2, 2016; Zwijnenburg, 2017).

The domination of multinational oil companies since World War I and that of the Seven Sisters over the oligopolistic oil market from the mid-1940s until the mid-1970s are partly related to their role in providing idiosyncratic investments in oil industry. The Middle Eastern states up until now can hardly appropriate oil without acquiring the required skill, know-how, machinery, equipment, and access to world market. However, they could be the major beneficiaries of petrol-rent as partners of major multinational oil companies compared to other sectors of the economy. A rentier state reliant on the oil revenue is not dependent on taxes from the private sector to develop its military apparatus and/or bureaucratic administration. Hirschman was one of the first economists who noted the 'enclave' characteristic of an economy dependent on oil revenue. By 'enclave', Hirschman (1977) meant a staple like oil and other similar mining activities that do not involve the rest of the economy and do not have any productive backward, forward, or final demand linkages.[13] In an enclave economy, *fiscal linkages* become particularly determinant.

It is precisely because of this absence of connections that the enclave becomes an obvious and comparatively easy target of fiscal authorities.

---

[13] I have defined backward, forward, and final demand linkages in the following terms: "*Backward* linkages lead to new investments in input-supplying facilities and influence the pattern of investment activity, notably transport for collection of the staple. *Forward* linkages are a measure of the inducement to invest in industries using the output of the export industry as an input; they often stimulate processing and service industries. Together with the *final demand* linkage, which measures the derived demand for consumer goods from staple production, these relationships determine the strength of the spread effects from the staple to the economy as a whole" (Vahabi, 2018, p. 399).

"Being a foreign body, often owned by foreigners to boot, the enclave has few defenders of its interests once the state acquires the will and authority to divert toward its own ends a portion of the income stream originating therein" (Hirschman, 1977, p. 74). In this sense, strong fiscal linkage in an enclave economy is in contradiction with other forms of linkages. In fact, if there was a productive activity with many direct links to the rest of economy, either because of strong backward and forward linkages or, more simply, because it is carried on in the central region of a country by producers with intimate ties to a dense network of traders and townspeople, then fiscal linkage would be difficult. "Clearly, with so many friends in court this activity is not likely to be subjected to significant special taxation. The situation that is brought to mind here is that of coffee-growing countries such as Brazil and Colombia" (Hirschman, 1977, p. 75).

Interestingly, similar to Hirschman, Mitchell (2011) opposes coal to oil's supposedly curse-like properties from the viewpoint of production process. He gives pride of place to the power of coal miners to strike as the basis for gaining the rights to vote, to organize, and to create political parties to democratize European countries in the late nineteenth and early twentieth centuries. The linkage effect in the coal industry is explored throughout the strike movement that spread to an array of interconnected industries of coal mining, railways, docking, and shipping sectors. In the same vein, Mitchell notes that the oil mines had similar effects in the early twentieth century. For example, the oil industry in Baku (presently called Azerbaijan) launched protests that would eventually result in the 1905 Russian Revolution. The ripple effect in oil industry in Baku was due to the fact that "The proximity of wells, workshops, pumps, power supplies and refineries created a concentrated labor force with the ability to disrupt supplies of energy across a broad region" (Mitchell, 2011, p. 34).

According to Mitchell, international oil companies and governments learnt from these early movements. They restructured the management of oil extraction to eschew worker pressures. For example, given the distance between oil mines and industrial centers, they exploited ethnic divisions or emigrant workers to insulate the oil industry in many countries. Moreover, various types of transport (maritime, pipeline, etc.) were developed to protect the delivery of oil in case of workers strikes. Although some social historians do not always agree with Mitchell's diagnostic of the workers' movement in oil industry (see, e.g., Atabaki et al., 2018), his contribution is an addition to staple theory[14] by identifying a new linkage effect, namely *industrial conflict.*

Overcoming the 'enclave' oil economy, forward and backward linkages should be created between the oil sector and other sectors in national economy. This diversification process strengthens the private sector and the basis for a fiscal state. The choice between a *rentier* and a *fiscal* state is a political choice. In Iran, this political choice was on the agenda of rulers after the World War II particularly during the early 1950s. The national government of Dr. Muhamad Mossadegh, the Iran's Prime Minister, opted for the nationalization of the Iranian petrol in 1951 to create a *fiscal* state and terminate with the 'enclave' economy, establishing linkages between the oil sector and other sectors. The first step in controlling a tyrant reliant on oil revenue was to tie the oil industry to other sectors so that the new interest groups in other economic sectors would be incentivized to support a *constitutional* monarchy and avoid *absolute* monarchy. In doing so, the state could not only count on its coercive force but should behave as an 'industrial and merchant' state, that is, a state monitoring industrial extraction, training the national technocratic and engineering staff to gain the skill, know-how, and the networking capacity for trading the oil in the world market.

The monarch's choice was a *rentier* state since it could strengthen his autonomy from all social classes by leaning on the partnership with multinational oil companies. Mossadegh's project failed because of the economic embargo and the American-British coup d'état covertly supported by the court, the bureaucracy, and certain Shiite religious leaders in 1953. The economic embargo against the Iranian oil showed that the appropriation of a mixed captive asset on the sole basis of sovereignty rights is considerably costly.

Generally speaking, the brutal force is insufficient to appropriate the idiosyncratic assets requiring specific investments in production, exploration, development, distribution, and marketing networks (Vahabi, 2011, 2015, 2016). The economic embargo caused arrear payments for the state employees and provoked contradictory reactions. While some supporters of Mossadegh massively bought the state's bonds to finance the depleted treasury, certain layers of the state employees grew dissatisfied with the government. The embargo paved the road to coup d'état that led to the

---

[14] For a detailed critical review of the staple theory and its relationship with natural resource curse, see Vahabi (2018).

failure of Mossadegh's goal to create a 'fiscal state' as the basis of a constitutional monarchy. Of course, he never employed the term 'fiscal state', but his idea of an "economy without oil" was describing an economy in which the state relies on tax acquisition rather than oil rent. The former could link the state to social classes including the nascent national bourgeoisie, whereas the latter would strengthen the state's autonomy from social classes and consolidate the Shah's personal rule.

A year after the overthrow of Mossadegh's government, the Shah's regime concluded an agreement with a new consortium of international oil companies called Iranian Oil Participants Ltd. (IOP) according to which while the National Iranian Oil and gas Company (NIOC) preserved the formal ownership of Iran's natural resources, it had to pass the effective control over the resources to this new consortium. To put it differently, the NIOC kept *de jure* sovereignty rights while IOP exercised de facto *usufructus* property rights including the production, exploration, and development of oil fields. The consortium put an end to the British monopoly over Iran's oil, since the formerly AIOC (Anglo-Iranian Oil Company) newly baptized as the British Petroleum's share was reduced to 40%. Five American companies[15] each having 8% gained 40% of the total share; Royal Dutch Shell won 14% and the French oil companies (later called Total) also gained 6%. It was not until 1973 that NIOC came into its own as an operator, both in governance and with regard to capabilities.

During the whole period of 1954–1973, the NIOC was granted a stronger position in owning the installations, exploitation, and sale management, and gradually achieved the know-how, skill, and required capabilities to manage the whole industry. The consortium solution was in line with the Shah's political ambition to establish an absolute monarchy independent from the pressure of internal forces. However, while the coup crushed the organizational backbone of the pro-Soviet Tudeh Party and deprived the Iranian national bourgeoisie from political power, the situation after the coup d'état was still far from unrestrictive power of the autocrat. The high-ranking military officers in the army, the upper echelons of Shiite clergy, and the big landowners gained autonomous political power before and right after the coup. For example, two of the top military

[15] These companies included Gulf Oil and the four Aramco partners, namely Standard Oil of California, later named Chevron; Standard Oil of New Jersey, named later as Exxon, then Exxon Mobil; Standard Oil Co. of New York, later called Mobil and then ExxonMobil; Texaco, later called Chevron.

intelligence officers (Timur Bakhtiar and Muhammad-Vali Gharani) have been accused of conspiring against the Shah. The failure of Gharani's putsch plot in 1959 was a turning point in the Shah's grip over the army and its pressure on the U.S. to eschew any contacts with dissidents or oppositional forces in Iran[16]. The Shah personally controlled all the nominations, rotation, firing, and promoting of high military officers, and he took all the necessary precautions to avoid any political influence of high commanders in the army.

After establishing its control over the army and securing the loyalty of his security forces by the means of the SAVAK,[17] the Shah could attack the landowners' authority in the rural regions that had extended their local powers due to years of weak centralization: "In the rural areas government control was very weak in the 1950's. For the most part, power in the countryside was monopolized by the large absentee landlords, especially those who lived in the major provincial towns" (Hooglund, 1982, p. 46). This was also true for the Khans or the chieftains of nomadic tribes such as Qashqai and Bakhtiari. Landlords' rural power base was a source of centrifuge political currents in the major provincial towns where they lived. In addition to large landlords and tribal chiefs, high Shiite clergy centered in

---

[16] The American relationship with this plot is still unclear. For instance, the full memorandum of the meeting of three members of the US embassy in Tehran (Fraser Wilkins, minister counselor of the embassy, Colonel Baska, and Lieutenant Colonel Braun) with the General Gharani on January 22, 1958, at the house of Esfandiar Bozorgmehr is still classified as "sensitive", not releasable to Foreign Nations (Milani, 2011, pp. 209–210). "On February 27, in an angry communique the Iranian government announced that 39 Iranians, including general Gharani, had been arrested for attempting to overthrow the government and that an 'unnamed foreign power was involved.' The reference to the 'foreign' power was, according to the British embassy in Tehran, 'intended to give the American a freight'. In later versions of the communique, the reference to foreign powers was deleted" (Milani, Ibid, p. 210). Following this event, the Shah pushed the Americans to shun contacts with the Iranian political opposition and dissidents inside Iran. The U.S. vigorously rejected the idea at the time, but later accepted it to the point that on the verge of the Iranian revolution, the U.S. had not its independent channels to know about the Iranian oppositional parties and dissidents' activities in Iran.

[17] SAVAK or Organization of Intelligence and National Security was the secret police, domestic security, and intelligence service created in 1956. General Timur Bakhtia was the first director of the agency from 1957 until 1961. He was dismissed in 1961 and Hassan Pakravan (1961–1965) was nominated as the new director. In 1965, Nematollah Nassiri replaced Pakravan until the eve of revolution (1965–1978). Finally, Nasser Moghadam directed the agency during the revolutionary year of 1978–1979 (see Keddie & Gasiorowski, 1990, pp. 148–151, 154–155).

the city of Qum who implicitly supported the Shah in the coup d'état against Mossadegh were the new autonomous center of power. They were against the westernization trend that threatened their religious and traditional culture. Moreover, the clergy's strategic interest was against a strong absolute monarch that could endanger their autonomy from the state as a religious caste. While big landowners and some influential Shiite clergy were in support of coup d'état, the urban civil society particularly students, workers, and some strata of the middle classes were against the coup and were striving for independence, freedom, and social justice.

Considering these independent power centers, what was the role of the agrarian reform in the Shah's strategy of consolidating its absolute monarchy? To what extent this reform can be regarded as a strategy of an inclusive predatory state? This question brings us to study the relationship between predation and production.

8.4   Complementarity between Predation and Production: The Shah's Political Capitalism

Predation is not necessarily an impediment to production; it can be complementary to it. An *inclusive* predatory state adopts strategies that can enhance production. An emblematic illustration is the Shah's regime that was both despotic and rentier. However, the Shah's despotic rentier state was an inclusive predatory regime that contributed to the development of capitalist mode of production. His land reform in the sixtie1960s that ended landlordism in Iran, extended his personal power in the countryside and accelerated the domination of capitalism based on the petroleum revenue. Political capitalism or profit-making through non-market avenues that had been launched since the inception of the Pahlavi's dynasty by its founder Reza Khan on December 15, 1925, was particularly accentuated under his son's reign, the late Muhammad Reza Shah. The oil rent provided the material conditions for political capitalism. In this sense, there is no rupture between the Shah's regime and the Islamic Republic of Iran (IRI). Political capitalism and reliance on oil revenue are their shared characteristics. However, Islamic political capitalism exemplifies an *exclusionary* predatory regime provoking many obstacles to production and capital accumulation. In this section, I will focus on the Shah's inclusive predatory regime and will identify its principal differences with the IRI.

The combination of the agrarian reform and the industrialization through oil revenue gave rise to the Shah's unchallenged autocracy that can be described as an *inclusive* predatory state.

The principal reason behind the Shah's motivation for land reform was seemingly both the extension of his monopoly power over rural areas and the dispossession of his political adversaries particularly progressive and left from one of their major reform platforms. Indeed, after the forced abdication of Reza Shah by the Anglo-Soviet invasion of Iran on September 16, 1941, and the ensuing power vacuum, the large absentee landlords dominated the rural areas wherever the pro-Soviet Tudeh Party or the Democratic Party of Azerbaijan were not influential among peasants. Following the dismantlement of these two parties, the landlord's monopoly of power in the countryside was unchallenged. The deposition of landlords by land redistribution could terminate their political power and extend the Shah's power in the villages. But the political defeat of landowners was only one side of the coin. The other side was that by taking the initiative of land reform, the Shah could thwart its progressive and left opposition. Retrospectively, the Shah claimed that his land distribution project was not tolerated by Mossadegh and accused him of jeopardizing it (Pahlavi, 1961/1974, p. 85).

Land reform was also the Shah's winning card against the National Front in the early 1960s. The latter had no reform program, and its main slogan was "free elections". They could not even believe in Amini-Arsanjani's land distribution program. When the reform adopted in January 1962 and implemented in the summer 1962, the National Front leaders were completely disarmed, and as one of their leaders, Allah-Yar Saleh, said later, they adopted the policy of "Patience and Waiting". Except for the Shiite clergy who opposed the Shah's reform in defense of its traditional and retrograde interests, all other political parties were confused and paralyzed in face of land reform. Students manifesting massively in the early 1960s, instinctively reacted to the Shah's reforms by voicing "Yes to the reform, no to dictatorship!"

There were three other reasons behind the Shah's motivation for pursuing an agrarian reform.

First, land distribution was the central piece of the Shah's claim for a "revolution from above" (*White* revolution[18]) as opposed to a "revolution from below" (*Red* revolution). We knew by the end of the 1970s that that there was no threat of peasant revolution or even peasant rebellions in the 1950s or the 1960s in Iran in dire contrast to many other countries such as Algeria, Angola, China, Cuba, Greece, Indonesia, Philippines, and Vietnam. As Kazemi and Abrahamian (1978, p. 260) correctly noted: "The social scientist studying Iran, however, is struck not by the importance but by the conspicuous absence of any large-scale peasant rebellions in the modern era." While In Iran, the urban movements were the source of "revolution from below", peasant movements were present in certain regions during 1949–1953. More importantly, the Americans' perception at the time was that such kind of movements could endanger the regime's political stability. Retrospectively, it can be said that in the early 1960s, contesting movements included some vigorous demonstrations by students and reached its climax in a widespread teachers' strike. Workers, particularly workers of brick forges, printing houses, and taxi drivers in Tehran also went on strike, but there was not a revolutionary situation in the countryside.

Second, land reform could create a social-political base among peasants supporting the Shah. Indeed, land reforms initiated from 'above' by the central government in other countries like Prussia have created such a social basis for the charismatic leaders.

Finally, land redistribution could gain the American's support in contrast to the British government who was still supporting landlords as its social base in Iran. In fact, after World War II and notably since the Kennedy administration, the United States regarded land reform as a panacea to developmental problems in Asia and America. An agrarian reform was recommended for motivational reasons notably to shun peasant rebellions or revolution.

---

[18] The identity of the inceptor of the term 'White Revolution' is controversial in the Iranian modern historiography. The Premier Minister, Amini, employed it in the course of answering a journalist's question a few months after his appointment. It has also been claimed that the term was coined by Chester Bowles, the American official sent to Tehran by Kennedy in 1962. However, quoting a report by the British Embassy in Tehran in 1958, Milani (2011, p. 290) attributes this expression to Alam: "Alam went to the embassy and offered a 'program of reform which he said he wanted the Shah to adopt. He used the now much quoted phrase 'White Revolution'. It is possible that in voicing these views Mr. Alam was acting as a 'sounding board' for some of the Shah's own ideas.'"

Kennedy actively pushed for an important administrative reform, a rationalization of the military expenditure and an improvement in the relationship between the Shah and the growing urban middle classes. These points have been clearly acknowledged in the Shah's interview on March 6, 1961, with *U.S. News & World Report* (pp. 64–65): "For my regime is always called 'corrupt' in the Western press, despite the fact that there is corruption in all countries. We have fired more than 4000 Government officials and Army officers in the past 18 months for corrupt practices, yet Westerners keep assuming nothing is done here about 'corruption'" (cited in Amini, 2009, p. 222).

Since 1956, the Shah was 'ruling' instead of 'reigning'. The Americans wished a strong Prime Minister, like Qavam, Razmara, or even Zahedi, for assuming full responsibility for his government, insisting that the Shah be separated from such responsibility. This separation was more compelling in case of the Iranian monarch since the military forces were under his command, not of the civilian chief of state. The American's paradox was that while they actively participated in overthrowing Mossadegh because of their economic interests in Iranian oil, they wished to control the Shah so that his rule could not be too personal and arbitrary. The Americans finally revised their strategy: they accepted the Shah's personal power but tried to train and control the Iranian technocracy. The education and training of highly qualified technocrats were given to the Americans and the Office of Planning, and the Budget Organization was run by Harvard educated technocrats.

What were the principal consequences of land reform? First, while land reform substituted the central state's power for that of the landlord, it did not strengthen independent small peasant landowners. The first phase of land reform[19] was conducted speedily under the supervision of Arsanjani whose goal was to replace subsistence agriculture for profit-oriented farming. The landownership was limited to one six-*dang*[20] village; all property in excess of this amount had to be sold to the government. The price of

---

[19] For a more detailed analysis of land reform, see Vahabi (2018).

[20] The unit basis of land reform was 'village' and not square meters surface, since the agricultural activities were dispersed among villages separated from each other by far distance. A 'dang' was a share of property over the village; each village having six 'dangs'. The whole property over a village meant to possess all six 'dangs'. A restriction was imposed over the owner's property that could not possess more than a village or six dangs. However, the landowners detoured the rule by transferring the property title to their relatives to avoid the limit of six dangs.

the land was determined by the value included in tax declaration. The land then had to be resold to each *nasagh*-holder peasant[21] who had recently been assigned to the land. The results achieved in land distribution during the first 18 months of the program were never seen during the remaining three phases: "By September 1963, a total of some 8,042 whole and partial villages had been purchased by the government and transferred to 271,026 peasants. At that time, it was estimated that at least half of the villages subject to the law had been affected" (Hooglund, 1982, p. 60).

The expeditious distribution of land provoked a strong enthusiasm and dynamic among peasants that could have produced a revolution from below. The Shah felt the 'danger' of an *independent* smallholder peasants taking power in the villages parallel to the deposition of large landlords. Not only Hasan Arsanjani was removed as Minister of Agriculture, but he was succeeded by a military officer, General Ismail Riahi. The pace of redistribution was halted so that independent peasant initiatives could be stopped totally, and the government could be able to consolidate its authority in rural areas. As Lambton (1969, p. 215) aptly remarked: "As the efforts of those who aimed at the creation of an independent self-reliant peasantry, were attended by an increasing measure of success, those holding the reins of power began to realize that the emergence of an independent peasantry might constitute a new factor in the political situation and threaten their own power." The second phase of the reform affecting over two-thirds of villages was launched: it was largely oriented toward a tenancy reform. This phase should be viewed as "an attempt to prevent the power-base of the landlords from being occupied by a strong independent peasantry, while the landlords themselves had been sufficiently weakened" (Katouzian, 1974, p. 228).

Second, the Shah did not need merchants and bankers to finance his industrialization program. The oil revenues could provide the required financing. In this context, merchants, bankers, and industrialists could not use their exit option as a bargaining means with the despot. Quite to the contrary, the despot could consent fiscal exoneration to these social groups having access to 'fugitive' and mixed assets. The lack of combativity of the Iranian nascent industrial bourgeoisie should be attributed to their *lack of exit option*. Generally speaking, in an oil reliant country, asset mobility has less restraining effect on tyranny during 'normal' or 'booming' periods of oil revenues. However, it has a direct political effect during 'bust' or

---

[21] They were the peasants who had the 'right' to cultivate the land.

negative oil shocks. A significant decrease in oil revenue reduces the state budget and expenditures, and consequently those social groups having access to fugitive and mixed assets would gain significant bargaining power in their relationship with the ruler. In such case, they might push a strong pressure on tyrant for political concessions. The *political* implication of oil cycles will shrink with growing economic diversification. This brings me to formulate a fundamental assumption: a political stable tyrant reliant on oil revenues tends to diversify the economy to the point that oil revenues downfall during 'busts' could be politically neutral. I call this the tyrant's limited diversification tendency for political stability.

By political instability, I mean a level of capital flight (KF) that could undermine the tyrant's monopoly of power. An example can cast light on this process. After the creation of consortium and the reactivation of the oil industry late in 1954, the Iranian economy experienced a great leap forward. The annual rate of investment was at least 20%, and the rate of economic growth was around 5–6% The rising oil royalties, a succession of good harvests, and substantial American loans and grants generated this rapid growth. During the period of 1952–1962, the United States loans amounted to over 200 million dollars, whereas economic and military grants reached 850 million dollars. During 1956–1957, "one third of new investment was from private sources; spread in the fields of industry; construction; agriculture; and trade and banking-in that order of percentage. For the first time the industrial investment exceeded that in construction, traditionally the main area for private capital" (Young, 1962, p. 280). The economic boom was related to an 'agricultural oil-exporting country' in which different layers of capitalism, that is, merchant, financial, but also industrial were growing. While oil export was becoming the major source of revenue, the loan and grants were still playing a considerable role.

The open-door policy combined with easy and uncontrolled credit furnished the conditions for large sums of expenditure on imported *luxury goods* exclusively accessible to the rich and higher echelons of the modern middle class as well as an economic growth based on shoestring capital. As soon as the oil barrel price decreased from 84 cents to 80 cents in 1960 and the rial's exchange rate for the American dollar decreased, the economic recession ensued. The recession lasted throughout the period 1958–1961, and it was the first oil-revenue cycle. The economic recession had strong economic and monetary origins. From a *monetary* or short-run viewpoint, it was an *illiquidity crisis* or *credit inflation* marked by the depletion of foreign exchange reserves. From an *economic* long-run perspective, the recession was related to the limited size of the market, confined to luxury goods and a tiny industrial sector. The merchant and banking capital were still the principal forms of capital accumulation, but oil-financed capitalism was growing in Iran independently of the other sectors. Landlord relationships were hindering the extension of markets for this growing capitalism. An agrarian reform in conjunction with developing capitalism reliant on oil revenues could enhance the growth of services and industry although it was detrimental to a prosperous agricultural sector capable of exportation.

In fall of 1960, the government was forced to adopt a stabilization program under the pressure of the IMF and World Bank refusing otherwise to consent further loans. To conserve foreign exchange, the government prohibited exchange of some 200 super-luxury imports, imposing a fourfold custom duty on many other items and abolishing strictly all travel abroad except in force major cases. More importantly was the political implication of this economic recession since Kennedy administration refused to consent any loan or military grants without the Shah accepting to appoint his favorite Prime Minister Ali Amini.

The vulnerability of economic growth reliant on oil revenue was linked to its political implication during the contraction phase. To avoid such consequences, a politically stable regime had to diversify the economy by broadening the industrial and service sectors during the oil booms. The Shah's regime was not limited to captive assets, it included mixed and fugitive assets by developing oil industry, non-oil industry, services, and investing heavily on training highly skilled technicians, and talented managerial technocratic cadre. His inclusive predatory state was based on a combination of land reform and oil-financed capitalism.

8.5   Predation Versus Production: Islamic Political Capitalism

The symbiotic relationship between predation and production under the Shah's regime in the 1960s and the early 1970s has been replaced by a contradictory relationship between them under the Islamic political capitalism. A few significant indicators highlight this difference.

The first two indicators are the average rate of annual economic growth and the per capita rate of national income. A solid base for our comparisons might be 1977 (1355 Iranian year), a normal year just before the outbreak of the 1979 Revolution and 2020 (1399 Iranian year). According to Consumer Price Index of Central Bank Statistics, 2752 units of 2020 currency has the Purchase Power of one unit of 1977 currency and therefore the GDP per capita of 37,770,000 tomans for 2020 equals 13,808 tomans in 1977. Considering the GDP per capita of 17,818 tomans in 1977, the purchasing power of Iranians has reduced a third during 1977–2020 (Mansoor, December 19, 2020, *Independent Persian*, https://www.independentpersian.com/node/107166, retrieved on July 11, 2022). Moreover, the average rate of annual growth during 1965–1977 was 10–11% (see https://www.macrotrends.net/countries/IRN/iran/gdp-growth-rate, retrieved on July 11, 2022), whereas the economic growth has been for the last decade with negative rate for 2012, 2013, 2015, 2018, and 2019.

A third major indicator is the ratio of the formation of fixed capital to GDP. This ratio should be around 30% to secure the replacement of the physical and technical depreciation of capital and extend the reproduction base. While this ratio had been in average 25–30% during 1963–1977, the average rate for the period 2010–2020 (calculated on fixed prices of 1390/2011) was around 16% with a maximum of 20% in 2011 and a minimum of 11% in 2019. The average annual growth rate of Gross Fixed Capital Formation (GFCF) has been minus 3.6 (see Mansoor, February 13, 2021, *independent Persian*, https://www.independentpersian.com/node/122631, retrieved on July 11, 2022).

These indicators[22] clearly confirm, respectively, the contradictory(complementary) relationship between predation and production under the IRI and the Shah's regime.

Three major reasons underlie this contradictory relationship that will be reviewed below: (A) capture of oil revenue by an oligarchy, (B) confiscatory regime, and (C) patrimonial development.

A) Capture of oil Revenue by an Oligarchy

One of the underpinning tenets of the IRI was to build an economy non-reliant on oil revenues. This never happened. Not only this reliance

---

[22] In addition to the afore-mentioned indicators, a fourth important one is the ratio of capital flight to the average formation of fixed capital (GFCF) that will be substantiated in Sect. 8.6.

persisted in the post-revolutionary period, but it was even accentuated because of oligarchic capture of the oil revenue.

During the Shah's regime, the Iranian petroleum revenue was managed by the Shah himself (see Chap. 4). Although the court, the army, and big industrialists and financiers were benefited from this revenue, it was centralized under the Shah's personal authority. The oil revenue financed the state's current expenditures and was also used for investment in the formation of fixed capital in the petroleum sector as well as in partial diversification of the economy. The political stability of the Shah's regime warranted this investment and partial diversification. The Shah's lion's share of the oil revenue was not necessarily contradictory with increasing investment and production. This centralized structure was superseded by an oligarchic capture of oil revenues under the IRI.

In fact, the oil industry in Iran is now only *formally* nationalized, but in reality, it is controlled by a new consortium in which at least six major actors, namely *Bonyad Mostazafan*, *Setad headquarters*, *Khatam al-anbiya*, *Bonyad Tavon Basij*, *Astan Ghods Razavi*, and the *Iranian formal state* have each their share. These economic magnates are run by a strong oligarchy related to *Anfal*, the Sepah, and the Basij. Nili and Associates (2015, p. 545, 548, 555) report the emergence of an oligarchy of parastatal and non-state public sectors after the privatization edict in July 2006. They relate the increasing role of this oligarchy to two factors: (1) state failure to control the non-state public sector and (2) the American economic boycotts that extended the influence of the oligarchy.

Rahman Zadeh Heravi (2018) referred to the statements of Ishaq Jahangiri, the first vice-president of Rouhani, in the conference titled 'Knowledge-based oil industry' on April 17, 2016, in which he alluded to the transfer of the right to sell oil to some revolutionary Islamic institutions during the American economic boycott. He said: "None of the institutions that got oil from the Ministry of petroleum to sell has returned back even one dollar to the state … the oil's sale should be only carried out by the Ministry of petroleum" (Jahangiri, 2016/2021). According to him, some security and military organizations had received oil from the Ministry of Petroleum to sell for 170 million dollars in 2012, but never paid the money to the state (Rahman Zadeh Heravi, 2018, p. 342). Maloney also underlined the rivalry among different institutions to prey on oil revenues by acquiring the right to sell it: "Rather than clashing on the fundamental shape of the economy and scope of state economic management, the most salient divide today within Iran concerns dividing up the spoils of the oil windfalls" (2015, p. 501).

While the Supreme Leader nominally wields ultimate authority, no single individual in Iran has uncontested or complete power. The Supreme Jurisconsult coordinates different institutional magnates, respecting their shares in economic activities and relative autonomy in spending their revenues. The oligarchic rivalry determines the distribution of spoils of the oil windfalls. The management of oil sale provides a salient example of the common-pool resources or "tragedy of the commons" (Hardin, 1968). The six principal beneficiaries of oil revenues use them to reproduce their authoritative resources and strengthen their political position. The oil revenues are used either on current expenditures of parallel Islamic institutions or sent abroad (capital flight) as part of personal wealth and cash hoarding of the religious and military leaders and their family members. This is known in economic literature as 'voracity effect' to which we will return in the next section. None of these six major benefactors has shown a genuine interest in using the oil revenue to invest in modernizing the machinery, equipment, engineering, or other skills of the oil industry. They have all behaved as competing oligarchs of a rentier state in the context of political instability since the IRI feeds on political instability rather than political stability as in the Shah's regime. This oligarchic rivalry explains why predation impedes production under the Islamic political capitalism.

B) Confiscatory Regime

It is often assumed that the Shi'i jurisprudence is consistent with the sanctity of private property. Maloney (2015, p. 501) repeats this idea widely shared by economists, political scholars, and jurists: "Ayatollah Khomeini was a reliably staunch defender of property rights and the role of the private sector, consistent with traditional Shi'a jurisprudence, which generally holds the sanctity of private property to be inviolable." As argued before, this assumption is wrong in light of *Anfal*. The sanctity of private property requires a separation between sovereignty and property. The IRI's confiscatory regime contradicts such sanctity.

I would add that even the late Shah was not an unconditional advocate of private property considering the fusion of sovereignty and property under his despotic rule. The Shah's discretionary power over the oil revenue and his statist policies have been underlined by many authors. For example, Abolhassan Ebtehaj,[23] the President of the Private Iranian's Bank, was one of the first who criticized the Shah's land reform for "confiscating property" and statist vision of the economy, where the state could and should become a Leviathan. According to Milani (2011, p. 263), Ebtehaj had correctly predicted, not long after the land reform, "the Shah proved willing to forcefully expropriate the country's only private television network, the first private university, and the country's richest private mine".

Similarly, Alikhani (2001, pp. 61–62), the first minister of the Iranian economy (1963–1969), mentioned in his oral interview[24] that the Shah was particularly inspired by the soviet's experience of Kolkhoz in launching Agricultural Stock Company during his agrarian reform in the 1960s. Moreover, he believed in the state priority in all major industrial sectors including metallurgy, petrochemicals, PVC manufacturing, and so on. Reviewing the third (1962–1967), the fourth (1968–1972), and the fifth (1973–1978) planning programs in the Iranian economy, Leilaz (2013, p. 69) also underlined the Shah's statism in controlling the industries such as tea, tobacco, fishing, petrochemicals, fertilizers, and steel plant.

Thus, both the IRI and the Shah's regime were based on the fusion of sovereignty and property. The sanctity of private property or the superiority of property over sovereignty was not consistent with *Anfal* nor with the Shah's despotic purview over the economy. However, the despotic monarch was more protective toward private property and private investment than *Velayat faqih*. The fundamental difference between the two political systems resided in the fact that the Shah's regime entertained close relationship with the USA and pursued an open-door policy to welcome massive foreign direct investment (FDI). Political stability was a necessary condition to maintain the capital flow. This explains why the

---

[23] Prominent banker, economic planner, and one of the most important and powerful figures in the economic history of Iran during the middle decades of the twentieth century (born in Rasht, November 29, 1899; died in London, February 25, 1999). He exercised a major influence on the development of the Iranian banking system and became a pioneer of economic planning in the country, earning international recognition for his vision and administrative competence. Ebtehaj was noted as a vocal critic of corruption and, later in his career, of what he considered to be the excessive military spending of the Shah's government (Encyclopedia   Iranica,   https://www.iranicaonline.org/articles/ebtehaj-abolhassan) retrieved on February 11, 2022.

[24] Alinaghi Alikhani (1929–2019) had an interview with Gholamreza Afkhami on behalf of the Foundation of Iranian Studies in December 1999 that was published in 2001.

monarchy acted as an inclusive predatory state following a strict protective policy toward property rights, whereas the IRI combined confiscatory regimes, with an anti-American policy eschewing foreign direct investment. The adoption of the Article 81 of the Constitution of the IRI reflected this structure, and the failure of efforts to relax that article during the presidencies of Hashemi Rafsanjani and Khatami[25] reinforced the closure of the domestic economy.

There exists another major difference between *Anfal* and the Shah's prerogatives. Like *Velayat faqih*, *Anfal* violates the people's sovereignty since all ownerless public properties (*res nullius*) are assumed to be the restrictive property of the Imam and not the people. By contrast, the Shah's despotic privileges were not justified in the name of the Shah's sovereignty over the people. In the Constitution born from the Iranian Constitutional revolution (1905–1911), which was contested by Ayatollah Shaikh Fazlollah Noori,[26] the founder of political Islam in Iran, the people's sovereignty has been explicitly stipulated and the Shah's royal power was supposed to represent the 'people's sovereignty'. The Shah's despotism was rather a de facto and not a *de jure* violation of the people's sovereignty.

There is another dimension to the confiscatory regime that should not be dismissed. It consists of corporate raiding, particularly central corporate raiding, that developed during the IRI whereas it was marginal during the Shah's regime. The issue of corporate raiding and its different types was systematically explored in the case of post-socialist transition in Russia and Hungary by Madlovics and Magyar (2021). The authors modelled corporate raiding or 'reiderstvo' practices as salient forms of post-Communist predation. They applied Vahabi's model of predation to central corporate raiding:

> Indeed, mobility and appropriability are useful aspects that can be used to develop a model of centrally led corporate raiding. According to Vahabi,

---

[25] See Chap. 5 regarding the Article 81 and the efforts to relax this article during Rafsanjani's and Khatami's presidencies.

[26] He was a prominent Shi'i theologian during the late nineteenth and early twentieth centuries (1843–1909). He was the founder of political Islam in Iran. Although he was shortly sympathetic to the Iranian Constitutional Revolution in the beginning for challenging the tyranny, he turned against it since he considered that the Constitutional Revolution aimed at a western-style democratic and secular government instead of a government with Islamic laws. The Constitutionalists executed him because of his treason to the revolution (see Kasravi, 2006).

mobility means the owners' ability to escape predation by removing their property from the reach of the predatory state. Escape may be accomplished by (a) hiding assets, for example by the various techniques of double accountancy and financial scheming used by small and medium-sized enterprises in Russia to escape predation (Ledeneva, 2006, pp. 142–163), or (b) moving the company geographically (Soós, 2017; Markus, 2017). Appropriability, however, is also determined by asset specificity, which in the case of a company means that 'the continuation of particular investments requires specific entrepreneurial capabilities, including marketing, financing, monitoring, coordinating and networking abilities', which the predator might not have (Vahabi, 2016, pp. 157–160) (Madlovics & Magyar, 2021, p. 256).

The authors identify three kinds of companies that would be potentially good targets for discretionary state intervention. They include: (1) market potential, (2) rent-seeking potential, and (3) kleptocratic potential. The first one consists of a single transfer or regulatory change that can raise the company's value. The second concerns the regulation of the market in which the company operates so that it could capture more rents. The third is related to companies that are suitable for illegal rent-seeking such as money laundering or capture of public procurement contracts at favorable prices (Madlovics & Magyar, 2021, p. 258). Central corporate raiding is a process that allows the predator to become a protector of the prey companies by "shelter providing" (Vahabi, 2015, pp. 69–76).

As discussed in Chaps. 6 and 7, the privatization decree in 2006 was a policy of swallowing the state enterprises by *Anfal*, the Sepah, and the Basij. In this sense, corporate raiding was organized centrally under the title of 'privatization' in the IRI. Moreover, in these chapters, we cited several methods of central corporate raiding under the IRI. Three major justifications have been advanced, namely the primacy of 'Islamic', 'revolutionary', and 'security' considerations. The predatory raiding has resulted in transforming many sectors and branches such as private banking, energy, telecommunication, and luxury cars into the chain food of predatory activity of parallel Islamic institutions. In fact, the primary question of operation for any potentially 'successful' private company in Iran is not whether it can remain in competitive markets, but whether it would become part of this predatory food chain. The vast discretionary powers of these institutions and their arbitrariness have strongly weakened the security of property rights and private investment under the IRI. According to Nili (2004, p. 113), "the investment in our country is very far from what is required for creating employment and income. The foreign investment is almost absent, and the state sector has serious financial problems in developing investment. Everything depends on the investment by private sector. However, it is commonly believed that the private sector needs *investment security* to invest."

The Research Centre of Islamic Legislative Assembly has overtly acknowledged the high security risk of private investment in Iran in its quarterly reports. This research center started its investigation on 'Business environment' and 'investment climate' in Iran[27] in fall 2011.

According to Sayyah (2016, pp. 26–27), based on the reports covering the period Fall 2010 to Summer 2015, the principal obstacles to business environment in Iran are not the lack of infrastructures such as roads, ports, or electricity, but rather the instability of macroeconomic factors, the lack of transparency, the economic unpredictability, corruption, and the lack of security for property rights.

The period 2017–2020 has also been under the scrutiny of the Research Centre of Islamic Legislative Assembly. The results of 13 quarterly reports are collected in Table 8.3. The quarterly rating of investment security is calculated based on perception of economic agents regarding 21 survey indicators as well as hard data. The highest figure indicating total insecurity is 10 and the lowest risk or perfect security is 1.

As Table 8.3 shows, the rating has always been close or over 6 confirming a chronic problem of investment security. Three worst indicators regarding the lack of security during all this period have been (1) national authorities reneging on their commitments, (2) provincial and local authorities reneging on their commitments, and (3) clientelist relationships violating the impartiality of official decisions. The ratings for all these three indicators have been systematically higher than 8.

The confiscatory regime and the lack of investment security are other factors explaining why predation impedes production under the Islamic political capitalism.

---

[27] I intentionally took the Iranian's official data to shun any excessive assessment of investment risk. I did not cite international ratings regarding 'Business climate rating' and 'Country risk rating' in Iran, since they all indicate a very critical situation for investment security. For example, based on Cofase indicators, Country risk rating is E and Business climate rate is D for Iran, see https://globaledge.msu.edu/countries/iran/risk/ retrieved on February 11, 2022.

Table 8.3   Quarterly rating of investment security

Year	Winter	Spring	Summer	Fall
2017	5.98	NA	NA	NA
2018	6.18	6.15	6.32	6.43
2019	5.84	6.07	6.07	6.12
2020	NA	6.16	6.46	6.37

Source: Author based on 13 quarterly reports of the Research Centre of Islamic Legislative Assembly

Note 1 The indicator is calculated on average for the whole country, but separate indicators are available for each province and each economic sector

Note 2 *NA*: Not available

C) Patrimonial Development

Patrimonial development describes the rationale of growth under the Islamic political capitalism. From an economic point of view, the contradictory relationship between predation and production is explicable by this pattern of development growth which is intrinsically linked to appropriation rather than production. What do I mean by 'patrimonial development'[28]?

The term 'patrimonial' refers to inherited property or assets (that may be 'abandoned' or 'confiscated' from a legal viewpoint) rather than new added value or income. Natural resources are also part of patrimonial assets. This is a type of accumulation in which the increase in capital is based on the re-evaluation of the market value of the already existing assets of corporations rather than new added value. Similarly, the growth of GDP is not generated by better economic performance, higher productivity, or efficiency of new investments. Moreover, the growth is not driven

[28] To my knowledge, the French economist, Michel Aglietta (1998), was the first to use the expression 'régime d'accumulation patrimonial' (a patrimonial accumulation regime) to describe an accumulation regime based on finance that replaced Fordism since the end of 1970s (1945–1979). In his opinion, while Fordism was based on wage/salary relationships, the new regime was dependent on monetary and financial relationships. Oliver Schlumberger (2008) coined a close expression "patrimonial capitalism" pertaining to structural economic reform, in a range of non-OECD countries, that has led to capitalist, yet non-market economies which differ qualitatively from competition-based market systems. Surprisingly, the author never referred to Max Weber's 'political capitalism' while his analysis of 'patrimonial capitalism' comes within the scope of 'political capitalism'. My usage of 'patrimonial development' is related to but different from both authors.

by the so-called Keynesian 'mass consumption' since the wealth-effect is more important than income-effect in explaining consumers' behavior. To put it differently, it is not mass consumption of wage/salary earners that enhances markets and economic growth. The consumption of elites, other property-holders in general, and subsidized products and services play a key role in extending markets.[29] Patrimonial accumulation is driven by maximizing the financial value of assets regardless of the level of profit-making or the creation of new added value by corporations. In sum, patrimonial accumulation maximizes rent-seeking rather than profit-making.

Many reports on the balance sheets of corporations have highlighted this point: "We know that a large share, probably 80 percent, of the capital increase in companies' balance sheets derive from a re-evaluation of their fixed assets and not from the new cash investment. Considering the level of productivity and efficiency, it can be said that not only the GDP has not increased because of an improvement in economic performance, but also experienced personnel of industries have lost their motivation to contribute to such an improvement. Rent-seeking behavior is spread everywhere" (Rahman Zadeh Heravi, 2018, p. 64).

Comparing financial speculative activities with productive activities, Maljoo (2017, p. 154) notes: "while the share of financial intermediation in the gross domestic product (*i.e.*, speculative economic activities) rose from 1.02% in 1996 to 2.78% in 2011, the share of capital formation in the private sector in the gross domestic product (*i.e.*, productive economic activities) decreased from 4.39% to 3.98% over the same period." Similarly, "the distribution of households' employed members in industry and mining declined from 23.7% in 1992 to 17.4% in 2014, while the percentage working in financial, insurance, proprietary, judicial, and commercial services rose from 2.6% to 8% over the same period" (Maljoo, Ibid., p. 155).

Nili and associates (2015) find that the economic growth has been a by-product of increase in oil revenue. This explains higher growth rates during Ahmadinejad's presidency with the extraordinary boom in oil receipts. However, such type of growth does not create new employment. Therefore, "since 2006, the Iranian economy has experienced growth without job creation accompanied by inflation" (2015, p. 117). The

---

[29] Many domestic markets including the market for necessary goods and services such as bread are reliant on subsidies. In this context, cutting subsidies does not necessarily add to the efficiency of markets but might end with 'dependent' markets.

concomitant increase of unemployment and inflation is not always related to stagflation,[30] but oil-derived growth.

Nili and associates (Ibid, p. 117) underline "the marginal role of private sector in production and economy". The special issue of the economic weekly, *Tejarat Farda* (May 2021), on the rate of investment and growth in Iran includes several papers documenting the low level of investment. Kaviani (2021) sums up the trend of investment in Iran in the recent period: "Almost since 2013, the stock of machinery capital has continuously diminished, and the slightly positive and low level of total capital increase has only been generated because of real estate construction. The latter was mainly due to the increase in real estate prices to store the value of assets." She also noted that not only the private investment but also state investment has decreased significantly during the same period.

In fact, the state was not even capable of covering its current expenditures. "In 2020, the government sold bonds worth of 125 thousand billion rials. Most of this amount was used to pay the salaries of state employees" (Kaviani, 2021). In economic literature, the emission of bonds by the state is known to have a 'crowding effect' on the private saving because private investment would be replaced by state debts. In this case, we are confronted by 'crowding effect' in its worst sense since the state mobilized private savings not to invest but to cover its current expenditures: "Presently, it is noteworthy that the issue is not the investment by the state sector, it is merely to finance its current expenditures to pay the salaries of the state employees by selling bonds … the decrease in state and private investments will in turn reduce further the level of investment in the country and the capacity of economic growth" (Kaviani, Ibid.). Symptoms of this lack of investment abound: systematic power cut during summer 2021,[31] systematic problem in extracting petroleum, or the non-renewal of equipment and machinery in almost all state enterprises.

Another dimension of the problem is the inefficiency of investment. Bjorvatn and Selvik (2007, p. 3) attributed the low returns to investment in Iran to "distortions in the allocation of capital caused by rent-seeking". These authors also noted the lack of property rights protection resulting

[30] Several episodes of stagflation with high rates of unemployment and inflation can be identified during the decade 2011–2021. For instance, the rate of growth in 2018 and 2019 were –4.9% and –7% respectively (Abdollahi, May 2021), and inflation rates were, respectively, 34.6% and 36.5% for the same years (*Atlantic Council*, July 8, 2021).
[31] See other causes of power cut in Sect. 8.8.

in less private investment at the aggregate level. Regulatory rents through development projects and subsidized loans are identified as the sources of the state's investment inefficiency (Ibid., p. 14).

An important dimension of patrimonial development is rent-seeking in commercial activities over multiple exchange rates that exemplifies capital accumulation without any production or newly added value.

There exist a host of exchange rates for the foreign currency, particularly the American and Canadian dollars, euro, and so on in Iran. The gap between the preferential official rate and the market rate has been a major source of rent-seeking since the first days of the IRI when foreign trade was nationalized until now.[32] One of the very recent examples of this gap is Rouhani's government offering American dollars to merchants for an official rate of 1 dollar=4200 tomans for so-called necessary goods. This currency was known as "Jahangiri's currency" alluding to the first vice-president of Rouhani, Mr. Ishaq Jahangiri.[33] The decision regarding "Jahangiri's currency" was made in a meeting comprising the heads of all three executive, legislative, and judiciary powers on August 4, 2018. The amount allotted to these 'necessary goods' was 15 billion dollars annually (Jahangiri, 2016/2021).[34] According to the ex-governor of the Iran's Central Bank (ICB), Abdonnaser Hemmati, although this amount varied several times since then, it was on average 12 billion dollars annually over the period 2018–2022 (*Khabar online*, January 18, 2022).

A simple calculation suggested by Akbar Turkan[35] (2020) reveals the immense amount of rent-seeking and systemic corruption. He assumed that on average the annual oil revenues amounts to 60 billion dollars. If in

---

[32] See Chap. 6 on 'dependent-government market' and privileged bazaaris in Iran during the 1980s.

[33] Ishaq Jahangiri served as the sixth first vice-president from 2013 until 2021 in Hassan Rouhani's government. Jahangiri was the minister of industries and mines from 1997 to 2005 under President Muhammad Khatami. Before that, he was the governor of Isfahan Province. He was also a member of parliament for two terms.

[34] All governments have adopted preferential currency rate. In Mir Hossein Mousavai's time (1981–1989), it was 7 tomans; in Rafsanjani's two terms presidency (1989–1997), the rate varied annually and reached first to 175 tomans, then 300 tomans, and finally to 800 tomans. During Khatami's two terms presidency (1997–2005), it varied from 175 tomans to 800 tomans. In Ahmadinejad's two terms presidency, the rate started at 800 tomans, rose to 1200 tomans, then to 2400 tomans, and finally attained 3000 tomans (see Jahangiri, 2016/2021).

[35] Akbar Turkan was the President Hassan Rouhani's chief adviser from 2013 to 2018. He was also the Minister of Defense and Minister of Roads and Transportation in the government headed by President Akbar Hashemi Rafsanjani

addition, we assume that the difference between the preferential and market rates of currency comes to 8000 tomans, the total difference would be 480 thousand billion tomans, which is twice the annual budget of the country. Turkan concluded the primacy of mercantilist over industrial interests in Iran. Without naming Turkan, his calculation was contested by Hemmati since the price of 'necessary goods' did not increase at the same rate as the difference between the market and preferential rates. But Hemmati's counterargument is not valid for many reasons.

First, the preferential rate could not stabilize prices of 'necessary goods'. More importantly, the preferential currency was not granted to procure only targeted goods but extended to luxury cars, cell phones, or 'ghost' products, that is, items that have never been imported but were used as fictive commodities to fill accounting books. In fact, the Rouhani government officially acknowledged that 5 billion dollars were 'lost', in the sense that its allocation could not be clarified. It is also noteworthy that Mehdi Jahangiri, the brother of Ishaq Jahaniri, was condemned in a tribunal for smuggling currencies on January 1, 2021 (see https://www.dw.com/fair/retrieved on February 13, 2022).

The scandalous issue of "Jahangiri's currency" was vastly used by Ebrahim Raisi to discredit Rouhani's government as a symbol of corruption. The abolition of 4200 tomans currency became a battle horse of the 13th government and new conservative Majles against the previous government of Rouhani. Its abrogation has become the controversial subject of the state budget in 2022.

In sum, while the oligarchic structure of capturing oil revenue and confiscatory regime explain the *institutional* aspects of a contradictory relationship between predation and production, patrimonial development casts light on the *economic* rationale of such relationship under the Islamic political capitalism.

8.6   Capital and Labor Flight as a Typical Economic Behavior

In economic literature, the economics of flight has been defined in various ways (Cuddington, 1986). The World Bank (1985) defines capital flight as the change in a nation's foreign assets. It captures the difference between the current account and official reserves, on the one hand, and the increase in recorded gross external debt and net foreign direct investment (FDI), on the other hand. Broadly speaking, this indicator measures the difference of FDI in Iran and the Iranians' investment abroad. Accordingly, capital flight (KF) can be defined by the following equation:

$$Capitalfligh(KF) = CurrentAccountBalance(CA)$$
$$+ NetForeignDirectInvesment(FDI)$$
$$+ ExternalDebt(ED) + ForignReserves(FR)$$

Considering the paucity of FDI during the Islamic Republic of Iran, the term FDI can be removed. External debt is the term that captures the foreign resource for financing. Applying this equation, it can be argued that capital flight started since 1984. Indeed, capital flight did not exist during the Shah's period. According to a study by the Research Centre of Islamic Legislative Assembly (May 2000), during the period 1973–1977, there was a 95 billion dollars surplus (calculated in terms of 1995 constant values). The surplus was drastically reduced during 1978–1983 to 24 billion dollars, and finally it became negative for the 1984–1993 period. The latter experienced a deficit amounting to 46 billion dollars. Annual capital flight was on average 4.6 billion dollars. According to the same study, the amount of capital flight during 1984–1993 is equivalent to the sum of Iranian oil and gas export revenues in 1991, 1992, and 1993 (Ibid, p. 13).

Borrowing the World Bank definition, Zobeiri et al. (2017) try to capture capital flight in Iran during 1981–2012. They find that capital flight has had an increasing tendency during the whole period, but "it has grown substantially from 2005 to 2007. After that, it began to decrease in 2008 and then, it rose significantly and reached to its peak in 2011 (38095.94 million dollars)" (Ibid, 2017, p. 418). To put it differently, capital flight is a specific feature of the political economy of the Islamic Republic of Iran that was vividly accentuated during Ahmadinejad's presidency and after Trump's withdrawal from the Joint Comprehensive Plan of Action (JCPOA).

Different national and international reports have been published regarding the average annual amount of capital flight from Iran during almost 40 years of the IRI. I will refer to some of the most significant ones; they all converge to 20 billion dollars annually. Farhad Ehteshamzadeh (2018), the chairman of the board of directors of the Federation of the Iranian Import, announced on April 18, 2018, that "capital flight during the last 40 years of the IRI amounted to 800 billion dollars" (*Iranjib*, April 18, 2018).[36]

Muhammad Reza Poor Ebrahimi, the president of the Economic Commission of the of Islamic Legislative Assembly, released some data on capital flight on June 17, 2018, according to which 30 billion dollars fled Iran by the end of 2017. The IMF's report on the Iranian capital flight also considered the year 2017 as a record year with 27 billion dollars. Considering the ICB's data over 2005–2017, it has been estimated that 180 billion dollars escaped the country (*Tejarat Farda*, June 17, 2018).[37] The Research Centre of Islamic Legislative Assembly (2018) also announced that during the two years 2016 and 2017, 59 billion dollars fled the country. According to this report, 39 billion and 200 million dollars escaped from Iran in 2017, comprising 83% of the non-oil Iranian export. The same research center estimated the amount of capital flight to be 20 billion and 200 million dollars in 2016.

All reports underline that the capital flight has been accompanied by emigration of asset-owners buying homes or investing in banks and stock exchange abroad. There are many different destinations such as Turkey, Canada, England, Georgia, Azerbaijan, and the United Arab Emirates. The emigrants apply for citizenship abroad wherever it would be possible. In this sense, capital flight includes labor flight, and it embraces not only rich or well-to-do people but also other non-rich layers of the population (*Radiofarda*, 28 May 2018).[38]

---

[36] The news code: 48180, see https://www.iranjib.ir/shownews/48180/%D8%AE%D8 %B1%D9%88%D8%AC-800-%D9%85%DB%8C%D9%84%DB%8C%D8%A7%D8%B1%D8 %AF-%D8%AF%D9%84%D8%A7%D8%B1-%D8%A7%D8%B2-%D8%A7%DB%8C%D8%B1%D- 8%A7%D9%86-%D8%AF%D8%B1-40-%D8%B3%D8%A7%D9%84-%DA%AF%D 8%B0%D8%B4%D8%AA%D9%87, retrieved on February 14, 2022. The persian sec- tion of the Deutsche Welle also diffused the news, see https://www.dw.com/fa- ir/%D8%AE%D8%B1%D9%88%D8%AC-%DB%B8%DB%B0%DB%B0-%D9%85%DB%8 C%D9%84%DB%8C%D8%A7%D8%B1%D8%AF-%D8%AF%D9%84%D8%A7%D8%B1- %D8%A7%D8%B2-%D8%A7%DB%8C%D8%B1%D8%A7%D9%86-%D8%AF%D8%B1- %DB%B4%DB%B0-%D8%B3%D8%A7%D9%84/a-43436169, retrieved on February 14, 2022.

[37] See:https://www.tejaratefarda.com/%D8%A8%D8%AE%D8%B4%D8%A7%DB%8C%D 8%B1%D8%A7%D9%86-%D8%A7%D9%82%D8%AA%D8%B5%D8%A7%D8%AF-41/27239- %D9%BE%DA%98%D9%88-%D8%A7%DB%8C%D8%B1%D8%A7%D9%86-%D8%B1%D8%A7- %D8%AA%D8%B1%DA%A9-%D9%85%DB%8C-%DA%A9%D9%86%D8%AF, retrieved on February 14, 2022.

[38] See https://www.radiofarda.com/a/f4_iran_parliament_organization_exit_capital_59_ billion_dollar/29255439.html, retrieved on February 14, 2022.

The figures for capital flight in 2018 and 2019 indicate that it constantly increased during these years. Masoud Khansari, the head of the Tehran's Chamber of Commerce, announced on February 21, 2021, that during the two years—2018 and 2019—100 billion dollars fled the country. Adding 59 billion dollars for 2016 and 2017, the total amount of capital flight over 4 years came to 160 billion dollars. This means that on average each year experienced 40 billion dollars of capital flight, twice the amount of the average annual capital flight over the last 40 years. To put it differently, Trump's economic boycotts doubled the capital flight that was already colossal. Khansari also highlighted that part of this capital was spent on buying home in neighboring countries notably in Turkey. The data released on January 15, 2021, showed that in 2020, 7200 homes were bought in Turkey by Iranians, ten times more than 2017, two times more than 2018, and one-third increase compared with the number of homes bought in 2019 (*Azadi faryade*, February 21, 2021).[39]

Among the Iranian emigrants, the children of leaders (known as 'Agha zadeh'[40]) related to both fundamentalist and the so-called reformist political factions have a special privileged status. Since Rafsanjani's presidency, they principally emigrated to North America (the USA and Canada) and to European countries (England, Germany, Austria, and Switzerland). Most of them are engaged in 'commerce'; they have bought very expensive houses and keep colossal amount of money in different North American and European banks. During recent years, the emigration to the USA has become more difficult for them, and they often have settled down in Canada (*Radio zamaenh*, September 7, 2018).[41]

The economist Saeed Leilaz (*Fararu*, September 4, 2019)[42] transposes the capital flight to other periods of Iranian history since the Safavid dynasty in the sixteenth century without providing any data or argument.[43]

---

[39] See https://azadi-faryade-irani.blogspot.com/2021/02/blog-post_970.html, retrieved on February 14, 2022.

[40] Literally speaking, it means 'born from masters' or masters' children.

[41] https://www.radiozamaneh.com/411043/ retrieved on 14 February 14, 2022.

[42] https://fararu.com/fa/news/410767/%D9%84%DB%8C%D9%84%D8%A7%D8%B2%D8%B3%D8%A7%D9%84%D8%A7%D9%86%D9%8710%D8%AA%D8%A720%D9%85%DB%8C%D9%84%DB%8C%D8%A7%D8%B1%D8%AF-%D8%AF%D9%84%D8%A7%D8%B1-%D8%AB%D8%B1%D9%88%D8%AA-%D8%A7%D8%B2-%D8%A7%DB%8C%D8%B1%D8%A7%D9%86-%D8%AE%D8%A7%D8%B1%D8%AC-%D9%85%DB%8C%E2%80%8C%D8%B4%D9%88%D8%AF, retrieved on February 14, 2022.

[43] It is also unclear how he could calculate capital flight during the Safavid period.

He also estimates an annual capital flight of 10–20 billion dollars during the last 50 years starting in 1972–1973 under the Pahlavi dynasty. The data provided in the report of Research Centre of Islamic Legislative Assembly (2000) does not support his statements. However, his claim corresponds to data regarding the post-revolutionary period in Iran. Leilaz also pretends that the amount of capital flight has always exceeded the capital investment in Iran. This does not hold true for the Iranian economy since Safavid dynasty, and not even for the Pahlavi dynasty during the 1960s and the first half of the 1970s, but it is certainly true for the IRI. According to Global Data Base (CEIC data), the average amount of 'formation of fixed capital' during June 1988–June 2018 has been 18.5 billion dollars, while the average amount of capital flight was 20 billion dollars. Since the tendency to capital accumulation domestically has always been less than the capital flight, it should be concluded that *de-investment rather than reinvestment of capital has been the stylized economic fact of the Iranian economy under the Islamic political capitalism.* Hoarding and more specifically cash hoarding is the typical economic fact of the Iranian economy. We will come back to this point in the next section, but it should be noted here that this phenomenon is closely related to capital and labor flight.

This macroeconomic estimation of capital flight has a purely *accounting* nature and suffers from two major shortcomings. First, it does not grapple capital flight as *a regular economic behavior* of agents (both prey and predators) in a predatory economy. Second, it does not capture the *illicit* capital exit.

Capital flight is not merely an *accounting equation;* it is a *behavioral regularity* describing agents' perceptions and expectations within a prey-predatory relationship. It pertains to all the lost opportunity costs related to the lack of security in capital investment and property rights. As indicated previously in Table 8.1, one of the distinctive characteristics of Islamic political capitalism in comparison with a Soviet-type system consists of capital and labor flight. While this constitutes a regular economic behavior of agents under the former, the latter might be characterized as a 'no-exit' economic system. Moreover, capital flight is present in a liberal market capitalism, but it is not necessarily opposed to domestic capital investment whereas in the Islamic political capitalism, it replaces reinvestment and result in de-investment.

Several dimensions of capital flight as an economic behavioral regularity are as follows:

1. *Brain drain and emigration*: As discussed in our theoretical framework (Sect. 8.2), human specific assets are fugitive assets detained by
experts and skilled workers. They massively emigrated from Iran during the post-revolutionary period. The brain drain has been a chronic
tendency that continues to this day (Research Centre of Islamic
Legislative Assembly, 1996, 2000; Torbat, 2002; Chaichian, 2012).
According to the *2009 Annual Report of the International Monetary
Fund*, Iran had the highest level of brain drain among 91 developing
and developed nations with the emigration of 150,000 to 180,000
educated and skilled individuals, costing the government an equivalent of $50 billion in foreign exchange currency. Moreover, the IMF
report also highlighted that more than 420,000 Iranians with higher
education degrees resided in the USA out of which 250,000 were
physicians and engineers (cited in Chaichian, 2012, p. 19). Recent
research on migration and brain drain from Iran indicates that the
total number of Iranian-born emigrants increased from about half a
million people prior to the 1979 Revolution to 3.1 million in 2019,
corresponding to 1.3% and 3.8% of the country's population, respectively. Overall, top destination countries for Iranian migrants include
the United States, Canada, Germany, and the United Kingdom
(Azadi et al., 2020, pp. 3, 8). The tendency of students for returning
to Iran has declined from upward of 90% in 1979 to less than 10% in
2020. As a proxy for the brain drain issue at large, the total number
of active scholars among the Iranian diaspora has undergone a ten-
fold increase since 2000 (Azadi et al., Ibid, pp. 3, 9–11).

2. *Transformation of specific assets into generic assets*: Many industrialists
dismantled their enterprises and sold the land, the machinery, and
the equipment separately because specific investments require a long
period of gestation. This means a preference for generic assets rather
than idiosyncratic assets. *Appropriative acquisition of resources prevails in an economy with generic assets rather than specific assets.* The
difference between these two types of economy, that is, productive
and redistributive, lies in the prominence of confiscatory policies in
redistributive economies. A confiscatory (predatory) regime results
in dismantling specific assets and transforming them into generic,
more liquid, and fugitive assets. Market forces then retreat from specific investments and leave it to economic sectors directly protected
by coercive forces. Specific assets require long-term relationships and
investments, secure credit lines, clearly defined property rights, and
extensive use of skilled labor. While the Iranian private sector has no

interest in contractual relationships involving specific assets, the parallel Islamic economic institutions prefer appropriating the oil revenue and importing ready-made products rather than investing in specific assets to produce such goods. Generally speaking, the added-value sectors do not develop due to the lack of contractual relationships involving specific assets. High protection and transaction costs are the ultimate cause of the lack of specific assets in physical capital and the high rates of brain drain.

3. *Cash hoarding as part of capital flight*: In multi-predators' system, every predator should 'hide' his/her booties from other predators. Hence, not only preys but also predators are massively engaged in capital flight. This may be called the paradox of predators: they should keep their booties somewhere safe. The 'baron thieves' should transform into 'new respectable gentlemen'. The ruling elite and their children spend a small fraction of their fortune on luxury homes and cars inside Iran, the bulk of their personal wealth is sent abroad. This has several advantages. First, considering the lack of domestic security for capital investment and property rights, and constant loss of value of national currency, cash (currency) hoarding could better store the value of assets. It is better to be debtor in rial and creditor in dollars. The Iranian elite hoard their money capital abroad and import commodities on easy bank credits. The amount of granted credits has been often bigger than the oil revenues (Al Yassen, 2014, pp. 198). Second, when there is a shortage of currency and strong devaluation of national monetary unit, the ruling elite sell its currency at the highest prices through the Iranian cambists abroad. It is not by chance that they have very close relationships with Iranian cambists in Canada and Dubai and dominate in and outflow of currency from and to Iran. Third, they often invest in real estate or keep their money in foreign banks, buy assets in stock exchange, and establish several companies abroad for diverse commercial activities including for money laundering, and facilitating cash circulation between Iran and abroad. Finally, the size of capital flight increases in the presence of an oligarchy. This is named 'voracity effect'.

4. *Voracity effect in the presence of oligarchic rivalry*: As underlined previously, in contrast to the Shah's regime, the Islamic Republic of Iran is characterized by competing powerful oligarchic groups. Lane and Tornell (1996, 1999) modelize the "voracity effect" that measures the extent of rent-seeking or appropriative activity of organized powerful groups following an increase in the rate of return of common resources such as oil. They show that any increase in the oil revenue

in countries like Venezuela, Nigeria, Trinidad, and Tobago where such powerful groups are dominant, provoke a voracity effect: the private consumption of these groups surpasses the amount of increase. The appropriative activity of powerful groups reduces growth rate due to the voracity effect. Lane and Tornell's model confirm Olson's result (1982, 1993) that if there exists only one long-lived powerful group, for example, a strong autocrat or a few powerful groups that can coordinate and act cooperatively, then the 'voracity effect' will disappear. A principal form of competing 'private consumption' of powerful groups is capital flight. The influential groups secure their fortunes by exporting them abroad. It is impossible to know the amount of capital flight related to the 'voracity effect' particularly when a country is sanctioned by the international community. One can give the example of the confiscation of 18.5 billion dollars of gold bullions and US dollars coming from Iran by Turkish authorities on October 7, 2008. Was this a way to flee capital related to *Anfal* and other parallel Islamic institutions? Or a way to detour international sanctions? Or other types of illicit financing by the Islamic Republic of Iran? Or a combination of all these elements?

5. *Preference for liquidity:* Although the biggest share of capital flight in form of cash hoarding belongs to the elite, any Iranian property-holder has an interest to keep his/her savings abroad in the absence of better options to reinvest the money capital inside the country. Even if by any chance, one's capital investment reveals to be profitable, the incentive to re-invest the profit instead of hoarding would be weak because of high risk of capital investment. The bigger the capital, the higher the probability of being raided by the Islamic parallel institutions.

Furthermore, in the absence of strong incentives to engage in long-term investment, any businessperson tries to maximize his/her profits in short-term projects, hoarding a good part of eventual profits in cash. Liquid assets such as foreign currencies, high ratio value-to-weight assets (antiquities, gemstones, precious old manuscripts, books and paintings, etc.) can escape more easily. Economic agents tend to hoard this type of assets rather than captive assets that can be easily confiscated. This tendency strengthens the diaspora's economic activity as an ally of capital flight. The Iranian diaspora in North America and in Gulf states plays a decisive role in capital flight. But the frontiers between legal and illegal flows of capital become blurred in the presence of massive capital flight.

Table 8.4 Estimation of annual average illicit capital flows for the period 1984–1993 (billion dollars)

Exit sources	Current prices	Prices calculated in terms of 1995 constant values
Deficit of foreign trade	-4	-4.6
Foreign currencies	-1.3	-1.4
Traditional and agricultural commodities	-2.3	-2.7
Total	-7.6	-8.7
Other commodities	?	?
Brain drain	?	?

Source: Research Centre of Islamic Legislative Assembly, May 2000, p. 22

6. *Illicit capital flows:* Capital flight is also defined as illicit capital flows (Cuddington, 1986). This definition precludes brain drain, but it includes the illicit flows of foreign currencies and commodities. For example, according to Research Centre of Islamic Legislative Assembly (May 2006, p. 18), two-thirds of the carpet exportation as well as the pistachio exportation, 90% of cumin's exportation and 80% of traditional and agricultural commodities' exportation (like caviar and dried fruits) are illicit. Table 8.4 provides an estimation of illicit capital flows.

This table excludes the amount of illicit capital flows with regard to antiquities, precious paintings, books, as well as brain drain. This estimation is very far from the amount of illicit capital flows if we take into consideration the fact that more than 60 unofficial maritime gates and airports belonging to Sepah were involved in non-recorded export and import of different types of commodities (Coville, 2017, p. 92).

8.7   Economics of Hoarding

The normal or typical state of any economy is described in terms of equilibrium in mainstream economics. The equilibrium position provides the *normative* rather than the *positive* state of the economy.[44] In reality, the normal state of any economy is often characterized by its distance from the

---

[44] In New Classical school, equilibrium state is not regarded as normative; any state is treated as an equilibrium state.

state of equilibrium or its specific chronic disequilibrium. For example, a competitive market economy can be described as a 'surplus economy', whereas a classical socialist economy might be depicted as a 'shortage economy' (Kornai, 1980, 2013).

What is the typical state of the economy under Islamic political capitalism? It can be defined as the economics of hoarding. Theoretically speaking, the Neoclassical school assumes that there exists an identity relationship between saving and investment both are assumed to be a function of interest rate: $S(r)=I(r)$. This identical equality postulates the Classical Dichotomy[45] or money *neutrality*. In other words, what is not consumed and saved will automatically be reinvested, and a chronic divergence between saving and investment is dismissed. By contrast, the economics of hoarding builds upon chronic disequilibrium between saving and investment. What is the background of the economics of hoarding and its place in economic literature?

Historically speaking, hoarding as the accumulation of possessions was negatively connotated in the Antiquity by Christianity (Merianos & Gotsis, 2017). In Islam, the term employed nine times in Koran for hoarding is al-*Kanz*. Surah 9 on "Repentance, Dispensation", verset 34, explicitly refers to *Kanz* as buried 'gold and silver' that is 'not spent in the way of Allah' and it is condemned as a 'grievous penalty'. There are many interpretations in Sunni and Sh'i Islam regarding *Kanz* (see the site of Ayotollah Makarim Shirazi,[46] and Darussalam, 2010). There are two broad readings: one insists on accumulating wealth without paying Zakat, and the other on accumulation of wealth beyond personal needs even after remitting the religious dues including Zakat. The latter is also ambiguous since it includes two different things: (1) any type of accumulation or (2) putting the wealth outside of the economic circuit. The second is closer to what is meant hoarding in economic literature.

In the medieval and early modern period, speculative hoarding of grain in turbulent times enriched local elites. However, hoarding was not limited to elites; all social strata were involved in it. The poorer sections of the population resorted to hoarding as a means of financial security. Hence, it

---

[45] The Classical Dichotomy entails the division of the economy into two parts: real and monetary, the latter reflects exactly the former. Money is assumed to be neutral as a means of exchange.

[46] http://www.makarem.ir/main.aspx?reader=1&lid=0&mid=101032&pid=253965 retrieved on March 28, 2022.

was not hoarding as such, but the amount of hoarded fortune and the particular drives behind its accumulation that made it economically or morally a despicable activity. Beyond hoarding of commodities, monetary hoarding and luxury spending were two alternative responses to a sudden increase in assets, which impacted the circular flows of wealth in mid-fourteenth-century Europe.

The concept of hoarding has particularly been scrutinized in economic literature since mercantilism. Mercantilists launched an analysis of hoarding from the viewpoint of capital theory. For example, David Hume (1752/1985) opposed banks and favored hoarding. He recommended hoarding of gold and silver by a public 100% reserve bank to lead to "the destruction of paper-credit", fostering economic growth by shunning inflation that could hinder exports (Paganelli, 2014).

The hoarding issue took a central place since the famous debate between Keynes and Hayek in the 1930s. The debate was focused on the relationship between hoarding and capital accumulation. In a nutshell, in 1932, Keynes, Pigou, and four other economists wrote and signed a letter in *The Times* newspaper in which they advised increasing effective demand instead of saving by augmenting public spending to compensate the deficit of the "reluctant" private sector. The letter was later known as the "paradox of thrift" (see Hayek, 1931/2008, pp. 131–139).

In response to this letter, Hayek, Robbins, and two other LSE economists retorted two days later in the same newspaper that although hoarding's deleterious effects were known to economists since the classics, it would be disastrous for the economy to favor consumption instead of saving through deposits in banks or securities. The modern analysis of the hoarding question through the lens of capital theory was shaped in this debate.[47] Although I will succinctly review the Keynesian and Hayekian standpoints, my line of inquiry in this section is not to explore who was right or wrong. My focus is to explore (1) what is meant by hoarding in this rich literature and (2) what is the originality of the hoarding issue in the context of the economics of escape?

---

[47] Another line of inquiry has explored the relationship between optimal consumption and real money holdings in time by introducing a "hoarding function" which specifies the rate at which the household saves in order to close the gap between actual real money holding and long-run desired money holdings (Dornbusch & Mussa, 1975). A host of post-Keynesian models assumed 'hoarding function', and this assumption has been questioned by advocates of a Circuit approach (Andersen, 2006).

Answering the first question, I should underline that both parties adopted the same terminology that has been suggested by Keynes. Hayek explicitly conceded: "Clearly recipients of income must make a choice: they may spend on consumption goods, or they may refrain from doing so. In Mr. Keynes's terminology, the latter operation constitutes saving. In so far as they do save in this sense, they have the further choice between what one would ordinarily call hoarding and investing or, as Mr. Keynes (because he has employed these more familiar terms for other concepts) chooses to call it, between 'bank-deposits' and 'securities'" (Hayek, 1931/2008, pp. 442–443).

According to Keynes, the total income is composed of two parts: consumption and non-consumption or saving: $Y=C+S$. Saving is the part of the income for which people prefer to sacrifice their present consumption for the prospect of increasing future consumption. This depends on people's time preference. Savings can take two main forms: investment or hoarding. Hoarding pertains to a process of withdrawal of money from active circulation by accumulating it or holding it in private in a 'state of idleness'. Hoarding is the part of saving which is neither consumed nor invested.

Hoarding does not increase the total volume of cash-holdings since all cash money is always held by somebody. Hoarding is a *decrease in the velocity of money*.[48] In fact, most of the phenomena that are usually supposed to stem from hoarding can be explained by a decrease in money velocity. However, money velocity is not a good candidate to clarify the hoarding issue since economists, in general, believe that "velocity is a meaningless *ex post* coefficient" (Emmer, 1959, p. 162). This observation motivated Emmer to suggest a new definition of hoarding as "the voluntary failure of any sector in the circular flow of income to pass on to another sector as much money as it receives from it. Dishoarding is the opposite phenomenon" (Ibid, p. 162).

Emmer identified three sectors, namely the consumer sector, the business sector, and the government sector. Each sector receives revenue (i.e., income broadly defined) from the other sectors by (1) the sale of services

---

[48] The velocity of money is a measurement of the rate at which money is exchanged in an economy. It is the number of times that money moves from one economic agent to another. It also refers to how much a unit of currency is used in a given period of time. In other words, it's the rate at which consumers and businesses in an economy collectively spend money. At an aggregate level, the velocity of money is usually measured as a ratio of gross domestic product (GDP) to a country's money supply defined in terms of M1 or M2.

of assets, (2) the sale of real or financial assets, and (3) borrowing or receipt of reimbursements of previous loans. In this context, "tax payments must be considered as payments for the services of government (thought of as an asset) and transfer payments by the government as a payment for past services rendered in a general sense" (Emmer, 1959, p. 163). In a country in which the state is reliant on oil revenue for more than 50% of its budget like Iran, the definition of sectors needs to be revisited. This requires a separation between the oil and non-oil sectors (comprising enterprises exporting non-oil products or importing products). The former will constitute the government sector, whereas the latter is part of the business sector.

According to Emmer's definition, hoarding can be defined at a sectoral and not merely at an individual level. For example, while a bank deposit by an individual might be described as 'investment', it does not imply that banks are exempt from hoarding. In fact, if there exists an excess of deposits in banks over loans, it results in cash hoarding. After this terminological clarification, we need to briefly introduce the Keynesian and Austrian positions on hoarding.

In the Keynesian theoretical framework, hoarding causes a reduction in effective demand and unemployment. According to Keynes, in an economic crisis, the economic agents will not engage in investment or consumption expenditure but will hoard their liquid assets. Thus, the propensity for liquidity preference grows. In this context, monetary policies would be inefficacious in stimulating the level of economic activity since new money will be hoarded in a deflationary momentum. In such cases, even if the interest rates decline to zero, it cannot remove the excess of deposits over loans, then we are in a situation of 'liquidity trap'. The liquidity trap has been a controversial subject among economists. One illustration is provided by Krugman (2013) in the recent decade in the USA, Europe, and Japan. In his opinion, the excess of deposits over loans in the banking sectors in these regions could not be removed by decreasing interest rates because they were experiencing a liquidity trap.

New research in Keynesian economics has questioned Keynes' conflation of *money* hoarding with *asset* hoarding in general. Rowe (2016) suggests drawing a demarcation line between saving in the form of money and saving in all other forms. The term 'hoarding' is reserved for monetary saving whereas saving of other liquidity assets is named as 'thrift'. For example, a fixed stock of gold that can be used as jewelery is a liquid asset but not money. In Rowe's opinion, hoarding this type of liquid asset does not generate a reduction in the effective demand, only monetary hoarding results in such a decrease and an equilibrium with unemployment. While Keynes (1936) emphasized both monetary and non-monetary hoarding of liquid assets as sources of potential crisis, Rowe (2016) identifies only monetary hoarding.

In the economics of escape, we are confronted with different types of hoarding, although cash (foreign currency) hoarding is the main drive. Does the Keynesian approach cast light on the economics of escape? My response is negative since the de-investment is not generated by the 'reluctance' of the private sector as suggested in the Keynesian approach. In fact, the private sector lacks the security of investment and property as indicated previously. The state expenditure is not an alternative to the lack of private investment either. The main problem is that saving is not re-invested since there exists massive capital flight particularly (but not limited to) in the form of currency hoarding. In other terms, the major issue is not increasing state expenditures or increasing effective demand but institutionalized state predation.

It can be argued that Keynes (1936) was studying hoarding within a closed economy, whereas capital flight assumes an open economy. A strand of literature explores the hoarding issue within the context of an open economy in the recent period of global financial crises. This literature establishes a relationship between international reserves (IR) hoarding and developments in the global economy. In the pre-global financial crisis (GFC) extending over 1999–2006, gross saving was associated with higher IR in developing and emerging markets (Aizenman & Lee, 2006). During the years 2007–2009, the trend changed and the propensity to import and gross saving had positive and larger effects on IR holding. Finally, during the period 2010–2012, new factors were in action: the macro-prudential policy tended to complement IR accumulation (Aizenman et al., 2015).

The significance of these findings on IR notwithstanding, the issue of capital flight related to state predation is not captured by IR hoarding. In this case, although capital flight should be addressed in the context of the global market, it is not related to its development. In fact, it derives from domestic limits in capital investment. In other words, capital flight as a means of monetary hoarding is neither purely domestic nor international. It is a way of regulating a limited international circuit that derives principally from domestic needs. *The Keynesian literature has not addressed the problem of hoarding liquid assets in the context of state predation and capital flight.*

By contrast, state predation is explicitly addressed in the Hayekian perspective. Moreover, the LSE economists' emphasis on saving rather than consumption is germane to my analysis. But how does Austrian economics deal with the hoarding issue? Austrian economics does not have a unique position on this problem.

Patruti's (2016) survey of the Austrian literature suggests a distinction between two contending positions. While Hayek acknowledged the destructive effect of hoarding on growth, Rothbard considered that the hoarding effect on the structure of production and economic growth was *neutral*: "[Hoarding] is simply an increase in the demand for money, and the result of this change in valuations is that people get what they desire, i.e. an increase in the real value of their cash balances and of the monetary unit.[...] No other significant economic relation-real income, capital structure, etc.-need be changed at all" (1962/2009. P. 776 cited by Patruti, 2016, p. 252).

Patruti suggests a compromising third approach according to which savings through investment and hoarding will both result in economic growth in the long run. However, in the short run hoarding is not neutral, since keeping money at home instead of depositing it at the bank causes a lagged adjustment of the market rate of interest. Hence, hoarding or "an increase in monetary capital accumulation" (in Patruti's terminology) (2016, p. 251) is a rather *suboptimal growth promoting tool*. But why should hoarding be considered an investment in the long run? In other words, why hoarding is assumed to be neutral in the long run?

It is said that when people hoard money, the "purchasing power of the monetary unit" will steadily increase and the price structure gradually changes (Patruti, 2016, p. 262). This argument is arguable since it assumes away any cumulative disequilibrium tendency between the so-called natural rate of interest and monetary rate of interest. The increased purchasing power of money leads necessarily to a corresponding gradual change in the *price structure*. It should be assumed that all ongoing economic tendencies stay the same before these gradual changes in price structure will realize all its effects. This specific interpretation of Austrian economics is similar to the conventional reason of the Neoclassical school regarding the equilibrating tendency of the market. Contrary to Patruti, Hayek never assumed that hoarding is neutral in long term and only effective in short run. This explains why all LSE economists including Hayek acknowledged the deflationary effect of hoarding.

Moreover, Patruti claims in a footnote (2016, p. 254) that while it is *theoretically* conceivable that hoarding can come from *disinvestment*, it is a rather improbable outcome. In his opinion, the only probable scenario is that the potential investor would need to make an imminent payment for a consumption good or another investment. This type of hoarding would be transitory and can be dismissed from the analysis. The problem with Patruti's argument is that he totally overlooks hoarding generated by the state predation which is *disinvestment and non-transitory*. Rothbard neutrality thesis and Patruti's distinction between the short and long term do not capture the probability of hoarding as disinvestment.

The originality of our contribution to the hoarding literature is to consider it as *disinvestment* related to capital flight deriving from state predation. Figure 8.1 describes the hoarding circuit under Islamic political capitalism. Hoarding is both in monetary and in non-monetary assets. Before explaining the economic circuit of hoarding under the IRI, I need to clarify the importance of monetary hoarding in foreign currency notably in the American dollar.

There exists a considerable literature on financial dollarization. It refers to a stylized fact in developing economies: their residents save and borrow in foreign currencies. This phenomenon was initially observed in the Latin America, but at the end of 2000, it was applicable to all developing economies, since the share of domestic bank deposits denominated in foreign countries was 35% on average in all these economies. The share was 44%

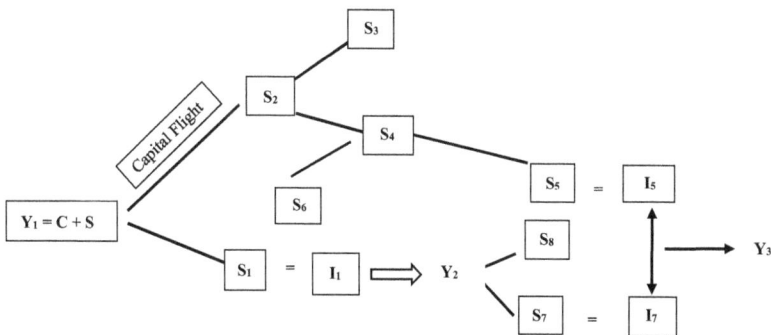

Fig. 8.1 Circuit of economics of hoarding

in those among them where dollar deposits were not illegal (Levy Yeyati & Rey, 2006, p. 63). Two explanations have been suggested for this phenomenon. The first one suggests dollarization is the result of currency substitution (the use of the foreign currency as medium of exchange) and the second defines it in terms of asset substitution (its use as store of value). In post-revolutionary Iran, financial dollarization can be observed and it is clearly related to asset substitution. The reason is rather *institutional*[49] in the sense that dollarization can be viewed as the collateral cost of low institutional credibility of rial and banking system in Iran. Although the relevance of dollarization is undeniable in Iran, it must be emphasized that this phenomenon is particularly intense in those countries with high level of official foreign debts in dollar, since the main source of liability dollarization is official debt. This does not apply to Iran although the monetary hoarding is principally in dollar.

Now, we can describe the hoarding circuit. The circuit starts with an initial income Y_1 that is either consumed or saved. The saved part is either invested in the domestic economy ($S_1=I_1$) or hoarded through capital flight (S_2). The source of income might be oil revenue or non-oil exporting goods. A fraction of S_2 can be either invested abroad S_3 (e.g., buying equities and real estate) or hoarded as cash money S_4. The hoarded money abroad might be reused for investment (S_5) or for precautionary hoarding (S_6) to reimburse domestic credit debts in rial. The invested part ($S_5=I_5$) targets the Iranian domestic market. This investment might take several forms: (1) importing products, (2) creating enterprises abroad for domestic money laundering, (3) creating enterprises for detouring economic boycotts, and (4) creating cambist agencies abroad particularly in Canada or Dubai to exchange foreign currencies for rials and vice versa.

The part of income saved and invested domestically ($S_1 = I_1$) will spawn new income Y_2 which, in its turn, will be either consumed or saved. The saved part is either hoarded (S_8) or reinvested ($S_7 - I_7$). This new investment generated domestically (I_7) and the investment initiated abroad out of capital flight (I_5), that is, de-hoarded part of capital flight, constitutes the total amount of investment ($I_5 + I_7$) inducing a new level of income Y_3.

---

[49] Three theories have been suggested to capture dollarization as asset substitution: (1) the portfolio view, (2) the market failure view, and (3) the institutional view (see Levy Yeati & Rey, 2006, pp. 76–83). All three theories have explanatory powers in the Iranian case, but the institutional view covers more readily the institutional failures in the Iranian banking system and monetary policies.

This process continues steadily. In other words, the reinvestment (de-hoarding) does not stop, but its total amount is less than the total amount of non-invested (hoarding) capital flight domestically ($S_2 - S_5 > S_1$). It is noteworthy that hoarding in the form of capital flight can be defined as *disinvestment domestically* but *reinvestment abroad*. This concerns S_3 which is reinvested internationally, but 'lost' domestically. It is noteworthy that while hoarding has a deflationary effect, de-hoarding has an inflationary effect. The de-hoarded S_7 is inflationary once it is exchanged in rial. The more rial is depreciated, the bigger will be the impact of de-hoarded capital in dollar. While the rate of inflation is chronically double digit, it would have been much higher in the absence of capital flight. Considering the deflationary impact of hoarding notably through capital flight, it becomes clear that the source of inflationary pressure in Iran is the state's colossal debts and the limited level of supply relative to demand due to the lack of investment in productive capacity.

There are several knots in this circuit that may be a source of speculative commodity hoarding. Capital flight derives from oil revenue as well as non-oil sectors, particularly the non-oil export sectors such as carpet, dried fruits, saffron, and so on. However, another major source of hoarding domestically is parallel markets in almost all types of factor and product markets. Regulated and black markets are everywhere side by side. Islamic parallel institutions related to *Anfal* and the Sepah dominate all regulated markets. They have privileged positions in acquiring bank credits, authorization for importing 'necessary goods' with preferential exchange rates and exporting natural and mineral resources. While in the regulated markets, the price is fixed by the state, and 'shortage' prevails; in the black market, there is an abundance or 'surplus' of the same goods at market price. Speculative hoarding is generalized in all parallel markets. The typical state of economics of hoarding can be characterized by both 'shortage' (in regulated markets) and 'surplus' (in black markets).

The price gap between these two markets is determined by the difference between the state or preferential exchange rate and the market exchange rate of dollar. Speculative hoarding of non-monetary commodities follows this gap. To put it differently, monetary hoarding plays a key role in regulating other forms of hoarding. The economic agents are highly sensitive to the exchange rate of dollar and more importantly to the gap between the official and market rates of foreign currency.

8.8   *Anfal* and Ecological Disaster

An analysis of the Iranian's diverse ecological issues warrants an entire book. Although different dimensions of the problem cannot be captured by this short section, I try to introduce a new perspective that has not been explored by other researchers. In my approach, the structure of *property rights* and *governance* over 'ownerless' public resources (*res nullius*) are determinants in explaining the acuteness of ecological disasters under the IRI compared to the Shah's period. In post-revolutionary Iran, *Anfal* or the specific property of the Supreme jurisprudent over *res nullius* has been the principal enhancer of ecological disasters. We have already studied its incidence on Mount Damavand in Chaps. 6 and 7. We will further explore this line of investigation in the present section.

It is noteworthy emphasizing that Iran's severe environmental problems under the IRI are numerous: water shortages or drying water resources (Abbaspour & Sabetraftar, 2005; Bijani & Hayati, 2011; Kowsar & Nader, 2019; Khazani & Bulos, 2021; *Nature*, 2021), increased air pollution (Soroush & Madani, 2014/2021; Schwartzstein, 2019; Moghtaderi et al., 2020), biodiversity losses (Schwartzstein, 2020), desertification (UNDP, 2017), and deforestation (Kooch et al., 2020). On this long list, water shortage and biodiversity losses have been the sources of many mass protestations by deprived farmers, urban people, and environmentalists since 2011. The conservationists and environmentalists were imprisoned and accused of espionage in 2018,[50] and popular protests were violently repressed by the Iranian Revolutionary Guards Corps (IRGC) and the Basiji in different Iranian provinces, especially in

---

[50] The arrests of Iranian environmentalists including nine of the country's leading big cat biologists from the Persian Wildlife Heritage Foundation (PWHF), and their imprisonment in the notorious Evin prison provoked a wave of protestations. These biologists were accused of being of espionage, in part because of their use of specialized equipment, such as camera traps, to record rare species particularly Asiatic Cheetah. Among these prominent conservationists, Kavous Seyyed-Emami, the foundation's manager and a prominent sociologist, died soon after in circumstances that his family sees as suspicious; Abdolreza Koohpayeh, a conservationist and wildlife photographer, was released in March 2018 (Schwartzstein, November 12, *National Geographic*).

2011[51]and summer 2021.[52] This section will be concentrated on water shortages and biodiversity losses.

Water shortage due to over-extraction of groundwater has been documented extensively (Bijani & Hayatti, 2011; Bradbury, 2020; Kowsar & Nader, 2019; Soroush & Madani, 2014/2021; *Nature*, 2021), particularly because it has resulted in several natural catastrophes.[53] For example, Lake Urmia, situated in northwestern Iran, revered by ethnic Azeris as "the turquoise solitaire of Azerbaijan", has mostly withered away. It was formerly second only to the Caspian Sea as the largest saltwater lake in the Middle East, a haven for birds and bathers (Weiss, April 3, 2018; Schmidt et al., 2021). Since the early 1970s, its size started to dwindle because of natural and ecological (human induced) disasters that reduced it to about 80% over the past 30 years. The flamingos, the pelicans, the egrets, and the ducks are mostly gone. Scientists have identified the share of climate change notably intensified droughts and elevated hot summer temperatures in speeding up evaporation. But this is not the whole story. Engineers and water experts have pointed out that the lake in this semiarid region suffered from a proliferation of dams, irrigation projects, water transfers, and thousands of illegal wells.

The same happened to lake Bakhtegan, a Salt Lake in Fars Province, southern Iran, once the second largest in the country. It was fed by the Kor River. The construction of several dams on the Kor River had significantly diminished the water flow into the lake, augmented its salinity and eradicated the lake's populations of flamingos and other migratory birds. The lake is now completely dry, and the living species have either extirpated or emigrated to other regions.

At Isfahan, the Zayandeh Rud river,[54] springing from the Zagros Mountains in the west and ending in the Gavkhooni wetland in central Iran, seldom flows anymore, reshaping the city's famous arched Syoseh

---

[51] *Human Rights Watch* reported on peaceful protests over Lake Urmia's destruction on September 10, 2011, and the arrest of hundreds in Azerbaijan (see https://www.hrw.org/news/2011/09/10/iran-allow-peaceful-protests-over-lakes-destruction/   retrieved   on March 10, 2022).

[52] I will refer to these recent protests later in this section.

[53] Over-extraction of groundwater leads to land subsidence, the sudden sinking of the ground, usually due to water depletion. A 2019 land fissure caused by drought and excessive water pumping in Malard, west of Tehran, is a sign that the area around Iran's capital is literally sinking.

[54] In Persian, Zayandeh Rud means life-giver. It was the reason for the centuries of the prosperity of the magnificent city of Isfahan, the capital of Iran during the Safavid dynasty in the sixteenth century.

Pol Bridge[55] now totally dry (Schwartzstein, January 25, 2019, *National Geographic*). Similar stories occurred to Karkheh and Karun rivers in Khuzestan, an oil-rich province with a large population of ethnic Arabs in the South of Iran (State Department report, September 28, 2018).

In fact, an analysis of national data from Iran's groundwater monitoring system during the period extending over 2002 and 2015 by Roohollah Noori at the University of Oulu in Finland and his associates indicates that Iran is using more groundwater than can be naturally recharged during that period, the number of wells and other locations that tap into groundwater nearly doubled. Yet the amount of groundwater extracted declined by 18%. Nationwide, the groundwater table dropped by an average of almost half a meter per year (*Nature*, June 16, 2021). Two major sources of over-extraction have been the construction of dams and the increasing number of wells.

In the 40 years since the revolution, the number of wells in Iran has climbed from 60,000 to almost 800,000 (Kowsar and Nader, *Foreign Affairs*, 25 Feb 2019). According to the State Department report (2018), since 1979, Iran has built about 600 dams, an average of 20 per year. By comparison, before the revolution, Iran had 7 ancient dams and 14 modern ones. Quoting the official Iranian Press, IRNA, Ghobadi (2021) reports that there exist now 1330 dams in various stages of operation, implementation, and study. But why so many dams and wells?

Historically, the Iranians developed a special system of irrigation through qanats that sustained their water sources in an arid country. A qanat is a system for water transportation from an aquifer to the surface through an underground aqueduct. This system was governed by people at the local level in a decentralized manner. Many authors (Goldsmith, 1968; Wilson, 2008) attributed the invention of qanat technology to ancient Iran in the early first millennium BCE that spread from there gradually to Eastward and Westward.

Before its nationalization in July 1968, water in Iran was a sustainable resource, with 34 million Iranians relying on millennia-old, natural underground qanats for their drinking water. There existed more than 50,000

---

[55] Syoseh pol (meaning 33 bridges in Persian) or Allahverdi Khan Bridge is a double-deck arch bridge over Zayandeh Rud river that was constructed under the supervision and expense of Allah Verdy Khan, one of the famous commanders of Shah Abbas Safavid I. Its construction started in 1599 and ended 1602. The bridge is 298 meters long and almost 14 meters width.

hand-excavated underground qanats with a length of up to 70 km and a depth of up to 300 meters (Tavakoli, 1987, p. 522). The piecemeal and fragmented water laws that developed down the generations were blamed partly for the inefficiency of irrigation farming in the country (Mohandes, 1965). In line with concentrating all power in his hands, Muhammad Reza Shah Pahlavi decided to nationalize all water resources and legislated a comprehensive body of water laws, known as the *Nationalization of Water Resources Act* (NWRA).

The main thrust of the Act was oriented toward a highly centralized authoritative system for the allocation and use of water resources. For example, Articles 6, 7, 8, 13, 14, 16, and 17 gave unlimited authority to two government agencies, namely the Ministry of Water and Power and the Ministry of Agriculture, to utilize and manage the water resources. The NWRA granted all the managerial responsibilities, from investment to the allocation of water, to a central body and deprived farmers of all decision-making power in governing water resources. Accordingly, the nationalization of water put an end to the qanats systems and introduced a new dynamic. Kowsar and Nader underlined this point: "The Shah of Iran sparked the current water crisis by nationalizing the country's water resources, before the revolution" (*Foreign Affairs,* 25 Feb 2019).

Although the authors correctly trace back the problem of over-extraction of water to the NWRA, they dismiss two major differences between the Shah's nationalization of water resources and the IRI's governance.

The first one is that water was nationalized during the Shah's era and its management was concentrated in two ministries: (1) the Ministry of Water and Power and (2) the Ministry of Agriculture. By contrast, water is part of *Anfal* in the IRI. As explained in Chap. 5, the Shi'i jurisprudence is unanimous to consider that *Anfal* includes, "Barren lands, all lands that have no owner, forests, reed beds, seas, lagoons and lakes, rivers, sea bores, the summit of a mountain." These public properties do not belong to all Muslims or people; it is the reserved property of the Imam or the Supreme Jurisconsult. The Imam can give any of them to any individual or organization. This opens the door for the oligarchic governance of all the above-mentioned resources. The Supreme Leader has granted the use of rivers, forests, seas, lagoons, and lakes to Bonyad, Setad, and the Sepah. The first major difference between the Shah's regime and the IRI in governing water resources resides in the fact that the former concentrated all the management in two ministries of a highly centralized and authoritative state, whereas the latter introduced oligarchic management of the resources due to *Anfal*.

There exists a second major difference. The late Shah shunned the intervention of the army in the management of natural resources. Even in the cases of protected lands, he supported Eskandar Firouz, a charismatic aristocrat and big game hunter, in the 1960s to keep off the military of protected lands (Schwartzstein, November 12, 2020, *National Geographic*). Starting in the 1960s, Firouz created the most extensive national park networks anywhere in the world and preserved several rare animal species including the Asiatic cheetah. In an achievement of international significance, he contributed to the conclusion of the *Ramsar Convention* in 1971[56] regarding the protection of wetlands. The creation of a new institution called the Department of the Environment (DoE), Firouz could help conservationists to mitigate some of the worst effects of rampant development which has been accelerated, thanks to the boom ensued by the first major petroleum shock in 1973.

Imprisoned after the Revolution because of his close relationship with the late Shah, Firouz was incarcerated for six years, but national parks could still resist the return of livestock. It was the eight-year war with Iraq that devastated the biodiverse-rich border and led to the conscription of park rangers. The war definitively erased conservationism from the political agenda of the new leaders and terminated with the DoE.

Contrary to the Shah's regime, the IRI ushered in a new era that is characterized by securitization of environmental issues. "The environment is being securitized because it's a potential unifier," says Kaveh Madani, an environmental scientist at Yale University, who previously served as deputy head of the Iranian DoE. He fled Iran in 2018 due to security issues. "If you talk about religion, about the hijab, you have people on both sides, but the environment unifies people. That's why it's a problem for part of the system" (Schwartzstein, November 12, 2020, *National Geographic*). Everything from Tehran's water quality to major river levels is effectively a 'system' (*Nezam*) secret. The total opacity over the environmentalist issues is related to *Anfal* and its oligarchic governance system involving the IRGC.

---

[56] Ramsar Convention is a convention on wetlands that was signed in 1971 in the Iranian city of Ramsar. The negotiations for the convention started in the 1960s by the different countries and NGOs for the protection of wetlands and their resources. Finally, it came into force in 1975. There are 42 Ramsar Sites in India listed under Ramsar Convention.

There exist strong economic interests in keeping the secret, since the main stakeholders in dams' construction and proliferation of wells are *Bonyad*, *Setad*, and *Khatam al-anbiya*. As explained in Chaps. 6 and 7, the intervention of the IRGC in economic activities started by constructing dams since 1990 under the pretext of combatting water shortages and resolving the drinking water problem in central Iran. Dams were not only lucrative contracts for the Sepah, but they also served as propaganda opportunities for the IRGC and its economic undertakings. The Sepah gradually monopolized the construction of all dams and water transfers in Iran. The State Department's report quotes Abdollah Abdollahi, the commander of *Khatam al-Anbiya* Construction Headquarters, the IRGC's engineering arm, that in December 2017, 62 dams, accounting for half of Iran's damming capacity were constructed by his holding (State Department report, September 28, 2018).

According to the same report, building numerous dams around Lake Urmia in the 1990s slowly siphoned off its water supply. The benefactors of these projects were contractors from the IRGC, individuals close to the Ministry of Energy, and large agribusinesses, who all got rich as the lake drained. The National Geographic remarked that Lake Urmia now looked more like a crime scene, its beautiful waters that were once immortalized in Persian poetry turned to salt, which fills Iran's asphyxiating dust storms.

Constructing dams has often been coupled with transferring water to run industrial plants. The principal stakeholders in water transfers have been Bonyad, Setad, and the IRGC. For example, the IRGC has transferred Karun's water to Isfahan, central Iran, under the pretext of helping agriculture and resolving the drinking water issues. However, the recent farmers' protests in Isfahan in December 2021 demonstrated that they were totally deprived of their right to irrigation.[57] In fact, the drive behind the water transfer to Isfahan by the IRGC has been the huge water consumption of the Mobarakeh Steel plant, which is one of the IRGC's largest industrial complexes. A similar story holds true for the incidence of the water transfer in southwestern Khuzestan province.

The two large rivers, Karun and Karkhe, belong to this oil-rich province Khuzestan. However, the construction of multiple dams on these reserves and water transfer projects depleted the water, causing farmers and other people to suffer from water shortages. The state-run *Aftab-e Yazd* daily on

---

[57] See "Iran-Isfahan water shortage protests" on December 25, 2021, https://apa-ice.org/2021/12/25/iran-isfahan-water-shortage-protests/ retrieved on March 10, 2022.

July 17, 2021, reported: "Dams have caused rivers to dry up in Khuzestan province. We built the dams in places where there was no need, and now the result is water shortages. When a dam is built, a lake is created on one side, which increases water evaporation. The amount of evaporation has augmented due to the construction of dams, which dissipates about a quarter of the water we consume. These lakes behind dams generate wastes about 25 percent of the country's water resources." Recurrent water shortages provoked protests by thirsty people of Khuzestan against the regime that lasted for more than a week and were violently suppressed by the military forces. *Aljazeera* reported on the number of deaths and the role of illegal water transfer projects from river forks and stealing water from the source of the rivers by 'water mafias'. Power outages also exacerbated the situation as many utilize electricity-powered pumps to get water inside their homes (Motamedi, July 21, 2021, *Aljazeera*).

The multiplication of popular protests in summer 2021 drew public attention not only to the number of dams but also water transfers by authorities particularly the IRGC. There is ample evidence that the transfer is related to the use of water for generating electricity. On July 19, 2021, the official *Fars News Agency* acknowledged this fact: "The first reason for the loss of water resources in the last two years is using dams from water resources management facility to electricity generator. According to the then CEO of Iran Water Resources Management Company, hydropower plants located in the country's dams generated electricity 9% more than their goal." Fars News added: "This means that water resources from the 2020 floods were diverted to downstream areas to generate electricity and were eventually wasted."

Thus, Iran is currently the third biggest dam builder in the world (Soroush and Madani, *Guardian*, Nov 21, 2014/2021), with consequent overuse of fossil groundwater sources, drying of its major rivers, and destruction of wetlands. This stemmed from *Anfal* and its oligarchic governance of water resources by the Sepah under the pretext of securitization of environmental issues. The disastrous impacts of *Anfal* on Iran's water resources and mountains have never been experienced before the 1979 Revolution. In fact, although *Anfal* is an old doctrine of Shi'i jurisprudence regarding public finance, its practice is an entirely new institutional innovation of the IRI.

When Caponera (1954) presented his detailed study of customary laws concerning the allocation of water in Muslim countries, he insisted on the improvised nature of these laws. His findings showed that the laws as they emerged and developed through a long historical process were strongly influenced by the geographic and climatic conditions of the different parts of the Muslim world. Furthermore, he considered that the fundamental problem with Islamic law, in general, was the lack of administrative policies for the implementation of the principles. However, Caponera's study begs further scrutiny in light of the recent experience of post-revolutionary Iran. The Islamic jurisprudence might strongly influence the customary practices and even contradicts the nationalization of water as practiced during the late Shah's regime. *Anfal* is neither privatization nor nationalization of 'ownerless' natural resources. It is the dispossession of people from their public properties by the Imam.

8.9   CONCLUSION

In this chapter, we started by recapitulating the three fundamental institutions (the three first blocks of the economic system) of Islamic political capitalism. They included *Velayat Faqih*, *Anfal*, and destructive coordination. The focus of this chapter was to disentangle the way these fundamental institutions determined the typical economic behavior of agents (block 4) and the typical economic state of the economy (block 5) in Islamic political capitalism.

Before exploring blocks 4 and 5, we returned to the relationship between 'mode of coordination' and 'mode of production' as discussed in Chap. 2. We argued that this relationship cannot be defined in terms of the primacy of production over appropriation. The relationship between them can be characterized as cumulative causation.

A predatory economic regime can be an enhancer or an impediment to production and economic growth. My theoretical framework on predation lent credence to a distinction between an inclusive and an exclusionary predatory state. The Shah's inclusive predatory state based on a combination of agrarian reform and oil-financed capitalism during the period 1962–1971 was an enhancer of production, whereas the IRI as an exclusionary predatory state acted as an impediment to production. Three major factors have been identified to explain this contradictory relationship between predation and production in the latter case: the capture of oil revenue by an oligarchy instead of a highly centralized despotic system, confiscatory regime, and patrimonial development.

We then elucidated capital and labor flight as the behavioral regularity of economic agents under Islamic political capitalism (block 4). This typical behavior leads to the economics of hoarding (block 5).

The emergence of the economics of hoarding under Islamic political capitalism shows a striking example of the contradiction between reality and normative ideal. While the public finance under the IRI has been inspired and tailored based upon the Shi'i jurisprudence regarding *Anfal*, its upshot in a capitalist economy has been the exact opposite of what Islamic economics always recommended, that is, hoarding. All strands of Sunni and Shi'i Islam with no exception have condemned strongly 'hoarding', but the implementation of *Anfal* in the context of a capitalist economy resulted in economics of hoarding. In other words, the principles of Islamic economics cannot necessarily secure in reality an ideal Islamic economic system.

Finally, I elucidated the deleterious impact of Islamic political capitalism as an economic system on the natural environment. Although the complex issue of environmental problems requires a whole book, I briefly suggested the property and governance structure of natural resources under the IRI as the immediate underlying causes of ecological disasters in today's Iran. The inception of the current water crisis might be traced back to the nationalization of water resources in July 1968 under the Shah's regime, but its pernicious present forms stem directly from *Anfal* and securitization of environmental issues.

REFERENCES

Abbaspour, M., & Sabetraftar, A. (2005). Review of Cycles and Indices of Drought and Their Effect on Water Resources, Ecological, Biological, Agricultural, Social and Economical Issues in Iran. *International Journal of Environmental Studies, 62*(6), 709–724.

Aglietta, M. (1998). *Le capitalisme de demain*, note de fondation Saint-Simon.

Aizenman, J., Cheung, Y.-W., & Ito, H. (2015). International Reserves Before and after the Global Crisis: Is There no end to Hoarding? *Journal of International Money and Finance, 52*, 102–126.

Aizenman, J., & Lee, J. (2006, December). Financial Versus Monetary Mercantilism: Long-run View of Large International Reserves Hoarding. *IMF Working Paper.*

Alikhani, A. (2001). *Siast va siasat gozari eqtesadi dar Iran, 1340-1350, mosahbeh ba Alinaghi Alikhani, virastar Gholamreza Afkhami (Economic Politics and Policy-Making in Iran during 1961-1971, Interview with Alinaghi Alikhani Edited by Gholamreza Afkhami)* (Vol. 7). Foundation of Iranian Studies. (in Persian).

Amini, I. (2009). *Bar bal bohran: zendegi siasi Ali Amini (On the Wing of Crisis: The Political Biography of Ali Amini).* nashre Mahi (in Persian).

Andresen, T. (2006). A Critique of a Post Keynesian Model of Hoarding, and an Alternative Model. *Journal of Economic Behavior and Organizations, 60*, 230–251.

Atabaki, T., Bini, E., & Ehsani, K. (Eds.). (2018). *Working for Oil: Comparative Social Histories of Labor in the Global Oil Industry*. Palgrave Macmillan.

Azadi, P., Mirramezani, M., & Mesgaran, M. (2020, April). Migration and Brain Drain from Iran. *Stanford Iran 2040 Project*, Stanford University, Working Paper No. 9.

Barzel, Y. (1977). An Economic Analysis of Slavery. *Journal of Law and Economics, 20*(1), 87–110.

Barzel, Y. (1997). *Economic Analysis of Property Rights* (2nd ed.). Cambridge University Press.

Barzel, Y. (2015). What Are 'Property Rights', and Why Do They Matter? A Comment on Hodgson's Article. *Journal of Institutional Economics, 11*(4), 719–723.

Bijani, M., & Hayati, D. (2011). Water Conflict in Agricultural System in Iran: A Human Ecological Analysis. *Journal of Ecology and Environmental Sciences, 2*(2), 27–40.

Bjorvatn, K., & Selvik, K. (2007, February 14). Destructive Competition: Factionalism and Rent-Seeking in Iran. *SAM 8, Discussion Paper*, Norwegian School of Economics and Business Administration.

Caponera, D. A. (1954). *Water laws in Moslem countries*. Food and Agricultural Organization, U.N.

Chaichian, M. (2012). The New Phase of Globalization and Brain Drain: Migration of Educated and Skilled Iranians to the U.S. *International Journal of Social Economics, 39*(1/2), 18–38.

Cole, D., & Grossman, P. (2002). The Meaning of Property Rights: Law Versus Economics? *Land Economics, 78*(3), 317–330.

Cooter, R., & Ulen, T. (2012). *Law and Economics* (6th ed.). Addison-Wesley.

Coville, T. (2017). "The Economic Activities of Pasdaran" In Vahabi, Mehrdad and Coville, Thierry (Dir.), L'économie politique de la République islamique d'Iran, *Revue internationale des études du développement*, No. 229, mai, pp. 87–107.

Cuddington, J. T. (1986). *Capital Flight: Estimates, Issues and Explanations*. Princeton Studies in International Finance, No. 58.

Dean, M. (2008). *Robbing the Jews, the Confiscation of Jewish Property in the Holocaust, 1933–1945*. Cambridge University Press.

Demsetz, H. (1964). The Exchange and Enforcement of Property Rights. *Journal of Law and Economics, 7*, 11–26.

Dornbusch, R., & Mussa, M. (1975). Consuption, Real Balances and the Hoarding Function. *International Economic Review, 16*(2), 415–421.

Ehteshamzadeh, F. (2018). Iranjib, The news code: 48180, see https://www.iranjib.ir/shownews/48180/%D8%AE%D8%B1%D9%88%D8%AC-800-%D9%85%D
B%8C%D9%84%DB%8C%D8%A7%D8%B1%D8%AF-
%D8%AF%D9%84%D8%A7%D8%B1-%D8%A7%D8%B2-

%D8%A7%DB%8C%D8%B1%D8%A7%D9%86-%D8%AF%D8%B1-40-%D8%B3%D8%A7%D9%84-%DA%AF%D8%B0%D8%B4%D8%AA%D9%87, retrieved on 14 February 2022. The persian section of the Deutsche Welle also diffused the news, see https://www.dw.com/fair/%D8%AE%D8%B1%D9%88%D8%AC-%DB%B8%DB%B0%DB%B0-%D9%85%DB%8C%D9%84%DB%8C%D8%A7%D8%B1%D8%AF-%D8%AF%D9%84%D8%A7%D8%B1-%D8%A7%D8%B2-%D8%A7%DB%8C%D8%B1%D8%A7%D9%86-%D8%AF%D8%B1-%DB%B4%DB%B0-%D8%B3%D8%A7%D9%84/a-43436169, retrieved on 14 February 2022.

Ellickson, R. (1991). *Order Without Law, How Neighbors Settle Disputes*. Harvard University Press.

Ellickson, R. (1993). Property in Land. *Yale Law Journal, 102*, 1317–1400.

Emmer, R. (1959, May). A Concept of Hoarding. *The Review of Economics and Statistics, 41*(2, Part 1), 162–169.

Ghaninejad, M. (2022, January 29). Charxesh be chap (A turn to the left). *Tejarat Farda*, Number 442.

Goldsmith, E. (1968). The Qanats of Iran. *Scientific American, 218*(4), 94–105.

Hardin, G. (1968). The Tragedy of the Commons. *Science, New Series, 162*(3859), 1243–1248.

Hirschman, A. (1977). "A generalized linkage approach to development, with special reference to staples," *Economic Development and Cultural Change, 25*, 67–98.

Hodgson, G. (2015). Much of the 'Economics of Property Rights' Devalues Property and Legal Rights. *Journal of Institutional Economics, 11*(4), 683–709.

Hohfeld, W. (1913). Some Fundamental Legal Conceptions as Applied in Judicial Reasoning. *Yale Law Journal, 23*, 16–59.

Hooglund, E. J. (1982). *Land and Revolution in Iran 1960-1980*. University of Texas Press.

Jahangiri, I. (2016/2021). Nagofteh-hay Jahangiri az door zadan tahreemha va arz 4200 tomani (Jahangiri's unsaid report on detouring economic boycotts and the 4200 tomans currency). *Ensafnews*, 14 March 2021, http://www.ensafnews.com/286750/, Retrieved February 13, 2022 (in Persian).

Kasravi, A. (2006). *History of the Iranian Constitutional Revolution: Tārikh-e Mashrute-ye Iran, Volume I, translated into English by Evan Siegel*. Mazda Publications.

Katouzian, M. A. (1974). Land Reform in Iran, A Case Study in the Political Economy of Social Engineering. *The Journal of Peasant Studies, 1*(2), 220–239.

Kaviani, Z. (2021). Dar ahmyaat roshd nerkh sarmyeh gozari, avamel moasser bar roshed eqtesadi saal 1400 kodamand (On the Importance of the Rate of Investment: What Are the Factors Influencing the Growth Rate in 2021–2022?)", *Tejarat Farda*, No. 404. 1 May (in Persian).

Kazemi, F., & Abrahamian, E. (1978). The Nonrevolutionary Peasantry of Modern Iran. *Iranian Studies, 11*(1/4), 259–304.

Keddie, N. R., & Gasiorowski, M. J. (Eds.). (1990). *Neither East nor West: Iran, the United States, and the Soviet Union.* Yale University Press.

Keynes, J. M. (1936). *The General Theory of Eemployment, Interest and Money.* Macmillan.

Khazani, O., & Bulos, N. (2021, August 2). As Water Table Lowers, Tehran and Much of Iran are Slowly Sinking. *Los Angels Times,* Retrieved March 8, 2022, from https://www.latimes.com/world-nation/story/2021-08-02/lower-water-table-climate-change-tehran-iran-sinking.

Klein, B., Crawford, R., & Alchian, A. (1978). Vertical Integration, Appropriable Rents, and the Competitive Contracting Process. *Journal of Law and Economics, 21*(2), 297–326.

Kooch, Y., Azizi Mehr, M., & Hosseini, S. M. (2020). The Effect of Forest Degradation Intensity on Soil Function Indicators in Northern Iran. *Ecological Indicators, 114,* 106324. https://doi.org/10.1016/j.ecolind.2020.106324

Kornai, J. (1980). *Economics of Shortage.* North-Holland.

Kornai, J. (1992). *The Socialist System. The political economy of Communism.* Princeton University Press and Oxford University Press.

Kornai, J. (2000). What the Change of System from Socialism to Capitalism does and does not Mean? *The Journal of Economic Perspectives, 14*(1), 27–42.

Kornai, J. (2013). *Dynamism, Rivalry, and the Surplus Economy: Two Essays on the Nature of Capitalism.* Oxford University Press.

Kowsar, N., & Nader, A. (2019, 25 February). Iran Is Committing Suicide by Dehydration. *Foreign Policy.* Retrieved March 8, 2022, form https://foreign-policy.com/2019/02/25/iran-is-committing-suicide-by-dehydration/.

Krugman, P. (2013, April 11). *The Conscience of a Liberal, Monetary Policy in a Liquidity Trap.* Retrieved February 22, 2022, from https://krugman.blogs.nytimes.com/2013/04/11/monetary-policy-in-a-liquidity-trap/.

Lambton, A. K. S. (1969). *The Persian Land Reform.* Clarendon Press.

Lane, P., & Tornell, A. (1996). Power, Growth, and the Voracity Effect. *Journal of Economic Growth, 1,* 213–241.

Lane, P., & Tornell, A. (1999). The Voracity Effect. *American Economic Review, 89,* 22–46.

Ledeneva, A. V. (2006). How Russia really works: The informal practices that shaped post-Soviet politics and business. New York: Cornell University Press.

Leilaz, S. (2013). *Mooj dovam, tajodod ameraneh dar Iran, Tarikh barnameh-hay omrani sevoom ta panjom (The Second Wave, the Authoritarian Modernity in Iran, the History of the Development Planning from the Third to the Fifth).* Niloofar publication. (in Persian).

Levy Yeyati, E., & Rey, H. (2006). Financial Dollarization: Evaluating the Consequences. *Economic Policy, 21*(45), 63–118.

Madlovics, B., & Magyar, B. (2021). Post-Communist Predation: Modeling Reiderstvo Practices in Contemporary States. *Public Choice, 187*(3-4), 247–273.

Maljoo, M. (2017). "The Vicious Circle Trapping Iranian Workers since the 1990s", in Vahabi, Mehrdad and Coville, Thierry (Dir.), L'économie politique de la République islamique d'Iran, *Revue internationale des études du développement*, No. 229, mai, pp. 135–160.

Maloney, S. (2015). *Iran's Political Economy since the Revolution*. Cambridge University Press.

Markus, S. (2017). "The Atlas that has not shrugged: Why Russia's oligarchs are an unlikely force for change." *Dædalus—Journal of the American Academy of Arts & Sciences, 146*, 101–112.

Marx, K. (1859/1977). *A Contribution to the Critique of Political Economy*. Progress Publishers. Retrieved from https://www.marxists.org/archive/marx/works/1859/critique-pol-economy/preface.htm. Accessed July 15, 2019.

Mazaheri, R. (2018, June 20). How Iran got Economically Socialist, and then Islamic Socialist. *The Saker*. Retrieved February 2, 2022, from https://thesaker.is/how-iran-got-economically-socialist-and-then-islamic-socialist/.

Merianos, G., & Gotsis, G. (2017). *Managing Financial Resources in Late Antiquity, Greek Fathers' Views on Hoarding and Saving*. Palgrave Macmillan.

Milani, A. (2011). *The Shah*. Palgrave Macmillan.

Mitchell, T. (2011). *Carbon Democracy: Political Power in the Age of Oil*. Verso.

Moghtaderi, T., Alamdar, R., Rodríguez-Seijo, A., Naghibi, S. J., & Kumar, V. (2020). Ecological Risk Assessment and Source Apportionment of Heavy Metal Contamination in Urban Soils in Shiraz, Southwest Iran. *Arabian Journal of Geosciences, 13*, 797. https://doi.org/10.1007/s12517-020-05787-9

Mohandes, A. (1965). *Water Resources of Iran*. Tehran University, Faculty of Law, Political Science and Economics.

Motamedi, M. (2021, 21 July). Violence Escalates in Water-Shortage Protests in Iran's Khuzestan. *Aljazeera*. Retrieved March 10, 2022, from https://www.aljazeera.com/news/2021/7/21/violence-intensifies-after-six-nights-of-water-crisis-protests-in.

Nature. (2021, 24 June). Water Shortage: Iran Is Draining Its Aquifers Dry. *Proceedings of the National Academy of Sciences of the United States of America, 594*, 476. https://www.nature.com/articles/d41586-021-01604-9

Nili, M. (2004). *Eqtesad Iran va moamayee toseh nayaftegi (Iranian Economy and the Puzzle of Non Development)*. danshegah Sanaati Shareif.

Nili, M., & Associates. (2015). *Iqtesad Iran be koja miravad? Kholaseh tarh motaleati tahleel avamel taseergozar bar amalkard myan moddat iqtesad Iran (Where the Iranian Economy Is Going? A Summary of Study Project Regarding the Analysis of Factors Impacting the Performance of the Iranian Economy in Medium Term)*. Intesharat Donyai Iqtesad (in Persian).

Paganelli, M. (2014). David Hume on Banking and Hoarding. *Southern Economic Journal, 80*(4), 968–980.

Pahlavi, M. R. (1961/1974). *Mission for My Country*. Hutchinson & CO LTD

Pareto, V. (1927/1971). *Manual of Political Economy*. A.M. Kelley.

Patruti, A. (2016). An Analysis on the Relationship Between Hoarding, Investment and Economic Growth. *The Quarterly Journal of Austrian Economics, 19*(3), 248–266.

Plato. (2013). *Sophist* (Benjamin, J., Hazelton, P.A. Trans.). An Electronic Classics Series Publication. http://www2.hn.psu.edu/faculty/jmanis/plato/sophist.pdf

Rahman Zadeh Heravi, M. (2018). *Negahi be Iqtesad Siasi Iran az Daheh 1340 ta 1395 (A Glimpse over the Political Economy of Iran from 1961 until 2016)* (1st ed.). Nashr Akhtaran. (in Persian).

Research Centre of Islamic Legislative Assembly. (1996, July). Fasli darbareh farar maghzha (A Chapter on Brain Drain). Report code: 4001510.

Research Centre of Islamic Legislative Assembly. (2000). *Adam amnyat eqtesadi va farar sarmayeh (The lack of economic security and capital flight in Iran)*, May, Report code: 2405543.

Rowe, N. (2016). Keynesian Parables of Thrift and Hoarding. *Review of Keynesian Economics, 4*(1), 50–55.

Sayyah, S. A. (2016). Amoozehay 16 doreh arzyabi fasli moheet kasb oo kar dar Iran tei paeez 1389 ta tabestan 1394 (Lessons of 16 Cycles of Assessing Business Environment in Iran over the Period Starting in Fall 2010 to Summer 2015). *Majles va Rahboord, 23*(85), Spring (in Persian).

Schlumberger, O. (2008). Structural Reform, Economic Order, and Development: Patrimonial Capitalism. *Review of International Political Economy, 15*(4), 622–649.

Schmidt, M., Gonda, R., & Transiskus, S. (2021). Environmental Degradation at Lake Urmia (Iran): Exploring the Causes and Their Impacts on Rural Livelihoods. *GeoJournal, 86,* 2149–2163.

Schwartzstein, P. (2019, January 25). Drought Turns Part of Iran into a New Dust Bowl. Retrieved March 8, 2022, from https://www.nationalgeographic.com/environment/article/drought-climate-change-turn-iran-sistan-and-baluchestan-into-dust-bowl.

Schwartzstein, P. (2020, November 12). Environment Movement. *National Geographic.* Retrieved March 8, 2022, from https://www.nationalgeographic.com/environment/article/how-iran-destroying-once-thriving-environmental-movement.

Scott, J. (1998). *Seeing Like a State, How Certain Schemes to Improve the Human Condition Have Failed.* Yale University Press.

Scott, J. C. (2009). *The Art of Not Being Governed, An Anarchist History of Upland Southeast Asia.* Yale University Press.

Soós, K. A. (2017). "Tributes paid through special taxes: Populism and the displacement of "aliens"". In B. Magyar & J. Vásárhelyi (Eds.), Twenty-five sides of a post-communist mafia state (pp. 259–278). Budapest: CEU Press.

Soroush, N., & Madani, K. (2014/2021, November 21). Every Breath You Take: The Environmental Consequences of Iran Sanctions. *The Guardian.* Retrieved March 8, 2022, from https://www.theguardian.com/world/iran-blog/2014/nov/21/iran-environmental-consequences-of-sanctions.

State Department Report. (2018, September 28). Iran's environmental issues, Chapter 7. Retrieved March 8, 2022, from https://iranprimer.usip.org/blog/2018/oct/04/state-department-report-7-irans-environmental-issues.

Stringham, E. (2015). *Private Governance, Creating Order in Economic and Social Life*. Oxford University Press.

Tabibian, M. (2022, January 29). Noskheh Irani polit bureau (The Iranian version of polit bureau). *Tejarat Farda*.

Tavakoli, A. (1987). Nationalization and Efficient Management of Water Resources in Iran. *Journal of Water Resources Planning and Management, 113*(4), 522–532.

Tiebout, C. (1956). A Pure Theory of Local Expenditures. *Journal of Political Economy, 64*(5), 416–424.

Tilly, C. (1985). War Making and State Making as Organized Crime. In P. B. Evans, D. Rueschemeyer, & T. Skocpol (Eds.), *Bringing the State Back in, Cambridge* (pp. 169–191). Cambridge University Press.

Torbat, A. (2002). The Brain Drain from Iran to the U.S. *Middle East Journal, 56*(2), 272–295.

UNDP. (2017, June 17). *Iran and UNDP Strengthen Efforts to Combat Desertification*. Retrieved March 8, 2022, from https://www.ir.undp.org/content/iran/en/home/presscenter/articles/2017/06/17/iran-and-undp-strengthen-efforts-to-combat-desertification.html.

Vahabi, M. (2011). Appropriation, Violent Enforcement and Transaction Costs: A Critical Survey. *Public Choice, 147*(1), 227–253.

Vahabi, M. (2015). *The Political Economy of Predation: Manhunting and the Economics of Escape*. Cambridge University Press.

Vahabi, M. (2016, September). A Positive Theory of the Predatory State. *Public Choice, 168*(3–4), 153–175.

Vahabi, M. (2018). The Resource Curse Literature as Seen Through the Appropriability Lens: A Critical Survey. *Public Choice, 175*(3–4), 393–428.

Vahabi M. (2020). "Introduction: a symposium on the predatory state", *Public Choice, 182*(3–4), 233–242.

von Hayek, F. (1931/2008). *Prices and Production and Other Works*. Ludwig von Mises Institute.

Weiss, K. (2018, April 3). Iran's Tarnished Gem. *National Geographic*. Retrieved March 8, 2022, from https://www.nationalgeographic.com/photography/article/lake-urmia-iran-drought.

Wilson, A. (2008). Hydraulic Engineering and Water Supply. In J. P. Oleson (Ed.), *Handbook of Engineering and Technology in the Classical World* (pp. 290–293). Oxford University Press.

World Bank. (1985). *World Bank Report 1985*. World Bank.

Young, C. (1962). Iran in Continuing Crisis. *Foreign Affairs, 40*, 275–292.

Zobeiri, H., Akbarpour Roshan, N., & Shahrazi, M. (2017). Capital Flight and Economic Growth in Iran. In *19th International Scientific Conference on Economic and Social Development*, Melbourne, Australia, 9–10 February.

Zwijnenburg, W. (2017, August 11). No Country for Oil Men: Tracking Islamic State's oil Assets in Iraq. *bellingcat*. Retrieved February 3, 2022, from https://www.bellingcat.com/news/mena/2017/08/11/no-country-oil-men-tracking-islamic-states-oil-assets-iraq/.

CHAPTER 9

Epilogue

Understanding endogenous crises necessitates a theory of economic systems. Economic processes are socially instituted, and they comprise four moments: production, distribution, exchange, and consumption. The last moment terminates the whole cycle. The sum of distribution and exchange can be defined as 'transaction'. Two broad approaches to economic processes are *productive* and *transactional* (or distributional). Accordingly, two levels should be distinguished in analyzing economic systems: distribution and production. While *institutional* factors are determinants in the emergence of economic systems at the *distribution* level, *technological* progress is crucial in deciding economic systems at the *production* level.

Table 9.1 shows the relevant significance of institutional factors at distribution and production levels.

Modes of appropriation/coordination capture economic systems at the distribution level, whereas modes of production describe economic systems at the production level. In the former case, an economic system is defined by the political/ideological power, property form, and the way different modes of production are articulated or dis-articulated with each other. These three fundamental institutions determine economic processes. Four ideal-typical modes of coordination are market, authoritative, cooperative, and destructive. The preponderant role of destructive coordination reflects disarticulation of coordination mechanisms in a critical order.

M. Vahabi, *Destructive Coordination, Anfal and Islamic Political Capitalism*, https://doi.org/10.1007/978-3-031-17674-6_9

375

Table 9.1   Economic processes and institutional primacy

Economic process	Institutional factor[a]	Technological factor[b]	Temporal horizon
Distribution	Principal	Secondary	Long term
Production	Secondary	Principal	Very long term

Source: Author

[a]Institutional factors include economic, political, ideological, juridical, and religious factors

[b]Technological factors contain all material processes of production notably technical progress and innovations

Applying the general theoretical framework elaborated in Chaps. 2–4 to the Islamic Republic of Iran (IRI), I identified an original and coherent model of Shi'i political capitalism that can be characterized by three fundamental institutions:

1. Political/ideological institution: *Velayat faqih* or the jurisconsult of the vicegerent.
2. Preponderant property form: *Anfal* or the specific ownership of the Supreme Jurisconsult over *res nullius*.
3. Dominant coordination mechanism: destructive coordination.

These three institutions shape the behavioral regularity of agents and the normal state of the economy at the distribution level. They contain:

4. Capital and labor flight as behavioral regularity of economic agents.
5. Economics of speculative hoarding as the normal state of the economy under this specific system, and patrimonial development as its dynamics.

Shi'i political capitalism is an original economic system at the distribution level that cannot be reduced either to state populism or liberal capitalism. Contrary to a dominant discourse among the economists specialized in Iranian and Islamic economics, the political economy of the IRI cannot be summarized by a shift from state populism (Islamic socialism) in the first decade of the 1979 Revolution to a liberal economy (Islamic capitalism) since the end of the eight-year war with Iraq in 1989. This misleading discourse fails to notice the *Islamization* of the economy throughout the whole post-revolutionary period.

By 'Islamization', I mean the emergence, expansion, and domination of *Anfal* as the underlying tenet of the public finance in the Shi'i jurisprudence. After elaborating on *Anfal* in Islamic jurisprudence and the constitution of the IRI in Chap. 5, I substantiated in Chaps. 6 and 7 the evolution of *Anfal* in *practice* through three phases.

The first phase of *Anfal* started under the first Supreme Leader, the founder of the IRI, Ayatollah Ruhollah Khomeini, in February 1979. Article 45 of the constitution of the IRI conflated *Anfal* with state properties in general although *in practice* the giant economic holdings related to *Anfal* such as *Bonyad Mostazafan* (the Foundation of the downtrodden) were organized separately from other state organizations under the purview of the Imam as 'Islamic revolutionary' organizations. These new institutions were the outcome of confiscating the late Shah's properties and 53 industrialists and financiers. *Anfal* stabilized and spawned under the pretext of Islamic non-profitable charities for the sake of the 'downtrodden' although it was closely involved in profit-making and rent-seeking through non-market mechanisms since its inception.

The second phase began in the post-war period in 1989 by Khomeini's injunction on guardianship of 'ownerless' properties and the enforcement of Article 49 of the constitution regarding a universal confiscatory regime. The nomination of the second Supreme Leader, Seyyed Ali Khamenei, after Khomeini's death on June 3, 1989, lacking the religious credentials weakened the position of the jurisconsult and strengthened temporarily the role of the presidency during Hashemi-Rafsanjani's two terms presidencies (1989–1997) followed by a wave of reformist movement incarnated by Seyyed Muhammad Khatami (1997–2005). The coalition of the new Supreme Leader with the Sepah was formed in their common struggle against the reformist movement for enhancing the political and economic position of Islamic parallel institutions. This transitional phase of *Anfal* lasted until the presidency of Mahmud Ahmadinejad and the issuance of the privatization decree in July 2006.

Setad headquarters, a second major *Anfal* conglomerate, were created in the second phase. *Anfal's* giant holdings could spread and achieve a dominant position in the economy through two channels. First, the edict on the so-called privatization of banks that transformed the parallel Islamic loan funds into official non-state, Islamic banks linked to Bonyad, Setad, the Sepah, and the Basij. These funds were not controlled by the Iranian Central Bank even though they were operating as de facto Islamic banks, since they opened deposit accounts, issued checks, and created money.

They had their own 'central bank', known as *Sazman Iqtesad Islami* (the Organization of the Islamic Economics). The second channel was a coalition with the Sepah which was actively interfering in economic activities as the privileged subcontractor of the state in building infrastructures such as dams, roads, subways, railroads, shipping, and exploiting oil fields or selling petroleum. It was also in this period that the Sepah developed its affiliated economic institutions notably *Khatam* headquarters in addition to *Tavoon* (the Sepah's cooperative).

Finally, the third period of *Anfal* was launched by Khamenei's decree on 'General policies pertaining to Article 44 of the constitution of the Islamic Republic of Iran' in July 2006. *Anfal* in coalition with the Sepah and the Basij swallowed the bulk of state enterprises in the name of privatization. Moreover, *Anfal* was explicitly extended to natural resources such as mountains, rivers, lakes, and forests. It ushered in a new era of Islamic economic revolution.

The key ingredient of Islamization has been the promotion of *Anfal*. This process entailed state predation and political capitalism or profit-making and rent-seeking through non-market mechanisms. Parallel to the extension of *Anfal*, resources were appropriated ever-increasingly by destructive coordination while the share of market, authoritative, and cooperative coordination drastically shrank. Moreover, the failure of these principal forms of coordination was reflected in their structural distortions. For example, markets were divided into state-dependent and parallel black markets. Authoritative coordination lost its ability to centralize resources, provide social services and public goods, and enforce rules and regulations. Cooperative coordination was suppressed since 1982 and any independent cooperative movement was censored for the sake of parallel Islamic corporatist organizations.

The failure of all principal modes of coordination to secure their role as mediators between fundamental institutions and economic processes, on the one hand, and the increasing share of parallel Islamic institutions under the exclusive purview of the Supreme Leader in resource appropriation, on the other hand, culminated in the predominance of destructive coordination. Oil revenue and its booms only reinforced state predation and accelerated the mechanisms of Shi'i political capitalism.

This coherent economic system induced specific behavioral regularity among households and enterprises that can be characterized as capital and labor flight detrimental to the formation of fixed capital domestically. Capital flight has been one of the major causes of the economics of speculative hoarding comprising both monetary and commodity hoarding with 'shortages' in state-dependent markets and 'surplus' in black markets. The chronic deviation between saving and investment was sustained by hoarding as partial disinvestment through capital flight.

There exists a hierarchical causal link among the afore-mentioned five principal institutional and economic blocks. The political system, *Velayat faqih* causes *Anfal*, which in turn leads to the dominance of destructive coordination. This type of coordination with state predation and parallel institutions generates capital flight, and the latter results in the economics of hoarding. The Shi'i political capitalism depicts an economic system at the distribution (appropriation) level.

The capitalist productive system that dominated the Iranian economy since the land reform in the 1960s under the Shah's monarchy, was maintained during the IRI. In post-revolutionary Iran, capitalist production was threatened only during the years 1979–1982 when workers tried to impose their control over production and assume the management wherever they were forced to because of the institutional vacuum provoked by owners and employers' flight.

Khomeini's edict in eight articles issued on December 12, 1982 strictly condemned any kind of confiscation or control of movable and immovable assets by workers or any other social groups except the qadi's orders in religious tribunals (see Article 4, 5, and 6).[1] This edict was issued following the suppression of workers' independent councils and the domination of Islamic corporatist organizations particularly Islamic labor Councils (*Shoorhay islami kar*) and Islamic labor associations (*Anjomanhay islami*) in the summer 1982.

While capitalist productive system was kept intact under the IRI, the Shi'i political capitalism hindered its development by enhancing state predation. The curse was not the oil income or *natural resources* but *institutional* stemming from this type of capitalism preying on oil income that resulted in retarding the productive capacity.

Table 9.2 recapitulates the major differences between Shi'i political capitalism with both classical socialism and liberal market capitalism.

[1] See the site Tabnak, related to the IRGC, February 12, 2018, that has republished Khomeini's edict, https://www.tabnak.ir/fa/news/364936/%D9%85%D8%AA%D9%86-%DA%A9%D8%A7%D9%85%D9%84-%D9%81%D8%B1%D9%85%D8%A7%D9%86-%DB%B8-%D9%85%D8%A7%D8%AF%D9%87-%E2%80%8F%D8%A7%DB%8C%D8%A7%D9%85%D8%A7%D9%85%D8%AE%D9%85%DB%8C%D9%86%DB%8C, retrieved on March 23, 2022.

Table 9.2 A comparative study of Shi'i political capitalism with classical socialist system and liberal market capitalism

Blocks	Classical socialism	Islamic political capitalism	Liberal market capitalism
1. Political/ ideological	Undivided power of the Communist party	*Velayat faqih* (jurisprudence of the vicegerent)	Liberal political pluralism based on electoral system
2. Dominant form of property	State property	*Anfal* (the Imam's property over *res nullius*)	Private property
3. Preponderant form of coordination	Authoritative coordination	Destructive coordination	Market coordination
4. Behavioral regularity of economic actors	Soft budget constraints and weak responsiveness to prices	Capital and labor flight and strong responsiveness to multiple exchange rates	Hard budget constraints and strong responsiveness to prices
5. Normal state of the economy	Economics of shortage	Economics of hoarding	Economics of overproduction
6. Normal or critical	Normal	Critical	Normal

The term 'normal' warrants a caveat. By 'normal', I do not imply an equilibrium state but specific chronic disequilibrium prevailing in an economic system (Vahabi, 1998). Thus, in classical socialism, the normal state is *shortage* while in market capitalism, *surplus* represents a normal state. However, the existence of chronic disequilibrium does not imply 'crisis'. The disequilibrium should bypass a tolerance threshold reaching a level of intensity to be considered critical. In Shi'i political capitalism, the normal state is not just chronic disequilibrium, but rather persistent crisis concretized by capital flight and speculative hoarding.

This explains why people feel that they do not live in a *normal* economic system or a 'normal' capitalist system. How to become 'normal' economically and politically is always related to solving or at least managing conflicts with the 'world community' on nuclear power, international terrorism, the respect for human rights, etc. In such a context, reforming the economic system often implies 'normalizing' the system through the resolution or management of conflicts. The Joint Comprehensive Plan of Action (JCPOA) provides an emblematic figure of such efforts in 'normalizing' direction permitting the removal of American economic sanctions.

Is Shi'i political capitalism reformable? If by 'reform', one means engaging in bargaining over deals targeting 'normalization', my answer is *conditionally* affirmative. All deals that can secure the longevity of the IRI and sustain *Velayat faqih* are welcome even if they explicitly contradict the Islamic principles. This is what is called the 'Expediency' of the system (*maslahat nezam*). As reminded in Chap. 2, Khomeini was categorical about the priority of keeping the power by clergies over the respect of Islamic principles. *Velayat Mutlaqah faqih* (the absolute power of the Supreme Jurisconsult) entails the primacy of the expediencies of the Islamic state over Islamic norms. To put it differently, if keeping the power requires the contravention of Islamic norms, including non-praying or lying, the norms should be suspended[2] (Schirazi, 1997; Fujinaga, 2018). However, this is not what I mean by reform. Reforms consist of institutional changes to improve coordination mechanisms within fundamental institutions of an economic system. A reform in Shi'i political capitalism does not aim at undermining *Velayat faqih* and *Anfal*, its objective is to introduce institutional changes that increase production, economic growth, and labor productivity within the existing order.

Two types of reforms have been attempted within the IRI. The first attempt happened during the two-term presidency of Hashemi Rafsanjani (1989–1997). The reform was principally *economic* and not political. It was inspired by the Chinese and Malaysian economic reforms to 'open the doors' by revising Article 81 of the constitution of the IRI regarding foreign direct investment (FDI) and elevating the importance and social value of experts in the state bureaucracy.

The second attempt occurred during the two-term presidency of Muhammad Khatami (1997–2005). His reformist initiative was rather *political* than economic. It targeted at a 'dialogue between civilization' (an opening toward the West) and a 'dialogue with civil society' through a

[2] Khamenei metaphorically spoke of 'heroic flexibility' in accepting JCPOA. This type of acrobatic gestures is easily justifiable if the 'expediencies' of the system force it to the Supreme Leader.

limited press freedom domestically (Karimian, 2009).[3] From an economic viewpoint, Khatami followed Rafsanjani's privatization program notably in the banking sector and relaxing Article 81 to attract FDI (see Chaps. 6 and 7).

Rafsanjani's economic reforms were launched during the 'reconstruction' era envisaging industrial growth based on two Five-Year Plan, creation of an 'efficient' technocratic state bureaucracy, reducing budget deficit, stopping, and reversing capital flight by reopening the economy to foreign direct investment (FDI) and capital investment of the Iranian diaspora, and encouraging exportation of non-oil products. Rafsanjani's plan for economic reforms has been the most comprehensive one until now although he never called himself 'reformist' but rather 'pragmatist'.

Achieving industrial growth instead of mercantilist accumulation was its main objective. In doing so, he introduced the following economic measures.

1. *Rehabilitation of technocracy*: He intended to rehabilitate professional technocratic classes based on 'expertise' (*takhaso*'s) instead of privileging 'Islamic and revolutionary commitments' (*ta'ahod*). This has been a fundamental contradiction and dilemma of the Shi'i political capitalism from its inception. The crux of the problem was a contradiction between 'science' (*elm*) in the Islamic sense (knowledge of *fiqh*) and 'science' in the modern Western and technical sense (technocratic expertise). Contradictions and dilemmas around this issue have been multiple: education system built upon seminaries versus modern universities, recruitment based on ideological-

---

[3] Khatami served twice as minister of Culture and Islamic Guidance, the second time was in 1989, when censorship restrictions on press loosened, and the number of newspapers published in Iran rose to about 550 in 1992–1994. These newspapers contributed largely to Khatami's popularity and resulted in his presidential victory in 1997. The black lash came from conservatives especially the Guardian Council, the judiciary power, the Sepah, and the paramilitary forces of the Basij. The press came again under attack and censorship from 1998 to1999. In August 2000, reformists introduced a bill to the sixth Majles aiming at reversing the newspapers closures and arrests of journalists. According to this bill, publishers rather than journalists could come under legal action giving immunity to writers and journalists. However, the bill was removed from the agenda of the parliament by the Speaker of the parliament, the cleric Karoubi upon the reception of a decree from the Supreme Leader warning against "the enemies of Islam, the revolution and the Islamic system taking the press in their hands" (Karimian, 2009, p. 16). Thus, the judiciary power could finish its job by closing more newspapers and the incarceration of many more journalists.

religious versus competencies criteria, Islamic 'equity' versus Western 'efficiency', clerics versus technocrats as cadre and managers of the state administration and corporations. The emergence of a new political formation, namely *Kargozaran-e Sazandegi* (servants of construction), was closely related to Rafsanjani's policy to foster a technocratic culture and a new social base among the middle class.

Theoretically, this policy had to rebuild the formal state and strengthen authoritative coordination. However, in practice, the ex-revolutionary functionaries were transformed into new partners of bazaaris and other parallel Islamic institutions in enriching themselves and their families in the post-war period. They used their networks, influence, and insider information within the state hierarchy and parallel Islamic institutions at the municipal and central levels to accumulate wealth and status. They profited from the state administration as a corporation to sell in black markets through provisions bought for the ministry with the ministry's funds to make monetary profit. They benefited from their access to foreign currencies at the official exchange rate to sell them to their networks at rates close to the market. They also created front state companies to perform subcontracting for the contracts granted to Bonyad and Setad by municipal or central state administration. In other words, they became new partners of parallel Islamic institutions in preying on the state's resources. The reformist technocrats were not necessarily clerics, they were often titled 'Doctor', 'Mohandes' (engineer), but these 'experts' who were allegedly against inefficiencies and lack of expertise were economic partners of *Anfal*, the Sepah, and the Basij.

2. *Reduction of budget deficits*: Rafsanjani was the initiator of conducting the Sepah to economic activities under the pretext of reducing the state's budget deficit after the end of the war. The financial autonomy of the Sepah had to rebalance the state's budget. In this way, the disappointment of the young Hezbollahis (committed revolutionary and Islamic soldiers of the God) released from war fronts mobilized in the Sepah and the Basij to secure a better future for themselves by benefiting from their years of serving at fronts either as newly enrolled university students without passing the entrance exams or engaging in economic activities of the Sepah. Rafsanjani's reform program was contradictory since it reinforced the same parallel organizations that impeded the reconstruction of the formal

state and privatization. It is noteworthy that Khatami's administration also granted major state contracts to the Sepah and increased its budget although the Sixth Majles adopted a ruling to tax parallel economic institutions under the purview of the Supreme Leader. This ruling was never enacted and limited to rhetorical effect.

3. *Privatization and open-door policy*: as discussed in Chap. 7, Rafsanjani's privatization policy provoked much enthusiasm at the start but ended with parasitic privatization in favor of his family and close associates. Individual enrichment was reached its zenith in Rafsanjani's time, and the famous phenomenon of *Aghazadeh* (children of the master) has been tied to his name. Familial nepotism replicating hereditary inequalities in power and wealth from one generation to another prevailed while the titles changed: the fathers were Hojatolislam and Ayatollah, whereas the children were carrying the title of 'Doctors' or 'Mohandes'! The children or *Aghazadeh* were now students at the universities in the USA, England, and Canada, having double nationalities with copious banking accounts, while their parents pulled the political and economic strings in Tehran, Qum, and Mashhad.

Rafsanjani's family epitomized this new political and business empire covering his brother as head of the state television broadcast, his two sons involved in managing multi-billion-dollar construction of the Tehran's subway system and significant petroleum contracts, and Rafsanjani's two daughters serving one as a parliament member and the other as head of a prominent charity organization. Other members of the family also had their shares of booties. Widespread corruption of the privatization campaigns discredited his initiative for attracting FDI and Iranian capital abroad. *Anfal*'s institutions benefited from factional struggles of traditional bazaaris and pragmatists to capture the lion's share of privatization.

Although corruption was one of the important reasons for the failure of the reform program, the fundamental reason was what I called the impossible trinity of *Anfal* in Chap. 7. The impossible trinity states that it is impossible to have more than two of the three following policy positions: (a) *Anfal* and economic openness, (b) *Anfal* and privatization, and (c) privatization and economic openness. Option (b) corresponds to what has happened after 2006 and option (c) was tried and defeated both under the Rafsanjani's and Khatami's presidencies. The internal coherence of Islamic political capitalism as an economic system has been displayed in this impossible trinity.

In other words, Rafsanjani's reform program based on a combination of the open-door policy and privatization was contradictory with keeping *Anfal* intact. It was doomed to failure even if it could be implemented without major corruption and scandals. The empirical evidence for the impossible trinity of *Anfal* has been provided during Khatami's presidency when the Sepah occupied by force Khomeini's international airport to cancel contracts with Turkish companies in the name of 'national security' one day after its inauguration in the presence of President Khatami on May 8, 2004 (see Chap. 6 for details).

4. *Reversing capital flight and exporting non-oil products*: The reform program could not achieve its objectives. Not only industrial growth did not happen, but also it failed in macroeconomic stabilization, since the inflation rate averaged 19% during the first Five-Year Plan, more than 25% during the second Five-Year Plan, and the record rate of 49% in some years (Maloney, 2015, p. 255). Capital flight persisted and accentuated particularly because a high percentage of currency from the exportation of non-oil products never returned to the country (see Chap. 8, Table 8.4).

Rafsanjani tried to reform the system while keeping the fundamental institutions intact. The final outcome of his economic reforms was not the rehabilitation of authoritative or market coordination. The reforms did not terminate parallel institutions, but established a new partnership between fundamentalists and reformists to prey on state resources. Of course, the reforms incorporated some cosmetic and half-measured changes. For example, expert technocrats having even Ph.D. from high-rank American universities were added to the impotent formal state administration and replaced sometime 'committed revolutionary Hezbollahis'. But these reforms could not stop capital flight or increase industrial growth and productivity. Instead, they generated more inconsistencies and incoherence in the system.

Indeed, the coherence of Shi'i political capitalism undermines its reformability and lends credence to the need for a transformation of the whole system. Interestingly, at the end of his second-term presidency, Rafsanjani intimated the idea of constitutional revisions to allow a third-term presidency for himself, but he was not successful in his political maneuvers. He then retreated and prepared his post-presidential status within the Expediency Council. The pragmatist president never tied his economic reforms to a fundamental political change questioning *Velayat faqih* or *Anfal*.

Khatami epitomizes the reformist approach in the IRI; he has even been called 'the leader of the reformist movement'. After the ostensible failure of Khatami as 'president of reforms', the reformist movement split into several groups. Despite their varieties, they can be broadly classified into two major categories: governmental reformism and reformist movement outside government. The latter led the massive popular protests against the results of the highly controversial 2009 Iranian presidential elections disputing victory by Ahmadinejad and supporting two leading opposition candidates, Mir Hossein Mousavi and Mehdi Karoubi. The main slogan of the protesters was: "Where is my vote?"

The protests were nationwide starting from 2009 into early 2010. The contesting movement was titled the 'Green Movement' (*Jonbesh-e Sabz*) echoing Mousavi's selected color for the electoral campaign. The movement was labeled as 'velvet revolution' plotted by 'foreign conspirators' in a cohort with 'western-educated, north-Tehrani elite'. The movement was brutally repressed by the Basiji and other military forces (Ansari, 2010, pp. 24–25; Ritter, 2015, p. 188).

As explained in Chaps. 6 and 7, Mousavi and Karoubi were both farouche supporters of Ayatollah Khomeini; the former served as the last Prime Minister of Iran from 1981 to 1989, and the latter, a Shi'a cleric, leader of the *National Trust Party* who served as the Speaker of the parliament from 1989 to 1992 and then the Speaker of the Sixth parliament with a majority of reformist representatives from 2000 to 2004.

While Mousavi had a populist statist economic program during his premiership, Karoubi remained loyal to *Anfal* and advocated some populist programs such as distributing the oil's revenue among people. The leaders of the reformist movement who were previously the followers of Imam Khomeini and staunch advocates of statism during the first decade of revolution gradually distanced from statism without elaborating any alternative economic program. Khatami backed privatization programs during his presidency. Indeed, the reformist movement was rallied around a central political idea, namely strengthening elective republican institutions of the IRI against dominant nominative institutions.

The reformists never advocated the removal of *Velayat faqih*. In their opinion, the Supreme Leader should be the unificatory figure of the IRI, and the reformist movement had to win his support in order to advance its platform. The reformist political agenda can be summarized in terms of establishing a Constitutional *Velayat faqih* similar to a Constitutional Monarchy. The coalition of the Supreme Leader and the Sepah bloodily suppressed the pacific protests of the 'Green Movement' and put Mousavi, his wife Zahra Rahnavard and Karoubi under house arrest, and interdicted the publication of any interview or image of the ex-president Khatami.

After the violent crackdown of the reformist movement, it was radicalized and started to critically assess its position toward *Velayat Faqih*. At its inception, the reformist strategy consisted of combining 'political pressure from below' and 'negotiation from above'. In this strategy, the popular movements had to be strictly shunned from questioning the whole political and economic system and be directed to push for those demands that could be implemented within the system (Vahabi and Mohajer, 2004). This tamed social movement could be a platform for reformist leaders to negotiate with fundamentalists for a bigger share of political power.

In practice, this strategy has never been realized, but it castrated independent popular movements transforming them to the social basis of one of the political factions inside the IRI. Governmental reformism rendered a big service to fundamentalists: it could represent the 'opposition' discrediting the radical opposition struggling for the transformation of the whole system (Vahabi & Mohajer, 2011). This political strategy was discredited by ousting governmental reformism from political power and violent suppression of popular protests. Disappointed by repeated failures of impotent reformist strategy, the social protests carried a new slogan since 2018: "Eslah talab. Osoolgara, digeh tamom majera" (It is the end of both reformists and fundamentalists) (see Asemi, June 16, 2021, *BBC*, *Persian section*).

While the reformist movement lost its momentum and tended toward a radical strategy of transforming the whole system, governmental reformism tried to stick to governmental positions by coming closer to moderates and conservatives such as President Rouhani and the conservative Larijani. For these governmental reformists, the major concern has always been to sustain their rent-seeking privileges by possessing governmental positions in the central state administration, municipalities, parliament, or city councils. Islamic political capitalism provided multiple opportunities of rent-seeking for all fractions of IRI including governmental reformists.

The non-reformability of the system is closely related to its inner coherence; reforms do not remove the fundamental problems of the system regarding capital investment, economic growth, and increase in productivity. The improvement of dynamic economic efficiency requires an institutional revolution. Transformation rather than reform is warranted to enhance economic development and eschew ecological disasters in Iran by putting an end to *Velayat faqih, Anfal,* and destructive coordination.

Shi'i political capitalism describes the rationale of a specific type of predatory or confiscatory regime closely related to *Anfal* and the Shi'i hierocracy. It provides an economic system supporting a critical order. The emergence of parallel institutions derives from an endogenous crisis that reflects the failure of principal forms of coordination like market, authoritative and cooperative. However, the crisis cannot be transformed into an order unless new institutional and economic forces could fill the institutional vacuum. The Shi'i Ulema with their historical networks and roots in the Iranian society were one of these sources. Further studies need to be conducted on other forms of destructive coordination and specific economic systems fostering them.

References

Ansari, A. (2010). *Crisis of Authority: Iran's 2009 Presidential Election.* Chatham House.

Fujinaga, A. F. (2018). Islamic Law in Post-Revolutionary Iran. In A. M. Emon & A. Rumee (Eds.), *The Oxford Handbook of Islamic Law.* Oxford University Press.

Karimian, R. (2009, Spring). The Reformist Moment and the Press. *Middle East Report, 250,* 16.

Maloney, S. (2015). *Iran's Political Economy since the Revolution.* Cambridge University Press.

Ritter, D. (2015). *The Iron Cage of Liberalism.* Oxford University Press.

Schirazi, A. (1997). *The Constitution of Iran: Politics and the State in the Islamic Republic.* I.B. Tauris.

Vahabi, M. (1998, September). The Relevance of the Marshallian Concept of Normality in Interior and in Inertial Dynamics as Revisited by G. Shackle and J. Kornai. *Cambridge Journal of Economics, 22*(5), 547–573.

Vahabi, M., & Mohajer, N. (2004). *Az eslahat ta barandazi: tangnaha va cheshm andazha (Islamic Republic of Iran, Paradoxes of Reform and Prospects of Rebellion).* Nashr Noghteh. (in Persion).

Vahabi, M., & Mohajer, N. (2011). Islamic republic of Iran and Its Opposition. *Comparative Studies of South Asia, Africa and the Middle East, 31*(1), 110–119.

References

Abadi, K., & Hossein, S. A. (1973). *Vaghayieh al-saneen va al-awam (The events of the years and masses)*. Entesharat Elsamieh.

Abazari, Y., & Zakeri, A. (2019, February 24). Three Decades of Coexistence of Religion and Neoliberalism in Iran. *Critique of Political Economy* (in Persian).

Abbaspour, M., & Sabetraftar, A. (2005). Review of Cycles and Indices of Drought and Their Effect on Water Resources, Ecological, Biological, Agricultural, Social and Economical Issues in Iran. *International Journal of Environmental Studies, 62*(6), 709–724.

Abdollahi, M. R. (2021). Roshd hast vali kam hast (The Growth Exists but it is Low). *Tejarat Farda*, 1 May, No. 404 (in Persian).

Abrahamian, E. (1993). *Khomeinism.* University of California Press.

Abrahamian, E. (2008). *A History of Modern Iran.* Cambridge University Press.

Abrahamian, E. (2009, Spring). Why the Islamic Republic Has Survived. *Middle East Report, 250*, 10–16.

Adamiyat, F. (1972). *The Politics of Reform in Iran 1858-1880, in Persian.* Entesharat Kharazmi.

Agamben, G. (1998). *Homo Sacer: Sovereign Power and Bare Life.* Stanford University Press.

Agamben, G. (2005). *State of Exception.* The University of Chicago Press.

Aglietta, M. (1998). *Le capitalisme de demain*, note de fondation Saint-Simon.

Ahmadi, M. (2019). *Inqlab va Naft, Revayat Vaziran Jomhouri Islami az Iqtesad Siasi Naft (The Revolution and Oil, Interviews of Ministers of the Islamic Republic Regarding the Political Economy of Petroleum), in Persian.* Intesharat Donyai Iqtesad. (in Persian).

Ahmadi Amooei, B. (2004). Interview with Engineer Ezatullah Sahabi. In *The Political Economy of the Islamic Republic* (pp. 9–58), Gam-e No. (in Persian); Interview with Dr. Mohsen Nourbakhsh. In *The Political Economy of the Islamic Republic* (pp. 59–140), Gam-e No. (in Persian); Interview with Dr. Massoud Roghani Zanjani. In The Pol*itical Economy of the Islamic Republic* (pp. 141–232), Gam-e No. (in Persian); Interview with Hossein Adeli. In *The Political Economy of the Islamic Republic* (pp. 435–495), Gam-e No. (in Persian).

Ahmadi Amooei, B. (2018). *Iqtesad siasi sandooqhay qarz al-hasaneh va mossasat etebari, sooghoot yek ideology (The Political Economy of the Islamic Charitable Funds and Financial Institutions, the Demise of an Ideology)*. Ketab Parseh. (in Persian).

Ahmadov, A. (2014). Oil, Democracy, and Context a Meta-Analysis. *Comparative Political Studies, 47*(9), 1238–1267.

Aizenman, J., Cheung, Y.-W., & Ito, H. (2015). International Reserves Before and after the Global Crisis: Is There no end to Hoarding? *Journal of International Money and Finance, 52*, 102–126.

Aizenman, J., & Lee, J. (2006, December). Financial Versus Monetary Mercantilism: Long-run View of Large International Reserves Hoarding. *IMF Working Paper*.

Al Yaseen, A. (2014). *Tarikhcheh barnameh rizi tooseh dar Iran (The History of Development Planning in Iran)*. Markaz Nashr Sahar. (in Persian).

Albats, Y. (1994). *The State Within a State, the KGB and Its Hold on Russia-Past, Present and Future*. Farrar, Strauss, Giroux.

al-Hilli (al-Muhaqqiq), J. I. H. (1988). *Shara'i' al-Islam fi masa'il al-halal wa l-haram (Islam Sharia Regarding Halal and Haram)* (Vol. 1, 2nd ed.). Entesharat Esteqlal. (in Persian).

Alikhani, A. (2001). *Siast va siasat gozari eqtesadi dar Iran, 1340-1350, mosahbeh ba Alinaghi Alikhani, virastar Gholamreza Afkhami (Economic Politics and Policy-Making in Iran during 1961-1971, Interview with Alinaghi Alikhani Edited by Gholamreza Afkhami)* (Vol. 7). Foundation of Iranian Studies. (in Persian).

Al-Samhudi, N. a.-D. A. b. A. (2001). *Wafa al-Wafa bi akhbar Dar al-Mustafa (The Fulfillment of Faithfulness on the Reports of the City of the Chosen One), edited and annotated by Qasim Al-Sammarai in five volumes*. Al-Furqan Islamic Heritage Foundation.

Al-Tabari, A. J., & Jarir, M. B. (1987). *The History of al-Tabari, the Foundation of the Community* (Vol. VII). State University of New York Press.

Amable, B. (2003). *The Diversity of Modern Capitalism*. Oxford University Press.

Amazon News. (2002, July 18). *Rosewood, a Sweet Aroma that Could Fade Away*.

Amini, I. (2009). *Bar bal bohran: zendegi siasi Ali Amini (On the Wing of Crisis: The Political Biography of Ali Amini)*. nashre Mahi (in Persian).

Amuzegar, J. (1992). The Iranian Economy Before and After the Revolution. *Middle East Journal, 46*(3), 413–425.

Amuzegar, J. (1993). *Iran's Economy under the Islamic Republic.* Tauris.

Amuzegar, J. (2007, Fall). Islamic Social Justice, Iranian Style. *Middle East Policy, 14*(3), 60–78.

Anderson, P. (1974). *Lineages of Absolutist State.* Verso.

Anderton, C. H., & Carter, J. R. (2009). *Principles of Conflict Economics, A Primer for Social Scientists.* Cambridge University Press.

Andreff, W. (2017). Post-Soviet Privatization in the Light of Coase Theorem: Transaction Costs and Governance Costs. In A. Oleinik (Ed.), *The Institutional Economics of Russia's Transformation.* Taylor and Francis. Chapter II.4, pp. 191-212.

Andresen, T. (2006). A Critique of a Post Keynesian Model of Hoarding, and an Alternative Model. *Journal of Economic Behavior and Organizations, 60,* 230–251.

Anonymous, "US National Policy", Office of Science and Technology Policy. Available at: www.ostp.gov/html/US%20National%20Space%20Policy.pdf.

Ansari, A. (2010). *Crisis of Authority: Iran's 2009 Presidential Election.* Chatham House.

Ansari Shushtari, M. (1886–7/1990). *Makasib (Islamic Commercial Law)* (vol. 4, Translated in Persian by Seyyed Muhammad Djavad Zehni Tehrani). Hazeq (in Persian).

Arrow, K. (1951/2012). *Social Choice and Individual Values.* Yale University Press.

Arrow, K. J. (1972). Gifts and Exchanges. *Philosophy and Public Affairs, 1*(4), 343–362.

Arrow, K. J. (1997, June). Invaluable Goods. *Journal of Economic Literature, XXXV*(2), 757–765.

Artières, P., & Lascoumes, P., (dir.) (2004). *Gouverner, enfermer, La prison, un modèle indépassable?* Presses de Sciences Po.

Artières, P., Lascoumes, P., & Salle, G. (2004). Introduction: Gouverner et enfermer, La prison, un modèle indépassable? In Artières Ph. et Lascoumes P. (dir.) [2004], pp. 23–51.

Asemi, F. (2021). "Eslah talab. Osoolgara, digeh tamom majera" (It is the end of both Reformists and Fundamentalists), June 16, BBC, Persian section. Retrieved March 26, 2022, from https://www.bbc.com/persian/iran-57496978.

Aslaksen, S. (2010). Oil and Democracy: More than a Cross-Country Correlation? *Journal of Peace Research, 47*(4), 421–431.

Atabaki, T., Bini, E., & Ehsani, K. (Eds.). (2018). *Working for Oil: Comparative Social Histories of Labor in the Global Oil Industry.* Palgrave Macmillan.

Auty, R. (1993). *Sustaining Development in the Mineral Economies: The Resource Curse Thesis.* Routledge.

Azadi, P., Mirramezani, M., & Mesgaran, M. (2020, April). Migration and Brain Drain from Iran. *Stanford Iran 2040 Project*, Stanford University, Working Paper No. 9.

Babookani, E. A. A., Saadi, H., & Tabeebi Jabali, M. (2018, Summer). Pajooheshay Fqih-i. *Persian, 2*, 405–427.

Bahadori, F. (2010, January 5). *Modir 'Amel-e Mo'aseseye Mali va E'tebari-ye Mehr Taqir kard* (The Director of the Mehr Credit and Finance Institute was changed), Donya-e Eqtesad. Retrieved December 11, 2021, from www.donya-e-eqtesad.com/news/590033/ (in Persian).

Bahramitash, R., & Salehi Esfahani, S. (2011). The Transformation of the Female Labor Market. In R. Bahramitash & S. Salehi Esfahani (Eds.), *Veiled Employment, Islamism and the Political Economy of Women's Employment in Iran* (pp. 123–165). Syracuse University Press., Chapter 4.

Bahro, R. (1978). *The Alternative in Eastern Europe*. New Left Books/Verso.

Barnett, A. (2006, August 27). Special Report: The New Piracy. *The Observer*, p. 9.

Barzel, Y. (1977). An Economic Analysis of Slavery. *Journal of Law and Economics, 20*(1), 87–110.

Barzel, Y. (1997). *Economic Analysis of Property Rights* (2nd ed.). Cambridge University Press.

Barzel, Y. (2015). What Are 'Property Rights', and Why Do They Matter? A Comment on Hodgson's Article. *Journal of Institutional Economics, 11*(4), 719–723.

Bataille, G. (1967). *La part maudite précède de la Notion de dépense*. Les Editions de Minuit.

Bayat, A. (1987). *Workers and Revolution in Iran: A Third World Experience of Workers' Control*. Zed.

Beaud, M. (2018). L'indiscernable début du capitalisme. *Revue internationale de la philosophie, 285*, 279–275.

Behdad, S. (1989). Property Rights in Contemporary Islamic Economic Thought: A Critical Perspective. *Review of Social Economy, 47*(2), 185–211.

Behdad, S. (1994). A Disputed Utopia: Islamic Economics in Revolutionary Iran. *Comparative Studies in Society and History, 36*(4), 775–813.

Behdad, S. (1995). The Post-Revolutionary Economic Crisis. In S. Rahnema & S. Behdad (Eds.), *Iran after the Revolution: Crisis of an Islamic State* (pp. 97–128). London and New York.

Behdad, S. (2006). Islam, Revivalism, and Public Policy. In S. Behdad & F. Nomani (Eds.), *Islam and the Everyday World: Public Policy Dilemmas* (pp. 1–37). Routledge.

Behdad, S., & Nomani, F. (2012). Women's Labour in the Islamic Republic of Iran: Losers and Survivors. *Middle Eastern Studies, 48*(5), 707–733.

Bello, W. (2000). The Asian Financial Crisis: Heroes, Villains, and Accomplices. In W. Paul & R. L. Edwin (Eds.), *Principled World Politics: The Challenge of*

Normative International Relations (pp. 181–190). Rowan and Littlefield Publishers, Inc.

Bello, W. (2004). *The Anti-Developmental State: The Political Economy of Permanent Crisis in the Philippines, by Walden Bello, Herbert Docena, Marissa de Guzman, and Marylou Malig.* Department of Sociology, University of the Philippines and Focus on the Global South.

Benigo, O. (2012). *The Kurds of Iraq: Building a State Within a State.* Lynne Rienner.

Bertalanffy, L. (1950). An Outline of General System Theory. *British Journal for the Philosophy of Science, 1*(2, August 1959), 136–165.

Best, S. (2004). *The Fugitive's Properties: Law and the Poetics of Possession.* Chicago University Press.

Bhattacharya, P., Mitra, D., & Ulubaşoğlu, M. (2019). The Political Economy of Land Reform Enactments: New Cross-National Evidence (1900–2010). *Journal of Development Economics, 139,* 50–68.

Bijani, M., & Hayati, D. (2011). Water Conflict in Agricultural System in Iran: A Human Ecological Analysis. *Journal of Ecology and Environmental Sciences, 2*(2), 27–40.

Binmore, K. (1990). *Essays on the Foundations of Game Theory.* Basil Blackwell.

Bjorvatn, K., & Selvik, K. (2007, February 14). Destructive Competition: Factionalism and Rent-Seeking in Iran. *SAM 8, Discussion Paper,* Norwegian School of Economics and Business Administration.

Bookchin, M. (1977). *The Spanish Anarchists: The Heroic Years, 1868–1936.* Free Life Editions.

Bookchin, M. (1991, October). Libertarian Municipalism: An Overview. *Green Perspectives,* No. 24, Burlington, VT.

Boroujerdi, M., & Rahimkhani, K. (2018). *Postrevolutionary Iran: A Political Handbook.* Syracuse University Press.

Boughton, J. (2003). On the Origins of Fleming-Mundell Model. *IMF Staff Papers, 50*(1), 1–9.

Boulding, K. E. (1962). *Conflict and Defense: A General Theory.* Harper and Brothers.

Bradbury, C. (2020). *"The Water Crisis in Iran,"* 10 September, *The Borgen Project.* Retrieved March 8, 2022, from https://borgenproject.org/ water-crisis-in-iran/.

Braudel, F. (1977). *Afterthoughts on Material Civilization and Capitalism.* Johns Hopkins University Press.

Braudel, F. (1983). *Civilization and Capitalism 15th–18th Century, vol. 2, The Wheels of Commerce.* Book Club Associates.

Brezis, E., & Cariolle, J. (2019). The Revolving Door, State Connections, and Inequality of Influence in the Financial Sector. *Journal of Institutional Economics, 15*(4), 595–614.

Bright, C. (1994, November). Who owns indigenous peoples' DNA? *World Watch*, 7(6), 8.

Bromley, D. W. (1992). The Commons, Common Property, and Environmental Policy. *Environmental and Resource Economics*, 2, 1–17.

Brown, V. (2009). Social Death and Political Life in the Study of Slavery. *American Historical Review*, 114(5), 1231–1249.

Brunner, R. (2010). Shiʿite Doctrine ii. Hierarchy in the Imamiyya. *The Encyclopedia Iranica.* https://www.iranicaonline.org/articles/shiite-doctrine-ii-hierarchy-emamiya

Burawoy, M. (1985). *The Politics of Production: Factory Regimes under Capitalism and Socialism.* Verso.

Bush, W. (1972). Individual Welfare in Anarchy. In Tullock G. (ed.), 1972, pp. 5–18; see also, Stringham E. (ed.) [2005], Chapter 2, pp. 10–23.

Bush, W., & Mayer, L. (1974). Some Implications of Anarchy for the Distribution of Property. *Journal of Economic Theory*, 8, 401–412.

Calder, N. (*2010*). *Islamic Jurisprudence in the Classical Era.* Cambridge University Press.

Caldicott, H. (2002). *The Nuclear Danger, George W. Bush's Military-Industrial Complex.* The New Press.

Calvin, D. (2021). *Entrepreneurial Communities: An Alternative to the State.* Book Villages.

Caponera, D. A. (1954). *Water laws in Moslem countries.* Food and Agricultural Organization, U.N.

Carvalho, J.-P. (2013). Veiling. *The Quarterly Journal of Economics*, 128(1), 337–370.

Chabas, F. (1995). *Les accidents de la circulation.* Dalloz.

Chaichian, M. (2012). The New Phase of Globalization and Brain Drain: Migration of Educated and Skilled Iranians to the U.S. *International Journal of Social Economics*, 39(1/2), 18–38.

Chaudhry, M. S. (*1992*). *Taxation in Islam and Modern Taxes.* Impact Publications International.

Chaudhry, M. S. (1999). Retrieved August 29, 2021, from www.muslimtents.com.

Chen, J. (2006). There's No Such Thing as Biopiracy…and It's a Good Thing Too. *McGeorge Law Review*, 37, 1–32.

Clinton, B. (2005). *My Life* (Vol. 2). Vintage Books.

Coase, R. (1960, October). The Problem of Social Cost. *The Journal of Law and Economics*, III, 1–44.

Coid, J., Babbington, P., Brugha, D., Jenkins, R., Farrell, M., Lewis, G., & Singleton, N. (2002). Ethnic Differences in Prisoners: Criminality and Psychiatry Morbidity. *British Journal of Psychiatry*, 181, 473–480.

Cole, D., & Grossman, P. (2002). The Meaning of Property Rights: Law Versus Economics? *Land Economics*, 78(3), 317–330.

Collier, P. (1999). On the Economic Consequences of Civil War. *Oxford Economic Papers, 51*(1), 168–183.

Collier, P., & Bannon, I. (2003). *Natural Resources and Violent Conflict: Options and Actions*. World Bank.

Collier, P., & Hoeffler, A. (1998). On the Economic Causes of Civil War. *Oxford Economic Papers, 50*, 563–573.

Commons, J. (1899–1900/1965). *A Sociological View of Sovereignty by John R. Commons [1899–1900]*. Augustus M. Kelley, Bookseller.

Commons, J. (1924/1995). *Legal Foundations of Capitalism* (With a New Introduction by Jeff Biddle & Warren J. Samuels). Transaction Publishers.

Commons, J. R. (1931). Institutional Economics. *American Economics Review, 21*, 648–657.

Commons, J. (1970). *The Economics of Collective Action*. University of Wisconsin Press.

Cooter, R., & Ulen, T. (2012). *Law and Economics* (6th ed.). Addison-Wesley.

Correa, C. (2000). *Intellectual Property Rights, the WTO and Developing Countries: The TRIPS Agreement and Policy Options*. Zed Books.

Coville, T. (2002). *L'Economie de l'Iran Islamique: Entre ordre et désordres*. L'Harmattan.

Coville, T. (2013). How to Transform a Rent-Seeking Economy: The Case of Iran. In H. E. Chehabi, F. Khosrokhavar, & C. Therme (Eds.), *Iran and the Challenges of the Twenty-First Century Essays in Honour of Muhammad-Reza Djalili*. Mazda Publishers.

Coville, T. (2017). "The Economic Activities of Pasdaran" In Vahabi, Mehrdad and Coville, Thierry (Dir.), L'économie politique de la République islamique d'Iran, *Revue internationale des études du développement*, No. 229, mai, pp. 87–107.

Cowen, T., & Sutter, D. (2007). Conflict, Cooperation and Competition in Anarchy. In E. Stringham (Ed.), *Anarchy and the Law, The Political Economy of Choice* (pp. 315–321). Transaction Publishers.

Coyne, C. (2005). Social Interaction Without the State. In E. Stringham (Ed.), *Anarchy, State and Public Choice* (pp. 49–59). Edward Elgar.

Crettez, B. (2020). Pareto-Minimality in the Jungle. *Public Choice, 182*, 495–508.

Cronk, L., & Leech, B. L. (2013). *Meeting at Grand Central: Understanding the Social and Evolutionary Roots of Cooperation*. Princeton.

Csaba, L. (2022). Illiberal Economic Policies. In S. Holmes et al. (Eds.), *Routledge Handbook of Illiberalism* (pp. 674–691). Routledge.

Cuaresma, J., Oberhofer, H., & Raschky, P. (2011). Oil and the Duration of Dictatorships. *Public Choice, 148*(3/4), 505–530.

Cuddington, J. T. (1986). *Capital Flight: Estimates, Issues and Explanations*. Princeton Studies in International Finance, No. 58.

Da Siva, N. (2020). Mutualité et capitalisme entre 1789 et 1947: de la subversion à l'intégration. *RECMA, 357,* 36–51.

Dabashi, H. (2016, March 10). Babak Zanjani and the Complicity of Iran. Aljazeera. https://www.aljazeera.com/opinions/2016/3/10/babak-zanjani-and-the-complicity-of-iran/

Dago, J. (2012). *L'Investissement Direct Etranger en Côte d'Ivoire, Economie Politique et Changement Institutionnel.* l'Harmattan.

Dana, L., & Wright, R. (2015). Bazaar Economies, Modern Networks and Entrepreneurship. In Wright, R. (ed.), Wiley Encyclopedia of Management, 2015 - Wiley Online Library. https://doi.org/10.1002/9781118785317.weom030005

Dareini, A. A. (2008, August 31). Iranian Conservative Attacks President on Economy. *Worldnews.* Retrieved December 18, 2021, from https://article.wn.com/view/2008/08/31/Iranian_conservative_attacks_president_on_economy/.

Darrussalam, A. Z. (2010). *The concept of al-Kanz in Qur'an (The Thematic Analysis of Qur'anic Verses).* A Thesis in Partial Fulfillment of the Requirements for the Degree of Sarana Theologi Islam (S.Th.I) of the Faculty of Ushuluddin and Philosophy of UIN Alauddin Makassar, Indonesia.

Dawood, N. J. (2014). *The Koran* (Translated with notes by N.J. Dawood). Penguin Books.

Dean, M. (2008). *Robbing the Jews, the Confiscation of Jewish Property in the Holocaust, 1933–1945.* Cambridge University Press.

Deleuze, G. (1996). *"Post-scriptum sur les sociétés de contrôle", dans Pourparlers* (pp. 240–247). Minuit.

Demsetz, H. (1964). The Exchange and Enforcement of Property Rights. *Journal of Law and Economics, 7,* 11–26.

Dornbusch, R. (1991). Experiences with Extreme Monetary Instability. In S. Commander (Ed.), *Managing Inflation in Socialist Economies in Transition* (Economic Development Institute of the World Bank, EDI Seminar Series) (pp. 175–196). The World Bank., chapter 8.

Dornbusch, R., & Mussa, M. (1975). Consuption, Real Balances and the Hoarding Function. *International Economic Review, 16*(2), 415–421.

Dostoyevsky, F. ([1861–62] 2003). *The House of the Dead.* Penguin Books.

Dreyfus, M. (2001). *Liberté, Égalité, Mutualité: mutualisme et syndicalisme, 1852-1967.* Éditions de l'Atelier.

Dunmore, T. (1980). *The Stalinist Command System: The Soviet State Apparatus and Economic Policy, 1945-1953.* Macmillan.

Economist. (1993, September 25). *For the Oppressed,* vol. 328.

Economist. (2021, August 28th-September 3rd). *Where Next for Global Jihad?*

Eftekhari, A. (2004, Summer). "Shari sazi ghodrat siasi; daramadi bar jaygah amnyat dar andisheh va amal foghahay shia dar asre safavi" (The Islamization of the Political Power; A Prelude to the Place of Security in the Thought and

Deed of the Shi'i Faqih During the Safavid Era). *Faslnameh Motaleeat Rahboordi, 7*(2), 275–298 (in Persian).

Ehsani, K. (2009, Spring). Survival Through Dispossession: Privatization of Public Goods in the Islamic Republic. *Middle East Report, 250,* 26–33.

Ehsani, K. (2013). The Politics of Property in the Islamic Republic of Iran. In S. Amir Arjomand & N. Brown (Eds.), *The Rule of Law, Islam, and Constitutional Politics in Egypt and Iran* (pp. 153–178). SUNY Press., Chapter 5.

Ehteshami, A. (2010). *Dynamics of Power in Contemporary Iran.* Emirates Centre for Strategic Studies and Research.

Ellickson, R. (1991). *Order Without Law, How Neighbors Settle Disputes.* Harvard University Press.

Ellickson, R. (1993). Property in Land. *Yale Law Journal, 102,* 1317–1400.

Emmer, R. (1959, May). A Concept of Hoarding. *The Review of Economics and Statistics, 41*(2, Part 1), 162–169.

Enayat, H. (1982). *Modern Islamic Political Thought.* University of Texas Press.

Encyclopedia Iranica. (1987). "Bonyad Chahid," Costa Mesa, Mazda, pp. 360–361.

Engels, F. (1877/1966). *Herr Eugen Dühring's Revolution in Science (Anti-Dühring),* International Publisher.

Engels, F. (1883/1993, March 17). *Speech at the Grave of Karl Marx Highgate Cemetery, London.* Transcribed: by Mike Lepore. https://www.marxists.org/archive/marx/works/1883/death/burial.htm

Engels, F. (1887/1968). *The Role of Force in History, a Study of Bismarck's Policy of Blood and Iron.* International Publisher.

Erdbrink, T. (2013, October 4). To This Tycoon, Iran's Sanctions Were Like Gold. *The New York Times.* Retrieved December 10, 2010, from https://www.nytimes.com/2013/10/05/world/middleeast/to-this-tycoon-iran-sanctions-are-like-gold.html

Esping Andersen, G. (1990). *The Three Worlds of Welfare Capitalism.* Polity Press.

Esposito, J. L. (1995). The Islamic World: Past and Present. *Oxford Islamic Studies Online.* Retrieved August 27, 2021.

Fanselow, F. (1990). The Bazaar Economy or How Bizarre is the Bazaar Really? *MAN, New Series, 25*(2), 250–265.

Farahmand, M. (2004, September 21). "*Monaghesheh-ye Majles va Dowlat-e Iran bar sar-e dow sherkat-e torkiyeh-ie* (The Quarrel between the Majles and the Government Regarding Two Turkish Companies). *BBC. Persian.* Retrieved December 13, 2021, from www.bbc.co.uk/persian/business/story/2004/09/040921_mf_turkcell.shtml. (in Persian).

Fararu. (2009, May 12). Mowjoodi-ye Hesab-e Zakhireh-ye Arzi haft milyard dollar ast (The balance of the Currency Reserve Fund is 7 billion US dollars). https://fararu.com. (in Persian).

Fassihi, F. (2020, June 7). A Daughter Is Beheaded, and Iran Asks if Women Have a Right to Safety. *Los Angeles Times*. Retrieved March 20, 2022, from https://www.nytimes.com/2020/06/07/world/middleeast/honor-killing-iran-women.html.

Filkins, D. (2012, March 12). The Deep State. *The New Yorker*. Retrieved January 6, 2022.

Financial Times. (1997, July 17). *State Foundations Dominate Economy*, p. 4.

Findlay, R. (1990, March). The 'Triangular Trade' and the Atlantic Economy of the Eighteenth Century: A Simple General Equilibrium Model. *Essays in International Finance*, No. 177, Princeton University, Department of Economics.

Floor, W. (2001). *Safavid Government Institutions*. Mazda Publishers.

Forozan, H. (2016). *The Military in Post-Revolutionary Iran, the Evolution and Roles of the Revolutionary Guards*. Routledge.

Foucault, M. (1975). *Surveiller et punir*. Gallimard.

Foweraker, J. (1987). Corporatist Strategies and the Transition to Democracy in Spain. *Comparative Politics, 20*(1), 57–72.

Friedman, D. (2007). Law as a Private Good: A Response to Tyler Cowen on the Economics of Anarchy. In Stringham E., pp. 284–291.

Frisch, R. (1933). Propagation Problems and Impulse Problems in Dynamic Economics. In *Economic Essays in Honour of Gustav Cassel* (pp. 171–205). George Allen & Unwin.

Fudenberg, D., & Tirole, J. (1986, July). A Theory of Exit in Duopoly. *Econometrica, 54*(4), 943–960.

Fujinaga, A. F. (2018). Islamic Law in Post-Revolutionary Iran. In A. M. Emon & A. Rumee (Eds.), *The Oxford Handbook of Islamic Law*. Oxford University Press.

Galbraith, J. K. (2004). *The Economics of Innocent Fraud, Truth for Our Time*. Houghton Mifflin Company.

Galbraith, J. (2009). *The Predator State, How Conservatives Abandoned the Free Market and Why Liberals Should Too* (Paperback ed.). Free Press.

Gambetta, D. (1996). *The Sicilian Mafia*. Harvard University Press.

Garnett, R. F., Jr., Lewis, P., & Ealy, L. T. (Eds.). (2014). *Commerce and Community: Ecologies of Social Cooperation (Economics as Social Theory)*. Routledge.

Geertz, C. (1978). The Bazaar Economy: Information and Search in Peasant Marketing. *American Economic Review, 68*(2), 28–32.

Geoloso, V., & Leeson, P. (2020). Are Anarcho-Capitalists Insane? Medieval Icelandic Conflict Institutions in Comparative Perspectives. *Revue d'Economie Politique, 130*(6), 957–974.

Gernet, J. (1962). *Daily Life in China on the Eve of Mongol Invasion, 1250–1276*. Stanford University Press.

Ghaninejad, M. (2022, January 29). Charxesh be chap (A turn to the left). *Tejarat Farda*, Number 442.

Ghartabi, M. i. A. (1973). *Tafsir Ghartabi (Ghartabi's exegesis)* (Vol. 8). Markaz Etellat va Madarek Islami. http://dl.islamicdoc.com/site/catalogue/457506

Ghosh, P. (2013, May 5). Iran's Supreme Leader Ayatollah Khamenei…A Multi-Billionaire and BMW Car Dealer? *International Business Times*. Retrieved December 5, 2021, from https://www.ibtimes.com/irans-supreme-leader-ayatollah-khamenei-multi-billionaire-bmw-car-dealer-1233899.

Gide, C. (1898/2018). *Principes d'Economie Politique* (6th ed.) Hachette-livre BNF.

Gobadi, S. (2021, July 25). How IRGC Created and Amplifies Iran's Water Crisis. *The National Council of Resistance of Iran (NCRI)*. Retrieved March 8, 2022, from https://www.einnews.com/pr_news/547176674/video-how-irgc-created-and-amplifies-iran-s-water-crisis.

Goldberg, E., Wibbels, E., & Myukiyehe, E. (2008). Lessons from Strange Cases: Democracy, Development, and the Resource Curse in the U.S. States. *Comparative Political Studies, 41*, 477–514.

Goldsmith, E. (1968). The Qanats of Iran. *Scientific American, 218*(4), 94–105.

Goldstone, J. (1998). Introduction. In G. Jack (Ed.), *The Encyclopedia of Political Revolutions* (pp. xxxi–xxxviii). Congressional Quarterly Inc.

Goodey, C. (1980, June). Workers' Councils in Iranian Factories. *MERIP Reports*.

Gunning, P. (1972/2005). Towards a Theory of the Evolution of Government. In Stringham E., pp. 60–66.

Haavelmo, T. (1954). *A Study in the Theory of Economic Evolution*. North-Holland.

Hall, E. (1989, July 12). Iran Names Two for Presidential Poll; Rafsanjani favourite. *Reuters*.

Hall, P., & Soskice, D. (2001). *Varieties of Capitalism: The Institutional Foundations of Comparative Advantage*. Oxford University Press.

Hamilton, C. (2006). Biodiversity, Biopiracy and Benefits: What Allegations of Biopiracy Tell Us About Intellectual Property. *Developing World Bioethics, 6*(3), 158–173.

Hanke, S., & Krus, N. (2013). World Hyperinflations. In R. Parker & R. Whaples (Eds.), *Routledge Handbook of Major Events in Economic History* (pp. 367–377). Routledge., chapter 30.

Hardin, G. (1968). The Tragedy of the Commons. *Science, New Series, 162*(3859), 1243–1248.

Hargreaves Heap, S. P., & Varoufakis, Y. (1995). *Game Theory, a Critical Introduction*. Routledge.

Harris, K. (2012). *The Martyrs Welfare State: Politics of Social Policy in the Islamic Republic of Iran*. PhD dissertation, The John Hopkins University, Baltimore, Maryland, August.

Harris, K. (2013). The Rise of the Subcontracting State: Politics of Pseudo-Privatization in the Islamic Republic of Iran. *International Journal of Middle East Studies, 45*, 45–70.

Harris, K. (2017). *A Social Revolution Politics and the Welfare State in Iran.* University of California Press.

Hart, O. (1995). *Firms, Contracts, and Financial Structure.* Clarendon Press.

Hart, O. (2017). Incomplete Contracts and Control. *American Economic Review, 107*(7), 1731–1752.

Hashemi Rafsanjani, A. A. (2007, December 29). *Etemad* (in Persian).

Hashemi Rafsanjani, A. A. (2008, December 11). Rafsanjani Criticizes Government Bodies for not Implementing Article 44. *Fars New Agency.* (in Persian).

Hassan-Yari, H. (2005, August 5). Iran: Defending the Islamic Revolution—The Corps of the Matter. *RadioFreeEurope, RadioLiberty.* Retrieved December 13, 2021, from http://www.rferl.org/content/article/1060431.html (in Persian).

Hau, C. (2017). What Is Crony Capitalism? *Emerging State Project (EPS) Grips,* Retrieved July 7, 2022, from http://www3.grips.ac.jp/~esp/en/event/what-is-%E2%80%9Ccrony-capitalism%E2%80%9D/.

Hazleton, L. (2010). *After the Prophet: The Epic Story of the Shia-Sunni Split in Islam.* Anchor Books.

Hemmati, A. (2022, January 8). Hoshdar arzi Hemmati be dowlat Raisi, chera dowlat davazahom arz tarjihi ra hazf nakard? (Hemmati's Warning to Raisi's Government, Why the 12th Government did not Abolish Preferential Currency Rate). *Khabaronline.* Retrieved February 13, 2022, from https://www.khabaronline.ir/news/1590360/. (in Persian).

Hess, J. R., & Schmidt, P. J. (2000, January). The First Blood Banker: Oswald Hope Robertson. *Transfusion, 40,* 110–113.

Hirschman, A. (1970). *Exit, Voice, and Loyalty.* Cambridge University Press.

Hirschman, A. (1977a). A Generalized Linkage Approach to Development, with Special Reference to Staples. *Economic Development and Cultural Change, 25,* 67–98.

Hirschman, A. O., (1977b/2013). *The Passions and the Interests: Political Arguments for Capitalism before Its Triumph.* Princeton University Press.

Hirshleifer, J. (1995). Anarchy and Its Breakdown. *Journal of Political Economy, 103,* 25–52.

Hirshleifer, J. (2001). *The Dark Side of the Force, Economic Foundations of Conflict Theory.* Cambridge University Press.

Hodgson, G. (2015). Much of the 'Economics of Property Rights' Devalues Property and Legal Rights. *Journal of Institutional Economics, 11*(4), 683–709.

Hogarthy, T. (2005). Cases in Anarchy. In Stringham E. (ed.), pp. 98–112.

Hohfeld, W. (1913). Some Fundamental Legal Conceptions as Applied in Judicial Reasoning. *Yale Law Journal, 23,* 16–59.

Holcombe, R. (2007). Government: Unnecessary but Inevitable. In Stringham E. (ed.), pp. 354–370.

Holcombe, R. (2015). Political Capitalism. *Cato Journal, 35*(1), 41–66.

Holcombe, R. (2018). *Political Capitalism, How Economic and Political Power Is Made and Maintained.* Cambridge University Press.

Honneth, A. (2018). 'Capitalism' - Economy, Society or a Form of Life? Greatness and Limits of Marx' Theory of Society,' Lecture Delivered at the Hamburger Institut für Sozialforschung 4.5.2018, https://www.youtube.com/watch?v=BB6epE9YVz0

Hooglund, E. J. (1982). *Land and Revolution in Iran 1960-1980.* University of Texas Press.

Hoominfar, E., & Zanganeh, N. (2021). The Brick Wall to Break: Women and the Labor Market Under the Hegemony of the Islamic Republic of Iran. *International Feminist Journal of Politics, 23*(2), 263–286.

Hosseini, S. R., & Sadeghi Fadaki, S. J. (2019). "Anfal", *Daerotal-maref Koran Karim* (The Encyclopedia of the Koran) in Persian, *5*, 15–24. (in Persian).

Houba, H., Luttens, R. I., & Weikard, H.-P. (2017). Pareto Efficiency in the Jungle. *Review of Economic Design, 21*(3), 153–161.

Humphreys, M. (2005). Natural Resources, Conflict and Conflict Resolution. *Journal of Conflict Resolution, 49*, 508–537.

Ibn Al-Mufid, M., & Ibn Noman, M. (1989). *Al-Muqni'ah (The Legally Sufficient)* (2nd ed.). Daftar Entesharat Islami.

Ibn Ishaq. (2004, June 25). The Earliest Biography of Muhammad. https://web.archive.org/web/20040625103910/ http://www.hraic.org/hadith/ibn_ishaq.html#khaybar#khaybar

Ilyess, E. K. (2012). Ethnic Minorities and Integration Process in France and the Netherlands: An Institutionalist Perspective. *American Journal of Economics and Sociology, 71*, 151–183.

Inikori, J. (2017). The Development of Capitalism in the Atlantic World: England, the Americas, and West Africa, 1400–1900. *Labor History, 58*(2), 138–153.

International Monetary Fund. (1998, April). *Islamic Republic of Iran. Recent Economic Developments,* IMF, Staff Country Report n 98/27, Washington DC.

International Monetary Fund. (2010, April). *World Economic Outlook Database.* Online. Available at: www.imf.org/external/pubs/ft/weo/2010/01/weo-data/index.aspx. Retrieved December 27, 2021.

Iordachi, C., & Bauerkämper, A. (Eds.). (2014). *2014, The Collectivization of Agriculture in Communist East Europe, Comparison and Entanglements.* Central European University Press.

Iran (Islamic Republic of)'s Constitution of 1979 with Amendments through 1989, constituteproject.org, Retrieved June 28, 2021.

Issawi, C. (1950). *An Arab Philosophy of History; Selections from the Prolegomena of Ibn Khaldun of Tunis (1332–1406)* (Translated and arranged by Issawi). John Murray.

Jafari, P. (2013, Fall). Reasons to Revolt: Iranian Oil Workers in the 1970s. *International Labor and Working-Class History, 84,* 195–217.

Jafari, P. (2018). Fluid History: Oil Workers and the Iranian Revolution. In T. Atabaki, E. Bini, K. Ehsani, & K. (Eds.), *Working for Oil: Comparative Social Histories of Labor in the Global Oil Industry* (pp. 69–98). Palgrave Macmillan.

Jafari, P. (2021). The Showras in the Iranian Revolution, Labour Relations and the State in the Iranian Oil Industry, 1979–82. In P. Brandon, P. Jafari, & S. Müller (Eds.), *Worlds of Labour Turned Upside Down Revolutions and Labour Relations in Global Historical Perspective* (pp. 252–285). Brill, chapter 9.

Jahangiri, I. (2016). Nagofteh-hay Jahangiri az door zadan tahreemha va arz 4200 tomani (Jahangiri's unsaid report on detouring economic boycotts and the 4200 tomans currency). *Ensafnews,* 14 March 2021, http://www.ensafnews.com/286750/, Retrieved February 13, 2022 (in Persian).

Jahanguiri, I. (2016). Discourse in the Conference on Knowledge-Based oil Industry. *Sharq,* 17 April, No. 2561 (in Persian).

Janos, K. (1998). The Place of the Soft Budget Constraint in Economic Theory. *Journal of Comparative Economics, 26,* 11–17.

Jebrayli, S. Y. (2018). *Revayat Rahbari, monasbeat jomhooryat va islamyat dar intekhab Valieh Faqih (The Story of Leadership, the Relationship between Republic and Islam in Electing the Supreme Jurisprudent).* Intesharat Islami. (in Persian).

Jensen, N., & Wantchekon, L. (2004). Resource Wealth and Political Regimes in Africa. *Comparative Political Studies, 37,* 816–841.

Johns, D. (2006). *The Crimes of Saddam Hossein, 1988 The Anfal Campaign.* Frontline World. Retrieved July 17, 2022, from https://www.pbs.org/frontlineworld/stories/iraq501/events_anfal.html.

Jordan, J. (2006). Pillage and Property. *Journal of Economic Theory, 131*(1), 26–44.

Juma, C. (1989). *The Gene Hunters: Biotechnology and the Scramble for Seeds.* Zed Books.

Kani, M., & Reza, M. (2000). *Anfal va asar an dar Islam (Anfal and its effects in Islam).* Bostan ketab Qom. (in Persian).

Karaki, Ali ibn Hossein ibn Abdol-Ali Ameli. (1510/1992). *Ghat al-lejaj fi tahghigh hal al-Kharaj (Ending with Obstinacy Regarding an Inquiry into the Solution of Tribute Issue).* Moasseseh Nashr Islami.

Karimian, R. (2009, Spring). The Reformist Moment and the Press. *Middle East Report, 250,* 16.

Karl, T. L. (1997). *The Paradox of Plenty: Oil Booms and Petro-States.* University of California Press.

Karshenas, M. (2021). *Minimum Wages, Labor Market Institutions, and the Distribution of Earning in Iran.* The Economic Research Forum, Working Paper No. 1478 August.

Kasravi, A. (2006). *History of the Iranian Constitutional Revolution: Tārikh-e Mashrute-ye Iran, Volume I, translated into English by Evan Siegel*. Mazda Publications.

Katouzian, M. A. (1974). Land Reform in Iran, A Case Study in the Political Economy of Social Engineering. *The Journal of Peasant Studies, 1*(2), 220–239.

Katzman, K. (1993). *The Warriors of Islam: Iran's Revolutionary Guard*. Westview Press.

Katzman, K. (2006, August 6). Iran's Bonyads: Economic Strengths and Weaknesses. *Emirates Center for Strategic Studies and Research*.

Kaviani, Z. (2021). Dar ahmyaat roshd nerkh sarmyeh gozari, avamel moasser bar roshed eqtesadi saal 1400 kodamand (On the Importance of the Rate of Investment: What Are the Factors Influencing the Growth Rate in 2021–2022?)", *Tejarat Farda*, No. 404. 1 May (in Persian).

Kazemi, F., & Abrahamian, E. (1978). The Nonrevolutionary Peasantry of Modern Iran. *Iranian Studies, 11*(1/4), 259–304.

Keddie, N. R., & Gasiorowski, M. J. (Eds.). (1990). *Neither East nor West: Iran, the United States, and the Soviet Union*. Yale University Press.

Keen, D. (2012). *Useful Enemies, When Waging Wars Is More Important than Winning Them*. Yale University Press.

Keshavarzian, A. (2007). *Bazaar and State in Iran, the Politics of the Tehran Marketplace*. Cambridge University Press.

Keynes, J. M. (1936). *The General Theory of Eemployment, Interest and Money*. Macmillan.

Khalaji, M. (2011). *Nazm-e Novin-e Rohaniat Dar Iran (The New Order of the Clerical Establishment in Iran)*. H&S Media (in Persian).

Khazani, O., & Bulos, N. (2021, August 2). As Water Table Lowers, Tehran and Much of Iran are Slowly Sinking. *Los Angels Times*, Retrieved March 8, 2022, from https://www.latimes.com/world-nation/story/2021-08-02/lower-water-table-climate-change-tehran-iran-sinking.

Khomeini, R. (1970). *Velayat Fqih*. Daftar Nashre Falagh. Translated in 1981, *Islam and Revolution, Writings and Declarations of Imam Khomeini*. Mizan Press.

Khomeini, R. (2000). *Ketab Al-Bey (The Book of Sale)* (Vol. 3). Moassesseh tanzeem va nashr asar al-Imam al-Khomeini.

Kimbrell, A., (1995, July/August), "The Body Enclosed, The Commodification of Human 'Parts'", *The Ecologist*, Vol. 25, No. 4, pp. 134–141.

Klebnikov, P. (2003, July 21). Millionaire Mullahs. *Forbes*.

Klein, L. (2006). Ragnar Frisch's Conception of the Business Cycle. In S. Strom (Ed.), *Econometrics and Economic Theory in the 20th Century*, Cambridge Collections Online, Cambridge University Press.

Klein, B., Crawford, R., & Alchian, A. (1978). Vertical Integration, Appropriable Rents, and the Competitive Contracting Process. *Journal of Law and Economics, 21*(2), 297–326.

Knight, F. (1947). Human Nature and World Democracy. In *Freedom and Reform* (pp. 308–310). Harper and Bros.

Kolko, G. (1963). *The Triumph of Conservatism: A Reinterpretation of American History, 1900–1916.* The Free Press of Glencoe.

Kolko, G. (1965). *Railroads and Regulation 1877-1916.* Princeton University Press.

Kooch, Y., Azizi Mehr, M., & Hosseini, S. M. (2020). The Effect of Forest Degradation Intensity on Soil Function Indicators in Northern Iran. *Ecological Indicators, 114,* 106324. https://doi.org/10.1016/j.ecolind.2020.106324

Kornai, J. (1971a). *Anti-Equilibrium, On Economic Systems Theory and the Tasks of Research.* American Elsevier Publishing Company, Inc.

Kornai, J. (1971b). Economic Systems Theory and General Equilibrium Theory. *Acta Oeconomica, 6*(4), 297–317.

Kornai, J. (1979). Resource-Constrained Versus Demand-Constrained Systems. *Econometrica, 47*(4), 801–819.

Kornai, J. (1980). *Economics of Shortage.* North-Holland.

Kornai, J. (1983). The Health of Nations: Reflections on the Analogy between the Medical Sciences and Economics. *Kyklos, 36*(2), 191–212.

Kornai, J. (1984). Bureaucratic and Market Coordination. *Osteuropa Wirtschaft, 29*(4), 306–319. Reprinted in: Kornai Janos (1990). *Vision and Reality, market and state, contradictions and dilemma revisited.* Routledge, pp. 1–19.

Kornai, J. (1990a). The Affinity between Ownership Forms and Coordination Mechanisms: The Common Experience of Reform in Socialist Countries. *Journal of Economic Perspectives, 4*(3), 131–147.

Kornai, J. (1990b). *The Road to a Free Economy: Shifting from a Socialist System: The Example of Hungary.* W.W. Norton.

Kornai, J. (1992). *The Socialist System. The political economy of Communism.* Princeton University Press and Oxford University Press.

Kornai, J. (1994). Transformational Recession: The Main Causes. *Journal of Comparative Economics, 19*(1), 39–63.

Kornai, J. (2000a). What the Change of System from Socialism to Capitalism does and does not Mean? *The Journal of Economic Perspectives, 14*(1), 27–42.

Kornai, J. (2000b). *Ten Years After 'The Road to a Free Economy': The Author's Self-Evaluation.* Paper for the World Bank 'Annual Bank Conference on Development Economics-ABCDE', April 18–20, Washington, DC.

Kornai, J. (2010). Innovation and Dynamism: Interaction between Systems and Technical Progress. In G. Roldand (Ed.), *Economies in Transition, Studies in Development Economics and Policy* (pp. 14–56). Palgrave Macmillan.

Kornai, J. (2013). *Dynamism, Rivalry, and the Surplus Economy: Two Essays on the Nature of Capitalism.* Oxford University Press.

Kornai, J. (2016). The System Paradigm Revisited, Clarification and Additions in the Light of Experiences in the Post-Socialist Region. *Acta Oeconomica, 66*(4), 547–596.

Kowsar, N., & Nader, A. (2019, 25 February). Iran Is Committing Suicide by Dehydration. *Foreign Policy.* Retrieved March 8, 2022, form https://foreignpolicy.com/2019/02/25/iran-is-committing-suicide-by-dehydration/.

Krätke, M. (2020). Capitalism. In M. Musto (Ed.), *The Marx Revival. Key Concepts and New Interpretations.* Cambridge University Press.

Kreps, D. M. (1990). *A Course in Microeconomic Theory.* Princeton University Press.

Kreps, D. M. (1991). *Game Theory and Economic Modelling.* Oxford University Press.

Kristof, N. (2011, 27 October). *Crony Capitalism Comes Home.* The New York Times. Retrieved July 7, 2022, from https://www.nytimes.com/2011/10/27/opinion/kristof-crony-capitalism-comes-homes.html.

Krugman, P. (2013, April 11). *The Conscience of a Liberal, Monetary Policy in a Liquidity Trap.* Retrieved February 22, 2022, from https://krugman.blogs.nytimes.com/2013/04/11/monetary-policy-in-a-liquidity-trap/.

Krugman, P., & Obstfeld, M. (2003). *International Economics, Theory and Practice* (6th ed.). Addison Wesley.

Kulayni, M. I. Y. (1988). *Al-Kafi (Extant)* (Vol. 1, 4th ed.). Dar al-kotob al-islamieh.

Kuran, T. (2001). The Provision of Public Goods under Islamic Law: Origins, Impact, and Limitations of the Waqf System. *Law and Society Review, 35*(4), 841–897.

Kuran, T. (2005). The Absence of the Corporation in Islamic Law: Origins and Persistence. *The American Journal of Comparative Law, 53*(4), 785–834.

Kuran, T. (2018). Islam and Economic Performance. *Journal of Economic Literature, 56*(4), 1292–1359.

Kurtis, G., & Hooglund, E. (Eds.). (2008). *Iran, A Country Study.* Washington DC.

Küttler, W. (2008). *Kapitalismus. Historisch-Kritisches Wörterbuch des Marxismus 7.1* (pp. 238–272). Argument-Verlag.

Lambton, A. K. S. (1969). *The Persian Land Reform.* Clarendon Press.

Lane, P., & Tornell, A. (1996). Power, Growth, and the Voracity Effect. *Journal of Economic Growth, 1,* 213–241.

Lane, P., & Tornell, A. (1999). The Voracity Effect. *American Economic Review, 89,* 22–46.

Lange, O. (1958). The Role of Planning in Socialist Economy. *Indian Economic Review, 4*(2), 1–15.

Lawson, G. (2019). *Anatomies of Revolution.* Cambridge University Press.

Le Billon, P. (2001). The Political Ecology of War: Natural Resources and Armed Conflicts. *Political Geography, 20*(5), 561–584.

Leeson, P. T. (2007). Anarchy, Monopoly, and Predation. *Journal of Institutional and Theoretical Economics (JITE), 163,* 467–482.

Leeson, P. T. (2009). The Laws of Lawlessness. *Journal of Legal Studies, 38,* 471–503.

Leeson, P. T. (2014). *Anarchy Unbound: Why Self-Governance Works Better than You Think*. Cambridge University Press.

Leeson, P., & Stringham, E. (2007). Is Government Inevitable? Comment on Holcombe's Analysis. In E. Stringham (Ed.), *Anarchy and the Law, the Political Economy of Choice* (pp. 371–376). Transaction Publishers.

Leilaz, S. (2013). *Mooj dovam, tajodod ameraneh dar Iran, Tarikh barnameh-hay omrani sevoom ta panjom (The Second Wave, the Authoritarian Modernity in Iran, the History of the Development Planning from the Third to the Fifth)*. Niloofar publication. (in Persian).

Leilaz, S. (2019). Salaneh 10 ta 20 miliard dollar az keshvar kharej mishavad (10 to 20 billion Dollars Fled the Country Annually). *Fararu*, 4 September 2019 (in Persian).

Lenin, V. I. (1917/1964, April). The Dual Power. In *Collected Works* (Vol. 24, pp. 38–41). Progress Publishers.

Lenin, V. I. (1920/1975–1979). "Report on the Work of the Council of People's Commissars" (December 22, 1920). In *Collected Works* (Vol. 36). Progress Publishers.

Leshem, D. (2016). What did the Ancient Greeks mean by Oikonomia? *Journal of Economic Perspectives, 30*(1), 225–231.

Levy Yeyati, E., & Rey, H. (2006). Financial Dollarization: Evaluating the Consequences. *Economic Policy, 21*(45), 63–118.

Lindblom, C. E. (1977). *Politics and Markets: The World's Political Economic Systems*. Basic Books.

Locke, J. (1690/1952). *The Second Treatise of Government* (Edited with an introd. by Thomas P. Peardon). The Liberal Arts Press.

Love, J. (1991). *Antiquity and Capitalism: Max Weber and the Sociological Foundations of Roman Civilization*. Routledge.

Lupton, S. (2011). *Économie des Déchets. Une Approche Institutionnaliste*, Collection "Ouvertures économiques", Bruxelles, De Boeck.

MacCallum, S. H. (2003). The Entrepreneurial Community in Light of Advancing Business Practices and Technologies. In MacCallum, Spencer Heath, D. Klein, & F. Foldvary (Eds.), *The Half-Life of Policy Rationales*. New York University Press. chapter 12.

Madlovics, B., & Magyar, B. (2021). Post-Communist Predation: Modeling Reiderstvo Practices in Contemporary States. *Public Choice, 187*(3-4), 247–273.

Magyar, B. (2016). *Post-Communist Mafia State: The Case of Hungary*. CEU Press.

Mahamed, A. (2012, Spring). "Tafsir Tatbeeghi Ayeh Sharifeh Anfal" (*A comparative interpretation of the honorable verse of Anfal*). *Faslnameh Motalleat Tafsiri, 3*(9), 81–104. (in Persian).

Mahdavy, H. (1970). The Patterns and Problems of Economic Development in Rentier States: The Case of Iran. In M. Cook (Ed.), *Studies in economic history of the Middle East* (pp. 428–467). Oxford University Press.

Makarem Shirazi, N. (2016). *Tafsir Nemoneh (Exemplary exegesis)* (Vol. 7). Ali in Abi Taleb.

Maljoo, M. (2017). "The Vicious Circle Trapping Iranian Workers since the 1990s", in Vahabi, Mehrdad and Coville, Thierry (Dir.), L'économie politique de la République islamique d'Iran, *Revue internationale des études du développement*, No. 229, mai, pp. 135–160.

Maloney, S. (2000). Agents or Obstacles? Parastatal Foundations and Challenges for Iranian development. In P. Alizadeh (Ed.), *The economy of Iran: The dilemma of an Islamic State* (pp. 145–176). I.B. Tauris Publishers.

Maloney, S. (2015). *Iran's Political Economy since the Revolution.* Cambridge University Press.

Mandel, E. (1995). *Long Waves of Capitalist Development: A Marxist Interpretation* (2nd revised ed.). London and New York: Verso.

Mann, M. (1986). *The Sources of Social Power, vol. 1, A History of Power from the Beginning to A.D. 1760.* Cambridge University Press.

Mansoor, H. (2020a, 19 December). Tolid servat dar iqtesad dar-ol-islam chera baz istad? (Why did the Creation of Wealth Stop in the Economy of the Islamic Country?). *Independent Persian.* Retrieved July 11, 2022, from https://www.independentpersian.com/node/107166.

Mansoor, H. (2020b, 13 February). Sevomeen charkheh namoozon iqtesad Iran: tolid melli va anbasht sarmyeh" (The Third Cycle of Iranian's Economic Disequilibrium: National Production and Capital Accumulation). *Independent Persian.* Retrieved July 11, 2022, from https://www.independentpersian.com/node/122631.

Markoff, J. (2006). Violence, Emancipation, and Democracy: The Countryside and the French Revolution. In G. Kates (Ed.), *The French Revolution, Recent Debates and New Controversies* (2nd ed., pp. 165–197). Routledge.

Marshall, T. (1963). *Sociology at the Crossroads and Other Essays.* Heinemann.

Marx, K. (1847/2009). *The Poverty of Philosophy.* Progress Publishers, 1955; Transcribed: by Zodiac for Marx/Engels Internet Archive (marxists.org) 1999; Proofed: and corrected by Matthew Carmody, 2009.

Marx, K. (1857a–8/1964). *Pre-capitalist Economic Formations.* Translated by Jack Cohen, https://www.marxists.org/archive/marx/works/1857/precapitalist/ch01.htm

Marx, K. (1857b/1971). Introduction to a Contribution to the Critique of Political Economy. In *A Contribution to the Critique of Political Economy*, translated from the German by S. W. Ryazanskaya, Appendix I, London: Lawrence & Wishart, pp. 81–111. https://www.marxists.org/archive/marx/works/1859/critique-pol-economy/appx1.htm

Marx, K. (1859/1977). *A Contribution to the Critique of Political Economy.* Progress Publishers. Retrieved from https://www.marxists.org/archive/marx/works/1859/critique-pol-economy/preface.htm. Accessed July 15, 2019.

Marx, K. (1867/1978). *Capital, a Critique of Political Economy* (Vol. 1), Progress Publishers.

Marx, K. (1973). *Grundrisse*. Vintage Books.

Mauss, M. (1967). *The Gift: Forms and Functions of Exchange in Arabic Societies*. Norton.

Mazaheri, R. (2018, June 20). How Iran got Economically Socialist, and then Islamic Socialist. *The Saker*. Retrieved February 2, 2022, from https://thesaker.is/how-iran-got-economically-socialist-and-then-islamic-socialist/.

McAuliffe, J. D. (2006). *The Cambridge Companion to the Qur'an*. Cambridge University Press.

Mcelroy, D. (2013, 2 May). Iran's Ayatollah Khamenei Embroiled in German Car Dealer Row. *The Daily Telegraph*. Retrieved December 5, 2021, from https://www.telegraph.co.uk/news/worldnews/middleeast/iran/10034051/Irans-Ayatollah-Khamenei-embroiled-in-German-car-dealer-row.html.

McGuirk, E. (2013). The Illusory Leader: Natural Resources, Taxation and Accountability. *Public Choice, 154*, 285–313.

Megginson, W., & Netter, J. (2001, June). From State to Market: A Survey of Empirical Studies on Privatization. *Journal of Economic Literature, 39*(2), 321–389.

Menard, C., Kunneke, R., & Groenewegen, J. (2021). *Network Infrastructures: Aligning Technologies and Institutions*. Cambridge University Press.

Merianos, G., & Gotsis, G. (2017). *Managing Financial Resources in Late Antiquity, Greek Fathers' Views on Hoarding and Saving*. Palgrave Macmillan.

Mesbahi Moghaddam, S., Ghyasi, M., & Nakhli, S. R. (2011, Fall). "Osool va siasathay hakem bar masraf Anfal va daramadhay hasel az an dar dowlat islami," (*The Governing Principles and Policies Regarding the Expenditure of the Income Originated from Anfal in the Islamic State*), *Faslnameh pajoohesh-hay eghtesadi Iran, in Persian, 48*, 193–221 (in Persian).

Milani, A. (2011). *The Shah*. Palgrave Macmillan.

Milanovic, B. (2019). *Capitalism Alone, the Future of the System that Rules the World*. Belknap Press of Harvard University Press.

Mingardi, A. (2018). P.T. Bauer and the Myth of Primitive Accumulation. *Cato Journal, 38*(2), 613–630.

Minutes of the discussions of the Majles on the final version of the Constitution of the Islamic Republic of Iran, in 4 Volumes, in Persian. Retrieved September 1, 2021., from https://www.shoragc.ir/fa/news/2098/%D8%B5%D9%88%D8%B1%D8%AA%D9%85%D8%B4%D8%B1%D9%88%D8%AD-%D9%85%D8%B0%D8%A7%DA%A9%D8%B1%D8%A7%D8%AA-%D9%85%D8%AC%D9%84%D8%B3%D8%A8%D8%B1%D8%B1%D8%B3%DB%8C%D9%86%D9%87%D8%A7%DB%8C%D9%82%D8%A7%D9%86%D9%88%D9%86%D8%A7%D8%B3%D8%A7%D8%B3%DB%8C%D8%AC%D9%85%D9%87%D9%88%D8%B1%DB%8C%D8%A7%

D8%B3%D9%84%D8%A7%D9%85%DB%8C-%D8%A7%DB%8C%D8%B1%D
8%A7%D9%86.

Mitchell, T. (2011). *Carbon Democracy: Political Power in the Age of Oil*. Verso.

Mitchell, L. (2012). *The Color Revolutions*. University of Pennsylvania Press.

Mobarak, A. M., & Purbasari, D. (2005, July 9). *Political Trade Protection in Developing Countries: Firm Level Evidence from Indonesia*. Available https://ssrn.com/abstract=770949 or https://doi.org/10.2139/ssrn.770949

Mobarak, A., & Purbasari, D. (2006). *Corrupt Protection for sale to Firms: Evidence from Indonesia. Unpublished Working Paper*. University of Colorado at Boulder.

Moghtaderi, T., Alamdar, R., Rodríguez-Seijo, A., Naghibi, S. J., & Kumar, V. (2020). Ecological Risk Assessment and Source Apportionment of Heavy Metal Contamination in Urban Soils in Shiraz, Southwest Iran. *Arabian Journal of Geosciences, 13*, 797. https://doi.org/10.1007/s12517-020-05787-9

Mohajer, N. (2020). *Voices of a Massacre: Untold Stories of Life and Death in Iran, 1988*. Oneworld Publications.

Mohandes, A. (1965). *Water Resources of Iran*. Tehran University, Faculty of Law, Political Science and Economics.

Moin, B. (1999). *Khomeini: Life of the Ayatollah*. I.B. Tauris & Co.

Moinfar, A. A. (2014, 24 January). Interview Regarding the Nationalization of the Banks and Industries Under the Provisional Government of Bazargan. *Tejarat Farda*, No. 74.

Momen, M. (1985). *An introduction to Shi'i Islam, the history and doctrines of Twelver Shi'ism*. Yale University Press.

Montazeri, H.-A. (1984). *Al-Khoms va Al-Anfal (Khoms and Anfal)* (2nd ed.). Mossasseh al-nashr al-Islamie.

Montazeri, H.-A. (1987). *Darasat fi velayet al-faqih va feqhe al-dowlah al-islamieh (Studies on Velayat faqih and the Jurisprudence of the Islamic State)* (Vol. 1, 4). Al-markaz al-alemi il-darasat al-islamieh.

Morrison, K. (2007). Natural Resources, Aid, and Democratization: A Best-Case Scenario. *Public Choice, 131*(3/4), 365–386.

Moss, L. (1974). Private Property Anarchism: An American Variant. in Tullock G. (ed.), 1974, pp. 1–31; see also, Stringham E. (ed.) [2005], Chapter 12, pp. 123–152.

Motamedi, M. (2021, 21 July). Violence Escalates in Water-Shortage Protests in Iran's Khuzestan. *Aljazeera*. Retrieved March 10, 2022, from https://www.aljazeera.com/news/2021/7/21/violence-intensifies-after-six-nights-of-water-crisis-protests-in.

Mouloud, L. (2006). "Chaque Prison a Son Petit Guantanamo…" *Journal l'Humanité*, le 21 décembre.

Mousavi Nik, S. H. (2009). *Gozar az Iqtesad dowlati be shebh dowlati (The Transition from State to Parastate Economy)*. The Research Centre of Islamic

Legislative Assembly, November, Serial number 9915, subject code 220 (in Persian).

Najafi Khah, M. (2016, Winter). "Marz-e myan bakhsh omomei va bakhsh khosousi dar hoghogh Iran ba takeed bar barnameh khosousi sazi va broon separi," (*The Delineation of the Public and Private Sector in the Iranian Law with the Emphasis on the Privatization Program and Outsourcing*). *Faslnameh elmipajooheshi Shapa, 21*(4), 101-133 (in Persian).

Naseri, S. (2006). *30 Darsad-e eqtesad-e Iran dar ekhtiar-e bonyadha ast* (The Foundation's Control Over 30 percent of the Economy), *Sarmayeh,* June 10, No. 195. Retrieved December 11, 2022, from www.magiran.com/npview.asp?ID=1096929 (in Persian).

Nature. (2021, 24 June). Water Shortage: Iran Is Draining Its Aquifers Dry. *Proceedings of the National Academy of Sciences of the United States of America, 594,* 476. https://www.nature.com/articles/d41586-021-01604-9

Netz, R. (2004). *Barbed Wire: An Ecology of Modernity.* Wesleyan University Press.

Neuberger, E., & Duffy, W. (1976). *Comparative Economic Systems, A Decision-Making Approach.* Allyn & Bacon, Incorporated.

New York Times. (1995, January 8). *Iranian Foundation Head Denies Accusations of Corruption,* p. 18.

Nili, M. (2004). *Eqtesad Iran va moamayee toseh nayaftegi (Iranian Economy and the Puzzle of Non Development).* danshegah Sanaati Shareif.

Nili, M., & Associates. (2015). *Iqtesad Iran be koja miravad? Kholaseh tarh motaleati tahleel avamel taseergozar bar amalkard myan moddat iqtesad Iran (Where the Iranian Economy Is Going? A Summary of Study Project Regarding the Analysis of Factors Impacting the Performance of the Iranian Economy in Medium Term).* Inteharat Donyai Iqtesad (in Persian).

Nomani, F., & Behdad, S. (2006). *Class and Labor in Iran: Did the Revolution Matter?* Syracuse University Press.

Noori, H. (1990). Hookomat islami and naghsh *Anfal (The Islamic Government and the Role of Anfal),* *Hawza,* in Persian, Numbers 37 and 38.

North, D. (1977). Markets and Other Allocation Systems in History: The Challenge of Karl Polanyi. *Journal of European Economic History, 6,* 703–716.

North, D. (1981). *Structure and Change in Economic History.* W.W. Norton and Company.

North, D. (1990a). *Institutions, Institutional Change and Economic Performance.* Cambridge University Press.

North, D. (1990b). A Transaction Cost Theory of Politics. *Journal of Theoretical Politics, 2*(4), 355–367.

North, D., Wallis, J., & Weingast, B. (2009). *Violence and Social Orders: A Conceptual Framework for Interpreting Recorded Human History.* Cambridge University Press.

Nowroozi, S. (2016). Does the Problems of oil Contracts Solve with EIKO. *BBC News, Perisan Section*, October 6. Retrieved December 5, 2021.

Nowroozi, M. D., & Nemati, M. (2017). Roykardi moghaysehi beh andisheh siasi 'Muhaqqiq Karaki' va Agustine (*A Comparative Approach to the Political Ideas of Muhaqqiq Karki and Saint Augustine*), two parts, *Faslnameh Hokomat Islami*, Number 80 (in Persian).

Nozick, R. (1974). *Anarchy, State, and Utopia*. Basic Books.

OECD (Organisation for Economic Co-operation and Development). (2009). *Revolving Doors, Accountability and Transparency*. Public Governance Committee.

Ogilvie, S., & Carus, A. W. (2014). Institutions and Economic Growth in Historical Perspective. In P. Aghion & S. N. Durlauf (Eds.), *Handbook of Economic Growth* (Vol. 2, pp. 403–513). North Holland, Chapter 8.

Olmsted, J. (2013). Gender and Globalization. In Bahramitash, Roksana and Salehi Esfahani, Salehi (Eds.), 2011, *Veiled Employment, Islamism and the Political Economy of Women's Employment in Iran* (pp. 25–52). Syracuse University Press, Chapter 1.

Olson, M. (1965/1980). *The Logic of Collective Action, Public Goods and the Theory of Groups*. Harvard University Press.

Olson, M. (1982). *The Rise and Decline of Nations: Economic Growth, Stagflation, and Social Rigidities*. Yale University Press.

Olson, M. (1993). Dictatorship, Democracy, and Development. *American Political Science Review, 87*, 567–576.

Omidvar, K. (2009, September 23). *Sepah-e Pasdaran-e Iran bank mizanad* (The Iranian Revolutionary Guards Corps Opens Bank). *BBC News Farsi*. Retrieved December 11, 2021, from www.bbc.co.uk/persian/business/2009/09/090923_ka_bankansar_sepah.shtml, (in Persian).

Osborne, J. (2005). Jungle or Just Bush? Anarchy and the Evolution of Cooperation. In Stringham E. (ed.), pp. 24–35.

Paganelli, M. (2014). David Hume on Banking and Hoarding. *Southern Economic Journal, 80*(4), 968–980.

Pagano, U. (2011). Interlocking Complementarities and Institutional Change. *Journal of Institutional Economics, 7*(3), 373–392.

Pahlavi, M. R. (1961/1974). *Mission for My Country*. Hutchinson & CO LTD

Papaioannou, E., & Gregorios, S. (2008). Economic and Social Factors Driving the Third Wave of Democratization. *Journal of Comparative Economics, 36*, 365–387.

Pareto, V. (1927/1971). *Manual of Political Economy*. A.M. Kelley.

Parker, G. (1988). *The Military Revolution, Military Innovation and the Rise of the West, 1500–1800*. Cambridge University Press.

Patruti, A. (2016). An Analysis on the Relationship Between Hoarding, Investment and Economic Growth. *The Quarterly Journal of Austrian Economics, 19*(3), 248–266.

Patterson, O. (1985). *Slavery and Social Death. A Comparative Study*. Harvard University Press.

Paxton, R. (1998). The Five Stages of Fascism. *The Journal of Modern History, 70*(1), 1–23.

Paxton, R. (2004). *The Anatomy of Fascism*. Alfred A. Knopf.

Peckham, R. (2013). Contagion: Epidemiological Models and Financial Crises. *Journal of Public Health, 36*(1), 13–17. 2014, March.

Peres-Cajias, J., Torregrosa-Hetland, S., & Ducoing, C. (2020). Resource abundance and public finances in five peripheral economies, 1850–1939. *Lund Papers in Economic History*, No. 216, Department of Economic History, Lund University.

Pérotin-Dumon, A. (1991). The Pirate and the Emperor: Power and the Law on the Seas, 1450–1850. In J. D. Tracy (Ed.), *The Political Economy of Merchant Empires* (pp. 196–227). Cambridge University Press.

Pesaran, H. (2000). Economic Trends and Macroeconomic Policies in Post-Revolutionary Iran. In P. Alizadeh (Ed.), *The Economy of Iran: The Dilemmas of an Islamic State*. I.B. Tauris & Co.

Pesaran, E. (2014). *Iran's Struggle for Independence, Reform and Counter-Reform in the Post-Revolutionary Era*. Routledge.

Peters, F. E. (1991). The Quest of the Historical Muhammad. *International Journal of Middle East Studies, 23*(3), 291–315.

Philippon, T. (2019). *The Great Reversal: How America Gave Up on Free Markets*. Harvard University Press.

Piccione, M., & Rubinstein, A. (2007). Equilibrium in the Jungle. *Economic Journal, 117*(522), 883–896.

Pierson, P. (1996, January). The New Politics of the Welfare State. *World Politics, 48*, 143–179.

Pierson, P. (2000a). Three Worlds of Welfare State Research. *Comparative Political Studies, 33*, 791–821.

Pierson, P. (2000b). Increasing Returns, Path Dependence, and the Study of Politics. *The American Political Science Review, 94*(2), 251–267.

Piryaei, S. (2018, March). *State of Perpetual Emergency: Legally Codified State Violence in Post-Revolutionary Iran and the Contemporary U.S*. PhD Thesis in Comparative Literature, University of California Riverside.

Pistor-Hatam, A. (2019, Winter). Religious Minorities in the Islamic Republic of Iran and 'The Right to Have Rights'. *Iran Namag, 3*(4).

Plack, N. (2013). The Peasantry, Feudalism, and the Environment, 1789–93. In P. McPhee (Ed.), *A Companion to The French Revolution* (pp. 212–227). Wiley Blackwell Ltd.

Plato. (2013). *Sophist* (Benjamin, J., Hazelton, P.A. Trans.). An Electronic Classics Series Publication. http://www2.hn.psu.edu/faculty/jmanis/plato/sophist.pdf

Polanyi, K. (1944). *The Great Transformation*. Farrar and Rinehart.

Polanyi, K. (1957/1968). *Primitive, Archaic and Modern Economies*. Doubleday.

Polanyi, K. (1965). *Trade and Market in the Early Empire; Economies in History and Theory*. Free Press.

Pryor, F. L. (2009). The Political Economy of a Semi-Industrialized Theocratic State: The Islamic Republic of Iran. In M. Ferrero & R. Wintrobe (Eds.), *The Political Economy of Theocracy* (pp. 243–270). Palgrave Macmillan.

Radin, M. J. (1996). *Contested Commodities*. Harvard University Press.

Rahman Zadeh Heravi, M. (2018). *Negahi be Iqtesad Siasi Iran az Daheh 1340 ta 1395 (A Glimpse over the Political Economy of Iran from 1961 until 2016)* (1st ed.). Nashr Akhtaran. (in Persian).

Rahnema, S. (1992). Work Councils in Iran - The Illusion of Worker Control. *Economic and Industrial Democracy, 13*(1), 69–94. https://doi.org/10.1177/0143831X92131004

Rahnema, S. (1995). Continuity and Change in Industrial Policy. In S. Rahnema & S. Behdad (Eds.), *Iran after the Revolution: Crisis of an Islamic State* (pp. 129–149). London and New York.

Rahnema, S., & Behdad, S. (1995). Introduction. In R. Saeed & S. Behdad (Eds.), *Iran after the Revolution Crisis of An Islamic State* (pp. 1–18). London, New York.

Rajabi, M. H. (2009, Spring and Summer). "Arae Faqihan asr Safavi darbareh-I tamool ba hookomatha" (*The Faqihs' Viewpoints on the Relationship with Governments During the Safavid era*). *Tarikh va Tamadoon Islami, 5*(9), 53-80. (in Persian).

Rasmusen, E. (1992). *Games and Information, An Introduction to Game Theory*. Blackwell.

Razi, F. (1992). *Tafsir Kabir (The Great exegesis)* (Trans to Persian by Asghar Halabi). Tehran (in Persian).

Razo, A. (2021, January). Network Structure and Performance of Crony Capitalism Systems Credible Commitments Without Democratic Institutions. *Public Choice, 189*, 115–137.

Renani, M. (2010). *Bazaar ya na-bazaar (Market or non-Market)*, Third Edition (first edition: 1997, Second edition: 2005). Moasseseh aali amoozesh, pajohesh modiriyat va barnamehrizi (in Persian).

Research Centre of Islamic Legislative Assembly. (1996, July). Fasli darbareh farar maghzha (A Chapter on Brain Drain). Report code: 4001510.

Research Centre of Islamic Legislative Assembly. (2000). *Adam amnyat eqtesadi va farar sarmayeh (The lack of economic security and capital flight in Iran)*, May, Report code: 2405543.

Research Centre of Islamic Legislative Assembly. (2017). *Payeesh amneyat sarmayeh gozari be tafkeek ostanha va hoozehay kary (Investment Security According to Provinces and Secor of Activities)* (1), Winter, Code subject 220, Serial number 16061.

Research Centre of Islamic Legislative Assembly. (2018a). *Payeesh amneyat sarmayeh gozari be tafkeek ostanha va hoozehay kary (Investment Security According to Provinces and Secor of Activities)* (2), Spring, Code subject 220, Serial number 16187.

Research Centre of Islamic Legislative Assembly. (2018b). *Payeesh amneyat sarmayeh gozari be tafkeek ostanha va hoozehay kary (Investment Security According to Provinces and Secor of Activities)* (3), Summer, Code subject 220, Serial number 16400.

Research Centre of Islamic Legislative Assembly. (2018c). *Payeesh amneyat sarmayeh gozari be tafkeek ostanha va hoozehay kary (Investment Security According to Provinces and Secor of Activities)* (4), Fall, Code subject 220, Serial number 16526.

Research Centre of Islamic Legislative Assembly. (2018d). *Payeesh amneyat sarmayeh gozari be tafkeek ostanha va hoozehay kary (Investment Security According to Provinces and Secor of Activities)* (5), Winter, Code subject 220, Serial number 16619.

Research Centre of Islamic Legislative Assembly. (2019a). *Payeesh amneyat sarmayeh gozari be tafkeek ostanha va hoozehay kary (Investment Security According to Provinces and Secor of Activities)* (6), Spring, Code subject 220, Serial number 16820.

Research Centre of Islamic Legislative Assembly. (2019b). *Payeesh amneyat sarmayeh gozari be tafkeek ostanha va hoozehay kary (Investment Security According to Provinces and Secor of Activities)* (7), Summer, Code subject 220, Serial number 16926.

Research Centre of Islamic Legislative Assembly. (2019c). *Payeesh amneyat sarmayeh gozari be tafkeek ostanha va hoozehay kary (Investment Security According to Provinces and Secor of Activities)* (8), Fall, Code subject 220, Serial number 16990.

Research Centre of Islamic Legislative Assembly. (2019d). *Payeesh amneyat sarmayeh gozari be tafkeek ostanha va hoozehay kary (Investment Security According to Provinces and Secor of Activities)* (9), Winter, Code subject 220, Serial number 17131.

Research Centre of Islamic Legislative Assembly. (2020a). *Payeesh amneyat sarmayeh gozari be tafkeek ostanha va hoozehay kary (Investment Security According to Provinces and Secor of Activities)* (10), Spring, Code subject 220, Serial number 17400.

Research Centre of Islamic Legislative Assembly. (2020b). *Payeesh amneyat sarmayeh gozari be tafkeek ostanha va hoozehay kary (Investment Security According to Provinces and Secor of Activities)* (11), Summer, Code subject 220, Serial number 17433.

Research Centre of Islamic Legislative Assembly. (2020c). *Payeesh amneyat sarmayeh gozari be tafkeek ostanha va hoozehay kary (Investment Security According to Provinces and Secor of Activities)* (12), Fall, Code subject 220, Serial number 17578.

Research Centre of Islamic Legislative Assembly. (2020d). *Payeesh amneyat sarmayeh gozari be tafkeek ostanha va hoozehay kary (Investment Security According to Provinces and Secor of Activities)* (13), Winter, Code subject 220, Serial number 17842.

Rezai, M. (2006). "Mohsen Rezai dar jam-e khabarnegaran : 100 hezar Milliard Toman az malekyat-e dowlat beh mardom va bakhsh khosousi vagozar mishavad" (Mohsen Rezai Among Reporters: 100 Thousand Billion Tomans of State Property will be Transferred to the People and the Private Sector), Fars News Agency,   July   5   (14   Tir   1385).   http://www.farsnews.net/newstext,php?nn=8504140273 (in Persian).

Ritter, D. (2015). *The Iron Cage of Liberalism.* Oxford University Press.

Rodinson, M. (1973). *Islam and Capitalism* (Trans from the French by Brian Pierce, First American ed.). Penguin Books Ltd.

Rosenthal, R. (1981). Games of Perfect Information, Predatory Pricing, and the Chain-Store Paradox. *Journal of Economic Theory, 25,* 92–100.

Ross, M. (1999). The Political Economy of the Resource Curse. *World Politics, 51*(2), 297–322.

Ross, M. (2009). *Oil and Democracy Revisited.* University of California-Los Angeles.

Ross, M. (2012). *The Oil Curse: How Petroleum Wealth Shapes the Development of Nations.* Princeton University Press.

Ross, M. (2015). What Have We Learned about the Resource Curse? *Annual Review of Political Science, 18,* 239–259.

Rothbard, M. (1973/1996).*For a New Liberty: Libertarian Manifesto.* Fox and Wilkes.

Rothbard, M. (1977). *Power and Market: Government and the Economy.* Sheed, Andrews and McMeel, Second Edition.

Rowe, N. (2016). Keynesian Parables of Thrift and Hoarding. *Review of Keynesian Economics, 4*(1), 50–55.

Rubin, R. E. (2003). *In an Uncertain World: Tough Choices from Wall Street to Washington.* Random House.

Sadr, M. B. (1961/1978). *Iqtisade ma (Our economics)* (Trans to Persian in two volumes, vol. II). Entesharat-e Islami (in Persian).

Saeidi, A. (2004). The Accountability of Para-Governmental Organizations (Bonyads): The Case of Iranian Foundations. *Iranian Studies, 37*(3), 479–498.

Sahih Muslim. *The Book of Jihad and Expedition,* Book 32, Hadith 1765. Retrieved August 29, 2021, from https://sunnah.com/muslim:1765.

Salem, M., & Mostaghim, R. (2022, February 9). *Iranian Husband Beheads Teenage Wife, Authorities Say, Shocking the Country*. CNN. Retrieved March 20, 2022, from https://www.cnn.com/2022/02/09/middleeast/iran-teenage-wife-beheaded-intl/index.html.

Samuelson, L. (1997). *Evolutionary Games and Equilibrium Selection*. The MIT Press.

Sattari, N. (2020). Women Driving Women: Drivers of Women-Only Taxis in the Islamic Republic of Iran. *Women's Studies International Forum, 28*, 102324. www.elsevier.com/locate/wsif

Savoia, A., & Sen, K. (2021). The Political Economy of the Resource Curse: A Development Perspective. *Annual Review of Resource Economics, 13*, 203–223.

Say, J.-B. (1841). *Traité d'économie politique, ou simple exposition de la manière dont se forment, se distribuent et se consomment les richesses*, Osnabrück, O. Zeller, 6ᵉ édition, disponible sur le site http://fr.wikisource.org/wiki/Livre:Say; English translation: Say, Jean-Baptiste, 1821/1964, *A Treatise on Political Economy or the Production, Distribution and Consumption of Wealth*, 6 ed., New York, Claxton, Remsen & Haffelfinger.

Sayyah, S. A. (2016). Amoozehay 16 doreh arzyabi fasli moheet kasb oo kar dar Iran tei paeez 1389 ta tabestan 1394 (Lessons of 16 Cycles of Assessing Business Environment in Iran over the Period Starting in Fall 2010 to Summer 2015). *Majles va Rahboord, 23*(85), Spring (in Persian).

Sazegara, M. (2006, July 23). "Sepah va seh enheraf" (The IRGC and three aberrations). Retrieved December 2, 2021, form http://www.sazegara.net/persian/archives/2006/07/060723_154435.html (in Persian).

Schanche, D. (1989, June 4). Ayatollah Khomeini dies at 86: Fiery Leader Was in Failing Health Following Surgery. *Los Angeles Times*. https://www.latimes.com/archives/la-xpm-1989-06-04-mn-2499-story.html

Schelling, T. (1963). *The Strategy of Conflict*. A Galaxy Book, Oxford University Press. Scheuer [1994], *Focus*, pp. 99–101.

Schirazi, A. (1997). *The Constitution of Iran: Politics and the State in the Islamic Republic*. I.B. Tauris.

Schlicht, E. (1998). *On Custom in the Economy*. Clarendon Press.

Schlumberger, O. (2008). Structural Reform, Economic Order, and Development: Patrimonial Capitalism. *Review of International Political Economy, 15*(4), 622–649.

Schmidt, M., Gonda, R., & Transiskus, S. (2021). Environmental Degradation at Lake Urmia (Iran): Exploring the Causes and Their Impacts on Rural Livelihoods. *GeoJournal, 86*, 2149–2163.

Schmitter, P. (1974, January). Still the Century of Corporatism? *Review of Politics, 36*, 102–110.

Schumpeter, J. A. (1939). *Business Cycles: A Theoretical, Historical, and Statistical Analysis of the Capitalist Process*. McGraw–Hill Book Company Inc.

Schwartzstein, P. (2019, January 25). Drought Turns Part of Iran into a New Dust Bowl. Retrieved March 8, 2022, from https://www.nationalgeographic.com/environment/article/drought-climate-change-turn-iran-sistan-and-baluchestan-into-dust-bowl.

Schwartzstein, P. (2020, November 12). Environment Movement. *National Geographic*. Retrieved March 8, 2022, from https://www.nationalgeographic.com/environment/article/how-iran-destroying-once-thriving-environmental-movement.

Scott, J. (1998). *Seeing Like a State, How Certain Schemes to Improve the Human Condition Have Failed*. Yale University Press.

Scott, J. C. (2009). *The Art of Not Being Governed, An Anarchist History of Upland Southeast Asia*. Yale University Press.

Seabright, P. (2010). *The Company of Strangers: A Natural History of Economic Life*, Revised Version. Princeton University Press.

Shahid Jamal Rizvi, S. (2014, November 10). *Khutba E Fadak (The Fadak Speech)* Vol.2. Koran O Itrat Foundation (in Persian).

Shiva, V. (2001). *Protect or Plunder? Understanding Intellectual Property Rights*. Zed Books.

Siddiqa, A. (2007). *Military Inc. Inside Pakistan's Military Economy*. Pluto Press.

Simon, H. (1951). A Formal Theory of the Employment Relationship. *Econometrica, 19*(3), 293–305.

Skocopol, T. (1982, May). Rentier Sttae and Shi'a Islam in the Iranian Revolution. *Theory and Society, 11*(3), 265–283.

Smith, A. (1776/1961). *An Inquiry into the Nature and Causes of the Wealth of Nations*. Methuen.

Smith, M. (1982). *Evolution and the Theory of Games*. Cambridge University Press.

Smith, B. (1997, January 18). Dual Control. *The Economist, 342*(8000).

Smith, B. (2007). *Hard Times in the Land of Plenty: Oil Politics in Iran and Indonesia*. Cornell University Press.

Sodagar, M. (1990). *Rooshd ravabet sarmayehdari dar Iran (The Development of the Capitalist Relationships in Iran)*. Shooleh Andisheh. (in Persian).

Sombart, W. (1902). *Der moderne Kapitalismus*. Duncker& Humblot.

Soroush, N., & Madani, K. (2014/2021, November 21). Every Breath You Take: The Environmental Consequences of Iran Sanctions. *The Guardian*. Retrieved March 8, 2022, from https://www.theguardian.com/world/iran-blog/2014/nov/21/iran-environmental-consequences-of-sanctions.

Springborg, R. (2013). Learning from Failure: Egypt. In T. Bruneau & F. C. Matei (Eds.), *The Routledge Handbook of Civil-Military Relations* (pp. 93–109). Routledge.

State Department Report. (2018, September 28). Iran's environmental issues, Chapter 7. Retrieved March 8, 2022, from https://iranprimer.usip.org/blog/2018/oct/04/state-department-report-7-irans-environmental-issues.

Stecklow, S., Dehghanpisheh, B., & Torbati, Y. (2013). Khamenei Controls Massive Financial Empire Built on Property Seizures. Three Parts. *Reuters Investigates*, 11, 12, 13 Nov., http://www.reuters.com/investiates/iran

Stewart, D. (2001). Islamic Juridical Hierarchies and the Office of Marjiʿ al-Taqlid. In L. Clarke (Ed.), *Shiʿite Heritage: Essays on Classical and Modern Traditions* (pp. 137–157). Binghamton.

Stewart, E. C. (2007, February). The Sexual Health and Behaviour of Male Prisoners: The Need for Research. *The Howard Journal of Criminal Justice, 46*(1), 43–59.

Stillman, N. (1979). *The Jews of Arab Lands: A History and Source Book*. Jewish Publication.

Stoker, B. (1897/1997). *Dracula*. Norton and Company.

Stringham, E. (Ed.). (2005). *Anarchy, State and Public Choice*. Edward Elgar.

Stringham, E. (Ed.). (2007). *Anarchy and the Law, The Political Economy of Choice*. Transaction Publishers.

Stringham, E. (2015). *Private Governance, Creating Order in Economic and Social Life*. Oxford University Press.

Sweezy, P., & Magdoff, H. (1979). Iran: New Crisis of American Hegemony. *Monthly Review, 30*(9), 1–24.

Szurek, S. (2004). Guantanamo, une prison d'exception. Artières Ph. et Lascoumes P. (dir.), pp. 201–223.

Tabarsi, F. I. H. (1973). *Majma Al-bayan (Speech collection)* (Vol. 6, Trans to Persian by Ahmad Behshti and Moosavi Dameghani). Farhani (in Persian).

Tabatabei, S. M. H. (1995). *Al-Mizan (The Measurement)*, Vol. 9 (*on Anfal and Repentance*) (Trans to Persian by Mosavi Hamedani, Seyyed Muhammad Bagher). Jame Modaresseen Hozeh Elmieh Qom (in Persian).

Taber, G. (1980, April 21). A Case of Crony Capitalism. *Time Magazine*.

Taber, G. (2015, November 3). The Night I Invented Crony Capitalism. Knowledge @ Wharton. Retrieved July 7, 2022, from http://knowledge.wharton.upenn.edu/article/the-night-i-invented-crony-capitalism/.

Tabibian, M. (2022, January 29). Noskheh Irani polit bureau (The Iranian version of polit bureau). *Tejarat Farda*.

Tasnim, Maqsood az Anfal chist? (What does it mean Anfal)? 12 September 2017. Retrieved January 9, 2022, from https://www.tasnimnews.com/fa/news/1396/06/21/1516015, (in Persian).

Taubes, G. (1995, November 17). Scientists Attacked for 'Patenting' Pacific Tribe. *Science, 270*, 1112.

Tavakoli, A. (1987). Nationalization and Efficient Management of Water Resources in Iran. *Journal of Water Resources Planning and Management, 113*(4), 522–532.

Taylor, S. (2003). *Rape in Prison: A Need for Support Systems and Prison Sex*. http://www.stetay.com

Tedlock, B. (2006). Indigenous Heritage and Biopiracy in the Age of Intellectual Property Rights. *Explore, 2*(3), 256–259.

Tiebout, C. (1956). A Pure Theory of Local Expenditures. *Journal of Political Economy, 64*(5), 416–424.

Tilly, C. (1985). War Making and State Making as Organized Crime. In P. B. Evans, D. Rueschemeyer, & T. Skocpol (Eds.), *Bringing the State Back in, Cambridge* (pp. 169–191). Cambridge University Press.

Titmuss, R. (1971). *The Gift Relationship: From Human Blood to Social Policy.* London and New York.

Torbat, A. (2002). The Brain Drain from Iran to the U.S. *Middle East Journal, 56*(2), 272–295.

Trotsky, L. (1932). *The History of the Russian Revolution*, vol. 1, Chapter 11 (Max Eastman, Trans.). Marxist Internet Archive. https://www.marxists.org/ebooks/trotsky/history-of-the-russian-revolution/ebook-history-of-the-russian-revolution-v1.pdf

Tullock, G. (Ed.). (1972a). *Explorations in the Theory of Anarchy.* Center for the Study of Public Choice.

Tullock, G. (1972b/2005). The Edge of the Jungle. In Stringham (ed.), pp. 36-48.

Tullock, G. (Ed.). (1974a). *Further Explorations in the Theory of Anarchy.* University Publications.

Tullock, G. (Ed.). (1974b). *The Social Dilemma: The Economics of War and Revolution.* University Publications.

Turkan, A. (2020). *Bourgeoisie tejari keshvar ra edareh mikonad (The mercantile bourgeoisie manages the country)*, Unpublished Manuscript, 2 June (in Persian).

Turner, B. (1974). *Weber and Islam: A Critical Study.* Routledge and Kegan Paul.

Turner, T. (1980). Iranian Oil Workers in the 1978–79 Revolution. In P. Nore & T. Turner (Eds.), *Oil and Class Struggle* (pp. 272–292). Zed Press.

Tusi, M. I. H. (1955). *Al-Iqtisad (Economics).* Ketabkhaneh Jamee Chehl Sotoon.

Tusi, M. I. H. (1984). *Al-Mabsoot (Comprehensive Study of the Shi'i Fqih)* (Vol. 2). Mortazavi.

Tyrou, E., & Vahabi, M. (2021). *A Critical Survey on Land-Grabbing: Land as a Source of Power and Profit.* Manuscript.

UNDP. (2017, June 17). *Iran and UNDP Strengthen Efforts to Combat Desertification.* Retrieved March 8, 2022, from https://www.ir.undp.org/content/iran/en/home/presscenter/articles/2017/06/17/iran-and-undp-strengthen-efforts-to-combat-desertification.html.

Vacca, V. (2012). Nadir, Banu'l. In P. Bearman, Th. Bianquis, C.E. Bosworth, E. van Donzel, W.P. Heinrichs (Eds.). *Encyclopedia of Islam Online.* Brill Academic Publishers. Retrieved August 29, 2021, from http://dx.doi.org.myaccess.library.utoronto.ca/10.1163/1573-3912_islam_SIM_5714

Vahabi, M. (1997). A Critical Survey of K.J. Arrow's Theory of Knowledge. *Cahiers d'Economie Politique, 29*, 35–65.

Vahabi, M. (1998, September). The Relevance of the Marshallian Concept of Normality in Interior and in Inertial Dynamics as Revisited by G. Shackle and J. Kornai. *Cambridge Journal of Economics, 22*(5), 547–573.

Vahabi, M. (2001). The Soft Budget Constraint: A Theoretical Clarification. *Recherches Economiques de Louvain (Louvain Economic Review), 67*(2), 157–195.

Vahabi, M. (2002). From the Walrasian General Equilibrium to Incomplete Contracts: Making Sense of Institutions. *Economie et institutions (Economics and Institutions), 1*, 99–143.

Vahabi, M. (2004). *The Political Economy of Destructive Power*. Edward Elgar.

Vahabi, M. (2009). An Introduction to Destructive Coordination. *American Journal of Economics and Sociology, 68*(2), 353–386.

Vahabi, M. (2010). "Ordres contradictoires et coordination destructive: le malaise iranien" (Contradictory Orders and Destructive Coordination: The Iranian Disease). *Revue Canadienne d'Etudes du Développement (Canadian Journal of Development Studies), 30*(3–4), 503–534.

Vahabi, M. (2011a). Appropriation, Violent Enforcement and Transaction Costs: A Critical Survey. *Public Choice, 147*(1), 227–253.

Vahabi, M. (2011b). Economics of Destructive Power. In D. Braddon & K. Hartley (Eds.), *The Elgar Handbook on the Economics of Conflict* (pp. 79–104). Edward Elgar., Chapter 5.

Vahabi, M. (2012). Political Economy of Conflict - Foreword. *Revue d'Economie Politique, 122*(2), 151–167.

Vahabi, M. (2014a). Soft Budget Constraint Reconsidered. *Bulletin of Economic Research, 66*(1), 1–19.

Vahabi, M. (2014b). "Contrainte budgétaire lâche et le secteur paraétatique" (Soft Budget Constraints and Parastatal Sector). In M. Makinsky (Ed.), *L'économie réelle de l'Iran* (pp. 147–176). L'Harmattan.

Vahabi, M. (2015a). *The Political Economy of Predation: Manhunting and the Economics of Escape*. Cambridge University Press.

Vahabi, M. (2015b, December 22). Jaygah Sepah dar Eqtesad Iran (The Place of Sepah in the Iranian Economy). *Mihan*, No. 6. Retrieved December 11, 2021, from http://mihan.net/1394/10/01/562/ (in Persian).

Vahabi, M. (2016, September). A Positive Theory of the Predatory State. *Public Choice, 168*(3–4), 153–175.

Vahabi, M. (2018a). The Resource Curse Literature as Seen Through the Appropriability Lens: A Critical Survey. *Public Choice, 175*(3-4), 393–428.

Vahabi, M. (2018b, March). *Coercive State, Resisting Society, Political and Economic Development in Contemporary Iran, Dr Sadighi Lecture Series*. International Institute of Social History and Leiden University. https://socialhistory.org/en/events/lecture-political-and-economic-development-contemporary-iran

Vahabi, M. (2020a). Introduction: A Symposium on the Predatory State. *Public Choice, 182*(3–4), 233–242.

Vahabi, M. (2020b, August 10). Neoliberalism and Inflation Control. Akhbar-Rooz. نئولیبرالیسم و مقابله با تورم مهرداد وهابی - اخبار روز - سایت سیاسی خبری چپ (akhbar-rooz.com) (in Persian).

Vahabi, M., Batifoulier, P., & Da Silva, N. (2020). A Theory of Predatory Welfare State and Citizen Welfare: The French Case. *Public Choice, 182*(3–4), 243–271.

Vahabi, M., & Coville, T. (2017). Introduction: L'Economie Politique de la République islamique d'Iran. *Revue Internationale des Etudes du Développement, 229*, 11–32.

Vahabi, M., & Mohajer, N. (2004). *Az eslahat ta barandazi: tangnaha va cheshm andazha (Islamic Republic of Iran, Paradoxes of Reform and Prospects of Rebellion)*. Nashr Noghteh. (in Persion).

Vahabi, M., & Mohajer, N. (2021). A Critical Reflection on Neoliberalism. *Critique, 48*(4), 461–503.

Vahabi, M., & Nasser, M. (2011). Islamic Republic of Iran and Its Opposition. *Comparative Studies of South Asia, Africa and the Middle East, 31*(1), 110–119.

Vahabi, M., Philippe, B., & Nicolas, D. S. (2020). The Political Economy of Revolution and Institutional Change: The Elite and Mass Revolutions. *Revue d'Economie Politique, 130*(6), 855–889.

Valadbaygi, K. (2021). Hybrid Neoliberalism: Capitalist Development in Contemporary Iran. *New Political Economy, 26*(3), 313–327.

Veccia Vaglieri, L. (2012). Fadak. In P. Bearman, T. Bianquis, C. E. Bosworth, E. van Donzel, W. P. Heinrichs (Eds.). *Encyclopedia of Islam Online*. (2 ed.). Brill Academic Publishers. Consulted online on 29 August 2021 http://dx.doi.org.myaccess.library.utoronto.ca/10.1163/1573-3912_islam_SIM_2218

von Hayek, F. (1931/2008). *Prices and Production and Other Works*. Ludwig von Mises Institute.

von Hayek, F. (1937, February). Economics and Knowledge. *Economica, New Series, 4*(13), 33–54.

von Hayek, F. (2014). In B. Caldwell (Ed.), *The Collected Works of F.A. Hayek, Vol. 15-The Market and Other Orders*. Chicago University Press.

von Hayek, F. (2017). In V. J. Vanberg (Ed.), *The Collected Works of F.A. Hayek, Vol. 14-The Sensory Order and Other Writings as the Foundation of Theoretical Psychology*. University of Chicago Press.

von Mises, L. (1946). *Bureaucracy*. Yale University Press.

Vukovic, V. (2021). The Politics of Bailouts: Estimating the Causal Effects of Political Connections on Corporate Bailouts During the 2008–2009 US Financial Crisis. *Public Choice, 189*, 213–238. https://doi.org/10.1007/s11127-020-00871-w

Walras, L. (1874/2003). *Elements of Pure Economics or the Theory of Social Wealth* (William Jaffé, Trans.). Routledge.

Wantchekon, L. (2002). Why do Resource Dependent Countries Have Authoritarian Governments? *Journal of African Finance and Economic Development, 2*, 57–77.

Weber, M. (1905/1985). *The Protestant Ethic and the Spirit of Capitalism* (Talcott Parsons, Trans.). Unwin.

Weber, M. (1922/1978). *Economy and Society* 1, University of California Press.

Weber, R. (2001). *Swords into Dow Shares, Governing the Decline of the Military-Industrial Complex.* Westview.

Wehrey, F., Green, J., Nichiporuk, B., Nader, A., Hansell, L., Nafisi, R., & Bohandy, S. R. (2009). *The Rise of the Pasdaran, Assessing the Domestic Roles of Iran's Islamic Revolutionary Guards Corps.* Rand Corporation.

Weiss, K. (2018, April 3). Iran's Tarnished Gem. *National Geographic.* Retrieved March 8, 2022, from https://www.nationalgeographic.com/photography/article/lake-urmia-iran-drought.

Williamson, O. (1985). *The Economic Institutions of Capitalism. Firms, Markets, Relational Contracting.* Free Press.

Wilson, A. (2008). Hydraulic Engineering and Water Supply. In J. P. Oleson (Ed.), *Handbook of Engineering and Technology in the Classical World* (pp. 290–293). Oxford University Press.

World Bank. (1985). *World Bank Report 1985.* World Bank.

Yazdani, K. (2021). !8th-Century Plantation Slavery, Capitalism and the *Most Precious Colony* in the World. *Vierteljahrschrift für Sozial-und Wirtschaftsgeschichte, 108*(4), 457–503.

Yokota, J. (2000). Tumor Progression and Metastasis. *Carcinogenesis, 21*(3), 497–503.

Young, C. (1962). Iran in Continuing Crisis. *Foreign Affairs, 40*, 275–292.

Zaitlen, R., & German, J. B. (2000a, June). Of Mice and Men. *Modern Drug Discovery, 3*(5), 63–66.

Zaitlen, R., & German, J. B. (2000b, July/August). "Of Mice and Men" (Part II). *Modern Drug Discovery, 3*(6), 67.

Zandi, R. (2006, June 8). Qarardad-e bozorg miyan-e Vezarat-e Naft va Sepah-e Pasdaran mon'aqed shod (A Big Contract Was Signed Between the Oil Ministry and the IRGC). *Sharq.* Retrieved December 12, 2021, from wwwmagiran.com/npview.asp?ID=1095191

Zandi, R. (2011, August 8). Sardar Qassemi barnameh-ye Vezarat-e Naft ra e'lam kard (General Qassemi Announced the Oil Ministry's plan. *Sharq.* Available at: http://old.sharghdaily.ir/news/90/05/17/7693.html.   Retrieved January 7, 2022.

Zingales, L. (2015). Presidential Address: Does Finance Benefit Society? *The Journal of Finance, 70*(4), 1327–1363.

Zingales, L. (2017). Towards a Political Theory of the Firm. *The Journal of Economic Perspectives, 31*(3), 113–130.

Zobeiri, H., Akbarpour Roshan, N., & Shahrazi, M. (2017). Capital Flight and Economic Growth in Iran. In *19th International Scientific Conference on Economic and Social Development*, Melbourne, Australia, 9–10 February.

Zwijnenburg, W. (2017, August 11). No Country for Oil Men: Tracking Islamic State's oil Assets in Iraq. *bellingcat*. Retrieved February 3, 2022, from https://www.bellingcat.com/news/mena/2017/08/11/no-country-oil-men-tracking-islamic-states-oil-assets-iraq/.

Index[1]

A

Abadi, Khatoon, 163
Abazari, Yousef, 197
Abbas ibn Abd al-Muttalib, 158
Abbasid caliphs, 159
Abbaspour, M., 360
Abdollahi, Abdollah, 365
Abdollahi, Muhammad Reza, 340n30
Abrahamian, Ervand, 5, 208n22, 209, 210, 326
Abu Abbas Abdullah al-Saffah, 159
Abu Bakr Siddiq, 148n4
Abu Dharr, 184
Abu Ghraib prisons, 81n6
Abu Jahl b. Hisham, 149
Abu Sufyan ibn Harb, 148
Abusus, 15, 16, 52, 74, 94, 99
Accumulation of capital primitive/original, 49, 93, 98, 118
Adamiyat, Fereydoun, 137
Adjustment mechanisms, 61
Adjustment Programs, 256

Affinity thesis, 53, 54
Afghanistan, 2, 49, 54, 209, 281
Afghan Mujahideen, 145
Agamben, G., 74, 83
Aggressive coordination, 44, 45, 64
Agha zadeh, 345
Aglietta, Michel, 338n28
Ahmad Ibn Muhammad Ardabili, 168
Ahmadi, Mehdi, 132
Ahmadi Amooei, Bahman, 203, 216–218, 231, 232, 233n45, 257, 258, 260, 261
Ahmadinejad, Mahmoud, 6, 186, 197, 197n6, 203, 226n37, 228, 232, 234n46, 239, 240, 254, 258, 263, 267–270, 273, 279, 283, 301, 339, 341n34, 343, 377, 386
Ahmadov, A., 2n1
Aizenman, Joshua, 355
Akrami, Rahmattolah, 200
Albats, Yevgenia, 45, 47
Al-Fai, 147n2

---

[1] Note: Page numbers followed by 'n' refer to notes.

M. Vahabi, *Destructive Coordination, Anfal and Islamic Political Capitalism*, https://doi.org/10.1007/978-3-031-17674-6

Milton Keynes UK
Ingram Content Group UK Ltd.
UKHW010029211223
434710UK00001B/30

9 783031 176755